Biographical Directory of
Negro Ministers

by

Ethel L. Williams

The Scarecrow Press, Inc.
New York and London   1965

Foreword

The role of Negro ministers in the revolution now gripping the Nation is a crucial one. They are demonstrating religion in action in the true Christian sense. The author of this book provides a readily available resource for biographical data concerning them. Included are familiar names but also can be found many ministers whose names and roles will be unknown generally. All, however, are active and influential in local or national affairs.

James M. Nabrit, Jr.
President
Howard University
Washington, D.C.

Contents

Preface

The idea of compiling a book of biographical sketches of living Negro ministers came to me as a result of my inability as a librarian to answer the requests received for this type of material over a long period of years. These requests have doubled in volume during the last few years because of the present social revolution in America and the responsible leadership role that the minister has assumed in all phases of this movement.

Existing publications containing biographical and directory material are either out-of-date, limited in number of Negroes included or inaccessible and scattered in numerous denominational annual reports and yearbooks.

It is hoped that in addition to serving as a much needed reference book on the American Negro and the clergy, this volume will prove useful as a source for national, state, city and county government officials in cooperation with the community in selecting and appointing ministers in their localities to serve on various types of community organizations and projects.

The editor wishes to emphasize that this volume is not a "Who's Who" in the strict sense. An effort was not made to evaluate or endorse the ministers included or to include all the ministers who are rendering valuable service to their parishioners, denominations and the community. This is rather, a beginning and the editor feels that one of the objectives in this publication of this first volume has been achieved if it induces further lists of ministers from church officials, librarians, congregations and others. Such new material will be used in the preparation of the supplements to be published biennially. Many ministers did not return their questionnaires with the information requested of them in time for publication and it is hoped that they will be included in the next edition.

Information regarding ministers not listed, and corrections of material included should be addressed to the Librarian, School of Religion Library, Howard University, Washington, D. C. , 20001. Also, the user should know that the biographies included in this first edition were sent to the publisher with a minimum of editing and that limitations in finances, staff and the time did not permit verification by the biographee before printing.

The index has been added to increase the usefulness of the book and lists ministers whose current addresses were secured but who either did not return the information or who were not contacted because of the limitations mentioned above. It is hoped that the index and the bibliography will serve to increase the usefulness of the book and will be a means for users to secure more information.

I am grateful to all who have assisted in making this volume possible, to those included who have generously furnished the information requested. To the officials, Dr. James M. Nabrit, Jr. , President of Howard University, Dean Daniel G. Hill and the faculty and staff of the School of Religion for granting me sabbatical leave and for various other forms of assistance provided me while engaged in this compilation.

Grateful acknowledgment is made to Mrs. Louise J. Tankerson, Library Assistant in the School of Religion Library, who has been most helpful in every phase of the project. I also wish to express my gratitude to Mr. Hyun Chil Kim, student in the School of Religion who typed most of the manuscript, to Mrs. Alice H. Williams, for securing sources of information and assisting in many other ways.

Ethel L. Williams

The Negro Clergy

An asterisk (*) indicates that the biographee is an alumnus of Howard University, School of Religion, Washington, D. C.

Abbreviations

The following list includes the most uncommon abbreviations used in the biographies; those which are generally used and known are not included.

A. A.	Associate in Arts
A. B.	Bachelor of Arts
Amer.	American, American
A. M.	Master of Arts
A. M. E.	African Methodist Episcopal
A. M. E. Z.	African Methodist Episcopal Zion
Assn.	Association
b.	born
B. A.	Bachelor of Arts
B. S.	Bachelor of Science
B. T. U.	Baptist Teachers Union
B. Th.	Bachelor of Theology
Bapt.	Baptist
Bd.	Board
Bn.	Battalion
Br.	Branch
B. W. I.	British West Indies
B. Y. P. U.	Baptist Young Peoples Union
Cath.	Catholic
Ch.	Church
Chmn.	Chairman
C. M. E.	Christian Methodist Episcopal
Coll.	College
Com.	Committee
Conf.	Conference
Congr'l	Congregational
Conv.	Convention

CORE	Congress of Racial Equality
D. D.	Doctor of Divinity
dau.	daughter
del.	delegate
D. Litt. or	
L.H. D.	Doctor of Literature
Denom.	Denomination
Dept.	Department
D. H.L.	Doctor of Human Letters
D. S.T.	Doctor of Sacred Theology
Dir.	Directors
Div.	Division
Ed.	Education
Ed. D.	Doctor of Education
Ed. M.	Master of Education
Elks	Protective Order of Elks
E. T.O.	European Theatre of Operations
Exec.	Executive
FOR	Fellowship for Reconciliation
Hdqtrs.	Headquarters
Hon.	Honorary
Hosp.	Hospital
Inst.	Institute
K. of P.	Knights of Pythias
L. H.D.	Doctor of Humane Letters
Litt.D.	Doctor of Letters
Luth.	Lutheran
LL. B.	Bachelor of Laws
LL.D.	Doctor of Laws
LL. M.	Master of Laws
m.	married
M. A.	Master of Arts
Mason	Free and Accepted Masons or Prince Hall Masons
M. D.	Doctor of Medicine
M. D. S.	Master of Dental Surgery
M. S.	Master of Science
Meth.	Methodist
M. R. E.	Master of Religious Education

x

NAACP	National Association for the Advancement of Colored People
NSS and BTUC	National Sunday School and Baptist Training Union Congress
Nat., Nat'l	National
Odd Fellows	Grand United Order of Odd Fellows
Ph. D.	Doctor of Philosophy
pres.	President
Presbyn.	Presbyterian
rep.	representative
s.	son
sch.	school
sec.	secretary
sem.	seminary
soc.	society
S.T. B.	Bachelor of Sacred Theology
theol.	theology
treas.	treasurer
Univ.	University
U. P.	United Presbyterian
vice pres. or v. p.	vice president

Biographical Directory of Negro Ministers

ABNEY, Albert, b. Marshall, Texas, Dec. 18, 1914; s.
Hayes and Annis (Devers) A.; B. Th., Providence Bapt.
Theol Scm., Los Angeles, Calif., 1961; m. Elvie Richardson; 1 dau. Albert Deloris (Robinson); pastor, Mt.
Carmel Holy Assembly Bapt. Ch., 1947--; mem. Progressive National Bapt. Conv., Inc. Home: 1342 W. 103
st., Los Angeles, Calif. 44 Church: 254 E. 94 St., L.A.
3, Calif.

ACKERMAN, Amos Abraham, b. Walterboro, S.C., May 12,
1917; s. Asbury and Alice (Gones) A.; Th. B., Malone
Coll., 1949; m. M. Ruth Glover; children--Patricia A.,
Ruth Yvonne; asst. pastor, St. Paul's African Methodist
Episcopal Zion Church, Cleveland, Ohio, 1936-50; church
school teacher, 25 years; current pastor, Bethel African
Methodist Episcopal Zion Ch., Cleveland, Ohio; Mem.,
Ohio Annual Conference, 1937--; Mayor's Committee;
Operation City of Cleveland; A.M.E. Zion Ministers Union; National Council of Churches; Cleveland Church Federation; NAACP; Urban League; Inter-denominational Ministers Ass'n; YMCA Board; Glenville Community Council
of Cleveland; Mason; Home: 10915 Lee Ave., Cleveland
6, Ohio; Office: 1428 E. 110th St., Cleveland 6, Ohio

ADAIR, Joseph H., b. Chester, S.C., Dec. 30, 1924; s.
Aton A. and Margaret (Jones) A.; A.B., Johnson C. Smith
University, 1941-43; B.D., 1948-51; m. Justine Godley;
children--Daisy Ellen, Godley Maurice; pastor, Mattoon
Presbyterian Ch., Greenville, S.C., 1951-58; Walker's
Chapel United Presbyterian Ch., Reidsville, S.C.; Bower's
Chapel United Presbyterian Ch., Wellford, S.C., 1958-63;
Served in U.S. Navy 1943-46, Pacific Theatre; Home:
Route 4, Box 577, Greenville, S.C.

ADAMS, James A., b. Holly Springs, Miss., April 12, 1898;
A.B., Lane Coll.; B.D., Gammon Theol. Sem., 1951-53;
Graduate courses, Fisk Univ. and Garrett Bibliocal Inst.;
m. Augusta Person; pastor, Christian Methodist Episcopal
Churches, McKensie, Jackson, Brownsville, Tenn.; cur-

rent pastor, Farmer Chapel C. M. E. Ch., Brownsville,
Tenn.; Prof., Phillips Sch. of Theol., 1944-58; Mem.,
Judiciary Count, C. M. E. Ch.; Home: 351 Berry St.,
Jackson, Tenn.

ADAMS, John H., b. Columbia, S. C.; s. Eugene A. and
Charity A.; A. B., Johnson C. Smith Univ., Charlotte,
N. C.; S. T. B., Boston Univ. Sch. of Theology; S. T.M.
Boston Univ., Boston, Mass.; Further study: Harvard
Univ. Sch. of Human Relations, Cambridge, Mass.;
Union Theological Seminary, NYC; D. D. (Hon.) Wilber-
force Univ., 1956; D. D., Campbell Coll., Jackson,
Miss., 1959; m. Dolly Jacqueline Deselle; children--
Gaye Desselle, Jann Hurst; asst. pastor, Charles Street
African Methodist Episcopal Church, Boston, Mass.,
1947-49; pastor, Bethel A.M. E. Church, Lynn, Mass.;
prof., Historical Theology, Payne Theological Seminary,
Wilberforce, Ohio, 1952-56; pres., Paul Quinn College,
Waco, Tex.; pastor, First A.M.E. Church, Seattle,
Wash., 1962--; Former State Education Director of
NAACP; mem., Seattle Council of Churches and Washing-
ton Northern Idaho Council of Churches; Denominational
Representative to Southwest Conference on the Christian
World Mission; Connectional Stewardship Committee of
The A. M. E. Church; Connection Pension and Retirement
Commission of A. M. E. Church; chairman, Central Area
Committee on Civil Rights; Mem. Board NAACP, Seattle
Branch; Mem., Board of Seattle Urban League; award:
"Man of Year" Award; Home: 1020 Wash. Pl., E. Seattle,
Wash. 98102;   Office: 1522 14th Ave., Seattle, Wash.,
98102

ADAMS, L. Bryant, b. Henderson, Tex., Jan. 7, 1907; s.
Gus and Amy (Montgomery) A.; B. A., Bishop Coll.,
1934; B. D., Southern Theol. Sem., Fort Worth, 1940; m.
Fern Kurkendall Crutehfield; children--Maxine Merle
(Mrs. Williams Walker).; pastor, Mt. Olive Bapt. Ch.,
Albuquerque, N.Mexico; Mt. Zion Bapt. Ch., Sweetwater,
Tex.; Mt. Zion Bapt. Ch., Brownwood, Tex.; current
pastor, Second Bapt. Ch., El Paso, Texas, 1953--;
former civilian chaplain, Camp Bowe, 6 years; teacher,
Sweetwater, Texas, 1949-51; Mem., Community Develop-
ment Assn., Sweetwater; dean, Original West Texas Dist.
S.S. & B. T. U. Congress; Mem., NAACP; Bd. Mem. of
the McCall Day Nursery; Public Relations Chairman, Inter-
denominational Ministerial Alliance; former pres., El
Paso Ministerial Alliance; editorial staff, Bishop Bears;

Albert, L. B.

Brownwood Community News Letter; contributing editor,
Southwest Trade Guide (The Interpreter) El Paso, Texas;
Home: 311 South Tornillo St., El Paso, Texas 79901; Office: Second Baptist Church, 401 South Virginia St., El
Paso, Texas

ALBERT, Xavier Robert, b. Houston, Texas, Sept. 10,
1931; s. Robert and Cora (Tillman) A.; B.S. Pharmacy,
Texas Southern Univ.; Loyola Univ.; Bellarmine College;
Wayne State U., Passionist Seminary; Ordained priest,
Roman Cath. Ch., May 26, 1963; Home: 23300 Davison
Ave., W., Detroit, Mich. 48223.

ALEXANDER, Lloyd Matthew, coll. prof.; b. Meredithville,
Va., June 3, 1903; s. William Alexander and Millie
(Brown) A.; St. Paul's Jr. College (Now St. Paul's College), Lawrenceville, Va., 1929-31; St. Augustine's College, Raleigh, N.C., 1931-33, B.A.; B.D., Bishop Payne
Divinity School, Petersburg, Va., 1933-36; Union Theological Seminary and Teachers Coll., Columbia University,
NYC, M.A., 1938, 1946; m. Helen Eugenia Arrant; children--Junita Lucille, Lloyd Matthew, Jr., Leonard Arrant; chaplain, Ft. Valley School, Ft. Valley, Georgia,
1937-40; Priest-in-charge, St. Mark's Episcopal Church,
Bracey, Va., 1940-43; chaplain, Armed Forces (Captain
in 5th Air Force), 1943-46; chaplain, St. Augustine's
College, Raleigh, N.C., 1947-49; Priest-in-charge, St.
Cyprian's, Hampton & St. Augustine's, Newport News,
1950-60; vicar, St. Augustine's Newport News, 1960;
teacher, Ft. Valley School; teacher of philosophy at St.
Augustine's College, Raleigh; award: Man of the Year in
Hampton, Virginia (Omega Psi Phi); Home: 1207 Aberdeen
Road, Hampton, Va.; Office: 2515 Marshall Ave., Newport News, Va.

ALEXANDER, Robert Henry, Sr., b. Camilla, Ga., Feb.
14, 1914; s. Moses Taylor and Mariah Androna (Melver)
A.; A.B., Morris Brown Coll., 1940; B.D., Turner
Theol. Sem., 1942; S.T.M., Boston Univ., 1948; m.
Ruby Artelia Johnson; children---Sheila Ann (Mrs. Lavonneo,
Robert Henry, James Avery; Ordained to ministry, African Methodist Episcopal Church, 1935; pastor, Rock Temple, Conyers, Ga., 7 yrs.; pres., Shorter Coll., North
Little Rock, Arkansas, 1948-52; pastor, Avery Church,
Oklahoma City, 1952--; Mem., General Bd., Publication
Bd., Com. on Education, 12th Episcopal Dist., A.M.E.
Ch., 1952---; US Army, Chaplain Corps, Maj., 1942-46;

Mem., Oklahoma City Council of Churches (pres., 1957-
59; v.p. 1953-57); Oklahoma City Interdenominational
Ministerial Alliance (pres. 1954-59); director, Urban
League, 1952-58; Mason; Home: 1109 NE 17th St., Oklahoma City 11, Okla.; Office: 1425 N. Kelham Ave., Oklahoma City 17, Okla.

ALEXANDER, William Alphonso, Sr., b. Newport News,
Va., Dec. 20, 1921; s. Samuel Roscoe and Carrie
(Allen) A.; A.B., Fisk University, 1949; M.A., 1957;
B.D., McCormick Theological Seminary, Chicago, Ill.,
1951; m. Fay Janet Hampton; children--William, Jr.,
Paul Garvin, Peter Hadley; associate pastor, St. Augus-
tine Presbyterian Church, Bronx, N.Y.; pastor, St.
Andrew Presbyterian Ch., U.S.A.; pastor, Nashville,
Tennessee, Dec. 1951--; Moderator of Nashville Presby-
tery, 1961; Visit monthly since 1956, to State Prison
(Nashville); chaplain, Fisk General Alumni Assn.; chap-
lain, Davidson County Independent Political Council
(Nashville, Tenn.); chaplain, Frontier's International
Nashville Chapter, 1956---; Home: 901 37th Ave. N.,
Nashville 8, Tenn. Office: 949 37th Ave. N. Nashville
8, Tenn.

ALEXANDER, William Peter, b. Columbus, Miss., Aug.
5, 1897; Douglas Univ., Coll. of Rel., 1927-28; McKen-
dree Coll., 1932; Univ. of Ill., 1941; Midwest Bible
Coll., 1959-60; D.D. (hon.) Central Miss. Coll., 1957;
Ark. Bapt. Coll., 1963; 6 children; pastor, Mt. Olive
Bapt. Ch., East St. Louis, Mo., 1927-39; Mt. Nebo
Bapt. Ch., 1939-44; current, New Hope Bapt. Ch.,
1944---; dean, East St. Louis Extension, Amer. Bapt.
Sem.; moderator, New Salem Bapt. District Assn, 1953-
63; pres., Ill. Bapt. General State Congress of Christian
Ed.; instructor, Adult Div. Nat. Sunday Sch. and B.T.U.
Congress; Mem., East St. Louis Chamber of Commerce;
former pres., NAACP; Bd. of Governors and Bd. of
Directors, United Fund of Greater East St. Louis; Mem.,
All America City Steering Com.; East St. Louis Centen-
nial Com.; vice chairman, East St. Louis Human Rela-
tions Com.; Appointed by Major, Illinois Emancipation
Centennial; Mason; Home: 4247 Piggott Ave., East St.
Louis, Ill.; Office: 2122 Missouri Ave., East St. Louis,
Ill.

ALLEN, Frank Muphy, b. Tray, Alaska, April 17, 1908;
s. John Wesley and Josephine Allen; Philander Smith

Univ.; A. B., Livingstone College; B. D., Hood Theological
Seminary, 1961; m. Flora Mae Stringer; children--two
boys, two girls; pastor, Greater Gesthemane A. M. E.
Zion Church, Charlotte, N. C.; Mem., NAACP; YMCA;
Mason; Office: 325 Cemetery Ave., Charlotte 8, N. C.

ALLEN, John Claude, bishop; b. Talladega, Alab., April
5, 1899; A. B., Talladega Coll.; 1 dau. Claudia Mae
(Shannon); Licensed to preach, Detroit, Mich., 1926;
Admitted into S. E. Missouri and Ill. Conf.; pastor,
Christian Methodist Episcopal Ch., Mich.; pastor,
Israel C. M. E. Ch., Gary, Indiana; presiding elder,
Chicago District, C. M. E. Ch.; Treas., S. E. Missouri
& Ill. Conf.; sec., Kingdom Extension C. M. E. Ch.,
1946-58; Established and pastored C. M. E. Churches in
Pacific Coast area; Bd. Mem., Bd. of Education, Pub-
lic Schools, Gary, Ind.; Elected 28th bishop C. M. E.
Ch., Memphis, Tenn., May 1954; Home: 755 West 26th
Ave., Gary, Ind.

*ALSTON, Charlie, b. Warren County, N. C., Oct. 17,
1921; s. Wayman and Elizabeth (Jordan) A.; A. B., Va.
Union Univ., Richmond, Va., 1951; Graduate work, Univ.
of Alaska, 1956; B. D., Howard Univ. Sch. of Rel.,
Wash., D. C., 1963; specialized training: Clinical Pas-
toral Training; Children's Center; Dept. of Public Wel-
fare, D. C.; Laurel, Md.; Personnel Supervision; Air
Training Command; Scott Air Force Base, Ill.; pastor,
St. John's Baptist Church, Fairbanks, Alaska, 3 years;
minister of education, Pilgrims Baptist Church, Wash.,
D. C., 2 years; juvenile counselor, Children's Center,
Dept. of Public Welfare, D. C.; Laurel, Maryland; instructor, Systematic Theology, The Washington Baptist
Seminary, Wash., D. C. 3 years; institutional chaplain,
Council of Churches of Greater Washington, Wash., D.
C.; senior clinical chaplain, Milledgeville State Hospital,
1963---; pres., NAACP, Alaska; 1st Amer. Negro to
pastor a Southern Baptist Convention Church; Mem.,
Fairbanks Ministers Ass'n, Alaska; The Executive Com-
mittee of the Alaska Baptist Convention; US Air Force,
three years active duty as Air Transportation Technician;
four years active duty as Personnel Supervisor; Mem.,
Urban League; NAACP; Georgia Public Health Ass'n;
Campaign medal with three bronze stars; Home: P. O.
Box 725, Milledgeville, Ga. 31061; Office: Milledgeville
State Hospital, Milledgeville, Ga.

ALSTON, Edward Deedom, b. Norfolk, Va., Sept. 29,
1911; s. Deedom and Berderlee (Redden) A.; 1935-B.S.
North Carolina College, Durham; 1942, B.D. Bishop
Payne Divinity School, Petersburg, Va.; m. Elouise
Williams A.; children: Edward Deedom, Jr., Virnal
Jeffery; St. James Episcopal Church, Emporia, Va.;
St. James Episcopal Church, Portsmouth, Va.; Our
Merciful Saviour Episcopal Church, Louisville, Ky.;
Activities: Home visitor, Staff, Louisville Municipal
Housing Commission; Ky. Committee on Illegitimacy;
Mayor's Com. on Human Relations; Board, Chestnut St.
Branch YMCA.; Ky. Civil Liberties Union; mem. Fron-
tiers of America; Kapha Alpha Psi; Home: 1016 S. 43rd
St., Louisville 11, Ky.; Church: 473 S. 11th St. Louis-
ville 3, Ky.

ALSTON, Justus M., b. Oxford, N.C., April 15, 1905; s.
L. L. and Mary A.; A.B., Johnson C. Smith University,
1928; B.D., Johnson C. Smith University, 1931; D.D.
(hon.), Johnson C. Smith Univ., 1940; m. Nannie Mc
Clure; children---Jeffery Myron; Former moderator
Catawba Presbytery; present pastor, New Hampton United
Presbyterian Church; Mem.: Mason, Phi Beta Sigma;
Former: Master, Myersville Lodge, F & A.M.; Pres.,
Johnson C. Smith Alumni; Home: 2012 Oaklawn Ave.,
Charlotte 8, N.C.

ALSTON, Percel Odel, Sr., church official; b. Norfolk,
Va., Jan. 27, 1926; s. Robert James Sr. and Louise
(Harrison) A.; A.B., Va. Union Univ., 1950; B.D.,
Andover Newton Theol. School, 1954; S.T.M., Andover
Newton Theol. Sch., 1954; m. Maybelle Helena Kelly;
children---Taitu Zawdu, Karen Louise, Percel Odel,
Jr.; pastor, Midway Congregational Church (United
Church of Christ), McIntosh, Ga.; director, Dorchester
Cooperative Center, McIntosh, Ga., 1954-56; minister,
Christian Education, Convention of the South; United
Church of Christ, Greensboro, N.C., 1956-64; sec.,
Leadership Development, Division of Christian Education,
Bd. of Homeland Ministries, United Church of Christ,
1964----; Mem., Com. on Administration and Leader-
ship, Div. of Christian Ed., National Council of Churches;
consultant, The Church and Urbanization, United Church
of Christ; consultant, Education for Vocational Decision
for Ministry Group Youth Work Party, Technological
Revolution; Office: 1505 Race St., Philadelphia 2, Pa.

ALLEYNE, Lawrence Edward D., teacher; b. Brooklyn,
N. Y., June 14, 1928; a. Edward C. and Wilhelmina
(King) A.; Jordan Seminary, Menominee, Mich; Mother
of the Savior Seminary, Blackwood, N. J.; Catholic Univ.
of America, Wash., D. C., 1954-57; B. A., 1956; Ordained priest, Roman Cath. Ch., 1960; Instructor, Greek
Latin, Religion, Mother of the Savior Seminary, Blackwood, N. J., 1960--; Treasurer of Seminary, 1961---;
Home and Office: Mother of the Savior Seminary, Blackwood, N. J.

ALLISON, Johnathan William, b. Leavenworth, Kansas;
s. John William and Lona (Oden) A.; took courses at:
Campion Academy, Loveland, Colorado; Oakwood Coll.,
Huntsville, Ala.; B. A., Emmanuel Missionary Coll.; fur-
ther courses at Univ. of Calif.; m. Bessie Lou Coit;
children-Frederick Dan, Carole Anne, John William,
Camille Yvonne. Pastored at the following Seventh-Day
Adventist Churches: Beacon Light, Phoenix, Arizona,
1940-43; Capitol Ave., Indianapolis, Ind., 1945-47;
Hartford Ave., Detroit, Mich., 1947-54; present: Univer-
sity Church, Los Angeles, Calif., 1954- . Member,
Lynwood Academy Board, 1954-63. Home: 1147 W. 39th
Place, L. A., 37, Calif. Office: 1135 W. Santa Barbara
St., L. A., 37, Calif.

AMOS, Walter Hansel, bishop; b. Milan, Tenn., March 16,
1908; s. E. F. B. and Alice E.; Lane Coll.; A. B., Univ.
of Wisconsin; B. D., Garret Biblical Institute; M. A.,
Univ. of Chicago School of Divinity; Wayne Univ.; Ph. D.,
Univ. of Michigan; Admitted on trial Christian Methodist
Episcopal Ch., 1935; Ordained deacon, 1936; Full correc-
tion, 1936; Ordained Elder, 1938; Elected 32nd bishop,
Christian Methodist Episcopal Ch., St. Louis, Mo., May
1962; Home: 2111 La Salle Gardens, So., Detroit 6,
Mich.

ANDERSON, Herbert Forgys, b. Jamaica, B. W. I., May 31,
1884; s. Henry Dorman and Frances Augusts; A. B.,
S. T. B., Lincoln Univ., 1916, 1931; m. Luevinia Buroll
Sullivan; pastor, Timothy Darling Presby. Ch., USA,
Oxford, N. C., 1919-20; Cumberland Presby. Ch., Va.,
1920-21; Helbrook St. Presby. Ch., 1921-23; Chestnut St.
Presby. Ch., 1923-24; 9th St. Bristol, Tenn. St. Mark
Rogerville, 1924-31; Christ Presby. Ch., Augusta, Ga.,
1931-64; teacher, Oxford, N. C.; Danville, Va.; Bristol,

Tenn.; Rogerville, Tenn.; mem., Omega Psi Phi; former
treas., Hodge Presby. Ch., 1945-60; moderator, commissioner, General Assembly, 1939, 1948, 1945; mem.,
Interdenominational Alliance, Augusta, Ga.; Advisory
Bd., U.S.A., Augusta, Ga.; home; 1136 Cecelin St.,
Augusta, Ga. 30901; office: 1316 Gwinette, Augusta, Ga.
30901.

ANDERSON, Jesse Fosset, b. Plainfield, New Jersey,
April 3, 1910; s. Jefferson Charles and Mary (Fosset)
A.; A.B., Lincoln University, 1932; S.T.B., General
Theological Seminary, 1935; m. Elizabeth Reynolds
Jackson; children---Jesse, Jr., John, Louis; curate, St.
Philips Church, New York City, 1935-38; priest-in-
charge, St. Philips Church, Grand Rapids, Mich., 1938-
42; priest-in-charge, St. Matthews Church, Wilmington,
Del., 1942-44; rector, St. Thomas Church, Philadelphia,
Pa., 1944---Mayors Commission on Higher Education
(Phila. Pa.); Mem. Diocesan and National Offices; Stand-
ing Committee (Bishop's Council of Advice); Executive
Committee of Diocese; Dept. of Christian Social Rela-
tions; Dept. of Missions; Committee on Racial Understand-
ing; Board of Episcopal Community Services; Twice dele-
gate, Diocese to National General Convention; Teacher,
Provincial and Diocesan Adult and Youth Conferences;
Home: 1427 No. 56 St., Phila. 31, Pa.; Office: 52nd
& Ponish Sts., Phila. 39, Pa.

ANDERSON, Leslie Otto, b. Steelton, Pa., November 5,
1933; s. John Richard and Mamie Cordella (Caldwell)
A.; B.A., Oakwood Coll., 1959; M.A., Andrews Univ.,
1960; m. Mary Alyce Branche. Present: District Pastor,
Muskegon-Grand Rapids-Idlewild, Michigan, 1960- .
U.S. Air Force, 1952-56; National Defense Award; Good
Conduct (military). Home: 715 Paris Ave., S.E., Grand
Rapids, Mich. 49503. Office: 111 Graham St., S.W.
Grand Rapids, Mich.

ANDERSON, Louis Lloyd; b. Stuberville, Ohio, Jan. 1,
1922; s. Cecil H. L. and Maggie Beachum A.; A.B.,
Univ. of Pittsburgh, 1948; B.S., M.A., Religious Education; Courses Ph.D., Univ. of Chicago; m. Pauline
Dinkins; pastor, Metropolitan Bapt. Ch.,. Pittsburgh, Pa.,
1940-43; Calvary Bapt. Ch., Duluth, Minn., 1950-52;
North Montgomery Bapt. Ch., Montgomery, Ala., 1954-
55; current pastor, Tabernacle Bapt. Ch., Selma, Ala.,
1955---; mem., Dallas County Voters League, Southern

Christian Leadership Conference; Home: 817 First Ave.,
Selma, Ala.; Office: 1431 Broad St., Selma, Ala.

ANDERSON, Vinton Randolph; b. Somerset, Bermuda, July
11, 1927; s. C. L. Rabberay (foster parents) and Francis;
B.A., Wilberforce Univ., 1952; B.D., Payne Theo.
Seminary, 1952; M.A., Kansas Univ., 1962; D.D. (hon.),
Paul Quinn Coll., 1964; m. Vivienne Louise Cholmondeley;
children--- Vinton R. Jr., Jeffrey Charles, Carlton Law-
son; pastor, St. Mark African Methodist Episcopal Church,
Topeka, Kan., 1952-53; Brown Chapel A.M.E. Church,
Parsons, Kans., 1953-55; St. Luke A.M.E. Church,
Lawrence, Kan., 1955-59; St. Paul A.M.E. Church,
Wichita, Kan., 1959-64; St. Paul A.M.E. Church, St.
Louis, Mo., 1964---; Mem.: General Board of Educa-
tion of the A.M.E. Church; First vice pres., Wichita
Branch of the NAACP; Church work chairman NAACP;
Kansas; pres., Board of Trustees, Wichita Council of
Churches; Mem., Bd. of Dir. Christian Stewardship for
the Kansas-Nebraska Conference of the A.M.E. Church;
Zeta Sigma Pi National Honorary Social Science Frater-
nity; Alpha Phi Alpha; delegate, World Methodist Confer-
ence, Oslo, Norway, 1961; Mem., President's Comm.
on Equal Employment Opportunities, 1963; representative,
A.M.E. Church to the Commission of Higher Education
of the National Council of Churches in the USA; Mayor!s
Committee; Episcopal Committee of the A.M.E. Church;
Attended Yale Univ. Conf. for the Ministry; Home: 5357
Batmeer St., St. Louis, Mo.; Office: 1260 Hamilton,
St. Louis, Mo.

ANDREWS, Richard Taylor, Jr.; b. Houston, Texas, Sept.
8, 1912; s. Richard Taylor and Julia (Sommerville) A.;
A.B., Fisk Univ., 1932; B.D., Sch. of Rel., Howard
Univ., 1953; m. Marjory Jackson; children-- Stephen B.,
Richard Taylor III. Pastor, Mt. Zion Congregational
(United Church of Christ), Cleveland, Ohio, 1953-present.
(Consultant, Social Action Comm. of United Ch. of
Christ; vice-moderator, Ohio Synod of United Church of
Christ; board member, N.A.A.C.P. (Cleveland Branch)
1956-60; board mem., Y.M.C.A., 1959-present. Honor-
able discharge, World War II.; Omega Psi Phi; Citizen's
League; Consumer's League; all in Cleveland, Ohio.
Article published in Social Action, 1962. Home: 9703
Parmelee Ave., Cleveland, Ohio. Office: 10723 Magnolia
Dr., Cleveland, Ohio.

*ANONYE, Albert Chinedozi, college professor; b. Alaenyi
Ogwa, Nigeria, West Africa, June 9, 1925; s. Aaron M.
and Isabella Eleonu (Nwachukugwobi) A.; B.A., Central
State Coll., Wilberforce, Ohio, 1953; M.A., Boston
Univ., Boston, Mass., 1954; B.D., Sch. of Religion,
Howard Univ., 1961; m. Archiong Ewa Ewa Eke; chil-
dren--Anita Chinwe, Stella Ulunma, Betty Ngozi, Colum-
bus K., Theodosia, Rose. Professor, Aggrey Mem.
Coll., Arochuku, Nigeria, 1955-56; principal, Emmanuel
College, Owerri, E. Nigeria. 1957-59; missionary pastor,
Twelfth Street Christian Church, Wash. D.C., 1960-63;
present: associate prof., and chairman, History Dept.,
Talladega Coll., 1963- . Former Secretary-General,
N'Dian Estate Branch of Calabar Mercantile Workers'
Union; founder, Ndi-Uhu Village Family Union, Nigeria,
1956; pres., International Relations Club, Inc. of N.
America, 1952-53; Office: 2260 Bathgate Avenue, Bronx,
New York, 10458

ANTHONY, Irving; b. Trinidad, West Indies; s. Alexander
A. and Martha (Jemmott) A.; A.B., M.S., College of
the City of New York, 1927, 1938; m. Cicely Olivia.
Curate: St. Ambrose Church, N.Y.C., 1945; St.
Andrew's Church, N.Y.C., 1946-49; St. Phillip's Ch.,
N.Y.C., 1949-60; rector, St. Andrew's Ch., N.Y.C.,
1960-present. Teacher, N.Y.C. Public Schools; advisory
board, Harlem Hospital School of Nursing; mason. Mas-
ter's thesis: "Factors Influencing Truancy Among Boys
of Junior High School Age". Home: 2588 Seventh Ave.,
N.Y. 39 N.Y. Office: 2067 5th Avenue., N.Y., 35,
N.Y.

*ARMSTRONG, Ernest W., chaplain; b. Bluff Route, Soper,
Okla., May 1, 1915; s. Giles H. and Vinnie (Jones) A.;
A.B., Dillard Univ., 1942; B.D., M.A., Howard Univ.,
1946, 1947; m. Luella Whitaker; children-- Ernest W.,
Jr., Earl M., Everett W. Chaplain to Baptist students at
Howard Univ. and assistant pastor, Shiloh Bapt. Ch.,
Washington, D.C., 1946-48; college minister and assoc.
prof., social science, Savannah State Coll., Savannah,
Ga., 1948-49; present: U.S. Army chaplain, 1949- .
Bronze Star (V) medal; American Defense medal: German
Occupation medal; 10 years U.S. Army Reserve medal;
U.N. Campaign medal; Korean War medal. Member,
Omega Psi Phi; Mason; cited "Mason of the Year" by the
Oklahoma Grand Lodge, 1962; received "Scroll of Honor",
Omega Psi Phi, 1964 for "outstanding achievement in the

field of International Brotherhood"; Deputy Sovereign
Grand Commander, Scottish Rite Masonary in Europe,
Southern Jurisdiction. Home: 1545 E. Apache St., Tulsa
6, Okla. Office: The Post Chapel, Ft. Sill, Oklahoma.

ARTIS, George Henry; b. Wilmington, N.C., July 2, 1931;
s. George H. and Hazel (Smith) A.; B.A., St. Mary's
Seminary, Techny, Ill., 1952-58; Divine Word Seminary
Bay St. Louis, Miss., 1948-52, 1958-62; Springhill Col-
lege, Mobile, Ala; Catholic U. of Amer., Wash., D.C.
Ordained March 17, 1962, priest, Roman Cath. Ch.;
Asst. Pastor, The Immaculate Heart of Mary Church,
Lafayette, La.; Home: Wilmington, N.C.; Office: Im-
maculate Heart of Mary Church, P.O. Box 2398, Sur-
rey & 12th Street, Lafayette, La.

ASBURY, Howard DeGrasse, coll. prof.; b. Boston, Mass.,
Aug. 28, 1907; s. Jasper DeGrasse and Adelaide (Hart)
A.; A.B., Clark Univ., Atlanta, Ga., 1936; M.A.,
S.T.B., Boston Univ., 1936-39; m. Doris Wade; chil-
dren---Shirley Evone (Mrs. Robert H. Downs); pastor,
Main St. Meth. Ch., Ronceverte, W.Va., 1939-41;
Trinity Meth. Ch., Fairmont, W. Va., 1941-43; coll.
minister, prof., Samuel Huston Coll. (later Huston-
Tillotson Coll.), Austin, Texas, 1943-54; current pastor,
St. Paul Meth. Ch., Jamaica, New York, 1954---; Mem.,
Alpha Phi Alpha; Phi Kappa Theta; Sons of Union Veter-
ans of the Civil War; chaplain, New York Dept., Camp
No. 20; Home: 104-20 189 St., Hollis, L.I., 12, New
York; Office: 173-01 108 Ave., Jamaica, New York

ATCHISON, Wallace William, presiding elder; b. Edgefield,
S.C., Mar. 31, 1876; s. Jarrett and Charity A.; Paine
College, Augusta, Ga., 1908; m. Mahala Field. Pastored
Christian Methodist Episcopal Churches in Ga., Ky.,
Tenn., Okla., Arkansas, Ala., and New Jersey, 1907-
35; presiding elder, Jersey City District and Camden,
New Jersey District, 1935-64; Retired April 1964. Home:
1588 W. Front St., Red Bank, N.J.

BABER, George W., bishop; b. Cleveland, Ohio, Aug. 29,
1898; s. William and Emma Effie (Griffin) B.; A.B.,
Payne Theol. Sem.; B.D., Chicago Theol. Sem.; D.D.
(hon.), Wilberforce Univ.; Morris Brown Coll.; Shorter
Coll.; Payne and Campbell Coll.; m. Alma Marie Wims
(deceased); children--June (Mrs. Woodson), Flora A.

(Mrs. J.S. Benn, III), George W., Benjamin S., Bar-
bara (Mrs. Crawford); pastor, African Methodist Epis-
copal Churches, Indiana, Michigan, 1924-27; Elected
bishop, 1944; current, presiding bishop of the First
Episcopal District; founder, Camp Baber, Cassopolis,
Mich.; organizer, The Pastors Seminar; Young People's
Congress; Trustee of Bd. and chairman of Finance Bd.
Payne Sem.; Mem., Detroit Interracial Com.; Welfare
Bd., Flint, Mich.; Home Federal Savings & Loan Assn.;
NAACP; sec., General Bd., Bishops' Council, 1959-60;
pres., Bishops' Council, 1960-61; chmn., General Bd.,
Bishops' Council, 1961-62; delegate, World Meth. Conf.,
Oxford, England, 1951; delegate, World Meth. Conf.,
Oslo, Norway, 1961; World Council of Churches, New
Delhi, India, 1961; Mem., Advisory Bd., Amer. Bible
Society, 1962---; Home: 7508-16th St., N.W. Washington,
D.C.

BAGWELL, Clarence W. b. Onancock, Va. Oct. 12, 1907;
s. Clarence P. and Hazel Rose (Bushrod) B; A.B.
Clark College, B.D. Gammon Theological Seminary,
D.D. Miller University; m. Cora Collins; Children:
Clarence H., Carroll Stephen. Ministry: Ferry Avenue
Methodist Church, 1961 to present, Camden, Mem.:
Mason; Chaplain, N.J. Civil Defense Corp. Home: 768
Ferry Avenue, Camden, N.J. Office: 8th & Ferry Ave.
Camden, N.J.

BAILEY, Jack Simpson, b. Brunswick, Ga., June 2, 1937;
s. Henry D. and Sylvia (Williamson) B.; A.B., Johnson
C. Smith Univ., 1960; B.D., 1963; Graduate Work at
Chicago Theological Seminary, 1963---; m. Mary Roberts;
student pastor Ceadar Grove & Bethpage Presbyterian
Churches, Kannapolis & Concord, N.C.; 1961-62; student
pastor Second Presbyterian Church, Cheraw, S.C., 1962-
63; asst. pastor, Lawndale Presbyterian Church, Chicago,
Ill. (post graduate intern); mem.: Chicago Urban League,
Alpha Kappa Mu and Sigma Rho Sigma National Honor
Societies, Pni Beta Sigma Fraternity; Home: 5751 S.
Woodlawn Ave., Chicago 37, Ill.; Ch.: 1908 S. Millard
Ave., Chicago 23, Ill.

BAILEY, John Henry, b. Lancaster, S.C., May 22, 1910;
s. Nathaniel and Carry (Spring) B.; A.B., B.D., Johnson C. Smith U., Charlotte, N.C., 1950-56; m. Mary
Stinson; 2 sons, John Henry, Nathaniel; 9 daus., Mary
Lee B. Herron, Alice B. Smith, Mamie B. Crawford,

Flossie B. Woodards, Carrie B. Wiley, Sallie Ann,
Virginia, Betty Ann and Patricia Ann; Pastor, Nazareth
Baptist Church and The Cross Road Bapt. Ch., Rock
Hill, S. C.; Dean, Christian Ed., York County, S. C.;
Vice-Pres., State Sunday School Conv., York County,
S. C.; Mem., Trustee Bd., Friendship Jr. College
Rock Hill, S. C.; Democrat; Home: 929 N. Davidson St.,
Charlotte, N. C. 28202 Church: RFD 1, 5 Rock Hill,
S. C.

BALL, William Franklin, bishop; b. Mt. Pleasant, S. C.,
Aug. 3, 1906; s. Charles F. and Delia (Blake) B.; A.
B., Bd., Edward Waters Coll., Walker Business Coll.,
Wilberforce Univ.; D. D. (hon.), Edward Waters Coll.;
LL. D. (hon.), Wilberforce Univ.; m. Agnes Marie
Moton; children--Frankie (Mrs. Harold), William F.,
Jr.; pastor, African Methodist Episcopal Churches, Mis-
sion Churches in Fla., Ky., Tenn.; presiding elder,
West Jacksonville Dist.; Elected bishop, 1956; current,
bishop 11th District; chairman, Bishops' Committee on
Evangelism; Committee on Compilation of the Discipline;
delegate, World Council of Methodism; Mem., Mason;
Phi Beta Sigma; former evangelistic preacher and held
many revivals; Home: 7530 NW 10th Ave., Miami, Fla.

*BANKS, Allen A., Jr. b. Bryan, Tex.; s. Allen A. and
Idell (Turner) B.; A. B., Bishop Coll., 1937; B. D., M.
A., Howard Univ., Sch. of Rel., 1938; 1943; D. D.,
Arkansas Baptist Coll., 1955; m. Victoria Allen; chil-
dren--Allen Arthur, III, Teta Victoria; current pastor,
Second Baptist Church, Detroit, Mich., 1947---; pres.,
Wolverine State Missionary Baptist Convention, 1960-64;
Corresponding sec., Metropolitan Missionary Baptist
Ass'n; Former member, General Board, National Coun-
cil of Churches; vice pres., Michigan Council of Churches;
vice pres., Detroit Council of Churches; Mem., Michigan
State Civil Rights Commission; Detroit Commission on
Children and Youth; Detroit Urban League; YWCA; Higher
Education Opportunities; Kappa Alpha Psi; Pioneer Club;
Home: 2340 Chicago Blvd., Detroit, Michigan 48206; Of-
fice: 441 Monroe Ave., Detroit, Mich. 48226

BARBER, Jesse Belmont, b. Charlotte, N. C., Nov. 2,
1893; s. Henry and Cecelia (Lyles) B.; A. B., Lincoln
University, 1915; S. T. B., 1918; M. Th., Auburn
Theological Seminary, 1936; D. D., Lincoln Univ., 1940:
m. Mae Valeria Fortune; children---Jesse Belmont, Jr.;

pastor, Grace Presbyterian Church, Seattle, 1918-22;
supervisor, S. S. Missions, Presbyterian U. S. A., 1922-
26; pastor, Leonard Street Presby. Ch., Chattanooga,
Tenn., 1926-43; dean, Theol. Sem., Lincoln Univ.,
Penna., 1943-50; sec. Presbyterian Work in the South-
Div. of Evangelism until retirement, 1960; minister of
visitation, 1961---; co-chairman, Presbyterian Institute
on Racial and Cultural Relations, 1946-48; leader, preaching missions in Mexico, Cuba, Puerto Rico, and Domin-
ican Republic, 1954-59; Member, Bd. of Dirs. of Red
Cross, Advisor to Housing Authority, YMCA; mem.:
Mason Fraternity; Alpha Phi Alpha; Alumni Association
of Lincoln, Auburn and Union; Editor, THE NEW AD-
VANCE; author: Climbing Jacob's Ladder; Home: 24-50
Gilmore Street East Elmhurst 69, New York.

BARBER, William Joseph, teacher, social worker; b. Free
Union Community, Jamesville, N. C., Mar. 21, 1927;
A. B., St. Augustine's College, Raleigh, NC; B. D. &
M. S., Butler Univ., Indianapolis; Courses: Elementary
Ed., Radio-technology; also courses⌐College of the Bible;
m. Eleanor Lucille Patterson; children---William Joseph,
II; pastor, Market Street Christian Ch., Carthays, Ind.;
supply pastor, Indiana Missouri and North Carolina; cur-
rent pastor-director, Hillside Christian Center, Indianapolis
Indiana; teacher, Warrenton High School, Ga.; Social case
worker, Martion Co., Dept. of Pub. Welfare; Counselor,
Eastside Christian Center; Staff Asst., Flanner House;
Field worker, Washington (N. C.), Norfolk (Va.); Disciples
of Christ; Mem.: Alpha Phi Alpha; United College Fund;
Disciples of Christ, Historical Society; Indianapolis Social
Workers Club; Indiana Registry of Social Workers; author:
"A History of the Origin and Development of a Rural
Negro Church Group in Eastern N. C., " "The Disciple
Assemblies of Eastern North Carolina, " "A Partial History
of the Free Union Community. " Home: Hillside Christian
Church Center Parsonage, 1731 Ingram St., Indianapolis,
Indiana 46218; Off.: Hillside Christian Church Center,
1731-37 Ingram St., Indianapolis, Indiana 46218

*BARNES, Frederick William, b. Washington, D. C., Janu-
ary 2, 1920; s. William Richard and Annie (Quander) B.;
A. B., Howard Univ., 1949; B. D., Sch. of Rel., 1958;
m. Vivian Elizabeth Thomas; children--Cynthia, Michael,
Ivan, Candas. Asst. pastor, John Wesley African Methodist
Episcopal Zion Ch., 1952-56; pastor, Contee A. ME. Ch.,
1956-present. Pres., Adams Elem. School PTA, 1960-

1962. Army Air Force, 1943-46. Kappa Alpha Psi;
treasurer, Far Northeast Ministerial Alliance; vice-pres.,
Methodist Ministers Assn., Wash., D.C. Home: 36 53rd
Place, S.E., Wash., D.C. Office: 903 Division Ave.,
N.E., Wash. D.C.

*BARNES, Kenneth Pearle, b. Wayside, P.O. Charles
County, Maryland, Sept. 6, 1904. s. William Humphrey
and Mary Jane (Thomas) B.; B.S. Howard U. 1926, D.D.
Howard U. Sch. Of Rel. 1934; m. Mildred Lois North;
Children: Kenneth William, Barrington Benton, Barbara
Lois V. Smith; Teacher, Douglas High School, Stanton,
Va. 1926-27, Ministry: Upper Marlboro, Md. 1935, Brook-
ville, Md. 1947, Mt. Vernon, Washington, D.C. 1939, Up-
per Marlboro, Md. 1941, Jones Methodist, Wash. D.C.
1943, Alexandria, Va. 1953, Present: Superintendant of
West Baltimore District of the Washington Annual Conference of The Methodist Church (since 1959); President of
Brown Junior High PTA Wash. D.C. 1951-52, Member:
Elks, Odd Fellows, Masons, Eureka Lodge, Wash. D.C.
and Omega Psi Phi Fraternity; Post-graduate work in Psychiatry and Education. Home: 3702 Dennlyn Road, Baltimore 15, Md. Office: 828 N. Carrollton Ave. Baltimore 17,
Md.

BARNES, William Heard, Sr. b. Grenada, Miss., June 15,
1918; s. Wm. Edward and Mary (Allen) B.; B.S., Campbell Coll.; B.D., Wilberforce Univ. Payne Theol. Seminary, N.Y.; D.D. (hon.), Campbell Coll., Jackson, Miss.;
m. Louise Trigg; children-- Sylvia Louise, Wm. H. Jr.,
Valarie V., Frederick Van Douglas; pastor, African
Methodist Episcopal Churches, Miss., Pa., S.C., 1937-
63; current pastor, Bethel A.M.E. Church, Kingston,
S.C., 1963---; Trustee Mem., Allen Univ., Columbia,
S.C.;Mem.: The Interdenominational and Inter Faith Ministerial Alliance; vice pres., The Connectional Dept. of
A.M.E. Church; Mem., Alpha Phi Alpha; Mason; Demo-
crat; Editorial Borad Mem., The Christian Recorder of
A.M.E. Church; Home:300 West Main St., Kingstue, S.
C.; Office: same.

BARNETTE, James William, b. Pineville, N.C., April 25,
1913; s. William W. and Tetsie (Thompson) B.; B.A.,
Johnson C. Smith University, Charlotte, N.C., 1937; B.D.
1940; m. Etta P. Lee; pastor, Miranda Presbyterian
Church, Charlotte, N.C.; pastor, Central Presbyterian
Church, Lynchburg, Va., 1940-43; Rocky Mount, North

Carolina, Mout Pisgah Presbyterian Church (1943-54);
Bethesda Church, Nottoway, Va. (1954-1960); Goodwill
Presby. Ch., 1960-62; and Presbyterian Ch. of Our
Saviour, Wilmington, Delaware 1962---; present-Delaware-
Inner City Project; Legal Redress Chairman of the local
Chapter in NAACP, Rocky Mount, N.C.; Member, Mason;
the Order of Eastern Star; Home: 1013 E. 27th Street,
Wilmington, Delaware; Ch.: 1017 E. 27th Street, Wilming-
ton, Delaware.

BARRETT, William Emanuel, Sr., b. Quinque, Va., Sept.
16, 1925; s. Stephen Emanuel and Ethel Clisten (Moten)
W.; A.B., Virginia Union University, 1950; B.D., 1953;
Lutheran Theological Seminary, Philadelphia, 1960-61; m.
Loretta Katherine Williams; William E. and Katherine
Denise; pastor, Antioch Baptist Church, Culpeper, 1949-
53; pastor, Mt. Zion Baptist Church, Staunton, Va., 1953-
57; pastor, Mt. Calvary Baptist, New Kensington, Pa.,
1957-60; pastor, Tabernacle Lutheran Church, Philadelphia,
1961---; consultant and lecturer, Philadelphia Psychiatric
Institute, 1963---; pres., 18th District Youth Referral
Committee, Philadelphia, 1962-63; Chairman Education
Committee, Cobbs Creek Civic Association, 1963; Board
of Directors, 1964; Member, NAACP; Member, Philadelphia 400 Ministers, Member, Philadelphia Fellowship
Commission; State Representative of the Lutheran Church
to the Council of Churches; Service in the US Army, 1943-
46; award: American Theater; Good Conduct; Home: 5933
Pine Street, Philadelphia, Pa.; Ch.: 59th and Spruce
Streets, Philadelphia, Pa.

BARRON, Richard Edward, b. Newark, N. J., Nov. 29,
1931; s. Edward and Cora (Crowell) B.; B.A., Oakwood
College, 1962; Andrews Univ., 1963; D.D., College Divine
Metaphysics, 1963; m. Vivian Virginia Steele; children-
Teresa Ann, Shelley Renee, Carol Marie. Present: New
Hope Seventh-Day Adventist Church, Pueblo, Colo., 1963-
U.S. Army, 1952-54; Good Conduct medal; N.A.A.C.P.
award, Newark, N.J. Branch for religious activities,
1958. Home: 1448 Stone Ave., Pueblo, Colo. Office: 714
Arroya St., Pueblo, Colo.

BASKIN, Lee Roy, presiding elder, teacher; b. Bullock
County, Ala., Sept. 29, 1897; s. Lee Roy and Ibbie
(Curry) B.; B.S. Ed., Alabama State College, 1917; B.S.,
Tuskegee Institute, 1918; M.A. Ed., University of Cincinnati,
1934-35; m. Johnnie Mae Pickett; children---Lee M.

Myrtle, Bennie E., Warren E.; pastor, A. M. E. Zion
Church, 1921-47; teacher, the School System, 23 years;
Presiding elder, 17 years; US Forces, 1918-20 (1st Lt.);
Mem.: Democrat; Chairman, Adult Committee; Sec.,
Budget Commission, A. M. E. Zion Church, Alabama;
Delegate, General Conf., A. M. E. Zion Church for 48
years; Home: Rte 2, Box 125, Tuskegee, Alabama

BASS, Richard Oliver, b. Nashville, Tenn., June 24, 1923;
s. D. W. and Ethel M. (McCorkle) B.; A. B., Lane Col-
lege; Wichita Univ.; B. D., Garrett Bible Inst., Evanston,
Ill.; m. Edith V. Thomas; children-- Richard O., Jr.
Claude Anderson; pastor, Christian Methodist Episcopal
Churches, Fla., Kansas, S. C., Ind.; current pastor,
Lewis Metropolitan C. M. E. Church, Los Angeles, Calif.;
teacher, Leadership Training Schools, Ohio, N. C., S. C.,
Ga., Kansas, Miss., Calif.; Has served as pres. of var-
ious Ministerial Assoc.; pres., National Youth Conf. -
C. M. E. Church, 1944-48 (Greenville County); Partici-
pated actively in interracial activities in all communities;
operating commissioner, U. S. O.; Mem., Board of Urban
League, Gary, Ind.; YMCA, Wichita, Kansas & Evanston,
Ill.; awards: Michigan-Indiana Conf. -C. M. E. Church for
Fellowship & Cooperation among Churches; Los Angeles
County Board of Supervision; Mem., Alpha Phi Alpha;
Mason; Democrat; Frontiers of America; Home: 1632
49th Los Angeles, Calif. 90062; Office: Lewis Metropolitan
C. M. E. Church, 4900 So. Western Aven., Los Angeles,
Calif. 90062

BATEMAN, Melvin, b. Indianapolis, Indiana, June 17, 1924;
s. George Hall and Julia Mae; Th. B., The Bethel School
of Theology, Detroit, Mich., 1953; m. Beatrice Laverne
Anderson; children---Jack, Melanie, Gregory, Donielle,
Marcia; pastor, Bethlehem Temple, Terre Haute, Indiana,
3 years; St. Paul A. M. E. Zion Church, Covington, Ky.,
1 year; Findlay St. Church, 1960-64; Secy., the Ministerial Fellowship (Scioto County), Portsmouth, Ohio; Handwriting Expert-Grapho-Analyst (The science of reading the
personality through the handwriting); Work with Ministers
and Business Organizations; Professional Ventriloquist -
2 dummies, Ike and Mike, Radio and TV Programs, WCPO-
TV, Cincinnati, WHTN-TV Huntington, W. Va., Channel
10, Columbus, Ohio, WCIN - Radio, Cincinnati. "Let
Youth Be Heard." Originated and moderated program in
Portsmouth; Organized the Community Recreational
Society. Have national award for outstanding work with

the Red Cross and also Award from the city for a Race
Relation Program titled "An Approach to Understanding,"
Served in the Medical Corps 2 yrs and 4 months of the
Air Force; Good Conduct Medal; Home: 1009 13th St.,
Portsmouth; Ohio.

BEANE, John Solomon, assistant presiding bishop, Bible
Way Church of our Lord Jesus Christ World-Wide, Inc.;
b. Boons Mill, Va., May 23, 1888; s. Joe and Elzina
(Napper) B.; A.B., Bluefield College 1905; D.D. (hon.),
American Bible College, 1957; assistant presiding bishop,
Bible Way Church; m. Miranda Jannie Carter, June 13,
1906; 1 daughter (deceased); Mem., Odd Fellows, NAACP,
Petersburg Virginia Civic and Political Groups; Home:
614 Harding St., Petersburg, Va.; Office: 459 Harding
St., Petersburg, Va.

BEARDEN, Harold Irvin, bishop; b. Atlanta, Ga., Mar. 8,
1910; A.B., Morris Brown Coll.; B.D., Turner Theol.
Sem.; D.D. (hon.), Morris Brown Coll.; Campebell Coll.;
Kittrell Coll.; LL.D. (hon.), Daniel Payne Coll.; Mon-
rovia Coll.; Wilberforce Univ.; m. Lois M. Mathis,
children---Mrs. Jo Ann B. Vickers, Harold Irvin, Jr.,
Mrs. Gloria B. Pearson, Lloyd Colbert, Sharon
Delores, Richard Louis; pastor, Foundation Chapel Afri-
can Methodist Episcopal Ch., Atlanta, Ga.; St. John
A.M.E. Church, Atlanta, Ga.; Austell Circuit, Austell,
Ga.; Greater Bethel A.M.E. Ch., Blandtown, Ga.;
Turner Chapel A.M.E. Church, Marietta, Ga.; First
A.M.E. Church, Athens, Ga.; St. James A.M.E. Church,
Columbus, Ga.; St. Paul A.M.E. Church, Atlanta, Ga.;
Big Bethel A.M.E. Church, Atlanta, Ga.; Trustee, Mor-
ris Brown Coll., 1933-64; pres., Atlanta Branch, NAACP,
1958-59; Civic Leagues: Marietta, Athens, Columbus,
Atlanta, all in Georgia; Elected Bishop May 17, 1964,
A.M.E. Church, 17th Episcopal District; Home: 644
Skipper Drive, N.W., Atlanta, Ga., 30318

BEASLEY, Louis James, b. Florence, Ala., April 18, 1907;
s. Rufus and Mary (Sneed) B.; A.B., Clark Coll., At-
lanta, Ga., 1935; B.D., Gammon Theol. Sem., Atlanta,
Ga., 1936; m. Lauvenia C. Minor; children---George F.,
Louis J. Jr., Sadye M., Winnie C., 1944; pastor, Rush
Memorial Congregational Ch., Atlanta, Ga., 1934-39;
First Congregational Ch., Marietta, Ga., 1936-39; cur-
rent chaplain, US Army: 24th US Infantry Regiment; 9th
US Calvary; 92nd Infantry Div.; Post Chaplain Hq USAG

Ft Devens, Mass; Deputy Chaplain USA COMZEUR (France);
Bronze Star, Purple Heart, Army Commendation with one
oak leaf cluster; Office: Chaplain Division, Hq USACOM-
ZEUR, APO 58, New York, New York

*BEASLEY, Moses W., church official; b. Memphis, Tenn.,
April 16, 1906; s. Moses P. and Irene (Potts) B.; A.B.,
Lane Coll., Jackson, Tenn., 1938; B.D., Howard Univ.
Sch. of Rel., 1941; M.A., New York Univ., Sch. of Ed.;
m. Hattie Mae Walton; children--- Moses, Muriel L.
(Mrs. Julian Bertran), Louise (Mrs. Wm. Steward),
Jacquelyn (Mrs. John Henry), William Nathaniel; asst.
pastor, Mt. Carmel Bapt. Ch., 1939-46; current pastor,
Shiloh Bapt. Ch., Alex., Va., 1948---; pres., Va. State
Bapt. Educational Congress; organizer National State Bapt.
Educational Congress; vice pres., Nat. Bapt. B.T.U. and
S.S. Congress, U.S.A., Inc.; Bd. Mem., Mental Health
Assn., 15 years; Alexandria Branch, 10 years; Third Vice
Moderator, Northern Va. Bapt. Assn; teacher, D.C. Public
Schools, 1950---; Nat. Bapt. S.S. and B.T.U. Congress,
U.S.A., Inc.; Exec. Bd., NAACP, Alexandria; pres.,
Lane Coll. Alumni, Washington, D.C.; Mem., N.E.A.;
D.C.E.A.; Mason; Mu Lambda Chapter of A/A; Republican;
tour leader, Europe and Holy Land; Five years with the
Nat. Negro Opera Company; Home: 647 Franklin St., NE,
Wash., D.C. 20017; office: 1401 Duke St., Alexandria,
Va.

BENNETT, Robert Avon, Jr., b. Baltimore, Md., Jan. 11,
1933; b. Robert Avon (deceased) and Irene (Harris) B.;
1954 B.A. (Phi Beta Kappa), Kenyon College; 1954-55;
Fulbright Fellowship, Univ. Copenhagen, Denmark; 1958,
S.T.B., General Theological Seminary, (N.Y.C.); m.
Patrica Ann (Greig) B.; children: Mark Robert, Ann
Elizabeth; Graduated, General Seminary, 1958; Ordained
Deacon, Episcopal Church, 1958; Priest, 1959; Ass't
Priest, St. James's Episcopal Church, Balt., Md., 1958-
63; Episcopal Chaplain, Morgan State College, 1959-63;
at present, tutor (faculty Ass't) General Theological Sem-
inary, 1963 Episcopal Chaplain, Provident Hospital; Balto,
Md., 1959-63; mem: Christian Social Relations Commis-
sion, Episcopal Diocese of Maryland, 1959-63; Phi Beta
Kappa, Kenyon, College); NAACP.; Episcopal Society for
Cultural & Racial Unity; Home: 175 Ninth Ave., New York,
N.Y., 10011

BENTON, Elijah, b. Mayersville, Miss., Nov. 4, 1896; s.
Lewis and Lubertha (Pitts) B.; B.T.H., Amer. Bapt.
Theol. Sem. & Sch. of Rel., Detroit, Mich., 1947; D.D.
(honorary) Greenville Industrial Coll., Greenville, Miss.,
1959; m. Fannie Howard; Ordained Baptist Minister, 1924;
Pastor, Mt. Zion Bapt. Ch., Toledo, O., 1928--; Mem.
Bd. Dirs., Nat. Bapt. Conv., USA, Inc.; Mem. Coopera-
tive Bd., Nat. SS and BTU Pub. House, Nashville, Tenn.;
Pres., Ohio State Baptist Convention, Inc.; Marr. Coun-
selor; Instr., Ohio Bapt. State Institute; Mem. Bd. of
Community Relations; Sel. Serv. Bd. #8, Toledo, O.;
Vet. World War I (10 mos., France); Mason; Home: 706
O'Brien, Toledo, Ohio 43602; Church: 701 Vance, Toledo,
Ohio.

BIBBONS, Jeffery Clarence, b. New Orleans, La. Dec. 12,
1907; s. Simon and Albertine (Pardo) B; Straight U.
1926-28, Tuskegee, 1929-1930, A.B. Dillard U. 1945-
1949, Certificate, Religious Education, Garrett Theological
Seminary; m. Evelyn Skillings; Children: Jeffreda An-
toinette; Social Worker, 1949-1958, Pastor: 1941-present;
President of Dunbar Community Civic League, 1959 to
present, 33rd degree Mason, member of Democratic
Party, Secretary, Methodist Ministers Alliance; Home:
9014 Palm Street, New Orleans, Louisiana, Office: 2001
Simon Bolivar Ave. New Orleans, La. 70113.

BILLOUPS, Edward Doyle, church official; b. West Baton
Rouge, Dec. 16, 1896; s. Luke and Julia Prince B.;
B. Th., Baton Rouge Coll., 1912; Leland Coll., 1931-
34; D.D. (hon.), Leland Coll., 1947; LL.D. (hon.),
Natchez Coll., 1952; m. Helen Rucker; m. L.E., Mildred
Ceola, Norma; pastor, Second Bapt. Church; New St.
John Bapt. Ch., Baton Rouge, La., 1922---; pres., 4th
District Bapt. Assn, 1946-64; pres., La. Bapt. State Con-
vention, 1949---; pres., Interdenominational Alliance,
Baton Rouge, La., 1948---; pres., Leland Coll. Trustee
Bd., 1951---; Mem., Bi-racial Com. Baton Rouge, La.;
vice pres.-at-large, National Baptist Convention U.S.A.
Inc.; Advisory Bd., Union Theol. Sem., New Orleans,
La., 1953; Advisory Bd., United Theol. Sem., Monroe,
La., 1955; Certificate of Appreciation from Pres. F.D.
Roosevelt, 1942; Mem., NAACP; Mason; Democrat; Home:
1678 79th Ave., Baton Rouge, La.; Office: 908 North 33rd
St., Baton Rouge, La.

*BIRCH, Adolphus Augustus, b. British Honduras, Feb. 28,
1898; s. Joshua and Ella (Franklin) B.; Hampton Coll.,
1919; Bishop Payne Divinity School; B.Th., Howard Univ.;
Va. Theol. Sem.; m. Mary Jefferson; children-- Adolpho,
Kennard. Entered ministry in 1926; pastored Protestant
Episcopal Churches in Virginia, Texas, and Washington,
D.C.; present: rector, St. George's Protestant Episcopal
Ch., Washington, D.C.; pres., Clericus, 1948. Chaplain,
Freedmen's Hosp., Wash., D.C.; former chaplain, Epis-
copal Students, Howard Univ., Alumni award, Sch. of Rel.,
Howard Univ. Republican. Home: 1933 2nd St., N.W.,
Wash. 1, D.C. Office: Second and You Sts., N.W., Wash-
ington, D.C.

BIRCHETTE, John Fletcher, Jr., b. Asheville, N.C., June
4, 1915; s. John Fletcher and Carolyn (Goodrum) B.; A.
B., Morehouse Coll., 1937; Atlanta U., 1938-39; Eckels
Coll. of Mortuary Science, 1946-47; m. Bessie Allen Hurt:
1 son, John Fletcher, III.; Pastored, St. John A. Baptist
Church, Asheville, N.C., 1949-51; Thankful Baptist
Church, Johnson City, Tenn., 1951---; Teacher, Franklin
City., Fla. Pub. Sch., 1939-42; Allen-Birchette Funeral
Home, Asheville, N.C., 1949-63; Birchette Mortuary,
Johnson City, Tenn., 1959--; Mem. Mayor's Adv. Comm.,
Mayor's Comm. on Human Relations; Trustee, Owen Col-
lege; S/Sgt, U.S. Army, 1942-44; Mem. Omega Psi Phi;
Frat. Home: 807 North Boone St., Johnson City, Tenn.
Church: 219 E. Millard St., Johnson City., Tenn.

BIRD, Van Samuel, b. Waycross, Ga., Sept. 6, 1924; A.B.,
Fort Valley State Coll., 1948; B.D., Seabury-Western
Sem., 1951; Diploma, St. Augustine's Coll., Canterbury,
England, 1958; courses: John Hopkins Univ., Summer
1963; m. Eva Ruth Brown; Children-- Amanda D., Van S.
Lesley S. Curate, St. Thomas Episcopal Ch., Phila., Pa.,
1951-53; founder and vicar, Holy Trinity Episc. Ch.,
Baltimore, Md., 1953-present. Omega Psi Phi. Home:
909 N. Bentalou St., Baltimore, Md. Office: Lafayette
& Wheeler Ave., Baltimore, Md.

*BISHOP, Cecil, b. Pittsburg, Pa., May 12, 1930; s. Ross
Mance and Diana Briggs (Wilson) B.; A.B., Knoxville
Coll., Knoxville, Tenn., 1954; Hood Theol. Sem., 1954-
56; B.D., Sch. of Rel., Howard Univ., 1958; S.T.M.,
Wesley Theol. Seminary, 1960; m. Wilhelma Jones. Pastor
Center Grove African Methodist Episcopal Zion Ch.,
Tobaccoville, N.C., 1954-56; asst. Pastor, John Wesley

A. M. E. Zion Ch. , Wash. , D. C. , 1956-58; pastor, Clinton
A. M. E. Zion Ch. , Rockville, Md. , 1958-60; present:
pastor, Trinity A. M. E. Zion Church, Greensboro, N. C. ,
1960-   . Lecturer, Board of Directors, United Southern
Christian Fellowship Foundation, A & T College. Member,
Board of Management, Hayes-Taylor Y. M. C. A. , Greens-
boro, N. C. ; mem. , former pres. , Greensboro Ministers'
Fellowship. Home: 2011 Asheboro St. , Greensboro, N. C.
Office: 445 E. Washington St. , Greensboro, N. C.

BLACKMAN, Herman Elliott-Constantine, b. Bridgetown,
Barbados, T. W. I. , Dec. 25, 1912; s. Joseph Constatine
and Amanda (Barrow) B. ; Barbados & St. Vincent (The
West Indies) London & Oxford Univ. , Bishop Payne
Divinity School, Union Theological Seminary, B. A. , M. A. ;
Post Grad. lectures from Union Theol. Sem. & Virginia
Thel. Sem. ; m. Henrietta Vinton Henry; Since ordination
worked only in the Diocese of Long Island; teacher, Lay
Reader; Deacon, 1949; Priest, 1949; curate, St. Augustine's,
Brooklyn, NY; vicar, St. Martin's, Diocesan Missioner;
rector, St. Stephen's & St. Martin's; Past secy. and vice
pres. , Long Island Clericus; teacher: Dept of Religious &
Psychological Theraphy; The Anglican Society; Dept of
Christian Social Relations in the City of the New York;
Member, Scholarship Examining Board of Gil Hodges
Foundation Inc. ; Academy of Religion and Mental Health;
The Fellowship of the Institute for Religious and Social
Studies; Served for the British forces, 1940-46; Mem. :
Brooklyn Democratic Club, Masonic Lodge & Mechanics
Lodge, Bermuda Benevolent Society, West Indian League,
Dept. for the Racial & Cultural improvement of Minority
Races, Church Historical Society; Nat. Geographical
Society; author: "The Being of God" 1954 Research work
on "Existentialism" by Jean P. Sartre; Editor of the
"Church Steeple" magazine: Home: 541 Franklin Ave. ,
Brooklyn, New York: Off. : 809 Jefferson Ave. , Brooklyn,
New York.

BLAKE, Charles Carols, b. Patterson, Ga. , June 9, 1918;
s. Sam and Emma B. ; A. B. , Morris Brown College,
Atlanta, Ga. ; B. D. , Turner Theo. Seminary, Atlanta,
Ga. ; M. A. , Boston Univ. Sch. of Theology, Boston,
Mass. ; D. D. (hon.), Jackson Theo. Seminary, North
Little Rock, Ark. ; m. Ruth Furgerson; children---Yvonne
Eith, Brenda Joyce, Charles Jr. ; pastor, A. M. E.
Churches, Mass. , New York, Ga. ; current pastor,
Bethel African Methodist Episcopal Church, Richmond

Hill Ave., Stamford, Conn. Civilian Chaplain; Clinical
training of Protestant Council of Churches; Six months
Connecticut State Hospital at Middletown, Conn; Six
months Riverside Hospital New York City; Two years
Resident protestant Chaplain at Riverside Hospital, North
Brother Island for adolescences, drug addicts in New York
City; Mem., Mason, Kappa Alpha Psi, Elks, Connecticut
Council of Churches, pres. of National Alumni Ass'n,
Turner Theo. Seminary; Educational Director of Institute
for the First District of the A. M. E. Church; Director of
Ministerial Institute for the first Episcopal District; Mem.,
Kiwanis Club; Mem., Bd. of Dir., Family & Children
Center, Comm. Civil Rights for the State of Connecticut,
author: "Hand Books For Members of the A. M. E. Church";
Home: 94 Richmond Hill Ave., Stamford, Connecticut; Of-
fice: 150 Fairfield Ave., Stamford, Conn.

BLAKELY, George Wayman, bishop; b. Ashley County, Ark.,
Aug. 30, 1905; s. Richard and Alice B.; A. B., Western
Univ., Quindaro, Kansas, 1924; B. D., Iliff Sch. of Theol.
Denver, Colo., 1928; D. D. (hon.), Payne Theol. Sem.,
Wilberforce, Ohio, 1948; Daniel Payne Coll., Birmingham,
Ala., 1948; Monrovia Coll., Monrovia, Liberia, 1953;
Kittrell Coll., Kittrell, N. C., 1963; m. Annie Marion
King (deceased), Vera Corrine Doyle; children---George
Wayman, Jr., Alyce Vera; pastor, Turner Mission Afri-
can Methodist Episcopal Church, Kansas City, Mo., 1923-
24; Mt. Olive A. M. E. Ch., Sheridan, Wyoming, 1924-25;
Ward Mission A. M. E. Ch., Denver, Colo., 1925-28; Ward
Chapel A. M. E. Ch., Junction City, Kans., 1928-29;
Bethel A. M. E. Ch., Leavenworth, Kans., 1929-30; St.
John A. M. E. Ch., Pine Bluff, Ark., 1930-31; Visitors
Chapel AME Ch., Hot Springs, Ark., 1931-35; Carter
Chapel, Helena, Ark., 1936-37; Big Bethel A. M. E. Ch.,
Little Rock, Ark., 1939-53; St. Paul A. M. E. Ch., St.
Louis, Mo., 1953-1964; presiding elder, Monticello Dist.,
1935-36; Pine 1964, Bluff Dist., 1937-38; Little Rock
Dist., 1938-39; Elected and consecrated Bishop, A. M. E.
Ch., Cincinnati, Ohio, May 17, 1964, 16th Episcopal
Dist. (Carribean - South American Area; delegate, World
Council of Churches, Amsterdam, Holland, 1948; Evanston,
Ill., 1954; fraternal delegate, General Conf., of Meth.
Church, Boston, Mass., 1948; delegate and mem., World
Meth. Council, Oslo, Norway, 1962; Mem., Bd. of Trustee,
Wilberforce Univ., Wilberforce, Ohio; Bd. of Directors,
Douglas Hospital, Kansas City, Kans.; Exec. Com., Seni-
tor Citizens Home, Kansas City, Kans.; pres., Inter-

denominational Ministers Alliance, two terms, Little Rock,
Ark. ; Exec. Committee, Fraternal Council of Churches;
Exec. Com. , Urban League; YMCA: NAACP; Exec. Com. ,
Metropolitan Ch. Federation, St. Louis, Mo. ; Grand Jury,
Pulaski County, Ark. , Being one of the first Negro mem-
bers since reconstruction days; chairman, Citizens Com.
for equalization of salaries of Negro teachers, Pulaski
County, Ark. ; chairman, Committee that organized USO,
YMCA, Little Rock, Ark. ; One of the first Negro mem.
of State Central Com. Republican Party, Ark. ; pres. ,
Interdenominational Alliance; vice pres. , Metropolitan
Church Federation Ministerial Alliance, St. Louis, Mo. ;
representative, Interdenominational Alliance, March on
Washington; Mem. , Mason; Kappa Alpha Psi; Home: 4940
Northland Place, St. Louis, Mo.

BLAKEY, Durocher Lon, publisher; b. Macon City, Ala. ;
June 14, 1909; s. Frank Robert Blakey and Watty Ann
(Walker) B. ; A. B. , Livingstone College, Salisbury, N. C. ,
1947; Johnson C. Smith University (Summers) 1945, 1946;
further study at Miles College, Birmingham, Ala. , 1955;
Hood Theological Seminary, 1947-50; 1952-53; B. D. ,
Southeastern Baptist Theological Seminary, Forest, N. C. ,
1961-63; m. Etta Florine Carter; pastor, North Alabama,
Western North Carolina, Georgia, Arkansas, and North
Carolina Conference of the A. M. E. Zion Church, current,
General manager, African Methodist Episcopal Zion Church,
Publishing House, Charlotte, N. C. , 1963---; Pastoral
counseling, St. John A. M. E. Zion Church; teacher, Walter
Southland Institute, Lexa, Ark. , 1950, 51 and Public
School Systems in Fayette, Ala. , 1958-60; Nash and Edge-
combe counties, N. C. , 1963-64; Mem. ; Elks, Masons,
Knights of Pythians; Rocky Mount Voters and Improvement
League, Rocky Mount Ministers' Fellowship, N. C. Council
on Human Relations, N. C. Joint Council on Health and
Citizenship, Southern Christian Leadership Conference,
NAACP, YMCA, YWCA, Pres. Livingstone College
Alumni Assoc. of Rocky Mt. , N. C. ; Citizenship award by
the Alpha Omicron Chapter, Fraternity, 1963; Home: 908
Leggett Road, Rocky Mount, N. C. ; Office: St. John A. M.
E. Zion Church, Rocky Mount, N. C.

BLASSINGAME, James Matthew, b. Anderson County, S. C. ,
Jan. 13, 1913; s. Moses and Maggie B. ; Paine Coll. ,
1935-36; Benedict Theological Seminary, Columbia, S. C. ,
1941-43; B. D. , Virginia Theol. Sem. , 1945; m. Hester
Lee Thompson. Pastor, Christian Methodist Episcopal

Chs., South Carolina, Virginia, N. Carolina; present:
pastor, Beebe Mem., Episcopal Church, Wash., N.
Carolina. Former instructor, Christian Institute, Winston-
Salem, N.C.; chairman, Committee on Admissions, C.
M.E. Ch. President, N.A.A.C.P. (Polk County, N.C.),
3 years; Interdenominational Ministers Alliance; council-
man, scoutmaster; executive board, Washington United
Fund, N. Carolina. Office: P.O. Box 300, Washington, N.
Carolina.

BODLEY, Simon, Jr., b. Camden, Ala., June 5, 1932; s.
Simon and Bella (Ethridge); Concordia Lutheran College,
Forth Wayne; Immanuel Lutheran Seminary; m. Jemima
Sessons; children---Chenita Maria, Simon Lemoyre, Kelvin
Derell missionary at large, 1957-60; pastor, Alabama Vic-
tory Lutheran Church, Youngstown, Ohio, 1960---; Home:
350 Falls Ave., Youngstown, Ohio; Ch.: Victory Lutheran
Ch., 336 Blender, Youngstown, Ohio.

BOHLER, Lewis Penrose, Jr., b. Augusta, Ga., Nov. 28;
s. Lewis P., Sr. and Margie A. (Fisher) B.; Hampton
Institute, 1944-46; W. Va. State Coll., 1949-51, A.B.;
B.D., Oberlin School of Theology; Kenyon Coll.; m.
Gloria Elizabeth Jackson; children---Carmen LeJeune,
Stephen Craig; pastor, St. Augustine's Episcopal Ch.,
Youngstown, Ohio, 1955-61; current rector, Episcopal
Church of the Advent, Los Angeles, Calif., 1961---; con-
sultant, Psychology of Race Relations, Episcopal Diocese
of Los Angeles; vice pres., Wilshire Community Coordinat-
ing Council; Mem., NAACP; Urban League; USO; Com. on
Human Relations; US Air Force, 1946-49; Good Conduct
Medal; Marksman; Soldier of Year; Mem., P.T.A.; Ex-
Disc Jockey; Ex-Boxer; Republican; Appears frequently
on TV and Radio; Home: 1739 Buckingham Pl., Los
Angeles 19, Calif.; Office: 4976 W. Adam's Blvd., Los
Angeles, Calif. 90016

BOLINGS, Blaine Arlington, b. Esmont, Va., June 13, 1919;
s. Joseph F. and Mamie (Wagner) B.; Wiley College,
1950-53; m. Edith Joseph; 5 sons, Blaine Jr., Lemie,
Beryl, Joseph, David; 3 daus., Mamie, Sheryl, Maude;
Pastored Anahuae Circuit, Anahuae, Texas, 9 years.
Marshal Circuit, Marshall, Texas, 3 years; mem. P.T.A.;
Boy Scouts; Military service, 1941-45; P.O. Box 483,
Anahuae, Texas.

BONNER, Isaiah Hamilton, bishop; b. Camden, Ala., July
27, 1890; s. Richard and Prescilla B.; A. B., Knoxville
Coll., 1912; B. D., 1914; D. D. (hon.), Payne Coll.,
1942; m. Nannie Jones; children---Isaiah Hamilton Jr.,
Helen Maric; Samuel; pastor, African Methodist Episcopal
Churches in Uniontown, Mobile, Dothan, Montgomery,
Selma, Ala.; presiding elder, Montgomery Dist., 1937;
Elected bishop, 1948; current, presiding bishop 9th Dist.;
Trustee, Daniel Payne Coll., 1929---; chairman, Mis-
sionary Bd., A. M. E. Church, 1952-56; Mem., Civil
League, Montgomery, Ala.; pres., State Interdenomina-
tional Alliance, 3 years; sec., Bishops' Council, A. M. E.
Church, 1960; pres., Bishops' Council, 1961; Home:
1721 Sylvan St., Selma, Ala.

*BOOKER, Merrel Daniel, b. July 9, 1908; A. B., Howard
Univ.,; B. D., Howard Univ. Sch. of Rel.; Union Theol.
Sem., New York; New York School of Social Work; Wash-
ington School of Psychiatry; Boston Univ., S. T. M.; Insti-
tute of Pastoral Care, Mass. General Hospital, Boston,
Mass.; Pastoral Clinical Training: Mass. Memorial Hos-
pital; Charlestown State Hospital for the Mentally Ill, Nor-
ristown, Pa.; Bellevue Hospital, New York; Gallinger
Municipal Hospital, Wash., D. C.; m. Erma E.; children---
Merrel, Sue; pastor, Fountain Bapt. Ch., Summit, N. J.
6 1/2 years; dean of men, Talladega Coll., Talladega,
Ala.; staff member, Washington Federation of Churches,
Wash., D. C.; resident chaplain, Freedmen's Hospital,
Wash., D. C.; Federal Correctional Institution, Chillicothe,
Ohio; chairman, Division of Religion, Bishop Coll., Mar-
shall, Tex.; pastor, New Hope Bapt. Ch., Dallas, Tex.,
1952-56; pastor, St. Timothy's Community Ch., Gary,
Indiana, 1956---; feature writer, Informer Chain of News-
papers, Minister Speaks His Mind; mission magazine,
International Pulpit and Parsonage Exchange; Home: 7007
So Creiger St., Chicago, Ill.

BOONE, Theodore Sylvester, educator, author; b. Winchester,
Texas, Dec. 28, 1896; s. Alexander Lorenzo and Ida
(Chaney) B.; A. B., Des Moines Coll., 1918; B. A.,
Sioux Falls Coll., 1918; LL. B., Chgo. Law Sch., 1922;
A. M. Arkansas Bapt. Coll., 1924; Other schools and
colleges, Prairie View, 1915; Bishop Coll., 1915-17;
U. of Iowa, 1918-20; U. of Chgo., 1920-21; Perfect
Voice Inst., Chg., Ill., 1929; Houston Coll., 1930 LL. D.
(honorary); Moody Bible Inst., Chgo., 1930; U. of Mich.,
1949-50; m. Ruby Beatrice Alexander; Pastor, 8th St.

Bapt. Ch., Temple, Texas, 1924-31; Mt. Gilead Bapt.
Ch., Fort Worth, Texas, 1931-36; Greater Mt. Gilead
Bapt. Ch., 1936-44; King Solomon Miss. Bapt. Ch., Det.,
Mich., 1944---; Lecturer, Bishop Coll., 1938-45; Spec.
Instr., Southwestern Bapt. Theol. Sem., 1941-43; Lec.,
Instr., Nat. S. S. & B. T. U. Cong., 1921-62; Progressive
Nat. SS & BTU Cong. Inst., 1963--; Dean, Okla. Sch.
of Rel. 1943-44; Instr. Negro Hist. Lexington U., 1943-
44; Dir. Historical Commission and Historiographer, Nat.
Bapt. Conv., USA, Inc., 1939-53; Pres., Ft. Worth Sch.
of Rel., 1933-36; Bible Instr., I. M. Terrell High Sch.,
1937-38; Editor, Western Star, Bapt. Miss. & Edu. Conv.,
Texas; Fort Worth Light; Open Door, Women's Aux.,
B. M. & E. Conv., Texas; Flaming Sword; Practiced law,
Indianapolis, Ind., 1922-24; 1st. Pres., Corpus Juris
Club; Recipient, Most Famous Negro Citizen Award, Fort
Worth, 1933; Distinguished Service Plaque, Citizen's
Comm., Detroit, Mich; Alumni Plaque, Bishop College,
1963; mem. Knights of Pythian, Odd Fellows, United
Brothers of Friendship, Elks, Masons, Kappa Alpha Psi,
Author: The Philosophy of Booker T. Washington, Racial
Development, Baptists, Know Yourselves and Others,
What Baptist Should Know and Do, and many others books;
Home: 590 E. Boston Blvd., Detroit, Mich. Church: 6125
Fourteenth St., Detroit 8, Mich.

*BOOTH, Lavaughn Venchael, b. Collins, Miss., Jan. 7,
1919; s. Frederick D. and Manie (Powell) B.; A. B.,
Alcorn A & M Coll., Miss., 1940; B. D., Howard Univ.,
Sch. of Rel., 1943; L. H. D., (Hon.), Wilberforce Univ.,
1963; m. Georgia Anna Morris; children-- Lavaughn V.,
Jr., William D., Anna M., Paul M., Georgia A.; Pas-
tored: First Baptist Ch., Warrenton, Va., 1942-43; First
Bapt. Ch., Gary, Indiana, 1944-52; present: Zion Bapt.
Ch., Cincinnati, 1952-   ; lecturer, Nat'l Bapt. Conv.
Inc., Women's Aux., 1946-62; founder, Nat'l Prayer League,
Inc.; founder, and Ex. Sec. Progressive Nat'l Bapt. Conv. Inc.
Author: Showers of Blessing (book of sermons), and several
songs, including Brothers Joined In Heart (1960) And You Need
Not Walk Alone (1963). Editor, Who's Who in Baptist America,
1960; Protestant Scout Committee; Citizens' Committee on
Youth; Committee of Management, Y. M. C. A., Republican.
Master's Thesis - Christian Philanthrophy and the Uplift of the
Negro in the South, 1865-1900. Home: 3415 Dury Ave., Cin-
cinnati 29, Ohio. Office: 630 Glenwood Ave., Cincinnati 29,
Ohio.

BORDERS, William Holmes, educator; b. Bibb County, Ga.
Feb. 24, 1905; s. James B. and Leila (Birdsong) B.;
A.B., Morehouse Coll., 1929; B.D., Garret Theol. Sem.,
1932; M.A., Chgo. U., 1936; Honorary degrees: D.D.,
Morris Brown Coll., 1940; Shaw U., 1942; Gammon Theol.
Sem., 1947; L.H.D., Wilberforce U., 1962; M. Julia
Pate; 1 son, William Holmes, Jr.; 1 dau., Mrs. Juel
Borders Benson; Pastor, 2nd Bapt. Ch., Evanston, Ill.,
1937; Wheat Street Bapt. Ch., Atlanta, Ga., 1937---;
Prof., Psych., Morehouse Coll., 1937-39; Active Y.M.
C.A. worker; Recipient, Omega Psi Phi Frat., Man of
The Year Award, 1950; Phi Beta Sigma Frat., Social
Action Achievement Award, 1949; Nat. S.S. and B.T.U.
Award, 1955; mem. Masons, Prog. Nat. Bapt. Conv.,
Bapt. World Alliance, NAACP (life), Kappa Alpha Psi
Frat.; Author: Follow Me, 7 Minutes at the Mike in the
Deep South, Thunderbolts (religious poems) "I'm Some-
body!", Men Must Live As Brothers, and others; Home:
1426 Mozley Drive, S.W., Atlanta, Ga., 30314. Church:
18 Yonge Street, N.E., Atlanta, Ga. 30312.

BOTTOMS, Lawrence Wendell, church official, b. Selma,
Alabama, April 9, 1908; s. Wilbur McDonald and Gussie
Adolphus (Shivers) B.; A.B., Geneva College, Beaver
Falls, Pa.; B.D., The Reformed Presbyterian Sem.,
Pittsburgh, Pa; further study: Atlanta Univ.; m. Elizabeth
Loutisha Stallworth; children---Lawrence Wendell, Jr.,
Jean (Mrs. Julian Perry), Letisha (Mrs. DeWitt Alfred),
Janice; Ordained by Presbytery of Illinois, Ref. Presby.
Ch., Nov. 18, 1936; pastor, Reformed Presbyterian
Church, Selma; Received into Presbyterian, U.S., Church,
1938; pastor, Grace Presbyterian Ch., Louisville, Ky.,
1938-49; While serving Grace Church, served as part
time Regional Director, Christian Education, Snedecor
Memorial Synod, Presbyterian, U.S., 1938-49; Served as
full time Director, 1949-51; Asst. Sec., Division of Negro
Work, Presbyterian, Director, 1949-51; Asst. Sec., Divi-
sion of Negro Work, Presbyterian, U.S., Board of Church
Extention, 1951-52; sec. in full time, 1953---; asst. sec.,
Division of Home Missions, Board of Ch. Extention
Presbyterian Church, U.S.; Mem., The Council of
Churches, Louisville, Ky.; Mem., Bd. of Christian Edu-
cation and Bd. of World Missions; Mem., The Commis-
sion on Missionary Education of the National Council of
Churches; moderator, Synod of Kentucky, 1962-63; As-
sociate editor, Presbyterian Outlook; 1960 Distinguished
Service Award from Geneva College, Beaver Falls, Pa.;

author: "The Policies and Rationale Underlining the Support of Negro College and Schools maintained by the
Presbyterian Church in the United States. " Home: 182
Chicamauga Place, S. W. Atlanta 14, Georgia; Office:
341 Ponce de Leon Ave. , N Atlanta 8, Georgia.

BOURNE, Charles Nathaniel, b. Cambridge, Mass. , Dec.
7, 1918; s. Joseph T. and Beatrice (Wilson) B. ; Eastern
Nazarene Coll. , 1948-52; A. B. , Wollaston, Mass. ; S.
T. B. , Boston Univ. Sch. of Theology, Boston, Mass. ,
1952-55; D. D. (Hon.), Kittrell Coll. , N. C. , 1957;
m. Marjorie Earmine Burke; children---Charlene,
Carmella, Charles, Jr. ; passt. pastor, St. Paul A. M. E. ,
Church, Cambridge, Mass. , 1946-48; pastor, St. James
A. M. E. Church, Jamestown, Rhode Island, 1948-50;
pastor, Bethel African Methodist Episcopal Church, Ply-
mouth, Mass. , 1950-52; pastor, Bethel A. M. E. Church,
Lynn, Mass. , 1952-55; pastor, Bethel A. M. E. Church,
Cambridge, Md. , 1955---; US Army and European
Theater, 1942-46; Member Bi-Racial Commission, City
of Cambridge, 1960-62; Vice Pres. , Dorchester County
Inter-racial Minister's Ass'n, 1960-62; Exec. Board,
Dorchester County NAACP, 1960---; Substitute teacher,
Cambridge Md. , Elementary Schools; Member, Mason;
Special articles to A. M. E. Church Review; Home: 621
Pine St. , Cambridge, Dorchester Co. , Md. ; Office:
Bethel A. M. E. Church, 623 Pine St. , Cambridge, Dor-
chester, Co. , Maryland.

BOWEN, Kenneth Athelston, educator; b. Boston, Mass. ,
Jan. 2, 1922; s. Rufus Wm. and Martha (Payne) B. ;
B. A. , Gordon Coll. , Beverly Farms, Mass. , 1949;
B. D. , Andover-Newton Theol Sem. , Newton Mass. ,
1952; m. Sylvia Glendora Clark; 1 son Kenneth A. , Jr. ,
2 daus. Yvonne A. , Elaine L. ; 1st Bapt. Ch. , Saugua,
Massa. , 1946-49; Messiah Bapt. Ch. , Brockton, Mass. ,
1949-52; Exec. Dir. Hickory St. Christian Educ. Center,
Buffalo, N. Y. , 1953-58; Pastor, Mount Moriah Bapt.
Ch. , Milwaukee, Wis. , 1958--; Eng. Instr. , 1st Negro
faculty mem. , Seneca High, Buffalo, N. Y. ; Pres. , Buf-
falo Br. NAACP, 1953-55; Recipient, Mayor's Annual
Award, Outstanding Community Serv. , Buffalo, N. Y. ,
1955 mem. , City of Milwaukee Bd. of Review, Cty.
Milwaukee, Comm. on Human Relations (Chrmn. Prog.
Planning Comm.); Comm. on Evangelism, Council of
Churches; Near Northside Non-Partisan Conf. , North-
side Inventory Conference Housing Committee: (Life)

NAACP; Frontiers International; Thi Beta Sigma Frat.;
Faculty mem., Nat. Bapt. SS & BTU Cong. and Nat.
Laymen's Conv.; Ch. Editor, Milwaukee Star. Church:
2747 N. 4th St., Milwaukee, Wisc.

BOWIE, Harry John, chaplain; b. Long Branch, New Jersey,
Nov. 12, 1935; s. Walter William and Esther (Lester)
B.; B.A., Hobart College, 1954-58; S.T.B., The General Theological Seminary, 1958-61; present rector,
Chapel of the Annunciation, Lawnside, New Jersey,
1961---; St. John's Episcopal Church, Camden, New
Jersey, 1961---; Episcopal Chaplain-Camden Hospitals,
1961-62; N.J. State School for the Mentally Retarded,
1962---; Mem.: Planning Board Borough of Lawnside,
1962; Phi Beta Kappa; Lawnside Jaycees; Home: 16
Warwick Road, Lawnside, New Jersey.

BOYD, Braxton Julian, teacher; b. Princeton, Kentucky,
Jan. 21, 1921; s. Hugh Lee and Margaret (Duke) B.;
A.B., Garrett Biblical Institute, 1942; B.D., St. Paul
Methodist Seminary, 1947; further study, Northwestern
Univ., 1962-63; m. Dorothy Harrison; children---
Kaaren, Braxton II, Thurston, James. Pastor, Christian
Methodist Episcopal Churches in Arkansas, Texas,
Michigan, Illinois, Missouri, and District of Columbia,
1948-64; present: pastor, Israel Metropolitan C.M.E.
Church, Washington, D.C. Teacher, Walker High School,
Magnolia, Arkansas; Flint, Michigan; Decatur, Illinois.
U.S. Navy - World War II. Member, Omega Psi Phi;
Mason; State's chairman, Columbia Democratic Voters
League, 1948-50; secretary, Voters Registration 1948-50;
youth council advisor, K.C., Mo.; N.A.A.C.P. Advisory
Council, K.C., Mo.; member, American Civil Liberties
Union, K.C., Mo. and POAU. Home: 632 Randolph St.,
N.W., Washington, D.C. Office: 557 Randolph St., N.
W., Washington, D.C.

BRADFORD, Charles Edward, Church official; b. Washing-
ton, D.C., July 12, 1925; s. Robert Lee and Etta
Elizabeth (Littlejohn) B.; Oakwood College, Huntsville,
Ala., 1946; special course, S.D.A. Theological Seminary;
m. Ethel Lee McKenzie; children-Sharon, Charles, Jr.,
Dwight. Pastor: New Orleans, La., 1946; Berean S.D.A.
Church, Baton Rouge, La., 1946-51; Oakland Ave., S.
D.A. Church, Dallas, Texas, 1951-52; Berean S.D.A.
Church, St. Louis, Mo., 1953-57. Secretary, Home
Missionary Department for Central States Conf. of S.D.

A., Kansas City, Mo., 1952-53; secretary, Home Missionary Department Northeastern Conf. and pastor of the
City Tabernacle S.D.A. Church, New York City, 1957-
61; president, Lake Region Conf., Chicago, Ill., 1961- .
Member: Lake Union Conf. executive committee; Andrews
Univ. Board; Oakwood College Board, Review and Herald
Publishing Association Board, Washington, D.C.: Hinsdale Hospital Board, Hinsdale, Ill.; Riverside Hospital
Board, Nashville, Tenn. Contributing editor, The Message Magazine, Nashville, Tenn.; contributed article to
the S.D.A. Encyclopedia on History of the Lake Region
Conf. of S.D.A. Home: 8560 S. Kenwood St., Chicago,
Ill. Office: 8517 S. State St., Chicago, Ill.

BRADFORD, Ernest Marvin, b. East St. Louis, Ill., April
21, 1927; s. Shelby and Leora (Barnes) B.; B.A.,
Morehouse Coll., 1952; B.D., Morehouse Coll. Sch. of
Rel., 1958; m. Adnee Marie Byrom; children---Althea
Bettye, Aleta Marie (Twins); pastor, Mt. Pisgah Presbyterian Church, U.S.A., Hartsville, S.C., 1960-62;
current pastor, Northern Heights Presbyterian Church,
Selma, Ala., 1962---; Mem., County Improvement Assn;
US Army Chaplain Asst., 1946-47; Home: 1571 Range
St., Selma, Ala.; Office: 1575 Range St., Selma, Ala.

BRADLEY, David H., editor, college prof.; b. Franklin,
Pa., Sept. 20, 1905; s. Daniel F. and Cora A. (Brewer)
B.; A.B., Livingstone College, 1929; A.M., University
of Pittsburgh, 1932; Graduate course: New York University, 1940-42; m. Harriette Marie Jackson; children---
Laverne Findlay (Mrs. George), David, Jr.; pastor,
Mercer, Pa. West Bridgewater, Pa. Bellevue, Pa.,
Altoona, Pa.; Professor of History, Livingstone College,
1933-35; pastor, Ridgewood, N.J., 1935-49; current editor, A.M.E. Zion Quarterly Review, 1948; Sec., A.M.
E. Zion Historical Society, 1956---; Conference director,
Christian Education, N.J., 1936-48; Denominational Director Ministers Institutes, 1938-55; Asst. Sec., Christian and Leadership Education Schools, 1949-55; Bergen
Co. T.B. Society; National Council of Churches Comm.
on Ed. Evangelism, Home Missions; Ad. and Leadership;
Mem.: Methodist Historical Society; Phi Beta Sigma
Mason, Republican, author The Federal Elections Bill
of 1890 (1932); History of the A.M.E. Zion Church,
(1956), Contributor, Dictionary of Christian Education,
by Cully, 1964; Home: P.O. Box 146, Bedford, Pa.

*BRADLEY, Fulton Obadiah, coll. prof.; b. Bishopville,
S. C., Dec. 23, 1926; s. Henry Herbert and Florence
(Ruth) B.; m. Lettie Myrtle Powell; children---Fulton
Adrian, Raymond Arnold; B. A., Morehouse Coll.,
Atlanta, Ga., 1947; B. D., Howard Univ. Sch. of Rel.,
Wash., D. C., 1950; M. A., Howard Univ. Sch. of Rel.,
1957; Further study: American Univ., Wash., D. C.;
Student Interm Pastor, Friendship Baptist Church, New
York City, N. Y., 1950; pastor, First Institutional Baptist
Church, Winston-Salem, 1951-54; First Baptist Church,
West Wash., D. C., 1954-62; dean, Dept. of Theology,
Va. Union Theol. Sem. and Coll., Lynchburg, Va.,
1950-51; dean, Baptist Ed. Congress, D. C.; faculty
mem., National Baptist Sunday School and Baptist Train-
ing Union Congress, National Baptist Convention, USA,
Inc., 1956; instructor, Howard Univ., Sch. of Rel.,
Wash., D. C. 1958-62; Former Mem., Board of Re-
ligious education, National Baptist Convention, USA,
Inc.; Board of Trustees, Stoddard Home, Wash., D. C.;
current mem., Religious Education Ass'n of US and
Canada; Mem., Ministerial Advisory Comm., Planned
Parenthood Ass'n of Detroit; Metropolitan Dist. Ass'n;
Wolverine State Baptist Convention; Booker T. Washing-
ton Business Ass'n; Baptist Ministers' Conference of
Detroit and Vicinity; Metropolitan YMCA, Fisher Branch;
Detroit Council of Churches; Pastors' Union, Evangelism
Comm., Detroit Council of Churches; Interdenominational
Ministerial Alliance, Detroit; Comm. of Management,
Fisher YMCA; co-chairman, Membership Campaign,
Fisher Branch, YMCA; contributing editor, Baptist
Teacher, Sunday School Publishing Board, National Baptist
Convention, USA, Inc., Nashville, Tenn.; Institute of
Rel., Howard Univ. Sch. of Rel., Wash., D. C., Fron-
tiers International; Home: 3814 Leslie St., Detroit 38,
Mich.; Office: 6125 Beechwood St., Detroit 10, Mich.

*BRADY, Crawford Wm. b. Milwaukee, Wis., Feb. 15,
1924; s. William and Sedalia Lovings (Trent) B.; Religion
Training Institute, Columbus, Ohio, 1947; B. S., Mar-
quette Univ., Milwaukee, 1954; B. D., Howard Univ. Sch.
of Rel., 1955-58; m. Well Harper; children---Clifford,
William; pastor, Walls Memorial A. M. E. Zion Church,
Toledo, 1961-62; St. Paul's African Methodist Episcopal
Zion Church, Blairsville, Pa., 1962-64; Aide to Congressman, 84th Congress; editor: Milwaukee Defender, 1951-
55; US Air Forces, 1943-45; Writer's Award, 1954
(Defender); Mem., Alpha; Home: 5423 13th St., NW,

Wash., D. C.

BRANCH, George Murray, clergyman, sem. prof. and
dir., b. Prince Edward Co., Va., April 18, 1914; s.
George McGuffie and Annie Pearl (Clark) B.; B.S.,
Virginia Union Univ., 1938; B.D., Andover Newton
Theol. Sch., 1944; M.A., Drew Univ., 1946; courses:
Hebrew Union Coll., 1952; Drew Univ., 1952-53; 1962-63;
m. Jamima Wall; children--- Dianne Everett; pastor,
Peoples Bapt. Ch., Portsmouth, N.H., 1940-41; First
Bapt. Ch., Madison, N.J., 1941-44; field sec., National
Student Council of YMCA, Southern Area, 1944-47; asst.
prof., Morehouse Coll., Atlanta, Ga., 1947-56; asso.
prof., 1956-59; current asso. prof., Interdenominational
Theol. Center, Atlanta, Ga., 1959---; director, More-
house Sch. of Religion in I.T.C., 1963---; Mem.,
Campus Work Com., Southern Area Council of YMCA,
1947-60; Advisory Com., West Side Branch, Butler St.
YMCA, 1963---; Advisory Com., Area I, Atlanta Public
Sch., 1955-56; Bd. of Directors, Atlanta Branch, Amer-
ican Civil Liberties Union, 1964---; Mem., American
Academy of Religion, Society of Biblical Literature and
Exergesis, American Sch. of Oriental Research, Society
for the Scientific Study of Religion, Howard Univ. In-
stitute of Religion, American Assn of Univ. Prof.,
Society for Religion in Higher Education, Kappa Alpha
Psi; Home: 841 Fair St., SW, Atlanta, Ga. 30314; Of-
fice: 645 Beckwith St., SW, Atlanta, Ga. 30314

*BRANTFORD, Gerald Henry; b. Lorain, Ohio, Dec. 28,
1919; s. Ernest and Mary (Perkins) B.; A.B., Western
Reserve Univ., Cleveland, Ohio, 1949; B.D., Howard
Univ. Sch. of Rel., 1953; m. Georgene Sweatt; children
--- David Alan;assoc. pastor, Asbury Meth. Ch., 1953-
55; director, Wesley Foundation, Howard Univ., 1955-
57; pastor, St. James Meth. Ch., Milwaukee, 1957-62;
Exec. sec., Lexington Conf., Bd. of Ed., The Meth.
Ch., 1962-64; pastor, Ingleside-Whitfield Meth. Ch.,
Chicago, Ill., 1964---; former mem., Exec. Bd.,
NAACP, Milwaukee; Milwaukee Commission on Human
Rights; Home: 924 East 76th St., Chicago, Ill. 60619:
Office: 929 East 76th St., Chicago, Ill. 60619

BREEDING, M.L., Miles Coll., Ala.; Paine Coll., Ga.;
Howard Univ. Sch. of Rel.; pastor, Christian Methodist
Episcopal Churches, Wash., D.C., Chicago, Pittsburgh,
Asheville, N.C., Dayton and Cleveland, Ohio and Indiana;

currently, General Sec., Bd. of Missions of the Christian Meth. Episcopal Churches (Home and International
Missions); Mem., Com. on Cooperation and Council
between the Meth. Ch. and the C. M. E. Ch.; Mem.,
General Com. on Chaplains and Armed Forces Personnel; Mem., Mason; Office: 307 Berkeley Rd., Indianapolis 8, Ind.

BREWER, Harold Cole; b. Kansas City, Missouri; s. John
Cole and Evelyn B. (Wright) B.; B. A. Oakwood College,
Union College, 1957; M. A., Andrews Univ., 1958; m.
Gaynell Tyler B.; daughter - Deanne M.; pastor-evange-
list, Central States Conference of Seventh-Day Adventist;
pastored: Pueblo, Colo., 1958; St. Joseph, Mo. and
Leavenworth, Kansas, 1959; St. Joseph, Mo., 1959-62;
Atchinson, Kansas, 1959-63; present:pastor, Topeka,
Kansas Seventh-Day Adventist Church, 1962- . Member:
American Temperance Society, N. A. A. C. P., Ministerial
Association. Home: 3304 Colfax Street, Topeka, Kansas.
Office: 954 College Street, Topeka, Kansas.

BRIGHT, John Douglas, bishop, Americus, Ga., Oct. 11,
1917; s. Turner and Estella (Williams) B., A. B. Wilberforce (O.) U., Th. B., Payne Seminary, 1942; honorary
degrees-- Daniel Payne, Allen U., and Wilberforce U.;
m. Vida M. -   ; children - John Jr. and Gwendolyn;
pastor, A. M. E. Churches, South Charlston, Ohio Ch.,
1937-38; Wayman Ch., Hillsboro, Ohio, 1938-40; Wayman Ch., Bainbridge, O., 1938-40, Shorter Chapel,
Greenfield, O., 1940, Lee Chapel, Cincinnati, O.,
1940-42, St. Paul Ch., Lima, O., 1942-43, Bethel Ch.,
Pittsburgh, 1943; elected bishop African Methodist Episcopal Church, May 1960, Los Angeles, Calif.; first as-
signm. as bishop was to Central Africa, 1960-1962;
12th Episcopal Dist. comprising Arkansas and Oklahoma,
1962-64; 1st Episcopal Dist., May 1964- ; Member of
the World Council of Churches, the World Conf. of
Methodism, Nat. Council of Churches, Mason, Elks, NAACP;
published articles in Southern Christian Recorder, Pittsburg,
Courier. Home or Office: 6608 Lincoln Drive, Philadelphia, Pa.

BRIGHTMAN, Edward Scipio, b. Charleston, S. C., Jan.
26, 1914; s. Peter Jackson and Katie (Johnson) B.;
B. A., College of the City of New York, 1949; B. D.,
Virginia Episcopal Theological Seminary, Alexandria,
Va., 1957; m. Lucy Frasier; children--- Laura,
Edwina, Edward, Jr., John, Samuel, James. Assistant

in charge, St. Philip's Episcopal Ch. , Brooklyn, N.Y. ,
1952-53; Priest in charge: St. Simon's Episc. Ch. ,
Springfield, Mass. , 1953-55; Christ Episc. Ch. , Hailfax,
Va. , 1955-57; St. Thomas Episc. , Ch. , Tulsa, Okla. ,
1957-61; curate, All Saints Episc. Ch. , St. Louis, Mo. ,
1961-63; rector, St. Philip Episc. Ch. , 1963-present.
Home: 2009 Locust St. , Omaha, Nebraska. office: 2532
Binney St. , Omaha, Nebr.

BRONSON, Oswald Perry, sem. prof. ; b. Sanford, Florida,
July 19, 1927; s. Uriah Perry and Flora (Hollinshed)
B. ; B.S. , Bethune Cookman Coll. , 1950; B.D. , Gam-
mon Theol. Sem. , 1959; Ph.D. courses: Northwestern
Univ. ; m. Helen Carolyn Williams; children---Josephine
Suzette, Flora Helen, Oswald Perry, Jr. ; pastor, The
Methodist Churches: St. Joseph, Deland, Fla. , 1948-50;
St. John, Ft. Pierce, Fla. , 1948-50; Keeney Chapel,
Tempa, Fla. , 1952-53; Rocky Ford Circuit, Rocky Ford,
Ga. , 1955-59; Jesup-Baxley Circuit, Ga. , 1959-60;
Church of the Redeemer, and Ingleside-Whitfield Meth. ;
1960-1964; current Director of Field Education & As-
sociate Professor of Christian Education at Interdenomina-
tional Theol. Center, Atlanta, Ga. ; Rehabilitation worker,
Fla. State Tuberculosis Rehabilitation Center, Marianna,
Fla. ; chaplain, Southwest State Tuberculosis Hospital,
Tampa, Fla. , 1952-53; Mem. , Alpha Kappa Mu Honor
Society; Home: 9 McDonough Blvd. , Atlanta, Ga. 30315;
Office: 671 Beckwith St. , Atlanta, Ga. 30314

BROOKINS, Houston Daniel, b. Yazoo County, Miss. , July
24, 1910; s. J.A. and Georgia Ann B. ; A.B. , Alcorn
Coll. , Miss. , 1932; M.R.E. , Tuskegee Inst. , Ala. , 1934;
m. Maggie Wade; Ordained Deacon African Methodist
Episcopalian Ch. , 1934; Ordained Elder, A.M.E. Ch. ,
1936; pastored in Oklahoma and Arkansas, the following
churches: St. Paul A.M.E. Ch. , Dover, Okla. , 1935-
36; Allen Temple A.M.E. Ch. , 1936-41; St. Paul A.M.
E. Ch. , Arkadelphia, Ark. , 1941-46; St. Luke Forrest
City, 1946-48; Carter Chapel Helena, Ark. , 1948-52;
Bethel A.M.E. Stuttgart, Ark. , 1952-56; Gates Chapel,
1964---; Most valuable citizens award, Crossett, Ala. ,
1960; pres. , Negro group for civil rights, Crossett;
Mem. , P.T.A. ,; Democrat; Trustee Mem. , Shorter
Coll. , North Little Rock, Ark. ; Hon. Mem. , City
Council, Crossett, Ala. ; Mem. , NAACP; Home: 400
N. Alabama St. , Crossett, Ark. 71635; Office: 305
West Third Ave. , Crossett, Arkansas 71635

BROOKS, Charles DeCatur, Church official; b. Greensboro,
North Carolina, July 24, 1930; s. Marvin B. and Mattie
(Reaves) B.; B.A., Oakwood College, 1951; m. Walter-
ene L. Wagner; children--- Diedra Yvonne, Charles
DeCatur, Jr. Pastored Seventh-Day Adventist Churches:
Wilmington, Delaware, 1951-52; Chester, Pa., 1951-53;
Camden, N.J., 1953-56; Columbus, Ohio, 1956-1960;
Cleveland, Ohio, 1960-63; present: secretary and
revivalist, Columbia Union Conf. of Seventh-Day Adven-
tists, 1963-   . Member, Pine Forge Institute Board,
1960-63 and Executive Committee, Columbia Union Conf.,
1963-present. Home: 1728 Varnum St., N.W., Washington, D.C. Office: 7710 Carroll Ave., N.W., Takoma
Park 12, D.C.

BROOKS, David Henry, chaplain; b. Decatur, Georgia, Dec.
6, 1908; s. Joseph Wood and Fort Sumter (Smith) B.;
Morehouse College, 1927-30; Virginia State College,
1945-47; Bishop Payne Divinity School, 1944-47; B.D.,
1949; A.B., Florida Agricultural and Mechanical Univer-
sity, 1948; m. Vivian Lucia Stallsworth; Ordained Deacon,
1947; Ordained Priest, 1948 (The Episcopal Church
Diocese of Florida); priest-in-charge, St. Michael and
All Angels Episcopal Church; Episcopal chaplain, Florida
A & M. University, Tallahassee, Fla., 1947---; Mem.:
The College Commission; Dept. of Mission; Church Ex-
tension of the Diocese of Florida; local and state officer;
NAACP; Member, Phi Beta Sigma Fraternity; teach,
Sociology, Florida A & M Univ., 1948-51; Omega Phi
Psi; Citizen of the Year Award; Member, Democrat; B.
D. Thesis: Community Determinations For Church Action
- In the City of Hampton, Va., 1947; Home: 2019 Owens
St., Tallahassee, Fla.; Off.: 1405 Melvin St., Talla-
hassee, Fla.

BROOKS, Elemit Anthony, b. Norfolk, Va.; A.B., Lincoln
Univ., 1950; B.D., Drew Univ. Theol. Sem., 1953;
courses: John Carroll Univ., Human Relations, 1956;
m. Doris Kearsley; daughter---Bethella Annete; pastor
Christian education and youth pastor, First Presbyterian
Ch., Oxford, Pa.; Trinity and Metropolitan Meth. Ch.,
New York City; youth advisor, Methodist Students,
Cleveland Church Fellowship, 1956-58; pastor, Werner
Methodist Ch., Cleveland, Ohio, 1953-58; pastor (as-
sociate), Bushwick Ave. Meth. Ch., Brooklyn, N.Y.,
1960-63; pastor, First Meth. Ch., Bronx, N.Y.,
1963---; Bd. Mem., Ministerial Training & Qualifica-

Brooks, H.C. 49

tion; Bd. of Hospitals and Homes; Bd. of Directors, N.
Y. East Conf., Health Care Agency; Bd. of Directors,
Brooklyn-Long Island Church Society; Mem. Bd. of
Managers, New York City Meth. Ch., 1964---; Bd. of
Managers of the Protestant Council, Bronx Division;
Mem., Local School Board; chmn. the South Bronx
Housing Com.; the Mayors Comn. on Religious Leaders
of New York City; Bd. of Managers of the Neighborhood
Advisory Service; chmn, the Mott Haven Citizen Com.;
Mem., The Advisory Committee of the National Council
Negro Woman, Bronx Division, Community Education
Committee; Mem., NAACP; Urban League; Home: 401
E. 141 St., Bronx, N.Y.

BROOKS, Henry Curtis, sem. prof.; b. Alexandria, Va.
May 7, 1929; s. Houston George, Sr. and Evelyn
(Lemon) B.; B.A., Storer Coll., 1950; B.D., S.T.M.
Andover Newton Theological Sch., 1954; Ph.D., Boston
Univ., 1964; m. Aeolus Jones; children---Steven Jeffrey;
Ordained, American Baptist minister, 1953; asst.
minister, Shiloh Bapt. Ch., West Medford, Mass.
1953-54; pastor, Saint John's Bapt. Ch., Waburn, Mass.,
1954-58; visiting lecturer, Andover Newton Theo. Sch.,
Newton, Mass., 1958-64; asst. prof., Andover Newton
Theol. Sch., 1964---; protestant chaplain, Boston City
Hospital, Boston, Mass., 1955---; chaplain supervisor,
The Andover Newton Theo. Sch. Summer Sch. of Clinical
Training at the Boston City Hospital, 1955-61; asst. di-
rector, the Summer Sch., 1961---; sec., Bd. of Governors,
Institute of Pastoral Care; vice pres., Board of Directors
Protestant Youth Center, Baldwinville, Mass.; Adult Pro-
gram Committee of New England Area Council of YMCA;
Committee on Juvenile Delinquency of the Dept. of Social
Relations of the Mass. Council of Churches; Social Con-
cerns Com. of the Newton Council of Churches; Assn.
of Sem. Profs. in the Practical Field; Accredited Hospital
Chaplain by the American Protestant Hospital Assn; Ac-
credited Chaplain Supervisor by the Institute of Pastoral
care; Home: 31 Paul St., Newton Centre, Mass. 02159;
Office: 210 Herrick Rd., Newton Centre, Mass. 02159.

BROOKS, Jerome Bernard, educator; b. Houston, Texas,
Mar. 20, 1932; s. Osburn B. and Agnes (Harrison) B.;
M.A. Eng., Notre Dame Univ.; Columbia U.; Loyola,
Los A.; College teaching, 1962---; Week-end parish
worker; Author, "The Negro Priest in White Parishes,"
Religious Education (Jan-Feb. 1964): Home and Office:

5700 N. Harlem Ave., Chicago, Ill., 60631.

*BROOKS, Thomas Howard, b. Annapolis, Md., Nov. 22,
1919; s. Thomas and Ethel (Osborne) B.; B.S., Morgan
State Coll., 1944; B.D., Sch. of Rel., Howard Univ.,
1947; candidate for Master's degree in Rel. Ed.; m.
Myrtle Holloway. Pastored: Ridgely-Huntsville Methodist
Ch., Seat Pleasant, Md., 1945-48; Upper Marlboro, Md.
Union Methodist Ch., 1948-50; St. James Methodist Ch.,
White Sulphur Springs, W. Va., 1950-53; Sharp St. M.
Ch., Sandy Spring, Md., 1953-61; present; Jerusalem
M. Ch., Rockville, Md., 1961- . Pres., Board of Ed-
ucation of Washington Conf., Methodist Ch.; vice-pres.,
Montgomery County N.A.A.C.P.; vice-pres., Rockville
Ministerial Alliance; mem., Board of Directors, Wesley
Foundation, Howard Univ. Mason. Home: 17 West Wood
Lane, Rockville, Md., Office: 21 W. Wood Lane, Rock-
ville, Md.

BROWN, Benjamin Harrison, teacher; b. Roberson County,
N.C., May 28, 1888; s. Angus and Mary Jane B.; B.
S., Johnson C. Smith, 1915-1919; B.D., 1920-1922; m.
Mamie Phar; children---Mary Harriet, Chasten, Atmos
Chasten, Benjamin A. Jr., Barbet Chasten; pastor,
Faison Memorial United Presbyterian Ch., Clinton, N.
C.; teacher Hayswood School, 1923-24; pastor, The
Second Presbyterian Church, 1926-40; teacher the County
& Bladen C.H.S. for eight years; commissioner from
Cape Fear Presbytery, Catawba Synod to the General As-
sembly of the United Presbyterian Ch., Cincinnatti,
Ohio; Home: PO Box 393 W&D Elizabethtown, N.D.; Ch.:
Faison St. United Presbyterian Ch., Clinton, N.C.

BROWN, Dillard Houston, b. Marietta, Ga., June 20, 1912;
s. Dillard Houston and Anna Rebecca (Robinson) G.;
A.B., Morehouse Coll., Atlanta, Ga., 1932-36; M.
Th., Univ. of South Calif., 1939; General Theol. Sem.,
1939-40; S.T.D. (Hon.), 1962; D.D. (hon.), Cuttington,
Coll., Suacoco, Liberia, 1961; m. Sarah Virginia Ross;
children---Bette Regina, Virginia Ann; curate, St.
Martin's Ch., N.Y., 1940-42; vicar, Church of Incar-
nation, Jersey City, N.J., 1943-46; rector, St. Luke's
Church, Wash., D.C., 1946-61; bishop coadjustor,
Republic of Liberia, 1961-64; bishop, Liberia, 1964---;
Home: Bishop's House, Monrovia, Liberia, W. Africa.

BROWN, Henry, clergyman, junior bishop; b. Orangeburg,
S.C., Jan. 5, 1914; s. John and Henretta (Muller) B.;
Public School, Orangeburg, S.C., Bible Way Training
School; m. Minnie Lee Onabitt; children---Valarie, La
Vonne, Henry Lewis, Joe Nathan, Maxine; pastor,
Bible Way Church World Wide, Prince Frederick, Md.,
Organizer and Builder; Junior Bishop, Diocese in Eastern
N.C.; Member, The Apostolic Inter-organizational Fel-
lowship Conference; Organized Recreation Area, Prince
Frederick, Md.; Home: Route 1, Box 66-A, Prince
Frederick, Md.

BROWN, James Walter, b. Edisto Island, S.C., August 14,
1932; s. Benjamin J. Sr. and Viola (Searbrook) B.; A.
B., Johnson C. Smith University, 1952-56; B.C., 1956-
59; m. Katherine Hope; children---Veronica Oveta, Alton
Tyrone, Jacqueline Nina; pastor Hopewell and Aimwell
United Presbyterian Churches of Walterboro, S.C.,
1958-59; Sunday School Missionary at Headquarters at
Spartanburg, S.C.; current pastor, the Ladson United
Presbyterian Ch., Columbia, S.C.; Home: 1401 Gregg,
Columbia, S.C.; Church: 1720 Sumter, Columbia, S.C.

BROWN, Johnny Mack, b. Selma, Ala., Aug. 23, 1928;
s. Ruben and Buela (Steel) B.; Alabama Lutheran College, 1946; Immanuel Lutheran College, Greensboro,
N.C., 1951; m. Janet Odessa Colemon; children---Mat-
tie, Johnnie, Debra; current pastor, Holy Cross Lutheran
Church (Mo. Synod), Camden, Alabama; Home: P.O. Box
N. Camden, Alabama.

BROWN, Philip Rayfield, III; educator; b. New Orleans,
La., Oct. 7, 1917; s. Philip R., Jr. and Eleanora B.;
A.B., Xavier U., 1939; B.Th., Union Theol. Sem.,
1943; D.D. (honorary), United Theol. Sem., 1964; m.
Bertha Duckett, 1938; 2 sons, Lt. Philip R., IV, James
Elliot; 2 daus., Eleanor Brown Miller, Norma Brown
West; Pastor, Pleasant Grove Bapt. Ch., N.O., La.,
1947-59; Calvary Miss. Bapt. Ch., W. Monroe, La.,
1959---; Instr., Nat. S.S. & B.T.U. Cong., 1942---;
Instr., United Theol. Sem., Monroe, La.; Pastor,
Travelers Rest Miss. Bapt. Ch., Tallulah, La., 1962;
Pres., Ideal Bapt. SS & BTU Cong., N.O., La., 1942-
59; Dean, La. State Bapt. Conv., Dept. Chrtn. Edu.,
1945--; Dir. Pub. Rel., La. Bapt. Conv., 1950--; Dean,
Chrtn. Edu., 10th Dist. Bapt. Assoc., Northeast, La.;
Dean, Twin City Leadership Training Institute, Monroe-

West, La.; Pres., Monroe Chap. NAACP, 1959-62; Spec.
Investigator, City of N.O. Utilities Dept., 1950-59;
Sec., Bd. Trustees, United Theol. Sem., Monroe, La.;
Recipient Highest Merit Award, City of N.O., La.; Of-
fice: Calvary Miss. Bapt. Ch., Ninth & Linderman Sts.,
West Monroe, La.

BROWN, Robert Leslie, social worker; b. Little Rock Ark.,
May 26, 1927; s. William R. and Verlie (Acklin) B.
1944, B.A. Jarvis Christian College, Hawkins, Texas;
m. Vera Mae (Bowser) B.; children: Robert Jr., Carol
William Arthur; pastor-1948-50, 12th St. Christian
church, Austin, Texas; 1951 (present) Maple St., Christian Church, Lockland, Ohio; Social worker-1959 (present) Hamilton County Welfare Dept., Cincinnati, Ohio;
mem. Pride of the Valley Prince Hall Masonic Lodge
(Master); Interdenomination Ministerial Alliance of
Greater Cincinnati; Social Service Assoc. of Greater
Cincinnati; NAACP.; Home: 608 Maple St., Lockland 15,
Ohio- 45215.

BROWN, Theophile Waldorf, teacher; b. Richmond, Va.
Aug. 24, 1925; s. Thomas Harvey and Sarah Etta (Tay-
lor) B.; B.A. Ed., Classics, Phil., St. John's U.
Collegeville, Minnesota, 1952; M.A., Latin, Univ. of
Ottawa, Canada, 1961; Ordained priest, Roman Cath.
Ch., 1956; Chairman of Classics, St. Augustine's Col-
lege, Nassau, 1957---; Monastery Organist and choir
director; Home: St. John's Abbey, Collegeville, Minnesota.

BROWN, Thomas Emerson, b. Crystal Springs, Miss.,
Dec. 7, 1888; s. Augustus G. and Lula (Scott) B.;
Moody Bible Institute, Chgo, Ill.; m. Clarinda Bridges;
Olivet Bapt. Ch., Chgo., Ill., 1916; Lily Dale Bapt.
Ch., 1918; Progressive Bapt. Ch., Chgo., Ill., 1919;
mem. Bd. Dir., Providence Hospital, Chgo., Ill.,
1945-55; Bd. Dirs., Chgo. Bapt. Institute, 1958; Bd.
Dirs., M. I & E Ministerial Coll., West Point, Miss.;
Recipient, Citation for Human Brotherhood, Citizen's
Salute, Station WBEE; mem. NAACP; Home: 3616 Went-
worth Ave., Chgo., 9 Ill. Church: 3658 Wentworth Ave.,
Chgo 9, Ill.

BROWN, William Henry, teacher; b. Rockford, Ill., April
2, 1915; s. Harry Leslie and Mary Magdaline (Cross-
wright) B.; 1948, A.B. Wasburn Univ.; 1960, North
Carolina, University; m. Ruth Margaret (Bynes) B.;

children: Jessie Curtis, Gerald Andrew, Rosemary,
William Jr. , Willa Ruth; pastor; 1935-39; Second Christian
Church, Atchison, Kansas; 1939-48; Second Christian
Church, Topeka, Kansas; 1942, Third Christian Church
Kansas City, Kansas; 1948-49; Ninth Street Christian
Church, Des Moines, Iowa; 1949-53, Cleveland Ave.
Christian Church, Winston Salem, N. C. ; 1953-56,
Jones Street Christian Church, Bluefield, West. Va. ;
1956 (present), Minister General Program, Piedmont
Tri-State District. Teacher: Director of Night School
for Adults, Reidsville, N. C. (typing, shorthand, Busi-
ness English); Kappa Alpha Psi; Home: 703 Melrose St. ,
Reidsville, N. C. church 1103 Ware St. , Reidsville,
N. C.

BRYANT, Harrison James, bishop; b. Georgetown, S. C.
Nov. 20, 1899; s. Richard and Annie B. ; A. B. , Allen
Univ. , 1932; B. D. , Payne Theol. Sem. , 1935; D. D.
(hon.), Payne Theol. Sem. ; Wilberforce Univ. , Ohio;
Kittrell Coll. , N. C. ; LL. D. (hon.), Campbell Coll. ,
Jackson, Miss. ; Monrovia Coll. , Liberia, W. Africa;
m. Edith Drusesella Holland; children---Cynthia Ann,
Hazel Joan, Harrison J. , Jr. , John Richard, Eleanor
Louise; pastor, Jones Chapel African Methodist Episcopal
Ch. , Lexington County, S. C. , 1926-27; Chappell Station
A. M. E. Ch. , Columbia, S. C. , 1927-32; First A. M. E.
Ch. , Xenia, Ohio, 1932-35; dean, Jackson Theol Sem.
and pastor of River View A. M. E. Ch. , 1935-36; St.
Paul A. M. E. Ch. , Zanesville, Ohio, 1936-39; St. Paul
A. M. E. Ch. , Lexington, Ky. , 1939-42; St. John's A. M.
E. Ch. , Baltimore, Md. , 1942-49; Bethel A. M. E. Ch. ,
Baltimore, Md. , 1949-64; Elected bishop, A. M. E. Ch. ,
May 1964; vice pres. , Md. Council of Churches, 1960-
62; Mem. , Exec. Bd. , Baltimore Branch NAACP, 1964
---; chaplain, Mason; Home: 3513 Dennlyn Rd. , Balti-
more 15, Md.

*BRYANT, Lawrence Chesterfield, college professor; b.
Battleboro, N. C. , Feb. 16, 1916; s. Emitt and Gattie
Bland (Cooper) B. ; B. S. , Shaw Univ. , 1940; B. D. , Sch.
of Rel. , Howard Univ. , 1950; M. A. , New York Univ. ,
1950; Ed. D. , Univ. of Va. , 1959; m. Ila Thomas; chil-
dren--- Lawrence Michael, Cynthia Ann. Pastored:
First Baptist Ch. , Mount Hope, W. Va. , 1950-51; First
Baptist Ch. , Harrisonburg, Va. , 1953-56; Florida Memor-
ial College, 1956-60; New Mount Zion Baptist Ch. ,
Orangeburg, S. C. , 1960-61. Professor of Education:

Jackson College, Jackson, Miss., 1956; Fla. Memorial
Coll., St. Augustine, Fla.; Present, Professor, Ed.
South Carolina State College, Orangeburg, S.C., 1960-64;
Alpha Phi Alpha, Palmetto Education Assn., Nat. Ed.
Assn., American Teachers Assn., American Personnel
and Guidance Assn. Chairman, Research Committee;
managing editor, Exploration in Education (Research
Journal at South Carolina State Coll.) Home: Box 1615,
College Station, Orangeburg, S.C.

BUDFORD, Kenneth Leroy, b. Pulaski, Va., Aug. 17,
1917; s. C. Jordan and Marie (Jenkins) B.; A.B., City
College, New York, 1939; B. Th., Bloomfield School of
Religion, Newark, N.J., 1942; D.D., Miller University,
Phila. Pa., 1960; m. Lillian M. Glanton; children---
Selma L. (Mrs. D. Ross Turpeau); Kenneth Leroy, Jr.,
Lawrence J. Thompson (Step-son); Myron H. Thompson
(Step-son); pastor, Brighton Rock A.M.E. Zion Church,
Portsmouth, Virginia, 1939-41; St. James A.M.E. Zion
Church, Matawan, N.J., 1941-45; St. Luke A.M.E.
Zion Church, New Castle, Pa., 1945-47; Martin Chapel
A.M.E. Zion Church, Los Angeles, Calif., 1947-56;
Butler Chapel, A.M.E. Zion Church, Tuskegee, Alabama,
1956---; Vice pres., Tuskegee Civic Assoc. and Chair-
man of its Community Welfare Comm.; Mem., Tuskegee,
Alabama, Bi-Racial Committee; Member, Macon County
County (Alabama) Progressive Democratic Committee;
A.M.E. Zion chaplain to students, Tuskegee Institute;
Chairman, Committee on Counseling - Religious Life
Council, Tuskegee Institute; Member and Past President,
Tuskegee Ministers' Council; Mem., Board of Trustees,
Christian Education Department; Member, Home and
Church Division, Christian Education Department; Mem-
ber, Connectional Budget Board; Member, Episcopal
Committee; Trustee, Lomax Hannon Jr. College, Green-
ville, Alabama; Chairman, Board of Examiners, Alabama
Conference Chairman, Budget Committee, Alabama Con-
ference; Office: Butler Chapel A.M.E. Zion Church
Tuskegee, Alabama

BULLOCK, Richard David, Jr. educator; b. Drewry, N.C.,
May 6, 1908; s. Richard D. and Mary (Burwell) B.;
Shaw University, Raleigh, N.C., 1929-34; North Carolina
Coll., Durham, N.C., 1948; m. Verlena Rowland (dec.);
1 dau., Ernestine V. Boon; Malnaye Bullock; Pastored
Children's Chapel Cong. Ch., Graham, N.C., 1946-52;
Corinth Cong. Ch., Youngsville, N.C., 1959-64; present

pastor, Mt. Zion Cong. Ch., Henderson, N.C., 1960-
64; Principal, Sandy Grove Elementary School, 1934-38;
Principal, Nutbush School, Manson, N.C., 1938-52;
Mem. N.C. Teacher's Assoc.; Steering Committee on
By-Laws and Constitution, United Church of Christ.
Home: Box 25, Manson 4, N.C. Office: Route 1, Drewry,
N.C.

BUNTON, Henry Clay, bishop; b. Tuscaloosa Co., Ala.,
Oct. 19, 1904; s. Isaac and Sarah L.B.; B.D., Fla.
A. & M. Col., Tallahassee, Fla., 1941; T.M., Iliff
Sch. of Theology, Denver, Colorado, 1952; D.D. (hon.)
Texas Coll., Tyler, Tex., 1955; m. Estelle McKinney,
Alfreda Gibbs; children---Mattye Lou, Marjorie, Henry C.
Jr., Joseph Ronald; pastor, C.M.E. Church, Ala., Fla.
Ark., Tex., Denver Colo. & Memphis, Tenn. (Christian
Methodist Episcopal Church): Elected Bishop, C.M.E.
Church, May 1962; Now serving Seventh Episcopal District,
C.M.E. Church, 1962---; Mem., C.M.E. Bd. of Chris-
tian Education; director, Adult and Youth Work for the
General Bd.; dean, Fla. School of Christian Workers;
director, Christian Education for Jackson- Memphis Tenn.
Annual Conference; Bd. of Directors of Henderson Coll.;
Mem., Southern Christian Leadership Conference; Trustee
of Miles College; Bd. of Trustees, Paine Coll. Fraternal
Organizations; Mason; Phi Beta Sigma; Chaplain, US Army,
1943-46, 1948-50, Major; 3 Battle Stars Awards from:
The Citizens Non Partisan Registration Committee,
Memphis, Tenn.; The Interdenominational Ministers Al-
liance, Memphis, Tenn.; NAACP, Memphis, Tenn.;
Award of Merit, Radio Station WDIA, Memphis, Tenn.;
Democrat; asst. editor, Christian Index and Sunday School
Lesson writer for the C.M.E. Church (Formerly), now
chairman of the Publishing Bd. of the C.M.E. church;
Home: 6524 16th St. NW, Wash. 12, D.C.

BURGESS, John Melville, Bishop; b. Grand Rapids, Mich.,
Mar 11, 1909; s. Theodore Thomas and Ethel Inez
(Beverly) B.; B.A., M.A., Univ. of Michigan; B.D.,
Episcopal Theol. Seminary, 1934; LHD (hon.), Univ. of
Mich., 1963; LLD., Augustine's College, 1963; m.
Esther Taylor; children---Julia; Margaret; Priest-in-
charge: St. Philip's, Grand Rapids, Mich., 1934-39;
St. Simon of Cyrene, Woodlawn, Cincinnati, O., 1938-
46; Episcopal Chaplain, Howard U., Washington, D.C.,
1946-56; Canon, Washington Cathedral, 1951-56; Arch-
deacon of Boston, Supt., Episcopal City Mission, 1956-

62; Suffragan Bishop of Mass. 62--; Del. Central. Com.
World Coun. Chs., India, 52--; Del. World Coun. Chs.,
New Delhi, 61; Dep. Gen. Conven. Epis. Ch., 1951-61;
Special lecturer, Episcopal Theological School; Trustee,
St. Paul's College, Lawrenceville, Va.; chairman,
Boston Committee on Race and Religion; Home: 46 Ber-
wick Road, Newton Centre 59, Massachusetts; Ch.: One
Joy Street, Boston 8, Massachusetts.

BURGESS, Monroe Abel, Church official; b. Baltimore,
Maryland, June 19, 1910; s. Monroe Abel and Gertrude
(Anderson) B.; Oakwood College, Huntsville, Ala.; Union
College, Lincoln, Nebraska; m. Willie Mae Herbin; chil-
dren:- Monroe A., III, James Edward. Pastored: Calvary
Seventh-Day Adventist Church, Norfolk Virginia, 1933;
Gill Street, S.D.A. Church, Petersburg, Va., 1936;
Ethan Temple S.D.A. Church, Pittsburgh, Penna., 1941;
Ebenezer S.D.A. Church, Philadelphia, Penn., 1948-52.
Teacher, Washington Union Academy, 1932; Departmental
secretary, Allegheney Conf. of S.D.A., 1945-47 and
1952-56; present: departmental secretary, Central States
Conf. of S.D.A., 1956-   . President, Interdenomina-
tional Ministers' Alliance, 1961-63; Church secretary,
N.A.A.C.P.- Region IV, 1961-63; committee member:
K.C. Council on Religion and Race, Citizens Co-ordinat-
ing Committee, Operation Alphabet. Democrat; Independent
Voters Association, Kansas City, Mossouri. Home: 3028
Agnes Street, Kansas City, Missouri 64128. Office: 2528
Benton Boulevard, Kansas City, Mo. 64127.

BURKE, DeGrandval, teacher; b. Matthews, N.C., Dec.
25, 1909; s. Crawford A. and Florence (McCauley) B.;
1934-38, B.S., 1944, B.D. (Seminary), Johnson C.
Smith University; 1946-47, M.A., McCormick Theological Seminary; m. Mattie Cannon; Child, DeGrandval, Jr.;
Teacher, 1944-61; Boggs Academy, Keysville, Ga.; Pastor, Emmanuel United Presbyterian Church, Charlotte,
N.C.; Co-pastor, 1961-63; Biddleville-Emmanuel United
Presbyterian Church; Instructor, Religious Education,
J.C. Smith Univ. 1946-50, 1962; Awards: "Minister
of the Year" of Catawba Synod-1956; mem. Alpha Kappa
Mu National Society; Phi Beta Sigma; Republican; Initiated
two special projects in Christian Education, which were
published in our Church's National magazine, and were
adopted by the Synod of Catawba as part of its adult work
program. They were known as Project 20 and the Alpha
Chi Omega Christian Fellowship; Home: 1414 Onyx Street

Charlotte 8, N.C.; Office: Box 314, Johnson C. Smith,
Univ. Charlotte 8, N.C.

BURKS, Olliw Allen, presiding elder; b. Montgomery,
Miss. Sept. 3, 1883; s. Sylas and Mary Ann (Johnson)
B.; Campbell Coll., Jackson, Miss., 1919-21; D.D.
(hon.), Payne Theol Seminary, 1925; m. Madora Harris;
children--- Marjorie May Tutus Sims; pastor, African
Methodist Episcopal Churches, Miss., Ohio, West Va.,
N. Carolina, W. Va.; current presiding elder, A.M.E.
Church; Mem., Democratic Party; Mason; Oddfellow;
Pythian; Home: P.O. Box 1265 Logan, West Va.

BURNS, Charles Dixon, teacher; b. Greenville, Miss.,
June 23, 1932; s. Washington and Charlie (Dixon) B.;
B.A., Divine Word Seminary, Techny, Ill., 1958; M.A.
Catholic Univ., Wash. D.C., 1963; Divine Word Semin-
ary, Bay St. Louis, Miss. (4 yrs. theol.); Ordained
priest, Roman Cath. Ch., March 17, 1962; Vocation
Dir., Divine Word Missionaries Southern Province;
Editor, The Divine Word Messenger; Mem., N. Amer.
Liturgical Apostolate, Miss. Council on Human Relations;
Home: Divine Word Seminary, Bay St. Louis, Miss.,
39520.

BURRUS, Lloyd Andros, b. Fairfield, N.C., June 29, 1920;
s. George B. and Mallissia (Johnson) B.; B.A., Shaw
Univ., 1945; B.D., Crozer Theol. Sem., Chester, Ph.,
1949; further study: McGill Univ., Canada; m. widower;
children---Celicia Elizabeth; asst. pastor, Queen Street
Baptist Church, Norfolk, Va., 1942-45; pastor, Zion
Bapt. Ch., Camden, New Jersey, 1949-54; Ebenezer
Bapt. Ch., Newburgh, N.Y., 1954-58; founder and
pastor, Zion Temple Bapt. Ch., Jamaica, N.Y., 1958--;
chairman, Home Missions Bd., Progressive Nat'l Bapt.
Convention, Ind.; teacher, Bordentown school, N.Y.,
1950-51; guest lecturer, O.T. History, Camden, N.Y.,
YMCA, 1953; consultant, South Jersey Bd. of Probation
& Parole, 1950-53; pres., Newburgh, New York Branch
NAACP, 1955-57; organizer, Newburgh, New York Citi-
zens' Committee, 1956; one of 12 honorees for 1952
Afro-American Newspapers, Camden, N.J. and Pa. Area;
Democrat; Mem., Phi Beta Sigma; Home: 1147 Noble
Ave., Bronx, N.Y.; Office: Zion Temple Bapt., Van
Wyer Express Way, 105th Ave., Richmond Hill, Jamaica,
N.Y.

BURTON, H. L., editor; A. B. Lane College; North Western
College.; Th. M., School of Religion - Butler University;
D. D. (Hon.) Lane College; further studies at Catholic
University of America. Pastor, 6 years, Mt. Olive, S.
Carolina, St. Mathew (N. Carolina - 6 months); Israel
Metropolitan, Wash., D. C., 9 1/2 years; present:
pastor, Phillips Temple Christian Methodist Episcopal
Church, Indianapolis, Ind. Annual Conf. secretary-
treasurer, C. ME. Ch.; Dean, director, teacher, Leader-
ship Training Schools, C. M. E. Ch. Member, executive
board, Church Federation, Indianapolis, Indiana and
vicinity; president, Interdenominational Ministers Al-
liance. Plaque award, Lane College. Branch president,
N. A. A. C. P.; Basileus; Chapter Omiga Psi Phi; Mason;
Elk. Editor, C. M. E. Official magazine and The Eastern
Index, 1954-62. Office: 1226 North West St., Indianapolis,
Ind. Home: 135 W. 21st St., Indianapolis, Inc.

BUTLER, Charles William, educator; b. Dermott, Ark.,
May 4, 1922; B. A. Philander Smith Coll., Little Rock,
Ark.; B. D., Union Theol Sem., NYC.; res. Ph. D.,
Columbia U.; Further study, U. of Nancy, Nancy, France,
Wayne State U., Clinical Training, Harper Hosp., Det.,
Mich., Merrill Palmer Inst., Det., Mich.; m. Helen
Odean Scoggins; 3 sons, Charles, Jr., Keith, Kevin; 1
dau. Beverly; Military Service, World War II, 4 Cam-
paign Stars; Asst. Pastor, St. James Presbyterian Ch.,
N. Y.; Released Time Instr., N. Y. City Miss. Society;
Instr., Bapt. Center, N. Y.; Instr., Biblical Lit & Rel.,
Morehouse Coll., Atlanta, Ga., 1951-54; Pastor, Metro-
politan Bapt. Ch., Det., Mich., 1954-63; Pastor, New
Calvary Bapt. Ch., Det., Mich., 1963--; Supervisor,
Gen. Div., Nat. Bapt. S. S. & B. T. U. Cong., Chrmn.,
Christian Edu. Commission, Wolverine Bapt. State Conv.,
Mich., mem. Theol. Study Commission. Priorities Eval-
uation Commission Bd., Met. Det. Council of Churches,
Mayor's Comm., Commission on Children & Youth (Det.)
Mich. Council of Churches, Interdenominational Minister-
ial Council, Ministerial Council, Home Fed. Savings &
Loan Assoc., Det., Boy Scouts, YMCA, Nat. Negro
Bus. League, Booker T. Washington Bus. Assoc., the
Pioneers, Alpha Phi Alpha; Office: 3975 Concord Avenue,
Detroit, Mich., 48207.

*BURRELL, Emma Pinkney, teacher; b. Prince Geo. Co.,
Md., Aug 9, 1912; s. Arthur Phillip and Florence
Butler P.; A. B., Howard Univ.; Miner Teachers Coll.,

1924-26; B.D., Howard Univ., 1959; m. George W.
Burrell; principal, Fanguire High Sch., Irvin, Va.,
1932-34; teacher, D.C. Eve. School and substitute
teacher, 1934-40; Government employee, 1940-58; pastor,
St. Mary's Larger Parish, 3 years; St. Luke Methodist
Church, Jackson, 1956-63; asst. pastor, Asbury Meth.
Ch., Wash., D.C., 1954-55; pastor, Mt. Vernon Meth.
Ch., 1963---; First woman in Central Jurisdiction to
receive full clergical status; Home: Rt. 1 Box 306-A,
Jessup, Md. 20794; Office: Mt. Vernon Meth. Church,
1910 W. Va. Ave N.E., Washington D.C. 20002.

BUTLER, Ernest Daniel, b. Connersville, Ind., Oct. 11,
1913; s. Daniel and Margaret Lucile B.; Franklin
Coll., 1933; Moody Bible Sch., 1935; Payne Theol.
Sem., 1936; m. Mary Louise Jones; 5 sons, Ernest E.,
Robert J., William D., Albert R., James L.; 2 daus.
Grayce L. Florence (Mrs.), Mary Ann; Pastored, Mt.
Zion Bapt. Ch., Connersville, Ind.; First Bapt. Ch.,
Noblesville, Ind., 1949-59; Second Bapt. Church, Bloom-
ington, Ind., 1959--; Dir. Southeastern Dist. Youth
Camp, 1946-49; 1960-64; Dir. Youth Work, Ind. Bapt.
State Conv., 1964; Chrmn., Southeastern Dist., Benevo-
lent Bd., 1962--; Dir., YMCA, Indiana U., 1962-65;
mem. Bd. Dir., Bloomington Family Counciling Agency,
1963--; Chrmn., Bloomington Fair Housing Committee,
1960-64; Vice-Chrmn., Bloomington, Mayor's Human Re-
lations Com.; Vice-Chrmn., Indiana Citizens Fair Housing Committee, 1963--; Rec., Service Award, Boy Scout
Activities, 1962-63; mem. Campus Ministers, Ind. U.,
Inter-Faith Council, Ind. U.; Author, The Church Looks
At Sex, 1963; Home: 509 W. 8th, Bloomington, Ind.
Church: 321 N. Roger St., Bloomington, Ind.

BUTLER, Joseph LeCount, b. Washington, D.C., s. Xavier
and Edith (Davis) B.; B.A., Union College; m. Noetta
Melvene Keller; children- Joseph, Jr., Davis Meredith,
Joel Kenneth. Pastored Seventh-Day Adventist Churches
in: Lincoln, Nebraska, 1 year; Topeka, Kansas, 6 years;
Wichita, Kansas, 5 years; present: Omaha, Neb. Home:
2114 Sprague St., Omaha, Nebraska 68110. Office:
3028 Bedford St., Omaha, Nebr.

BUTLER, J. Ray, educator; b. Roseboro, N.C., Aug. 5,
1923; s. Amos D., Sr. and Mary F.B.; A.B., Shaw
U., 1951; B.D., Shaw Div. Sch., 1953; D.D. (honorary)
Friendship Coll., Rock Hill, S.C., 1964; m. Marion

Ceola Lucas; 4 sons; Pastorates: Mt. Olive Bapt. Ch.,
Fayettesville, N. C. (2 yrs); First Bapt. Ch., Creedmoor,
N. C. (6 yrs) New Christian Bapt. Ch., Rose Hill, N. C.
(3 yrs); Ebenezer Bapt. Ch., Wilmington, N. C., 1954--;
Pres., Interdenominational Ministerial Alliance, Wil-
mington & Vicinity, 1956-58; Sec. 1960--; Pres., Wil-
mington Civic League, 1960--; mem. Adv. Bd., Phyllis
Wheatley YWCA, Exec. Bd. mem., Wilmington Adult
Chap. NAACP; mem. Alpha Phi Alpha; Vice Chrmn.,
Gen Bd., Gen. Bapt. State Conv., N. C., Inc., 1960--;
mem. Extension teaching Staff, Shaw U., In-service
Ministers, 1957--; Moderator, Western Union Assoc.,
1956--; mem. Exec. Bd., Theol. Alumni Assoc., Shaw
U., Raleigh, N. C.; mem. Exec. Bd., Lott Carey Bapt.
For. Miss. Conv., Inc.; Exec. Bd., Hampton Minister's
Conf.; Bapt. For. Miss. Conv., Inc.; Exec. Bd., Hamp-
ton Minister's Conf.; Nat. Bapt. Conv. USA, Inc.;
Home: 211 S. Seventh St., Wilmington, N. C. Church:
209 S. Seventh St., Wilmington, N. C.

BYRD, Cameron Wells, b. Ithaca, New York, Nov. 10,
1935; B. A., Univ. of Buffalo, New York, 1953-57; B. D.,
Howard Univ. Sch. of Rel., 1957-60; Certificate Clinical
Pastoral Care, Andover Newton Theol. Sch.; m. Maxine;
children-- two; research aide, Bd. of Redevelopment,
Buffalo, New York, 1954; chaplain of Migrant Agricul-
tural Workers, New York State Council of Churches,
1958; pastor, Bradley Mem. Bapt. Ch., Oak Bluffs,
Mass., 1959; advisor, Student Christian Assn., Howard
Univ., 1958-59; student asst., Peoples Cong. Ch., Wash.
D. C., 1960-62; asst. pastor, Peoples Cong. Ch., Wash.
D. C., 1960-62; director of Halfway House, Plymouth
Cong. Ch., Detroit, Mich., 1962-63; current pastor,
Christ Church, United Church of Christ, Detroit, Mich.;
award: Fellow of The American Assn. of Theol. Schs in
the US and Canada, 1959; mem., Camp Management
Com., Detroit Metropolitan Assn., United Ch., of
Christ; Commission on Social Concerns, Mich. Conf.,
UCCC; Christian Ed. Com., Detroit Assn., UCC; Chris-
tian Education Fellowship, UCC; Audio-Visual Review,
Detroit Council of Chs.; Greater Detroit Ministerium
Detroit Council of Chs.; Inter-denominational Ministers'
Alliance of Greater Detroit; Southwest Detroit Inter-Faith
Redevelopment Project; Legislative Principles Com.,
Mich. Council of Churches; Div. of Christian Ed., Na-
tional Council of Churches; World Service Com., Down-
town YMCA; Youth Com., Downtown YMCA; Ministerial-

Advisory Com., Planned Parenthood League, Inc.; chmn.
Grass Roots Organization Workers (GROW) of Southwest
Detroit; Bd. of Directors, Protestant Community Serv-
ices, Detroit, Mich.; home: 19440 Mendota, Detroit
21, Mich.; office: Christ Church, United Church of
Christ, Detroit, Mich.

BYRD, Vernon Randolph, b. Enoree, S. C., July 1, 1931;
s. Syfellas and Josephine; A. B., Allen Univ. 1949-51;
Boston Univ., 1951-63; B. D. (hon.), Kittrell Jr. Col-
lege; m. Theora Lindsey; children---Michele, Vanesa
Dawn, Vernon Jr., Christopher Paul; asst. pastor,
Charles Street African Methodist Episcopal Church,
Roxbury, Mass., 1951-53; pastor, Macedonia A. M. E.
Church, Seaford, Delaware, 1954-59; pastor, St. Paul's
African Methodist Episcopal Church, Hamilton Bermuda,
1959---; pres. Ministerial Ass'n, Bermuda; arbitrator,
between government and local Bermuda Industrial Union;
Mem., Phi Beta Sigma; Mason; Home: 196 Sharpnack,
Phila., Pa.; Office: St. Paul A. M. E. Church Box 361
N. Shore, Pembroke West, Hamilton, Bermuda.

BYRD, William Theodore Jr., b. Mocksville, N. C. Dec.
22, 1921; s. Wm. Theodore and Mattie (Wilson); A. B.,
Lincoln University 1941; S. T. B. 1944; m. Perzealia
(Holmes); dau. Cecilia Alice; sons-Wm. Theodore 3rd.
(deceased), Paul Anthony, Director of Friendship House,
Lockawanna, N. Y., 1944-'49; Minister of Grace Pres-
byterian Church, U. S. Louisville, Ky. 1949-1960; Minis-
ter of Lawrence Chapel United Presbyterian church and
Bethel Presbyterian, 1960, Dandridge, Tenn. mem.
N. A. A. C. P., Ministerial Alliances, Morristown Assoc.
(Interracial and Interdenomination); President-Louisville
Branch N. A. A. C. P. -1957; President-Ministerial Alliance-
Morristown, 1964; mem. Omega Psi Fraternity; I. P. B.
O. E. of Elks; Knight of Pithian Lodge; Sermons published
(newspaper) and Radio broadcasts. Home: 414 Harrison
St., Morristown, Tenn. Office: Lawrence Chapel United
Presbyterian Church-414 Harrison St., Morristown,
Tenn.

CABEY, Edwin Herbert, b. Montserrat, West Indies, Aug.
17, 1930; s. John Matthew and Alfredine (Donoghue) C.;
A. B. Phil, Divine Word Seminary, Techny, Ill., 1958;
S. T. B., S. T. L., Pontifical Gregorian Univ., Rome,
Italy, 1959-63; Pontifical Biblical Institute, Rome, Italy,

1963---; Ordained priest, Roman Cath. Ch., March 17,
1962; Home: Divine Word Seminary, Bay St. Louis,
Mississippi; Office: Collegio del Verbo Divino, Roma-
Ostiense 5080, Italy.

CADDELL, Gerwood Lincoln, b. Woodbrook, Trinidad W. I.,
Jan. 10, 1906; s. Benjamin Christopher and Margaret
(Ashby) C.; A. B., Wilberforce Univ.; B. D., Payne
Theological Seminary, 1936; B. S., Coll. of Steuberville,
1956; D. D. (hon.), Payne Theol. Seminary, 1946; m.
Virginia Jane Jackson; children---Karen Ashby; pastor,
Bethel African Methodist Episcopal Church, N. Y. C.;
Chief secretary, North Ohio Conference, 1943-51; pastor,
St. Luke A. M. E. Church, Alliance, Ohio, 1943-47; St.
Paul A. M. E. Church, Lima, Ohio, 1947-50; Reeds
Chapel A. M. E. Church, Youngstown, Ohio, 1950-51;
Quinn Memorial A. M. E. Church, Steuberville, 1951-59;
current pastor, St. Paul A. M. E. Church, Akron, Ohio,
1959---; dean of theology, Campbell Coll., Jackson,
Miss., 1937-38; pres., Ohio Valley Ministers' Alliance,
Steuberville, 1953-57; Mem., Akron Ministerial Ass'n,
1959---; Substitute teacher, Akron Public School System,
1959---; Mem., Bd. of Directors, Payne Theol. Sem.,
1961---; pres., Intergroup Goodwill Council, Steuberville,
1954-57; vice pres., Alumni Ass'n of the Coll. of Steuberville, 1957-59; Elected Trustee Mental Health Ass'n
of Summit County Inc., 1962---; Mem., Council of
Greater Akron; vice pres., Trustee Board of Council of
Churches of Greater Akron, 1963---; Exec. Committee
Wilberforce Univ. National Alumni Ass'n, 1961---; Wil-
berforce Univ. Alumni Citation of Honor, 1956; Special
Award Payne Theol. Seminary, 1959; Life Member Ohio
Pastors Convention of the Ohio Council of Churches,
1962; Mem., Phi Beta Sigma; NAACP; Democrat;
Associate Mem., Ohio Education Ass'n; author: Barbara
Heck: Pioneer Methodist, Pathway Press, Cleveland,
Tenn., 1961; Home: 746 Kolb Akron 44307 Ohio; Office:
St. Paul A. M. E. Church, 739 St. Clair, Akron 44307
Ohio.

CALDWELL, John Martin, b. Henry County, Ky., Sept.
15, 1902; s. John Martin and Anna (Hobbs) C.; A. B.,
Evansville Coll., 1949; B. Th., Simmons Univ., 1930;
D. D. (hon.), Simmons Univ., 1945; m. Maude Alice
Johnson; children---James, Naomi, John R., Evelyn
Ruth, Gloria D., James Martin, Ann Mary; pastor,
Riverview Bapt. Ch., Louisville, Ky., 1 year; Pleasant

Point Bapt. Ch.; 2 1/2 yrs; Zion Bapt. Ch., Evansville,
Inc., 1932---; moderator, Southern District Ass'n; State
Dean of Religious Education of Indiana, 14 years; teacher,
National Baptist Congress, 15 years; vice pres., Bi-
racial Minister's Ass'n; Citation by Pres. Roosevelt for
service on the draft bd. in World War II; pres., NAACP,
Evansville Branch, 15 years; Mem., Mason; author:
Zion Pulpit (annual pamphlet of sermons); Home: 830 East
Gum, Evansville, Ind.; Office: 1800 South Governor,
Evansville, Ind.

CALHOUN, Clyde Livingston, b. Marlboro Co. South Car-
olina, Feb. 20, 1926; s. Hugh Livingston and Isadora
(Stubbs) C; A.B. Claflin Coll, 1951, B.D. Gammon
Theological Seminary, 1955; m. Birdadean Jamison;
Ministry: Walhalla, S.C. 1954-56, Barberg, Ct., 1957-
1959, Jefferson Charge, Jefferson, S.C. 1960-63, Pre-
sent, Old Bethel Methodist Church, Charleston, S.C.
Member: Mason; Home: 20 Felix Street, Charleston
South Carolina, Office: 222 Calhoun Street, Charleston,
S.C. 29403

*CALHOUN, Raymond L.; b. Ennis, Texas, Mar. 27, s.
Carl C. and Sallie (Warner) C.; B.S., Lane Coll.,
1942; B.D., Howard Univ., Sch. of Rel., 1945; MSW
Catholic Univ., Wash., D.C., 1959; m. Mary U. Jack-
son; children---Carl, Raymond, Marilyn; pastor, Williams
Temple Christian Methodist Episcopal Church, Phila.,
Pa., 1945; instructor, Texas Coll., Tyler, Tex., 1947;
pastor, Hopps Memorial C.M.E. Church, Syracuse,
N.Y., 1948-55; Miles Memorial Church, Wash., D.C.,
1956-59; Williams Inst. C.M.E. Church, New York,
N.Y., 1959-63; Director Program & Service, Congrega-
tional Church, Broadway, N.Y., N.Y., 1963---; Mem.,
Alpha Phi Alpha; Bd. Mem., NAACP; former pres.,
NAACP; Thesis: Action Research In Community Planning;
Office: 211 W. 56 St., New York, N.Y. (Broadway
Congregational Church).

CALHOUN, William Edward, b. Carrollton, La., Dec. 26,
1932; s. Fred D. and Henrietta (Hill) C.; Morehouse
College, 1949-53; The School of St. Philip Neri for
Delayed Vocations, Latin Cert., 1957; Catholic Univ.,
Wash., D.C., Grad. studies, 1963--; Ordained priest,
Roman Cath. Ch., May 25, 1963; Served U.S.A.F.,
1952-56; Mem. Alpha Phi Alpha; Home: 135 Griffin, N.
W., Atlanta, Ga.; Office: Caldwell Hall, Box #74, Catholic
Univ. of Amer., Wash. D.C. 20017.

64

Cath. U. of Amer., Wash., D.C., 20017.

CALLENDER, Eugene St. Clair, b. Boston, Mass., Jan.
21, 1926; s. Arthur St. Clair and Eva Valeria (Graham);
A.B., Boston Univ., 1947; B.D., Westminster Theol.
Sem., 1950; graduate studies: Union Theol. Sem.,
1953-55; m. Lemoine DeLeaver; children---Renee,
William, Leslie; assoc. pastor, Second Christian Re-
formed Ch., Patterson, N.J., 1950-53; Founder of The
Mid-Harlem Community Parish, 1955-59; assoc. pastor,
Church of Master, 1959-61; current pastor, Church of the
Master, 1961---; consultant to the Taconic Foundation,
N.Y.; chmn, Harlem Neighborhoods Assn; moderator,
The Presbytery of New York City United Presby. Church;
Mem., The Bd. of Directors, Sneltering Arms Children
Service; vice pres., New York Branch, NAACP; Bd. of
Harlem Youth Opportunities Unlimited; Omega Psi Phi;
Mason; Home: 2160 Madison Ave., New York 37, N.Y.;
Office: 360 Morningside Ave., New York 27, New York.

CALVIN, Willie James, b. Dallas, Tex. March 31, 1913;
s. Will and Lula (Page) C.; B.D., Bishop Coll.; m.
Bernice Fields; children---Sylvia, Willette; pastor,
Galilee Baptist Church, Marshall, Tex., 10 years; Mt.
Zion Bapt. Ch., 1961---; Mem., Bapt. Missionary and
Educational Convention; contributing editor, National
Voice, Nat. Baptist Conv., Inc.,; Mem., Bd. of Urban
League, Milwaukee; dean, Wisconsin State Congress,
Nat. Bapt. Conv.; Mem., Mason; Home: 4346 N. 16 St.,
Milwaukee, Wis. 53209; Office: 210 Garfield, Milwaukee,
Wis.

CAMERON, Johnnie Earl, b. Hattiesburg, Miss., June 11,
1932; s. A.C. and Courtney; B.S., Rust Coll., 1957;
B.D., Amer. Bapt. Sem., 1956; m. Mrs. Johnnie Earl
Cameron; children--Jonetta, John Earl, Jr.; pres. Nat.
Bapt. Student Union, 1954; Ambassador to Republic of
Panama for 10 weeks, 1954; pastor, Second Baptist Ch.,
Oxford, Miss., 1955-56; New Hope Bapt. Ch., Meridian,
Miss., 1958-59; Calvary Bapt. Ch., Laurel, Miss.,
1960-63; current pastor, Faith Tabernacle Bapt. Ch.,
Hattiesburg, Miss.; candidate, US Fifth Congressional
District, 1964; director, Hattiesburg Ministers' Project
for the National Council of Churches; Mem., Assn for
Civil Improvement; chairman, Hattiesburg Assn for Civic
Improvement; Mem., Southern Leadership Conf.; Home:
401 Ashford St., Hattiesburg, Miss.

CAMPBELL, Jeffrey, teacher; A.B., B.D., St. Laurence University, 1933, 1935; ordained, Minister Unitarian Universalist Church, 1935. Present: teacher, Putney School, Putney, Vermont. Office: Putney School, Putney, Vermont.

CAMPBELL, Stephen Calhoun (Dynamo), educator, administrator; b. Newberry, S.C., June 6, 1895; s. Major and Melinda C.; Morris College, A.B., B.Th., 1920; D.D. (honorary), 1959; Benedict Coll., A.B., 1931; B.D., 1933; Wayne State, Ed.M., 1947; A.M., 1956; m. Beulah Clinkscales (1st); Pauline Finley; 5 sons, Stephen, Jr., Finley C., Major C., Anthony C., Russell C.; 1 dau., Ansonia; Minister, 1911; Teacher, 1920; Pastor, St. Paul Bapt., 1924-42; Pastor Russell St. Bapt. Ch., Det., Mich., 1942--; Pres. Edu. Conv., Abbeville-Greenwood, 1922-42; Sec. Bapt. State Conv., S.C., 1931-36; Moderator, Rocky River Bapt. Assoc., 1927-43; Dean, State S.S. & BTU Cong., S.C., 1931-43; Dean, Wolverine State Cong., Mich., 1944-60; Sec., Met. Dist. Assoc., Mich., 1944-60; Dir., Christian Edu., Bapt. State Conv., Mich., 1963--; Pres., State Cong. of Christian Edu., 1962--; Recipient, Church Leadership Award, 1954; Educational Leadership, 1962; Public School Leadership, 1963; mem. Phi Delta Kappa, Alpha Kappa Delta, The Academy of Rel. and Mental Health, Soc. for Scientific Study of Rel.; Author, A Baptist Church Organized for Action; and several other publications; Editor, Sr. B.T.U. Manual; Home: 301 Boston Blvd., Detroit 2, Mich. Church:8700 Russell St., Detroit 11, Mich.

CANNON, James Alexander, Jr. b. Gastonia, N.C. Mar. 13, 1920; s. U.S. and Emma (Grant) C.; Johnson C. Smith University, A.B. 1942; M.A. 1960; B.D. McCormick Theological Seminary, 1945; m. Edna Mae (Jones) C.; sons: James, Charles, Joseph; dau. Merrie Sue. 1945-52 College Minister, North Carolina at Durham, N.C.; 1955, Ass't Minister, Presbyterian Church of the Covenant, Detroit, Mich.; 1954-60, Pastor, Lawndale Presbyterian Church, Chicago, Ill.; 1960-62; Calvary Presbyterian Church, Asheville, N.C.; Current: Director of the Westminster Foundation of the Sonod of Catawba of the United Presbyterian Church, U.S.A.; State of North Carolina of the United Campus Christian Ministry; Mem. Asheville and Buncombe County Citizens Organization-1961-62; N.A.A.C.P. Award: Omega Psi Phi Fra-

ternity Man of the Year in Community Service; Mem.
Omega Psi Phi; North Carolina Human Relation Coun-
cil; Home: 1102 Gorrell Street, Greensboro, N.C.
Church: 1102 Gorrell Street, Greensboro, N.C.

CAREY, Archibald J., Jr., lawyer; b. Chicago, Ill., Feb.
29, 1908; s. Bishop Archibald J. and Elizabeth (Davis)
C.; A.B., Lewis Inst., Chgo, Ill., 1928; B.D., Northwestern U., 1932; LL.B. Chgo., Kent Coll. Law,
1935; D.D. (hon.) Wilberforce U., Ohio, 1943; LL.D,
Campbell Coll., Jackson, Miss., 1950; LL.D. (hon.)
John Marshall Law School, 1954; m. Hazel Harper, Jan.
31, 1931; children---Caryolum Eloise; Ordained to ministry, A.M.E. Ch., 1930; pastor, Woodlawn A.M.E. Ch.,
Chgo., 1930-49; Quinn Chapel A.M.E. Ch., Chgo.,
1940---; Admitted to Ill. bar, 1936--; mem. Prescott,
Taylor, Carey & Cooper; dir., counselor, Unity Mutual
Life Ins. Co.; dir-pres. Ill. Fed. Sav. & Loan Assn.;
Elected alderman, 3d Ward, Chgo., 1947, 51; Rep.
nominee 1st Ill. Dist. U.S. Congress, 1950; Chrmn.
Pres.'s Comm. on Gov. Employment Policy, 1957-61;
vice chrmn, 1955-57; mem. U.S. del. 8th Gen. Assembly, US, 1953; Received 1st prize. Daily News Oratori-
cal Contest, 1924; Edmund W. Burke law scholarship,
1935. mem. Chgo. Council Against Racial and Religious
Discrimination; Am. Brotherhood (Chgo br. Natl Conf. of
Christians and Jews); Alpha Phi Alpha Award of Honor,
1953; Abraham Schwartz Award for Human Relations,
1954; "Useful Citizen" Award, 1954; Northwest Sertoma
Club of Chgo "Service to Mankind" Award, 1956; Order
of Eastern Star National Citation, 1960; Home: 4934
S. Mich. Ave., Chgo, Ill. Office: 188 W. Randolph St.,
Chgo, Ill.

CARPENTER, Charles William, b. Stanford, Ky., May 1,
1886; s. James and Amanda C.; Tuskegee Normal and
Industrial Institute, 1909; Garrett Biblical Institute,
Evanston, Ill., 1917; Payne Theol. Sem., Wilberforce,
Ohio; m. Linnia H. Hopkins; pastor, African Methodist
Episcopal Ch., 18 years, New Duluth, Minn., Joliet,
Ill., Crawfordville, Inc., French Lick, Ind., Marion,
Ind., Muncie, Ind., Toronto, Ontario, Canada; pre-
siding elder, Ontario Conf; pastor, Second Baptist Ch.,
1929---; vice pres., Ann Arbor Ministerial Ass'n, 3
years; Community Fund, YMCA Board, Ann Arbor;
Home: 216 Beakes, Ann Arbor, Mich. 48104

CARRINGTON, Charles L., b. Austin, Texas, Oct. 27,
1909; s. Essex and Palice (Langham) C.; A.B., Samuel
Houston Coll., Austin, Tex., 1930; B.D., Gammon Theol.
Sem., Atlanta, Ga., 1933; M.A., Drew Univ., Madison,
N.J., 1934; Columbia Univ.; New York Univ.; m. Muriel
Jervis; children---Charles Langham C. Jr.; asst. pastor,
director of Rel. Education, St. Mark's Meth. Ch., New
York City, 1934-36; Ordained Elder, The Meth. Ch.,
West Texas Conf., 1936; director, Adult Guidance Bureau,
New York City Bd. of Education, 1936-38; pastor, Butler
Memorial Meth. Ch., Bronx, New York, 1938-48; pastor,
Brooks Memorial Meth. Ch., Jamaica, New York, 1941-
64; Exec. Sec., Bd. of Missions, The New York Conf.,
The Meth. Ch., 1964; Mem., Delaware Conf., 1937-64;
dean, Conference of Meth. Youth Fellowship Assembly,
6 yrs; Dean of Area Pastor's School, 13 yrs.; chmn,
Conf. of Bd. of Christian Social Concerns; Organizer
and chairman, Citizens' Com. on Juvenile Problems;
Organizer and chairman, Citizens' Com. on Juvenile Prob-
lems; Exec. Mem., Pres. (former), Jamaica Branch,
NAACP; Charter and Board Me., Community Council of
South Jamaica; vice pres., Queens Federation of Churches,
Mem., New York Metropolitan Area Planning Com., The
Meth. Church; Home: 223-43 111th Ave., Queens Village,
29, New York; Office: 1228 North Ave., New Rochelle,
New York.

CARRINGTON, John Elmer, b. New Rochelle, New York,
Nov. 18, 1926; s. William O. and Pearl M. (Robinson)
C.; B.S., New York Univ., 1950; B.D., Drew Univ.,
1952; Union Sem., New York City, 1956; New York Univ.,
1958-59; m. Virginia T. De Pass; children---Marlene
Diane, Jeanette Elaine; pastor, St. Luke African Methodist Episcopal Zion Church, Westfield, N.J., 1949-50;
Wallace Chapel A.M.E. Zion Ch., Summit, N.J.,
1950-59; Willis Ave. Meth. Ch., Bronx, N.Y., 1959-
63; Springfield Gardens Meth. Ch., New York City,
1963---; chaplain, Harlem Hospital, New York City
Dept. of Hospitals, 1960---; director, Christian Education, N.J. Annual Conf., A.M.E. Zion Ch., 1951-
57; Mem., New York City Local Sch. for District, 15,
16, 1962-63; US Army Air Corps, 1944-46; Home: 131-
29 Farmers Blvd., Jamaica, New York 11434; Office:
same.

CARRINGTON, William Orlando, b. Georgetown, British

Guiana, Oct. 30, 1879; m. Pearl Robinson; Began pas-
torate 1906 in So. Tenn. Conf. African Methodist
Episcopal Zion Ch.; pastor, First A.M.E. Zion Ch.,
Brooklyn, N.Y., 1936--; Retired 1964; former prof.,
Hood Theol. sem.; Howard Univ. Sch. of Rel.; author:
Carry A Little Honey (book of sermons); Home: 480
Tompkins Ave., Brooklyn, New York.

CARROLL, Edward Gonzalez, chaplain, ch. official; b.
Wheeling, W. Virginia, Jan. 7, 1910; A.B. Morgan Col-
lege, 1930; B.D., Yale Univ., 1933; M.A., Columbia
Univ., 1941; m. Phenola Valentine; children---Edward
Jr., Nansi Ethelene; pastor, St. Andrews Methodist Ch.,
Mt. Washington, Md., 1933-34; pastor, John Wesley
Meth. Ch., Salem, Va., 1934-35; pastor, Methodist
Church, Grafton, W.A., 1936-37; Instructor in Bible
and Philosophy at Morgan College, 1937-41; US Army
Chaplain, 1941-45; Associate Sec. Student Y.M.C.A.,
1945-49, in New York City; Associate pastor, St. Marks
Meth. Church, N.Y. City, 1949-53; pastor, Epworth
Meth. Church, N.Y.C., 1953-55; pastor, Sharp Street
Memorial Methodist Church, Baltimore, Md., 1955-62;
District Supt. Washington District Methodist Ch., Wash-
ington, D.C., 1962---; Mem., Provident Hospital Board
Baltimore, Md., 1960-62; Mem. Governor's Comm. for
the Employment of the Handicapped; Board of Baltimore
Urban League and NAACP, 1955-62; Citation by the
Governor's Safety Committee, 1961; Masons; author:
The Military Chaplaincy," in book "We have this Ministry."
Home: 1710 Varnum NW, Washington 11, D.C.; Office:
110 Maryland Ave., NE, Washington 2, D.C.

CARTER, Churchill, b. Louisville, Ky., July 30, 1922;
s. Churchill and Ethel (B.) C.; B.S., Wilberforce Univ.,
1945; B.D., Payne Theol. Seminary, 1945; M. Litt.,
Univ. of Pittsburgh, 1947; m. Alice Edwina Roston;
children---Toinette Ernestine, Kimberly Ann, Stephen
Earl; pastor, St. James African Methodist Episcopal
Church, 1945-47; pastor, Mallory Chapel A.M.E.
Church, Edenborn and Masontown, 1947-48; St. Mark
A.M.E. Church, Wilkinsburg, 1948-50; pastor, Bethel
A.M.E. Church, Canonsburg, Pa., 1950, St. James A.
M.E. Church, Erie, 1950-57; current pastor, Park
Place A.M.E. Church, Homestead, Pa., 1957---;
Parole Advisor, Penn. State Parole Board; Former
Probation Officer, Juvenile Court, City of Pittsburgh;
Part time physical ed. instructor; Salvation Army

(former); Exec. sec. , Tawawa School of Religion, Wilber-
force Univ. ; Mem. , Governor Lawrence's State Juvenile
Commission; Chairman, Republican Party, Borough of
Homestead, Pa. , 1963-64; Bd. of Directors, Homestead
Community Center, 1959-64; Bd. of Directors, Payne
Theo. Seminary, 1960-64; Mem. , Exec. Bd. , Penna.
Council of Churches, 1958-62; Former Dean, Tawawa
School of Religion, Wilberforce Univ. ; Mem. : Phi Beta
Sigma, Mason, Frontiers International; Republican;
Home: 215 East Tenth Ave. , Homestead, Penna. ; Office:
Park Place. A. M. E. Church, Homestead, Pa.

CARTER, Grover Hester, editor; b. Lishon, La. , Jan. 14,
1889; s. William J. and Cora E. C. ; A. B. , Walden Univ. ,
B. D. , Paine Coll. 1919; D. D. (hon.), Paine College;
principal, Minden High School, 1915-   ; pastor,
Mountain View Ch. of the Christian Methodist Episcopal
Church, Iva. , S. C. ; Holsey Temple C. M. E. Church,
Atlanta, Ga. ; Holsey Temple, Macon, Ga. ; Mitchell
Street, Atlanta, Ga. ; editor, Eastern Index, C. M. E.
Church, Pastor of Trinity C. M. E. Ch. , Augusta, Ga. ;
Publishing Agent of C. M. E. Church, Jackson, Tenn.
pres. , NAACP, Augusta, Ga. ; Mem. , YMCA Board of
Directors, Atlanta, Ga; Trustee Board, Paine Coll. ,
Augusta, Ga. ; Republican; Instrumental in defeating the
Speaker of the House as representative, 1947; Also as
president of the NAACP, revived the Negro vote in
Augusta; Home: 109 Shannon, Jackson, Tenn. ; Office:
109 Shannon, Jackson, Tenn.

CARY, William Sterling, b. Plainsfield, N. J. , 1929; A. B.
Morehouse College; B. D. Union Theol. Sem. ; m. Marie
Belle Phillips, 1952; 2 daus. , Yvonne Eileen, Denise
Marie; 1 son, William Sterling, Jr. ; Pastor, Grace
Congregational Church, Harlem; Mem. UCC Comm. on
Racial Justice Now; UCC Bd. of Homeland Ministries;
Former Vice-Pres. , Protestant Council of N. Y. (Man-
hattan Division). Home: 111-29 196th St. , Hollis 12,
N. Y. Office: 310 W 139th St. , New York, N. Y.

*CATCHINGS, Lincoln Maynard, YMCA sec. ; b. Houston,
Tex. , Oct. 30, 1914; s. Robert M. , Sr. , and Bessie G.
(Maynard) C. ; B. S. , Prairie View Coll. , Texas, 1935;
B. D. , Howard Univ. , 1941; M. A. , Howard Univ. , 1942;
Univ. of Chicago, summer sessions; m. Rose M. Withers;
children--Lincoln M. , Jr. ; teacher, Jackson High Sch. ,
Rosenberg, Texas, 1936-38; Southern Regional Sec. ,

National Student YMCA, 1942-44; "Common Ground"
worker, special consultant for churches and religious
organizations, Dept of Race Relations, American Missionary Assn; pastor, Plymouth Congregational Ch.,
Wash., D.C., 1947-53; asst., Dept. of Social Science,
Fisk Univ., 1945-47; chaplain, Congregational Christian
Students, Howard Univ.; National Assoc. Sec., Commission on Interracial and Intercultural Relations, National Student Council YMCA, 1953---; Mem., Bd. of Public Welfare for the District of Columbia, 1952---; Bd.
of Directors, Wash. Urban League; chairman, Commission on Community Life of the Wash. Federation of
Churches; Director of Education, Eastern Region of Alpha
Phi Alpha; Bd. of Trustees, United Community Services
of the D.C.; Bd. of Directors, Wash. Federation of
Churches; The Jesse Mitchell Club; Nominating Com-
mittee of Family and Child Welfare, Section of United
Community Services; Commentator: "Religion in the
News" - Newscast over WCPM; Awarded Plaque for out-
standing community service by Wash. Afro-American
Newspaper; Mem., Bd. of Trustees, Planned Parenthood
Assn., Wash., D.C.; Exec. Committee, Family and
Child Welfare Section, U.C.S.; Philosophy Club, Howard
Univ.; Institute of Religion, sponsored by Sch. of Rel.,
Howard Univ.; Bd. of Freedom Rally, Inc.; Fact Finding
Committee of Interdenominational Ministers Alliance
(chairman); chairman, committee to draft statement to
Pres. Eisenhower on elimination of segregation for Fra-
ternal Council of Churches; Mem., Nominating Committee
of the General Council of Congregational Christian
Churches; Christian Citizenship Committee of the Council
for Social Action of the Congregational Christian Churches;
National Advisory Committee on Race Relations, Ameri-
can Missionary Assn; assoc. director, International
Work Camp in La Chambon, France, 1950; Exec. Council of Christian Action; Exec. Com. of the Fellowship of
Southern Churches; Alpha Kappa Delta; Citation by Bd. of
Commissioners of Wash., D.C. for distinguished public
service; Office: Malayan Council of YMCA, A. Orchard
Rd., Singapore 9, Malaya.

CAUTION, Tollie LeRoy, Sr., church official; b. Baltimore,
    Md., Aug. 20, 1902; s. Gustave Orville and Blanche
    (Johnson) C; A.B., Cum Laude, Lincoln Univ., Penn.,
    1926; S.T.B., Magna Cum Laude, Phila. Div. Sch.,
    1929; M.A., Univ. of Penn., 1929; D.D. (hon.), Lincoln
    Univ., 1947; D.D., Phila. Div. School, 1954; m. Cora

Marie Gosnell; children---Tollie LeRoy, Jr.; Ordained
1930; vicar and rector, Parishes in Md., Pa. and N.Y.;
asst. sec., Home Dept., Nat'l Council of the Protestant
Episcopal Church working with Negroes, Orientals,
Puerto Ricans and Mexican Americans, 1945---; Trustee
St. Augustine's Coll., Raleigh, N.C.; Trustee, Voor-
hees Coll., Denmark, S.C.; Bd. of Trustee, Okolona
Coll., Okolona, Miss.; Bishop Payne Divinity School;
Phila. Divinity School; Fort Valley Coll. Center, Fort
Valley, Ga.; secy., Amer. Church Institute; director,
Summer Schools of Religious Education for St. Augustine's,
Voorhees and Okolona Coll.; Comm., Episcopal Nat'l
Council; Committee, Nat'l Council of Churches of Christ,
USA; Mem., Mason; Kappa Alpha Psi; Rural Workers
Fellowship; Life Mem., NAACP; Mem., Southern Chris-
tian Leadership Conference; Southern Conference Educa-
tion Fund; author: A Decade of Progress in Negro Work;
The Protestant Episcopal Church:Policies and Rationale
Upon Which Support Of Its Negro Colleges Is Predicated;
Home: 549 West 123rd St., NYC 10027; Office: 815
Second Ave., NYC 10017

CHAMBERS, James Coolidge, s. John and Mary Elizabeth
(Cunningham) C.; A.B., Virginia Union Univ.; B.D.,
Yale Divinity School, Recipient Jesse Hayes Fellow at
Yale; m. Yolande Hargraves; children---Esther, James
and Timothy; pastor, Organizing minister Covenant Presbyterian Ch.; Norfolk Presbytery, Norfolk, Va.; Organized Community United Presbyterian Ch., Presbytery
of Virginia, United Presbyterian Ch., Portsmouth, Virginia; current: St. John's Presbyterian Ch., Detroit,
Mich.; mem.: chmn. United Negro College Fund Financial Drive in Virginia; Detroit Fellowship of Urban Ch.
chmn. Steering Committee for Central City Redevelopment Corporation Housing Commissioner, City of Detroit,
Mich.;Home: 2326 Atkinson, Detroit, Mich.; Office: 1410 Jos
Campau, Detroit, Mich.

CHAMBERS, Timothy Moses, b. Mt. Pleasant, Texas,
June 19, 1899; s. C.C. and Jeraline C.; Bishop Coll.,
Marshall, Texas; Princeton Theol. Sem., 1921; S.T.D.
(honorary) Princeton U.; D.D. (honorary), Coleman
Coll.; m. Hazel Thomas; 2 sons, Timothy, Jr., Jonnie
Madlock; 1 dau., Eunice M.; Dir. Extension Work,
Ark. Bapt. Coll., Pine Bluff, Ark.; Pres., Bapt. Miss.
& Ed. Conv., Texas, 1946-50; Pastor, Zion Hill Baptist
Conv. of Amer., Inc., 1962--; Instr., Ministers' In-

stitute, Ark. Bapt. Coll.; mem. Seminar & Preacher's
Staff, Nat. L. K. Williams Institute, Bishop Coll.; Instr.
Sch. of Leadership Training, West. Bapt. Conv., Calif.
and Bapt. Minister's Union, S. Calif.; Pres., Inter-
denominational Minister's Alliance, L. A. & Vicinity;
Trustee, Bishop College; "Minister of the Year", 1960;
Rec., Distinguished Service Award, Bishop Coll.;
Church Administration Award, Southern Bapt. Conv.;
Democrat; Speaker, Bapt. World Alliance, Copenhagen,
Denmark, 1947; Author: Chambers at the Blackboard,
The Revival Pattern, The Petical Mouthpiece; Home:
3890 6th Ave., Los Angeles, Calif. Church: 5025 S.
McKinley Ave., Los Angeles 11, Calif.

CHAMBLISS, Carroll Randolph, chaplain; b. Jackson,
Miss. May 29, 1925; s. Jesse Rudolph and Noro Viola
(Robinson) C.; A. B., Wilberforce Univ., Ohio, 1951;
B. D., Payne Theo. Seminary, Wilberforce, Ohio, 1951;
Further study: Washington Univ., Concordia Seminary,
St. Louis, Mo.; m. Christene Helen Knew; children---
Randolph, Francis, Christopher, Philip A.; pastor, St.
Matthew African Methodist Episcopal Church, St. Louis,
Mo., 1951-56; US Navy Chaplain, 1956---; American
Theatre, Asiatic Pacific, World War II Victory Medal;
Home: 903 Langford St., Oceanside, Calif. 92054; Office:
USS Prairie Yofpo San Francisco, Calif. 96601

CHANDLER, James Cleveland, b. State-line, Miss., June
20, 1911; s. Bose and Lucy (Lang) C.; A. B., Dillard
Univ.; Th. M., Union Bapt. Sem.; m. Hallowene Inez
Reed; children--- Charles E. James C., Jr.; pastor,
St. Elmo Bapt. Ch., Laurel, Miss.; pres., East
Sunday School & Bapt. Training Union Congress; State
vice pres., National Sunday School and B. T. U.; instruc-
tor, East Miss. District S. S. & B. T. U. Congress;
leader, Voter Registration Movement, Hattiesburg,
Miss., 1961; Mem., National Bapt. Conv., USA, Inc.;
NAACP; Phi Beta Sigma; Mason; Home: Laurel, 512 S.
6th Laurel, Miss. 39440, Office: 512 S. 6th Ave.,
Laurel, Miss. 39440

*CHAPPELLE, Ezekiel Emerson, Jr., sem. prof.; b.
Greenwood, S. C., May 31, 1915; s. E. E. and Susie A.
C.; A. B., Benedict Coll., 1937; B. D., Howard Univ.,
1940; S. T. M., Oberlin Graduate School of Theology,
1941; D. R. E., Central Baptist Sem., 1958; m. Thelma
Dunston; children---Charles Wesley, Bernice Virginia;

Second Baptist Church, Elyria, Ohio, 1 year while in
school at Oberlin; pastor, First Baptist Church, Suffolk,
Va., 4 years; Second Baptist Church, Kansas City, Mo.
1946---; teacher, Western Baptist Coll., 12 years;
Mem., Advisory Bd., Queen of World Hospital; Rehabilitation Institute; Council of Churches; vice moderator, Fellowship District Ass'n; author: The Voice of God,
by the Carlton Press, N.Y.C.; Home: 3224 E. 29th Kansas City, Mo.; Office: Second Baptist Church, 39th
Monroe, Kansas City, Mo.

CHAPPELLE, Thomas Oscar, dean; b. Sapulpa, Okla., Oct.
15, 1915; S. Peter A. and Sacannah B.; A.B., Bishop
Coll., 1934; B.Th., American Baptist Theol. Sem.,
Nashville, Tenn., 1936; m. Elizabeth Louise; children---
Flora, Thomas, Carlos; director, Christian Education
Third Baptist Toledo, Ohio, 1937-40; dean, Oklahoma
Sch. of Religion, 1940-42; pastor, Morning Star Baptist
Ch., Tulsa, 1942---; owner, Rest Haven Nursing Home,
Tulsa, Okla.; pres., Moton Memorial Hospital Bd.; pres.
Oklahoma Baptist Congress of Christian Education;
assoc. director, General of the National Sunday School
and B.T.U. Congress; D.D. (hon.), Wright Sch. of
Rel., Morris Booker Baptist Coll., Birmingham Baptist
Coll.; Distinguished Service Award, Tulsa Council of
Churches; Mem., NAACP; Tulsa Urban League; The
Prince Hall Masonic Lodge; Democrat; author: How We
Do It, 1960; Home: 1136 E. 26 Pl. N., Tulsa 6, Okla.;
Office: 1014 East Pine St., Tulsa 6, Okla.

*CHASE, Lendall Warren, b. Wash., D.C.; s. Berry Ray-
mond and Carrie (Jackson) C.; A.B., Lincoln Univ.,
Pa., 1937-42; B.D., Howard Univ. Sch. of Rel., Wash.,
D.C., 1950; m. Elnora Elizabeth Ellis; children---
Lendall W. Jr., Patricia G., Larry W., Percy R.,
Elaine E.; asst. pastor, Tabernacle Baptist Church,
Wash., 1949-53; pastor, High Street Baptist Church,
Danville, Va., 1953---; Bd. of Manager, Brodnax
Branch YMCA, 1954-56; vice pres., Danville Minister-
ial Ass'n, 1953-60; pres., Ministerial Alliance of Dan-
ville & Vicinity, sec., Chr. of Civic Affairs Comm.;
substitute teacher, Pittsylvania County School System;
Mem., Bd. of Danville Branch NAACP; pres., Danville
Christian Progressive Ass'n (affiliate of Southern Christian Leadership Conference); US Army, 1942-45; Home:
632 High St., Danville, Va.; Office: 630 High St., Danville, Va.

CHEATHAM, William Lee, Church official, b. Belzonia,
Miss., August 25, 1899; s. William and Lydia (Dixon)
C.; Oakwood College, Huntsville, Ala., 1921; m.
Laura Elizabeth Muir; 6 sons and 2 daughters. Pastor:
Dover and Wilmington, Delaware, 1937-44; Berea Tem-
ple, Baltimore, Md., 1944-53. President, Allegheny Conf.
of Seventh-Day Adventists; chairman, Board of Pine
Forge, Pa. Academy, 1953-63; vice-chairman, Board of
the Hadley Hospital, Washington, D.C.; trustee, River-
side Hospital Board, Nashville, Tenn. Member:- Trustee
Board of Oakwood College, Huntsville, Ala., Columbia
Union Coll., Washington, D.C., Charles F. Kettering
Memorial Hospital, Dayton, Ohio. Member:- Human Re-
lations Committee, General Conf. of S.D.A., Washington, D.C.; Executive Committee, Columbia Union Conf.,
Takoma Park, Md. Home: Manatawny Road, Pine Forge,
Penna. Office: P.O. Box 21, Pine Forge, Penna.

CHERRY, Charles Alexander, b. Anderson, S.C.; s.
Charles E. and Florence C.C.; A.B., Benedict Coll.,
1935; B.D., Oberlin Graduate Sch. of Theology, Ohio,
1949; m. Verna Mungin; children---Ruth Deborah, Charles
A., Jr.; pastor, Dunn's Creek Baptist Church, Ware
Shoals, S.C., 1940-44; chaplain, US Army, 1944-46,
served at Camp Ellis, Ill., Camp Howrah, Calcutta,
India; coll. pastor, Benedict Coll., 1949-58; pastor,
Central Baptist Ch., Charleston, S.C., 1951-53; cur-
rent, field representative, Benedict Coll. and pastor,
Liberty Hill Baptist Ch., Catawba, S.C., teacher, public
schools of S.C., 1935-44; decorations: Asiatic-Pacific
Campaign Medal; American Campaign Medal; World War
II Victory Medal; Mem., Omega Psi Phi; Home: Benedict
Coll, Columbia, S.C.

CHERRY, Henry C., b. Benoit, Miss., March 20, 1905;
s. Nealy Cherry; Eng. Bible Diploma, Miss. Bapt. Sem.,
Inc.; D.D. (hon.) Natchez College, Natchez, Miss.; m.
Rachel Simmons; 1 son, Archie L. Adams; Pastored,
Strangers Home Bapt., Shaw, Miss.; First Bapt.,
Memphis, Tenn.; Macedonia Bapt. Ch., Benoit, Miss.;
Mod. Bolivar Co. Gen. Bapt. Assoc.; Vice-Pres. at
large, Progressive Bapt. State Conv., Miss.; Trustee,
Miss. Bapt. Sem., Inc.; Mem. Bd. Management, Tabor-
ian Hosp., Mound Bayou, Miss; Trustee, Natchez Coll.,
Natchez, Miss.; Church: Box 123, Benoit, Miss.

*CHERRY, Maurice Stallworth, b. Cordele, Ga., Dec. 2,
1932; s. Jeffery Lee and Olivia (Dean) C.; B.A., Paine
Coll., 1952; B.D., Howard Univ. Sch. of Rel., 1955;
m. Joyce Lundy; Director of Youth Work, Christian
Methodist Episcopal Churches of Ga., 1955-59; pastor,
Davisboro Circuit C.M.E. Church, 1955; pastor,
Montezuma Circuit C.M.E. Church, 1955-59; chaplain,
Paine Coll., 1959-61; chaplain and dean of men, Paine
Coll., 1961; graduate study in O.T., Emory Univ.,
1963---; counselor, Paine Coll. Student Movement,
1960-63; Mem., American Academy of Religion; Board
of Christian Education, C.M.E. Church, 1956-60; pres.,
National Christian Youth Fellowship, C.M.E. Church,
1956-60; home: 851 Clifton Court Circuit Apt. 7, Atlanta,
Ga. 30329.

*CHRISTIAN, George Benjamin, b. Winston-Salem, N.C.,
Dec. 8, 1908; s. Joseph Benjamin and Hattie (Patterson)
C.; B.S., Shaw Univ., Raleigh, N.C.; B.D., Howard
Univ. Sch. of Rel., Wash., D.C. 1949; m. Margaret
Delores Odom; children---Randolph Harrison; teacher,
Public School, W-Salem, N.C., 1930-38; US Employment
Service, Interviewer, 1938-41; Youth Counselor, Nat'l
Youth Adm., 1941-42; War Manpower Recruiting Officer,
US Employment Service, Eastern, N.C., 1942-44; Pro-
gram Director, U.S.O., Norfolk, Va., 1944-46; chaplain
and organizer, Westminster Foundation, Howard Univ.,
1949-51; director, Knox Community Center, Baltimore,
1951-53; pastor, Bethel Presbyterian Church, Plainfield,
N.J., 1953---; Bd. of Directors, Red Cross, Plainfield
Chapter, 1955-50; Bd. Directors, Community Service
Council, 1956---; Bd. of Directors, Neighborhood House,
1957-58; Mayor's Civil Rights Commission, 1958-63; cur-
rent mem., Mayor's Commission on Human Rights; Staff
of Chaplains, Veterans Hospital, Lyons, N.J.; Trustee
Presbytery of Elizabeth; moderator, Presbytery of
Elizabeth (former); Certificate of Appreciation, Red
Cross, Plainfield Chapter, for 5 years service, 1960;
Mem., Phi Beta Sigma; Frontiers; International Service
Club; Mason; Fellow-Institute of Religious Studies, Jewish
Theol. Seminary, N.Y.C.; Alumnus, Rutgers Human Re-
lations Workshop; Home: 751 Webster Pl., Plainfield,
N.J.: Office: 300 E. 5th St., Plainfield, N.J.

CHRISTIAN, Gerald Chilton, b. Antigua, B.W.I., Feb. 28,
1916; s. Joseph Martin and Maria (Frances) C.; A.B.,
City Coll., New York, 1939; B.D., Chicago Theol.

Sem., 1943; M.A., Drew Univ., 1947; pastor, St. Luke
Congregational Church, Little Rock, Ark., 1939-43; St.
Luke's Congregational Church, 1947-52; Oak Park United
Church of Christ, Sacramento, Calif., 1952---; sec.,
Urban League, Little Rock, Ark.; pres., Boys Work,
YMCA, Ark.; pres., Neighborhood Council; moderator,
Sacramento Valley Assn, United Church of Christ; Oral
Panel Bd. Member, State of California; Mem., Mason;
Phi Beta Sigma; Ministerial Assn; Licensed Religious Ed.
Teacher, National Council of Churches; Home: 2761
Santa Clara Way, Sacramento 17, Calif.; Office: 3308
4th Avenue, Sacramento 17, Calif.

CLAIR, Matthew Walker, Jr., bishop; b. Harpers Ferry,
W.Va., Aug. 12, 1890; s. Matthew Wesley and Fannie
Meade (Walker) C.; Syracuse Univ., 1909; B.A., Howard
Univ., 1915; S.T.B., Boston Univ., 1918; S.T.M., Iliff
Sch. of Theol., 1927; D.D. (hon.), Morgan Univ., 1934;
Gammon Theol. Sem., 1936; m. Ethel C. Smith, Nov.
25, 1920; children--Phyllis Ann, Ethel Maxine (Mrs.
Jasper Wilson); Ordained to ministry, Meth. Ch., 1917;
prof. practical theology, Gammon Theol. Sem., 1936-40;
pastor, St. Mark Meth. Ch., Chgo; bishop, Meth. Ch.;
Council Bishops, N.Y.C.; Mem., Bd. of Directors, E.
Stanley Jones Union; chaplain, 380 Labor Bn., US Army,
World War I; Mem., Ch. Federation of Greater Chgo.;
Gen. Conf. Com Ministerial Training of Meth. Ch.; Pi
Gamma Mu; Alpha Phi Alpha; Home: Box 234 Main Post
Office, St. Louis 66, Mo.

CLANCY, Bryant Edward, b. Catherine, Alabama, Jan.
23, 1937; s. Bryant and Ida (Clark) C; Immanuel
Lutheran College & Seminary, Greensboro, N.C., 1956-
61; 1958, AlB. (Magna Cum Laude) 1961 Diploma of
Graduation from Seminary (Cum Laude); m. Elma
Pearl Neely; vicar, St. Andrew Lutheran Church, Char-
lotte, N.C., Grace Lutheran Church, Concord, N.C.,
1953-62; pastor, St. Andrew's Lutheran Church, Char-
lotte, N.C.; Member, Lutheran Human Relation Associa-
tion of America; Member, NAACP; Member, Democratic
Party; sec., Tri-Circuit Conference, sec. Charlotte
Lutheran Urban Church Study Committee; treasurer,
Charlotte Lutheran Ministerial Association: Home: 2607
Abelwood Road, Charlotte 8, N.C.; Ch.: 213 N. Mc
Dowell, Charlotte 6, N.C.

CLARK, Isaac Rufus, sem. prof.; b. New Castle, Pa.,
Feb. 15, 1925; s. James H. and Lillian (Alexander) C.;
B. A., Wilberforce Univ., 1951; B. D., Payne Theol.
Sem., 1952; Th. D., Boston Univ. Sch. of Theology,
1958; post-doctoral studies, summers of 1959, 1962,
1963, Union Theol. Sem., N. Y.; m. Betty Jane Clark;
children---Isaac R. Jr., Karen E.; pastor, Bethel
African Methodist Episcopal Church, Lynn, Mass., 1952-
53; Bethel A. M. E. Ch., New Bedford, Mass., 1953-55;
asst. & assoc. prof., Systematic Theology, Payne Theol.
Sem., Wilberforce, Ohio, 1955-60; dean & assoc. prof.,
Paul Quinn Coll., Waco, Tex., 1960-62; current prof.,
Interdenominational Theol. Center, Atlanta, Ga., 1962--;
director, Field Education, Interdenominational Theol.
Center; Religious News Broadcasting Each Sunday over
WAOK, Atlanta; director, Kitty Haven Nursery School,
1960; US Navy, 1943-46; Conduct and Asiatic-Pacific
Medals from Navy; Mem. (former), Nat. Assn of Col-
legiate Deans & Registrars; Mem., Alpha Kappa Mu
Honor Society; Assn of Texas Coll. and Univs.; Assn.
of Field Work Directors of Theol. Sems.; AAUP;
NAACP; Democrat; YMCA; Collaborating with profs. in
Homiletics at Candler and Columbia Sems. on Value of
Television Media in the teaching of Homiletics, work
done at Protestant Radio and TV Center; home: 157
Ct., Atlanta, Ga.; office: 671 Beckwith SW, Atlanta,
Ga.

CLARK, James I., bishop; b. Trinidad B. W. I., Sept. 6,
1906; s. William and Alberta (James) C.; Governor
School, Elen. 1921, W. I. Shelton College, National
Bible Inst. 1936-43, Certificate and Th. B. College of
Paterson, 1945-47, Bloomfield College, 1949, American
Bible College, Chicago, Th. D., D. D., 1952; Further
study: General Jewish Theological Seminary; m. Rachel
Johnson; children--- James I, Jr., William S., Mrs.
Albertha Thomas, Alvin Thomas, Benjamin W., Joseph
Alan, Mary, Hubert, Henretta, Lois, Frances; Ordained
1932 in the Bible Way Church of Our Lord Jesus Christ
World-Wide, Inc., 1932 after 2 years of evangelistic
work; pastor, Bible Way Church, Patterson, New Jersey,
1941-55; dean, The Bible Institute, 1955-58; pastor,
Straight Gate Church, Mamaro, N. Y., Overseer, States
of North Carolina and Connecticut; Organized, Christ
Temple Church; Consecrated Bishop of Diocese of New
York and West Indies, 1962---; Conducts: Bible School
for Training of Christian Workers, in Westchester

County, New York; Member: Mason: Interdenominational
Ministers Conference, N.Y.; YMCA; Chairman, Board
of Education, Protestant Council, N.Y.; Home: 25-63
98 St. E. Elmhurst 69 L.I., N.Y. Office: 507-09 West
125th St., N.Y., N.Y.

CLARK, Moses Julius, b. Catherine, Ala., July 4, 1925;
s. Madison and Lola (Funish) C.; Alabama Lutheran
Academy; Immanuel Lutheran College, Greensboro, N.C.;
1950-55; m. Lucille E. Dale; m. Miriam Marie, Moses
J. Jr., Lydia L., Cynthia D.; pastor, St. Matthew
Lutheran Church, Arlington, Ala., St. Luke Lutheran
Church, Laminson, Ala., 1955-57; St. Paul Lutheran
Church, Oak Hill, Ala., 1957-63; Christ Lutheran
Church, Rosebud, Ala.; Gethsemane Lutheran Church,
Hamburg, Ala.; St. Mark Lutheran Church, Ackerville,
Ala.; Augustana Lutheran Church, Alexandria, La.; St.
Paul Lutheran Church, Mansura, La.; Service, US Air
Force, 1943-46; awards: America Service, Good Conduct
World War II Victory Medal; Ch.: Augustana Lutheran
Church, Alexandria, La.

CLARKE, Aloysius Roland, teacher; b. Washington, D.C.
Oct. 17, 1928; s. William Lownes and Lottie (Johnson)
C.; St. Augustine Seminary, Bay St. Louis, Miss., 1945-
49; B.A., S.T.B., Benedictine Mission Seminary,
Newton, N.J., 1950-59; Univ. of Wurzburg, 1960-61;
Fordham Univ. (NYC), 1961-63; M.A.; Prefect and Instr.
Benedictine Mission Seminary, 1959-60; Asst. Pastor,
St. Charles Borromeo Ch., NYC, 1962, Instr. Bene-
dictine Mission Seminary, 1962--; Vice-Pres., Sussex
City., Community Relations Council, 1963--; Home:
St. Paul's Abbey, Newton, New Jersey.

CLARKE, Elisha Salathiel, b. Miami, Fla., July 30, 1921;
s. Elisha Salathiel and Theodora (Johnson) C.; A.B.,
St. Augustines Coll., Raleigh, N.C., 1945; B.D., Bishop
Payne Divinity Sch., Petersburg, Va., 1948, m. Julia
Rebecca Smith; children---Sheila Coleen, Elisha
Salathiel III, Alison Trienette; rector, St. Matthew's
Episcopal Ch., Delray Beach, Fla.; St. James Episco-
pal Ch., Tampa, Fla.; The Ch. of the Incarnation,
Miami, Fla.; The Church of the Transfiguration, Opa
Locka, Fla.; Mem., Bd. of Directors; James' E. Scott
Community Assn; Alpha Psi Alpha; Home: 1984 NW 153rd
St., Opa Locka, Fla.

CLARKE, Jimmy Ed., librarian; b. Tuler, Texas, Feb.
20, 1934; s. Junius and Lillie (M.) C.; B.S., Texas
College, Tyler, Texas, 1954; Perkins School of Theology
S.M.U., 1954-55; B.D., North Texas State University,
Denton, Summer 1959; M.S., Illinois 1962; m. Norma
Jean Tilley; 1 son: Chandran Edward. Public School
teacher, Kerens, Texas, 1955-57; pastor, Powell
Chapel C.M.E. Church, Kerens, Texas; Brookins C.M.
E. Church, Malakoff, Texas, 1953-57; circulation librar-
ian, Bridwell Library, Perkins School of Theology,
Southern Methodist Univ., 1959-62; pastor, Magnolia C.
M.E. Church, Dallas, 1962-1964; present, Librarian,
Interdenominational Theol. Center; Atlanta, Ga., 1964.
Instructor in the Texas Pastor's School each summer at
Texas College, Tyler, Texas; member: Board of Chris-
tian Education of the Dallas-Fort Worth Conf. of the
C.M.E. Church, and the Advisory Council of the Dallas
Youth Council of the C.M.E. Church; chairman, Leader-
ship Education Section of the National Christian Educa-
tion Council of the C.M.E. Church; Asst. secretary,
Dallas C.M.E. Ministerial Alliance; secretary-treasurer,
Board of Directors, Youth Opportunities Incorporated.
Awarded a Lilly Fellowship to study at Illinois; Kappa
Alpha Psi Beta Kappa Chi in undergraduate science.
Office: Interdenominational Theol. Sem., Atlanta, Ga.

*CLATER, Bobbie Daniel, coll. dean; b. Dallas, Texas,
April 3, 1927; s. Marshall and Pauline Lillian W.; A.
B., Bishop Coll., 1948; M. Ed., Bishop Coll., 1951;
B.D., Howard Univ. Sch. of Rel., 1954; m. Virginia
Alice Douglas; children---Brian Daniel, Robert Douglas;
pastor, New Hope Bapt. Ch., Como, Texas; Liberty
Bapt. Ch. and St. Mark Bapt. Ch., Marshall, Tex.,
1945-51; asst. pastor, Lane Christian Methodist Ch.,
Wash., D.C.; dean of Men and Teacher in Religion,
Bishop Coll., 1949-51; Dean of Students and Chairman
of Dept. of Practical Theol., Oklahoma Sch. of Rel.,
Langston, Okla., 1954-56; director, Bapt. Student Work
and Chair of Bible, Lincoln Univ., Jefferson City, Mis-
souri, 1956-63; Current pastor, Mt. Zion Baptist Ch.,
Bunceton, Mo., 1963---; Mem., Missouri Council of
Social Welfare, Council on Religion and Race, NAACP;
National Council on Family Life; pres., Ministerial Al-
liance, 1965---; dean, S.S. and B.T.U. Congress, Mt.
Carmel District, Mo.; mem., Council of Religion and
Race; Omega Psi Phi; Democrat; home; 413 N. 5th
St. Columbia, Missouri; office: Second Bapt. Ch., 4th

and Broadway, Columbia, Missouri

CLAY, W. Benjamin, b. Yazoo City Miss., Feb. 16,
1927; s. Rev. Henry C. Sr. and Clara C; A. B. Rust
College, B. D. Gammon Theological Seminary, D. D. Na-
tional Bible School; m. Ruth D. Clay; Children: W.
Benjamin, Jr. Jonathan, Margo; Present: Pastor of
Gammon Methodist Church, Chicago, Ill.; President of
Interracial Methodist Group, Y. M. C. A. Home: 229 S.
Central Park, Chicago 24, Ill Office: 1959 W. Maypole
Avenue, Chicago 12, Ill.

CLAYTON, Robert Louis, Jr. b. Pensacola, Fla., Feb.
25, 1934; s. Robert L. Sr. and Louise Clayton (Hardy);
A. B., Talladega Coll., 1955; Gammon Sem., 1955-56;
B. D., Hood Sem., Livingstone Coll., 1959; Emory
Univ., 1964; S. T. M. Candidate, Interdenominational
Theol. Center, 1963-64; m. Minnie Harris; children---
Robert Joel, Myrna Audiness; Ordained pastor, The
A. M. E. Ch.; pastor, Union Temple A. M. E. Ch.,
Athens, Ga., 1955-56; Pleasant Grove, Cheraw, S. C.,
1958-59; Tenn. Valley Community Ch., Florence, Ala.,
1961-63; asst. dean of Chapel, Dillard Univ., New Or-
leans, La., 1957-58; acting chaplain and instructor,
Alabama A & M Coll., Normal, Ala.; current instructor
and director of publicity and placement, Interdenomina-
tional Theol. Center, Atlanta, Ga.; youth consultant,
Christian Education Convention; Advancement chairman,
Monto Sano Dist., Boy Scouts of America; Football and
Basketball official for high schools; pres., Graduate
Chapter of Fraternity initiating Adult Literacy programs
for Voter Registration, 1962-63; worked in Harris Home
for Children Program; Mem., Ala. Interscholastic Ath-
letic Assn; Ala. Sociologist and Anthropologist Assn;
Ala. State Teachers Assn; Alpha Phi Alpha; American
Teachers Assn; Assn for the Coordination of Univ. Re-
ligious Affairs; Boy Scouts of America; Nat. Assn of
Coll. and Univ. Chaplains; National Education Assn;
Religious Education Assn; Southern Intercollegiate Athletic
Assn; NAACP; The Passive Revolution of Jesus, The
Many Faces of God, and The Person of Christ In The
New Testament are lectures now being used Nkawkaw
Training Coll., Ghana, W. Africa; The Danforth Founda-
tion Seminary Internship Award, 1957; home: 653 Beck-
with St., Atlanta, Ga. 30314

CLEAGE, Albert Buford, Jr., b. Indianapolis, Inc., June
13, 1911; s. Albert Buford and Pearl (Reed) C.; A. B.,
Wayne State Univ., Detroit, Mich., 1937: B.D., Oberlin
Grad. Sch. of Theology, Oberlin, Ohio; Univ. of Southern
Calif., Los Angeles, Calif.; Wayne State Univ. Graduate
Sch.; m. Doris Graham; children---Kristin, Pearl; case
worker, Detroit Dept. of Public Welfare, 1937-38; pastor,
Chandler Memorial Congregational Ch., Lexington, Ky.,
1942-43; Fellowship Ch. of All Peoples, San Francisco,
Calif., 1943-44; St. John's Congregational Ch., Spring-
field, Mass., 1946-51; St. Mark's Community Ch.,
Detroit, Mich., 1951-52; current, Central Congregational
Ch., Detroit, Mich., 1952---; chairman, Housing Com.,
Exec. Bd., NAACP, 1948-51; Mem., Round Table Conf.
of Christians and Jews, Springfield, Mass., 1950-51;
NAACP Exec. Bd., Detroit, Mich., 1951, 1963---;
Group on Advanced Leadership Exec. Bd., Detroit,
Mich., 1962---; The Freedom Now Political Party,
Michigan State Chairman, 1963---; The United Ch. of
Christ Ministerium, Detroit, Mich., 1964; The Congrega-
tional Ministers Assn., Detroit, Mich., 1953-63; assoc.
editor, Metro-Newsweekly, Detroit, Mich., 1959-60;
contributing editor, The Illustrated News, Detroit, Mich.,
1962---; Home: 2042 Calvert, Detroit 6, Mich.; Office:
7625 Linwood, Detroit, Mich.

CLEMENTS, George Harold, b. Chicago, Ill., Jan. 26,
1932; s. Samuel G. and Aldonia (Peters) C.; Quizly
Preparatory Seminary, 1945-50; B.A., M.A., S.T.B.,
St. Mary of the Lake; Asst. Priest, St. Ambrose, 1957-
62; St. Dorothy, 1962-64; Mem. Cath. Interracial Council, NAACP, Urban League, H.O.M.E.; Home: 450 E.
78 St., Chgo. 19, Ill.

*CLIFFORD, Richard Lorenzo, b. Romney, W. Va., April
23, 1916; s. Earl Overton and Ruth (Fisher) R.; A.B.,
Clark Coll., 1940; A.M., W. Va. Univ., 1952; B.D.,
Howard Univ. Sch. of Religion, 1963; m. Robertine
Lewis; children---Sharon Louise; Linda Marie; Nancy
Kay; pastor, The Methodist Church, Johnstown, Pa.,
1940; Prostburg, Md., 1941; Grafton, Morgantown, W.
Va., 1946-47; Wheeling, W. Va., 1946-53; Washington,
D.C., Simpson, 1953-55; Centenial, Baltimore, Md.,
1955-59; current supt., The Va.-Washington Dist. of the
Washington Annual Conf. of the Meth. Ch.; current exec.
sec., Bd. of Christian Education, N.C., Va. Conf. of
Meth. Ch.; visiting clergy service, Johns Hopkins Hospi-

tal, Baltimore, Md., 1955-59; Bd. of Directors, Wesley
Foundation, Howard University, 1960---; mem., Amer-
ican Sociological Society; Society for the study of Social
Problems; Office: 4016 W. Broad St., Richmond, Va.

COAN, Josephus Roosevelt, sem. prof., b. Spartanburg,
S.C.; Nov. 26, 1902; s. Andrew Johnson and Mary Ann
(Foster) C.; A.B., Howard Univ., 1930; B.D., Yale
Divinity School, 1933; M.A. Yale University Graduate
School, 1934; D.D. (hon.), Morris Brown Coll., 1938;
Ph.D., Hartford Seminary Foundation, 1961; m. Sammye
Elizabeth Fuller; pastor, Rhode Island, 1933-34; Adairs-
ville, Ga., 1935; Dallas, Ga., 1936; Morris Brown Coll.,
Atlanta, 1934-38; 1948---; missionary, South and Central
Africa, 1938-47; associate editor, A.M.E. Journal of
Religious Education; Writer of Adult Sunday School
Quarterly; Head of the Division of Philosophy and Re-
ligion, Morris Brown College; current prof., Christian
Education & Missions, Interdenominational Theological
Center, Atlanta, Ga.; Director of Religious Education,
A.M.E. Church in Ga.; Mem., Exec. Comm. of the Ga.
Council Churches; NAACP; AAUP, AHA, AMSAC, Theta
Phi, Phi Beta Sigma, MABI, NACUC, REA; author:
Daniel Alexander Payne: Christian Education, 1935; Ph.
D. Dissertation, The Expansion of Missions of the
A.M.E. Church in South Africa, 1896-1908; Education
Among the Bantu People of South Africa; 1949; Home:
244 W. Lake Ave., Atlanta 14, Ga.; Office: 671 Beck-
with St., SW, Atlanta 14, Ga.

*COBB, Charles Earl, coll. chaplain; b. Durham, N.C.,
Sept. 28, 1916; s. James Samuel and Mary (Cox) C.;
A.B., N.C. Coll., 1940; B.D., Howard Univ. Sch. of
Rel.; S.T.M., Boston Univ.; Residential requirements
for Th.D., Boston Univ.; m. Martha Bea Kendrick;
children---Charles E. Jr., Ann C., M. Adrienne,
Janet E.; pastor, St. John's African Methodist Episcopal
Church, Frankfort, Ky., 1947-51; St. Mark Congrega-
tional Church and Social Center, Boston, Mass., 1944-
47; chaplain and dean of men, Kentucky State Coll.,
1947-51; present, pastor, St. John's Congregational Ch.,
1951---; organizer, School of Civic Responsibility,
Springfield, Mass; director, Dramatics, St. John's
Players, St. John's Congregational Church, Springfield,
Mass.; chairman, Legal Redress Committee, Publicity
Committee, Springfield Branch, NAACP; organizer and
first pres., Springfield Civic Ass'n; Executive Committee,

Citizen's Action Commission (By Major) Springfield,
Mass.; commissioner, Public Welfare Commission,
Springfield, Mass.; pres., Eisenhower's Committee on
Government Contracts, Religious Leaders Conference,
Wash., D.C.; Award: New England Regional Conference,
NAACP Award 1958, Maine, New Hampshire, Vermont,
Conn., Mass., Rhode Island; Pastor's Council (Spear-
head and Fought - Rec'd Plaque) "For distinguished serv-
ice in attacking the barriers of discrimination and in
uniting the spirits of men in understanding and brother-
hood, done according to the highest democratic ideals
and motivated with the living spirit of true Christianity;"
Annual Award Brotherhood Club, Greenfield, Mass.,
"Distinguished Award for Outstanding Community Service
and High Standards in your profession;" Man of the Year,
Omega Psi Phi Fraternity, New England Region, 1954;
Bd of Directors, Hampden County Mass. Ass'n for Retarded Children; Bd. of Directors, Child and Family
Service, Springfield, Mass.; Exec. Bd., Mass. Council
of Churches, Boston, Mass.; Exec. Bd., McKnight Civic
Ass'n, Springfield, Mass.; Exec. Committee, Springfield
Branch, NAACP, Springfield, Mass.; chairman, Committee
on Ministry, Hampden Ass'n of Congregational Christian
Churches; Committee on Urban Church, Mass. Congrega-
tional Christian Conference; Inter-racial Action Committee,
Greater Springfield Council of Churches; Steering Com-
mittee, Scholarship Clearing House; Comm. for Students
of Prince Edward County, Va.; Mem., Greater Spring-
field Ministers Ass'n, Springfield Mass.; Congregational
Ministers Club; Pastors Council, Springfield; NAACP,
Springfield Branch; Urban League, Springfield; Omega
Psi Phi Fraternity; Delta Chi Chapter, Springfield;
Meridan Sun Lodge, No. 26 Free and Accepted Masons;
Hampden Ass'n Congregational Chr. Churches; Home:
117 Buckingham, Springfield 9, Mass.; Office: 643
Union St., Springfield, Mass.

COBHAM, Dudley DeCosta, b. New York City, New York,
April 5, 1922; s. Clement Leroy and Ruth Naomi
(Waithe) C.; B.A., Lincoln University, 1945; B.D.,
General Theological Seminary, 1949; Ordained Deacon,
1949; Ordained Priest, 1950; curate, St. Philips, 1949-
52; vicar, St. Clement's, 52-54; Rector, St. Clement's,
1954---; chaplain, Mt. Vernon New York Police Dept.,
1959---; Board of Directors Mental Hygiene Assoc. Mt.
Vernon, New York; Board of Directors of the Boys Club
of Mount Vernon, New York; Board of Directors of the

Community Chest, Mount Vernon, New York; Board of
Directors of the Community Center, Mount Vernon, New
York; Chairman, Education Committee, NAACP, Mount
Vernon, New York Chapter; Mount Vernon Ministerial
Association; mem.: Phi Beta Sigma Fraternity; Progres-
sive Lodge No. 64 F. & A. M.; Men's Of St. Clement's
Church; Priest Association S. S. J. E.; New York Confirma-
tion Commission Appointed by the Bishop; Research on
the History of Confirmation for the Confirmation Com-
mission with particular emphasis on Youth; Home: 42
North High Street, Mount Vernon, New York: Office:
126 South Ninth Avenue, Mount Vernon, New York.

COCHRAN, Morris Bartlett, teacher; b. Charlotte, N. C.,
June 19, 1910; s. Arthur Myron and Sarah J. (Bly) C.;
B. A., Fisk University, 1932; B. D., Bishop Payne
Divinity School, 1937; m. Carrie Watson; children---
Janeice Farrar, Brenda Louise, Morrisena Bartlett,
Carol Ann; chaplain, Gaudet Normal and Industrial Sch-
New Orleans, La., 1937-38; chaplain and teacher, the
Gailor Industrial Sch-Mason, Tenn., 1938-40; priest-in-
charge, St. Timothy's - Daytona Beach, Fla., & St.
John's, Orlando, Fla., 1945-49; instructor, Business
Department of Bethune Cookman College, Daytona Beach,
Fla., 1947-49; Rector of St. Margaret's Protestant Epis-
copal Church - Dayton, Ohio, 1949---; secy., the
Memphis Chamber of Commerce, 1942-1944; Member,
The Dayton Urban League Board, 1950-61; Member,
Social Health Board, 1954-59; present member, The
Human Relations Commission of Dayton, Ohio; campaign
coordinator, Dayton United Negro College Fund Campaign,
5 years; former secy. and pres., the Dayton Ministerial
Association; award from the National United Negro Col-
lege Fund - Citation for services to the Dayton &
Montgomery County Social Hygiene Assoc.; award from
the Eta Phi Beta Sorority, for services in Religion,
Education etc.; Home: 6380 Germantown Pike, Dayton,
Ohio; Office: 3010 McCall Street, Dayton, Ohio

COLE, Wilbert C., b. Miss.; Attended, Amer. Baptist
Theol. Sem., Nashville, Tenn.; Storer Coll.; United
Theol. Sem., N. Y.; current pastor, St. Philips Bapt.
Ch., Wash., D. C., 1945---; Organizer, National
Capital Bapt. Convention; Mem., Walter H. Brooks Bd.
of Directors; vice moderator, Mt. Bethel Baptist Ass'n;
active in politics, Wash., D. C.; Office St. Phillips Bapt.
Church, 10 K. St. NE, Wash., D. C.

COLEMAN, David Cyrus, b. Thomasville, Ga., Jan. 24,
1901; s. J. E. and Creacy C.; Florida State College,
1926-28; Lane College, Jackson, Tenn., 1932; Florida
Memorial College; D. D., Liberia, Africa, 1945; m.
Tennie Mildred Anderson; one son, David Cyrus, Jr.;
R. W., E. H., Mildred; pastor, Greater Bethel African
Methodist Episcopal Church, Jackson, Tenn., 1932-36;
Bethel A. M. E. Church, Knoxville, Tenn., 1937; busi-
ness manager, Shorter College, 1939; principal, High
School Live Oak, Fla., 1929-30; Committeeman 10th
Dist. Tucson, Arizona, 1945-46; Chaplain, Central
Democratic in Same City Worked Hon. Steward Udal and
Gov. McFallen of Arizona; Member, NAACP, pres., The
East Denver Ministerial Alliance; current pastor, Camp-
bell Chapel A. M. E. Church, Denver, Colo; Mem., Gen-
eral Board of A. M. E. Church; Mem., Mayors Advisory
Committee and Executive Board Denver Area Council of
Churches; Mem. YMCA; Mem., George Washington Day
Nursery; Home: 2815 Dahlia St. Denver, Colo.; Office:
1500 East 22nd Ave., 80206 Colo.

COLEMAN, Frederick Douglass, Jr., c. physician; b.
Louisville, Ky., Jan. 25, 1921; s. Frederick Douglas,
Sr. and Jamye (H.) C.; Fisk University; Meharry Medi-
cal College, M. D., 1944; D. D., Monrovia College,
Liberia, 1955; m. Ann Gleaves; children---FriedaAnn,
Frederick Douglass III; pastor, African Methodist Epis-
copal Church, Hartsville Circuit, 1940-42; Trinity,
Nashville, 1942-45; presiding elder, Clarksville District,
1956-64; practicing physician, Clarksville, Tenn.,
1945---; staff physician, Memorial Hospital, Clarksville,
Tenn., 1956---; examiner, Metropolitan Life Insurance
Co., 1958---; Mem., Montgomery County Medical
Society (integrated); Tenn. Med. Association; American
Medical Association; National Medical Association; US
Army, Medical Corps, captain, 1953-55; Commanding Of-
ficer, 765th Med. Detachment; Chief Physical Examiner
US Army Hosp. Ft. Campbell; Battalion Surgeon 47th
Armoured Med Bn 1st Armored Division; representative,
A. M. E. Church Medical Missions Board National Coun-
cil Churches; Mem., Mason; American Legion; Home:
847 Woodwart Dr., Clarksville, Tenn.; Office: 224
8th St., Clarksville, Tenn.

COLEMAN, Harry Alexander, b. Piedmont, West Virginia;
s. Paul Abraham and Marguerite
(Howard) C; Johnstown Center, University of Pittsburgh,

1953-1955, A. B. University of West Virginia, 1955-57;
STB Boston University School of Theology; m. Helen
Threasa Price; Ministry: Asst. Pastor, Trinity Meth.
Ch. Johnstown, Pa. , 1953-1955, Asst. to Pastor, Jones
Meth. Ch. Morgantown, W. Va. 1957, Asst. to Pastor,
Warren Methodist Church, Pittsburgh, Pa. summers of
1957 and 1958, Minister to Youth of First Methodist
Church, Everett, Massa. , 1958-1960, Pastor, Logan
Memorial Methodist Church, Parkersburg, W. Va. 1960-
1962, Pastor Ebenezer Methodist Church, Huntington,
W. Va. 1962-1964, Charleston District, Director of
Youth Work, 1960-1964; Member: N. A. A. C. P. Chair-
man, Legal Defense Fund of N. A. A. C. P. 1963-1964,
Secretary, Brotherhood of Christians and Jews, 1961-
1962; U. S. Army, 1951-1953; Member of W. Va. University Philosophical Society; Sigma Theta Epilson Fraternity; Home: 1647 Eighth Avenue, Huntington, W. Va.
25703

COLEMAN, William Hannan, Jr. , teacher; b. Detroit,
Mich. Jan. 5, 1926; s. Wm. J. , Sr. and Willie C. ;
Livingstone College, 1943-45; Detroit Institute of Tech-
nology, 1945-46; University of California, 1947-48; A. B. ,
San Francisco State, 1949; Graduate study: University
Southern California, Los Angeles State; children---
Stephanie Cornelius, David William (deceased), Paul
Frederick; pastor, Shiloh A. M. E. Zion Church, Mon-
rovia, 1950-52; First A. M. E. Zion Church, Pasadena,
Calif. , 1952-57; Martin Chapel A. M. E. Zion Church,
Los Angeles, 1957-58; Second A. M. E. Zion, Los Angeles,
1958---; teacher, John Muir Junior College, Pasadena,
1953-54; Wilson High School, Pasadena, 1955-57; Los
Angeles School System, 1957-58; office manager, Com-
mercial Express Trust of Arcadia, Calif. , 1951-52;
Fourth Vice-pres. , Ministers & Laymen's Assoc. (A.
M. E. Zion Church); faculty member, San Francisco
Council of Churches Dept. of Christian Education; faculty
member, West Coast Conferences, A. M. E. Zion Church
Leadership Training Institute; area director, Christian Education; chmn. of Conf. Board; director of youth (presently)
secy. , District Conference; sec. ,the Budget Committee of
the South West Rocky Mountain Conference; chairman,
Committee on Admissions and Conference field secretary
of the Committee on Social Action (A. M. E. Zion Church).
Outstanding Community Award for service by the Consolidated Realty Board of Los Angeles, 1964; Recommended for Education Award for Los Angeles Ministers

Awards Annual Event, 1961; Mem.; Democrat, Alpha Phi
Alpha Phi Alpha, Civil Right Non-Violent Workers Com-
mittee, Inc., NAACP, Urban League, UCRC Education
Committee, Friends of Student Non-Violent Cordinating
Committee; research area: Howard Becker's Sacred
Secular Theory, 1963 (unpublished); Social Teachings of
John Wesley and Black Muslims in the U.S.A.; Home:
2117 1/2 Palm Grove Ave., Los Angeles, Calif.; Office:
1201 East 43rd St., Los Angeles, California.

COLERIDGE, Clarence Nicholas, b. Georgetown, British
Guiana, S. Africa, Nov. 27, 1930; s. Charles and Ina
(De Weever) C.; Lincoln Univ., 1950-51; B.S. Howard
Univ., 1951-54; B.D., Drew Univ. Sch. of Theol.,
1960; Gen. Theol. Sem., 1960-61; curate, St. Philip's
Ch., N.Y.C., 1961; curate, St. George's Episcopal Ch.,
Brooklyn, N.Y., 1962---; Home: 845 Putnam Ave.,
Brooklyn 21, N.Y.; Office: 800 Marcy Ave., Brooklyn
16, N.Y.

*COLES, Joseph Carlyle, Jr., b. Wash. D.C., Feb. 15,
1926; s. Joseph Carlyle and Rubie (Banks) C.; A.B.,
B.D., Howard Univ., Wash., D.C., 1947, 1950; m.
Geneva Rose Hamilton; children---Rubie, Jocelyn; pastor,
St. Paul Christian Methodist Episcopal Church, Halifax,
Va., 1949-50; Ebenezer C.M.E. Church, South Boston,
Va., 1950-53; Lane Metro. C.M.E. Church, Cleveland,
Ohio, 1953-63; Williams Institutional C.M.E. Church,
New York City, N.Y., 1963---; dean, The Ohio Leadership
Training School (C.M.E.), 1955-59; Mem., Cleveland
Bd. of Education, 1962-63; pres., Methodist Ministers
Alliance, Cleveland, Ohio, 1959-61; Exec. Comm.,
NAACP, Cleveland, O.; Picture appeared in Ebony
Magazine in 1955 under caption "Bright Young Men of
God"; Mem., 11th Ward Democratic Club, Cleveland,
Ohio, 1961-63; Alpha Phi Alpha; Former Contributing
Editor, The Christian Index (official organ of the C.M.
E. Church); Home: 1270 E. 222nd Bronx 69, N.Y.;
Office: 2225 7th Ave., New York 27, N.Y.

COLLINS, George Napoleon, bishop; b. Quincy, Fla., June
8, 1899; s. Charles C. and Fannie (Armstead) C.;
A.B., Edward Waters Coll., 1926; B.D., B.F. Lee
Sem., 1926; D.D. (hon.), Shorter Coll. 1944; Moody
Bible Institute, Chicago, 1943-45; m. Lottie Phyllis
Miller (deceased), Oneida B. Mickens; children---
George N. Jr., Charles C., William L.; pastor, Sun-

bean African Methodist Episcopal Ch., Mirroui, 1919;
St. Paul A. M. E. Ch., May Port, Fla., 1919-24; St.
James A. M. E. Ch., Commers Mill, Jacksonville, Fal.,
1925-26; St. James A. M. E. Ch., Miami, Fla., 1926-
28; Mt. Moriah A. M. E. Ch., Cocoa, Fla., 1928-29; St.
Mark A. M. E. Ch., Orlando, Fla., 1929-31; Mt. Zion
A. M. E. Ch., Dayton Beach., Fla., 1931-33; Mt. Her-
mon A. M. E. Ch., Ft. Lauderdale, Fla., 1933-40;
St. Paul A. M. E. Ch., Tampa, 1940-41; Visitors Chapel
A. M. E. Ch., Hot Springs, Ark., 1945; Elected bishop,
1964, 18th Dist.; pres., Interdenominational Council;
Mem., Race Relation Council of Hot Springs; Mason;
NAACP; Elk; Alpha Phi Alpha; author: Practical Junior
Church Work; Home: 4426 So. Liberty St., New Orleans,
La. 70115

*COOK, Payton Brailsford, b. Griffin, Ga., March 10,
1931; s. Marucs E., Sr. and Mary (Daniel) C.; A. B.,
Paine Coll., Augusta, Ga., 1953; B. D., Howard Univ.,
Sch. of Rel., Wash., D. C., 1959; Graduate Study in
Sociology, The Graduate School; Howard Univ., Wash.,
D. C., 1960; certificate; Univ. of Ga., Southeastern Sch.
for Alcohol Studies, 1964; m. Mary Prudence Murray;
children---Pamela Yvonne, Lisa Del Nell, asst. pastor,
First Bapt. Ch., Wash., D. C., 1959-62; Migrant chap-
lain, New York State, Council of Churches, Camden,
New York, 1958-60; counselor, Children's Center,
Laural, Md., 1960-63; Senior Clinical Chaplain, Milledge-
ville State Hospital, 1963---; Mem., National Assn. for
the Advancement of Colored People & National Urban
League; US Army, 1953-55; Good Conduct Medal; Defense
Medal; Mem., Ga. Public Health Assn; The American
Correctional Chaplain's Assn; American Protestant
Correctional Chaplains Assn; Home: 548 Boundary St.,
Milledgeville, Ga.; Office: Milledgeville State Hospital,
Milledgeville, A.

COOLEY, James Franklin, teacher; b. Rowland, N. C.,
Jan. 11, 1926; s. James F. and Martha (Buie) C.;
A. B., Johnson C. Smith University, 1953; B. D. Johnson,
C. Smith Univ. Theol. Sem., 1956; m. Lourenia Mc
Callum; children---Virginia Mae, James Francis,
Gladys,   Franklin D.; pastor, Grant Chapel Presbyterian
Ch., Darien, Ga., 1956-57; current pastor, St. Andrews
Presbyterian Church, Forest City, Ark., 1956---;
teacher, Lincoln Jr. High School, Forest City, Ark.,
1957---; Advisor to Youth Group (Conference), Stillman

Coll., Tuscaloosa, Ala., 1956---; Mem. Civic League;
delegate, State-side Meetings on Community Service Pro-
grams, Juvenile Problems, US Forces, 1944-46; Award
and Decorations: E. T. O. Ribbon; P. T. O. Ribbon, Ribbon
for Liberation of France & Philipines; Good Conduct
Medal; two battle stars; Mem.: Omega Psi Phi; Mason;
Ark. Teachers Assn; Forrest City Professional Teachers
Assn; Ministerial Alliance; Forrest City Professional
Teachers Assn; Ministerial Alliance, Juvenile Probation
Officer, Juvenile Board & Forrest City Voters league;
Special recognition in newspaper for Juvenile Work;
Ex-official member of public welfare dept.; Lion Club
consultant with Juvenile, municipal, and circuit courts
on all Negro violators; Home: 222 S. Beach St., Forrest
City, Ark.; Office: 715 S. Center St., Forrest City,
Ark.

COOPER, Austin Rellins, b. Miami, Florida, Aug. 8, 1933;
s. Benjamin Leon, Jr., and Louise (Bethel) B.; 1953-
57, B. A. St. Augustine's College, Raleigh, N. C.; 1957-
60, B. D. Evanston, Ill.; m. Patricia Ann Hopkins;
son: Austin, Jr.; Ordained Deacon, 1960; ordained
priest, 1961; Vicar, Church, Transfiguration & St.
Andrew's Episcopal Church, Hollywood, Fla., July '60-
Sept. '60; Vicar, St. Matthew's Episcopal Church, Delray
Beach, Fla., & St. Mary's Church, Deerfield Beach,
Fla., Oct. 1960-Feb. 1962; Curate, St. Simon's Roches-
ter, N. Y., Mar. 1962-Oct. '62 Vicar and Headmaster-
St. Augustine's Episcopal, Dallas, Texas Activities:
Pres., Delray Beach (Fla.) branch NAACP., July 1961
Feb. 1962; mem. Dallas (Tex.) branch NAACP; Dallas
Committee for Full Citizenship, Educ. Committee;
American Civil Liberties Union.; Alpha Phi Alpha;
Home: 3940 N. Hampton Rd., Dallas 12, Texas; church
3930 N. Hampton Rd., Dallas 12, Texas.

*COOPER, John, Jr., b. Jonesville, Tex. Feb. 28, 1928;
s. John and Sue Milla Owen; A. B., B. D., Howard Univ.;
m. Eleanor J. James; asst. pastor, Shiloh Bapt. Ch.,
Wash., D. C., 1942-55; First Bapt. Church, Lexington,
Va., 1955-58; current pastor, New Monumental Bapt.
Ch., Chattanooga, Tenn., 1958---; teacher, Bible
Center, Chattanooga, Tenn.; sec., Chattanooga Minis-
terial Alliance; pres., Bapt. Minister's Alliance, Chat-
tanooga; pres., Interdenominational Ministers Alliance;
Democrat; Mem., NAACP; Home: 1112 East Fifth St.,

Chattanooga, Tex.

COOPER, Quincy Darnell, b. Republic, Pa., Feb. 14,
1938; b. Lafayette S. and Jannie C.; A. B., Maryland
State Coll., 1956-60; S. T. B., Wesley Theol. Sem.,
1960-63; m. Deborah Lynn; pastor, Lewes Charge,
Lewes, Delaware, 1958-63; assoc. pastor, Salem Meth.
Ch., New York City, 1963-64; pastor, John Wesley
Meth. Ch., Brooklyn, New York, 1964---; research
director, Morningside Teen Council, 1963-64; Community
Voters Assn Inc., Brooklyn, New York City; Mem., Har-
lem Branch YMCA, Bedford Branch YMCA; Protestant
Council of Brooklyn; Rockefeller Foundation Award for
Theological Students; Mem., Kappa Alpha Psi; Mason;
Kappa Alpha Mu Honor Society; Home: 378 Nostrand
Ave., Brooklyn 16, New York City; Office: 260 Quincy
St., Brooklyn 16, New York City.

COOPER, Theodore Walter, b. New Orleans, La., April
28, 1929; s. Walter and Irene C.; m. Margie Luvada
Thompson; children---Monica; pastor, St. Andrews
Lutheran Church; pastor, Bethlehem Lutheran Church,
New Orleans, La.; pastor, St. John Lutheran Church,
Kansas City, Mo.; pastor, New Hope Lutheran Church,
Detroit, Michigan; Member, Board Directors, Lutheran
Human Relations Council; Home 4055 Seebaldt, Detroit
4, Michigan; Ch.: 1658 Holden, Detroit 4, Michigan.

COSTEN, James Hutten, b. Omaha, Nebr., Oct. 5,
1931; s. Wm. Theodore and Mary (Brookings) C.; A. B.,
Johnson C. Smith Univ., 1953; B. D., Johnson C. Smith
Univ., 1956; Th. M., Southern Baptist Theol. Sem.,
1963; m. Melva Wilson Costen; children---James Hutten,
Jr., Craig Lamont, Cheryl Leatrice; pastor Mount
Pisgah United Presby. Ch., Rocky Mount, N. C., 1956-;
mem. Mayor's Good Neighbor Comm., Rocky Mount,
N. C., pres. NAACP, Secretary Voters League, Dir.
T. B. Assn.; awards: United Fund Award 1961 for Out-
standing Citizenship, Rocky Mount, N. C.; Citizen of the
Year Award 1962 by Alpha Omicron Chapter Omega Psi
Phi Fraternity; mem. Alpha Phi Alpha Fraternity;
Home: 312 Park Ave., Rocky Mount, N. C.; Ch. 614
Goldleaf Street, Rocky Mount, N. C.

*COURSEY, John Henry, b. Marshall, Tex., Sept. 22,
1931; s. Wm. and Mackie (Ford) C.; B.A., B.D.
Howard Univ., Sch. Thel., 1955, 1963; pastor, Liberty

Town Meth. Charge, Liberty Town, Md., 1960-61;
Atholton Meth. Charge, Simpsonville, Md., 1961---;
instructor, Cortez Peters Business School, Wash., D.
C., 1962-63: Mem., Bd. of Directors, Tsugo Day Camp,
Guilford, Md., 1964; Political Action Comm., NAACP
Howard County Branch, 1963---; 5th Dist. Democratic
Club, Howard County, Md.; Kappa Alpha Psi; chaplain,
Howard Univ. Business Alumni; author: "A Second
Look"; a play; Home: 501 Oglethrope NW,
Wash., D.C.; Office: Locust Meth. Ch., R&32,
Simpsonville, Md.

COUSIN, Lee Andrew, chaplain; b. Roxboro, N.C., Mar.
17, 1915; s. Nathaniel Theodore and Sadie Fisher (Dun-
can) C.; B.D., Payne Theological Seminary, 1936; m.
Mary Evelyn Lunsden; children---Myrna Lee (Choates),
Evelyn Elayne, Jesse Andrew, Joan Elizabeth; pastor,
A.M.E. Churches, Huntington, Pa., West Bridgewater,
Pa., Greensburg, Pa., Tampa, Fla., 1936-40; pastor,
Monessen and Wilkenburg, Pa., 1945; US Army Chaplain,
1943-45, 50; Service in the European Pacific Theatres
of operation during World War II; current, Deputy Staff
Chaplain of Fort Devens, Mass; Home: 7416 Race St.,
Pittsburgh 8, Penna.

*COX, Benjamin Elton, b. Whiteville, Tenn., June 19,
1931; s. Charlie and Ada C.; A.B., Livingstone Coll.,
Salisbury, N.C., 1954; Hood Seminary, Salisbury, N.C.,
1954-55; B.D., Howard Univ. Sch. of Rel., Wash.,
D.C., 1957; Courses: Episcopal Theol. School, Cam-
bridge, Mass., 1957; youth minister, Caldwell Chapel
African Methodist Episcopal Zion Church, Kankakee,
Ill., 1948-51; pastor, Jonesville, A.M.E. Zion Church,
Matthews, N.C., 1953-55; youth minister John Wesley,
A.M.E. Zion, Wash., D.C., 1955-56; lay reader, Saint
Luke's Episcopal Church, Wash., D.C., 1956-57; student
minister, All Saints' Episcopal, Church, Lyn, Mass.,
1957; current pastor, Pilgrim United Church of Christ,
High Point, N.C., 1958---; asst. chaplain, Boys' Village
of Md., Chetleham, Md., 1956-57; teacher, William Penn
High School, High Point, N.C., 1958-59; Bd. Mem.,
Carl Chavis YMCA, High Point, 1962; active in non-
violent protests; National Youth Secy. for NAACP, 3
months; field secy., CORE, 1961; One of the first 13
Freedom Riders; Jailed 17 times; Face sentence of 10
years if ever convicted by highest court; spent more
than 4 1/2 months in jails in N.C., Ark. and La.;

Home: 619 North Elwood Dr., High Point, N.C. 919-
8823754; Office: 600 Fairview St., High Point, N.C.
919-882-4222.

COX, James Alexander, educator; b. Pittsburgh, Pa., Aug.
17, 1913; s. Samuel R. and Mary Francis Mayo C.;
Va. Sem. & Coll. 1932-35; A.B., Va. Union U., 1937;
M.A., U. of Pittsburgh, 1957; Adv. Studies, Harvard
& Yale; Pastored, Mt. Zion Bapt. Ch., Bridgeport, O.,
1938-42; Act. Pastor, 2nd Bapt., Steubenville, O., 1943;
Pastor, Macedonia Bapt., Wheeling, W.Va., 1947-53;
Pastor, Calvary Bapt., Pittsburgh, Pa., 1953---; Prin-
cipal, Westmoreland Co., Va., 1937-38; Teacher, Lincoln
High Sch., Wheeling, W.Va., 1938-43; U.S. Army Chap.,
(Major), W.W. II., 1943-46; Recipient, Bronze Star
(action beyond call of duty); Achievement Award, Courier
WAMO, 1960; Salute Award, Station WZUM, Outstanding
Contribution to Community, 1964; Mr. Pastor Plaque
Award, Elks of World, 1957; Meritorous Service Placque,
Social Worker at Morals Court, Bapt. Ministers Conf.,
Pittsburgh & Vicinity, 1961; Social Worker, Moral Court,
Pittsburgh, Pa., 1954-60; Pres. Bapt. Ministers Conf.,
Pittsburgh & Vicinity, 1963---; mem. Bd. Dirs., NAACP;
Asst. Dean, Fac. Mem., Pittsburgh Extension, Amer.
Bapt. Theol. Sem.; mem., United Negro Protest Com-
mittee, Pittsburgh; Mason; Home: 512 Junilla Streets,
Pittsburgh, Pa., 15219, Church: 2629 Wylie Avenue,
Pittsburgh, Pa. 15319

COX, Milton Edward, teacher, b. Sanford, N.C., Nov. 10,
1921; s. Wm. Francis and Rosa (Smith) C.; A.B.,
Johnson C. Smith Univ., Charlotte, N.C., 1932-36;
B.D., Johnson C. Smith Univ., 1936-39; M.A., Mc
Cormick Theol. Sem., Chgo., Ill., 1947-48; m. Mar-
garet Elizabeth Robinson; pastor Logan-New Center
Churches, R.F.D., Statesville, N.C., 1937-41; Antioch
Presbyterian Ch., Eliz. City, N.C., 1941-43; Ladson
Presby. Ch., Columbia, S.C., 1943-60; Cheraw Second
Presby. Ch., Cheraw, S.C., 1960-62; Trinity Presby.
Ch., Tallahassee, Fla., 1962- ; instructor Benedict
College, Columbia, S.C., 1953-61; chaplain, Police
Dept., Columbia, S.C.; mem. of bd. of dir., Boys
Club, Columbia, S.C., mem. Advisory Bd.; mem Nat.
Foundation of Infantile Paralysis, Richland, mem. USA
Committee, pres. Interdenominational Ministerial Al-
liance, all of Columbia, S. S.; mem.: Ministerial Al-
liance of Tallahassee, Boy Scouts of America, Inter-

Civic Council, NAACP, and Kappa Alpha Psi Fraternity;
Home: 1901 S. Boulevard, Tallahassee, Fla.; Office:
Corner of Gore and Pasco, Tallahassee, Fla.

COX, Sherman Haywood, b. Baltimore, Md., Aug. 10,
1934; s. Squire Masco and Kathleen William (Hall) C.;
Morgan State College, 1957; B.A., Oakwood College,
1960; Andrews University, M.A., 1961; Doctor of
Divinity Degree from College of Divine Metaphysics,
1962; Pastor, Seventh-Day Adventist Church in Paducah
Kentucky, 1961; Seventh-Day Adventist Church, Lexing-
ton, Covington, Berea and Richmond. Present: - Pastor,
Hattiesburg, McComb, Laurel, Brookhaven, Soso and
Gulfport Seventh-Day Adventist Churches, Mississippi.
Member, Kentucky Board for Mental Health; Lexington,
Kentucky interracial Ministerial Association. Board
Member of one of the two mentally retarded schools for
Negroes in the State of Mississippi; Associate Director,
1964 March of Dimes for the Regional work in Hatties-
burg, Miss.; Lexington, Kentucky and Hattiesburg, Mississippi P.T.A. Editorial, Lexington Herald Leader in
1962; two articles in "The Message Magazine", 1961-
1963. Home: 209 Rose Ave., Hattiesburg, Miss.

*CRAIG, Benjamin Howard, b. Clanton, Ala., Oct. 1,
1907; s. Abraham and Mamie C.; A.B., Miles College;
B.D., Howard Univ., Sch. of Religion; courses for
M.A., American Univ.; m. Lillie Hendrieth; 1 daughter
Annette. Secretary, Y.M.C.A., Birmingham, Ala., 8
years; supply minister, Calvary Presbyterian Ch.,
Anniston, Ala., 1948; stated supply minister, Bethel
Presbyterian Ch., Alexandria, Va., 6 years; present:
pastor, Faith United Presbyterian Ch., Washington, D.
C., 6 years. Counselor and social worker, Dept. of
Pub. Welfare, D.C. Gov't., 9 years. Mem., S.E.
Civic Assn. and treasurer, S.E. Ministerial Assn.,
Washington, D.C.; former chairman, precinct 80 -
Democrat - Washington, D.C., Mem., Community Inter-
racial Committee. Home: 1629 Fort Davis Pl., S.E.,
Wash. 20, D.C. Office: 3129 20th St., S.E., Washing-
ton 20, D.C.

CRAIG, Lawrence Lauman, teacher; b. East St. Louis,
Ill., Feb. 4, 1938; s. Charles Ashley and Martha Fisher
(Sydnor) C.; B.A. Lane College, Jackson, Tenn., 1960
B.D., Iliff School of Theology, 1963; m. Zenobia
Yvonne Barge; children---Kennethia La Trace, Conchita

De Ella, Lawrence Lauman. Assistant minister, Jamison Memorial C. M. E. Church, 1954-56; associate
minister, St. Paul C. M. E. Ch. , Jackson, Tenn. , 1956-
57; minister, Spring Creek Circuit, 1957-60; and St.
Luke's C. M. E. Ch. , Denver, Colo. , 1960-1963; present:
minister, Miles Memorial C. M. E. Church, Washington,
D. C. , 1963- ; music teacher, Henderson, Tenn. Pas-
torial Counciling. Alpha Phi Alpha; Democrat. Home:
1104 Fairmont St. , N. W. , Wash. D. C. Office: 1110
Third St. , N. W. , Washington, D. C.

CRAWFORD, Evans Edgar Jr. , Dean, Professor; b.
Temple, Texas, July 2, 1923; s. Evans Edgar, Sr. and
Mary (Inge) C. ; A. B. Samuel Huston Coll. (now Huston-
Tillotson), Austin, Texas, 1943, STB. Boston University
School of Theology, 1946, Ph. D. Boston University,
Graduate School 1957; m. Elizabeth Pinder Bailey; Min-
istry: Student minister at Morgan Memorial Church of
All Nations, Boston, Mass. 1943-1946, Staff Pastor,
Church of all Nations, 1946-1949, Interim Minister,
Pond Street Baptist Church, Providence, R. I. 1949-
1954; Coordinator, Student Activities, Boston University
School of Theology, 1956-58, Asst. Professor of Prac-
tical Theology, Howard Univ. School of Religion, 1958,
Dean of Chapel, Howard University, 1959; Board
of Directors, Providence Urban League, 1953, Board of
Directors, John Hope Community Center, 1952; Member:
Alpha Phi Alpha Fraternity, N. A. A. C. P. Executive Com-
mittee, National Association of College and University
Chaplains, 1963; Home: 4130 Arkansas Ave. , N. W.
Wash. , D. C. Office: Howard University, Chapel Office,
Washington 1, D. C.

CRAWFORD, William Richard, b. Winston-Salem, N. C.
June 18, 1910; s. Walter and Henrietta (Evans) C. ;
A. B. , W. Va. State Coll. , 1937; B. D. , Gammon Theol.
Sem. , 1947; m. Givendolyn Scales; children---Gloria
Yvette; ordained elder, 1947; pastor, Mt. Pleasant
Methodist Church, Winston-Salem, N. C. , 1947--;
Mem. , The Mayor's Civic Betterment Committee, 1950-
51; Board of Aldermen, Winston-Salem, N. C. , 1951-
61; Board of Directors, United Fund; Div. chairman,
United Fund, 1951-53; Public Safety Comm. Bd. , Bd.
of Alderman; Winston-Salem Sch. Bd. ; Comm. of Man-
agement YMCA, chairman; Urban League-Welfare Comm. ;
Recreation Commission; Sec. , N. C. Annual Conference
of the Methodist Church; Bd. of Directors, The Eye Bank

for Restoring Sight, Inc.; Chief Warden, Civil Defense,
South Third Ward; PTA Council; N.C. School Bd. Ass'n;
Alcoholic Rehabilitation Comm.; Interdenominational Min-
isterial Alliance; The Forsyth Minister's Fellowship;
Alpha Phi Alpha; NAACP; Mason; Hon. Mem., Social
Promoters Club; Les Bonne Filles; vice pres. and
director, Safe Bus Inc.,; vice chairman, Exec. Comm.
Democratic Party of Forsyth County; Trustee, Winston-
Salem Teachers Coll.; Bd. of Directors, Memorial In-
dustrial Sch.; awards: "Man of the Year, 1953, Winston-
Salem Jaycees; Service and Civic Award, 1954, Omega
Psi Phi, Citation for Service Award, Patterson Ave.,
YMCA, 1954; The Nathan W. Collier Meritorious Serv-
ice Award, Florida N & I Coll.; article: Where Does
The Church Stand?, Central Christian Advocate; The
Church and Community Outreach, Central Christian Ad-
vocate; Home: 1701 Shadymount Ave., Winston-Salem, N.
C.; Office: 1003 E. 14th St., Winston-Salem, N.C.
27105

CREWS, William Hunter, b. Winston-Salem, N.C., March
18, 1932; s. Bynum Curlee and Ruth (Penn) C.; B.A.,
Va. Union Univ., 1955; M.A., New York Univ., 1964;
courses: Union Theol. Sem., New York City; m. June
Day; children---William H., Jr.; director of Christian
Education, Bethel African Methodist Episcopal Church,
Detroit, Mich.,1955-57; current pastor, The Mount
Pleasant Baptist Church, Norfolk Va., 1957---; chair-
man, Budget Comm., Norfolk Com for the Improvement
of Education; vice pres., Bapt. Minister Conf. of Nor-
folk; Mem., Omega Psi Phi; Interracial Fellowship,
Norfolk Com. for Improvement of Education; Home: 118
Mount Pleasant Ave., Norfolk 5, Va.; Office: 934 West
Little Creel Rd., Norfolk 5, Va.

CRISS, George Washington, Jacksonville, Tex., Oct. 17,
1919; s. Lum C. and Jessie (Cary) C.; B.D., Western
Sem., Kansas City, Mo.; D.D., Friendship Coll.,
1963; m. Doris Williams; children---George, Jr.; asst.
pastor, Highland Baptist Ch., Kansas City, Mo., 1945;
organized Friendship Baptist Ch., Kansas City, Mo.,
1949; Metropolitan Baptist Ch., N.Y.C., 1951-52; pastor
Providence Baptist Ch., Marlin, Tex., 1952-53; Marvella
a Park Baptist Ch., Calif., 1954-56; Sharon Baptist
Ch., L.A., Calif., 1956-61; current, Sharon Baptist
Ch., Bronx, N.Y.; Trustee, Interfaith Health Ass'n,
N.Y.C.; Home: 947 Grant Ave., Bronx 56, New York;

Office: 827 Forest Ave., Bronx 56, New York

CROSBY, Isaac, b. Bayspring, Miss., Feb. 21, 1936; s.
Obadiah and Flossie (Moncrief) C.; B.A., Stillman College, 1958; B.D., Union Theological Seminary (Presbyterian), 1962; m. Willirea Jackson; Director of Recreation Religious Activities, Summer, '58; Asst. pastor of
All Souls Presbyterian Church, 1958-59; current pastor,
Faith Presbyterian Church, 1962---; Director of United
Christian Fellowship, 1962---; awards: Highest Scholastic Average; State NFA Quiz Contest, 1953; Outstanding
Achievements Award upon graduation from college; Pres.
of Stillman College Alumni Association, 1960-61; Home:
913 North Cedar St., Pine Bluff, Arkansas; Office:
24 Watson Boulevard, Pine Bluff, Arkansas

*CROSSON, Calvin Perry, b. Clinton, S.C., May 25, 1921;
s. Calvin Luther and Eula S. (Murles) C.; A.B. Howard
Univ., 1956; B.D., Sch. of Rel., Howard Univ. 1961;
m. Ronetta Collyne Swann; 1 daughter: Delores C. (Mrs.
Phillip Jones). Pastor, Eastern Methodist Ch., Baltimore,
Md., 1956-present. World War II - Asiatic Pacific
Theater, 1942-45; Asiatic Pacific Theater ribbon; Philippine Liberation ribbon; Good Conduct medal. Mem., Interdenominational Ministers Alliance; Methodist Ministers
Wednesday Morning Fellowship; Methodist Ministers Fellowship; East Baltimore Clergymen's Association; Republican. Home: 1907 N. Wolfe St., Baltimore, Md. Office:
1609 N. Wolfe St., Baltimore, Md.

CUMMINGS, James L., b. Allensville, Todd County, Ky.,
Dec. 2, 1926; s. Andrew and Fannie Robbie C.; A.B.,
Lane Coll., Jackson, Tenn., 1948; Butler Univ. Sch.
of Rel., Ind., B.D., 1959; m. Norma J. Cravens; chil-
dren---Denise Marie; pastor, Trinity Christian Methodist
Episcopal Ch., Indianapolis, Ind., 1956---; Mem., Bd.
of Directors for Church Federation; pres., President of
Indianapolis Ministerial Ass'n; Interdenominational Ministerial Alliance; sec., The Ohio Annual Conference Christian Methodist Episcopal Church; Mem., Bd. of Indianapolis Zoning Appeals; City Council , Indianapolis, Ind.,
1963---; Fall Creek Parkway YMCA; Bd. mem. NAACP;
Federated Associated Club; Scout Award, Region Seven;
Democrat; Alpha "Man of the Year", 1960; Citation from
Crispus Attucks High School from "Hall of Fame" for
service to community, nation and profession, 1962; Mem.,
Mason, Alpha Phi Alpha; Office: 2253 Martindale Ave.,

Indianapolis, Ind.

CUNNINGHAM, Frank, coll. pres., b. Okolona, Miss., Oct.
10, 1912; s. Frank and I. B. C.; B. A., Mount Union Coll.,
Alliance, Ohio, 1937; M. A., Boston Univ., 1939; S. T. B.
Boston Univ. Sch. of Theol., 1940; Ohio State Univ.;
Ph. D., Boston Univ., 1951; LL. D. (hon.), Paul Quinn
Coll., 1952; m. Elizabeth Holmes; asst. prof., Wilber-
force Univ., 1942-45; dean, Turner Theol. Sem., 1945-58;
visiting prof., Atlanta Univ. Summer Sch., 1948-58;
assoc. pastor, Church of All Nations, Boston Univ.,
Mass., 1939-42; pastor, Community African Methodist
Episcopal Ch., Cleveland, Ohio, 1942; current pres.,
Morris Brown Coll., Atlanta, Ga., 1958---; pres., The
Ga. Philosophical Society and Psychology; Mem., Amer-
ican Philosophical Assn; Institute of Religion, Howard
Univ.; Phi Beta Sigma; Kappa Boule of Sigma Pi Phi;
Danforth Fellow in Philosophy, Univ. of Minnesota, 1958;
Fullbright Scholar in India, 1962; Office: Morris Brown
Coll., Atlanta, Ga.

CUNNINGHAM, Theodore Francis, b. Omaha, Neb., May
22, 1928; S. Theodore, Sr. and Lilly Mae (Addie) C.;
B. S. Phil., Greighton Univ., 1951; M. A. Eur. Hist.
St. Louis Univ., 1960; Conv. to Catholicism, Aug.
1948; Ordained priest, Roman Cath. Ch., June 11,
1964; Teacher: history, Eng. speech, dramatics, Creighton Prep, Omaha, 1957-59; Mem. Alpha Phi Alpha;
Home: St. Mary's College, St. Mary's, Kansas.

CURRY, John Wesley, b. Ashville, Alabama, Jan 10,
1908; s. James Arthue and Zilla (Arnold) C. A. B.
Claflin College, Orangeburg, S. C. 1927-1930, B. D.
Gammon Theological Seminary, Atlanta, Ga. 1930-1933,
Further Study: Garrett Seminary, 1955, D. D. Claflin
College, D. D. Gammon Theological Seminary; m. Willa
Mae Ogletree; children: John Wesley, Jr., James Adam
Curry; Ministry: St. Marks Methodist Church, Mayesville,
S. C. 1933-1938, Centenary Methodist Church, Charleston,
S. C. 1939-1945, Superintendant, Charleston District of
the South Carolina Conference, 1945-46, Florence District,
1946-51; Pastor, Cumberland Meth. Ch. Florence, S. C.
1951-57, Superintendant Florence District, 1957-62,
Pastor, Trinity Meth. Ch. Orangeburg, S. C. 1962 to
present; Member: The Methodist Ecumenical Conference,
Oxford, England, 1951; World Methodist Conference,
Norway, 1961; Delegate to the Methodist General and

Jurisdictional Conference, 1948, 1952, 1956, 1960, 1964;
Member: Co-ordinating Council of The Methodist Church,
1956-64; General Council on World Service and Finance,
1964, Treasurer of the South Carolina Annual Conference; Trustee, Claflin College, Member: Phi Beta Sigma,
Masonic Lodge, Executive Committee N.A.A.C.P.;
Author of Column: "Know Your Church" in the Central
Christian Advocate of The Methodist Church. Home:
191 Boulevard, N.E. Orangeburg, S.C.

CURRY, Morris Alexander, b. Magnolia, Ark., Apr. 17,
1913; s. Luther and Mattie E.C.; B.A., Ark. Baptist
Ch., 1945; M.A., Phillips Univ., Enid, Okla., 1962;
m. Zarah Mae Gholston; children---Morris Alexander,
Jr.; pastor, First Baptist Ch., Idabel, Okla., 1937-
51; Shiloh Baptist Ch., Camden Ark., 1951-54; Calvary
Baptist Ch., Oklahoma City, Okla., 1955---; dean,
Southeastern Dist. S.S. & B.T.U. Congress, 1941-46;
moderator, Southeastern Dist. Baptist Ass'n, 1949-51;
vice moderator, East Zion Dist. Ass'n, 1962---; vice
pres., NAACP, Okla. City Branch, 1959-61; Mem.,
House Comm. YMCA East Side Branch, 1961---; pres.,
Oklahoma City Interdenominational Minister's Alliance,
1960-62; Mem., Pythian; Mason; Democrat; Home: 1918
NE Grand Blvd., Okla. City 11, Okla.; Office: 300
North Walnut, Okla. City 4, Okla.

CURRY, Norris Samuel, bishop; b. Naples, Texas, Aug.
16, 1910; s. Lonnie and Fannie (Hervey) C.; A.B. Texas,
Coll., 1942; B.D., Drew Univ., 1947; LL.D., Texas Coll.,
1957; m. Mary Cleopatra Reynolds; children--Betsy Gail,
Norris Duane; Pastoral ministry began in 1928, East
Texas Conf., Central Texas Conf. to 1944; to New Jer-
sey through 1949 in Drew Univ. on leave via pastoral
duties; to Los Angeles, Calif. as pastor, Phillips Tem-
ple C.M.E. Church, 9 years; editor, Christian Index,
official organ of C.M.E. Church, 1958; Elected 31st
Bishop of C.M.E. Church in 1962 General Conf., St.
Louis, Mo.; Presently presiding bishop of the Fourth
Episcopal District, Louisiana and Mississippi, C.M.E.
Church, residing in New Orleans, La.; teacher, Texas
Coll., 1947; delegate, World and National religious
bodies; World Methodist Conf., National Council of
Churches General Assemblies; Faith and Order Conf., in
Europe and the United States; chairman, Mississippi Indus-
trial Coll. Trustee Board, Holy Spring, Miss.; Mem.,
Home Mission Div., National Council of Church; Trus-

tee Board, Phillips School of Theology, ITC, Atlanta,
Ga.; chairman, governing Board of General Bd. of
Lay Activities, C. M. E. Church; Mason; Democrat;
Home: 9141 S. Claiborne Ave., New Orleans, La.
70118.

DADE, Malcolm Gray, canon; b. New Bedford, Mass.,
Feb. 27, 1903; s. I. C. and Margaret (Warfield); B. A.,
Lincoln Univ.; Episcopal Theological Seminary, Cam-
bridge, Mass.; D. D. (hon.), Wilberforce University;
m. Bonnie Jwan Denham; children---Malcolm, Jr.,
Duwain, Margaret and Julie; rector, St. Cyprian Pro-
testant Episcopal Church, 1936---; Appointed Honorary
Canon of the Cathedral Church of St. Paul, Michigan;
Mem.: Mayor's Civic Commission (Mich.); Board of
Wayne County Training School, 1960-62; chaplain, De-
troit House of Correction, 1961-62; Delegate, Prot.
Episcopal General Convention; Chaplain Michigan State
Troops during World War II; Cited for distinguished com-
munity service by District-Historic Society and Omega
Psi Phi Fraternity; Major of Detroit, Proclaimed a
"Canon Dade Day."; Honorary Mem.; WAW-CIO (Local
600); author: Inside Michigan; Home: 18834 Charest,
Detroit 34, Mich.; Office: 6114 28th St., Detroit 10,
Mich.

DAMES, Jonathan Alexander, b. Key West, Fla., Feb. 9,
1883; s. R. H. and Malvina J. D.; Edward Waters College,
A. B. & B. D., Howard Univ., 1924; Graduate Work: But-
ler Univ., Indplis, and Union Theological Seminary, NY
City; D. D. & LL. D. (hon.), Douglas Univ., St. Louis
and Monrovia College, Monrovia, Liberia, West Africa;
m. Annie L. Dames; pastor, Lakeland Md., 1920-24;
Cambridge, Md., 1924-27; St. Paul African Methodist
Episcopal Church, 1928; pastor, Campbell A. M. E. Church,
Washington, D. C., 1928-29; pastor, St. James, A. M. E.
Church, St. Louis, Mo., 1929-40; Pasadena, Calif.,
1940-44; Bethel, Detroit, 1944-49; Bethel, Indianapolis,
Ind., 1949-57; Woodlawn A. M. E. Church, Chicago, 1957
---; Trustee Chairman, Indiana Conference, 1956-7;
Trustee, Wilberforce Univ., 1934-39; principal, School
at Thompsontown, Md., 1924-25; Organized Clerk Circle
in St. Louis seeking jobs integration; Interracial pastoral
activities in each city pastored, with emphasis on better
race relations; Men.: Phi Beta Sigma Fraternity, Mason;
Democrat; author, The A. M. E. General Budget Cate-

chism, Copyright 1957 (pamphlet); The Probationer's
Guide-published 1956 (pamphlet); Home: 7842 S. Mary-
land Ave., Chicago 19, Ill. Office: 6456 S. Evans Ave.,
Chicago 37, Ill.

DANIEL, Wilbur Nathan, b. Louisville, Ky., Jan. 2,
1918; s. Nathan Daniel and Fannie B.D.; Ft. Wayne
Bible Institute; B. Th., Amer. Bapt. Theol. Sem., Nash-
ville, Tenn., 1948; B.S., Tenn. State U., 1949; M.A.,
Austin Peay State Coll., 1957; m. Marguerite Richards;
2 sons, Wilbur Nathan and Richard Eugene; Pastored,
Macedonia Bapt. Ch., Garrett, Ind., 1944-47; Pilgrim
Emmanuel Bapt., 1947-49 (Nashville, Tenn); St. John
Bapt., Clarksville, Tenn., 1949-57; Antioch Miss.,
Bapt., Chgo., Ill., 1957---; Bd. Men., Chgo. Urban
League; Bd. Mem., NAACP; Vice-Chrmn., Chgo. Bapt.
Institute; Vice-Moderator, North Woodriver Bapt. Dist.
Assoc.; Pres., Chgo. Br. NAACP 1962; Cand. for
Cong., 1st Cong. Dist., Ill., 1964; Rec. "Minister
of the Year Award", 1960; D.D., Va. Theol. Sem. and
Coll., 1960; D.D., Arkansas Bapt. State Coll., 1961;
"Good American Award", Chgo. Comm. of 100 organiza-
tions, 1964; Home: 8445 S. Calumet, Chicago 19,
Illinois Church: 415 W. Englewood Ave., Chicago 21,
Illinois.

DANIELS, Reginald James, b. Orangeburg, S.C., Aug. 2,
1916; s. Malachi Samuel and Sallie Garret (Adams) D.;
B.S., S.C. State A & M Coll., 1937; S.T.B., Lincoln
Univ. Seminary, 1943; m. Marguerite Wade Younger;
children---Reginald II, Judith M., Freda A.; Served City
and Industrial Unit, Bd. of National Missions, Presbyterian Church, USA, Philadelphia, 1943; Dayton, Ohio, current pastor, Madison Ave. Presbyterian Church, Baltimore, Md., 1944---; teacher, Chester Co., S.C., 1937-
40; sec., Bd. of Christian Managers, Druid Hill Branch
YMCA, 1958; chairman, Advisory Com., Family and
Children's Society, 1954---; Bd. Mem., Family & Children's Society, 1963---; Office: Madison Avenue Presbyterian Church, Baltimore 17, Md.

DARBY, Walter A., Jr. b. October 22, 1922; s. Walter
A. and Iris (Newman) D.; B.A., Oakwood College, 1949;
m. Florence Burton; children-- Walter A. III, Edythe
Vanessa. Pastor, St. Petersburg and Palmetto, Fla.,
1949-50; director of 20th Century Bible School for the
South Atlantic Conference of Seventh-Day Adventist,

Atlanta, Ga. , 1950-51; manager of the South Atlantic Book
and Bible House, 1951-57; organized Church, Mt. Olives,
Athens, Ga. , 1957; Winston-Salem, 1957-59; Wilmington,
N. C. , 1959-61; Macon, Ga. , 1961-63; present: pastor,
S. D. A. Church, Wichita, Kansas, 1963- . Night School
teacher, Reid Business College, Atlanta, Ga. , 1955-56;
U. S. Army, 3 years; former member of Inter-denomina-
tional Ministerial Alliance. Home: 1639 North Volutsia,
Wichita, Kansas. Office: 1121 Wabash Ave. , Wichita,
Kansas.

DARNELL, Milner L. , sem. dir. , prof. ; b. Lamar City,
Ala. ; Paine Coll. , Augusta, Ga. ; Gammon Theol. Sem. ;
Grad. study: Hammond Theol. Sem. , Springfield; Fisk
Univ. ; D. D. (hon.), Miss. Industrial Coll. ; Lane Coll. ,
Jackson, Tenn. ; m. Harriet Goldston; children---Emma
Ione; pastor, Freeman Chapel Christian Methodist Epis-
copal Church, Kopkinsville, Ky. , 1948-55; Miles Chapel
C. M. E. Ch. , Little Rock, Ark. , 1955-59; director,
Phillips Sch. of Theol. , Atlanta, Ga. , 1959---; prof. ,
History & Polity of C. M. E. Ch. , Phillips Sch. of
Theology; Mem. , Adm. staff, director of C. M. E. students
Interdenominational Theological Center, Atlanta, Ga. ;
Mem. , Atlantic Council on Human Relations; former
mem. , Exec. Com. , Urban League, Little Rock; 1st vice
pres. , Interracial & Interdenominational Minister's Assn,
Greater Little Rock; US Army Chaplain, World War II,
1943-46; Major; Mem. , Dept. of the Ministry, Advisory
Committee, Southern Office, Atlanta, Ga. , Nat. Council
of Churches; North Arkansas Annual Conference; Office:
641 Beckwith St. , Atlanta 14, Ga.

DAVIES, Everett Frederick Samuel; b. Freetown, Sierra
Leone , Africa, July 21, 1902; s. Frederick and Eliza-
beth; B. A. , Talladega Coll. , 1927; B. D. , 1928; M. A.
Yale Univ. , 1930; Ed. D. , Columbia Univ. , 1946; m.
Marguerite Marion Buckner; Prof. , Bishop Coll. , 1932-
35; associate director, Detroit, Mich. Survey, 1935-36;
prof. and director of Religious Activities, Va. State
Coll. , Petersburg, Va. , 1936-46; professor, 1946---;
Mem. , 5-Man Town Committee, Ettrick, Va. ; 1st vice
pres. , Va. Council on Human Relations; Mem. , Editorial
Bd. of Psychology (Publication); Alpha Phi Alpha; sec. ,
Va. Philosophical Assn; Amer. Philosophical Assn; Fel-
low, Amer. Sociological Assn; sec. , Va. Philosophical
Ass; Editorial Bd. of Psychology; Home: 54 Third Ave. ,
Ettrick, Va. ; Office: 202 Va. Hall Va. State Coll. ,

Petersburg, Va.

*DAVIES, Lawrence Anderson, b. July 7, 1930. Houston,
Texas; s. Lawrence Anderson and Autrey (Thomas) D.;
B.S., Prairie View A & M Coll., 1949; B.D., Howard
Univ. Sch. of Rel., 1957; S.T.M., Wesley Theol. Sem.,
1961; m. Janice J. Pryde; children---Lauren Andrea,
Karen Michelle, Sharron Lynie; pastor, Good Samaritan
Bapt. Ch., Wash., D.C., 1956-61; asst. pastor and di-
rector of Rel. Ed., Shiloh Bapt. Ch., Wash., D.C.,
1961-62; current pastor, Shiloh (Old Site) Bapt. Ch.,
Fredericksburg Area Ministerial Assn, 1962---; pres.,
Fredericksburg Area Ministerial Assn; Bd. of Dir.,
Fredericksburg Area Counseling Service; 2nd vice pres.,
Pratt Chapter; mem., Va. Assn for Mental Health; Exec.
Bd., Lott Carey Foreign Missions Convention; Fredericks-
burg Area Personal Counseling Service; Christian Ed.
Div., Va. Council of Churches; pres., Walker Grant P.
T.A., Fredericksburg bi-racial Commission; Progressive
Nat. Bapt. Convention; U.S. Army, 1952-54; Certificate
of Commendation for service and counselor by Pratt
Chapter, Va. Mental Health Assn; mem., Alpha Phi
Alpha; home: 1205 Cardwell St., Fredericksburg, Va.
22401; office: 801 Sophia St., Fredericksburg, Va.

DAVIS, Abraham Eric, Teacher; b. New Orleans, La. Nov.
16, 1934; A.B. Southern University, 1954-58; Gammon
Theological Seminary (Interdenominational Theological
Center) 1958-1960; m. Muriel McCall; Children: four
daughters; Ministry: Student Asst. Pastor, Bowen Methodist Church, Atlanta, Ga. 1958-1959, Trinity Methodist
Church, 1960-63, St. Paul Meth. Ch. Shreveport, La.
1963 to present; Instructor and Counselor, Godman Ele-
mentary School, Baldwin, La., Sagen Brown Home for
Underpriviledged Children, Baldwin, La.; Member,
Louisiana Conference Board of Christian Social Concerns
of The Methodist Church, N.A.A.C.P., Citizens Com-
mittee of Shreveport; Received the Frank W. Clelland
Award; Member, Interdenominational Ministerial Alliance,
Institutional Representative Boy Scouts of America, Y.M.
C.A., Democratic Party; Home: 1852 Abbie Street,
Shreveport, La. Office: 1001 Pierre Avenue, Shreveport,
La.

*DAVIS, Arnor S., rel. educator; b. Ga., Dec. 30, 1919;
s. Alex and Bessie D.; B.S., Ga. State Coll., 1948;
B.D., Howard Univ. Sch. of Rel., 1953; M.A., 1958;

m. Virginia; children---Arnetta, Timothy, Alex; director,
Religious Education, Galbraith African Methodist Epis-
copal Zion Church, Wash. , D.C. , 1958-60; current
director, Rel. Ed. New Bethel Bapt. Church, Wash. ,
D.C. , 1960---; staff asst. Howard Univ. Community
Service Project, 1963; Mem. , Bd. of Directors, Iona
Whipper Home, Wash. , D.C. ; Clergymen's Advisory
Committee, Planned Parenthood, Wash. , D.C. ; US Army,
1942-46; Home: 631 Jefferson St. NE, Wash. , D.C. ;
Office: New Bethel Ch. , 812 S St. NW, Wash. , D.C.

DAVIS, Cyprian, teacher; b. Washington, D.C. , Sept. 9,
1930; s. Clarence Wm. and Evelyn (Jackson) D. ; A.B. ,
St. Meinrad College, 1953; S.T.L. Cath. Univ. of Amer. ,
1957; Licencie en sciences historiques, Universite Cath-
olique, Louvain, Belgium, 1963; Solemn vows as Benedictine monk, St. Meinrad, 1954; Ordained priest, Roman Cath. Ch. , 1956; Instr. , Church Hist. , Sch. of
Theol. , Instr. , French & Eur. Hist. , St. Meinrad College, 1963-64; Mem. Medieval Academy, The Cath. Historical Assoc. ; Home: St. Meinrad Archabbey, St. Meinrad, Indiana 47577.

DAVIS, Grady Demus, seminary dean; b. Pleasant Hill,
N.C. , Dec. 23, 1919; s. Willie E. and Elenora D. ;
A.B. Shaw U. , 1942; B.D. , Andover-Newton (Mass.),
1949; Ph.D. , Boston U. , 1953; m. Dorothy Mae Hicks;
2 sons, Grady D. , Jr. , Mahatma Gandhi; 3 daus. , Deryl
Gradette, Psyche Darzette, Crystal Tara; Student Pastor,
Ebenezer Bapt. Ch. , Boston; Zion Bapt. , Everett, Mass. ;
Pastor, Oberlin Bapt. , Raleigh, N.C. ; Pastor, Oberlin
Bapt. , Raleigh, N.C. , 1953-63; Union Bapt. , Durham,
N.C. , 1963---; Dean, Shaw U. Divinity Sch. , 1953--;
Pres. , Raleigh Citizens Assoc. , 1961; Candidate, House of
Representatives, Wake Co. , N.C. , 1960; Appointed Gov, 's
Comm. on Juv. Delinquency & Youth Crime, 1962; U.S.
Army, 1942-46; Recipient Raleigh's Negro Family of the Year
1959; mem. , Amer. Psychological Assoc. , N.C. Psych.
Assoc. , Amer. Assoc. Univ. Profs. , Soc. , for Scientific
Study of Rel. , NAACP, Phi Beta Sigma; lecturer, Col-
lege and University Religious Emphases Weeks and Re-
treats; Home: 802 Elizabeth St. , Durham, N.C. 27701
Church: 904 N. Roxboro St. , Durham, N.C. 27702

DAVIS, Hooker D. , ch. official; b. Hazlehurst, Miss.
Jan. 22, 1917; s. Brennon and Lucille (Christmas) D. ;
Rust Coll. , Holly Springs, 1935-36; A.B. , Alcorn A&M

Coll., Alcorn, Miss., 1939; S.T.B., Lincoln Univ.,
1944; m. Rovena Rita Mabines; children---Charles
Hooker; Beverly Ann; pastor of Delaware Conf., Meth.
Ch.; Methodist Ch., Townsend, Delaware; 3 years; White
Temple Meth Ch., Salisbury, Md., 5 years; Laurel,
Del., 3 years; Hamilton Memorial Meth. Ch., Atlantic
City, N.J., 10 years; current, District Superintendent
of The Easton District, The Meth. Ch.; asst. principal,
Lampton High Sch., Miss.; pres., Greater Atlantic City
Ministerial Assn; sec., Conference Missionary, 7 years;
pastor to migrants, Del. area, 17 years; Elected minis-
ter of Gen. Bd. of Missions, 1964; Mem., Bd. of
Managers, Atlantic County TB Assn; Mem., Bd. of Di-
rectors, Talbot County Mental Health; Phi Beta Sigma;
Home: 420 E. Dover St., Easton, Md.

DAVIS, John Candler, b. Webster, N.C., Sept. 12, 1907;
s. John Harden and Carrie (Love) D.; B.A., St. Augustine Coll., 1932; B.D., Bishop Payne Divinity Sch.,
1936; M.A., Western Reserve Univ., 1959; D.D. (hon.),
Wilberforce Univ., 1956; m. Ethel Norris; rector, St.
Matthias Ch., Asheville, N.C., 1936-39; curate, St.
Philips Ch., N.Y.C., 1939-42; prof., Bishop Payne
Divinity Sch., 1942-43; rector, St. Andrew's Ch., Cleve-
land, Ohio, 1942-58; chaplain, Cleveland State Hospital,
1945-58; Vicar, Meade Memorial Episcopal Ch., Alexan-
dria, Va., 1959; certificate in Clinical Training, Boston
State Hospital, 1950; certificate in Group Life Laboratory,
Bethel Maine, 1958; Mem., Academy of Religion and Men-
tal Health; Bd. of Trustee, Alexandria Welfare Council
Com. on Day Care, Greater Washington Area; Durant
Civic Assn, Alexandria, Va.; Mason; Shriner; Knight
Templar; Omega Psi Phi; Assn of Mental Hospital Chaplains; American Protestant Hospital Chaplains Assn; (Life)
NAACP; home: 382 Beacon Hill Road, Groveton, Va.
22306; office: 322 N. Alfred St., Alexandria, Va. 22314

DAVIS, Leon Houston, church official; b. East St. Louis,
Ill., May 8, 1920; s. James Roy and Viola (Reid) D.;
Oakwood Junior College, 1943; Emmanuel Missionary Col-
lege, 1945; m. Althea Lightner; 1 son: Leon Houston, Jr.
Pastored: Marion and Muncie, Indiana Seventh-Day Adven-
tist Church, 1945-46; Springfield and East St. Louis,
Illinois S.D.A. Church, 1946-49; youth director and edu-
cational superintendent (Lake Region Conf. of S.D.A.,
Chicago, Ill., 1949-54); present: youth director and edu-
cational superintendent - Northeastern Conf. of S.D.A.,

Davis, S. M.
105

New York City, N.Y., 1955- . American Temperance
secretary (Northeastern Conf., New York City); Civil
Defense secretary (Northeastern Conf., New York City);
National Selective servicemen representative; press secretary; committee member: Northeastern Conference Academy Board of S.D.A., 1955- . Northeastern Conf.
of S.D.A. - Executive Committee; Atlantic Union Board
Educational Committee, South Lancaster, Mass. Testimonial luncheon - Americana Hotel, Feb. 10, 1962, New
York City, for outstanding achievement as Youth Director
of Northeastern Conference of S.D.A.; Pathfinder Director; Victory Lake Camp; Youth Camp Director, Hyde
Park, N.Y. Home: 1257 Carroll St., Brooklyn, N.Y.
Office: 560 W. 150th St., N.Y. City, N.Y.

DAVIS, Samuel Matthew, b. Shortersville, Ala., Sept. 7,
1908; s. Alexander A. and Mahala D.; B.D., Daniel
Payne Coll., 1927; D.D. (hon.), Payne Coll., 1945;
LL.D., Monrovia Coll., W. Africa, 1955; LL.D., Daniel
Payne Coll., 1961; m. Alma D.; children---Rebecca
(Mrs. Ullessee Fletcher), Dorothy (Mrs. C.E. Murphy),
Coleman, Robert, Joseph, James, Solomon, Bester J.,
Walter; pastor, since 1928, African Methodist Episcopal
Churches; Cole Bluff, Miss.; St. Stephen, Crighton,
1929; Fairhope, 1930; Pinegrove Mobile, 1931; Thomas-
ton, 1932-33; Pleasant Hill, Magnolia, 1934; St. John
Swicha, 1935-36; Prattsville, 1937; presiding elder,
The Camden District, 1938; presiding elder, The Pratts-
ville Dist., 1939; pastor, St. James A.M.E. Church,
Pratt City, 1940; Jones Chapel, Clayton; St. Mark A.M.
E. Church, Toscaloosa, 1947; St. James Anniston, 1948;
presiding elder, Florence Huntsville Dist., 1949; current
pastor, St. Paul African Methodist Episcopal Church
Birmingham, Ala.; pres., Brotherhood of A.M.E.
Church; Trustee, Daniel Payne Coll.; pres., Smithfield
Civic League, 4 years; Mem., Episcopal Comm. A.M.E.
Church, 1952-56; pres., United Order of Brotherhood of
State of Ala.; Republican; Mason; Citation from Payne
Theol. Sem.; Award of Merit, Pi Lamba Sigma Honor
Society, 1962; Award, WENN (radio) in field of human
relations, 1963, Birmingham, Ala.; Home: 320 Ninth
Court West Birmingham 4, Ala.; Office: 300 Fourth
Court North, Birmingham, Ala.

DAW, Matthew Leonard, b. Youngstown, Ohio, Jan. 28,
1921; s. Lane and Myrtle (White) D.; A.B., Univ. of
Pittsburgh, 1947; B.D., Reformed Presbyterian Seminary,

1959; m. Lenore Estella Owens; children---Andrea, Matthew L., Alan Lane; Licensed to ministry, 1941; interim
pastor, Mt. Olivet Bapt. Ch., Newport, Rhode Island,
1943; New Hope Bapt. Ch., Braddock, Pa., 1947-49;
South Hills Bapt. Ch., Pittsburgh, Pa., 1950-51; pastor,
St. John Bapt. Church, Pittsburgh, Pa., 1951-52; Second
Bapt. Ch., Ford City, Pa., 1952-56; Triumph Bapt. Ch.,
Sweickley, Pa., 1956-62; Calvary Bapt. Ch., 1962---;
former social worker, Morals Court, Pittsburgh, Pa.;
area moderator, Kiski Valley Area (Auba), Pittsburgh, Pa.;
chairman, Bi-racial Committee, Spokane; Mem., Bd. of
Directors, Council of Churches, Spokane; Alpha Phi
Alpha; Home: East 207 Third Ave., Spokane 3, Wash.,
99202; Office: same.

DAWKINS, Maurice Anderson, b. Chicago, Ill., Jan. 29,
1921; s. Anderson Maurice and Marie Von (Dickerson)
D.; A.B., Columbia Univ., N.Y.C., 1943; M.A., Union
Theol. Sem. & Columbia Univ.; 1950; further study:
Columbia Univ.; D.D. (hon.), 1964; m. Doris Myrtle
Scott; children---Kimball Maurice, Susan Scott; minister
of Ed. & assoc. pastor, The Community Church of New
York, 1948-54; minister & director, People's Independent
Church of Christ, Nat. Council of Community Churches;
former pres., International Council of Community
Churches; Mem., Nat. Urban League, Western Regional
Board; American Leadership Conf. on Africa American
Assn; United Nations World Affairs Council; former
pres., NAACP (Los Angeles); founder and former pres.,
Western Christian Conf.; West coast coordinator, National
Day of Prayer, 1956; Prayer Philgrimage to Washington,
1957; Youth March on Washington, 1958, 1963; Governor's
Commission on Metropolitan Area Problems, 1959-63;
Atty. General's Advisory Com. on Constitutional Rights,
1959-63; Major's Com. on Human Rights, 1960-61;
California State Com. on Urban Policy; League Award for
Promoting Interracial Understanding; George Washington's
Carver Award for Human Rights; National Council of Negro
Women Award for Religious Leadership; Weekly Radio
broadcast Los Angeles, Column-"The Christian Answer"
in Calif. Eagle; Weekly guest columnist, Los Angeles
Sentinel; Office: Peoples' Independent Church of Christ,
1025 E. 18th St., Los Angeles, Calif.

*DeBERRY, David, b. Mainline, Pa., May 22, 1932; s.
Jonathan Robert and Mary Ellen (Thomas) D.; A.B.,
Va. Union Univ., 1952; courses, Sorbonne, Paris; M.S.,

Colorado Univ., 1962, B.D., Howard Univ., School of
Rel.; m. Clara Jayne Terry; migrant minister, Delaware
Nat. Council of Church; assoc. pastor, St. Paul Methodist
Ch., Laurel, Md.; pastor, Winchester Va. Methodist Ch.;
pastor, John Mann Meth. Ch.; Mem., Bd. of Missions,
The Meth. Ch.; counselor, Boys Scouts of Amer.; Mem.,
Civic Voters League, Roanoke, Va.; Roanoke Ministers
Alliance; former pres., Winchester NAACP; Mem.,
Omega Psi Phi; Served with United States Force (Korean
War); Home: 809 Madison Ave. NW, Roanoke, Va.; Of-
fice: 5th and Gilmore Sts., Roanoke, Va.

DeGRAFFENREIDT, Kermit Jesse, b. Durham, N.C.,
Oct. 3, 1937; s. Jesse Roscoe and Minnie (Ellis) D.;
A.B., North Carolina College, Durham; B.D., Hood
Theological Seminary, 1963; Course: Wesley Theological
Seminary, 1963---; m. Guytanna Maria Herton; asst.
pastor, St. Mark A.M.E. Zion Church, Durham, N.C.,
1958-60; Mt. Moriah, A.M.E. Zion Church, Henderson,
N.C., 1960-63; current pastor, Clinton A.M.E. Zion
Church, Rockville, Md., 1963---; NAACP participant in
N.C. demo., 1960-63; Vice pres. (Community Youth
Improvement Association of Rockville, 1964; Mem.:
Omega Psi Phi; Ministerial Alliance of Rockville & Wash-
ington District A.M.E. Zion Church; Home: 223 Eliza-
beth Ave., Rockville, 20850 Md.; Office: 814 Westmore
Ave., Rockville, Md.

DENNIS, Walter Decoster, b. Washington, D.C., Aug. 23,
1932; s. Walter Decoster, Sr. and Helen (Maddux);
Asst. pastor, St. Philip's Church, Brooklyn, NY., 1956;
Asst. pastor, The Cathedral of St. John the Divine,
1956-60; Adjunct Asst. Professor, American History,
Hampton Institute Consultant, National Council of the
Episcopal Church; Member, Board of Directors of Epis-
copal Society of Racial Cultural Unity; author: "Puerto
Rican Neighbors" "Mexican-American Neighbors"; Home:
551 East Mercury Blvd., Hampton, Virginia; Office: 55
East Tyler St., Kecoughtan Square, Hampton, Va.

DeVEAUX, John Allen, Jr., chaplain; b. Miami, Fla.,
May 26, 1909; s. John Henry and Allen Learnora (S.)
D.; A.B., Wilberforce Univ., 1932; B.D., Payne
Theological Seminary, Wilberforce, Ohio, 1930; m.
Della (NMI) Phillips; children--- Leanora (Mrs.
Orlando Vernon Brown), John A., Jr., William Phillips;
pastor, Ross Chapel African Methodist Episcopal Church,

1932; Pride Chapel A. M. E. Church, Clarksburg, W. Va.,
1932-34; Wayman A. M. E. Church, 1934-36; Bethel A. M.
E. Ch., 1936-38; Rodger Chapel A. M. E. Church, Wash-
ington C. H. Ohio, 1959-60; Payne Chapel A. M. E. Church,
Hamilton, Ohio, 1960-62; Quinn A. M. E. church, Steuben-
ville, Ohio, 1962---; Vice pres., NAACP, Hamilton,
Ohio Branch, 1961-62; Trustee Board Member, Payne
Theological Seminary, 1963---; Chaplain: 24th Infantry
Regt., 25th Inf. Regt.; 368th Inf. Regt. 93rd Inf. Div.
Chaplain; Chaplain 25th Inf. Combat Team; President US
Army chaplain Board; Headquarters Area Command Chap-
lain European Theater; Decorations of Service in World
War II: South Pacific Theater, China-Burma-India
Theater; European Theater; Mediterranian Theater;
"Legion of Merit" Medal for Action beyond the call of
duty in The Korean Conflict; Home: 524 Madison Ave.,
Steubenville, Ohio; Office: 515 North Steubenville, Ohio

DIAL, James Samuel, b. Darlington, S. C., Aug. 17, 1912;
s. Sammie S. and Mary (Burch) D.; Claflin Coll., 1930-
31; A. B., Clark Coll., 1950; B. D., Gammon Theol.
Sem., 1952; m. Gertrude Alma Brevard; children---
Michael Sylvester; pastor, Methodist Churches, Landrum,
S. C., 1932-33; Cowpens, S. C., 1934-35; Blacksburg, S.
C., 1936-37; South Greenville, S. C., 1958-62; Dist.
Supt., Beaufort Dist., 1963-64; Dist. Supt., Orangeburg,
S. C., 1964---; pastor (current), Mt. Zion Meth. Ch.,
Kingstree, S. C.; teacher, 11 years (elementary sch., 7
years, high sch., 4 years); Mem., Claflin Coll. Trustee
Board; chmn, S. C. Conf. Com. on World Service &
Finance, The Meth. Ch.; Mem., Mason; Home: 319 W.
Main St., Kingstree, S. C.

DICKERSON, Adolphus Summer, sem. prof.; b. Greenville,
Ga., May 25, 1914; s. Dixie and Mary Bessie (Ogle-
tree) D.; A. B., 1943, Clark Coll., Atlanta, Ga.; B. D.,
Gammon Theol. Sem., 1945; M. A. Atlanta Univ., S. T.
M., Boston Univ. School of Theology, 1960; m. Virginia
Griffin; pastor, Barnesville Methodist Ch., Ga., 1937-
38; St. Mark Meth. Ch., Augusta, 1938-40; Palen Meth.
Ch., Savannah, Ga., 1940-41; Centenary Meth. Ch.,
Atlanta, Ga., 1941-42; South Atlanta Meth. Ch., Atlanta,
Ga., 1942-48; Ariel Bowen Meth. Ch., 1948-54; Dist.
Supt., Atlanta South, 1954-60; 1960---; Professor, Gam-
mon Theol. Sem. and Interdenominational Theol. Center;
"Minister of Year" 1958; 1st negro chaplain to serve in
a Federal Prison, 1945---; columnist, Atlanta Daily

World; contributor, Central Christian Advocate; Home:
1507 Mozley Pl. SW, Atlanta, Ga.; Office: 583 Mitabell
St. SW, Atlanta, Ga.

DICKERSON, Noy Jasper, teacher; b. Elkhorn, West Vir-
ginia, Sept. 17, 1892; s. Charles Marion and Maria (Hig-
ginbotham) D.; 1932, B.S. Bluefield State College; 1942,
M.A. Michigan University; m. Frances Louise (Anderson)
D. teacher 1923-24 Mercer County Schools (W. Va.);
1925-37; McDowell County Schools (W.Va.); 1937-44;
Mercer County Schools (W.Va.) 1944-50, Interviewer:
W. Va. State Employment Service; pastor-1946-(now)
Community Christian Church; U.S. Army, 1918-19;
Home: 309 Allen St. Bluefield, West Virginia; Office:
315 Marshall St., Bluefield, West Virginia.

DICKS, Abel Joseph, b. Beaumont, Tex., Apr. 5, 1933;
s. Abel and Winnie (Premeau) D.; B.A., Divine Word
Seminary, Techny, Ill., 1959; Ordained priest of Ro-
man Cath. Ch., Mar. 19, 1962; Mem. Society of the
Divine Word; Home: 1025 Michigan Ave., N.E., Wash.,
D.C. 20017

DICKSON, Melvin Curtis, b. Texas, Oct. 25,1912; s.
David M. and Lizzie (De Laney) D.; A.B., Southern
Christian Institute, 1935; Butler Univ., 1935-93; m.
Eunice S. King; children--- Melvin, Joseph, Larry,
Brenda; pastor, Louden Ave. Christian Church, Roanoke,
Va., 1939-43; Forest Ave. Christian Ch., Texas, 1943-
53; Louden Ave. Christian Ch., Roanoke, Va., 1953-
56; current pastor, Forest Ave. Christian Ch., Dallas,
Tex., 1956---; pres., Texas Christian Missionary Com-
mittee, present: consultant, Youth Conf., Christian
Ch.; Mem., Civic Com.; Housing Com.; Democrat;
Home: 1814 Peabody, Dallas, Texas 75215; Office: 1802
Forest Ave., Dallas, Texas 75215

DIXON, James Inman, b. Nashville, Tenn., Oct. 10, 1910;
s. William Henry and Mary (Pitt) D.; M.S., A & I State
Teacher's Coll., Nashville, Tenn., 1935; M.A., Dept.
Psychology Religion, 1946; M.S., Butler Univ., Indianapolis, Ind.; m. Tommie Hinton; B.D., Gammon
Theol. Sem., 1938; served as a minister-in the pastor-
ate-30 years; Dist. Supt., 5 years; founder, 5 Methodist
Church bodies, and have developed much interest in
working with alcoholic patients, after receiving much
information in regards to working with alcoholic school

of Alcoholic Studies, Yale Univ., 1946, and at other
times; Pastor: South Atlanta Meth. Ch., 1939; Anderson
Indiana-Second Meth. Ch., 1942-47; Dayton, Ohio, Mc
Kinley Meth. Ch., 1947-52; founder Dixon Meth. during
this period, 1950; Indianapolis, Indiana, Simpson Meth.
Church; Established Christ Meth. Ch. while pastoring here;
Cincinnati, Ohio Dist. Supt., 1959---; current pastor,
Grace Meth. Ch., Cincinnati, Ohio; Given much time to
pastoral counseling, in family life, and etc.; Mem., Bd.
of Wesley Foundations in Colleges; pres., NAACP;
YMCA; Mason; writer of many articles to papers and
poems of a religious nature: Home: 830 Lexington Ave.,
Cincinnati 29, Ohio;

DOGGETTE, Jackson Michael, b. Virginia, December 11,
1930; s. Herbert Richard and Sally (Robertson) D.;
studied architecture, 1944-48; B.A., Oakwood College,
1954; doing graduate work at Andrews Univ.; m. Edythe
Marie Young; children- Linda, Jackson, Jr., James.
Pastored Seventh-Day Adventist Churches in: Lubbock,
Texas; Roswell, N. Mexico; El Paso, Texas, 1954-
55; Wichita Falls, Texas; Ardmore, Oklahoma, 1956-57;
present: pastor, S.D.A. Church, Santa Monica, Calif.,
1958-   . Member, School Board of Santa Monica Jr.
Academy and Glendale Academy. Home: 1904 19th St.,
Santa Monica, Calif. Office: 1845 20th St., Santa Monica,
Calif.

DONALD, Grady H., b. Belton, S.C., June 19, 1929; s.
Alonza C. and Ella (Calhoun) D.; A.B., Benedict Coll.,
Columbia, S.C., 1951; B.D., American Bapt. Theol.
Sem., Nashville, Tenn., 1954; m. Clara G. Phillips;
children---Grady H., Jr., Michael Thomas, Angelyn
Yvonne; pastor, Hopewell Bapt. Ch., Glasgow, Ky.,
1953-55; First Bapt. Ch., Murfreesboro, Tenn., 1955-
58; current, Kayne Ave. Bapt. Ch., 1958---; faculty
mem., American Baptist Theol. Sem. Extension School,
1963---; Missionary to Jamaica, 1951; teacher, National
Sunday School & B.T.U. Congress; associate dean-at-
large, Leadership Education Congress of Tenn. B.M. &
E. Convention; 1st vice pres., The Nashville Christian
Leadership Council; Mem., Bd. of Directors, South
Street Community Center; chartered mem., The Nashville
Coordinating Council for Civil Rights; Mem., The NAACP
and The Davidson County Independent Political Council;
Alumni Award, 1960, For Outstanding Service to Race,
Country and Church; Mem., Alpha Phi Alpha; Mason;

Home: 1423 Edgehill Ave., Nashville, Tenn. 37212; Office
1109 12th Ave. So. Nashville, Tenn., 37212

DOUGLAS, Jesse L., b. New Orleans, La., Aug. 19, 1930;
s. William and Isabella D.; Dillard Univ., 1952-56; A. B.
Lane Coll., Jackson, Tenn., 1957-59; B. D., Interdenominational Theol. Center, Atlanta, Ga., 1959-64; S. T. M.
candidate; m. Blanche Y. Gordon; children---Jesse L.,
Jr.; Assistant to the general Sec. of Evangelism of the
Christian Methodist Episcopal Church; Conference Soloist
for the Georgia Conf., 1959-62; current pastor, The
First C. M. E. Church, Montgomery, Ala.; Mem., Board
of Directors, Montgomery Improvement Ass'n; vice pres.,
Interdenominational Ministerial Alliance, Montgomery,
Ala.; A Commissioner's Committee on Community Af-
fairs; Home: 716 Glass St., Montgomery, Ala.; Office:
First C. M. E. Church, 776 So. Holt St., Montgomery,
Ala.

DOYLE, Bertram Wilbur, bishop; b. Lowndesboro, Ala.,
July 3, 1897; s. Henry Sebastian and Anna Magnolia
(Walker) D.; A. B., Ohio Wesleyan U., 1921; A. M., U.
Chgo., 1924, Ph. D., 1934; D. D., Lane Coll., 1934;
Doctor of Laws (honorary), Miles College, 1958; m.
Pansy Ray Stewart, August 12, 1918; children---Vera
Corinne, Annie Glenn, Grace Margaret, Pansy Henrieta,
Bertram Wilbur. Teacher, Samuel Houston Coll., 1921-
22, Claflin Coll., 1922-24, Clark Coll., 1924-26; dean
Paine Coll., 1925-27; Teacher, Fisk U., 1927-37, personnel
dean, 1928-30; ordained to ministry, of Christian M. E.
Ch., 1925; pastor Orangeburg, Allendale, S. C., Nash-
ville, Goodlettsville, Tenn.; faculty summer schs.
Atlanta U., 1939, Hampton Inst., 1940-41; dean Louis-
ville Municipal Coll., 1942-50; sec. edn. Christian M. E.
Ch., 1937-50; elected bishop 7th dist., 1950, 6th dist.,
1954, 8th dist., 1958; exec. com. Meth. World Conf.,
1951, mem. 1956, mem. Ecumenical Conf., 1951; mem.
exec. com. World Meth. Council, 1951---; chairman
Christian M. E. delegation to World Methodist Conference,
Oslo, Norway, 1961. Chairman bd. trustees Tex. Coll.
Mem. National Council Christians Chs. (gen. bd. 1950-
---; mem. constituting conv. 1950), Nat. Protestant
Council Higher Edn. (sec. exec. com. 1948-50), New
Deal Progressive League, Phi Beta Kappa, Kappa Alpha
Psi, Sigma Pi Phi. Author: Etiquette of Race Relation in
the South, 1937. Editor: A Study of Negro Business and
Employment in Louisville, 1944. Contributor articles

mags. Home: 1702 Heiman St., Nashville, Tenn.

*DRAYTON, Jerry, b. Savannah, Ga., June 15, 1918; s.
Solomon and Marie D.; certificate clinical psychiatry,
Bowman Gray School; A.B., Morehouse Coll., 1943;
B.D., Howard Univ. Sch. of Rel., 1946; D.D. (hon.),
Va. Theo. Sem., Lynchburgh, Va.; m. Susie E. Jones;
children---Jerry Alphonso, Jr.; pastor, New Bethel
Baptist Church, Winston-Salem, N.C.; pres., Forsyth
Ministers Fellowship, Winston-Salem, N.C.; vice pres.
Interracial N.C. Baptist Fellowship; chairman, Exec.
Bd. of Interracial Urban League, Winston-Salem, N.C.;
chairman, Comm. on Public Accommodations; Bd. Mem.,
Forsyth County Alcoholic Program; chairman, Education
Conn.; Executive Bd. of Interracial N.C. Council of
Churches; Counseling Staff of the Domestic Relations Court;
chairman, Interracial Committee studying complete desegre-
gation of all recreational facilities in Winston-Salem, N.C.;
Historian, Baptist State Convention, N.C.; vice pres., Exec.
Bd., NAACP; Education Board, National Baptist Convention,
Inc.,; Mem. Exec. Bd. Lott Carey Foreign Mission Conu.
Home: 2035 K Court Ave., Winston-Salem, N.C.; Office:
1016 North Trade St., Winston-Salem N.C, 27101.

DUDLEY, Charles Edward, Church official; b. South Bend,
Indiana, Feb. 1, 1927; s. Joseph and Julia (Talley) D.;
Emanuel Missionary College; B.A., Oakwood College,
1947; m. Etta Mae Maycock; children- Bonita Andrea,
Charles E. II, Albert Leroy; Pastored: Jackson and
Memphis, Tenn. Seventh-Day Adventist Churches, 1949-
1954; Montgomery, Alabama S.D.A. Church, 1954-55;
Baton Rouge S.D.A. Church, 1955-1958; Dallas, Texas,
City Temple, 1958-1962; Secretary-Treasurer, Southwest
Region Conference, summer of 1962 (Dallas); Present:
President, South Central Conference of S.D.A., Nashville,
Tenn.; Member: Riverside Hospital Board, Nashville,
Tenn., Madison Hospital Board, Madison, Tenn.; Exec-
utive Committee, Southern Union Conf., Decatur, Georgia;
Oakwood College Board, Huntsville, Alabama; Southern
Publishing Assn., Nashville, Tenn. Home: 1604 White's
Creek Pike, Nashville 7, Tenn. Office: 715 Young's Lane,
Nashville, Tenn.

DUNGEE, John Riley, Jr., chaplain, b. Roanoke, Va. Mar
6, 1900; s. John Riley, Sr. and Flossie Belle (Wingfield)
D.; A.B., Johnson C. Smith Univ., 1923; B.D., 1926;
D.D. (hon.), 1957; Courses-Union Theological Sem., New

York, Summer, 1946; pastor Green St. Presbyterian Ch.,
Morganton, N.C.; Trinity Presby. Ch., Marion, N.C.,
1923-26; Lebanon Presbyterian Ch., Rdgeway, S.C.,
1926-36; teacher Henderson Institute, Henderson, N.C.;
pastor, Townsville United Presby. Ch., Townsville,
N.C., 1936-42; chaplain US Army, 1942-46; pastor Cotton
Memorial United Presby. Ch., 1946- ; Stated clerk
Presbytery of Tenn. (U.P.) 1950-58; General Assembly
Commissioner-1931, 1940, 1947, 1950, 1953, 1957,
1961; Permanent Clerk Synod of Catawba, United Presby.
Ch., USA; pres. Vance County Branch, NAACP, 1948-
49; vi. pres., 1959; pres. Vance County Ministers' Al-
liance, 1952-58; pres. Vance County Voters' League,
1953-60; chaplain, US Army, 1942-46; awards: Ameri-
can Theater Ribbon, Asiatic-Pacific Theater Ribbon;
Certificate of Commendation, Army Service Forces Hq.,
Camp Shelby, Miss.; Certificate of Award for Meritorious
Service, General Commission on Army and Navy Chaplains; mem.: Charter president, Alpha-Omicron Chapter,
Alpha Phi Alpha Fraternity, Johnson C. Smith University, 1923. Junior Grand Warden, South Carolina Grand
Lodge, A.F. & A.M., Asst. Rabban, Cairo Temple,
A.E.A.O. Nobles of the Mystic Shrine, 1932-36; Home:
439 W. Rock Spring Street, Henderson, N.C.; Office:
Off.: 511 N. Chestnut St., Henderson, North Carolina.

DUNLAP, Theodore Roosevelt, b. Wewoka, Okla., April
21, 1903; s. Robert Green and Sylvia (Trotter) D.;
B.D., Union Theol. Sem., 1948; San Diego State Coll.,
San Diego, Cal., A.B., 1946; m. Sadie Altin Fields;
pastor, Oak Park Community Ch., Sacramento, Calif.,
1948-51; Chandler Memorial Congregational Church,
Lexington, Ky., 1951-54; Methodist Churches, Kentucky,
Tennessee, Arkansas, Kansas and Ill., 1954---; An
interim term on the Bd. of Hospitals and Homes, The
Meth. Ch., 1958-60; Mem., Mason; Home: 611 South
15th St., Springfield, Ill. 62703; Office: 15th and Edward
Sts., Springfield, Ill. 62703

DUNSTON, Alfred G., Jr., bishop; b. Coinjock, N.C.,
June 25, 1915; s. Alfred G. and Cora (McNair); A.B.,
Livingstone College & Hood Seminary; M.A., Drew
University, 1939-41; D.D. (hon), Allen Univ.; D.C.L.
Monrovia College, Liberia; children--- Carol,
Aingred, Armayne; Elected Bishop, Indianapolis, Ind.,
May 20, 1963, Twelfth Episcopal District; Mt. Sinai
A.M.E.Z. Advance, N.C., 1936-37; St. John A.M.E.Z.

Thomasville, N. C. , Wallace Temple A. M. E. Zion
Church, Bayonne, N. J. , 1939-41; Price Memorial A. M.
E. Zion Church, Atlantic City, 1941-43; Wallace Chapel,
Summit, N. J. , 1946-48; Logan Temple, Knoxville, Tenn. ,
1948-52; Big Wesley, Phila. , Pa. , 1952-63; Mother Zion
NYC, 1964; Member, Commission on Human Relation,
Phila. , Pa. , 1963; Member, Selective Patronage Program,
Phila. , 1960-63; Member, Bd. Directors Mercy-Douglas
Hospital, Phila. ; Co-Founder, Opportunities Industrializa-
tion Center, Phila. , 1963; Trustee, Berean College,
Phila. Pa. , 1956-64; Trustee, Shapp Scholarship Fund,
1960-63; Member, Bd. Directors, Western Community
House, 1954-64; Member, Bd. Directors, Phila. Council
of Churches, 1960-63; Chaplain, World War II, 92nd
Infantry Division Artillery; 92nd Infantry Division Citation
for meritorious Service in support of Combat Troops;
Mem. , Alpha Phi Alpha; Mason; Narrator of Film "The
Rising of Africa"- Produced by Trans-Continental Featured
in Television Documentary film "The Run From Race"
1963; Home: 5901 Cobbs Creek Pkway, Philadelphia, Pa.

DYKES, DeWitt Sanford, church official; b. Gadsden, Ala.
Aug. 16, 1904; s. Henry Sanford R. and Mollie Wade D. ;
A. B. , Clark Coll. , 1930; B. D. , Gammon Theological
Sem. , 1931; S. T. M. , Boston Univ. Sch. of Theology; m.
Viola G. Logan; children---Reida Belle (Mrs. George L.
Gardiner), DeWitt S. , Jr. ; pastor, Mt. Pleasant Methodist
Ch. , Marion, Va. , 1932-36; Wiley Memorial Meth. Ch. ,
1936-46; East Vine Ave. Meth. Ch. , Knoxville, Tenn. ,
1946-53; dist. supt. , Chattanooga Dist. , The East Tenn.
Conf. , 1953-64; Present, Staff Mem. of the Div. of Nat'l
Missions of the Bd. of Missions of the Meth. Ch. , Sec-
tion of Ch. Extension, Dept. of Finance and Field Serv-
ice, 1953---; pres. , Clark Coll. Alumni, 1942-44; Mem. ,
Alpha Phi Alpha; Home: 2139 Dandridge Ave. SE, Knoxville, Tenn. 37915; Office: same.

DYSON, William Andrew, radio announcer; b. Norfolk, Va.
May 20, 1935; s. Eddie E. and Leola (Jackson) D. ;
Virginia State Coll. ; Univ. of Bordeoue, France; Virginia
Theol. Seminary; Now engaged in historical research;
m. Mildred Marianne Saunders; children---Michael,
William Andrew II, San Deo Paul; business exec. Bar-
Charis, Recreational Facilities; asst. pastor, St. Paul's
Christian Methodist Episcopal Church, Norfolk, Va. ;
pastor, Walker Memorial C. M. E. Church, Spartanburg,
S. C. , 1963; current pastor, Metropolitan C. M. E. Church,

Phila., Pa.; radio announcer (before entering clergy),
WRAP, Norfolk, Va.; WLOW, Portsmouth; WBRG, Lynch-
burg, Va.; Mem., Va. Council Human Relations; US
Air Force (European area), 4 years; American Legion,
Merit award, while in High School; chaplain, Civil Air
Patrol Unit, Washington, D.C.; Mem., The National
Collegiate Panel of America; Contributing editor to
Mail-Mat, official organ of Interdenominational ministers
Council of America and the British West Indies; Home:
3432 North 17th St., Phila., Pa.

*EATON, Herbert Hoover, b. Creedmoor, N.C., Dec. 8,
1928; s. Hugh Dee and Flossie (Moss) E.; Hampton Institute, 1956; B.S., North Carolina Coll., Durhan,
1956; B.D., Howard Univ., Sch. of Rel., 1956; S.T.M.,
Boston Univ., 1957; m. Delores Costella Sankey; chil-
dren---Eric Renard; US Military Service (Army), 1951-
53; asistant pastor, Zion Baptist Church, Wash., D.C.;
student assistant to Dean of Andrew Rankin Memorial
Chapel, Howard Univ., 1954-56; director of student christian ass'n, Howard Univ., 1957-58; Adm. Assistant to
Dean of School of Rel. Howard Univ., 1957-60; current
pastor, Dexter Avenue Baptist Church, Montgomery,
Alabama, 1960-65; current pastor, Kenwood United Church of
Christ, 1965---; chairman, Board of Director, Montgomery
Improvement Ass'n, 1963---; Mem., City Commissioner's
Committee on Community Affairs; vice pres., Inter-Denomina-
tional Minister's Alliance of Montgomery, 1963; vice pres.,
Tuskegee-Montgomery; Howard Univ. Alumni Club, present;
Institute of Religion, Mason; Alpha Phi Alpha; Circulation
Manager, Journal of Religious Thought, 1957-60; Editor,
School of Religion "NEWS"; Office: 4608 So. Greenwood
Ave., Chicago 53, Ill.

*EATON, James Alonza, coll. chaplain, b. Portsmouth,
Va., Dec. 26, 1921; s. Lloyd R. and Mary (Massenburg)
E.; A.B., Virginia State Coll., 1943; B.D., Howard Univ.
Sch. of Rel., 1946; M.A., Boston Univ., 1952; Ed.D.
Columbia Univ., 1959; pastor, Wentz Memorial Con-
gregational Church, Winston-Salem, N.C., 1946-48;
chaplain, US Army, 1950-54; Acting chaplain, Tuskegee
Institute, 1954-55; associate pastor, Friendship Baptist
Church, New York City, 1955-58; director, Religious
Activities, Elizabeth City State Coll., Elizabeth City,
N.C., 1959-63; counselor to students, City Coll. of New
York, 1958-59; director of Testing and Guidance, Savan-

nah State Coll., 1963---; Mem.: Amer. Ass'n of Univ.
Professors; Southern Student Personnel Ass'n; American
Personnel and Guidance Ass'n; Amer. Psychological Ass'n;
Kappa Delta Pi Honor Society; Home: Box 188, Savannah
State Coll., Savannah, Ga. 31404

EDINGTON, Charles Arthur, b. Loudon, Tenn., April 10,
1889; s. Joseph and Sarah E.; A.B., Swift Memorial
Coll., 1906-10; S.T.B., M.A., Lincoln Univ., 1912-
15; D.D. (hon.), Johnson C. Smith Univ.; m. Della Mae
Reid; children--- Marie Alease (Mrs. Charles F. Chisolm),
Arthur Reid, H. Clifford, Sarah Elizabeth (Mrs. James
H. Houston); asst. pastor, Grace Presbyterian Church,
Pittsburg, Pa., 1915-17; pastor, St. Mark's Presbyter-
ian Church, Rogersville, Tenn., 1917-35; Calvary Pres-
byterian Ch., Asheville, N.C., 1935-39; Retired, Dec.
31, 1959; teacher, Swift Memorial Coll.; dean, Swift
Memorial Coll.; Concurrent with duties as pastor, St.
Mark's Presbyterian Ch.; stated clerk, Rogersville,
Presbytery; chmn, National Missions of Presbytery and
Synod; Bd. of Management, Market Street YMCA (Ashe-
ville, N.C.); Bd. of Directors, American Red Cross;
served as civilian chaplain at Camp Croft, S.C. (W.W.
II); home: Rt. 5, Box 182, Asheville, N.C.

EDMONDS, Edwin Richardson, teacher; b. Austin, Texas,
June 19, 1917; A.B., Morehouse Coll., 1938; S.T.B.
Boston Univ. Sch. of Theol., 1946; Ph.D., Boston Univ.
Grad. Sch., 1949; m. Maye Frances Bailey; 4 daus.
Lynette Edmonds Johnson, Karen, Cheryl, Toni. Pastor,
Dixwell Avenue Cong. Ch., New Haven, Conn., 1959-
64; Prof. Soc., Bennett College, 1956-59; Inst. Soc. and
Dean of Students, Delaware St. College, 1948-50; Asst.
Prof. Soc. and Dir. of Institutional Research, Langston
Univ., 1950-56; Instr. Soc. (part-time), Quinnipiac Col-
lege, New Haven, Conn.; Bd. of Dir., Community Pro-
gress, Inc., United Appeal, New Haven Council of
Churches; mem. Conn. Advisory Committee to the U.S.
Civil Rights Commission; Author: "Demographic Study of
the Negro of Oklahoma, 1910-1950", Annals, Oklahoma
Academy of Science, 1954; "A Program of Student Dis-
cipline", Negro Educational Review, Oct. 1953; "The
Myrdalian Hypothesis of Rank Order Discrimination",
Phylon, 2nd Quarter, 1955. Home: 40 Bellevue Road, New
Haven., Conn. Office: 100 Dixwell Avenue, ·New Haven,
Conn.

EDWARDS, Chancy Rudolph, b. Nash County, N.C., Feb.
28,   ; s. Buck Hilliard and Lucy Kearney E.; A.B.,
Shaw Univ., Raleigh, N.C., B.D., Shaw Divinity Sch.,
1949; D.D. (hon.), Shaw Univ., 1963; m. Luella Dickens;
children---Jewyl Anita; pastor, Spring Garden Bapt. Ch.,
Washington, N.C., 1948-53; First Baptist Ch., Fayetteville, N.C., 1953---; director, Roanoke Institute, Elizabeth City, N.C., 1950-53; current visiting pastor, Mc
Cain Sanitorium, McCain, N.C., 1963---; teacher, Dept.
of Religious Promotion, Shaw Univ.; Trustee, Shaw Univ.
Raleigh, N.C., 1960---; Democrat; Mason; Home: 312
Moore St., Fayetteville, N.C.; Office: 302 Moore St.,
Fayetteville, N.C.

EDWARDS, Joseph DuMaine, Sr., church official; b. St.
Louis, Mo., Mar. 27, 1907; s. Lewis James and Belle
(Berry) E.; A.B., B.Th., Douglas Univ., 1934-41;
m. Bessie Mae Johnson; children--Mrs. Lois M. Henry,
Joseph DuMaine, Jr.; professional baseball player, 1929-
30 (St. Louis Stars); professional musician, 10 years;
insurance salesman, waiter, cook, butler, laborer, con-
struction work, etc., 1930-39; began ministry as local
preacher, 1939; pastor, St. Charles Church, Mo., 1939-
42; Colo. People's Methodist Church, 1942-43; St.
Joseph Meth. Ch., Mo., 1943-45; Key Meth. Ch., 1945-
47; District superintendent South Nashville District,
1947-53; pastor, Pitts Methodist Ch., Springfield, 1953-
60; district superintendent The Meth. Ch. (Kansas City
District), 1960---; Office: Kansas City District Central
West Conf., The Methodist Ch., 3219 Lockridge, Kansas
City 28, Mo.

EDWARDS, Vinson Allen, educator, administrator; b. Craw-
fordville, Ga., July 12, 1897; s. Alexander and Fannie
B.E.; A.B., Morehouse Coll., 1927; B.D., Drew Theol.
Sem., 1930; M.A., Cornell U., 1940; m. Lillian Dixon;
Instr., Morehouse Coll., 1930-35; Sup. Adult Edu., Ga.
1935-36; Dean of Instruction, Forsyth Teach. Coll.,
1937-39; Dir. Rel. Ext., Home Missions Div., Nat.
Council of Chs., 1940-46; Dir. Rural Ch. Div. Nat.
Bapt. Conv. USA, Inc., 1946-52; Dir., Leadership Edu.
Div., Home Missions, Nat. Council of Churches, 1952-
64; Pastor, County Church, 1932-35; 1953-54; Instr.,
Amer. Bapt. Sem.; Colloborator U.S.D.A. in Rural
Areas Development; mem. Tuskegee Civic Assoc., 1952-
64; Nominated, Bd. of Revenue, Macon Co., Ala., 1964;
mem., Rural Sociological Soc., Masons, Democratic

Party; Ala. Council of Human Relations, Ala. Council of
Churches; Research: Study of Negro Leadership in Rural
Ga. , Negro Church in 5 Ala. Counties; Author: The
Church At Work in Rural Communities, and others;
traveled abroad (1956 sum.), Seminar on Study of Rural
Life in Europe; Home: P. O. Box 58, Tuskegee Institute,
Ala.

*EGGLESTON, George Watkins, b. Martinsville, Va. , Oct.
21, 1924; s. Raymond James and America (Payton) E. ;
A. B. , Va. State Univ. , Petersburg, Va. , 1951; M. A. ,
Va. State, 1952; B. D. , Howard Univ. , Sch. of Rel. ,
1960; journalist, Norfolk Journal and Guide, 1953-55;
Mem. , European Seminar for Christian Education (United
Ch. of Christ), 1956; asst. chaplain, United Christian
Fellowship; supply minister, Bethel Presbyterian Ch. ,
Alexandria, Va. , summers; current, asst. pastor, 15th
St. Presbyterian Ch.; instructor, Institute of Modern
Language, 1960-62; Va. State Citizenship Award; Howard
Shields Awards for Poetry, Va. State; recipient: Amer-
ican Foundation Scholarship for the Blind; Home: 1308
Clifton St. NW, Wash. , D. C. ; Office: 15th St. Presby-
terian Ch. , 15th & R St. NW, Wash. , D. C.

ELLIGAN, Irvin, Jr. , church official, b. Chattanooga,
Tennessee, Nov. 24, 1915; s. Irvin, Sr. and Annie
Ceola (Simmons) E. ; B. S. , Knoxville College, 1938;
Th. B. , Pittsburgh-Xenia (now Pittsburgh) Theological
Seminary, 1944; Special work at Union Theological Sem-
inary of Virginia, 1955, 56, 58, 60; m. Florence Jame-
sena Coston; children---Rachel Annette, Irvin, III; High
School science teacher, Camden Academy, Alabama,
1940-41; pastor, First United Presbyterian Church, Nor-
folk, Va. , 1944-48; First United Presbyterian Church &
College pastor, Knoxville College, Tenn. , 1948-52; pas-
tor, All Souls and Eastminster Presbyterian Churches,
Richmond, Va. , 1952-57; pastor, All Souls Presbyterian
Church, Richmond, Va. , 1952-63; current, Assoc. Sec.
Div. Christian Action, Board of Christian Ed. , Presby.
Ch. U. S. , 1963---; Teacher of Bilbe, Evangelism, and
Worship at various Church Leadership Schools; Member
Crusade for Voters, NAACP State Church Program Com-
mittee; Member, The Governor's (Virginia) Committee for
Youth; Former Bd. Mem. , The Richmond Area Com-
munity Council; Mem. Speakers' Bureau United Givers
Fund since 1960; V. Pres. Friends Ass'n for Children;
1962 Moderator Hanover Presbytery, Presbyterian, U. S. ;

Silver Beaver Award, R. E. Lee Council, Boy Scouts of
America, 1960; Five Year Service Pin, 1961, American
Red Cross of Richmond; Outstanding Citizen Awards;
Delver Woman's Club, 1962; Astoria Beneficial & Social
Club of Richmond, 1963; Chairman, Permanent Com-
mittee on Christian Relations, Presbyterian, U. S.;
Richmond Area Ministers Fellowship, Presbyterian
Ministers Fellowship; Member, "SILVER BEAVER" Committee, R. E. Lee Council, Boy Scouts of America; Member, St. James Fellowship, Presbyterian discussion
society of Richmond, Va.; Co-author of race relations
pamphlets: Two Major Issues; Race Relations (The Relationship Between the Races in the Area Served by the
Presbyterian Church, U. S.); Contributor to Presbyterian
Survey and Presbyterian Action, Church papers; Home:
2614 Lamb Avenue Richmond, Va. 23222; Office: Box
1176 8 N. 6th St. Richmond 23209 Va.

ELLIS, Thomas H., b. Farmville, Va., Sept. 2, 1918; s.
William E. and Clara (Anderson) E.; B. A., Morgan State
College, 1950; Colgate Rochester Divinity School, 1955-
58; m. Frances Anderson; 4 daus. Sylvania, Yvonne,
Geneva, Frances, 1 son, Thomas; Asst. Minister, First
Pentecostal Church, Chester, Pa., 1946-52; Minister,
Bethel Tabernacle Church, Buffalo, N. Y., 1952-57; Chap-
lain, Migrant Ministry, N. Y. State Council of Churches,
Niagara County, 1958; Minister, Lincoln Memorial Cong.
Ch., Chicago, Ill., 1959---; Vice-president, Woodlawn
Organization, 1962; Pres., Greater Woodlawn Pastors
Alliance, 1963; U. S. Navy, 1945-46 (R.); Home: 6329
St. Lawrence, Chicago 37, Ill. Office: 6454 Champlain
Ave., Chgo. 37.

ENWRIGHT, John Thomas, b. Birmingham, Ala., Sept. 20,
1904; s. Thomas Jefferson and Emma (Laws) E.; B. S.,
Clark College, Atlanta, Ga., 1929; B. D., Gammon Theol.
Sem., Atlanta, Ga., 1932; m. Eula Chatfield; 1 dau.,
Florence Marjorie Miller; First Cong. Ch., Athens,
Ga., 1935; Midway Cong. Ch., McIntosh, Ga., 1936-
37; First Cong. Ch., Greensboro, N. C., 1937-39;
Beecher Memorial Cong. Ch., New Orleans, La., 1939-
50; Plymouth Cong. Ch., Charleston, S. C., 1950---;
mem. Omega Psi Phi, Democrat; Home: 32 Bull, Charleston, S. C., 19401. Office: 124 Spring, Charleston, S. C.

*EUBANKS, John Bunyon, coll. pres.; b. Clinton, La.

Feb. 28, 1913; s. Frank and Ella (Collins) E.; Th.B.,
Howard Univ., Sch. of Rel., 1935, A.B., 1936; A.M.,
1938, Ph.D., 1947, Univ. of Chicago; Additional Study:
Harvard Univ.; Syracuse Univ.; children---Judith Anne,
John B., Jr., David; education sec., Senate Avenue
YMCA, Indianapolis, Ind., 1937-41; area sec., National
Council YMCA, 1941-43; professor and chairman, Social
Science, Morris Brown Coll., Atlanta, Ga., 1946-49;
pres., Jarvis Christian Coll., Hawkins, Tex., 1949-53;
community development officer, International Cooperation
Administration, Bagdad, Iraq, 1953-55; chairman and
professor, Social Science, Jackson State Coll., Miss;
professor of philosophy and fundations of education,
Tuskegee Institute, 1960---; Mem., Advisory Board of
Boggs Academy, Keyesville, Ga., 1963---; Mem.: General Education Board Fellow in Comparative Religions,
1943-44; Alpha Kappa Delta National Honorary Sociological Society; African Studies Ass'n; Academy of Religion
and Mental Health; Alabama Philosophical Society; Society
for Applied Anthropology; Society for International Development; Home: 624 South 15th St., Baton Rouge, La.

EVANS, Benjamin Bonaparte, teacher, b. Gloucester, Va.,
May 26, 1892; s. Ransom and Alice (Holmes) E.; B.A.
Knoxville College, 1920; B.D., Pittsburgh Theol. Sem.,
1925; Ed. M, Univ. of Pittsburgh, 1943; D.D. (hon.)
Knoxville College, 1950; m. Theresa Hamlet; pastor
United Presbyterian Church, Norfolk, Va., 1926-37;
Dir. of Rel., Knoxville College, 1937-44; current pastor
United Presby. Ch., Cincinnatti, 1944- ; mem.: Knox-
ville College; Bd. of Ministers, 1955; YMCA; NAACP,
1946; Cincinnati Mayors Friendly Relations Comm.; Home:
3549 Reading Rd., Cincinnati, Ohio.

EVANS, Charles Lawrence, administrator; b. Pleasantville,
N.J., May 2, 1908; s. Charles Lawrence and Florence
(Gray) E.; A.B., Lincoln U. (Pa.), 1933; S.T.B., Lin-
coln U. Sch. of Rel., 1936; A.M., Lincoln U.; D.D.
(honorary), Va. Union U., 1958; Minister, First Bapt.
Suffolk, Va., 1937-42; Zion Bapt., Petersburg, Va.,
1942-45; Exec. Sec., Bapt. Allied Bodies of Va., 1945
---; m. Alice Priscilla Rasin; 1 dau., Sandra Elizabeth;
mem. Exec. Bd., Va. Ch. Temperance Council, Va.
Council of Churches; Va. Negro Bapt. Children's Home,
Inc.; Lott Carey Foreign Mission Conv.; Publishing Bd.,
Nat. Bapt. Conv. of Amer., Inc.; Interdenominational
Religious Work Foundation; Pres., West End Civic &

Improvement League, Richmond, Va.; Author: S. S. Lessons, Norfolk Journal & Guide, 1939--; Tour Leader,
Europe and Holy Land, 1955 & 1963; South America,
1960; Home: Office: Virginia Union U., Richmond, Va.

EVANS, John Marvin, chaplain; b. Cincinnati, Ohio, Sept.
3, 1925; s. John Thomas and Addie G. (Smith) E.; B.
S., Howard Univ., 1950; American Univ., 1953-54; Epis-
copal Theol. Sch., 1955-58; m. Lillian M. Swann; one
son: John Edward. Pastor, All Saints Protestant Episc.
Ch., Toledo, Ohio, 1958-62; Army chaplain, 4th Inf.
Div. Support Command, Fort Lewis, Washington, 1963-
present. Federal employee, Bureau of Census, H. E. W.,
Dept. of Welfare, D. C., 1950-1955. Board mem., Planned
Parenthood League; businessman mem., Y. M. C. A.,
Toledo, Ohio; board mem., Group work division of Toledo
Council of Social Agencies and Toledo Chapter of Boy
Scouts; pres., Neighborhood Areas Council; membership
chairman and housing chairman and selective buying chair-
man, Toledo Chapter of N. A. A. C. P. official delegate,
Ohio Council of Churches for Diocese of Ohio, 1961-62;
mem., Housing Committee (State Level) of N. A. A. C. P.,
Ohio. Served in Europe and Pacific theaters of operations
World War II, 1944-46; enlisted man, 1/Lt. Chaplain of
4th Inf. Div. Support Command, 1962-present; battle star
- European campaign. Citizen's Certificate for community
work, Toledo Ohio, given by Frederick Douglas Community Center. Omega Psi Phi; Episcopal Soc. for Cultural and Racial Unity. One of the Episcopal clergymen
jailed in Jackson, Miss. during prayer pilgrimage, Sept.
1961. Home: Quarters 2546-E, Ft. Lewis, Wash. Office:
Chapel #2, Bldg. 1645, Ft. Lewis, Wash.

EVANS, Joseph Henry, b. Kalamazoo, Mich., Aug. 15,
1915; s. Charles A. and Etta (Hill) E.; A. B., Western
Mich. Univ., 1939; B. D., Yale Univ. Divinity Sch.,
1942; m. Harriette Clark; 3 daus., Lesley Annette,
Harriette June, Barbara Corin; Pastor, St. Luke's Cong.
Ch., Brooklyn, N. Y., 1942; Grace Cong. Ch., New York,
N. Y., 1942-46; Mt. Zion Cong. Ch., Cleveland, Ohio,
1947-53; Church of The Good Shepherd, Cong. Ch., Chi-
cago, Ill., 1953---; Assoc. Gen. Sec. Conn. Council of
Churches, 1946-47; Pres. Chicago Urban League, 1959-
61; Ad. Bd. Chicago Theol. Sem.; Advisory Bd. Mem.,
Chicago Cong. Association; Comm. on Church Assistance,
Illinois Cong. Chr. Conf.; Bd. of Dirs., Chicago City
Missionary Society; Chgo. Urban League (Bd. of Dirs.);

Bd. of Trustees, LeMoyne College; Moderator, Cong.
Chr. Conference, Illinois; Mem., Kappa Alpha Psi.
Home: 5712 Prairie Ave., Chicago 37, Ill.; Office: 5700
Prairie Ave.

EWING, Isaiah, b. Nashville, Tenn., Dec. 25, 1928; s.
Isaiah and Valine; A.B., Fisk Univ., 1949; B.D., Chi-
cago Theol. Sem., 1954; M.A., Fisk Univ., 1960; m.
Polly Ann Eslick;   children---James Waller, Benita
Cordellia, Waller; Ordained Elder African Methodist
Episcopal Church, 13th Episcopal Dist.; pastor, McGav-
ock Chapel, Charlotte, Tenn.; Salters Chapel, Waverly,
Tenn.; St. John, A.M.E. Church, McEwen, Tenn.; cur-
rent pastor, St. Paul A.M.E. Church, Fayetteville,
Tenn.; teacher, Public Schools, Nashville, Tenn. Waver-
ly, Tenn. and Fayetteville, Tenn.; Mem., National Ad-
visory Committee; Core; National Advisory Committee,
Southern Christian Leadership Council; US Army Chap-
lain, 1954-58; Mem.: Mason; Alpha Phi Alpha; Sigma
Pi Phi; Home: 326 West College, Fayetteville, Tenn.;
Office: 328 West College, Fayetteville, Tenn.

EXUM, John M., editor; b. Memphis, Tenn., Jan. 3, 1909;
s. John W. and Lena (Turner) E.; B.A., University of
Denver, 1947; M. Th., Iliff School of Theology, 1950; m.
Lola Thelma Gibbs; 1 daughter: Yvonne Lois. Pastored:
Rock of Ages Christian Methodist Episcopal Church,
Memphis, Tenn., 1942-44; Cleaves Mem. C.M.E. Ch.,
Denver, 1944-50; Jamison Mem. Temple, Kansas City,
Mo., 1950-59; Grace C.M.E. Ch., Detroit, Michigan,
1959-61; Carter Metropolitan C.M.E. Ch., Detroit,
1961- present. Director, Christian Education Kansas, Mo.
Conf. C.M.E. Ch., 1950-59 and Christian Education,
Michigan-Indiana Conf., 1960-   . Achievement award,
Omega Psi Phi fraternity, Kansas City, Mo., 1952.
Omicron Delta Sigma; Masons: Knights of Pythians. Edi-
tor, Eastern Index, C.M.E. Church. Home: 1804 W.
Grand Blvd., Detroit, Michigan. Office: 1512 W. Grand
Blvd., Detroit, Michigan.

*FARMER, James Leonard, organization official; b. Mar-
shall, Texas, Jan. 12, 1920; s. James Leonard;
B.S., Wiley College, 1938: B.D., Howard
University, 1941; m. Lula Peterson, 1949; 2 daus. Tami
Lynn, Abbey Lee. Race Relations Sec., Fellowship of
Reconciliation, 1941-45; participated organizing drive
in South of Upholster's Internant'l Union, 1946-48; del.

from Intern'l Confederation of Free Trade Unions to 15
African countries, 1958; Program Dir., NAACP, lec-
tured extensively; written articles for Crisis, Fellowship,
World Frontiers and Hadassah News. Organized first
chap. of Congress of Racial Equality (CORE), U. of Chgo.
1942; Is director (national) CORE; a director of American
Civil Liberties Union. Has pioneered such tactics as
Freedom Rides, sit-ins, stand-ins, and jail-ins; Howard
Univ. Alumni Award, 1964. Office: 490 Riverside Drive,
New York 14, N.Y.

FAULKNER, Robert Huntt, b. Garrard Co., Ky., March
22, 1899; s. A.W. and Ellen (Rayston) F.; A.B., B.D.,
D.D. (hon.), Simmons Univ., 1926, 27, 45; m. Genevieve
W. Warren (deceased), Nellie B. Hughes; children---
Genevieve (Mrs. Pritchett), Robert Huntt, Jr., Lauretta
(Mrs. Burleson), Barbara (Mrs. Lee Roach), Lois P.
(Mrs. Craig), Arthur, Patricia Ann (Mrs. Virgil Tharp);
pastor, Little Benson Bapt. Ch., Franklin Co., Ky.,
1922; Second Bapt. Ch., Bloomfield, Ky., 1926; First
Bapt. Ch., Nicholasville, Ky., 1929; First Bapt. Ch.,
Stanford, Ky., 1933; Alpha Bapt. Ch., Franklin, Ky.,
1939; director, Christian Education, Ky., 1944-49; pastor
Second Bapt., Ch., Bloomfield, Ky., 1949-51; dean, Cen-
tral Bapt. Theol. Sem., Indianapolis, Ind., 1951; St.
Paul Bapt. Ch., Marion, Ind., 1952---; State director,
Christian Education, General Bapt. State Convention of
Ind. (currently serving); current dean, State Bapt. Sunday
School and Bapt. Training Union Congress; pres., Bapt.
Fellowship, Marion and Anderson, Ind.; pres., Marion
Congress of Social Action; Mem., Exec. Bd., Urban
League; Exec. Bd., Congress for Religion and Race;
Commission of Chaplaincy Service; Marion Area Minis-
terial Assn; state chairman, Ten Million Dollar Educa-
tional Foundation of the Nat. Bapt. Conv., USA, Inc.;
Office: St. Paul Bapt. Ch., 1615 W. 7th St., Marion,
Ind.

FAULKNER, William John, dean of chapel; b. Society Hill,
S.C., Nov. 16, 1891; s. Lawrence and Hannah J. (Dobey)
F.; Normal Dept., Mayesville Coll., S.C.; Bachelor
of Humanics, YMCA Coll., Springfield, Mass.; A.M.,
Univ. of Chicago (Practical Theology); graduate courses,
Univ. of Pa.; D.D. (hon.), Chicago Theol. Sem., 1946;
m. Elizabeth Abele Cook; children--. William John, Jr.
(deceased), Mrs. Chas. H. Webster, Mrs. John O.
Brown; sec. YMCA, Phila. Pa. and Atlanta, Ga.; per-

sonnel placement sec., YMCA War Council (World War
I); pastor, First Congregational Ch., Atlanta, Ga.; dean
of men and ministers, Fisk Univ., 1934-42; dean of the
Chapel, 1942-53; pastor, Congregational Church of Park
Manor, Chicago, Ill., 1953-62; dean of the Chapel, Dil-
lard Univ., New Orleans, La., 1963-64; Promoted
"Build Better Homes" Movement for Negroes, Atlanta,
Ga.; Established first summer camps for Negro boys,
Phila. & Atlanta; former moderator, Tenn. State Conf.
of Congregational Churches; twice vice moderator, Gen-
eral Council, Congregational Christian Churches; Mem.,
Congregational Christian Churches; Social Action Com-
mittees; Church Extension Division; Race Relations Dept.;
former pres., Nashville Interdenominational Ministers
Alliance; former pres., NAACP; Univ. Chaplains Assn;
Edward W. Hazen Foundation; Bd. of Directors, Dis-
ciplined Order of Christ; Fellowship of Southern Churchmen; Southeastern Regional Council; former pres.,
NAACP, Nashville, 7 years; The suit to equalize
teachers, salaries, Nashville, Tenn.; won in 1942 under
presidency; Mem. Bd. of Directors, Welfare Council of
Metropolitan Chicago; Advisory Bd., Chicago Theol. Sem.,
vice chairman, Advisory Bd., Chicago Assn of Congregational Christian Churches; Bd. of South Chicago Community Center; Administrative Committee, Chicago Church
Federation; Grand Crossing Ministerial Alliance; Evangelism and Devotional Life Committee, Ill. State Conf.;
Mem., Apostles Club; Foreign Missions Conference of
North America; Contributes articles ed. and rel. magazines; Has recorded several folk stories for sale by Bd.
of Education, Meth. Church; Home: 128 West Roberts
Ave., Wildwood, N. J.

FAUNTROY, Walter E., b. Wash., D.C., Feb. 6, 1933;
s. William T. and Ethel V.(F); A.B., Va. Union Univ.,
Richmond, Va., 1951-55; B.D., Yale Univ. Divinity
School, 1955-58; graduate school, Catholic Univ., 1958-
59; 1959-60; pastor, New Bethel Bapt. Ch., Wash.,
D.C., 1959---; director, Washington Bureau, SCLC,
1964; regional representative, Southern Christian Leader-
ship Conference, 1961---; D.C. coordinator, for the
August 28, 1963 March On Washington For Job and
Freedom; Exec. Bd.; Washington Urban League Project;
Citizens Committee on Homes and Highways; Council
of Churches of Greater Washington; Howard Univ.
Community Service Project; Interreligious Com. on Race
Relations; Junior Citizens Corps; NAACP, D.C. Branch;

"Stay-In-School" Committee; Washington Action for Youth;
Wash. Home Rule Comm.; Wash. Planning and Housing
Assn; Bapt. Ministers Conf., Wash., D.C.; Central
Northwest Civic Assn; Kappa Alpha Psi; Leadership Conf.
on Civil Rights; Wash. Ministerial Assn; YMCA; Citizen
of the Year, 1963; Home: 4105 17th St. NW, Wash.,
D.C.; Office: 812 S. St. NW, Wash., D.C.

FEAST, James Floyd, b. Beaumont, Tex., Aug. 22, 1930;
s. Allen and Virginia (Feast) F.; A.B., Wiley Coll.,
Marshall, Tex., 1946-47; 1947-48; A.B.; Gammon Theol.
Sem., Atlanta, Ga., 1951; 1952-55; B.D.; m. Cecelia
Fagans; children---Reginald Eugene, Angelia Elaine,
Edwin Jeffrey; pastor, The Trinity Circuit, Huntsville,
Tex., 1955-56; Bethlehem Meth. Ch., Hempstead, Tex.,
1956-57; St. Paul Meth. Church, Galveston, Tex., 1957-
60; Grace Meth. Ch., Houston, Tex., 1960-63; current,
Union Memorial Meth. Ch., Houston, Tex., 1963---;
substitute teacher, Galveston Independent School Dist.,
1958-60; Dist. Director of Temperance, 1958-60; Bd.
Mem., Financial Sec., Gibson Branch YMCA Galveston
United Fund, American Heart Ass'n, Young Democrats;
former chairman, Meth. Ch. Bd. of Christian Social
Concerns; sec. Bd. of Pensions; Jurisdictional Repr.
South Central Jurisdiction, Bd. of Christian Concerns;
Mem., Local Ministerial Alliances, Houston; Mason;
Home: 4307 Wipprecht St., Houston, Tex. 77026; Office:
4712 Calvacade St., Houston, Tex. 77026

FEATHERSTONE, Rudolph Richard, b. Washington, D.C.,
Dec. 26, 1934; s. James Samuel and Annie Rebecca
(Brown) F.; B.A., Gettysburg College, 1952-56; B.D.,
Gettysburg Seminary, 1956-60; m. Carmella Delores
Walker; board missionary, St. Johns Lutheran Church,
Bronx; pastor, The Lutheran Church of the Incarnation,
Jamaica, N.Y., 1961---; Home: 119-41 Sutphin Blvd.
Jamaica 36, N.Y.; Office: 150-14 Foch Blvd. Jamaica 34,
N.Y.

FELDER, Clifford Samuel, coll. prof.; b. Douglas, Ga.,
Aug. 9, 1909; s. Isaac and Lillie (Buckin) F.; B.S.,
Fla. Memorial Coll., St. Augustine, Fla.; B.D.,
Detroit Divinity Institute, 1935; m. Vera Mitchell; chil-
dren---Cullen C., Clifford F., Leo W.; pastor, St.
Marys Baptist Ch., Ga.; Bapt. Ch., Titusville, Fla.
current pastor, Bapt. Ch., Petersburgh, Fla., 1941--;
instructor, Dept. of Rel., Fla. Memorial Coll., St.

Augustine, Fla.; dean, asst. to the pres., Fla. Memor-
ial Coll.; head teacher and supervisor, Adult Education
Euclid Center, De Laud, Fla.; pres., Fla. State Sunday
School and B.T.U. Congress; Bd. Mem. of the National
Congress, USA, Inc.; Mem., Mason; NAACP; Public
Relation Office; Citizen's Taxpaper Assn, Daytona Beach;
Inter-Racial Alliance, De Laude, Fla.; Ministers Al-
liance, Dayton, Fla.; author: Syllabus for Workers of
Religious Education; Home: 635 Bellevue Ave., Daytona
Beach, Fla.

FERGUSON, Clarence F., church official; b. Easley, S.C.,
Dec. 1, 1900; s. William and Amanda F.; A.B., Clark
College, 1921; B.D., Gammon Theological Seminary,
1925; D.D. (hon.), Gammon Theol. Sem., m. Etta J.
Brwer; children---William, Clifford, Mildred (Mrs.
Greer); present pastor, Mt. Mark Methodist Ch., S.C.;
Mem., The South Carolina Conference of The Meth. Ch.;
(former) two General Conferences of The Methodist Ch.;
Mem. of five the Central Jurisdictional Conferences of
The Meth. Ch.; General Bd. of The Meth. Ch., 12 years
District supt. S.C. Conference of The Meth.; Mem., Bd.
of Trustees, Claflin Coll.; Mason; NAACP; Home: 101
Hardale Lane, Greenville, S.C. Office: same.

FERRELL, Clarence J., teacher; b. Early Branch, S.C.,
Oct. 18, 1927; s. Clarence and Bessie (Williams) F.;
A.B., Benedict College, Columbia, S.C., 1957; m. Ninnie
Albany; children---Delores, Clarence, Pastored in Chris-
tian Methodist Episcopal Chs. in St. Peters, Walterboro,
S.C., 1960-63; and Canaan Fair, Williston, S.C., 1963-
present. Teacher of English and Speech, Estill Training
School, Estill, S.C., 1957-present. U.S. Army, 1952-55;
Good Conduct medal. Member, Progressive Educational
Association and the Palmetto Educational Association.
Home: P.O. Box 197, Estill, S.C. Office: Canaan Fair,
Post Office, Williston, S.C.

FERRELL, Horace Albion, b. Phila., Pa., April 11, 1913;
s. Isaiah P. and Lillian (Johnson) F.; B.S., N.J. State
Coll., 1932; Th.B., Phila. Divinity School, 1947; Th.M.,
1954; m. Sylena Anderson; vicar, Church of St. Mary
the Virgin, Pleasantville, N.J., 1947-50; Church of the
Ascension, West Chester, Pa., 1950-56; chaplain, Douglas
Hospital, Phila., Pa., 1947-52; Cheyney State Coll.,
Cheyney, Pa., 1950-56; episcopal chaplain, Howard Univ.,
faculty, Howard Univ. Sch. of Religion, 1956--; consultant,

Juvenile Court of Atlantic County, N.J., 1948-50; Bd.
Directors, Family Service Agency of Chester County,
Pa., 1953-56; Bd. of Directors Health and Welfare Coun-
cil, Chester County, Pa., 1954-56; Mem. District of
Columbia Parole Bd.; Five member bd., 1963; Omega
Psi Phi Fraternity, Beta Chapter; Distinguished Service
Award, 1949;Mem., Am. Acad. of Polit. and Social Sci.;
Negro Community Council of the National Capitol Area;
International Chaplain, Frontiers International, Inc.;
Wash. Urban League; NAACP; Ass'n of Professors of
Practical Theol. Pigskin Club of Wash.; Omega Psi Phi;
Acad. of Religion and Mental Health; Oxen Blades Golf
Club; Home: 2333 First St., NW, Wash., D.C.

FITZGERALD, Charles Harris, ch. official; b. Mandeville,
La.; A.B., B.D., Morehouse Coll.; M.A., Hartford
Sch. of Religion; courses: Gammon Theol. Sem.; Atlanta
Univ. Summer Sch.; m. Mary Elizabeth Shute; children---
Vivian Lisette, Karen Lavette; professor, registrar,
dean, Amer. Bapt. Theol. Sem., Nashville, Tenn., 1956-
64; pastor, Roger Heights Bapt. Ch.; current director,
Promotion, Tenn. Bapt. M & E Conv., Nashville, Tenn.;
former moderator, Stone River Dist. Assn, Nashville;
dean, Tenn. Bapt. Leadership Congress; director, The
Administration Workshop of the Nat. S.S. and Bapt.
Conv., U.S.A., Inc.; chairman, Program Comm. of the
Bd. of Directors, Bethlehem Center, Nashville, Tenn.;
Mem., Exec. Com. of the Joint Comm. of the Nat. Bapt.
Student Union, Nashville, Tenn.; Office: Tenn. Bapt.
M & E Convention, P.O. Box 5645 North Station, Nash-
ville, Tenn. 37208

FLACK, French Z., b. Alexander, N.C., April 6, 1896;
s. Berry Rollins and Mary Elizabeth; A.B., Knoxville
Coll., Knoxville, Tenn., 1918-20; B.D., Livingstone
Coll., Salisbury, N.C., 1920-23; D.D. (hon.), Miller
Univ., 1960; teacher, 1916-18; pastor, African Methodist
Episcopal Zion Churches, Kansas City, Mo., 1924-30;
Key West Fla., 1930-36; Bridgeport, Conn., 1936-37;
Indianapolis, Ind., 1937-41; Plainville, Conn., 1941-48;
Oklahoma City, Okla., 1948-52; pastor & presiding elder,
Bristol, Tenn. & Va., 1952-54; pastor, Kingsport,
Tenn., 1954-57; Phila., Penna., 1957-62; current pastor,
Small Memorial A.M.E. Zion Ch., Pa.; Office: 254 S.
Pershing Ave., York, Pa.

FLANAGAN, William Carl, b. Moundville, Ala., Nov. 6,
1909; s. Abe and Ethel F.; Miles Memorial College;
private tutorship in Theology; m. Ora Mae Moore; chil-
dren---William C., Samuel Lee, Ronald. Ordained minister of the Christian Methodist Church; pastored in Alabama, Kentucky, Ohio, Indiana, Virginia, Maryland; present: pastor, Central Metropolitan C.M.E. Church and
presiding elder, Jacksonville District Florida C.M.E. Annual Conference. Arrested twice in struggle for Civil
Rights in the City of Jacksonville, Florida. Home: 526
West 21st St., Jacksonville, Fla.; Office: 1079 Davis
St., Jacksonville, Fla.

FLEMING, John Wilson, sem. prof. b. Morganton, N.C.,
July 7, 1916; s. Wm. T. and Rebecca (Avery) F.; A.B.,
Shaw Univ., Raleigh, N.C., 1935-38, 1946-47; B.D.,
The Graduate School of Theology, Oberlin, Ohio, 1947-
50; S.T.M., 1950-51; m. Hortense Gilmore; children---
Sundar Wilson; Director of Christian Education, General
Baptist State Convention, 1951-53; instructor, Shaw Univ.,
1953-54; Gen. Bapt. St. Convention, 1955-63; pastor,
Brookston Bapt. Church, Henderson, 1961---; associate
professor, Humanities, Shaw Univ., 1964---; Director of
Religious Activities, Migrant Camps, two summers;
columnist, Norfolk Journal & Guide, 1959-60; reporter,
Associated Negro Press, 1963; founder and first pres.,
Raleigh Citizens Ass'n, 1960; pres., RCA; US Army,
1941-46; European Theater; Mem., NAACP; North Carolina Council of Churches; Conference on Race and Religion; Mayor's Advisory Committee; Phi Beta Sigma;
Young Democratic Club; editor, Baptist Informer, official
organ of Gen. Bapt. Conv. of N.C., 1956-60; Home:
1816 Charles St., Raleigh, N.C.; Office: Shaw Univ.,
Raleigh, N.C.

FLEMING, Maryland Taft, b. Henrico County, Va., Nov.
12, 1908; s. Claude Julian and Sarah Miles F.; A.B.,
Va. Union Univ., 1948; B.D., Va. Union Univ. Sch. of
Rel., 1950; D.D. (hon.), Va., Theol. Seminary & Coll.,
1962; m. Hattie L. Chamberlayne; children---Ruth, Loyd,
M.T., Jr., Geneva Dallas, John H., Dorothy B. Bradley; pastor, St. James Bapt. Ch., Jetersville, Va.,
1936-42; Shady Grove Bapt. Ch., Louisiana, Va., 1936-42;
St. Peter Bapt. Ch., Glen Allen, Va., 1939-55; Jerusalem Bapt. Ch., Doswell, Va., 1943-55; Bethany Bapt.
Ch., Montpelier, Va., 1952---; St. John Bapt. Ch.,
1942-55; Zion Bapt. Ch., Richmond, Va., 1955---; pres.,

Baptist Ministers' Conference of Richmond & Vicinity, 1954-
55; moderator, Tuckahoe Bapt. Ass'n, Va., 1948---;
Hampton Ministers Conference Exec. Bd., 1961-64; Mem.,
Trustee Bd. of Va. Bapt. Negro Children's Home, 1959--;
Broad Street Civic Club, Richmond, Va.; Baptist Ministers
Ass'n; Baptist Minister's Alliance, Richmond, Va.; Ma-
son; Home: 7302 W.Broad St., Richmond 29, Va.; Office:
2006 Decatur, Richmond, Va.

FLORENCE, Franklin D.R., Sr., b. Miami, Fla., Aug. 9,
1933; s. Henderson and Bertha (Bensley) F.; Nashville
Christian Institute; George Pepperdine Coll.; m. Mary
Edna; children---Franklin Jr., Clifford, Joshwyn M.;
pastor, Reynold St. Church of Christ, Rochester, N.Y.;
Non Violent Integrated Committee; Executive Board of
NAACP; Police Advisory Board for the City of Rochester;
vice pres. Love and Goodwill Corporation; Home: 37 Reynolds St., Rochester 8, N.Y.

FLOYD, Harris Limual, chaplain, b. Wilmington, N.C.,
May 15, 1929; s. Clarence Limual Thomas and Callie
(Floyd) T.; A.B., Shaw Univ., 1952; B.D., Berkeley
Baptist Divinity Sch., 1959; m. Ethel Lee Rogers; US
Army Chaplain, 1958-60; pastor, Mt. Zion Missionary
Baptist Ch., 1961---; auditor, North Pacific Bapt. Con-
vention, Washington and Idaho; vice moderator, Olympic
Ass'n, Bremerton, Port Angles, Port Townsend; Good
Conduct Medal; Defense Medal for service in the US
Army; Mem., Bremerton Ministerial Ass'n; Phi Beta
Sigma; Home: 420 Union Ave., Bremerton, Wash.;
Office: 4650 Werner Road, Bremerton, Washington.

FOGGIE, Charles H., teacher; b. Sumpter, S.C., Aug. 4,
1912; s. James Legree and Marie Louise F.; A.M.,
Livingstone Coll., 1936; S.T.B., S.T.M., Boston Univ.,
1939; D.D. (hon.), Livingstone Coll., 1949; m. Madeline
Sharpe; asst. pastor, African Methodist Episcopal Zion
Ch., Boston, 1931-32; pastor, Providence A.M.E. Zion
Church, Rhode Island, Cambridge, Mass., 1936-39; current, Wesley Center, A.M.E. Zion Church, Pittsburgh,
1944---; Mem., Board, Univ. Pittsburgh Religions Fellowship; Pittsburgh Courier Award in Religion; pres.,
NAACP (Pittsburgh); Alpha Phi Alpha; Frequent speaker
on TV and radio and colleges; Home: 3131 Evart Drive,
Pittsburgh, Pa.; Office: 2701 Center Ave., Pittsburgh
19, Pa.

FORBES, James Alexander, Jr. b. Burgaw, N.C., Sept.
6; s. James A. and Mable F.; B.S., Howard Univ.,
1957; B.D., Union Theol. Sem., N.Y., 1962; m. Bettye
Jeanne Franks; asst. pastor, Binkley Memorial Bapt. Ch.,
current pastor, Holy Trinity Baptist Ch., Wilmington,
N.C. and St. Paul Holy Baptist Church, Roxboro, N.C.;
instructor, Bible Training Institute, Goldsboro, N.C.;
Mem., Fellowship of Southern Churchmen; Home: 516
N. 4th St., Wilmington, N.C.; Office: Holy Trinity
Church, Corner of 4th and Campbell Sts., Wilmington,
N.C.

FORDHAM, Walter Wraggs, Church official, b. Charleston,
South Carolina, October 20, 1912; s. Henry Joseph and
Katherine (Wraggs) F.; Oakwood College, 1927-34; A &
I State Univ., 1931-32; Univ. of Pittsburg, 1940-41; A &
I State Univ., 1958-59; m. Maybelle Lois Winston; chil-
dren- Lois Frankie (Mrs. Charles R. Clay), Audrey
Elaine (Mrs. Robert L. Booker), Walter Wraggs. Began
ministry in New Jersey; pastored: Camden, Asbury Park,
Burlington, and Bridgeton, New Jersey, 1934-39; Pitts-
burg, Penna., 1939-42; State of Florida, Secretary of De-
partment of Evangelism, 1942-46; Southwest Region area
a conference president, 1946-54; present: conference
president of South Central Conference, Kansas City, Missouri, 1959- ; Riverside Hospital Board, Nashville,
Tenn.; Porter Hospital and Boulder Hospital Boards,
Denver and Boulder, Colorado, Oakwood College Board,
Huntsville, Ala.; Union College Board, Lincoln, Nebras-
ka; Pacific Press Publishing Board, Mountain View,
California; Loma Linda Medical Board, Los Angeles,
California; Human Relations Committee, General Conf.
of S.D.A., Washington, D.C. Chairman of Membership
Drive, Centre Avenue Branch of Y.M.C.A. - 1940,
received the Loving Cup Award; member, N.A.A.C.P.;
editorial Board of The Message Magazine published in
Nashville, Tenn. Home: 3501 Bellefontaine St., Kansas
City, Missouri 64128. Office: 2528 Benton Boulevard,
Kansas City, Missouri 64127.

FORTUNE, Allen Ethan, b. Mayesville, S.C., Sept. 9,
1899; s. Thomas J. and Rebecca; A.B., Johnson C.
Smith Univ., 1926; B.D., 1929; Harvard Univ., Cambridge, Mass.- chaplain's school, 1942; Columbia
Theological Seminary, Decatur, Ga., 1951; m. Annie M.;
children---Carolyn, Alleyne; Vice pres., Albian Academy,
Franklinton, N.C., 1929-30; teacher of sociology & psy-

chology, Haynes Jr. College, Augusta, Ga., 1930-32;
pastor, Grace Presbyterian Church, Winston, Salem,
N.C., 1932-37; pastor, United Presbyterian Church, Norfolk, Va., 1937-42; Army chaplain, 1942-46; Vice president, Chaplain Association, Atlanta, Ga., 1954-58; Chairman, Church Extension Committee, Georgia Presbytery,
1950-58; Chairman, "Minister and His Work," 1958---;
pres., Christian Interracial Group, Winston-Salem,
N.C., 1947-48; US Army chaplain, 1945-46; awards:
three battle stars, Certificate of award for meritorious
service; Mem., Omega Psi Phi; Home: 309 N. Sanborn St.,
Florence, S.C.

FOSTER, Richard A.B., b. Lawrenceville, Va., Dec. 19,
1900; s. Walter Scott and Mary M. (Vaughans) F.; A.B.,
Livingstone Coll., 1925; Hood Theol. Sem., 1927; Syra-
cuse Univ., 1930; Yale Divinity Sch., 1950-51; Indian
Central Coll.; Calif. State Coll.; m. Thelma Louise
Brooks; children---Ethel Jane (Mrs. Hillard), Mary Anne
(Mrs. Cobb), Richarda Louise, Lillian Brooks, Ellen
Eugenia; pastor, People's A.M.E. Zion Ch., Syracuse,
N.Y.; St. John A.M.E. Zion Ch., Wilson, N.C.; Varick
A.M.E. Zion Ch., New Haven, Conn.; current pastor,
Cooper African Methodist Episcopal Zion Ch., Oakland,
Calif.; Elected Alderman of 19th Ward, New Haven,
Conn.; chairman, Railroads and Bridges of Aldermatic
Bd.; Mem., Mayor's Committee on Education and School
Survey; New Haven Council of Churches; Rent Control Bd.
of State of Conn. & Oakland, Calif.; vice chairman,
Republican County Central Committee, 10 years; Bd. of
Directors and Vice Pres. of Oakland Council of Churches;
Trustee, Peralta Jr. Coll. Dist. of 6 cities including
Oakland; Trustee and Bd. Mem., Booth Hospital, Oakland
Calif.; Mem., National Council of Churches; Bd. of Di-
rectors, March of Dimes; Birth Defects Committee;
Mason; Elks; Alpha Phi Alpha; Republican;
Very active in civil rights; Mem., NAACP;
Founding Mem., Men of Tomorrow (Civic Organization);
Home: 1927 Filbert St. Oakland, Calif.; Office: Greater
Cooper A.M.E. Zion Ch., Oakland, Calif.

FOUNTAIN, Major Lee, b. Angus, Tex. (Navarro County),
Sept. 29, 1934; s. Jaycee and Pearline (Quarles) F.;
B.A., Jarvis Christian Coll., Texas, 1957; current,
Brite Divinity School, Texas, 1963---; m. Perlean Simp-
son F.; children---Bennie Lee, Laneda Jo, Donald Ray,
Linda Gale, Lydia Denise; pastor, 13th Ave. Christian

Church, Corsidana, Tex., 1955-57; Puget St. Christian
Ch., Dallas, Texas, 1958-60; Cedar Grove Christian
Church, Rockwall, Tex., 1960-62; current, East Annie
Christian Ch., Ft. Worth, Tex., 1963---; annual coun-
selor & instructor, Youth Groups at summer fellowships;
Home: 1312 E. Leuda St. Ft. Worth 4, Texas; Office:
1234 E. Annie St. Ft. Worth 4, Texas.

FOUSHEE, Warren Raymond, presiding elder; b. Bynum,
N. C. Mar. 31, 1907; s. John B. and Lula (Snipes) F.;
Berry O'Kelly Training School, 1938-41; Shaw Univer-
sity, 1941; Paine Coll. Summer Schools; Student Bible
Institute; m. Sylvia B. Roberson; children---Warren
Raymond, Jr.; pastor, Young Chapel Christian Methodist
Episcopal Church, Raleigh, N. C., 1938-41; Mt. Pleasant
& Piney Ridge Ch., Union Mills, N. C., 1941-43; Sweet
Spring Church, Holly Springs, N. C., 1943-45; St. Mat-
thew Church, High Point, N. C., 1945-47; Durham Dis-
trict N. C. Conference, Presiding Elder, 1947-48; pastor,
Brown Temple C. M. E. Church, Asheville, N. C., 1948-
54; Beebe Memorial Church, Washington, N. C., 1954-
55; St. Joseph C. M. E. Church, Chapel Hill, N. C.,
1955---; pres., Inter-racial Ministerial Ass'n; 1956-57;   *
Sec., Chapel Hill Ministerial Alliance, 1958-59; Mem.,
Chapel Hill City Planning Board, 1960-61; The Fellow-
ship for Better Schools, 1956-61; chairman, Citizen's
Committee for Schools, 1960-63; Mayor's Human Rela-
tion Committee, 1963---; vice pres., Chapel Hill Chapter,
NAACP, The Executive Comm. for Open Movies, 1960;
The Exec. Comm. for Open Business, 1961-63; The
Exec. Comm. for Integration, 1963---; chairman, The
Finance Comm. for building $50,000 Swimming Pool (The
Chapel Hill-Carrboro Swimming Pool Inc.), 1960---;
Board of Directors of Community Action, Chapel Hill,
N. C., 1963---; Mason; Royal Arch; Elks; Voter's Regis-
tration Comm.; Home: 520 W. Rosemary St., Chapel
Hill, N. C.

*FOWLER, Andrew, sem. prof.; b. Inman South Carolina, Feb.
  23, 1910; s. John C. and Ina (Nesbitt) F.; A. B., Tuskegee
  Institute, 1937; B. D., M. A., Howard Univ., 1940; 1943;
  D. D. (hon.), Lynchburg Sem. and Coll., 1960; m. Henrietta;
  Roberta Hatter; children: Andretta, Andrew H., Henrietta
  E. John; current pastor, Capitol View Bapt. Ch., 1941---;
  current prof. of Biblical Interpretation and English, Wash.,
  D. C. Bapt. Sem., 1949---; visiting lecturer, Howard Univ.
  Sch. of Rel., 1962---; director, Wash. Bureau, Nat. Fed-

eral Council of Churches, 1951; D. C. Chairman, Foreign
Missions Com. of Nat. Bapt. Cinv. Mission Bd.; Mem., Bd.
of Directors, Lott Carey Bapt. Foreign Mission Conv; Bd. of
Directors, D. C. Tuberculosis Assn; General Assembly,
Health Welfare Conv., D. C.; Bd. of Directors, Stoddart Bap-
tist Home; Mem., Society of Biblical Literature and Exegesis;
Bd. of Directors, New England Bapt. Missionary Bapt. Conv.;
Bapt. Conv., D. C. and Va.; former pres., Bapt. Conv.,
D. C. & vicinity; Cited by Nat. Fraternity Council of
Churches, 1962, Wash. D. C.; Home: 249 10th St. NE,
Wash., D. C.; Office: Division Avenue and Ames St.
NE, Washington, D. C.

FOWLIS, Ronald Preston, b. Springfield, Ohio, June 6,
1934; s. Charles O. and Edna (January) F.; Butler Univ.,
Indianapolis, Ind. m. Coralee Harper F.; children: Joy,
Rondalee, Connie; 1957-to date, pastor-Third Christian
Church, Warren, Ohio; Activities: counselor for Y. M.
C. A. Outpost; Club advisor, Warren Urban League;
mem.: Mayor's Housing Committee; Warren Urban
League Board; NAACP; Frontiers of America; Warren
Ministerial Assoc.; Trumbull County Ministerial Alliance;
Home: 849 Tod Ave., Warren, Ohio; Office: 241 1st St.
S. W., Warren, Ohio.

FOY, James Douglas, b. San Antonio, Tex. Sept. 10,
1907; s. Thomas H. and Ida L. F.; A. B., Samuel Huston
Coll.; B. D., Gammon Theol. Sem.; S. T. M. Boston
Univ. Sch. of Theology; Resident work for doctorate,
American Univ.; m. Venera R.; pastor, Aliquippa, Pa.,
1938; Lewisburgh, W. Va., 1939-41; Pittsburgh, Pa.,
1941-48; Georgetown, Washington, D. C., 1948-54; Dist.
Supt. of the Wash. Dist. of the Meth. Ch., 1954-55;
pastor, Asbury Methodist Church, 1955---; Mem., Phi
Beta Sigma; Mason; Wash. Annual Conf. Meth. Church;
frequent contributor to church publications; Home: 3801
So. Dakota Ave. NE, Wash., D. C. 20018; Office:
Asbury Meth. Ch., 11th & K Sts. NW, Wash., D. C.
20001.

FRANCIS, Joseph Abel, b. Lafayette, La.; s. Joseph Abel
and Mabel (Coco) F.; St. Augustine's Sem., Bay St.
Louis, Miss. 1936-41; St. Mary's College, Techny, Ill.,
B. A., 1942-1947; St. Augustine's Major Sem., Bay St.
Louis, Miss., 1947-51; M. A. Cath. U. of America,
1959; Mount St. Mary's Coll., Los. A., 1962; Loyola
Univ., Los. A., 1963; Xavier Univ., New Orleans;

Asst. Dir. Holy Rosary Inst., Lafayette, La.; Pastor,
Holy Cross Cath. Ch., Austin, Texas; Instr. Pius X
High School, Downey, Cal.; Prin. Verbum Dei High
School, Los Angeles, Calif.; Home: 3 St. James Park,
Los Angeles 7, Calif. Office: 11100 S. Central Ave.,
Los Angeles 59, Calif.

FREEMAN, Edward Anderson, church official; b. Atlanta,
Ga., June 11, 1914; s. James Henry Watts and Ollie
Watts F.; A.B., Clark Coll., Atlanta, 1939; B.D., Cen-
tral Bapt. Seminary, Kansas City, Kans., 1949; Th.M.,
1950; Th.D., 1953, Central Bapt. Seminary; m. Ruth
Anthony; children---Edward Anderson, Constance Marie,
William Norman; Ordained to ministry Bapt. Ch., 1935;
prin. Austell, Ga., Pub. Sch., 1939-42; pastor, First
Bapt. Ch., Kansas City, Kan., 1946---; pres., Mission-
ary Baptist State Convention of Kansas, 1957---; Mem.;
State vice pres., National Baptist Convention, USA, Inc.;
director, Kansas City, Kan. City Planning Commissions
Kansas City, Kansas Human Relations Commission;
Trustee, American Baptist Theol. Seminary, Nashville,
Tenn.; Western Baptist Bible Coll., Kansas City, Mo.;
Douglas Hospital, Kansas City, Kan.; The Greater Kan-
sas City, Mo.; Douglas Hospital, Kansas City, Kan.; The
Greater Kansas City Bapt. and Community Hospital Ass'n
Kansas City, Mo.; Kansas City, Kan. Bapts. Ministers'
Alliance; KCK Ministerial Inter-racial & Interdenominational Alliance; US chaplain Corps, 1942-46; 1st Lt. to
Major; Man of the Year, Wyandotte Council of Churches,
1949; Man of the Year, Nat. Baptists of South India,
1958; Candidate, Kansas City Bd. Edn., 1950, 54; candidate for rep. State Legislature, 1952; author: The Epoch
of Negro Baptists and the Foreign Mission Board, 1953;
paper: The Role of Integrated Seminaries in Meeting Educational Needs of Negro Students; Home: 3620 Oak Ave.,
Kansas City 4, Kansas; Office: Fifth & Nebraska, Kansas
City, Kansas.

FREEMAN, J.(ames) Jasper, educator; b. Bertie Co., N.C.,
Sept. 8, 1907; s. Maggie F.; A.B., Shaw U., 1937;
B.D., Shaw Theol. Sem., 1938; M.A. Ed., N.Y.U.,
1962; D.D. (honorary), Va. Theol. Sem., 1944; Sum.
studies, Columbia U., Union Theol. Sem., N.Y.,
Wheaton Coll., Ill.; m. Mary C. Taylor; 2 sons, James
J., Jr., Clarence Eugene; 3 daus., Gloria Beatrice,
Carolyn Elizabeth, Maggie Restora; Pastored: Brown's
Missionary Bapt., Clinton, N.C., 1934-39; New Mt.

Zion Bapt., Roxboro, N.C., 1935-39; 1st Bapt. (Lambert's Pt.), Norfolk, Va., 1939-49; Queen Street Bapt., Norfolk, 1949---; Teach. Pub. Schs., Bertie Co., 1929-31; Dir. Roanoke Institute, Shaw U. Unit, Elizabeth City, N.C., 1952-58; Instr., Roanoke Inst., 1959---; Evening Coll., Norfolk Div. Va. State U., 1955---; Trustee, Norfolk Community Hosp., 1947-62; Va. Theol. Sem. & Coll., Lynchburg, 1942---; Shaw U., 1961---; Bd. Management, Hunton YMCA, 1958-64; Sec., Lott Carey Bapt. Foreign Mission Conv., 1954---; Home:730 E. 28th Street, Norfolk, Va., 23504. Church: 413 E. Brambleton Ave., Norfolk, Va. 23510.

FREEMAN, Thomas F., prof.; b. Richmond, Va., June 27, 1920; s. Louis H. and Louise E. F.; A.B., Va. Union Univ., Richmond, Va.; B.D., Andover Newton Theol. Sch., Newton Center, Mass.; Ph.D., The Univ. of Chicago, Chicago, Ill.; further study: Boston Univ., Boston, Mass.; Harvard Univ., Cambridge, Mass.; m. Clarice Estell; children---Thomas F. Jr., Carter Evan, Carlotta Vanessa; assoc. minister, Concord Bapt. Ch., Boston, Mass., 1940; pastor, Pleasant St. Bapt. Ch., Westerly, R.I., 1941-42; assoc. pastor, Monumental Bapt. Ch., Chicago, Ill., 1942-44; pastor, Mt. Carmel Bapt. Ch., Richmond, Va., 1944-50; prof., Va. Union Univ., 1944-48; guest lecturer, Bishop Coll., Marshall, (current Prof.) Tex. Southern Univ., 1949---; Coach of the T.S.U. Debate Team, 1949---; advisor, Alpha Beta Chapter Alpha Kappa Mu, 1950---; Alpha Mu Omega Philosophical Fellowship, 1949---; Sigma Pi Alpha Symposium, 1949---; chmn, Com. on University Ushers, 1949---; chmn, Com. on Rel. Activities, 1949-54; and pastor, The Mt. Horem Bapt. Ch., Houston, Tex., 1951---; Frequently engaged as speaker for: Religious Emphasis Week Programs; Ministers Institutes; Honors Convocation; High Sch. and Coll. Baccalaureate Services; High School and Coll. Commencement Exercises; Community and Awards: The Kappa Gamma Chi Debate Key for 4 years Collegiate Debating; The Chick Scholarship for maintaining the highest scholastic standing for three consecutive years at Andover Newton; Turner Fellowship for Graduate Study from Andover Newton; Divinity Fellowship for Graduate Study at the Univ. of Chicago; Faculty Member of the Year, 1951, 1952; pres., Southern Intercollegiate Forensic Conf., 1951-55; Executive Sec., 1955---; Sec., Southwest Debate League, 1952-54; regional director, Region VII Alpha Kappa Mu National Honor

Society, 1954-62; National pres. , Alpha Kappa Mu, 1962;
Mem. , American Philosophical Assn; American Forensic
Assn; Southwest Philosophical Assn; Southern Speech
Assn; National Education Assn; Assn. of Higher Educa-
tion; National Assn. of Univ. Chaplains; American
Academy of Science; YMCA; National Bapt. Convention;
Home: 2522 Calumet St. , Houston, Texas; Office: 1915
Lockwood Drive, Houston, Texas.

FREEMAN, William Lee, presiding elder, b. Charleston,
S. C. , Nov. 11, 1906; s. Kitt and Elizabeth (K.) F. ;
The National Bible Institute, New York City, 1942 (Now
the Shelton College); D. D. (hon.), Payne College, Birmingham, Ala. ; D. D. (hon.), Monrovia College, Monrovia,
Liberia; D. D. , Allen Univ. ; D. D. Edward Waters College, Jacksonville, Fla. ; Mem. , Mason; Elk, Oddfellow;
Knights of Pythians; Mem. , General Conference of the
African Methodist Episcopal Church for the past 25
years; Home: 1928 Prospect Avenue, Bronx, New York
10457; Office: same.

FULFORD, Fergus Maurice, b. Norfolk, Virginia, March 21,
1917; s. James Edward and Annie (Brehon) F. ; B. S. ,
St. Augustine's College, Raleigh, N. C. ; B. D. , Bishop
Payne Divinity School, Petersburgh, Va. ; - Grad. School
of Applied Religion, Cincinnati, Ohio; Ordained deacon,
St. Paul's Chapel, Lawrenceville, Va. , 1941; Served
Mission Churches in Diocese of So. Va. ; Ordained Priest,
Novice-Order of St. Francis, Mt. Sinai, N. Y. , 1942-43;
Curate, Ch. of the Crucifixion, NYC, 1944-46; present
pastor, St. Barnabas' Church, Brooklyn, 1946---; Father
Benedict, Oblate Tertiary of the Order of Member,
Youth Consultant on Service of the Diocese of Long Is-
land; Member, Diocesan Youth Commission as Clerical
Advisor; Member, Executive Committee of Archdeaconry
of Brooklyn, Diocese of L. I. ; chaplain (Major) in US
Army Reserves; Member, American Church Union; New
York Catholic Club; Long Island Clerical League; NY
City Commission on Human Rights; Home 417 Elton St. ,
Brooklyn 8, NY; Office: St. Barnabas' Church - 727
Belmont Ave. , Brooklyn 8, N. Y.

FULLILOVE, Paul Allen, b. St. Louis, Mo. , Oct. 17, 1917;
s. Oliver V. and Elnora (Johnson) F. ; Amer. Baptist
Theol. Sem. , Nashville, Tenn. , 1941-42; B. Th. , Gordon
Coll. of Theology, Boston, Mass. , 1944-48; Hartford
Sem. , Hartford, Conn. , 1951-52; m. Josephine Daniels;

children--- Paul, Jr., Jo-Ethel; asst. pastor, Peoples
Bapt. Ch., Boston, Mass.; pastor, Union Baptist Ch.,
New Bedford, Mass., 1946-59; current, Third Bapt. Ch.,
Springfield, Mass., 1950---; Mem., Bd. of Directors,
Dunbar Community Center, Springfield, Mass; Bd. Mem.
at large, Child and Family Service, Springfield, Mass.;
NAACP; treasurer, United Bapt. Convention of Mass.
and Rhode Island; Bd. of Directors, National Bapt. Con-
vention, Inc. US.A.; treasurer, New England Bapt. Mis-
sionary Convention; treasurer, Pastor's Council of Greater
Springfield, Mass.; African Comm., National Council of
Churches; President Johnson's Baptist Joint Comm. on
Public Affairs; Syracuse Lodge; Knights of Pythias; Home:
150 Buckingham St., Springfield, Mass. 01109; Office:
151 Walnut St., Springfield, Mass. 01109.

FURBRLUR, Harold Alonzo, b. Boston, Mass., June 13,
1936; s. Harry A. and Beatrice (Johnson) F.; Cardinal
O'Connell Minor Seminary, Jamaica Plain, Mass.,
1954-56; St. John's Major Seminary, Brighton, Mass.,
1956-1962; Curate, St. John-St. Hugh's Parish, (Rox-
bury-Dorchester Sect.) Boston, Mass., 1962---;
Boy Scouts of America (volunteer), 1949---; Home: 62
Lincoln St., W. Medford 55, Mass., Office: 26 Lawrence
Ave., Dorchester 21, Mass.

*GANDY, Samuel Lucius, sem. dean, chaplain; b. Anderson,
S.C., Nov. 28, 1916; s. Charles F. and Belle Victoria
(Brock) G.; B.A., S.C. State Coll., 1935; B.D., Howard
Univ. Sch. of Rel., 1938; Ph.D., Univ. of Chicago,
1952; Post-doctoral, Danforth Fellow, 1958; m. Frances
Elizabeth Williams; asst. dean of men and asst. minister,
Fisk Univ., 1938-41; Acting pastor, Church of the Good
Shepherd, Chicago, 1941-44; director of religious activities
and prof. of religion, Va. State Coll., Petersburg, 1944-
55; dean of the chapel, Dillard Univ., New Orleans, La.,
1955-61; pastor, Kenwood United Ch. of Christ, 1961-64;
current, dean of School of Rel., Howard Univ., Sept.
1964---; consultant, Southern Regional Council. Mid-
West Round Table, National Conference of Christians and
Jews; director, European Seminar for Students Studying
the heritage of the Church, 1960; Bd. Mem., North Kenwood Oakland Community Conf.; Neighborhood consultant
to military establishments, especially Fort Lee, Va.;
Mem., Com. on Urban Renewal; Dialogue Group of Ministers; Rabbis and Priests, Chicago Chapter; Nat. Conf.

Christians and Jews; Bd. Mem., Mich. Ave. Hospital;
Peoples Co-op Credit Union; Nursing Sch., Provident
Hospital; Advisory Com., Bd. of Health Elementary Sch.
Girl Pregnancies; Urban Missions Com.; Rel. Ed. Assn;
Nat. Assn. of Coll. and Univ. Chaplains; Mem., Urban
League; NAACP; author: Chapel, publication of NACUC;
Booklet on Prayers in the Chapel; Research in urban
church activities; Office: School of Rel., Howard Univ.,
Wash. 1, D.C.

*GARDENER, Elijah Harris, b. Allendale, S.C., May 21,
1934; s. Elijah H., Sr. and Otha (Williams) G.; A.B.,
Morris Coll., Sumter, S.C., 1955; B.D., Howard Univ.,
Sch. of Rel., Wash. D.C., 1962; Graduate student,
Boston Univ. School of Theology, S.T.M., 1962---; m.
Hermenia Thecla Cooper; public school teacher, Jasper
High School, Ridgeland, S.C., 1955-57; Director of Public
Relations, Morris Coll., 1957-59; Graduate Counsel for
men, Howard Univ., 1960-62; pastor, Calvary Baptist
Church, Haverhill, Mass., 1962---;Reserve Chaplain
(1st Lt.) USAR, Asgn, 1030th ARSU School, Boston Army
Base, Mass., 1961; Kiwanis Appreciation Certificate;
Mem., NAACP; Palmetto Educational Ass'n; Civic Edu-
cation Club of Haverhill, Mass.; YMCA; Home: 9 Ash-
land St., Haverhill, Mass;

GARNER, Frank Travis, Jr., b. Cincinnati, O., Jan 30,
1924; s. Frank T. and Lillian (Wright); 1963, Bishop
College, Dallas, Texas; m. Mayme Carroll Watson;
children: two sons and two daughters; asst. pastor:
1953-55, Wehrman Ave. Christian Church, Cincinnati,
O.; pastor, Elm St. Christian Church, Oxford, O.;
1961-63, East Vine Ave. Christian Church, Knoxville,
Tenn.; currently: Denley Drive Christian Church, Dallas,
Tex., U.S. Army-1943-45; mem. Mason; American Legion
636; Home: 1407 Glen Ave., Dallas 16, Texas; Church:
1702 Denley Dr. Dallas 16, Texas.

GARTRELL, C.L., b. Washington, Ga., June 11, 1927;
s. George G. and Rosa (Wellmaker) G.; A.B., Johnson
C. Smith Univ., 1948; B.D., 1951; Further study: Ft. Val-
ley State; m. Gladys Maloy; pastor, Christian Methodist
Episcopal Churches, Union Mill, N.C., 1948-50; Forest
Chapel C.M.E. Church, Fair Forest, S.C., 1950-52;
Bethel C.M.E. Church, Macon, Ga., 1952-55; Trinity
C.M.E. Church, Milledgeville, Ga., 1955-57; chaplain,
State Mental Institution, Milledgeville, Ga.; current

pastor, Jeffersonville C. M. E. Church, 1957---; chairman,
Examining Board, Central Ga. Conf. C. M. E. Church;
teacher, Bettis Academy and Jr. Coll., 1951-52; elementary school, 1952-54; Ballard-Hudson Sr. High School,
1954---; Mem., Masons; Phi Beta Sigma; Alpha Phi
Omega; National Service Fraternity; Boy Scouts of America; NEA; ATA; PTA; Home: 409 Lilly Ave., Macon,
Ga.,

GASKINS, Walter Wesley, b. Middleburg, Va., Feb. 10,
1934; s. Dadley Scott and Martha (Lloyd) G.; Paine Coll.,
Augusta, Ga., 1 semester; m. Marion Fox Brown; chil-
dren---Walter Wesley, II; pastor, Monroe Chapel Chris-
tian Methodist Episcopal Church, Ashburn, Va., 1 year;
Lawrenceville circuit, 2 years; St. Stephen C. M. E.
Church, Winchita, 2 years; Williams Chapel & St. Paul
C. M. E. Church, Va.; active in the civic affairs of Front
Royal and Warren Co.; Mem., Human Relations Council;
Home: 15 E. Prospect St. Front Royal, Va.

GASTON, Joseph Alexander, church administrator, b.
Winnsboro, S. C., Jan. 3, 1928; s. John N. and Lilla
(Russell); A. B. & B. D., Johnson C. Smith Univ.; M. A.
Univ. of Denver; pastor Edward Webb Ch., Mt. Airy,
N. C.; First Presbyterian Ch., Boonsville, N. C., 1952;
Sunday School Missionary, United Presby. Ch., 1952-
56; Johnson C. Smith Univ., 1956- ; consultant Counsel-
ing and Guidance for Vocation and Church Occupations,
Catawba Synod; mem.: American Personnel and Guidance
Assoc., Nat. Assoc. of Personal Worker, Mental Health
Assoc., Omega Psi Phi Fraternity; Home: 301 Campus
St., Charlotte, N. C.; Office: Johnson C. Smith Univ.,
Charlotte, N. C.

GEORGE, Arthur Henry, dean, Camden, S. C., 1894; s.
Henry and Elvira (Beckham); A. B., Johnson C. Smith
Univ., 1917; S. T. B., J. C. Smith Seminary, 1920; S. T.
M., Western Theol. Sem., 1921; Auburn Sem., Union
Sem.; m. Minnie B. Jones; children---Arthur Allen,
Henry Hamilton, Bryant; pastor Calvary Presby. Ch.,
Wilson, N. C., 1921-29; Stated Clerk of Cape Fear
Presbytery; Shiloh Presbyterian Ch., Knoxville, Tenn.,
1930-34; prof. Homiletics, Johnson C. Smith Univ.,
1934; dean J. C. Smith Seminary, 1946-60; dean Emeritus
and prof. of homiletics, 1960---; Home: Johnson C.
Smith Univ., Charlotte 8, N. C.

GEORGE, Bryant, administrator, b. Wilson, N.C., Nov.
19, 1927; s. Arthur Henry and Minnie (Jones); B.A.,
Johnson C. Smith Univ., Charlotte, N.C., 1950; B.D.,
1953; m. Marion Frances Gater; children---Arthur
Henry, II; Fraternal Worker, UPUSA Church to Pakistan,
1953-57; associate General Sec. Pakistan Student Christian
Movement; Dir. of Youth Work Lahore Church Council.
Church Extension Board Presbytery of Church; asst. to
exec. dir. and sec. South Central Planning Council, 1957-
61; UPUSA Board of Nat. Missions; asst. dir. Dept. of
Urban Church, 1961-63; assoc. chrm. Division of Church
Strategy and Development, United Presbyterian Church,
U.S.A. 1963---; lecturer in Mission World Mission Insti-
tute Evanston, Ill., 1960; lecturer Home Missions Chris-
tian Theological Seminary, 1959; Spiritual Emphasis Week
Macalester College, 1964; mem. Bd. of Directors Engle-
wood Urban League (NJ), Bd. of Managers Commission
on Missionary Education (Friendship Press), Board of
Managers Urban Dept. Nat. Council of Churches; mem.,
Masons, Omega Fraternity, Elks, Home: 52 Beveridge
St., Teaneck, N.J.; Office: #1151, 475 Riverside Drive,
N.Y.

GEORGE, Carrie Leigh, sem. prof.; b. Winder, Ga., Sept.
28,   ; s. Elijah J. and Olian (Owens) L.; A.B.,
Clark Coll., 1932-36; M.A., Atlanta Univ., 1936-37;
B.D., Gammon Theol. Sem., 1948-54; P.C.R.E., New
York Univ., 1961; Ed. R.D. (hon.), Burton Coll. and
Sem., 1963; Ohio State U.,   1942; Hartford Sem. Founda-
tion, 1958, 59; Garrett Theol. Sem., Sum. 1960; Atlanta
Univ., 1963-64; m. Domotory T.; children---Faith Olian,
Donald T.; assoc. prof., Gammon Theol. Sem., Atlanta,
1954-57; Interdenominational Theol. Center, Atlanta,
1957---; minister of Rel. Ed., Antioch Bapt. Ch., At-
lanta, 1955-62; director, "People's Sch. of Christian
Education" at the Interdenominational Theol Center, 1964
---; instructor, Turner Theol. Sem. (Morris Brown
coll.), Atlanta, 1957-58; Head of Mathematics Dept.,
Samuel Howard Archer High Sch., Atlanta, 1957-58; in-
structor, Spelman Coll., 1959-60; dean, Mission Study
Institute, Mt. Hermon Assn, 1954-64; Mem., Com. on
Christian Education of Children, National Council of
Churches, 1962---; Recipient, Woman of the Year Award
in Religion, Iota Phi Lambda, 1956; Most Outstanding
Minister's Wife of the Year Award, Nat. Assn of Minis-
ters' Wives, 1954; delegate, World Baptist Alliance in
London, England and given a tour of eight other countries

including the Holly Land, 1955; author: What Matters
Most, 1948, Logan Press, Atlanta, Ga.; Mem., Ameri-
can Assn of Women Ministers; American Assn. of Univ.
Profs.; American Personnel and Guidance Assn; Rel.
Education Assn. of Grater Atlanta; American Assn of
Religious Educators; Mid-Eastern Assn of Religious Ed-
ucators; Bapt. Ministers' Wives' Coterier; YMCA; ITC
Women's Fellowship; Alpha Kappa Alpha Sorority; Home:
1652 Detroit Ave. NW, Atlanta, Ga. 30314; Office: 671
Beckwith St., Atlanta, Ga.

GERALD, William , church official, editor, radio announcer;
b. Fitzgerald, Ga., Dec. 15, 1918; s. Percy and Bitha
Wilcox (Collins) G.; Cortez Peters Business College,
1951; Howard University, 195 ; Bible Way Training
School, 1950-62; m. Fannie Mae Braxton; children---
Edmond, Clarence, Frank, Raymond; Member, Bible Way
Church Our Lord Jesus Christ World-wide, Inc., 1947---;
Sec. Pastor Bishop S.E. Williams, Exec. sec. Board of
Bishops of Bible Way Church World-wide Inc.; Editor,
official paper of organization, The Bible Way News Voice;
Chairman, Ministers and Elders Club; General manager,
Sacred Composers' United Council; Gospel and semi-
classic Song Composer; Music Arranger; Pianist; Organist;
Accordionist; Interior Decorator; Pastor of the Lighthouse
Church, Annapolis, Md., Artist; Sign painter; photographer;
visiting minister to area penal institutions in nearby Va.,
1951-58; author: musical composions-"My Hope Is Fixed
In Christ", "You Can Make It", "Have You Ever Been
Touched By The Master," "When I Get Through," (Gospel
songs); "My Ship Will Come In," "Tell Me Now," (Semi-
classic); religious drama: "Three Deaths," "Laughing At
Wisdom." Weekly broadcast (Annapolis, Md.); Home:
4708 Sheriff Rd., NE. Washington, D.C.; Office: Bible
Way Church, 1130 N.J. Ave., NW, Washington, D.C.

GIBBS, Carey Abraham, bishop; b. Madison, Fla., Mar. 20,
1892; s. Jack and Lila G.; A.B., Edward Waters Coll.,
1917; B.D., Payne Sem., 1923; D.D. (hon.), LL.D.
(hon.), Edward Waters Coll.; pastor, African Methodist
Episcopal Churches, Ohio, Fla., Missouri; presiding
elder, 13 years; pres., Edward Waters Coll., 1929;
Elected bishop, 1948; current, presiding bishop, 7th
Dist., A.M.E. Ch.; Mem., Gen. Bd., Nat. Council of
Churches; chmn. Trustee, Edward Waters Coll., 1932;
1936---; US Forces, World War I; Served as A.M.E.
bishop in Africa and West Indies; Mem., Mason; Pythian;

American Woodman; Republican; Elk; General Bd., Council of Churches; Home: 1011 W. 8th St., Jacksonville,
Fla.

*GILL, W.O.; B.D., Howard Univ. Sch. of Rel., 1941;
three children; pastor, United Christian Ch., Jackson,
Miss., 1956-62; dean of instruction & prof. of religion,
Jarvis Christian Coll., 1942-55; dean of students, Jackson State Coll., 1956---; current, Jackson Miss., Jackson State Coll.; Home: 1009 Eastview St., Jackson, Miss.

GILLESPIE, William George, b. Knoxville, Tenn., May 12,
1931; s. Matt Wm. and Virginia (McBrayer); B.S., Knox
ville College, 1948-52; B.D., Johnson C. Smith Theological Seminary, 1952-55; Concordia Seminary, 1958-59;
Washington Univ., 1962-63; m. Martha Bele Cox; chil-
dren---Vendetta Elizabeth, Wm. Edward, Harry Edmund;
pastor Davie Street Presby. Ch., Raleigh, N.C., 1955-
56; Cote Brilliante Presby. Ch., St. Louis, Mo., 1956-
; pres. Carver House of Directors, 1961- ; mem.: Alpha
Phi Alpha Fraternity, Frontiers International, Presbyterian
Interracial Council, Democrat; Home: 4665 Labadie, St.
Louis 15, Missouri; Church: 4673 Labadie, St. Louis 15,
Missouri.

GIPSON, Waymon Jefferson, b. Red Bay, Fla., Oct. 10,
1898; s. Finley Jefferson and Christiane Nellie (Mc
Clendon) G.; Stillman Institute, 1924-36; Dillard University, 1937-38; A.B., Southern University, 1945-46; B.D.;
Gammon Theological Seminary, 1956-57; m. Leard Arnes-
tine Powell; children---Hilda Marie; pastor, Berean Presbyterian Church, New Orleans, La., 1934-47; pastor,
Faith Presbyterian Ch., Jackson, Miss., 1947---; Served
on Committee on Negro Work General Assembly, Presbyterian Church, U.S., 1942-50; Stated clerk, Central
Louisiana Presbytery, 1936-50; Chairman, Christian
Education, 1950---; Trustee of Stillman College, 1952-
63; Mem. of Board of Farish St., YMCA Board Management, 1950-58; Home: 2407 Morton Jackson 3, Miss.;
Office: 2219 Morton, Jackson 3, Miss.

GIVENS, Howard Washington, b. Waynesdoro, Aug. 4,
1904; s. Howard W. and Ada (Handkerson) G.; A.B.,
Johnson C. Smith Univ., Charlotte, N.C., 1932; B.D.,
Johnson C. Smith University, 1935; A.M., Columbia
University, New York, 1949; D.D. (hon.), Johnson C.
Smith, 1960; pastor BenSalem and Lloyd Churches,

1935-40; (Presbytery of Catawba); Biddleville-Emmanuel
Presbyterian Church, Charlotte, N.C., 1940- ; Delegate
to General Assembly of United Presbyterian Church, U.
S.A. (three times); Stated clerk of the Synod of Catawba,
Presbyterian Church, USA, 1957- ; mem. Advisory Com-
mittee (Boggs Academy, Keysville, Ga., 1959-); Exec.
comm. Human Relations Council; exec. comm. Charlotte
Branch NAACP; pres. Mecklenburg Ministers Association,
1961; official representative the Synod of Catawba to
N.C. Council of Churches, mem. the Comm. on Desegre-
gation Comm. of Friends, 1960- ; Certificate of Recognition from NAACP (Charlotte Branch), 1960; mem.: Phi
Beta Sigma; Home: 401 Campus Street, Charlotte, N.C.;
Church: 403 Mattoon Street, Charlotte 8, North Carolina.

GLADNEY, Harvey Levi, teacher; b. Moundville, Alabama,
April 14, 1914; s. Lee Andrew and Nettie (Bishop) G.;
Stillman College, 1937-39; B.S., Rust College, 1945-47;
B.D., Johnson C. Smith, 1955: m. Gladys Miller; chil-
dren---Jean, Clevie, Edith and Beverly; pastor, Green-
field and McKinney Presbyterian Ch., 1940-48; pastor,
Bethel and New Liberty Presbyterian Churches, Dillon,
S.C., 1948-57; pastor, 2nd Presbyterian Church, Thomas-
ville, Georgia, 1957-59; current pastor, Carver Heights
Presbyterian Church, Columbis, Ga., 1959---; Public
school teacher and principal, 2 years in Miss., 2 years
in Dillon, S.C.; Home: 3313 Decatur St., Columbus 6,
Ga.; Office: Carver Heights Presbyterian Church, 8th
St. & Illges Rd., Columbus 6, Georgia

GLENN, Lawrence Talmadge, administrator, b. Winnsboro,
S.C., July 20, 1963; s. James W. and Mattie A.G.;
B.A., Johnson C. Smith Univ.; B.D., Theol. Sem.,
Johnson C. Smith Univ., 1947-54; S.T.M. Temple Univ.,
1954-56; Dir. St. John's Presbyterian Neighborhood
House, Detroit, Mich., 1956-58; Asst. on the Staff of the
Institute on the Church in Corporate Society, 1959-61;
pastor the Broadstreet United Presbyterian Church,
Detroit, Mich., 1961- ; mem.: Bd. of the Greater De-
troit Comm. for Fair Housing Practices; Home: 4082
Cortland, Detroit 4, Mich.; Church: 12065 Broadstreet,
Detroit 4, Mich.

GOLDEN, Charles Franklin, bishop; b. Holly Springs,
Miss., Aug. 24, 1912; s. L.W. and Mary P. (Tyson)
G.; A.B., Clark Coll., Atlanta, 1936; B.D., Gammon,
Theol. Sem., 1937; B.D. (hon.), 1958; S.T.M., Boston

Univ., 1938; grad. study, 1946-47; m. Ida Elizabeth
Smith; Ordainted to deacon, Meth. Ch., 1936; elder,
1938; pastor, Birmingham, Ala.; Atlanta, Cooksville,
Tenn.; Clarksdale, Miss., 1935-38; Wesley Ch., Little
Rock, 1938-42; prof., Dept. of Religion and Philosophy,
Philander Smith Coll., 1938-41; director, field service,
Dept. of Negro Work, Meth. Bd. Missions, 1947-52;
assoc. sec., Div. of National Missions, 1952-56; director, Div. of National Missions, 1956-60; bishop, Nash-
ville-Birmingham area, Meth. Ch., 1960---; representative, Div. of World Missions to India Centennial, Lucknow,
Ind., 1956; chairman, Bd. of Trustees, Gulfside Assembly,
Rust Coll.; trustee, Cottreel Coll., Morristown Jr. Coll.;
captain, Chaplains Corps, US Army, 1942-46; Mem. Interdenominational Ministers Alliance; National Council Church
of Christ in Am.; Meth. Rural Fellowship (Sec. 1952-
56); Contributor of articles to religious publications;
Home: 2533 Shreeve Lane, Nashville, Tenn.; Office:
1908 Grand Ave., Nashville 5, Tenna.

GOMEZ, Joseph, bishop; b. Trinidad, West Indies, Nov. 29,
1889; A.B., Wilberforce Univ., 1914; M.A., Eden Grad-
uate Sch. of Rel.; m. Hazel Thompson; children---Eula
Viviana, Annetta Louise; pastor, African Methodist Epis-
copal Churches; Mission field of Bermuda and Canada;
Elected bishop, 1948; current, presiding bishop 4th Dist.;
prof., Payne Theol. Sem.; chmn, Ration Board 11-18,
Auyahoga Co.; pres., Interdenominational Ministers Al-
liance; Mem., Exec. Com., Federal Council of Churches;
Bd. of Directors, Cleveland Church Federation; Trustee,
Wilberforce Univ.; chmn, Payne Theol. sem.; Bd. of
Directors, Cedar Branch, YMCA, Cleveland; Financial
Bd. A.M.E. Ch.; Corporation of Schauffer Coll. of
Rel. & Social Work; Mem., Kappa Alpha Psi; director,
St. James Literary Forum; delegate, World Conf. of
Methodism, 1956, 1961; World Council of Churches, New
Delhi, India; chmn, Connectional Com. on Missions, 1959-
60; sec., Council of Bishops; pres., Council of Bishops,
1960-61; Home: 11009 Wade Park Ave., Cleveland, Ohio.

GOODWIN, Kelly Oliver Perry, b. Washington, D.C., Dec.
24, 1911; s. Oliver Perry and Martha (Duncan) G.; A.
B., Howard U., Wash., D.C., 1935; B.D., United Theol.
Sem., Dayton, O., 1941; Grad. study, Temple U.,
Phila., Pa., 1941-42; Counselling Cert., N.C. Bapt.
Sch. of Pastoral Care, Bowman Gray Sch. of Medicine,
Winston-Salem, N.C., 1948; D.D. (Honorary), Shaw U.,

Raleigh, N.C., 1960; Ordained Bapt. Minister, 1936;
Pastored, Friendship Bapt. (student asst.), Wash., D.C.,
1935-36; Supply Pastor, Zion Bapt. Ch., Reading, Pa.,
1936; Pastor, Zion Bapt., 1937-47; Pastor, Mount Zion
Bapt., Winston-Salem, N.C., 1947---; Consultant & mem.
Exec. Comm., Town and Rural Institute, Ministers, N.
C.A. & T. Coll., Greensboro, N.C.; mem. The Amer.
Academy of Pol. & Soc. Science; mem., Nat. Assoc. of
Housing and Redevelopment Officials; Vice-Chrmn.,
Commissioner, Winston-Salem Housing Authority, 1958--;
Mem., Chaplain, Comm. of Management YMCA, 1960---;
Vice-Pres., Emancipation Assoc., Winston-Salem and
Forsyth Co.; 1961---; Coll. Chaplain, Winston-Salem
State Coll., 1958-59; mem. Omega Psi Phi ;
Masons,   IBPOE;   Traveled, N. Amer., Caribbean
Islands, Europe, West Africa; mem., Nat. Bapt. Conv.,
USA, Inc., 1945---; mem., Exec. Bd., Phyllis Wheatley
Home, Winston-Salem, N.C.; Home: 501-26th Street, N.
W., Winston Salem, N.C. 27105 Office: 1304 N. High-
land Ave., Winston Salem, N.C. 27101.

GORDON, Frank R., teacher, b. Hague, Va. Jan. 23, 1918;
s. John and Marie; A.B., Lincoln Univ., 1939; S.T.B.,
1942; m. Evelyn Crabb; children---Sandra Dale, Lee
David; pastor: Penna., Georgia, Missouri; current,
Shiloh Presby. Ch., Knoxville, Tenn.; Missouri; Bible
teacher Knoxville College; mem. Na. Comm. on Rel.
and Race, U.P. Ch., U.S.A.; Served as moderator of
the Presbytery and Synods; mem. Governor's Comm. on
Human Relations, Tenn.; Bd. of Managers-YMCA; Juvenile Court; 1954-57 pres. Knoxville N.A.A.C.P.;
pres. Tenn. State Conf., N.A.A.C.P. Branches; chairman Church Work Comm. of Ministers Southeast Region,
N.A.A.C.P.; leader School Integration, City of Knoxville;
mem.: Elk, Mason, Kappa Alpha Psi; Church: 1015 East
Church St., Knoxville, Tenn.

GORDON, Maxie Sylvester, educator, author; b. Greenville,
S.C., Dec. 10, 1910; s. John Oscar and Hattie (Byrd)
G.; A.B., Benedict Coll., Columbia, S.C.; B.D.,
Oberlin Grad. Sch. of Theol., 1937; M.A., 1938; S.T.
M., 1939; Addl. study, U. of Chgo, Sorbonne U., Paris,
France; D.D. (honorary), Benedict Coll., 1956; m.
Ethel Mae McAdams; 2 sons, Maxie S., Jr. (2d Lt.),
Thomas Asbury; Pastor, Royal Bapt., Anderson, S.C.,
1940-45; New 1st Calvary Bapt., Columbia, S.C., 1945-
Instr., Mod. Lang. & Rel., Friendship Jr. Coll., 1939-

42; Asst. then Assoc. Prof., Fr. and Bib. Lit., Benedict
Coll., 1942-60; Act. Dean, Starks Center of Training,
Benedict Coll., 1960---; Research scholar & author,
Flashlights, S.S. Pub. Bd., Nat. Bapt. Conv. USA;
S.C. Rep., Foreign Mission Bd., Nat. Bapt. Conv.;
Chrmn. Standing Comm. on Intercultural Relationships;
appeared in Who's Who In Amer. Education, Vol. 20,
1961-62; Who's Who In Colored America, 1950; mem.
(sub. life) NAACP; Coll. Lang. Assoc.; Nat. Assoc.
Bible Instrs; Council on Higher Education; Palmetto Edu.
Assoc.; Omega Psi Phi Frat.; Home: 2221 Marguerette
Street, Columbia 4, S.C. Church: 1401 Pine Street,
Columbia 4, S.C. School: Benedict College, 1618 Oak
St., Columbia, S.C.

GOPAUL, Paul Albert, educator; San Francisco, Calif.,
June 11, 1926; s. Paul Mortimer and Ivy Grace (Gibbs)
G.; B.A., St. Michael's, 1952; M.A., St. Michael's,
1954; Ph.D., U. of Ottawa, 1958; Ph.D. Cand., U. of
N. Mex., 1958---; Ordained priest Roman Catholic Ch.,
1952; Teach., Eng., Hist., Humanities, Rel., Phil., St.
Michael's; Med. Ethics, Marr., Jeanne Mance Sch. of
Nursing, Burlington, Vt.; Ch. Hist., Patrology, Pius
XII Maj. Seminary, Albuquerque, N. Mex.; Psych.,
Regina Sch. of Nursing, Albuquerque, N. Mex.; Founder,
co-curricular program in Communication Arts, St.
Michael's, 1957-58; Prof. Hist., U. of New Mex. New-
man Extension, 1962-63; Pius X High School, Alb. N.
Mex, 1962-63; U.S. Hist., Academic Counsellor, St.
Charles Borromeo Sem., El Paso, Texas, 1964; Priest-
hood: Weekend ministries, 40 hrs., Sodality, Days of
Recollection, Sisters' Renovation, Children's Retreats,
Vermont Cath. Hr., Columnist, Vermont Catholic Tri-
bune Editor, Sponsor Magazine, Newman Apostolate,
Vermont and New Mexico, Hospital Chaplain; Prof. Soc.;
Amer. Cath. Hist. Assoc., Amer. Hist. Assoc.; Life
Mem. Calif. Scholarship Federation, J.H. Card, New-
man Hon. Soc.; Asst. Pastor, Blessed Sacrament Church,
El Paso, Texas, 1963---; Assoc. Editor, Southwest
Cath. Register, El Paso, Texas, 1964; Home: 90-25
Diana Drive, El Paso, Texas. Office: 90-25 Diana Drive,
El Paso, Texas.

GOW, Francis Herman, bishop; b. Cape Town, S. Africa,
Sept. 29, 1896; s. Francis McDonald and Sarah Elizabeth
G.; A.B., Wilberforce Univ.; Tuskegee Institute; Miami
Univ., Ohio; Lane Theol. Sem.; D.D. (hon.), Morris

Brown Coll.; Wilberforce Univ.; LL.D., Allen Univ.; m.
Louise Ballon; children--- Teepho; pastor, Cincinnati
African Methodist Ch., Charleston, W. Va.; Cape Town,
S. Africa; presiding elder, Cape Town Dist.; supt., Cape
National Conf.; Elected bishop, 1952, 15th Episcopal Dist.,
S. Africa; Mem., Committee on Revision of the Discipline,
Education and Missions, A.M.E. Ch.; Omega Psi Phi;
Mason; Council of Christian Churches, S. Africa; pres.
African Peoples' Organization; chairman, Colored Ad-
visory Council; commandant, Civilian Protective Services,
S. Africa; pres., African Students Union; Home: 40
Prince George Drive, Wynberg, Capetown, S. Africa.

GRADY, James Crawford, b. New Hanover, Co., N.C.
Sept. 19, 1900; s. Luke and Rebecca (Aycock) G.; A.B.,
B.D., Kittrell Coll.; Further study: Harvard Univ.; Shaw
Univ., Cortez W. Peters School of Business; m. widower;
children---Marion (Rev. Reubenk Dicks), Charles; pastor,
Churches, North Carolina, Western N.C., Virginia,
Maryland; principal, Ross Hill, N.C. Elementary Sch.,
1929; Present pastor, St. John African Methodist Epis-
copal Church; Wilmington, N.C.; Mem., Exec. Board,
Wilmington, N.C., Chapter, NAACP; 1st Lt. Chaplain,
US Army, 1944-46; Commendation Award; Good Conduct
Award; Mem., Voters Registration; Mason, Civic League;
Mem., Writers Staff Second Episcopal District of the
A.M.E. Church; Home: 216 South 7th St., Wilmington,
N.C.; Office: St. John A.M.E. Church, Wilmington,
N.C.

GRANBERRY, James Madison, Jr., ch. official; b. Coweta,
Okla., April 29, 1914; s. James Madison Sr. and Naomi
Eva G.; A.A., Western Univ., 1934; A.B., Lane Coll.,
1936; D.D. (hon.), Campbell Coll., Jackson, Miss.,
1952; LL.D. (hon.), Monrovia Coll., Liberia, W. Africa,
1955; m. Ethel Lee Hymes; pastor, Brown Chapel African
Meth. Episcopal Ch., Bristow, Okla.; Bethel A.M.E.
Ch., Claremore, Okla.; St. Peter A.M.E. Ch., Clarks-
ville, Tenn.; St. John A.M.E. Ch., Nashville, Tenn.;
St. Paul A.M.E. Ch., Columbia, Tenn.; Served as
pastor churches in Oklahoma and Tenn. from 1939 to
May 1964; current, Sec.-Treas., Pension Dept., A.M.E.
Ch.; chmn, State Church work, NAACP, Tenn., 1962;
One of the organizers of the Brotherhood of the A.M.E.
Ch.; Mem., Ex. Bd., T.V.A.; Citizen of the Year,
Radio Station WVOL; outstanding minister's award from
Payne Theol. Sem., Wilberforce, Ohio; Citation from

Davidson County by Mayor Briley, Honorary Citizen of
Tenn.; home: 1131 E. Delmas Ave., Nashville, Tenn.;
Office: 414 Eighth Ave. S., Nashville, Tenn. 37203

GRAY, Arthur Douglas, b. Sheffield, Ala., Jan. 17, 1907;
s. William L. and Hattie (Shine) G.; A.B., Talladega
College, 1929; B.D., Chicago Theological Seminary, 1934;
D.D. (Honorary), Chgo. Theol. Sem., 1948; m. Edna
Brown; 1 dau., Clarice; Pastored, Plymouth Cong. Ch.,
Wash., D.C., 1934-44; Ch. of the Good Shepherd Cong.
Ch., Chgo., Ill., 1944-52; Park Manor Cong. Ch., Chgo.,
Ill., 1962---; Asst. to Pres., Talladega College, Ala.,
1930-32; Pres. Talladega College, 1952-62; mem. Alpha
Phi Alpha; Sigma Pi Phi; Home: 1450 E. 55th Place,
Chicago 37, Ill. Office: 7000 S. Park Ave., Chgo. 37,
Ill.

GRAY, L. Charles, b. Camden, N.J., May 3, 1915; s.
Jules and Georgia Ann G.; A.B., Lincoln Univ., 1935;
S.T.B., M.A., New York Univ., 1938; courses toward
Ph.D.; m. Maude E. Johnson; children---Charles Jr.,
Denis Jules; pastor, Faith Presby. Ch., Phila., Pa.,
1938-40; teacher and pastor, Swift Memorial Jr. Coll.,
Rogersville, Tenn., 1940-42; pastor, Gibson Chapel,
Springfield, Mo., 1942-43; St. Paul Presby. Ch., Kan-
sas City Lafayette Presby. Ch., Jersey City, 1951-62;
current pastor, Presbyterian Ch. of St. Albans, 1962---;
visiting lecturer, Lincoln Univ. Seminary, 1957-59;
teacher, Public Schools, Springfield, Mo., 1941-42;
English and Public Speaking, Synder High School, Jersey
City, N.J., 1960-62; chaplain, Hospital for Mental Diseases,
Secaucus, N.J., 1957-60; pioneer in summer camping
program for Junior and Senior High Schools in Synod of
Missouri for 11 years; former moderator, Presbytery of
Palisades; former pres., Jersey City Council of Churches,
Organized Operation Clean Up (St. Albans) by recognition
to serious housing problems; Honored by Long Island
Chapter of Omega Fraternity, 1964; mem., Core - arrested many times on picket line; Mem., Alpha Phi Alpha;
author: Plays - "Broken Threads" Three Acts, "A Rose
by Any Other Name", "Magnets and Magic"; home: 119-
11 190 St., St. Albans, N.Y.; Office: Presbyterian Ch.
of St. Albans, 190 St. and 119th Ave., St. Albans.

GRAY, William Herbert, Jr., educator, author, administrator; b. Richmond, Va., Sept. 25, 1911; s. Rev. William
H. and Mary (Smith) G.; B.S., Bluefield State Coll.,

W. Va., 1933; M. S., U. of Pa., Phila., 1934; Ph.D.,
U. of Pa., 1942; Temple U., Sch. of Theol., 1949-50;
D. D. (honorary), Edward Waters Coll., Jacksonville, Fla.
1952; m. Hazel Yates; 1 son, William Herbert, III; 1
dau, Marian Anne; Prof. Ed., Prin. Dem. Sch. and
Field Dir. of Extension, Southern U., Baton Rouge, La.,
1934-41; Pres., Fla. Normal & Industrial Coll., St.
Augustine, 1941-44; Pres., Fla. Agri. and Mech. U.,
Tallahassee, Fla., 1944-49; Editor, Phila. Afro-Amer.
Newspaper, 1949-51; Columnist, Phila. Daily News,
1952-55; Exec. Dir., Industrial Race Relations Com-
mission, Dept. Labor & Industry, Pa., 1952-55; Vice-
Pres., Pa. Council of Churches, Harrisburg, Pa., 1955-
60; Specialist, State Dept. of Pub. Instruction, Harris-
burg, Pa., 1960-62; Pastor, Bright Hope Bapt. Ch.,
Phila., Pa., 1949; Mem. Bd. Dirs., Citizens and
Southern Bank and Trust Co., Phila., Pa., 1956; mem.,
Phi Delta Kappa Frat., Alpha Kappa Mu Nat. Honor Soc.,
Alpha Phi Alpha Frat., Frontiersmen, Masons, Elks;
Recipient several awards including, Service Award,
Manassas Academy, Manassas, Va., 1952, Annual Top
Rung Award, Distinguished Service in Fields of Educa-
tion, Religion, and Civic Endeavor, Mitrana Sch. of Model-
ing, Phila., Pa., 1957, and 1st Annual Greater Phila-
delphia Award of Merit, 1960; Freedom Jubilee Award,
Pittsburgh, Pa., 1960; Author of several published
articles, "Vocational Guidance in Louisiana High Schools,"
Journal of Negro Education, 1939: "Broadening our Hori-
zons for Correctional Service," The Prison Journal, Vol.
XXXII, July 1952; et. al.; Vice-Pres., Phila. Fellowship,
Commission; Chrmn., Bd. Trustees, Berean Institute,
Phila., Pa.; Sec., Carver Loan and Investment Corp.,
Phila., 1950---; Sec.-Treas., Phila. Housing Authority,
1960---; Mem. Bd. Dir., NAACP, Phila. Branch; Mem.,
Bd. Dirs., Concord Park Homes (Interracial Housing
Development), Trevose, Bucks Co., Pa.; Exec. Sec.,
Police Advisory Bd., City of Phila. Home: 1511 N.
Sixteenth St., Phila. 21, Pa.

GREENE, Horace Henry, Sr., b. Louisville, Ky., Apr. 12,
1907; s. George Isaac and Eva (Bloomer) G.; B.Th.,
Gammon Theol. Sem.; m. Daisy Mae English; children---
Horace Jr., Elwood La Monte; pastor, Irvington, Ky.,
1929-31; New Zion, Ky., 1931-39; Gunn Meth. Ch.,
Lexington, Ky., 1939-48; Dist. Supt. Louisville Dist.,
Lexington Conf., 1948-52; Calvary Church, Cincinnati,
Ohio, 1952; Jones Temple Methodist Church, Louisville,

Ky., 1953---; pres., Louisville Ministerial Ass'n, 1961-
62; chairman, Bd. of Dir., Wesley Club, Ky. State
Coll., 1960---; Exec. Bd., Boy Scouts, 1956-62;
former pres., Interdenominational Ministers' Assn; chairman, Bd. of Evangelism, Lexington Conf.; chairman,
Common Conf. Relations; Central Jurisdiction Conf. The
Methodist Church, 1964; Home: 1816 W. Jefferson,
Louisville, Ky.; Office: 1921 W. Jefferson, Louisville
3, Ky.

GREENE, Sherman Lawrence, bishop; b. Vicksburg, Miss.
June 15, 1886; s. Henry and Delia (Wilson) G., student
Alcorn (Miss) College, 1900-02; A.B., Campbell (Miss)
Coll., 1916; B.D. Shorter Coll., Little Rock, Ark.,
1912; D.D., Allen U., Columbia, S.C., 1923; LL.D.,
Wilberforce (O.) U., 1932; m. Pinkie Beatrice Spencer,
June 21, 1905, deceased. m. Callie   1962. Chil-
dren-Sherman Lawrence, Jr., and Lillian V. Ordained
deacon, A.M.E. Ch., 1908, elder, 1910; consecrated
bishop, 1928; pastor St. James Ch., New Orleans,
1915-16, Bethel Ch., Little Rock, 1917-19; president
Shorter Coll., 1918-24; presiding elder Pine Bluff and
Little Rock dists., 1924-28; bishop Tenn. and West
Indies, 1928-32; Miss. and La., 1932-48; Ala., 1948-
51, Ga., 1951-62; D.C. 1962-64; elected pres. Council of
Bishops, 1952, pres. Nat. Conf.Ch. Leaders, 1936-40;
Del Ecumenical Conf. of Methodism, London, Eng.,
1951, State Chmn. Gen Commn Rural Edn. and Inter-
church Relations, 1940-44; member of exe. bd. Council
of Chs., USA, 1950-54; v.p. Ga. Council of Chs., 1953-;
Del. Nat. Rep. Conv., Phila., 1944; Trustee Wilberforce
U., 1924-, Atlanta U., 1953-, Mem Am. Acad. Polit
and Social Sci., Kappa Alpha Psi., Mason, Elk, K.P.
Home or Office: 1105 Fountain Drive, SW Atlanta, Ga.

GREGORY, Henry C., III, b. New York City, July 31,
1935; s. Henry C. and Louise A.G.; Howard Univ. Sch.
of Rel., 1951; A.B., Howard Univ., 1952-56; B.D.,
Drew Univ., 1957-59; asst. pastor, Shiloh Bapt. Church,
Wash., D.C. (currently); Mem., Eta Sigma Phi (National Honorary Classical Fraternity); Alpha Phi Alpha;
Home: 3915 13th NW, Wash., D.C. 20011; Office: 1500
9th NW, Wash., D.C.

GRIFFIN, Marvin Collins, church official; b. Wichita,
Kans. Feb. 20, 1923; s. Jessie and Beulah (Howell) G.;
B.A., Bishop Coll., 1943; B.D., Oberlin Coll., 1947;

M.R.E., Southwestern Theol. Sem., 1955; m. Lois Jesse
King; children---Marva Lois, Gaynelle, Ria Joy; Ordained
to ministry Baptist Church, 1942; professor, Oklahoma
Baptist Sch. of Rel., 1944-48; supt., City Missions,
Dallas, 1948-50; pastor, New Hope Baptist Ch., 1951---;
sec., Ministers' Conference of Missionary Bapt. General
Convention of Texas; Mem., Doris Miller Branch YMCA,
1952---; pres., Democratic Progressive Voters' League
of Waco and McLennan County, Tex., 1956---; Grass
Roots Committee of Waco, Tex., 1957---; Bd. of Directors, Texas Southern Univ.; author column, Historian,
National Baptist Convention of America, 1958---; Home:
1324 N. 6th Waco, Tex.; Office: 915 N. 6th Waco, Tex.

GRIFFIN, Theolia John, b. Fort Smith, Ark., Apr. 29,
1907; s. Butler John and Eliza (Simpson) G.; Philander
Smith College, 1927-31; A.B., Atlanta Univ., 1934; B.
D., Gammon Theological Sem., 1931-34; D.D., Shorter
College, 1941; LL.D., Natchez College, 1951; pastor,
Tenn., Okla. West Va. Ark. Ill. Ark. and again Tenn.
At which time edited newspapers and worked in the
NAACP; teacher, St. Louis Area Methodist Summer
School, 7 summers; Chaplain, Talf, Okla. Mental Hos-
pital; Member, Phi Beta Sigma; author: Book of Sermons;
Home: 268 Edsel Ave., Memphis, Tenn.; Off.; 1606 Kan-
sas St., Memphis 9, Tenn.

GRIFFIN, Thomas J., church official; b. Carroll Co.,
Miss., July 4, 1917; A.B., Jarvis Christian Coll.,
1947; B.D., Garrett Theol. Sem., 1947; courses, Columbia Univ. Sch. of Social Work, 1959; Seminars:
Economics, Politics, Education, Religion and United Nations; m. Geneva Brown; children---Robert Eugene;
Thomas J. II, Reginald De Koven, Rayford Galen; student
pastor, Fort Worth Christian Ch., Tex.; Muskogee Christian Ch., Oklahoma; Jacksonville Christian Ch., Tex.;
asst. pastor, Indiana Avenue Christian Ch., Chgo., Ill.;
pastor, East Sixth Christian Ch., Oklahoma City, 1950-
56; Nat. Field Sec., Christian Ch., Dept. of Christian
Action and Community Service, 1956-60; current pastor,
Univ. Christian Ch., Houston, Tex., 1960---; former
sec., International Christian Youth Fellowship, Christian
Ch.; former pres., Interdenominational Ministers Alliance;
Christian Exec. Bd., NAACP, Oklahoma City; organizer,
Houston Conf. on Religion and Race; Mem., editorial
staff, Social Action News Letter, Christian Ch., Publication; Mem., NAACP; Bd. of Houston Council of Human

Relations; co-chmn, Houston Conf. on Rel. and Race;
Mem., Dept. of Cultural and Community Relations, Texas
Council of Churches; Office: 3610 Southmore St., Houston,
Texas 77004

GRISHAM, Dubro Merriweather, church official; b. Murfrees-
boro, Tenn., Dec. 12, 1911; s. Henry and Alice Mariah
(Smith) G.; B.S., Tenn. A & I State Coll., 1938; B.D.,
Gammon Theol. Seminary, 1941; m. Frazelia Belle
Walker; children.--- Frazelia Metia, Daniel Wesley; pastor,
Brooks Chapel Methodist Ch., Brentwood, Tenn., 1933-
38; Clark Memorial Meth. Ch., Nashville, Tenn., 1941-
53; Centenary Meth. Ch., Memphis, Tenn., 1953-62;
Nashville Dist. Supt., Tenn. Conference, 1962---; pres.,
Trustee Bd. Gorine Coll., Memphis, Tenn.; Trustee Mor-
ristown Coll., Morristown, Tenn.; Mem., James A.
Myers Lodge; J.A. Henry Consistory; Home: 2207 Elliott
Ave., Nashville, Tenn. 37204; Office: same.

*GUILES, Samuel Everette, b. Pamplico, S.C., Oct. 17,
1921; s. William Samuel and Areta (Green) G.; A.B.,
Allen Univ., 1944; B.D., Howard Univ. Sch. of Rel.,
1947; Howard Univ. Law School, 1948; D.D. (hon.),
Kittrell Coll., 1950; m. Anne Gertrude Rowe; pastor,
Dent Chapel African Methodist Episcopal Church, Bladens-
burg, Md., 1947; Campbell A.M.E. Church, Wash., D.
C., 1949-56; current, Turner Memorial A.M.E. Church,
Wash., D.C., 1956---; Pastoral Clinical Training: Chap-
lain Intern, National Training School for Boys, D.C.;
D.C. General Hospital; St. Elizabeth's Hospital, Wash.,
D.C.; Mem., Coordinating Committee of Anacostia, D.C.
and Vicinity, 1950-55; Consolidated Parent Group, 1953-
54; Bd. of the Washington Federation of Churches, 1953-
56; Borad of Directors, Iona Whipper Home for Unwed
Mothers, 1959-63; D.C. Commissioner's Youth Council,
1959-63; Exec. Bd. of the D.C. Branch of the NAACP;
Institutional Chaplaincy Comm. of the Council of Churches,
National Capital Area; Bd. of Directors, The Washington
Urban League; Volunteer worker, United Givers Fund;
Citation, Coordinating Committee of Anacostia and Vicinity, for progressive community work, especially among
the youth, 1954; Citation of Appreciation as Volunteer
Worker for the United Givers Fund, 1957; Citation, Washington Urban League, for outstanding community work,
1959; Trophy Award from the International Dance Studios
for exemplary achievements in the field of Culture, especially amont the youth, 1964; Cited in Washington Post,

Jan. 11, 1964," Washington Church", for outstanding
pastoral work with youth; Mem., Republican State
Committee, D.C.; President's Committee on Government
Contracts (Under Eisenhower administration; Phi Beta
Sigma; Home: 1605 Crittenden St., NW, Wash., D.C.,
20011; Office: 600 I St., NW, Wash., D.C., 20001.

GUY, John Francis, b. Cleveland, Ohio; s. Frank L. and
Bertha L.G.; B.A., Andrew Univ., 1958; M.A. Andrews
Univ., 1960; m. Evelyn Alicia Phipps; son: John Kendall.
Assistant pastor, Shiloh Seventh- Day Adventist Church,
1960-61; present: pastor, Ecorse and Bellivelle S.D.A.
Churches, Ecorse, Mich. Member, Local Ministerial As-
sociation; Most Sportsmanship Award in basketball. Home:
3788 19th St., Ecorse, Mich. Office: 3834 10th St.,
Ecorse, Mich.

HADDEN, Thomas Paul, educator; b. Raleigh, N.C., May
31, 1929; s. Thomas Gary and Clarice (Mallette) H.; B.
A., St. Meinrad College, 1950-55; S.T.B., The Pontifical
Gregorian Univ. (Rome), 1955-59; Pastorates: Newton Grove
Cath. Ch., Newton Grove, N.C., 1959-60; Consolation
Cath. Ch., Charlotte, N.C., 1960-61; St. Theresa's
Cath. Ch., Durham, N.C., 1961-62; St. Joseph's Cath.
Ch., New Bern, N.C., 1962---; Teacher: Charlotte
Cath. High Sch., 1960; Wm. Gaston Cath. High Sch.,
New Bern, N.C., 1962---; Bd. of Dir., West St. Public
Library, New Bern, 1962---; NAACP Youth Council Ad-
visor, New Bern, 1963; N.C. Conf. on Race and Religion;
N.C. Cath. Clergy Cred. Union; Home: 306 Bern St.,
New Bern, N.C.

HAIG, Albert Randolph, publishing secretary; b. Jamaica,
West Indies, Oct. 9, 1903; s. Reginald and Hannah
(Feurtado) H.; "Jamaica Government Education Certificate,"
Jamaica, W.I., Government Elementary Preparatory,
1910-18; (Coll. Education Certificate" - West Indian
Training College (S.D.A. Denominational), 1923-27; At-
lantic Union College, Mass., extra-mural dept. (New
York Center) - Seminary Course; m. Marian Louise
Parchment; children---Iralyn Patrice (Mrs. Gladwin Trott),
Myrnelle Faunglow, Anne Alberga (Mrs. Albert Jahn);
Jamaica Conf. of Seventh-Day Adventists, Jamaica, W.I.,
publishing secretary, 1928-29; Bahamas Mission of S.D.
A., Bahamas, publishing secretary, 1929-30; Jamaica
Conf. of S.D.A., Jamaica, W.I., literature-evangelist,

1930-32; Jamaica Conf. of S.D.A., pastor-evangelist,
1932-40; Jamaica Conf. of S.D.A., publishing secretary, 1940-43; British, French and Dutch Islands and
Colonies of West Indies, publishing department secretary, 1943-46; British West Indies Union of Seventh-Day
Adventist, Jamaica, West Indies, publishing, educational,
youth-leader, temperance, home-missionary and sabbath-
school, secretary, 1946-56; publishing secretary, Northeastern Conference of S.D.A., N.Y.; current pastor,
Evangelist and Superintendent of "Hanson Place S.D.A.
Church," "Park Place S.D.A. Church," 1959---; Youth
movement organizer; Mem. of the following Boards;
Andrew's Memorial Hospital, West Indies College, and
Kingsway High School, all of Jamaica, W.I. Annual
Scholarship to West Indies Training College, Mandeville,
Jamaica, W.I., awarded for exceptional accomplishments
in religious literature salesmanship, 1921-26; Educational
scholarship to W.I. College awarded for faithfulness and
other accomplishments in pastoral-evangelism, 1936-37;
American Temperance Society; American Red Cross.
Home: 560 W. 150th St., N.Y., 31 N.Y. Office: 88
Hanson Pl., Brooklyn 17, N.Y.

HAIRSTON, Andrew Jasper, b. Clemons, N.C., July 9,
1932; s. James and Laura (W.) H.; B.A., Southwestern
Christian College, 1955; B.A., B.S., Paul Quinn,
1956, 57; B.D., Johnson C. Smith Univ.; Texas Chris-
tian Univ., 1960; Residence work completed for Th.M.;
m. Jeanne Turner; children---Kenneth Andrew, Norma
Jeannean, Kerr Lynn; current pastor, The Church of
Christ, Atlanta, Ga., 1962---; Member, Greater Atlanta
Council on Human Relations: NAACP; Home: 245 Simon
Terrace, East Atlanta, Ga.; Office: 810 Simpson St.,
N.W., Atlanta 14, Ga.

HAIRSTON, Samuel Henry, b. Henry County, Va., Nov. 24,
1891; s. Jack and Thenie H.; Diploma Ed. courses:
Hampton Institute, St. Paul, Va. State College; m.
Mamie Lee Foster; children: Mrs. Christiana Napper,
Mrs. Wilson Napper, Mrs. Irene Ramey, Mrs. Estes
Barnes, James C. Barnes; Present, pastor-Mt. Olive
Christian Antioch Christian Church, Meadow Christian
Christian Church, New Bethel Christian Church, 1916-
to date; teacher: Public Schools, Henry County, Va.
(50 yrs.); mem. Trustee Board, Community Hospital,
Martinsville, Va. honored; Samuel H. Hairston Con-
solidated Elementary School, Rt. 3, Martinsville, Va.
Former Editor, National Christian Messenger; Home:

R. F. D. 3, Box 156, Martinsville, Va.

HALL, James Harold, b. Brunswick, Georgia, June 20,
1928; B. A. , Talladega College, 1944-47; St. Augustine's
College, 1948-50; B. D. , Nashotah House Seminary,
1950-53; M. A. course, Montana State Univ.; pastor, St.
Matthew's Delray Beach, Fla. , 1953; pastor, St. Chris-
topher's P. E. Ch. , Fort Lauderdale, Fla. , 1955; Timothy's
Daytona Beach Episcopal Chaplain to Bethune-Cookman
College; Member: NAACP, Florida Council on Human Re-
lations, Mental Health Association of Volusia County;
Omega Psi Phi Fraternity; Home: 200 Agnes Avenue,
Missoula, Montana.

HALL, Laurence Edward, YMCA official ; b. Balto. , Md. ,
March 11, 1920; s. Wallace James and Lula Mae (Hall)
L. ; Jarvis Christian College, Hawkins, Texas - B. A.
Degree, 1950; M. A. , Southern Methodist University,
Dallas, Texas, 1952; Graduate Study, College of the
Bible, Philip's University, Enid, Okla. , 1953. Major,
Religious Education, American Church History; m.
Irene Deniese Watson; children---Thaddeus Waldof;
pastor, Romine Avenue Christian Church, Dallas, Texas,
1947-52; Vicar, St. Philip's Episcopal Church, Muskogee,
Oklahoma, 1952-56; Rector, St. Luke's Episcopal Church,
New Orleans, La. , 1957-62; Executive-Sec. , James
Rhodes YMCA Ft. Pierce, Fla. , 1963; adult education
teacher, New Orleans Public School System, 1958-62;
Mem. : The Commission of Social Action, Diocese of
Louisiana, 1960; The Northeastern Oklahoma Mental Health
Assn. , 1954; the Psychiatric Achievement Awards Com-
mittee, 1952-56; founder of the Interfaith A. A. Group,
New Orleans, La. , 1958, part-time chaplain, Taft State
Mental Hospital, Taft, Okla. , 1953-56; US Army during
World War II; 1/Lt. during Korean Conflict; awards:
Good Conduct Medal, US Army, World War II: Citizen-
ship Awards from Marylandand Louisiana; Mem. : Mason,
NAACP; Congress on Racial Equality; Radio speaker
WARN; Home: 1214 Ave. L. , Ft. Pierce, Fla. ; Office:
3100 Ave. G. , Ft. Pierce, Fla.

*HALL, Lloyd Dalton, coll. prof. b. Dallas, Texas, Sept.
11, 1935; s. Lloyd Dalton, Sr. and Elizabeth (Hayden)
H. ; B. A. , Bishop Coll. , 1959; B. D. , Howard Univ.
Sch. of Rel. , 1962; m. Virginia Ambler; children---
Clyde Allen, Lloyd Burnett; student pastor, Shiloh Bap-
tist Church, Wash. , D. C. ; Honeywell's Heiland Division,

Denver, Colo.; assoc. prof., Religion, Bishop Coll.,
Dallas, Texas; Rockefeller Theological Award, 1961-
62; Mem., Alpha Phi Alpha; Home: 3837 Simpson-Stuart
Rd., Dallas 16, Texas; Office: Bishop Coll. Dallas,
Texas.

HAMILTON, Charles Spencer, educator; b. Cedartown, Ga.,
May 12, 1927; s. Lindley D. and Clifford (Mozelle) W.;
A.B., Morehouse Coll., 1950; B.D., Morehouse Coll.
Sch. of Rel., 1953; courses: Fla. A. & M. Univ., 1954;
M.S.T., Interdenominational Theol. Center, 1964; m.
Sallye Butler; children---Ronald Spencer, Charletta Gale;
student pastor, First Baptist Ch.; pastor, The Arbor
Grove Baptist Ch., LaGrange, Ga.; The Woodward Bapt.
Ch., Atlanta, Ga.; The First Bapt. Ch., Thomasville,
Ga., 1953-56; Tabernacle Bapt. Ch., Augusta, Ga.,
1956---; teacher, The Boston High School, Boston, Ga.;
coach, girl's and boy's basketball; employee, The Atlanta
Life Ins. Co.; Mem., Bd. of Directors, Augusta Richmond County Voters League, 1962-64; Richmond County
Exec. Democratic Comm., 1962; State Advisory Comm.
of Commission on Civil Rights, 1962; US Merchant Mar-
ines, 1945-46; US Army, 1946-47; awards: Man of the
Year 1963, Omega Phi Fraternity; YMCA award for service, 1963; Augusta Richmond County Voters League Freedom award, 1963; Mem., Bd. of Directors, Shiloh Orphanage: YMCA; Bethlehem Center; Human Relation Council; Omega Phi Fraternity; vice pres., State Conference
of NAACP; pres., Augusta Chapter, NAACP; treasurer,
New Era Baptist Convention, Ga.; pres., The Gwinnett
Street Investment Company; Home: 1224 Gwinnett St.,
Augusta, Ga. 30901; Office: 1223 Gwinnett St., Augusta
Ga. 30901.

HAMILTON, McKinley John, b. Lake Charles, La., Nov.
24, 1921; s. Lincoln and Jennie (Keys) H.; A.A., Butler
Junior Coll., Tyler, Tex., 1941-43; A.B., Bishop Coll.,
Marshall, Tex., 1943-45; Crozer Theol. Sem., 1947;
B.D., Howard Univ. Sch. of Rel., 1955-58; m. Mary
Stone; pastor, New Hope Bapt., Alto, Tex., 1942-43;
St. James Bapt. Ch., 1942-43; The Good Samaritan Bapt.
Ch., Wash., D.C., 1955-57; asst. pastor, Shiloh Bapt.
Ch., Wash., D.C., 1947-58; First Bapt. Ch., Rocky
Mount, Va., 1958---; chaplain, Migrants, Lake Shore
area of Westfield, N.Y., 1957; vice pres., S.S. Conv.,
Franklin County, Va., 1962---; moderator, The Pigg
River Assn, Franklin County, Va., 1963---; pres. Lee

M. Waid PTA, 1962-63; vice district chmn, Algonquin
District of the Boy Scouts, 1960--; instructor, Week-
Day Religious Ed. , Lee M. Waid Sch. , 1964---; Mem. ,
Franklin County Minister's Assn; Virginia Council of
Human Relations, Roanoke, Va. ; Home: 137 Patterson
Ave. SE, Rocky Mount, Va. 24151; office: 137 Patter-
son Ave. SE, Rocky Mount, Va. 24151.

HANDY, James Albert, b. Tyaskin, Md. , June 1, 1881;
s. John and Julia (Hester) H. ; St. Paul Episcopal School
(Va.); Delaware State Coll. ; Morgan Coll. (Baltimore);
Honorary degree, Philadelphia School of the Bible;
widower. Present: presiding elder, Norfolk District,
Christian Methodist Episcopal Church; Church extension
secretary, 1957-63; one of the organizers of Community
Hospital, Norfolk, Va. ; member, International Union of
Gospel Missions. Founder and secretary, Seaview Hotel
and Beach Corporation; former Probation officer, Norfolk, Va. Home: 2527 Virginia Beach Boulevard, Norfolk, Va. Office: 408 Main St. , Norfolk, Virginia.

HANEY, William Riley, b. Cataula, Ga. , July 26; s. John
Henry and Celia H. ; A. B. , Central Univ. , Ind. , 1947;
B. Th. , 1941, B. D. , 1942 and D. D. (hon.), 1953, Bir-
mingham Bapt. Coll. ; graduate study: Wayne State Univ. ,
1949-54; Univ. of Michigan, 1954, 55; m. Anne Clara
Andrew; former pres. , Wolverine State Missionary Bapt.
Convention; Mem. , Editorial Staff, Sunday School Pub-
lishing Bd. of the National Baptist Convention, U. S. A. ,
Inc. ; Exec. Bd. , Wolverine State Missionary Bapt. Con-
vention; Bd. of Directors, Detroit Council of Churches;
Bd. of Directors Gleiss Memorial Center; pres. , Bd.
of Trustees, Bapt. Training School, Detroit; instructor,
National Sunday School and Bapt. Training Union Congress
in the Ministers' Division; corresponding sec. , Metro-
politan Dist. Assn; pastor (current), Dexter Ave. Bapt.
Church, 1946---; Mem. , Mason; Home: 4048 Fullerton
Ave. , Detroit 38, Mich. ; Office: 13500 Dexter Ave. ,
Detroit 38, Mich.

HARGROVE, Beverly Milton, II. , chaplain; b. Birmingham,
Ala. , Oct. 20, 1920; s. Beverly Milton and Ruth (Short-
ridge) H. ; A. B. , Miles Memorial Coll. , Birmingham,
Ala. , 1942; B. D. , Gammon Theol. Sem. , Atlanta, Ga. ,
1948; m. Blanche Day; children---Beverly III, William,
John, Gayle, Ruth; pastor, Ebenezer Methodist, Sparrows
Point, Md. , 1948-49; Eastern Methodist Ch. , Baltimore,

Md., 1949-52; Asbury Meth. Ch., Hagerstown, Md.,
1952-56; Buena Vista Meth. Ch., 1956-59; Simpson
Memorial Meth. Ch., Charleston, West Va., 1959---;
former teacher, Junior High School, Birmingham, Ala.;
current, director of the Wesley Foundation on the Campus
of West Va. State Coll., 1961---; Merit Award, NAACP;
Mem., Bd. of Ministerial Training of the Wash. Annual
Conf. Meth. Ch.; Bd. of Ministerial Training of the
Wash. Annual Conf. Meth. Ch.; Bd. of Education, Ministerial Training of the Wash. Annual Conf. Meth. Ch.;
Bd. of Christian Social Concerns, Ministerial Training
of the Wash. Annual Conf. Meth. Ch.; articles in the
Central Christian Advocate and local newspapers; Home:
212 Brooks St., Charleston, W. Va.; Office: 607 Shrews-
burg St., Charleston, W. Va.

HARGRAVES, James Archie, ch. official; b. Greensboro,
N.C., Aug. 2, 1916; s. Archie and Geneva (McCollum)
H.; B.S., N.C. Agricultural and Technical College,
1940; B.D., Union Theol. Sem., 1948; Columbia Univer-
sity, 1948-51; m. Inez Boger; 1 dau. Janet Delmanda;
Pastored: East Harlem Protestant Parish, NYC, 1948-
51; Lawndale Community Presbyterian Ch., Chicago,
1954-56; Nazarene Congregational Ch., Brooklyn, 1956-
61; Instr., Soc. Sciences and Dir., Pub. Relations, N.C.
Agr. and Tech. College, Greensboro, N.C., 1940-41;
Prof. Soc. Problems, Biblical Seminary, NYC, 1958-60;
Lecturer, Institute for Religious and Social Studies,
Jewish Theol. Sem., NYC, 1961-64; Dir., Westside
Christian Parish, Chgo., 1951-56; Sec., Urban Church,
United Ch. Bd. for Homeland Ministries, NYC, 1961-
64; Dir., Metropolitan Ministries, The Urban Training
Center for Christian Mission, Chgo., 1964---; Info.
Specialist, Office of Public Admin., Washington, D.C.,
1941-42; Sgt. 92nd Infantry Div., 1943-44; 2nd Lt., AOS
(Calcutta, India), 1945-56; Recipient, Gen. Alumni Award,
N.C. Agric. and Tech. Coll., 1962, Social Action Award,
Phi Beta Sigma, 1960, Y.M.C.A. Service Award, 1955;
mem. Religious Research Assoc., Long Range Planning
Committee, United Church of Christ, North American
Study Committee,   World Council of Churches; Delegate,
Third Gen. Assembly, World Council of Churches, New
Delhi, India, 1961; Author: Stop Pussyfooting Through A
Revolution, 1963; Office: 40 N. Ashland Avenue, Chicago,
Ill.

HARPER, Theophilus E. , b. Newberry, S. C. , Oct. 23,
1906; s. J.S. W. and Josephine (Sims) H.; A. B. , Allen
Univ. , Columbia, S. C.; D. D. (hon.), Wilberforce Univ. ,
Daniel Payne Coll. , Monrovia Coll. , W. Africa; m.
Callie (O) Bryant; Children---Theophilus E. Jr. , Brenda
Joyce, Linda Kay; pastor, Cherry St. African Meth.
Episcopal Ch. , Dothan, Ala. 1941-42; St. Paul A. M. E.
Ch. , Birmingham, Ala. , 1942-44; pres. , Daniel Payne
Coll. , Birmingham, Ala. , 1944-48; St. James A. M. E. Ch. ,
Atlanta City, N. J. , 1948-55; St. Matthew A. M. E. Ch. ,
Phila. , Pa. , 1955---; principal, Shiloh Jr. High Sch. ,
Prosperity, S. C. , 1933-36; asst. principal, Dothan Col.
High Sch. , 1941-42; pres. , Daniel Payne Coll. , 1944-48;
pres. , Atlantic City Branch, NAACP, 1951-52; chair-
man, Equal Housing Com. , Phila. , Fellowship Commis-
sion; Mem. , Urban League; Educational Bd. , A. M. E.
Ch. ; Home: 6212 Washington Ave. , Phila. , Pa. ; Office:
59th and Summer St. , Phila. 39, Pa.

*HARRIS, Charles Poindexter, b. Franklinton, N. C. , June
2, 1897; s. Caswell Powell and Elizabeth (Tharrington)
H.; Franklinton Christian Coll. , N. C. , 1914-18; B. D. ,
Howard Univ. , Sch. of Rel. , 1927; courses: Columbia
Univ.; Roanoke Coll.; D. D. , Shaw Univ. , 1946; m.
Mattie Louise Sears; children---Charles Warren; teacher,
Roanoke Institute, Elizabeth City, N. C. , 1921-22; pastor,
First Baptist Church, Warrenton, Va.; teacher, Washing-
ton Baptist Seminary, Wash. , D. C. , 1927-31; pastor, Mt.
Ararat Baptist Church, Rutherford, N. J. , 1931-38; cur-
rent, Calvary Baptist Church, Plainfield, N. J. , 1938---;
pres. , General Baptist Convention of N. J. , 1953-57;
exec. sec. , The Home Mission Board, The National Baptist Convention, USA, Inc. , 1958---; vice pres. , The
New England Baptist Missionary Convention, 1959---;
dean, National Baptist Sunday School and Training Union
Congress, 1947-52; director, Religious Education, 1943-
50; pres. , Plainfield, N. J. , Branch NAACP, 1950-52;
Mayor's Commission on Civil Rights, 1952-59; chairman,
Local Co-Ordinating Committee for Fair Housing, 1950-
51; vice pres. , New England Baptist Missionary Conven-
tion; exec. sec. , Home Mission Board, National Baptist
Convention, USA, 1928; editor: The Home Mission Journal
Home: 1283 East Second St. , Plainfield, N. J. ; Office:
Calvary Baptist Church, 1000 W. 4th St. , Plainfield,
N. J.

HARRIS, Elbert Ferdinand, teacher; b. Harriston, Miss.,
Sept. 26, 1933; s. Alvin E. and Alice (Porte) H.;
Epiphany Coll., Newburgh, N.Y., 1949-53; St. Joseph's
Sem., Wash. D.C., 1954-60; St. Michael's College,
Winooski, Vt., 1956-59; B.A., 1961; Cath. U. of Amer.
Wash., D.C., 1960; Assumption College, Worcester,
Mass., 1961; Sorbonne, Paris, France, 1962; Ordained
priest, Rom. Cath. Ch., 1960; Teacher, Latin, French,
Epiphany Apostolic Coll., Mem., Nat. Fed. of Modern
Lang. Teachers; Office: Epiphany Apostolic College, New-
burgh, New York.

*HARRIS, Henry Benton, b. Bloomfield, N.J., Oct. 17,
1898; s. Pleasant and Lucy (Roberts) H.; B.Th., Shaw
Univ., 1916; A.B., Talladega Coll., 1922; Drew Univ.,
1926; B.D., Howard Univ., Sch. of Rel.; B.D., Andover-
New Sch. of Rel., 1931; M.S.T., Boston Univ., 1938;
graduate studies: Harvard Univ. Divinity School; m. Icilmah
Athrin Thompson; pastor, Shiloh Baptist Church, Hartford,
Conn., 1928-30; Peoples' Baptist Church, Portsmouth,
N.H., 1930-38; Union Baptist Church, New Bedford,
1939-45; Bethlehem Community Church, Holyoke, Mass.
and Second Baptist Church, Greenfield, Mass., 1945-49;
John Street Baptist Church, Worcester, Mass., 1945-
49; Western Ave., Baptist Church, Cambridge, 1949-55;
US Army, 92nd Div., 350 Field Artillery Overseas (France),
1918-19; moderator, Franklin-Millers River (Mass.) Baptist
Ass'n; vice pres., Holyoke (Mass.) Ministers' Ass',; pres.
Worcester (Mass.) Ministers' Ass'n; moderator, Worcester
(Mass.) Baptist Ass'n; Mem., The Advisory Committee
(38 persons) of the City of Worcester, Mass. Planning
Board (appointed by mayor); Clerk of the Worcester
(Mass.) Baptist City Mission Board; Clerk of the Perman-
ent Council of the Worcester (Mass.) Baptist Ass'n;
Corresponding sec., United Baptist Convention of Mass.
and Rhode Island, 1942-52; pres., United Baptist Conven-
tion of Mass. and Rhode Island, 1952-54; counselor and
teacher, Royal Ambassador Boys' Camp, Ocean Park,
Maine, 1944-54; Member of the Finance Committee and
also member of the Board of the New England Baptist
Missionary Convention, 1950; Member of the Board,
Person-Simpson Rest Home, Worcester, Mass.; 1955;
Delegate to Federal Council of Churches, Cleveland, Ohio,
from the Greater Worcester Area Council of Churches;
Student on two occasions to the Town and Country School,
Green Lake, Wis.; Member of the Board, Greater Wor-
cester Area Council of Churches, 1955-56; Member of the

Board, Hampton Ministers' Conference, Hampton Institute,
1954-56; Member of the Institute of Religion, School of
Rel., Howard Univ., Wash., D.C.; delegate , Churchmen's
Seminar, Wash., D.C. (Social Action Committee of the
American Baptist Ass'n), 1955; Home: 168 Western Ave.,
Cambridge 39, Mass.; Office: Western Avenue Baptist
Church, 299 Western Ave., Cambridge.

HARRIS, Marquis Lafayette, bishop; b. Macon Co., Ala.
March 8, 1907; s. William Eugene and Estelle Marie
(Glen); B.S., Clark College, Atlanta, Ga., 1928; B.D.,
Gammon Theological Seminary, 1929; S.T.M., Boston
Univ., 1930; Studies, Phil. of Rel., Howard Univer-
sity, Psychology of Econ., Western Reserve Univ., Ohio;
Ph.D., Ohio State Univ., 1933; Fellow Nat'l College of
Canada, 1940; D.D. (Hon.), Gammon Theological Seminary,
1941; LL.D. (hon.), Southwestern College, 1960; m.
Geneva Magnolia Nelson; children---Ison, Marquis Laf-
ayette, Jr.; Elder, Methodist Ch., 1932; pastor, Colum-
bia and Martins Ferry, Ohio; Elected Bishop of The Meth.
Ch. Atlantic Coast Area, 1960; 7 years-Ex. Sec. Chris-
tian Ed., Lexington Conference; teacher: Clark College,
1927-29; Chaflin College, 1930-31; College dean and prof.,
Samuel Huston College, 1933; pres. and prof., Philander
Smith Coll., 1936-60; mem.: Gen. Board of Ed., Meth.,
Ch.; Gen. Conf. Comm. on Church Union; Member, the
Methodist Ecumenical Conference, Oxford, England, 1951;
Member, the World Methodist Conference, Oslo, Norway,
1961; Accredited delegate, The World Council of Churches,
Evanston, 1954; Member, International Conference on
Church Union, Chicago, 1954; Member, The Gen. Conf.
Committee on Rules, 1952; vice chairman, 1952 General
Cof. Comm. on Education; chairman, The Committee on
Education of the Jurisdictional Conferences of 1952 and
1956; Member, The Board of Trustees of The Methodist
Church; Executive Committee of the General Conf. Comm.
on Advance Projects, 1952-56; Member, The General and
Jurisdictional Conference of The Methodist Church, 1940,
44, 48, 52, 56, 60; Member, Board of Directors of the
Southwest Region of the YMCA, 1939-52; The Mid-Century
Conference on Children and Youth, 1950; Member, the
Arkansas State Conference on Child Welfare and Youth,
1950-54; The Mayor's Committee; Member, The State
Advisory Board of United Nations, Little Rock, Arkansas,
1951-54; The Executive Committee of the Pulaski County,
Arkansas Health Association; Governing Board of the
Council of Social Agencies and Community Chest, 1955-

58; sponsoring comm. of the 1955 South Wide Conference
on Integration in the public schools, elected Man of the
Year in Race Relations by the Urban League of Greater
Little Rock, and presented a certificate of merit on May,
1955; The Advisory Board on Teacher Education for the
State of Arkansas, the Little Rock Methodist Council, Vice
pres. of the Arkansas Council of Churches and founder and
President of the Gulf Coast Inter-collegiate Athletic
Conference, 1955; American Philosophical Association;
Southern Society of Philosophy and Psychology; Southwestern
Philosophical Society; American Mathematics Society; Amer-
ican Academy of Social and Political Science; Alpha Delta
Alpha, Alpha Phi Alpha, Beta Kappa Chi, Alpha Kappa
Mu, Sigma Pi Phi, Mason, Elk; Member, The Board of
Trustees of Atlanta University and the Interdenominational
Theological Seminary Chairman of the Boards of Trustees
Bethune-Cookman College (Fla.), Claflin College (South
Carolina), Clark College, Gammon Theological Seminary
(Georgia); Member, Federal Council of Churches, 1944-51;
Official voting member, National Council of Churches,
successor to the Federal Council of Churches, 1951;
Member (current), The General Board of Directors of
the National Council of Churches; author: Some Concep-
tion of God,   Values in One World,   Voice in the Wil-
derness,   Life Can Be Meaningful. Contributes to
magazines: Together; Central Christian Advocate; Adult
Teacher; The Methodist Story; Adult Student; Home: 250
Aurburn Ave. NE, Atlanta 3, Ga.

HARRIS, Odell Greenleaf, church official; b. Warren County,
N.C., Sept. 3, 1903; s. Robert L. and Susanna (Russell)
H.; A.B., St. Augustine's Coll.; B.D., Payne Divinity
School; Columbia University & Union Theol. Seminary,
A.M.; m. Lizzie Elnora Henderson; children---Odell
Greenleaf, Marion Elizabeth (Mrs. Mervin E. Perry);
rector, All Saint's Church, Warrenton, N.C., 1933-37;
Warden & Professor, Bishop Payne Divinity School,
Petersburg, Va. 1937-48; Archdeacon of Diocese, S.
Virginia, 1946-51; director-chaplain, Fort Valley Coll.
Center, Ft. Valley, Va., 1951-61; Archdeacon of Negro
Work-Diocese of Atlanta, 1956-61; rector, St. Peter's
P.E. Church, Richmond, Va., 1961---; Mem., Diocese
of Southern Va., 3 years; Exec. Committee of Diocese
of S. Va.; Dept. of Christian Education in Third Province;
Alternate to General Convention; pres., Petersburg Recre-
ation Ass'n, Petersburg, Pa. 1959-61; dean, St. Augus-
tine's Conf. on Christian Education, 1950-59; examining

chaplain, Diocese of Atlanta, 1952-56; director of camp
for boys and girls, Diocese of Atlanta, 1952-61; Exec.
Comm. in Diocese of Atlanta, 1958-61; Dept. of Missions
Diocese of Atlanta, 1957-61; Deputy to General Convention,
Diocese of Atlanta, 1958; Alternate to General Convention,
Diocese of Atlanta, 1961; Testimonial of Merit Certificate
Delta Omega Chapter, Omega Psi Phi Fraternity, for out-
standing community service, 1961; Mem., Alpha Phi
Alpha; Mason; Editor, Handbook of Objectives, Methods,
and Plans for Our Work, 1947-56, Protestant Episcopal
Ch.; Home: 1907 N. 23rd St., Richmond, Va.; Office:
1719 N. 22nd and X Sts., Richmond, Va.

HARRIS, Otha Carruthers, b. Norfolk, Virginia, Dec. 19,
1916; s. John Alexander and Julia (West) H.; A.B.,
Johnson C. Smith, 1939; B.B., 1942; M.A., McCormick
Seminary, 1946; M.A., Columbia University; m. Wyndell
Griffin; pastor, Trinity United Presbyterian Ch., Smith-
field, N.C., 1942-45; Mizpah Presbyterian Ch., South
Boston, Va., 1947-50; John Calvin United Presbyn. Ch.,
Petersburg, Va., 1953---; Associate in Religious Activities,
Virginia State College, Petersburg, Va., 1954---; Religious
and Cultural Seminar to Latin America; mem.: Virginia
Council on Human Relations, Parent Teachers Association,
NAACP; Virginia Social Science Assn., Southern Sociologi-
cal Society; Alpha Kappa Delta, National Sociology Honor
Society; author: History of Johnson C. Smith Seminary;
Home: 231 New Petersburg, Virginia; Ch.: Westminster
U. Presbyn. Ch., Petersburg, Virginia.

HARRIS, Robert Lee, b. Asheville, N.C.; s. John and Lessie
(Norris) H.; Southeastern Commercial Coll., Asheville,
N.C., 1950; B.D., New Era Theol. Institute, Phil., Pa.,
1953; Temple Univ., 1963; m. Clara Lee Lindsay; chil-
dren--- Robert, Ophelia, Henrietta, Paul, Gladys, James
Charles, Calvin, Minerva; assoc. pastor-Temple Meth.
Church, Asheville, N.C.; student supply pastor, James
Memorial Meth. Church, Phil., Pa.; current pastor, St.
Thomas Meth. Ch., Phil., Pa.; US Navy Reserve, 1942-
45; Home: 5539 Morton St., Phila. 44, Pa.; Office: 4701
Tackawanna St., Phila. 24, Pa.

HARRIS, William Henry, b. Selma, Ala., June 3, 1922;
s. William and Frances H.; Knox Academy, 1939; Selma
University High School, 1941; Daniel Payne College,
A.B., 1945; B.D., Ruffin Nicholas Theological Seminary,

1950; D. D. , Daniel Payne College, 1954; D. D. , Monrovia
College; m. Bertha King; children--- William Henry, Jr.;
pastor, St. Mary African Methodist Episcopal Church,
Piper, Ala. , 1942-45; Sadlers Chapel A. M. E. Church,
Bessemer, Ala. , 1945-50; Nicholas Temple A. M. E.
Church, Birmingham, Ala. , 1950-59; current pastor,
St. John A. M. E. Church, Montgomery, Ala. , 1959; Or-
dained Itinerant Deacon, 1942; Itinerant Elder, 1944; Mem. ,
A. M. E. Ministerial Alliance; General Board of the A. M.
E. Church; Interdenominational Ministerial Alliance; Legal
Board of Trustees, Daniel Payne Coll. ; Pastoral Council
by appointment; faculty member, Daniel Payne College
High School, 1949-51; Award of Merit for outstanding work
in Religion- Pi Lambda Sigma, 1963; Mem. , Democrat;
Home: 1928 Pearson Ave. , S. W. Birmingham, Ala. ;
Office: 809 Madison Ave. , Montgomery, Ala.

HARRISON, Earl Leonard, b. Alto, Texas, Jan. 23, 1891;
B. Th. , Bishop Coll. Theol. Sch. , 1919; Post-Grad.
studies, Union Theol. Sem. , NYC; D. D. (honorary)
Bishop Coll. , 1936; m. Eula Mae Anderson (dec.); Ella
B. Snell, 1948; 1 son, Earl; 2 daus. , Earline Zane
Sampson (Mrs.), Eulene Kay James (Mrs.); Pastored
rural churches Antioch Bapt. Ch. , Houston, Texas; Shiloh
Bapt. Ch. , Washington, D. C. , 1930---; Chrmn. Bd.
Trustees, Washington Bapt. Sem. , D. C. , 1958---; Pres.
Bapt. Conv. D. C. and Vicinity; Trustee, Butler Coll. ,
Tyler, Texas; Trustee, Bishop College, Dallas, Texas;
Pres. , Bishop Coll. , 1951-52; Republican, Mason; In
Who's Who Religious Leaders of Amer. , 1941-42; Home:
1743 Webster St. , N. W. , Washington, D. C. Church:
1500 9th St. , N. W. , Wash. , D. C.

*HARVEY, Raymond Francis, b. Hempstead, L. I. , New
York, June 20, 1918; s. Martin Luther, Sr. and Rosa
(Monroe) H. ; A. B. , Va. State Coll. , Petersburg, Va. ,
1940; B. D. , Howard Univ. Sch. of Rel. , Wash. , D. C. ,
1943; Courses, Sch. of Theology, Oberlin Coll. , Oberlin,
Ohio, 1943-44; D. D. (hon.), Birmingham Baptist Coll. ,
1964; m. Lillian Holland; children---Lind Kathleen, Paul
Timothy, Peter Charles; acting chaplain, Tuskegee Institute, Ala. , 1944-46, 1949-50; religious director, Interracial group of Southern Coll. Students to Danzig, Poland,
1946; Pastor, Bethesda Baptist Church, Opelika, Ala. ,
1950-54; Greenwood Missionary Baptist Church, Tuskegee
Institute, 1954.---; religious emphasis week speaker:
Florida A. & M. , Tuskegee Institute, Alabama A. & M. ;

Morehouse Coll., Prairie View A. & M.; Arkansas A. &
M.; Va. State Coll.; Miss. Vocational Coll.;visiting
preacher: Appalachian Preaching Mission; Howard Univ.,
Southern Univ., N.C. Coll.; Baptist State Convention of
N.C.; Home: 909 Washington Ave., Tuskegee Institute,
Ala.

HARVEY, Wardelle Green, b. Boonville, Ind., June 12,
s. Elner and Inez Mae (Green) H.; B.Th., Tri-State
Baptist Coll., 1955; D.D. (hon.), Baptist Theological
Center, Houston Tex., 1962; m. Josephine Boling; chil-
dren---Marion Jeanette, Wardelle Green, Jr.; pastor,
First Ebenezer Baptist Ch., Evansville, 1956-62; cur-
rent pastor, Harrison St. Bapt. Ch., Paducah, Ky.,
1962---; pres., Non-Partisan League; Mem., Local
Human Rights Commission; chaplain, Paducah Area Min-
isterial Fellowship; pres., Baptist Ministers Fellowship;
2nd vice moderator, The First District Baptist Conven-
tion of Ky. Baptist; Mason; Mem., publisher, Harrison
Street Messenger (newspaper), official organ of Harrison
Street Baptist Church and Community; Mayor's Advisory
Board, Paducah, Ky. Hone: 1126 Harrison, Paducah, Ky.;
Office: 1124 Harrison, Paducah, Ky.

HATCHER, Eugene Clifford, bishop; b. Eufaula, Ala. Sept.
12, 1902; s. Clarence George and Julia Ann (Watts) H.;
A. &T. Coll., Greensboro, N.C.; A.B., Daniel Payne
Coll.; D.D. (hon.), Payne Univ., 1930; D.D. (hon.),
LL.D. (hon.), Wilberforce Univ.; LL.D., Shorter Coll.;
Flipper Curry Coll., 1944; Morris Brown Coll.; J.U.D.
(hon.), Nasson Coll., Springfield, 1960; m. Oretha Mae
Tillman; children--- Rubye (Mrs. Crawford), Eugene
Clifford, Jr.; pastor, Wayman Chapel, African Methodist
Episcopal Ch., S. Jackson, Jacksonville; South St. African
Methodist Episcopal Ch., Dothan, Ala.; presiding elder,
1930, Fla. & Ozark Dists.; Elected bishop, 1952; Now
presiding bishop 3rd district; professor, Payne Univ. and
Bethel Coll.; Trustee, Daniel Payne Coll.; chairman,
Wilberforce Univ. Trustee Bd.; Mem., Wilberforce
Foundation; National Council of Churches; Phi Beta Sigma
NAACP; pres., General Bd. of Education (A.M.E.),
World Methodist Council; One of the chief celebrants
community services, Oslo, Norway, 1961 World Meth.
Conf.; Mem., Elks; Mason; editor: Southern Christian
Recorder, 1940-48; author: What We Saw, Heard and Ac-
complished In West Africa; Home: 110009 Wade Park,
Cleveland 6, Ohio.

HAWKINS, Alexander Amos, social worker; Gainesville,
Fla., Sept. 3, 1923; s. George Washington and Pearl
Williams; Cookman Coll., Bethune, 1942-44; Associates
of Arts, Morehouse Coll., 1944-46; B.A., Univ. of
Pittsburgh-Law School, 1946-47; Master of Social Work,
1949; Post-graudate courses: School of Social Work,
1953---; m. Mable Teola Emanuel; children--- Alexander,
A., Jr., Clinton M.; Public Assistance Case Worker,
1949-50; American Red Cross Caseworker, 1951-53; Va.
Hospital, Pittsburgh Psychiatric Social Worker, 1954-60;
Supervisor Correctional Services-Salvation Army, Pgh.,
1960-62; Director Social Service-Dept. of Justice-Bureau
of Correction-Central Office, 1962---; asst. pastor,
Brown Chapel African Methodist Episcopal Ch., Pitts-
burgh, 1955-56; asst. pastor, Calvary A.M.E. Church,
Braddock, Pa., 1956; Interim pastor, Bethel A.M.E.
Church, Greensburg, Pa., 1956-57; pastor, Quinn Chapel,
A.M.E. Church, Elizabeth, Pa., 1957-60; asst. pastor,
Bethel A.M.E. Church, Pittsburgh; pastor, Bethel A.M.
E. Church, Monroeville, Pa., 1960---; field instructor,
Univ. of Pittsburgh Social Work, 1960---; Adult Educa-
tion-Dept. of Public Instruction-Evening Correctional In-
service Training Program, 1960---; Mem., United Negro
College, Fund; sec.-treas., Pittsburgh Univ. Social Work
Alumni Ass'n; Past secy., Psychiatric Social Work Assn-
Pittsburgh; US Army, 1942-43; Mem., NAACP; National
Ass'n of Social Workers; Academy of Certified Social
Workers; National Conf. of Crime & Delinquency; Middle
Atlantic States Conf. on Correction; Pa. Ass'n on Proba-
tion, Parole and Correction; author of article: "Casework
in Corrections" The Quarterly; presently writing book,
"Principles & Practice of Social Work in the Bureau of
Correction;" Home: 253 Travella Blvd., Pittsburgh, Pa.,
15235; Office: Bethel A.M.E. Church, Box 365, Wilmerd-
ing, Pa.

HAWKINS, Elder Garnett, b. NYC, June 13, 1908; s. Albert
and Annie (Lee) H.; B.A., Bloomfield Coll., 1935; D.D.
(hon.), 1938; B.D., Union Theol. Sem., N.Y.C., 1960;
m. Thelma Burnett; children---Renee, Ellen; Ordained
to ministry, Presbyterian Ch., 1938; present pastor and
founder, St. Augustine Presbyn. Ch., N.Y.; moderator,
Presbytery, N.Y., 1958-60; vice moderator, Gen. Assembly United Presbyterian Church, U.S.A., 1960-61;
moderator, 1964; Mem., Bd. of Christian Education,
1959---; Bd. of Directors, National Big Bros. Am.,
Bronx Mental Hygiene Assn; pres., Bd. of Forest House,

Bronx; Advisory Com., Bronx Community Coll.; Awards:
American War Mothers; National Council Negro Women;
National Urban League; Bronx Borough President's Office;
Home: 834 E. 165th St., N.Y.C. 59; Office: St. Augus-
tine Presbyterian Ch., Prospect Ave., 165th St., Bronx 59,
N.Y.

HAWKINS, Reginald Armistice, dentist, b. Beaufort, N.C.,
Nov., 11, 1923; s. Charles C. and Lorena (Smith); B.S.,
Johnson C. Smith Univ., 1941-44; D.D.S., Howard Univ.,
1944-48; B.D., Johnson C. Smith Univ., 1953-56; LL.D.,
Johnson C. Smith Univ., 1962; m. Catherine Elizabeth
Richardson; children--- Paulette Charlene, Reginald
Armistice, Jr., Wayne Beauregard, Lorena Bernice;
Practicing dentist, 1948- ; captain in US Army Dental
Corps, 1951-53; pastor United Presbyterian Church, USA
(Minister at large of Catawba Presbytery) 1956---; mem.
Bd. of Mecklenburg County Tuberculosis and Health Assoc.,
Bd. of Charlotte-Mecklenburg Youth Council; Board of
Mecklenburg Men's Democratic Club, chrm. Democrat
Precinct #25; Executive Comm. of Bd. of Trustees of
N.C. College at Durham; Good Neighbor Comm. of
N.C.; captain, US Army Dental Corps, Korean Conflict,
1951-53; Decorations: 1961 Dentist-of-the-Year of Old
North State Dental Society (N.C.); 1962 Dentist-of-the-
Year of National Dental Society; Received Honorary Doctor
of Laws Degree from Johnson C. Smith University in
1962. mem.: Old North State Dental Society, National
Dental Society, Executive Committee of local Democratic
Men's Organization; Chairman of Mecklenburg Organiza-
tion on Political Affairs; United Presbyterian Church,
USA; NAACP; Kappa Alpha Psi Fraternity; author: "Status
of Negro Doctors in Municipal Hospitals," Featured in
feature article of Charlotte Observer, May 4, 1962;
Featured in feature article of Washington Post, November
1962; Featured in Howard University Journal, April 1963;
Interview on national CBS and ABC network feature on
civil rights; Interview on Radio Free Europe feature on
civil rights; Home: 1703 Madison Avenue, Charlotte, N.
C.; Office: 1218 Beatties Ford Road, Charlotte, 28208.

HAWKINS, Zachariah, teacher; b. Salisbury, N.C., Aug.
10, 1923; s. Wm. A. and Lou W. (Pogue) H.; B.S.,
Johnson C. Smith Univ., 1946; B.D., 1949; M.A., North
Carolina College at Durham, 1955; Post Graduate Work
at New York University and Rutgers Univ.; pastor Mebane
Second Presby. Ch., Nebane, N.C., 1949-55; Scott El-

liott Memorial Presby. Ch., Graham, N.C.; teacher Pub-
lic Schools, New Jersey, 1955-59; Public Schools, N.Y.,
1959-   ; mem. NAACP; Civic Assoc. of Wyandanch,
Long Island, N.Y.; Mem.: Omega Psi Phi Fraternity;
New York State Teachers Assoc.; Home: 804 Mount Avenue,
Wyandanch, Long Island, N.Y.

HAYES, Joshua William, b. Alabama, Aug. 2, 1905; s.
Joshu and Florence E.; A.B., Livingstone College, 1944;
m. Josephine Moore; 1 dau., Josephine Moore; pastor,
Trinity African Methodist Episcopal Zion Church, Birmingham, Alabama; One of the organizers of the Montgomery Improvement Association; Pres., Ensley Voter
League; Men., Christian Movement for Human Rights;
Democratic Preachers Party, Birmingham, Ala.; Active
in 1963 Birmingham demonstrations; Home: 1810 19th
St., Birmingham, Alabama; Office: 1800 19th St., Birmingham, Alabama.

HAYES, William A., b. Tuscumbia, Ala., June 15, 1928;
s. William and Estella (Coleman) H.; A.B., Indiana Central Coll., 1950; B.D., Colgate Rochester Divinity,
1953; co-pastor, Oak St. Christian Parish, New Haven,
Conn., 1954-55; asst. pastor, St. Albans Cong. Ch.,
1955-56; pastor, Lloyd's Memorial United Ch. of Christ,
Buffalo, N.Y., 1956---; Home: 31 Marine Drive Apt 5-H.
Buffalo 2, N.Y.

HAYGOOD, Lawrence Franklin, college prof.; b. Coffee
Springs, Ala., March 29, 1933; s. Roy W. and Venetta
(Tyrus) H.; Stillman College, Tuscaloosa, Ala., 1951-
55, B.A.; B.D., Union Theological Seminary, Richmond,
Va.; m. Bennie S. Taylor; children---Lawrence F., Jr.,
Rouetta, Jocasta, Chiquita Anastasia; pastor, Covenant
Presbyterian Ch., Norfolk, Va., 1959-62; present pastor,
Parkway Gardens Presbyterian Ch., Memphis, Tenn.,
1962---; instructor, The Dept. of English at the Norfolk
Division of Virginia State College, Norfolk, Va., 1961-
62; Mem., Health and Welfare Planning Commission for
Memphis & Shelby County; Mem., Memphis Committee
on Community Relations; Church Work Chairman of
Memphis Branch NAACP; Stillman College Alumni As-
sociation; Home: 1253 Worthington, Memphis, Tenn.;
Office: 1683 S. Parkway, E., Memphis, Tenn.

*HAYLING, Mapson Forkau, b. Grenada, West Ind., June
12, 1877; s. George and Rosetta H.; B.D., Howard Univ.

Sch. of Rel. 1912; children--- Mapson, Jr.; pastor, The
Methodist Church, 1911-50; Retired, 1950; current, vice
pres., Ministorium, Verona, Pa.; Mem., Mason; Home:
505 Church St., Verona, Pa.

HAYNES, Roosevelt, b. Summer County, Tennessee, Feb.
17, 1933; s. Henry Grant and Maude (Macmurry) H.;
A.B., Stillman College, 1959; B.D., Louisville Pres-
byterian Theological Seminary, 1962; m. La Pearl
Hamilton; children---Terrence De Wayne; student pastor,
Good Hope Presbyterian Church, 1957-59; Cecilia Pres-
byterian Church, 1959-61; student pastor at Bowling
Green, Kentucky; asst. pastor, Grace Presbyterian
Church, Louisville, Ky., 1961-62; pastor, Washington
St. Presbyterian Church of Dublin, Ga., 1962---; US
Army, 1953-55; National Defense Service Medal, United
Nations Service Medal, Korean Service Medal, Good Con-
duct Medal; Mem., Democrat; Home: 112 Carter St.,
Dublin, Georgia; Office: 975 S. Washington, Dublin,
Georgia.

HEACOCK, Roland Tilman, b. New Milford, Conn., Dec.
30, 1893; s. Stephen and Mary (Gregory) H.; B.A.,
Howard Univ., 1921; B.D., Yale Univ. Divinity Sch.,
1924; S.T.M., Boston Univ., 1925; D.D. (hon.), Amer.
International Coll., Springfield, Mass., 1951; m. Lucille
LaCour; children--- Don R., Mrs. Marshal Layton,
Mrs. Jean Musson; Ordained Congregational minister,
1924; pastor, Lincoln Congregational Ch., Brockton,
Mass., 1924-26; assoc. pastor, St. John's Congregational
Ch., Springfield, Mass., 1926-29; pastor, Community
Congr'l Ch., Phila., Pa., 1929-31; St. John's Congr'l
Ch., Springfield, Mass., 1931-45; pastor ad interim,
Stafford Springs Congr'l Ch., Stafford Springs, Conn.,
1948-49; pastor, Staffordville Congr'l Ch., Staffordville,
Conn., 1950-59; retired, 1959; National Conference of
Christians and Jews in Tulsa, Okla.; US Army, World
War I, 1917-18; chaplain, American Legion Post, Staf-
ford Springs, Conn., 1947-49; chaplain (captain), World
War II, 1942-45; citation by the Chicago Defender for
advance race relations in the past year; author of
articles in the religious press on race relations; chairman, Social Action Committee; Committee on the Ministry; pres., Springfield Congr'l Union, Springfield, Mass.;
director, Bd. of the Springfield Goodwill Industries;
arbitrator on a labor-management dispute; Mem., Jewish
Lecture Bureau on Race Relations; Mem., Alpha Chapter,

Omega Psi Phi, Howard Univ., 1920; Home: Hydeville
Rd., Stafford, Conn.

HEDGLEY, David Rice, b. Mobile, Ala., Apr. 22, 1907;
s. Noah M. and Pauline (Rice) H.; A.B., Va. Union
Univ., 1931; A.M., Univ. of Chicago, 1935; B.D.,
Northern Bapt. Theol. Sem., 1945; D.D. (hon.), Shaw
Univ., 1953, Va. Union Univ., 1955; m. Christine Kelly;
children---David, Jr., Christine Lunah; chaplain, Fla.
A. & M. Coll., 1936-44; pastor, First Baptist Ch.,
Winston-Salem, 1944---; moderator, Rowan Bapt. Ass'n,
1958-62; pres., Missionary & Educational Union; pres.,
Ministers Ass'n; Mem., Urban League Exec. Committee,
1957---; Mayor's Goodwill Committee, 1964; Mason;
Phi Beta Sigma; Democrat; Home: 901 13th NE, Winston-
Salem, N.C.; Office: 912 7th NE, Winston-Salem, N.C.

HENDERSON, James Franklin, Sr., b. Blackstock, S.C.,
Dec. 31, 1912; s. John Loyd and Carrie (Carylon) H.;
A.B., Allen Univ., 1933; B.D., Johnson C. Smith Univ.,
1936; D.D. (hon.), Johnson C. Smith Univ., 1958; Post-
graduate Work-Auburn Seminary in association with Union
Seminary (Columbia Univ. N.Y.) ; m. Frank Mildred Sim-
mons; James Franklin, Jr.; pastor Zion Presbyterian
Church, Charleston, S.C.; Allison United Presbyterian
Church, Little Rock, Ark.; pres. Ministers' Union,
Charleston, S.C. and Greater Little Rock Ministers'
Alliance of Little Rock, Ark.; vi. moderator The Okla-
homa-Arkansas United Presbyterian Synod; Served on Jury
First Division of Circuit Court of Pulaski County. As-
sociate Professor of Religion and Sociology at Philander
Smith College and Arkansas Baptist College; (current)
pastor Allison Memorial Presby. Ch., Little Rock, Ark.;
mem.; Mayor of Little Rock's Interracial Comm. Arkansas
Valley Presbytery; chrm. Interracial Ministerial Alliance
Comm. on Community and World Affairs; Advisory Bd.
Nat. Urban League; Florence Crittenton Home; Dir.
Canadian Summer Conference for Westminster Fellowship;
vi. pres. Quapaw Area, Boy Scouts of Amer.; Ad. Comm.
Presby. Men's Forum of Canadian Synod; moderator
Canadian Synod and White River Presbytery; Community
War Chest Campaign of Little Rock Merit Award, 1944;
author: The Way to Walk and The Light To Follow,   A
Report on Racial and Cultural Relations , A History of
The Negro in Zion Presbyterian Church. Home: 1620 W.
21st St., Little Rock, Arkansas; Church: 901 Gaines St.,
Little Rock, Arkansas.

HENDERSON, Jefferson Winston, b. Kansas City, Kansas,
Sept. 29, 1915; s. Roscoe C. and Ethel H.; B.A.,
Indiana Central Coll.; B.D., Payne Theol. Sem.; m.
Frances Marie Harris; children---Gloria (Mrs. Robert
Alford), Sylvia, Jefferson, Jr.; pastor, African Methodist
Episcopal Churches, Nashville, Tenn., 1942; Urbana,
Ohio, 1944; Pittsburgh, Pa., 1947; current, Cincinnati,
Ohio (Brown Chapel A. M. E. Church); draftsman, General
Electric Evansdale, 1951-53; Psychiatric Social Worker
(Univ. Pittsburgh); former pres., NAACP, Urbana, Ohio;
candidate for City Council, Cincinnati, Ohio, 1961;
Democrat; RCIN- Radio-Outstanding Cincinnati Citizen;
Mem., Mason; pres., A. M. E. Ministerial Alliance;
Home: 1711 Crane, Cincinnati 7, Ohio; Office: 2804 Alms
Peace, Cincinnati 6, Ohio.

HENDERSON, Lewis Duke, principal; b. Dallas, Texas,
June 2, 1924; s. Eddie and Francis (Hubbard) H.; B.A.,
Oakwood Coll., 1950; M.A., Texas Southern, 1953;
Hon. D.D., Union Baptist Theological Seminary, Houston,
Texas, 1955; m. Earnest M. Boss; children---Lewis, Jr.,
Carolyn Elaine, Ann Laverne, Lynda K.; Began ministry
in Forth Worth, Texas, 1950-51; teacher and pastor,
Seventh Day Adventist Church, Houston, Texas, 1951-55;
pastored; Lake Charles, La., 1955-62; present: pastor
and principal of school, Shreveport, La. U.S. Army Med-
ical Core, 1942-1944. Home: 1960 Anna Street, Shreveport, La. Office: 1143 Madison St., Shreveport, La.

HENRY, Vincent DePaul, teacher, librarian; b. Charleston, S. C.
Sept. 2, 1931; s. Freeman and Estelle (DeVeaux) H.;
St. Francis Seminary, 1949-51; Assumption Seminary,
1952-54; St. Anthony-on-Hudson Seminary, 1954-57;
S. T. L., Cath. Univ. of Amer., 1957-58; B. Mus., B.
Sac. Mus., Manhattanville College - Pius X School of
Liturgical Music; Res. Chap., Manhattanville College,
1958-59; Student, Manhattanville, 1958-60; St. John's
Grad. Sch. of Library Science, 1960-62; Teacher, Li-
brarian, Organist, St. Francis Sem. Staten Island, N. Y.
1960---; Dir., St. Louis Fraternity, Third Order of St.
Francis, Staten Island, N. Y.; Mem, Nat. Cath. Music
Educators Assoc.; Cath. Library Assoc.; Home and Of-
fice: St. Francis Seminary, Todt Hill Rd., Staten Island
14, New York.

HERRON, Vernon Mack, b. Charlotte, N. C., Oct. 7, 1928;
s. Samuel and Mamie (McPherson) H.; A. B., Shaw Univ.;

B. D., Johnson C. Smith Univ.; further study; Pittsburgh-
Xenia Graduate School; m. Louise Christine Oliphant; chil-
dren---Vernease Marcelinia; Leila McPherson; Frenshetta
Louise; pastor, First Baptist Church, Dallas, N. C., 1952-
55; Friendship Baptist Church, Pittsburgh, Pa., 1957-62;
prison chaplain, State Penitentiary, 1961---; Joliet, Ill.;
Trustee, Woodville State Mental Hospital, 1961; Mem.,
Alpha Phi Alpha; Home: 156 S. Joliet St. Joliet, Ill.

HEWLETT, Everett Augustus, Sr., b. Virginia; s. Augustus
and Adelaide (Sykes); A. B., Lincoln Univ., Chester County,
Penn., 1935-39; S. T. B., Lincoln Seminary, 1939-41; m.
Mary Still; children---Everett A. Jr.; Deborah A.;
Michelle K.; pastor First Presbyterian Ch., Richmond,
1941-43; US Army chaplain, 1943-46; South Pacific Board
of National Missions, Presbyterian Church, 1947; N. Y. C.
Sargent Memorial United Presby. Ch., U. S. A., 1948- ;
June, 1965 - Elected men., Dist. of Columbia, Bd. of
Education; 3rd vice pres., D. C. Citizens Council; vice
chmn, Washington, D. C. Presbyterian Com. on Race;
Mem., Nat. Capitol Area Presbyterian Council, Presbyn.
Interracial Council; Home: 4300 Ord St. NE, Washington,
D. C.; Church: Grant St. at 51st NE, Washington, D. C.

HICKMAN, Ernest Lawrence, bishop; b. Fayetteville, Tenn.,
June 8, 1903; s. Edgar and Lilla Ann (Brown) H.; B. D.,
Turner Coll., 1928; D. D. (hon.), Payne Theol. Sem.;
Shorter Coll., both in 1953; LL. D., Wilberforce Univ.,
1956; m. Cleopatra Watkins; children--- Bertha, Othella
(Mrs. Leroy Green); pastor, African Methodist Episcopal
Churches, Cleveland, Chattanooga, Memphis, Knoxville,
Fayetteville, Tenn.; presiding elder; Elected bishop, 1956;
Now presiding 13th Dist., A. M. E. Ch.; Mem., Civilian
Defense Council Chattanooga; Chattanooga Interracial Com.;
Nat. Fraternal Council of Negro Churches; Southern Re-
corder Bd., A. M. E. Ch.; vice pres., Pension Bd., A.
M. E. Ch.; vice pres., Bd. of Payne Theol. Sem.; Mem.,
Mason; NAACP; Urban League; Council of Churches;
YMCA; Mayor's Com., Louisville; Office: 451 Halden
Drive, S. W., Atlanta 11, Ga.

HICKS, Jessie May, evangelist; b. Grapeland, Texas, Sept.
28, 1915; s. James B. and Jeola H.; Mary Allen Jr. Coll.,
Crockett, Tex.; B. S., Tillotson Coll., Austin, Tex.;
B. D., Howard Univ. Sch. of Rel.; currently evangelist
National Bapt. Conv. of America; teacher, Sunday Sch.,
Zion Star Bapt. Ch., San Antonio; Mem., NAACP; Bd.

of Directors, Ella Orphanage Home; organizer and pres.,
San Antonio Bapt. Missionary Council; pres., Texas
Beauty Culturist League; vice pres., National Beauty
Culturist League; organizer and pres., San Antonio
Beauticians; founder and instructor, The Hicks Beauty
School; statistician, The Senior Auxiliary of the National
Bapt. Convention of America; Travels extensively, made
two trips to Liberia, Africa to secure deeds to 1000 acres
of land for the National Bapt. Conv. of America to do
mission and educational work; 1964 guest speaker, Jamaica
(National Bapt. Conv.); Toured the Holy Lands, 1956;
awards: Woman of the Year, Zeta Phi Beta Sorority;
Citation by Tillotson College; Awarded an honorary degree,
the Union Bapt. Sem., Houston, Tex.; Citation by the business Dept. of Tex. Teacher Assn; a community award by
San Antonio Chamber of Commerce for outstanding work;
a trophy by San Antonio Chamber of Commerce for outstanding business and religious personality; Home: 802
Dekota, San Antonio 3, Texas; Office: 922 New Branufels
Ave., San Antonio, Texas.

HICKS, John Josephus, b. Bronwood, Ga., Feb. 13, 1915;
s. Noble and Julia Mae Dasher; A.B., Paine Coll.,
Augusta, Ga., 1938; B.D., Gammon Theol. Sem., Atlanta
Ga., 1941; Th.M., Univ. of Southern Calif., 1944; D.
D. (hon.), Gammon Theol. Sem., 1956; m. Pollie Bledsoe;
children--- John, Jr., Eldon, Raiford, Paula, Emma;
Pastor, Barnesville Methodist Church, Ga., 1940-41; St.
Johns Meth. Ch., Los Angeles, Calif., 1941-55; Union
Memorial Meth. Ch., 1955---; prof., Reid Coll. of
Religion, 1952-54; pres., St. Louis Board of Education;
Mem., Bd. of Directors, Page Park; YMCA; awards:
Nat'l Ass'n of Coll. Women, 1962; Man of the Year 1959;
Ass'n of Colored Womens Clubs, 1964; Public Service
Award, St. Louis Argus; Mem., Phi Beta Sigma; Frontiers
of America International; Chi Alpha Fraternity; Home:
4160 Enright St., St. Louis 8, Mo.; Office: St. Mark's
Methodist Church, 49 Edge Comb Ave., New York City,
N.Y.

HICKS, Richard Louis, Jr., b. Alexandria, Louisiana; s.
Richard Louis, Sr. and Agnes (Moses) H.; B.A., Florida
A & M University, Tallahassee, Fla., 1949; M.A.,
Western Reserve Univ., Cleveland, Ohio, 1952; B.D.,
The Divinity School of Kenyon College (Bexley Hall),
1956; m. Pearly Mae Wilson; children---Cynthia Delores,
Patricia Agenes, William Joseph, Richard Lami; Instruc-
tor of Dramatics, Fla. A & M Univ., 1949-53; curate,

St. Andrew's Episcopal Church, 1956; chaplain, Cuttington
College & Divinity School, 1957-60; rector, Trinity Pro-
Cathedral, 1957-60; chaplain A & T and Bennett and
Priest-in-Charge, Church of the Redeemer, Greensboro,
N.C., 1960---; Chairman, Greensboro Ministers Forum,
1962---; Recording sec., Greater Greensboro Ministers
Fellowship; Member, Mayor's Special Bi-Racial Com-
mittee, 1962; Chairman, Greensboro Citizens Co-ordinating
Committee, 1962-; U.S Army, 1942-48; awards: Knight
Commander; Order of African Redemption (Liberian Govern-
ment); Member: Institute of Pastoral Care, Academy of
Religion and Health, Episcopal Overseas Missionary So-
ciety, Episcopal Society for College Work, NAACP; Omega
Psi Phi Fraternity; Article: Liberia: Land of Change;
Home: 1605 Lansdown Ave., Greensboro, North Carolina;
Office: 901 East Market Street, Greensboro, North Car-
olina.

HILDEBRAND, Richard Allen, b. Winsboro, S.C., Feb. 1,
1916; A.B., Allen Univ., 1938; B.D., Wilberforce Univ.,
1941; S.T.M., Boston Univ., 1948; D.D. (hon.), Wilberforce Univ., 1951; m. Anna B. Lewis; children---Camille;
pastor, in S.C., Jonestown and Akron, Ohio, Providence,
Rhode Island, New York, Wilmington, Delaware; current
pastor, Bethel African Methodist Episcopal Church, 1954--;
1st Negro pres., Manhattan Division of Protestant Council
of New York; pres., NAACP (N.Y.C.); Mem., Alpha Phi
Alpha; Mason; Home: 52 West 132nd St., New York, N.Y.
10037; Office: 54-60 West 132nd St., New York, N.Y.
10037.

HILL, Daniel Graxton, sem. dean, prof.,; b. Annapolis, Md.,
May 26, 1896; s. Daniel G., Sr. and Margaret (Peck) H.;
B.A., Lincoln Univ., Pa., 1917; B.D., Iliff Sch. of
Theology, Denver, Colo., 1928; social work, Univ. of
Oregon, 1930; M.A., 1932; S.T.M., Pacific School of
Religion, 1935; Th.D., Iliff School of Theology, 1946; D.
D. (hon.), Lincoln Univ., 1963; m. May Louise Edwards;
children---Jeanne M. (Mrs. Sidney Flateau), Margaret T.
(Mrs. Harry I. Martin), Daniel E., III, Doris M. (Mrs.
Salter Cochran); pastor, African Methodist Churches, Mo.
Colo., Oregon, Calif., 1921-45; Mem. faculty, School of
Religion, Howard Univ.; dean, Chapel, Howard Univ.,
1945-57; dean, School of Rel., Howard Univ. 1958-64;
pastor, Washington Conference Meth. Ch., 1950---;
teacher, Berean School, Phila., Pa., 1919-20; teacher,
History and Ethics, Western Univ., Kansas City, Kansas,

1923-24; probation officer, Court of Domestic Relations,
Portland, Oregon, 1930-33; case aide and supervisor,
State Relief Adm., Oakland, Calif., 1936-40; US Army,
1917-19, 2nd Lt.; Mem., Academy, Political and Social
Science; Nat'l Ass'n of Coll. and Univ. Chaplain; Alpha
Phi Alpha; editor, Well Springs of Life, book of chapel
sermons; contributor: Best Sermons, 1947; Article on
African Methodist Episcopal Church in the Encyclopedia
Americana, 1951; Home: 2946 Chain Bridge Rd. NW, Wash.
16, D.C.; Office: Howard Univ. Sch. of Religion, Wash-
ington 1, D.C.

HILL, Robert Arlander, church official; b. Sturgis, Ky.,
Aug. 16, 1913; s. Henry H. and Rebecca (Fortson) H.;
Evansville Coll., 1952; Tri-State Baptist Bible Coll.,
Evansville, Ind., 1955; m. Minnie Mary Dunlap; children--
Herman, George Sherman; pres., Central Dist. Ass'n,
Ind., 1957-64; pres., Mt. Olive State Sunday School & B.
T.U. Congress of Ind., 1956-64; financial sec., National
Baptist Song Leaders Convention, 1960---; pastor, Second
Baptist Church, Vincennes, Ind., 1954-64; current pastor,
Seventh St. Baptist Ch., 1964; Mem., Citizens Participa-
tion Committee & Special Committee, Minority Group
Housing, Vincennes, Ind., 1963---; Bd. of Chaplains,
Knox County Ministerial Alliance; Good Samaritan Hospital
Vincennes, Ind., 1962-63; Home: 903 Clark St., Paducah,
Ky.; Office: 504 South 7th Paducah, Ky.

HOARD, Samuel Lawrence, b. St. Louis, Missouri, April
16, 1927; s. Robert Lee, Sr. and Leah Belle (Brown) H.;
Concordia Junior Preparatory College, Ft. Wayne, Indiana;
Concordia Theol. Seminary, 1959; missionary, Atlantic
District, The Lutheran Church-Missouri Synod, 1957-58;
asst. pastor, Lutheran Church of St. John the Evangelist,
Brooklyn, N.Y., 1958-60; associate pastor, The Lutheran
Church of Our Savior, Brooklyn, N.Y., 1960---; Service
in Civil Defense Chaplain; Service in US Marine Corps;
currently, 1st Lt., US Army Reserve; Home: 190-06 117th
Rd., St. Albans 12, L.I., N.Y.; Office: 21 Covert St.,
Brooklyn 7, N.Y.

HODGES, Sloan Stanley, b. Hodges, S.C., May 15, 1913;
s. George and Malissa (Vaughns) H.; B.Th., Amer. Bap-
tist Theol. Sem., Nashville, Tenn., 1948; m. Martha
Ruth Treece; Licensed to preach in St. John Baptist
Church, Miami, Fla., 1939; Ordained at Sylvan St. Baptist
Ch., Nashville, Tenn., 1942; asst. pastor, Hartford Ave.

Baptist Ch., Detroit, Mich., 1940-44; First Bapt. Ch.,
Toronto, Canada, 1944-46; pastor, Thankful Baptist Ch.,
Johnson City, Tenn., 1946-50; current, Pilgrim Bapt.
Ch., Hamilton, Ohio, 1950---; relocation supervisor,
Hamilton Urban Renewal Agency, 1958-61; Trustee of
Fort Hamilton Hospital, Hamilton, Ohio, 1953---; pres.,
Second Ward Community Center Bd., 1960 and presently
a member of the Board; Mem., Goodwill Industry Advisory
Board of Hamilton, Ohio; The Mayor's Friendly Relations
Comm.; Home: 1028 S. Second St., Hamilton, Ohio,
45011; Office: 337 Chestnut St., Hamilton, Ohio 45011.

HOGGARD, Dennie W., b. Bertie County, N.C., June 5,
1897; s. Morgan and Alice (Rainer) H.; Roanoke Collegiate
Institute, Elizabeth City, N.C.; Moody Bible School; D.D.
(hon.), Va. Seminary, Lynchburg, Va.; m. Isabel E.
Ricks; children---Dennie W., Jr., Olga Elizabeth, Phyllis
Yolards, Watson; pastor, Calvary Baptist Ch., Plainfield,
N.J., 10 1/2 years; current pastor, Mt. Carmel Baptist
Ch., Phila., Pa., 30 years; former mem., States Legis-
lature for four terms, 8 years; chairman, Foreign Mis-
sion Bd., National Bapt. Convention, USA, Inc.; Mem.,
NAACP; Home: 558 North 58th St., Phila. 31, Pa.; Of-
fice: 5732-34 Pace St., Phila. 39, Pa.

HOLLOMAN, John Lawrence Sullivan, educator; b. Powells-
ville, N.C., Apr. 24, 1885; s. Turner and Amy (Free-
man) H.; A.B., Union Univ., Richmond, Va.; M.A.
Frelinghuysen Univ., Wash. D.C.; Pastorates, Hertford,
Bertie, and Northampton Cos., N.C.; Second Baptist
Church, Washington, D.C., 1917 to present. m. Rosa
Victoria Jones; 4 daus., Carolyn H. Troupe, Jessie H.
Jackson, Dr. Marjorie H. Parker, Miss Grace F., 1
son, Dr. J.L.S. Holloman, Jr.; Mem. four Bapt. World
Alliance congresses, Toronto 1928, Atlanta 1939, Cleve-
land 1950, London, Eng., 1955. Instr. Waters Normal
Institute, 1910-1917; Dean, Washington Baptist Seminary,
Wash. D.C. Home: 403 P St., N.W., Wash. D.C. Office:
816 3rd St., N.W., Wash. D.C.

HOLMES, Jacob Arthur, b. Georgetown, S.C., Oct. 20,
1921; s. Saul and Mary; A.B., Allen University, Columbia, S.C., 1945; B.D., Payne Theological Seminary,
Wilberforce Univ.; D.D. (honorary), Allen Univ.; m.
Edith Reynolds; children--- Edith Arthuretta, J. Arthur,
Jr.; pastor, Bethel, A.M.E. Church, 1948-49; asst.
pastor, Greater Trinity and White Hall Mission, Spartan-

burg, S.C., 1949-50; Presiding Elder of the Columbia
District of Columbia Conference, 1950-51; pastor,
Bethel A.M.E. Church, Columbia, S.C., 1951---;
prof., Religion, Allen University, Columbia, S.C.; teacher
Public Schools, S.C.; Mem., Exec. Bd., Allen Univ.;
Mem., Bi-Racial Committee of City Hall, Columbia, S.C.;
pres., The Interdenominational Ministers Alliance; Mem.,
State Hospital Board; Mem., Trustee of Allen Univ.,
Mem., Alpha Phi Alpha; Mason; Home: 2507 Waites Road,
Columbia, S.C.; Office: 1528 Sumter St., Columbia, S.C.

HOLMES, Willie Lawnsie, coll. pres.; b. Ealnor, Ala.,
Apr. 13, 1913; s. Joe and Elizabeth (Lewis); A.B., Univ.
of Louisville, 1950; B.D., Th.M., Southern Baptist Seminary, 1954, 1957; D.D. (hon.), Simmons Univ., 1959;
Cincinnati Theol. Sem., 1962; m. Annie Beatrice Woods;
pastor, First Baptist Eminence Ch., Eminence, Ky.,
1951-56; pres., Simmons Univ., Louisville, Ky., 1956---;
instructor, Simmons Univ., 1954---; Religious Advisory
Bd., Jefferson County Jail, Louisville, 1958---; chairman,
Bd. of Dir., Louisville Area Health Center; Counseling
Staff member, Jefferson County Jail, 1956---; Mem.,
Planned Parenthood Advisory Bd., 1961---; US Forces,
1943-45; Home: 900 South 42nd Louisville 11, Ky.; Office:
1811 Dumesnil St., Louisville, Ky. 40210

HOLMES, Zan Wesley, Jr., b. San Angelo, Texas, Feb. 2,
1935; s. Zan Wesley and Blakely Naomi H.; A.B., Huston-
Tillotson Coll., Austin, Tex., 1956; B.D., Perkins School
of Theology, Southern Meth. Univ., Dallas, Tex.; S.T.M.;
m. Dorothy Burse; pastor, Hamilton Park Meth. Church,
Dallas, Tex., 1958---; treasurer, Dallas Pastors Ass'n;
chairman, Conference Committee on Ministerial Recruitment; chairman, Conference "Our Mission Study" Study;
Mem., Board of Carnation Charity Home: Dallas Traffic
Commission; Dallas Chapter of American Red Cross;
Alpha Phi Alpha; Democrat; Dallas Pastors Ass'n;Methodist
Ministers Fellowship; Interdenominational Ministers Alliance, Dallas; Home: 8418 Bunche, Dallas 31, Tex.; Office:
11881 Schroeder, Dallas 31, Tex.

HOOD, Robert E., author; b. Louisville, Kentucky, Feb.29,
1936; s. G.R. and B. (Tubbs) H.; A.B., Ohio Wesleyan
Univ., 1957; Union Theological Seminary, 1957-59; S.T.
B., General Theol. Seminary, 1960; Oxford University,
England, 1962-63; asst. pastor, St. Philip's Church, New
York City, 1960-62; asst. pastor, Chapel of the Interces-

sion, Trinity Parish, New York City, 1962--; Mem.;
Society for Biblical Exegesis; Episcopal Society for Cultur-
al and Racial Unity; Beta Sigma Tau Fraternity; Omicron
Delta Kappa; Phi Beta Kappa; Theta Alpha Phi (dramatics
honorary); Delta Sigma Rho (Debate honorary), author: The
Absurdity of Corporate Worship (to be published in Fall,
1964); Home: 550 West 155th St., New York 32, New
York.

*HOPKINS, Thomas Ewell, social worker; b. Sontag, Va.,
Aug. 30, 1908; s. Daniel Thomas and Cora Ann H.; A.
B., W. Va. State Coll., 1933; B.D., Howard Univ., Sch.
of Rel., 1938; Grad. Sch. of Howard Univ., M.A., 1939;
m. Esther Harrison; children---Susan, Thomas, Jr.;
director, Religious Education, Vermont Ave. Baptist
Church, Wash., D.C.; pastor, First Baptist Church, West
Washington, D.C.; pastor, The Union Baptist Church,
Stamford, Conn.; Rockview-Brookside Community Church,
New Haven; teacher, Public School system, Va. & The
Washington Baptist Seminary; social investigator, Dept. of
Welfare, City of New Haven; exec. sec., Dixwell Minister's
Alliance; chaplain, Mason; Home: 77 Beers New Haven 11,
Conn.; Office: City Welfare Dept., 196 Bassett, New Haven,
11, Conn.

HORSLEY, Leroy, b. Kinston, N.C., Dec. 22, 1930; s. Wil-
liam and Beaddie (Rouse) H.; B.S., Fayetteville Teachers
College, Fayetteville, N.C., 1959; B.D., Johnson C.
Smith Univ., Charlotte, N.C., 1963; m. Geneva Louise
Knight; children---Cynthia; Edwin; current pastor, Mt.
Pelier Presbyterian Church, U.S., Rowland, N.C., 1962-
63; pastor, Anys Chapel Presbyterian Church, U.S., Max-
ton, N.C., 1963; pastor, Covenant Presbyterian Church,
U.S., Kannapolis, N.C., 1962-63; Bellefonte President,
UP USA Harrisburg, N.C., 1962-63; Arena Voluntary
worker for state vocational rehabilitation; Advisory to
Community Improvement Ass'n; US Army, 1951-52; Good
conduct medal; Mem.: NAACP, Elks, American Legion,
Republican; Home: Box 581 Rowland, N.C.

HOUSTON, Charles Edward, b. Benham, Ky., Jan 4, 1914;
s. John and Agnes (Bradley) H.; A.B., Morehouse Coll.,
Atlanta, Ga. 1939; B.D., Union Theol. Sem., NYC,
1942; Adv. Study, N.T. Greek, Union, 1949-50; m. Mary
Ann Patterson; 1 son, Charles, Jr.; 3 daus., Cornelia,
Mary, Jeanne; Ordained Bapt. Minister, 1942; Pastoral
Asst., Providence Bapt. Ch., Atlanta, Ga., 1935-39;

Field Work Stu., Church of the Master, NYC, 1939-41;
Salem Methodist Ch., 1941-42; Pastor, Shiloh Bapt. Ch.,
Tuckahoe, N.Y., 1946---; Mem. Faculty and Bd. Dir.,
Bapt. Edu. Center, N.Y., N.Y.; Chrmn., Christian Edu.
Comm., Empire Missionary Bapt. Conv.; Faculty and Bd.
Dir., Empire Miss. SS & BTU Congress; Commissioner,
Tuckahoe Housing Authority, 1957--- (Chairman, 1962);
Treas., Central Hudson Bapt. Assoc. (7 yrs.); Dean,
SS & BTU Aux. (7 yrs); Pres., SS. & BTU Aux. (8 yrs);
Home: 61 Washington St., Tuckahoe, New York. Church:
15 Marbledale Road, Tuckahoe, N.Y.

HOUSTON, William Eugene, Jr., church administrator; b.
Hot Springs, Ark., July 1, 1920; s. Wm. Eugene and
Abbie (Austin) H.; A.B., Johnson C. Smith U, 1941;
B.D., J.C. Smith, 1944; D.D., 1961; Johnson C. Smith
U., Charlotte, N.C.; m. Lilla M. Johnson; children---
Bjorn Lorenz, Cheryl Jeanne; pastor Rendall Memorial
Presbyterian Church, 1944---; chaplain N.Y.C. Hospital,
Welfare Island, 1950-57; chaplain Elmhurst General Hos-
pital, Queens, N.Y., 1957-60; chaplain Dept. of Sanita-
tion City of N.Y., 1960---; also vice moderator Presby-
tery of N.Y., 1960-62; moderator Synod of New York
U.P. Church, 1962-63; exec. dir. Commission on Religion
and Race, Presbytery of New York City, 1963; Board of
Directors, N.Y. J.B. Assoc., 1957---; Board of Pen-
sions United Presbyterian Church, U.S.A., 1960-66,
chairman Central Harlem Council for Community Planning,
1957-59; chairman Public Relations Committee, and Church
College Committee Synod of N.Y., 1963- --; chairman
Commission on Religion and Race, Presbytry of N.Y.C.,
1964; polemarch N.Y. Alumni Chapter of Kappa Alpha Psi
Fraternity, 1958-60; chairman Grand Chapter of Kappa
Alpha Psi Nominating Committee, 1958-62; chairman
Northern Manhattan Volunteers for Stevenson, 1952-56;
Board of Directors Henry Hudson Historical Society As-
sociation; pres. Presbyterian Ministers of N.Y. & N.J.,
1946-60. pres., Presbyterian Council of The North and
West, 1956-58; v.p. Interdenominational Ministers Meet-
ings of N.Y. & Vicinity, 1947- ---; pres., Johnson C.
Smith University Club of N.Y., 1945-48, 1956-58; treas-
urer N.Y. Tennis Association, 1960- --; Umpire in
Chief, N.Y. State Championships A.T.A., 1959- --; Al-
ternate Referee National Championships American Tennis
Association, 1962- --; mem.: Alpha Kappa Mu, Kappa
Alpha Psi, Chi Alpha, National Presbyterian Health and
Welfare Association, Academy of Religion and Mental

Health, Association of American Protestant Hospital
Chaplains, County Committee, Democratic Party, N. Y.
County, chaplain to N. Y. State Legislature, N. Y. City
Council and twice to Democratic State Committee; contribu-
tor to The Presbyterian, Presbyterian Tribune, Social Pro-
gress, Monday Morning, Football News, Social Whirl
Vanguard, (once Assoc. Editor) Presbyterian Life, Cross-
roads. Compositions: Agnus Dei, Ordination Prayer, and
and musical setting for the Eucharist. Home: 2255 Fifth
Ave., New York City 37, N. Y.; Church: 59-61 W. 137
Street, New York City 37, N. Y.

HOWARD, Lawrence Webster, Sr., clergyman, teacher; b.
Blount Co., Tenn., Sept. 23, 1920; s. George and Bertha
Elizabeth H.; Swift Memorial Jr. Coll., Rogersville,
Tenn., 1935-37; A. B., Knoxville Coll., Knoxville, Tenn.,
1943; Courses: Howard Univ. Sch. of Rel.; Lincoln Univ.;
m. Alice McIver Turner; children--- Bertha Alice Law-
rence W., Jr.; pastor, Sanders African Methodist Epis-
copal Zion Ch., East Tenn.; Jones Memorial A. M. E.
Zion Ch., Greenville, Tenn.; St. Paul A. M. E. Zion Ch.,
Maryville, Tenn.; Allenyen A. M. E. Zion Ch., Phila., Pa.;
A. M. E. Zion Churches, Harrisburg, Gettysburg, Allen-
town, Pa.; current pastor, St. Paul A. M. E. Zion Ch.,
Salisbury, Md.; County School teacher; pres., P. T. A.,
Salisbury, Md.; former pres., Ministerial Alliance; cur-
rent sec., Salisbury Ministerial Alliance; Mem., Mason;
Elk; Democrat; Scout Master; Home: 408 Delaware Ave.,
Salisbury, Md.

HUCLES, Henry Boyd, III, hospital chaplain; b. New York,
N. Y., Sept. 21, 1923; s. Henry Boyd and Alma (Lewis)
H.; B. S., Va. Union Univ., 1943; B. D., Bishop Payne
Divinity School, 1946; m. Manie Dalceda (Adams) H.;
children---Henry B. IV, Michael Edward; priest in charge,
Grace Protestant Episcopal Church, Millers Tavern, Va.;
St. Andrews Church, Upright, Va., 1946-49; rector, St.
George's Church, Brooklyn, N. Y., 1949---; senior pro-
testant chaplain, Brooklyn House of Detention for Men;
Mem., Bd. of Managers, St. John's Episcopal Hospital;
Brooklyn Protestant Council; Alpha Phi Alpha; Home: 255
Monroe St. Brooklyn 16, N. Y.; Office: 800 Marly Ave.,
Brooklyn 16, N. Y.

HUDSON, James, coll. prof.; b. Birmingham, Ala., Oct.
1, 1903; s. Berry Henry and Alta (Hawkins) H.; A. B.,
Morehouse Coll., 1926; Oberlin Coll., 1928-29; B. D.,

Colgate-Rochester Divinity School, 1929-31; A. M. , Ph. D. ,
Boston Univ. , 1935, 1946; m. Augustine Josephine Lagarde;
children---James Lagarde; Public School Teacher, Lincoln Jr. High School, 1927-28; teacher and coll. pastor,
Leland Coll. , Baker, La. , 1931-42; pastor, Bradley
Memorial Baptist Church, Oak Bluffs, Mass. , 1943-46;
teacher and chaplain, Fla. A. & M. Univ. , 1946---;
3rd Vice pres. , Fla. A. & M. Univ. Clinical Ass'n,
1963-64; Mem. , Exec. Bd. of Inter-Civic Council (Talla-
hassee, Fla. , 1956---;)); pres. , Tallahassee, Non Partisan
Voters Crusade, 1960---; Mem. , Exec. Committee of
Tallahassee Community Awakening Crusade, 1962---;
Mem. , Alpha Phi Alpha Scholarship Award; Phi Beta
Sigma Social Action Award from Chapter at Fla. A & M
Univ. , 1956; former pres. , Fla. Philosophical Ass'n;
American Teachers Ass'n; National Ass'n of Coll. and
Univ. ; Home: 712 Gamble St. , Tallahassee, Fla. ; Office:
Box 251 Fla. A. & M. Univ. , Tallahassee, Fla.

HUDSON, James Hammie, teacher; b. St. Charles, Lee Co. ,
S. C. , June 13, 1917; s. James and Jannie (Hudson) H. ;
Mayesville Institute, 1926-34; Coulter Memorial Academy,
Cheraw, S. C. , 1936-37; Coulter Jr. College, Cheraw,
S. C. , 1937-39; A. B. , Johnson C. Smith Univ. , Charlotte,
N. C. , 1939-41; B. D. , Seminary, 1946-49; m. Mozelle
Delois Peay; children--James Hammie, Jr. ; pastor
Pleasant Ridge U. Presby. Ch. , Lancaster, S. C. Page-
land 2nd U, Presby. Ch. , Pageland, S. C. , 1948-51;
Mt. Vernon U. Presby. Ch. , Palatka, Fla. and Mather-
Perit U. Presby. Ch. St. Augustine, Fla. , 1952; West-
minster U. Presby. Ch. , Spartanburg, S. C. , 1953-57;
Calvary U. Presby. Ch. and Shiloh 1st U. Presby. Ch.
Winnsboro, S. C. , 1957.   ; Dir. and Teacher of Rel. Ed.
Harbison Jr. College, S. C. , 1957-58; pres. Spartanburg
County NAACP branch, 1955-57; moderator Atlantic
Synod U. Presby. Ch. , 1962-63; moderator Fairfield,
McClelland and the merged Fairfield-McClelland Presby-
teries several terms; US Army 1941-46. 9 months over-
seas duty in the Southwest Pacific Theater-Okinawa;
awards: Good Conduct Medal, American Defense Service
Medal, American Campaign Medal, Asiatic-Pacific Cam-
paign Medal with Bronze Star, World War II Victory
Medal and Army of Occupation Medal with Japan Clasp;
mem. : Atlantic Synod, United Presbyterian Church in
U. S. A. ; Fairfield-McClelland Presbytery, United Presbyterian Church in USA; Jenkinsville, S. C. Branch NAACP;
Fairfield High School PTA; Sanctorium Lodge #25, Cheraw,

S. C. and Cairo Temple #125, Columbia, S. C.; Home:
501 W. Moultrie, Winnsboro, S. C.

HUDSON, R. T., Church official; b. Jackson, Miss., Decem-
ber 4, 1912; s. Joseph Bell and Anna Lee (Cotton) H.;
Oakwood Coll., 1930-34; Queens Coll., 1960-61; Andrews
Univ., 1961-62; m. Dorothy Mae Warren; children-
Romona Mouzon, Sharon Rose, Robbin Denise, Ricardo
Tilden; Pastor, Philadelphia Seventh-Day Adventist Church,
Des Moines, Iowa, 1935-41; secretary, Regional Work,
Texas Conference of S. D. A., 1941-45; minister, Allegheney
Conference of S. D. A., 1945-1955, pastoring in Pittsburg,
Pa., Washington, D. C., and Cleveland, Ohio; pastor,
Ephesus S. D. A. Church, 1955-62; former teacher,
Elementary School, Huntsville, Ala., 1933-34; present:
president, Northeastern Conference of S. D. A. Church,
1961;   Mem., Oakwood College Board, Atlantic Union
College Board; Atlantic Union Conference Executive Com-
mittee; New England Sanitarium Board; chair-
man, Northeastern Conference Executive Committee;
chairman, Northeastern Academy Board. Co-author, State
Paper presented to the New York Legislature assembly
on "The Fair Sabbath Law", Jan. 29, 1962. Home: 457
Lafayette Ave., Rockville Center, N. Y. Office: 560
W. 150th St., N. Y., 31, N. Y.

HUGHES, Carl Donald, educator; b. Indianapolis, Ind., June
10, 1918; s. Twidell and Lillian (Haslewood) H. Ford;
A. B., Ind. U., Bloomington, Ind., 1939; B. S., Bus.
Adm., W. Va. State Coll., Institute, W. Va., 1942; M. A.,
Finance, Wharton Sch. of Finance, U. of Pa., 1943;
B. D., Grad. Sch. Rel., Butler U., Indianapolis, 1957;
M. A., Grad. Sch. of Rel., Butler U., 1958; Sch. of
Law, Ind. U. (2yrs); Grad. work in Education, Wayne
State U. and U. of Det. (Mich); m. Louise Cox; 1
son, Carl D., Jr.; 2 daus., Karen Louise, Beverly Jean;
Teacher, Business Ed., Detroit Public Schools; Instr.,
Calvary Dist. Assoc., Det., Mich.; Wolverine State Conv.
SS & BTU Cong., Mich.; Nat. Bapt. SS & BTU Cong.;
Prog. Chrmn. Interdenominational Minister's Conf., Det.
Mich.; Recipient, 1st John L. Webb Award, Nat. Bapt.
Conv. USA, Inc., (contr. field of rel. ed.), Houston,
Texas, 1948; Who's Who in Amer. Coll. and U., 1943;
Who's Who in Colored Amer., 1950; Membership Comm.,
YMCA and NAACP; mem. Kappa Alpha Psi Frat., Mason,
Budg. Comm., Nat. Negro Bus. League; Ordained Bapt.

Minister, 1952; Second Baptist Ch., Lafayette, Ind.,
1952-56; Greater St. John Missionary Bapt. Ch., Det.,
Mich., 1956-60; Dir. C. Ed., Metropolitan Bapt. Ch.,
Det., 1960; Pastor, Bethel Baptist Ch., East, Det.,
1961---; Home: 258 Trowbridge Ave., Det., Mich.
48202 Church: 5715 Holcomb, Detroit, Mich. 48213

HUGHES, Henderson Randolph, b. Hemingway, S.C., Dec.
23, 1908; s. Silas M. and Hattie (M.) H.; A.B., Allen
Univ., Columbia, S.C.; B.D., Oberlin Graduate School
of Theology; D.D. (hon.), Allen Univ.; Daniel Payne
Coll.; m. Ruth Henderson; children---Henderson R.;
pastor, Shiloh African Methodist Episcopal Church, Charleston, 4 years; St. John A.M.E. Church, Birmingham, Ala., 8
yrs; Emanuel A.M.E. Church, 17 years; pres., Daniel
Payne Coll., Birmingham, 4 yrs.; teacher, Allen Univ.,
Columbia; Berkley County Training School; Mem., YMCA;
NAACP (Local Branch); Urban League; Mason, Elk;
Home: 400 Convent Ave., NY 31, N.Y.; Office: 37 W.
119th St. N.Y. 26, N.Y.

HUGHLEY, Judge Neal, coll. prof.; b. Columbis, Ga.,
Dec. 10, 1907; s. William Wilkins and Ozella (Jones) H.;
A.B., Morehouse Coll., 1929; M.A., Columbia Univ.; B.
D., Union Theol. Sem., 1932; Ph.D., Columbia Univ.,
1947; m. Sadie Sawyer; children---Mario Neal; prof.,
Bishop Coll., 1932-37; pastor, First Bapt. Ch., Okmulgee,
Okla., 1938-39; Mt. Calvary Bapt. Ch., Coffeyville, Kans.
1939-41; current prof., North Carolina Coll., Durham,
N.C., 194---; current pastor, Mt. Calvary Bapt. Ch.,
Durham, N.C., 1959---; chmn, Fellowship of Southern
Churchmen, 1947-49; Danforth Associate, 1955-65; mem.,
Selection Com. for Danforth Graduate Fellowships; Howard
Univ. Institute of Religion, 1942-65; Ex. Bd. N.C. Coun-
cil on Human Relations; Ex. Bd. N.C. Council of Churches;
author: Rethinking Our Christianity, Dorrance Press,
1942; Trends in Protestant Social Idealisms, Columbia
Univ. Press, 1948; Home: 203 Pekoe St. Durham, N.C.
27707; Office: North Carolina Coll., 312 Administrator
Bldg., Durham, N.C. 27707.

HUNT, Blair Theodore, teacher; b. Memphis, Tenn., Oct.
1, 1888; s. Blair Theodore and Emma (House) H.; B.A.
Morehouse College; T.H.B. & M.S., Tenn. State Univ.;
m. Ernestine (Jacobs) H.; children: Blair; Wilson;
Ernest; Present-pastor Miss. Blvd. Christian Church;
teacher: 46 yrs., Memphis Schools System, the last 27

years principal of B.T. Washington High Sch. (Retired in
1959); mem. Former Pres. of the National Convention of
Christian Churches; County Board of Ed., Shelby County,
Tenn.; Board of Trustee, Owen College, Memphis, Tenn.
and Tougaloo College, Tougaloo, Miss.; World War I,
1st Lieutenant; mem. Alpha Phi Alpha; Elks; Urban
League, NAACP; 1952, Weekly sermon for "The Memphis
World" (Newspaper); Home: 931 Hastings St., Memphis,
Tenn. Office: 978 Mississippi Bldv., Memphis, Tenn.

*HUNTER, Charles Alvin, teacher; b. Longview, Texas, May
7, 1926; s. Wallace Alvin and Ivernia (Fleming) H.; B.
A., Bishop College, 1947; B.D., Howard University, Sch. of
Rel., 1950; M.Th., 1954; Th.D., 1958; Divinity School, Phila.
Pa.; m. Annie Mary Alexander; children--- Alpha Angela,
Rhonda Fleming, Rhashell Debra, Byron Charles; Minister
Trinity Congregational Church, Athens, Ala., 1950-52;
teacher of Social Studies, Trinity High School, 1951-52;
teacher of Social Studies and Common Learning, Phila-
delphia Public Schools, Pa., 1954-57; Dir. of United
Campus Christian Fellowship, Fla. A & M Univ., 1959-
61; Minister Trinity United Presbyterian Church, Talla-
hassee, Fla., 1959-61; Assoc. Prof. of Sociology, Bishop
College, Dallas, Texas 1961-present; Minister Hope Presby.
Ch., 1962-present; Associate - American Sociological
Society, Southwest Regional Sociological Assn. Southwest
Philosophical Society. Home: 4425 Meadow St., Dallas,
Texas; Church: 4411 Meadow St., Dallas, Texas.

HUNTLEY, Thomas Elliott, b. Wadesboro, N.C. June 28,
1903; s. John P. and Lula (Brewer) H.; grad. Va. Theol.
Sem. and Coll., Lynchburg, Va., 1928; A.B., Morehouse
Coll., Atlanta, 1934; Atlanta Univ., 1937; Union Theol.
Sem., N.Y.; D.D. (hon.), Friendship Coll., Rock Hill,
S.C., 1943; Selma Univ., 1954; m. Kiffie Elizabeth Esther
Maddox; Ordained to ministry of Bapt. Ch., 1928; pastor,
St. Louis Bapt. Ch., 1942---; founder, Church on Wheels,
1947; leader, Nat. Ministers' Prayer March on Washington,
1948; Mem., Social Service Com., Nat. Bapt. Conv. Inc.,
1948-52; Hist. Com., 1956-58; former mem., Pastor's
Advisory Com., Nat. Council Religious Education; founder,
Nat. Bapt. Publication House of South India, 1956; chmn,
editorial Staff foreign publications of Bharath Social and
Cultural Trust, Publishers of South India, 1957; Mem.,
NAACP; Protestants and Other Americans United for
Separation of Church and State (v.p.), Phi Beta Sigma;
Mason; author: As I Saw It, 1954; Devil on the Moon;

When People Behave Like Sputniks; Sense and Common
Sense in a World of Non-Sense; A Baptist Manifesto in
Three Epistles; 1940, while in the pastorate at Pensacola,
Fla. he influenced (without organizational help) the editor
of the white daily Pensacola News Journal, to change his
policy of spelling the word "Negro" with a small "n";
1946, To curtail juvenile delinquency in St. Louis, founded
The Church on Wheels (A school bus, used as a church
house in the streets in blighted areas, with a staff of Sunday
School teachers, evangelistic and social workers; 1948,
Led Ministers' Prayer March on Washington in an effort
to influence and World Peace; 1955, His book As I Saw It
(Not communism but Commonism) was sold, for the first
time in a foreign land, by the Carey Kingsgate Press,
London, England; 1956, As I Saw It was translated and
published into three languages of India, with a preface,
in the Telugu language, by Dr. B. Pattabhi Sitaramayya,
(Governor Madhya Pradesh) who referred to the book as
"a great contribution to the advancement of the moral
and spiritual development of India;" 1956, he was cited
by The Hindustan Times of India as "a priest of the
highest type of liberalism and toleration instead of the
maximum, "My country right or wrong;" 1963, author:
Huntley's Manual for Every Baptist (Some Things Every
Member Should Know); Founded, The Family Fireside Institute (designed to teach children, at an early age, in
the home, the fundamentals of good citizenship as well as
Baptist doctrine; 1963, Through the October 25, 1963 edition of The St. Louis Argus, he made an appeal to the
Negro Citizens of St. Louis to withdraw their deposits
from most of the banks and establish a bank of their own,
upon an integrated basis, due to an accute "sit in" con-
troversy that was taking place at the Jefferson Bank over
hiring of Negroes -- a bank where most Negroes deposited
their money; 1964, His appeal materialized into the organization of the Gateway National Bank with 15 Negro
workers and one white chashier, two white board members; His book, Huntley's Manual for Every Baptist, was
adopted by the National Bapt. Convention, USA Inc. (in
its 1964 session at Detroit, Mich.) as a standard guide
in Bapt. Ch. administration -- the first such doctrinal
guide from a lone author ever to be adopted by this religious body; Cited and recommended for membership in
the International Platform Assn by the Committee on Associates; Lowell Thomas, Drew Pearson, Edgar Bergen,
and Hal Holbrook (The International Platform idea dates
back to the days of Aristotle and represents the highest

type of literary and artistic characters) He holds a mem-
bership certificate from this organization; Home: 4959
Cote Brilliant Ave., St. Louis 3, Mo.; Office: Central
Bapt. Church, 2842 Washington Ave., St. Louis 3,
Missouri.

HURDLE, Isaiah Q., teacher; b. Greenville, Texas, Aug. 12,
1886; s. Andrew J. and Viney J. (Sanders) H.; B.S.,
Prairie View State College, 1927; Graduate Study-Univ. of
Colorado, 1929; Graduate Study, University of Denver,
1937, later, at Prairie View and also Texas Southern
Theology, Brite College, Ft. Worth, Tex., 1960; m.
Erma (Bowser); children---Irving Q., Zenobia L., Jas.
R.; Ordained, 1912; Pres., Northeast Texas Christian
Theological and Industrial College, Palentiane, Texas,
1912ᵣ58; Served as school principal during the years of
ministerial work for 26 years; Interim preaching since
1958, when retired from Willow Park Christian Church,
San-Antonio, Texas; pastor, Holland Chapel, Holland,
Texas; Organized Crest View Christian Church, Temple,
1942, also New Hope in Marlin, Friendship Christian
Church, Taylor, Texas and Friendship Christian Church,
Davilla, Texas; Served as Parliamentarian for National
Christian Missionary Convention, Disciples of Christ;
Served as instructor Summer camps; Austin, Texas 1934-
36, Hiram College, Ohio, 1950, San Antonio, Texas,
1956-58; Church Schools and Evangelistic campaigns,
President of Texas Christian Missionary Convention, 1939-
45; Boy Scouts Commissioner, 1934-37; Scout Commissioner,
1934-37; Samuel Huston College (Summer School Director,
1922), Visiting Professor in Tillotson College, 1936,
Jarvis College, 1945-46 (Summer activities); Pres. Texas
Teachers State Association, 1936-37; Member, Board of
Trustees, Jarvis Christian College, 1945-57; current-
Interim Pastor, Friendship Christian Church, Davilla,
Texas; Forty Year service pen from National Christian
Missionary Convention, 1954; 50 year service medal from
the International Convention of Disciples of Christ; Dele-
gate from the US, the World Convention on Christian Edu-
cation, Toronto, Canada, 1950; current-recording sec., the
Most Worshipful St., Joseph Grand Lodge, Texas Juris-
diction, Scotish Rite Ancient Free and Accepted Masons;
Editor, The Texas Christian Evangelist, 1912-16; Editor,
Texas Standard, 1937-38; Home: 1416 E. 12 St., Austin
2, Texas.

HUTCHINS, Joshua, Jr., church official; b. Huntingtown,
Md., Apr. 6, 1937; s. Joshua and Lillian Brown H.;
B. S., St. Paul's Coll., 1960; B. D., Interdenominational
Theol. Center, Gammon Theol. Sem., 1962; m. Gloria
M. Walker; Licensed to preach, 1954, Chr. Board of
Ed., Washington Conference Methodist Church; Alpha
Phi Alpha Student Christian Movement, Crusade Scholar,
1961-63; Home Missions, 1962-63; pastor, Trinity Meth.
Church, 1962-64; Conference Youth Director, Church
Board of Ed., Methodist Church, Washington Conference,
1964---; pres., NAACP, Clarksburg, W. Va.; Mem.,
Alpha Phi Alpha; Republican; Office: Bd. of Education,
Wash. Conf., The Meth. Church, 1206 Etting St., Balti-
more, Md.

HYLTON, Samuel Wilbur, Jr., teacher; b. Roanoke, Va.
Feb. 14, 1927; s. Samuel W. and Idenia (White) H.;
1946-49, B. A. Morehouse College; 1951-54; B. D., Bos-
ton University; Butler Univ. (Christian Theological Sem-
inary); m. Mildred (McLeod) H.; children: Samuel Wilbur
III; Karen Elizabeth; Pastor: 1951-54; Second Christian
Church, Indianapolis, Ind. 1954-61; Cleveland Ave. Chris-
tian Church-Winston-Salem, N. C. 1961 (present) Centen-
nial Christian Church-St. Louis, Mo., mem. Faculty-
Winston-Salem Teachers College, Winston-Salem, N. C.;
Board of Managers, Patterson Ave. Y. M. C. A., Winston-
Salem, N. C.; Omega Psi Phi; Beta Chi Honorary Society;
Home: 771 N. Euclid Ave., St. Louis, Mo. -63108; church:
4950 Fountain Ave., St. Louis, Mo., 63113.

JACKSON, D. Manning, b. Monroe, La., July 5, 1906;
s. Gabriel and Mattie; A. B., Southern Univ., 1928;
Bishop Coll., 1934; D. D. (hon.), Conroe Coll., 1944;
m. Minnie Ruth Hawkins; pastor, Golden Gate Baptist
Ch., 1930-36; First Baptist Church, San Antonio, Tex.,
1936-39; First African Baptist Ch., Phila., Pa., 1949-
52; Fellowship Baptist Church, Phila., Pa., 1952-54;
Live Oak Baptist Ch., Beaumont, Tex., 1954-59; El
Bethel Baptist Church, San Francisco, Calif., 1959---;
dean of religion, Guadalupe Coll., 1941-45; director of
education, Phila. Pastors Conference; sec. Bills and
Accounts, National Baptist Convention of America, since
1958; author: Pulpit Meditations; Home: 127 Thrift St.,
San Francisco, Calif.

JACKSON, Edward Franklin, b. Pensacola, Fla., July 19,

1911; Florida A&M College, Edward Waters, Jacksonville,
Fla.; Further study, Tuskegee Institute and Univ. of
Buffalo; D.D., Livingstone College, 1948; m. Mildred
Dodson; children--- 3 sons, Edward, Jr., Cameron W.,
Darryl J.; 1 daughter, Floria J.; pastor, Alabama,
Tennessee, Buffalo, N.Y.; current pastor, John Wesley,
A.M.E. Zion Church, Washington, D.C., 1952---; 1955,
led Church Committee for NAACP Campaign; 1957, led
Ministers in successful effort to place Negroes in sales
positions in Downtown Dept. Stores; 1959, elected presi-
dent D.C. Branch NAACP; 1960, led campaign for Mr.
Frank D. Reeves as National Democratic Committeeman;
elected to Central Democratic Committee and elected
delegate to Democratic National Convention; vice pres.,
Central Democratic Committee; led and assisted in successful efforts to re-organize United States Employment
Service-District of Columbia and to place Negro drivers
on trucks of major oil companies; Vice chairman, Citizens Advisory Committee to Presidents Civil Rights
Commission; national president of the Ministers and
Laymen's Association of the A.M.E. Zion Church since
1953; Member: Board of Directors, Council of Churches;
Advisory Committee Northwest Settlement House; Committee of Management Y.M.C.A.; Board of Director United
Givers Fund; Steering Committee Inter-religious Committee
on Race; Chairman Person to Person Communication Sub-
Committee; National Speakers Bureau Democratic Party;
Mason, Omega Psi Phi; Elk; Awards: Afro man of the
year D.C. 1957; Recalled to Buffalo to receive citation
for outstanding service 1958; Chosen for 12th Street
YMCA's "1963 Outstanding Citizen's Award; Office: 1615
14th St., NW, Washington, D.C.

JACKSON, Henry Brown, music teacher; b. Alden Bridge,
Louisiana, Feb. 11, 1889; s. Silas and Sallie (Brown)
J.; A.B., Philander Smith Coll., 1919; studied medicine,
Howard University; studied law at Howard Univ.; studied
theology at Shaw Univ.; music, Detroit Conservatory of
Music; m. Elizabeth Reid; children---Henry Brown, Jr.,
Charles Lee. Minister, Christian Methodist Episc. Church;
member of three General Conferences; piano teacher for
fifty-one years; recording artist, O.K. Recording Co.,
N.Y.; present: minister, C.M.E. Ch., Spartanburg, S.
C. President, Interdenominational Ministerial Assoc.,
Spartanburg, S.C. Home: 176 Amos St., Spartanburg, S.
C.

*JACKSON, James Castina, b. Okla. City, Okla., Mar. 24,
1922; s. Wade D. and Rosie (Owens) J.; A.B., Morehouse
Coll., 1944; B.D., Howard Univ. Sch. of Rel., 1947;
Oklahoma School of Religion, D.D. (hon.), 1964; m.
Barbara Mae Sparks; children---Janice C., Meredith
Patrice; director, North Tulsa Baptist Center, Tulsa,
Okla., 1947-56; pastor, Paradise Baptist Church, Tulsa,
1956---; professor of preaching, Oklahoma School of Religion, Langston, Oklahoma, 1950-54; sec., Tulsa Branch
NAACP, 1954-60; Bd. of Directors, Tulsa County Ass'n
for Mental Health; Bd. of Directors, North Tulsa Co-
ordinating Committee; Bd. of Directors, Oklahoma School
of Religion; pres., Okla. State Baptist Pastors' Conference;
dean, Creek District Congress of Christian Education; Bd.
of Directors, Hutcherson Branch YMCA; Bd. of Directors,
Oklahoma Baptist State Convention; contributor: "Oklahoma
Eagle;" former editorial staff of the National Baptist
Sunday School Publishing Board; Home: 503 E. Young St.,
Tulsa, Okla.; Office: 507 E. King St., Tulsa, Oklahoma.

JACKSON, James Conroy, chaplain; b. Scranton, Pa., May
9, 1913; s. James Conroy and Ella Glascoe (Smith) J.;
B.S., Cheyney State Teachers College, Cheyney, Pa.,
1938; B.Th., Philadelphia Divinity School, 1949; m.
Daisy Louise Ledgister; children---Patricia Ann; Ordained
deacon in the Episcopal Church 1949; Priest, 1949; vicar,
St. Philip's P.E. Church, Dallas, Texas, 1949-56; priest-
in-charge, St. Simon's Church, Ft. Worth, Texas, 1949-
56; vicar, St. Philip's, P.E. Church, Little Rock, Ark.,
1956-62; St. Mary's P.E. Church, Hot Springs, 1956-
62; St. Andrew's P.E. Church, Pine Bluff, 1956-61;
St. Augustine's P.E. Church, Ft. smith, 1961-62; current
chaplain of Voorhees College; priest-in-charge of Philip's
Chapel, Voorhees College, Denmark, South Carolina;
pres. Greater Little Rock Urban League, Little Rock,
Ark., 1960-62; Served overseas in Solomon Island and the
Philippines during World War II, 1942-45; Member, Kappa
Alpha Psi Fraternity; American Church Union-Episcopal
Society; award: Good Conduct Award; Home: Voorhees Col-
lege, Denmark, S.C.

JACKSON, John Henry, Jr., b. Oakwood, Tex., Sept. 24,
1919; s. John Henry, Sr. and Aggie (Williams) J.; A.B.,
Samuel Houston Coll., Austin, Tex.; M.A., Atlanta
Univ., Atlanta, Ga.; B.D., Gammon Theol. Sem.; D.D.
(Hon.), Turner Sem., Kansas City, Kansas; m. Verna
Maude Worthy; children---Linda Joyce, La Verne, Janis

Harlene; pastor and principal of High School, Kynette
Forsyth Ga. for 16 years; Exec. Sec., Bd. of Ed. Central
West Conference Meth. Ch.; pastor (current), Scott Meth.
Ch., 1959---; Summer workshop leader, Oregon, Colo.;
former pres., East Denver Ministerial Alliance; pres.,
Rocky Mountain Ministerial Alliance; chaplain, House of
Representative, Denver, Colo.; Devotional Speaker for
Sunday morning Radio Program, KIMN Station; Certificate
from Governor Talmadge; Mem., Mason; Sigma Phi Beta;
Published two books of prayers given in House of Repre-
sentatives; Home: 2830 Eudera St., Denver, Colo. 80207;
Office: 2201 Ogden St., Denver, Colo. 80205.

JACKSON, Joseph Harrison, ch. administrator; b. Jonestown,
Miss., Sept. 11, 1900; s. Henry and Emily (Johnson) J.;
A. B., Jackson Coll., 1926; B. D., Colgate Rochester
Divinity Sch., 1932; M. A., Creighton U., 1933; D. D.
(honorary), Central State Coll., Wilberforce O., 1954;
LL. D. Bishop Coll., Marshall, Texa., 1956; m. Maude
Thelma Alexander, 1926; children---Kenny. Ordained,
Bapt. Ministry, 1922; pastor 1st Ch., Macomb, Miss.,
1925-27; Bethel Baptist Ch., Omaha, Nebr., 1927-34;
Monumental Bapt. Ch., Phila., Pa., 1934-1941; Olivet
Bapt. Ch., Chgo., Ill., 1941- ; Pres. Nat'l Bapt. Conv.,
Inc., 1953- -; Sec. Foreign Mission Bd., Nat. Bapt.
Conv., 1934-41; Mem. Bapt. World Alliance (Exec. Comm).
Mem. Nat'l Council Ch. (gen. bd.) Phi Beta Sigma,
Mason. Author: A Voyage to W. Africa and Some Reflec-
tions on Modern Missions, 1936; Stars In The Night,
1950. Home: 4937 Kimbark Ave., Chgo., Ill. Ch. Off.:
3101 S. Parkway, Chgo., Ill.

JACKSON, Lester Kendel, b. Fort Gaines, Ga., May 18,
1895; s. Edwin and Maria (Booyer) J.; Chatahoochie
Institute, Ga. State U.,Va. Theol. Sem. & Coll.; m.
Emma Lee Hawkes; 1 son, Lester K., Jr.; 3 daus.,
Mrs. Veora Maxine Proctor, Mrs. Joyce Estelle Swain,
Mrs. Sarah Yvonne McCall; Prof. Rel. Ed., Va. Theol.
Sem. & Coll., 1924-27; Bus. Manager, 1929-31; Pastor,
Rivermount Bapt. Ch., Lynchburg, Va., 1925-34; Ebenezer
Bapt. Ch., Passaic, N. J., 1934-36; Second Bapt. Ch.,
Long Branch, N. J.; 1936-42; St. Paul Bapt. Ch., Gary,
Ind., 1943---; Pres., Interdenominational Ministers Al-
liance, Gary, Ind.; Pres., Gary Fellowship of Ministers
(Interracial, Interfaith); Sec., Ind. Bapt. State Conv.; mem.
Gary Chamber of Commerce; Life Mem. NAACP; Life
Mem., Nat. Fraternal Council of Churches; Congress

Of Racial Equality; SCLC (Southern Leadership Confer-
ence), Republican; Recipient, Citation, Interdenominational
Minister's Alliance and Luther Morris Award, NAACP,
outstanding service in Civil Rights, 1962; Home: 2541
Madison St., Gary, Ind. Church: 1938 Adams St., Gary,
Ind.

*JACKSON, Moses Lester, b. Florence, S.C., Aug. 16,
1921; s. Moses L., Sr. and Alma (Williams) J.; electro-
tech. certificate, Milwaukee, Wis. School of Engineering,
1940-50; B.A., Va. Union Univ., 1958; B.D. Howard
Univ. Sch. of Rel., 1961; m. Cora Lee Moore; children
---; Velvenia Lestine, Timothy Demetrius; Ordained Mt.
Airy Baptist Church, D.C.; asst. pastor, Jr. Church,
1950-58, Mt. Airy Baptist Ch., Wash., D.C.; pastor,
Beulah Baptist Church, 1961---; Mem., NAACP; Baptist
Ministers Conference; Far North East Ministers Ass'n;
Director of Teen-age Problems for the Far North East
Civic Ass'n; US Coast Guard, Sea duty in South Pacific,
1943-46; General Services Administration Suggestion
Award, 1964; Home: 802 49th St., NE. Washington 19,
D.C.; Office: 5901 Dix St. NE, Wash. 19, D.C.

JACKSON, Theodore Clifton, Jr., teacher; b. Baltimore,
Maryland, Aug. 4, 1933; s. Theodore Clifton and Lucy
(Milbourne) J.; Howard University, College of Liberal
Arts, 1952-54; Virginia Theological Seminary, Lynchburg,
Va., 1955-57; A.B.; Howard University, School of Re-
ligion, 1957-59; Morgan State College, 1962-63; m. Mar-
lene Young; children---Patricia Ann, Carla Rae. Chaplain:
Anna Mae Hunter Home for the Blind, Baltimore, Md.,
1958; pastor: St. Matthews Christian Methodist Episcopal
Church, Washington, D.C., 1949-62; Present pastor,
Herberts Chapel C.M.E. Church, Baltimore, Md.,
1962---; Teacher, Baltimore City Public School System,
1960-64. U.S. Army, 86th Airborne; mason, Mt. Zion
Lodge #10; Kappa Alpha Psi; N.A.A.C.P.; Interdenomina-
tional Ministers Alliance; Methodist Youth Fellowship;
C.M.E. Ministers Alliance, Urban League. Home: 4019
Grantley Rd., Baltimore, Md. Office: 3300 Fairfield Rd.,
Baltimore, Md.

JACKSON, Walter Kinsley, b. Boley, Okla., Mar. 28, 1914;
s. Eddie and Adlade J.; A.B., Bishop Coll., 1937; B.Th.,
Okla. Sch. of Rel., Langston, Okla., 1947; D.D. (honorary), Morris-Booker Coll., Dermont, Ark., 1955 and
Okla. Sch. of Rel., 1964; Adv. Study, Union Theol. Sem.,

NYC, 1963-64; m. Eula Lee Wilhite; 1 dau., Waltine
Lynette; Pastor, Corinth Bapt. Ch., Ardmore, Okla.,
1937-45; St. John Bapt. Ch., 1945---; pres., Bapt. Minister's Ass'n, 1947-64; Pres., Citizen's Action Comm.,
1950-58; Seminar Leader, Ch. Admin., Bishop Coll.,
1952, 53, 53; Bd. of Regents, Okla. Sch. of Rel., 1960-
64; Serve, Governor's Human Relation Comm., 1962-64;
Urban League, NAACP, YMCA; mem., Boy Scouts of
Amer., Inc., Amer. Legion, Omega Psi Phi Frat., Demo-
cratic Pty; Moderator, East Zion Dist. Ass'n; Contr.
Editor, National Baptist Voice, Nat. Bapt. Conv. USA,
Inc., 1959---; Home: 1200 N. E. Euclid, Oklahoma City,
Okla. 73117   Church: 805 Northeast Second St., Oklahoma
City, Okla. 73104.

JAMES, Allix Bledsoe, Coll. dean; b. Marshall, Tex., Dec.
17, 1922; s. Samuel Horace and Tannie Etta (Judkins)
J.; A. B., Va. Union Univ., 1944; B. D., Sch. of Rel.,
Va. Union Univ., 1946; Th. M., Union Theol. Sem., Va.,
1949; Th. D., 1957; Special studies: Pa. State Univ.; Boston Univ. Drew Theol. Sem.; m. Susie Beatrice Nickens;
children---Alvan Bosworth, Portia Veann; pastor, Union
Zion Baptist Church, Gloucester, Va., 1942-50; Mt. Zion
Baptist Ch., Downings, Va., 1944-53; Third Union Bapt.
Ch., King William, Va., 1953---; instructor, Va. Union
Univ., 1947-50;dean of students, Va. Union Univ., 1950-
56; dean, Sch. of Rel., Va. Union Univ., 1956---; vice
pres., Va. Union Univ., 1960---; Mem., Mayor's Commission on Human Relations, Richmond, 1963-65; vice
pres., Richmond Area Ministers Assn; vice pres., Council on Theol. Education, American Bapt. Conv.; Alpha
Psi Alpha; Committee on Christian Education, Va. Council
of Education; Administrative Comm., Dept. of the Ministry,
Nat. Council of Churches; sec., Protestant Ministers'
Assn of Richmond; Home:608 Overbrook Rd., Richmond,
Va.; Office: 1500 N. Lombardy St., Richmond, Va.
23220

*JAMES, Bose Moses, b. Memphis, Tenn. Feb. 12, 1922;
s. Bose Moses and Beulah (Moss) J.; A. B., B. D.,
Howard Univ., 1953, 1959; m. Dorothy Elizabeth Cox;
children---Lois Michelle; pastor to migrants, N. Y. State
Council of Churches, 1956-57; asst. pastor, Canaan Bapt.
Ch., Wash., D. C., 1957-61; pastor, North Community
Reformed Ch., Kalamazoo, Mich., 1961---; chmn, Kalamazoo Community Religious Bd., Bd. of Education, Reformed Ch. in America; U. S. Army, 1942-43; home: 325

Norway Ave., Kalamazoo, Mich.; Office: 324 W. Frank
St., Kalamazoo, Mich.

*JAMES, Daniel Finney, b. Richmond, Va., June 23, 1911; s.
Nathaniel Loved and Missouri (Finney) J.; B.S., Va.
Union Univ., Richmond, Va., 1939; B.D., Howard Univ.
Sch. of Rel., Washington, D.C., 1955; m. Doris Courtney;
children---Joletta A., Wanda M., Daniel F., Jr.; staff
member, Shiloh Baptist Church, Wash., D.C., 1950-55;
White Rock Baptist Ch., Wash., D.C., 1956-60; asst.
pastor, Good Will Baptist Church, Wash., D.C., 1960---;
US Navy, 1943-45; Area Campaign Medal; W.W. II Vic-
tory Medal; Mem., Phi Beta Sigma; Democrat; Home: 804
Crittenden St., NE, Wash., D.C.; Office: 1862 Kalorama
Rd. NW, Wash., D.C.

JAMES, Eugene Marshall, b. Princess Anne, Md., Apr. 26,
1938; s. William Henry, Sr. and Pauline Ballard (Fields)
J.; Somerset Jr.-Sr. High Sch., 1956; A.B., Maryland
State College, 1956-60; B.D., Theological Sem., John-
son C. Smith Univ., 1960-63; Post Sem. Intern (for the
Bd. of Nat. Missions) at St. Augustine Presby. Ch.,
1963-64; mem: NAACP; Home: E. 172nd Bronx 59, New
York, N.Y.

*JAMES, Frederick C., b. Prosperity, S.C., Apr. 7, 1922;
s. Edward and Rosa (Lee) J.; A.B., Allen Univ., 1943;
B.D., Howard Univ., Sch. of Rel., 1947; further study;
Union Theological Seminary; Columbia Univ.; D.D. (hon.),
Allen Univ.; Monrovia Coll., West African Seminary, Al-
len Univ., 6 years; pastor, Friendship African Methodist
Episcopal Church, Irmo, S.C.; Bishop's Memorial A.M.
E. Church, Columbia, S.C.; Wayman A.M.E. Church,
Winnsboro, S.C. 3 years; Chappelle Memorial A.M.E.
Church, Columbia, S.C., 3 years; current, Mt. Pisgah
A.M.E. Church, Sumter, S.C., 10 years; author of the
1960 Social Action Bill which created The A.M.E. Com-
mission On Social Action; Elected the 1st Consultant-
Director, Social Action Commission, A.M.E. Church;
Mem., The General Board of The A.M.E. Church; Sec.,
Commission on Finance and Statistics of The A.M.E.
Church; superintendent, The A.M.E. Sunday Schools of
S.C.; Denominational Staff Council, National Council of
Churches; President's 30 member Commission on Religion
and Race; National Council of Churches, 1963; Home: 215
W. Bartlett St., Sumter, S.C.

JAMES, Goree Leon, b. Daingerfield, Texas, Sept. 5, 1930;
s. Aaron and Loan Mae (J.); Prairie View A & M College, 1949; A.B., Oklahoma City Univ., 1960; m. Kate
Lee McCann; children---Goree II, Kerwin Lemarr. Ordained as an Elder in the Christian Methodist Episcopal
Church, 1958; Present pastor, St. Mary's C.M.E. Ch.
1961---; private secretary to Bishop B. Julian Smith and
Bishop W.H. Amos; chairman, Conference Board of Christian Education, C.M.E. Church, 1961- ; vice-president,
Oklahoma Council of Churches; present: Dean of the Oklahoma City District Leadership Training School, 1963- .
Member: Oklahoma Council on Religion and Race; Speaker's
Bureau for the National Council of Christians and Jews;
chairman, committee on housing, Oklahoma City N.A.A.C.
P.; religious consultant, Oklahoma City Urban League;
member, Advisory Committee for the Oklahoma City Urban Renewal Authority, 1963-64; U.S. Army, 1950-53;
served in Korea 18 months; Korean Service medal; vice
president of the Interdenominational Ministerial Alliance,
Oklahoma City. Democrat. Home: 3332 NE 16th St.,
Oklahoma City, Oklahoma. Office: 1700 NE 4th St., Oklahoma City, Oklahoma.

JAMES, Samuel H., b. a native Texan; Tenn. State Coll.;
B.D. and S.T.M., Andover Newton Theol. Sem.; Grad.
Work, Boston U. and Harvard U.; D.D. (honorary), Selma,
U.; LL.D., Bishop Coll.; m. Catherine J. Lomans; 2 sons,
Samuel H., III; Carl Austin; 1 dau., Angela Inez; Former,
Dean of Men, Instr. Dept. of Rel., Bishop Coll.; Pastor,
Second Bapt. Ch., San Antonio, Texas; Moderator, La
Grange Bapt. Dist. Assoc., Texas; Vice-Pres., State Bapt.
Missionary and Ed. Conv., Texas and State SS & BTU
Cong., B.M. & E. Conv.; Mem. Bd. Dirs., Council of
Churches, Metropolitan San Antonio; Mem. Bd. Dirs.,
Community Welfare Council, San Antonio;Mem. Bd. Dirs.,
Central Br., San Antonio YMCA; Travelled, England,
Europe, Holy Land, Africa, Scandinavian Countries,
Switzerland and Russia; Mem. Planning and Zoning Com-
mission, City of San Antonio. Home: 430 North Pine St.,
San Antonio, Texas. Church: Chestnut & Center Sts., San
Antonio 2.

JAY, Grover Cleveland, b. Ocilla, Ga., Aug. 14, 1914; s.
John B. and Lizzie (Wells) J.; A.B., Paine Coll., Augusta,
Ga., 1941; B.D., Gammon Theol. Sem., 1948; m. Jonnie
Mae Mitchell; children---Grover Anthony; Ordained, 1942;
pastor, Church Hill Circuit, Webster Co., Ga.; pastor,

Scotts Mater Christian Methodist Episcopal Church, Americus, Ga.; Holsey Temple C. M. E. Church, Atlanta, Ga.;
Flat Rock Circuit, Elbertony District; current pastor,
presiding elder, Trinity C. M. E. Church, Augusta, Ga.;
teacher, Eatonton, Ga. Public School; Holsey Cobb Insti-
tute, Cordle, Ga.; director, Student Recruitment, Paine
Coll., 1932-64; Mem., Bd. of Trustees, Philip School of
Theology, Atlanta; Bd. of Trustees, Paine Coll.; vice
pres., Bd. of Christian Education, Christian Methodist
Episcopal Church; Augusta Richmond Co. Voters League;
Ga. Council on Human Relations; NAACP; Div. of Chris-
tian Ed., Nat. Council of Churches; Home: 731 Taylor,
Augusta, Ga. 30901; Office: 818 Eighth St., Augusta,
Ga.

JENKINS, Bradley Palmer, b. Wilcox County, Ala., July 17,
1916; s. Silas and Bessie J.; Snow Hill Institute, Snow
Hill, Ala., 1938; Immanuel Lutheran College and Seminary,
1954; Summer Courses Concordia Seminary, St. Louis,
Mo., 1955 & 60; m. Leila Scott; pastor, Faith Lutheran
Church, Mobile, Ala., 1954-61; pastor, St. Philip Luther-
an Church, 1962---; principal, Christian Day School,
Faith Lutheran Church, Mobile, Ala.; vi-pres., Alabama
Lutheran Conference, five years; Home: 803 Eddings St.,
Chattanooga, Tenn.; Ch.: 51 West 25th St., Chattanooga,
Tenna.

JENKINS, Charles Edward, St. b. Paris, Tenn., Aug. 24,
1928; s. Charles Atkins and Louis (George) J.; Lemoyne
College; Alabama A & M College; Union Bible Seminary;
D. D. (hon.), Monrovia College, Monrovia, Liberia, West
Africa; m. Lula Mae Reynolds; children--- Charliese,
Lunelle, Mary Louise, Charles Edward, Jr.; pastor, St.
Mary's African Methodist Episcopal Church, Sahillo, Tenn.,
1949; St. Mary and Lewis Chapel A. M. E. Churches, Lex-
ington & Parson, Tenn., 1949-50; pastor, Ebenezer A. M.
E. Church, Alarksville, Tenn., 1951-55; St. Paul A. M. E.
Church, Fayetteville, Tenn., 1955-60; St. Paul A. M. E.
Church, Chattanooga, Tenn., 1960---; St. Mark A. M. E.
Church, Rossview, Tenn., 1951-52; Kelso Ciacoit, Kelso,
Tenn., 1959-60; Radio speaker & programs on stations,
WTPR, Paris, Tenn., WDXI, WJZM, Clarksville, Tenn.,
WEKR, Fayetteville, Tenn.; Former pres., A. M. E. Al-
liance of Chattanooga; Former vice pres., Interdenomina-
tional Alliance, Chattanooga; Sec., Central Tenn. Confer-
ence, 1950-55; Delegate to General Conference of A. M. E.
Church, 1960-64; Contributing editor of A. M. E. Christian

Recorder; Home: 2524 Williams, Chattanooga 8, Tenn.;
Office: 2514 Williams, Chattanooga 8, Tenn.

JENKINS, John Dallas, Sr., teacher; b. Luray, Page Go,
Virginia, Oct. 12, 1919; s. Isaac Isaiah and Minnie
(Jeffries) J.; Studies: Storer College, Harper Ferry, W.
Va.; Capital, University, Columbis, Ohio; Conference of
Virginia Negro College on Rural Life, Virginia State Col-
lege, Etrricks, Va., 1947; American Bible College (B.
Th. - 1960; American Divinity School; D.D. (hon.), 1962;
m. Marian Elizabeth Dennis; children---Mrs. Grover
Cleveland Banks, Mrs. Lewis E. Dodley, Mrs. Richard
Vern Smith, John Dalls, Jr., Carver Robeson, Dennis
Lee; Ordained at Shepherdstown, W.V., 1938; pastor,
Baptist Churches in Shenandoah Valley of Virginia, 1938-
48; reordained Deacon and Elder in A.M.E. Zion Church,
1949; pastor, Poplar Street A.M.E. Zion Church, Philadelphia, Pa., 1949-52; pastor, A.M.E. Zion Church, Lis-
bon, Ohio, 1951-52; pastor, Aveery Memorial A.M.E.
Zion Church, Pittsburgh, Pa., 1952-54; pastor, Caldwell
Temple A.M.E. Zion Church, Columbus, Ohio, 1954---;
instructor, Central School of Religion, Columbus, Ohio;
instructor, Fourth District Institute; Resource Person,
General Convention on Christian Education; Chairman,
Church Committee, Columbus NAACP, 1959-60; Sec. Co-
lumbus Area Council of Churches, 1958-59; Member, Ad-
ministrative Board, Ohio Council of Churches, 1955-63;
Chairman, Commission to Study Evangelism in A.M.E.
Zion Church, 1964; President, A.M.E. Zion Ministers
Conference of Columbus, 1955---; Vice Pres., Interde-
nominational Ministers' Alliance of Columbus, 1960-63;
Member, Pastor's Section, NCCCUSA, 1962; Member,
Exec. Board, Women's Charity Council; Member, Exec.
Board, Poindexter Center, 1962-63; Chairman, Budget
Committee Ohio, A.M.E. Zion Church; Member, Steering
Committee Organic Union of A.M.E. Zion & C.M.E.
Churches; Chairman, Columbus Chapter, American Negro
Emancipation Centennial Authority; Extraordinary Service
Award in Christian Education, presented by the Christian
Education Department of the A.M.E. Zion Church, 1959;
Member, NAACP, Mason, Elks, YMCA, Urban League;
Author: "Toward Order" (a Handbook for Zion Methodists
on the Sacraments and Ordinances); Contributor, A.M.E.
Zion Quarterly Review (a homiletic journal); Home: 1750
E. Long, Columbus 3, Ohio; Office: 925 Bryden Road,
Columbus 5, Ohio.

JENKINS, Warren Marion, church official; b. Cowpens,
S. C., March 15, 1915; s. James E. C. and Maggie E. J.;
A. B., Claflin Coll., 1933-37; B. D., Gammon Theol. Sem.,
1944; M. A., Drew Univ., 1946; m. Alma Louise Williams;
children---Patricia Elaine; chaplain and teacher, Claflin
Coll., Orangeburg, S. C., 1946-49; chaplain, S. C. State
Coll., Orangeburg, S. C., 1949-53; pastor, Trinity Meth.
Ch., Camden, S. C., 1953-57; Cumberland Meth. Ch.,
Florence, S. C., 1957-61; Exec. Sec., S. C. Conf., Bd. of
Education, 1961---; Mem., Phi Beta Sigma; Mason; Bd.
of Ed., The Meth. Ch., 1956---; Mem., The Assn of Historical Society of the Meth. Ch.; Home: Muller St., Orange-
burg, S. C.; Office: Claflin Coll., Orangeburg, S. C.

JOHNS, Vernon, administrator; b. Darlington Heights, Va.;
s. William and Sally Branch (Price) J.; Va. Theol. Sem.
and Coll., Lynchburg, Va., 1915; Oberlin Coll. Grad.
Sch. of Theol, Oberlin, Oh., 1918; m. Altona Trent; 3
sons, Vernon, William, John; 3 daus., Adelaide, Enid,
Jean; Ordained Bapt. Minister, 1918; Pastored, Court
Street Bapt. Ch., Lynchburg, Va., 1920-26, 1941-48;
Holy Trinity Ch., Phila. 1933; First Church, Charleston,
W. Va., 1937-41; Dexter Avenue Bapt. Ch., Montgomery,
Ala., 1948-53; Dir., Bapt. Education Ctr., NYC, 1926-
29; Pres., Va. Theol. Sem. and Coll., 1929-33; mem.
Alpha Phi Alpha Frat.; Author, "Human Possibilities",
Best Sermons, 1926; Editor, Second Century Magazine,
1961---; Address: Box 418, Va. State College, Petersburg,
Va.

JOHNS, Paul, b. Bristol, Pa., Feb. 7, 1887; s. Reading
Beatty and Maria Caroline (Barney) J.; B. A., Howard
Univ., 1913; B. D., Yale Univ., 1918; m. Grace Alma
Wellmon; pastor, Congregational Churches, Knoxville,
Tenn., 1918-24; Newport, R. I., 1924-27; Philadelphia,
Pa., 1927-28; New Haven, Conn., 1928-30; Savannah, Ga.
1930-34; Retired, 1947; Teacher, Brewer Normal Sch.,
Greenwood, S. C., 1913-14; Gregory Institute, Wilmington,
N. C., 1914-15; Home: 173-54 103rd Road, Jamaica, New
York 11433.

JOHNSON, Andrew Lincoln, chaplain; b. Memphis, Tenn.,
Sept. 14, 1911; s. Aron and Sarah J.; B. A., Johnson C.
Univ.; B. D., Oberlin Graduate School of Theology; M. A.,
Oberlin College; D. D., Payne Theological Seminary; m.
Dora K. Kennedy; children---Dennis Harowe; Elder, Afri-
can Methodist Episcopal Church, North Ohio Conference;

Conference; Entered Reserve Chaplancy of US Army,
1938; Active Duty Chaplain, 1941---; Lt. Col., 1954;
Present assignment, Deputy Post Chaplain Fort Carson,
Colo., 1961---; First chaplain in 93rd Div. to earn
bronze star, 1944; Army Commendation Ribbon; Men.,
Alpha Phi Alpha; Mason; Home: 10523 Gooding Ave., Cleve-
land 8, Ohio; Office: Office Post Chaplain, Fort Carson,
Colo.

JOHNSON, Coolidge Milford, b. Honea Path, S.C., Dec.
30, 1923; s. Milford E. and Bertha (Mattison) J.;B.A.,
Benedict Coll., 1946; B.D., J.J. Starks School of Re-
ligion, 1949; D.D. (hon.) Friendship Coll., 1952; m.
Freeda Mae Moore; children---Freeda Lynne current
pastor, Majority Bapt. Ch., 1955---; pres., State Bapt.
Cooperative Convention, 1957---; sec., State Sunday School
and B.T.U. Congress, 1954---; principal, Greer High
School, Belton, S.C., 1950-52; teacher, Benedict School of
Rel. Extension Class; pres., Palmetto Voters League;
Bd. of Trustees, Morris Coll. and Friend Coll.; pres.,
Spartanburg Branch of CORE, 1957-60; Mem., NAACP,
1944---; State Youth Branch (college); Active in Boy Scouts
of America since 1948; chairman, Piedmont Div. of Boy
Scouts of America; Bd. of National Sunday School and B.
T.U. Congress, U.S.A., Inc.; Bd. of the Home Mission,
Nat. Bapt. Conv., U.S.A., Inc.; Silver Beaver Award,
1963; Mem., Mason; Omega Psi Phi; Home: 199 W. Park
Ave., Spartanburg, S.C.; Office: 199 W. Park Ave.,
Spartanburg, S.C.

JOHNSON, Gray Gould, chaplain; b. East Stroudsburg, Penna.
Oct. 27, 1922; s. Wm. Mck. and Josephine (Ray) J.;
Stroudsburg High School, Stroudsburg, Pa., 1940; B.A.,
Johnson C. Smith Univ., 1945; B.D., Theological Sem.,
Johnson C. Smith Univ., 1947; m. Helen Louise Smith;
children---Gray G. II, Bonnie Ray; pastor Second Presby.
Ch., Brunswich, Ga., 1947-48; chaplain US Army, 1948.
present serving as Lt. Colonel; Awards; UN Medal for
Korea; US Service Medal for Korea with 6 campaign at-
tachments; National Defense Medal; The Occupation Medal
for Japan and Germany; The Army Commendation Medal;
The Silver Star with the First Oak Leaf Cluster, The
Nations 3rd highest award for gallentry in action; Home:
APO, New York, N.Y.

JOHNSON, Harvey Eligah, chaplain; b. Atlanta, Ga., Apr.
19, 1898; s. Harvey, Sr. and Indiana M. (Oneal) J.;
B. D., Taladega Coll., Ala., 1923; B. S. L., Christian
Bible Coll., 1924; M. A., Atlanta Univ. Ga., 1939; D. D.
(hon.), National Spiritual School, 1960; m. Fannie Ram-
sey; children---Marcine A. (Mrs. Sylvester Hall); pastor,
First Congregational Church, Chattanooga, 1923-29; Rush
Memorial Congregational Ch., 1929-31; Beecher Congregational Ch., New Orleans, 1931-33; Talladega and Kymulga
Congr'l Churches, 1933-36; The First Congr'l Churches,
Montgomery and Selma, Ala., 1936-41; US Army Chaplain,
Lt. Colonel, 1941-54; instructor, High School, Lawrenceville, Ga. Notary Public; Mem., Mason; Home: 568 Auburn Ave., Atlanta 12, Ga.; Office: 18 South Jackson, At-
lanta 12, Ga.

JOHNSON, Julius Caesar, b. Baltimore, Md., Sept. 1894;
s. Julius Caesar and Lillie Virginia (Matthew) J.; Temple
Univ., 1911; Gammon Theol. Sem., 1916; graduate work:
Boston Univ., 1921, D. D. (hon.), Wiley Coll., Marshall
Tex.; m. Emma Pepper; son, John Henri Watkins; pastor,
Washington Conference Methodist Church, 1916; director,
Sharp St. Memorial Church Educational Center, 1920-21;
director, Community Center and Playgrounds, Lexington,
Ky. and part time pastors: Denver, Colorado, 1923-30;
Hot Springs, Ark., 1930-32; Nashville, Tenn., 1932-34;
Minister and Director of Christian Education, Tenn., Ark.,
and Okla., 1930; summer school instructor, Methodist
Ministers through Ministerial Training Methodist Church,
Philander Smith Coll., 16 years; Mem., Christian Board
Directors, South Street Community Center; Chaplains
Training School, World War I; Citation Plague, for serv-
ice in Public School by Cameron High School; Mem.,
Mason; Omega Psi Phi; Home: 1109 First Ave., So.
Nashville 10, Tenn.; Office: 1116 First Ave. So. Nash-
ville 10, Tenn.

JOHNSON, Lawrence Washington, teacher; b. Clifton, Tenn.,
Feb. 24, 1901; s. Frank and Ida (Briggs) J.; B. S., Tenn.
State Coll., 1937; M. A., Fisk Univ, 1946; m. Lucille
Jacison; children---Sharon, Ralph, Deborah, Roy; pastor,
Shorter Chapel African Methodist Episcopal Church, Frank-
lin, Tenn., 1951-52; Cedar Grove Circuit, Rutherford
County, Tenn., 1956-57; Lewisburg Circuit, Lewisburg,
Tenn., 1958, 1962-63; Woodfork Chapel A. M. E. Church,
Shelbyville, Tenn., 1959; St. Luke A. M. E. Church, Galla-
tin, Tenn., 1963---; principal, High School, Winchester,

Tenn. & Princeton, Ky., Trenton, Tenn., Midville, Ga.,
Rochell, Ga.; Mem., Amer. Legion and Brotherhood
Club; chaplain asst., US Army, 1943; Mem., Ministerial
Interracial Group; Home: 355 Blythe Ave., Gallatin, Tenn.;
Office: 357 Blythe Ave., Gallatin, Tenn.

JOHNSON, Mordecai Wyatt, univ. pres., b. Paris, Tenn.,
Jan. 12, 1890; s. Wyatt and Carolyn (Freeman) J.;
Academy of Roger Williams Univ., Nashville, Tenn. and
Howe Institute, Memphis; A. B., Morehouse Coll., Atlanta,
Ga., 1911; LL. D. (hon.), 1935; A. B., Univ. of Chicago,
1913; B. D., Rochester Theol. Sem., 1921; S. T. M.,
Harvard Univ., 1922; D. D., Howard Univ., Wash., D. C.
1923; Gammon Theol., Sem., Atlanta, Ga., 1928; LL. D.,
Delaware State Coll., 1955; Atlanta Univ., 1960; Va. State
Univ.; D. H. L., Temple Univ., 1954; D. C. L., University
Liberia, 1956; m. Anna Ethelyn Gardener; children---
Carolyn Elizabeth, Mordecai Wyatt, Archer Clement, Wil-
liam Howard, Anna Faith; prof., English, economics, his-
tory, Morehouse Coll., 1911-13; student pastor, Second
Bapt. Ch., Mumford, N. Y., 1913-16; student sec., International Comm., YMCA, 1916-17; Ordained Bapt. Ministry,
1916; pastor, First Bapt. Ch., Charleston, W. Va., 1917-
26; pres., Howard Univ., 1926-60, now emeritus; dir., del.
Atlantic Congress, NATO Parliamentaries Council, London,
1959; Mem., Advisory Council for the Virgin Islands; Adv.
Council, Nat. Youth Commn.; director, Nat. Council
United Negro Coll. Fund; general exec. bd. Nat. Religion
and Labor Found.; vice chmn., Nat. Council Prevention
of War; director, Nat. Council Christians and Jews;
Decorated Order of Varco Minez de Balboa, Panama;
Order of Star of Honor with Grand Cordon, Ethiopia;
Home: 1610 Buchanan St. NW, Wash. 11, D. C.

JOHNSON, Ned Howard, b. Wheeling , W. Va., Nov. 8,
1934; s. Arthur F. and Elizabeth (Jackson) J.; A. B.,
Clark Coll., Atlanta, Ga., 1957; B. D., Gammon Theol.
Sem., 1960; D. D. (hon.), The Coll. of Philosophy, Kan-
sas City, Miss., 1963; m. Sarah Hughes; children---Ned,
Jr., Geneva, Yvonne, Karen; pastor, First Congregational
Church, Marietta, Ga., 1956; First Congregational Church,
Macon, Ga., 1958-59; St. Paul Meth. Church, Montgomery,
Ala., 1959-60; Trinity Meth. Ch., Clarksburg, W. Va.,
1961-62; Ronceverte-White Sulphur Charge, Ronceverte, W.
Va., 1962---; Mem., Alpha Phi Alpha; Masons; Alpha
Kappa Delta Sociological Honor Society; Democrat; Home:
231 Main St., Ronceverte, W. Va. 24970; Office: same.

*JOHNSON, Richard Hanson, b. Balto, Md., Sept. 8, 1904.
s. Charles A. and Anna Elizabeth H.; A.B., B. Th.,
Howard Univ., Sch. of Rel., 1934; A.M., Howard Univ.,
1952; courses, Gammon Theol. Sem., 1959: m. Julia
Louise Taylor; children---Richard Hanson, Jr., Charles
Albert II, Beverly (Mrs. Kelly), Florence (Mrs. Richard
I. Ray), Joan M., Alexander P., Edgar A.; current Dist.
supt. Meth. Ch.; mem., Bd. of Pensions; Chaplains Com.;
Committee on Ministry to Neglected Areas; treas., Wesley
Foundation, Howard Univ.; mem., Omega Psi Phi; author:
Faith Through Victory, Washington, D.C. Campbell Press;
Home: 3208 Carlyle Ave., Balto. 16, Md.; Office: 828 N.
Carrollton Ave., Balto. 17, Md.

JOHNSON, Robert Josiah, b. Hartford, Conn., Oct. 12,
1884; s. Robert and Elnora (Hurb) J.; St. Augustine's Collegiate Institute, Raleigh, N.C., 1906; Bishop Payne
Divinity School, 1909; Attended College of Preachers,
Washington, D.C., 1945-52; D.D. (hon.), Shaffer Theological Seminary, Kansas City, Kans., 1930; m. Anna Turner
Burgess; children---Elnora, Robert, James, Ann, Theodore,
Fancis; vicar, St. Titus, Durbaur, N.C., 1909-13; St.
Auden's Peterson, N.J., 1919-23; Good Shepherd, Lynch-
burg, Va., 1913-19; St. Augustine's, Wichita, Kans.,
1923-25; Church of the Ascension, Kansas City, Kans.,
1925-30; St. Mary's, Hot Spr., Arkansas, 1930-40; All
Saint's, Warrenton, N.C., St. Mark's, Wilson, 1943-57;
Retired, 1957; Director of Young People's Groups of Con-
ferences Dioceses of N.C., 1945-56; Sec., Board of Trus-
tees of St. Augustine's College, 1957---; Member, The
Exec. Council of the Diocese of N.C., 1943-47; 1951-54;
Home: 1304 Fidewood, N. Wilson, N.C.; Office: Vicar
Emeritus of St. Mark's Church, Wilson, N.C.

JOHNSON, Robert Pierre, b. Jersey City, New Jersey,
1914; A.B. Bloomfield Coll., 1937, B.D. Union Seminary,
N.Y.C. 1940, Ed. M. University of Pittsburgh, Pa. 1947,
D.D. Bloomfield Coll., 1964; m. Florence V. Bond, 1941
(deceased, 1962); children---Lydia; Elayne; Alex; Deborah;
Ministry: Ordained by Presbytery of Jersey City, 1940,
Bethesda Presbyterian Ch. 1940-1950, Asst. Secretary
Department of City and Industrial Work - Board of Na-
tional Missions (Presbyterian) 1950-1954-; Pastor, Fifteenth
Street Presbyterian Church, 1954. Institute of Racial and
Industrial Relations - Co-founder, Pittsburgh, 1946, Com-
mittee of Reorganization of Presbytery, 1949-50; West-
minister Foundation, 1954-1960, 1961-1964; Chairman,

Pensions Committee, Washington Presbytery, 1956-1962;
General Council, 1959-1962, 1963; Moderator, 1964---;
102nd Synod Preacher, 1957; Teacher, Wilson Leadership
School, 1959-62; Chairman, National Missions, 1963;
Permanent Commission on Inter-Church Relations, 1955-
1958; Delegate, World Alliance of Reformed Churches
holding the Presbyterian Order, 1958-64; Trustee, Nation-
al Presbyterian Church and Center, 1962-64; Commissioner,
1953, 1963; Member: Board of Directors of Children and
Family Services, Pittsburgh, Pa. 1948-1950; Secretary,
Board of Directors, Council of Churches National Capitol
Area, 1958-1960; Chairman, Department of Social Welfare,
Council of Churches of National Capitol Area, 1960-1962;
President, Macfarland Parent Teachers Assoc., 1958-59;
Housing Committee, Washington Urban League, 1960;
Home: 4503 17th St., N.W. Wash. D.C.   Office: 15th
and R Streets, N.W. Wash. D.C.

JOHNSON, Robert Ross, b. Spokane, Wash., June 26, 1920;
s. John J. and Meha (Nickleberry) J.; B.A., Whitworth
Coll., 1939-43; B.D., Colgate Rochester Coll., 1943-
46; m. Ernestine N.; children---Michele, Stephen Ross,
John Ernest; instructor, Fla. Normal Ind. Coll., 1946-
47; pastor, 2nd Baptist Ch., LeRoy, New York, 1947-
48; co-minister, So. Congregational Ch., Chicago, Ill.,
1947-52; pastor, Nazarene Congr'l Ch., Brooklyn, N.Y.,
1952-56; St. Albans Congr'l Ch., 1956---; Mem., New
York City Dept. of Correction; Former Mem., Oakwood-
Kenwood Community Council; Hyde-Park Community Conf.;
Bd. Mem., Chicago Council Against Religious and Racial
Discrimination; vice pres., Church Federation of Chicago;
pres., Chicago Congr'l Minister's Union; pres., Ill. State
Conf. of NAACP; Bd. Mem., Chicago NAACP; chairman,
Christian Educational Dept., Brooklyn Prot. Council, 2
years; Bd. Mem., New York City Congr'l Church Assn;
Urban League of Jamaica, N.Y.; pres., Brooklyn-Long
Island Ministerial Alliance; Alpha Phi Alpha; chairman,
Com. on Church Extension and Home Missions of the New
York City Congregational Church Assn; Local Sch. Bd.
Dist. #50, Queens; Bd. of Jamaica Br., NAACP; Nation-
al Conf. of Christians and Jews; Queens Mental Health
Society; Queens Federation of Churches; Queens Center;
Queens T.B. and Guidance Health Assn; Home: 175-46
Murdock Ave., St. Albans 33, New York; Office: 172-17
Linden Blvd., St. Albans, N.Y.

JOHNSON, Samuel T., b. New York, N.Y., Oct. 20, 1925;

s. John L. and Carolyn (Russell) J.; N.Y.U., 1941-43;
B.A., Roosevelt Coll', Chgo, Ill., 1948; Th.B., Chgo
Bapt. Institute, 1951; B.D., N. Bapt. Theol. Sem.,
1955; m. Korin Clark; 1 son, Samuel T., Jr.; 2 daus.
Saundra Anita, Cheryl Dennese; Ordained, Bapt. Minis-
ter, 1954; Assoc. Minister, Union Evangelistic Bapt.
Ch., Chgo. Heights, Ill., 1951-54; Asst. Minister, Union
E. Bapt. Ch., Chgo, Heights, 1954-58; Pastor, New Mt.
Zion Bapt. Ch., Daytona Beach, Fla., 1958---; Faculty
staff, Nat. SS & BTU Congress, 1959---; Pres., Inter-
racial Council on Human Relations; Vice-Pres., Minister-
ial Alliance, (integrated), Halifax Area, Fla.; Officer
local NAACP (5 yrs); Coordinator, Assoc. Branch S.C.L.
C. (Southern Christian Leadership Conf.); Pres. (protem),
Council on Human Relations for Full Compliance to Civil
Rights Law, 1964; U.S. Army, Overseas (China, India,
Burma Theater), 1943-46; Recipient, Good Conduct Service Medal and Bronze Star; mem. Social Engineers (Pres.)
business and professional club for better community improvement. Home: 251 Weaver, Daytona Beach, Fla.
Church: P.O. Box 863, Daytona Beach, Fla.

JOHNSON, Ulysses Samuel, b. Fairfield County, S.C., Oct.
13, 1909; s. Robert and Ida (Sanders) J.; A.B., Livingstone College, 1938; B.D., Johnson C. Smith University,
Theological Seminary, 1942; D.D. (hon.), Livingstone Col-
lege, 1952; m. Marie Jennings; children---Norris Jennings;
pastor, St. Paul A.M.E. Zion Church, Hendersonville,
N.C.; Hunters Chapel A.M.E. Zion Church, Tuscaloosa,
Ala.; St. Luke A.M.E. Zion Church, Wilmington, N.C.;
current pastor, St. Johnson A.M.E. Zion Church, Wilson,
N.C.; Substitute teaching-instructor, Ministers & Laymen's
Institute, South Port, N.C.; Trustee, Clinton, N.C., Rock
Hill S.C.; Mem.: Men's Civic Club; Wilson, N.C.; NAACP;
Home: 119 Pender St., Wilson, N.C.; Office: St. John
A.M.E. Zion Church, Wilson, N.C.

JOHNSON, Wilbur R., b. Chicago, Ill., Sept. 28, 1920;
s. L.C. and Corinne A.; B.S., Wilberforce Univ., 1945;
S.T.B., Boston U. Sch. of Theology, 1949; m. Ernestine
Range; children---Gayle, Karen; pastor, Easter Hill Meth-
odist Church, Richmond, Calif., 1951-59; Normandie Ave.,
Methodist Ch., Los Angeles, Calif., 1959-61; Enterprise
Methodist Church, Compton, Calif., 1961-63; current,
Pueblo Gardens Methodist Church, Tucson, Ariz., 1963--;
Received world-wide news coverage over my appointment
as first Negro to be assigned as minister-in-charge of all

white church (as of July 1963); First Negro in Richmond,
Calif. Rotary Club; Mem. , Mason; Alpha Phi Alpha;
Democrat; NAACP; Christmas sermon in Pulpit Digest,
Dec. , 1963; Home: 2303 South Norris Ave. , Tucson,
Ariz. 85713; Office: 2520 South Plumber Ave. , Tucson,
Ariz. 85713.

JONES, Aubry, b. Texarkana, Ark. , Feb. 22, 1933; B. S. ,
Ark. A. M. & N. Coll. , Pine Bluff, Ark. , 1954; M. Ed.
Univ. of Ark. , Fayetteville, Ark. , 1961; Wesley School
of Theology, 1962; m. Joyce Young; children---Aubry
Jones, Jr. ; pastor, Smith Chapel Meth. Church, Sikeston,
Md. , 1960---; teacher, public school, 1956---; chairman,
The Recreational Committee, Sunset Chamber of Commerce;
US Army, 1954-56; Mem. , Kappa Alpha Psi; NEA; Mis-
souri Education Ass'n; Ind. Arts & Vocational Education
Ass'n; Home: 4680 Essex Pl. , St. Louis 15, Mo. ; Office:
200 Young St. , Sikeston, Md.

JONES, Bennie J. , b. Danville, La. , Nov. 12, 1909; s.
Billie and Edna Essie; Grambling Coll. , La. ; Bishop Coll. ;
Langston Univ. , B. S. ; m. Ada B. Hewitt; children---
Geneva, Marjorie, Bennie, Jr. ; teacher, 15 years; chap-
lain, World War II; pastor, First Bapt. Church; modera-
tor, S. E. District Bapt. Ass'n; dean, Okla. Bapt. Congress
of Christian Education; two battle stars; Mem. , Mason;
Home: 4 NW Enid St. , Idabel, Okla.

JONES, E. Theodore, B. A. , Va. Union Univ. , Richmond,
Va. ; B. D. , Crozier Theol. Sem. , Chester, Pa. ; M. A. ,
Univ. of Pa. , Phila. , Pa. ; Union Theol. Sem. & Columbia
Univ. ; m. Dorothy L. Rice; children---Cheryl Laconia,
Theodore B. , Eric Todd; pastor, Riverview Bapt. Ch. ,
Richmond, Va. ; dean of Chapel, Director of Student Chris-
tian Center, Va. Union Univ. ; Prof. of Soc. & Anthro. ;
current asst. director, Dept. of Schs. and Coll. , Ameri-
can Baptist Convention, Valley Forge, Pa. , 1962---; Office:
American Bapt. Convention, Dept. of Schs. and Coll. ,
Valley Forge, Pa.

JONES, James Miller, b. New York, N. Y. , Aug. 2, 1921;
s. (adopted) Mary Nelson Jones; B. S. Ed. , West Va.
State Coll. , 1949; S. T. B. , Boston Univ. Sch. of Theol. ,
1953; m. Margaret Rugh Howard; 2 daus. , Nathlie Eloise,
Valerie Teresa; Mig. Ministry, Home Miss. Div. , Nat.
Counc. of Chs. of Christ, U. S. A. , 51, 52, 1953-57;
Assoc. Chap. , Hampton Institute, Hampton, Va. , 1957-

61; Pastor, Lemuel Haynes Cong. Ch., Jamaica, N.Y.,
1961; Part-time Chaplain, Vet. Adm. Hosp., New York
City; mem. NAACP, Bd. of Dirs., Social Action Comm.,
United Church of Christ; U.S. Army, 33 mos. overseas
duty, 1942-45; Home: 160-35 119th Drive, Jamaica 34,
N.Y. Office: 146-09 116th Avenue, Jamaica 36, N.Y.

JONES, John Luke, b. White Plains, Va., Aug. 28, 1886;
s. Wilkins E. and Elizabeth (Tanner) J.; Downingtown
Industrial Sch., 1913; Lincoln Univ. Theol. Dept., Pa.
1917; Carswell Institute of Speech; m. Estella Rose Morgan; Former missionary of the Bethany Bapt. Assn, N.J.
1918; instructor, The Liberty Bapt. Institute, Camden, N,
J.; pastor, Union Bapt. Ch., Pawtucket, R.I., 1922-24;
Grace Temple Bapt. Ch., Lawnside, N.J., 1927-29; current pastor, Miller Memorial Bapt. Ch., 1936---; pres.
(former), UNIA, R.I.; Gospel Singer, 1910-18; Studied
as Crayon Artist, House and Sign Painting, Mail Order
Business, Compositor-Printer and Journalism; editor and
founder, Northwest Truth magazine; reporter, Bapt.
Ministers Conf. of Philadelphia; Mem., Evangelistic Bd.
of the Penna, Bapt. State Convention; Grand Order Moses;
NAACP, Fellowship Commission; Crime Prevention Assn;
The Wharton Center Assn; Home Mission Dept. of the
National Council of Christ in America; Home: 2225 North
College Ave., Phila. 21, Penna.; Office: 22nd St. above
Jefferson St., Phila., Pa.

JONES, Lawrence Neale, educator; b. Moundsville, W. Va.,
Apr. 24, 1921; s. Eugne Wayman and Rosa (Bruce) J.;
B.S. Ed., West Va. State Coll., 1942; M.A., Univ. of
Chgo., 1948; B.D., Oberlin Sch. of Theol., 1955; Ph.D.,
Yale University, 1961; m. Mary Ellen Cooley; dau. Mary
Lynn, son, Rodney Bruce; West Salem Charge Evan.
and Ref. Ch., 1953-55; Student Chr. Movement, Middle
Atlantic Region, 1957-60; Dean, Fisk Univ. Chapel, Nash-
ville, Tenn., 1961---; U.S. Army, 1943-46; 1947-53;
ROTC Asst. Prof. of Military Science, Va. State Coll.;
Captain, U.S. Army, Europe, 1951-53; mem. Bd. Dirs.,
Nashville NAACP, 18th Ave. Comm. Ctr., Nashville
Assoc. for United Nations; Vice-Pres., Nashville Human
Rel. Council; mem. Soc. Action Comm., Tenn. Council
of Churches; Pres., United Church Fellowship of Campus
Ministry; mem., Commission on Higher Education, Nat.
Council of Churches; Recipient, Rosenwald Scholarship,
Lucy Monroe Scholarship, Rockefeller Doctoral Fellowship;
Home: 908 17th Ave., North, Nashville, Tenn. 32708. Of-

fice: Fisk Union Church, Fisk University, Nashville, Tenn.,
37208.

JONES, Leon Cooper, social worker; Laurel, Miss., Apr.
16, 1919; s. Robert Franklin and Addie (Mobley) J.;
certificate, Cornish Musical Conservatory, Seattle, Wash.,
1952; B.A., Seattle Pacific Coll., 1962; m. Rubye Brown;
children---Kathryn Louise; asst. pastor, Mt. Olive Baptist
Ch., Seattle, Wash., 1957-60; pastor, Second Baptist Ch.,
Everett, Wash., 1960---; caseworker, Washington State
Dept. of Public Assistance; Mem., Mason; vice moderator,
Cascade Ass'n, American Baptist Churches of Pacific
Northwest, 1963; US Navy, 1938-46; Defense Medal; Good
Conduct Medal; Asiatic Pacific Ribbon; Phillipines Cam-
paign; World War II Victory Medal; The American Theater
Medal; Home: 1424 31st Ave., Seattle 22, Wash.; Office:
Second Baptist Ch., 2807 Virginia, Everett, Washington.

JONES, Major J., coll. prof., church official; b. Rome,
Ga.; A.B., Clark Coll., Atlanta, Ga.; B.D., Gammon
Theol. Sem.; S.T.M., Oberlin Coll., Ohio; Th.D., Bos-
ton Univ., Mass.; m. Mattie P.; children---Chandra J.;
pastor, college professor, conference director of Chris-
tian education in The Methodist Church; current supt.,
The Knoxville Dist. of the East Tenn. Conference of The
Methodist Church; Mem., 1964 General Conference, The
Methodist Ch.; 1964 Central Jurisdictional Conference of
The Methodist Church; General Bd. of Education of The
Methodist Church; The Commission on Standards for Wes-
ley Foundations of The Methodist Ch.; The Chattanooga
Mayor's Bi-Racial Committee; Chattanooga Chamber of
Commerce; Bd. of Director, Tenn. Council on Human Re-
lations; The Bd. of the Committee of Southern Churchmen;
The Bd. of the Southern Christian Leadership Conference;
The Committee of Management of the YMCA; The Bd. of
the Chattanooga Area Literacy Movement; The Bd. of the
National (Chattanooga) Conference of Christians and
Jews; Office: 3709 Rogers Rd., Chattanooga, Tenn.

JONES, Matthew Aureluis, Sr., teacher; b. Bethel, N.C.
Aug. 17, 1913; s. Henry Fred and Isabella (Payton) J.;
1937, A.B. St. Augustine's College; 1947, B.D. Bishop
Payne Divinity School; m. Oliva Beatrice Browning; chil-
dren: Matthew, Jr., Marshall R., Rose J. Hicks
(Thomas H. Hicks, Jr.) Brenda J. (Mrs. Clarke S.
Frazier); Headmaster, John Moncure High School 1937-
38 (Millers Tavern, Va.); Principal-teacher, Marie Mc

Iver High School, 1939-43, Littleton, N.C.; Chaplain,
Voorhees, School & Jr. College, 1947-51, Denmark, S.
C.; Priest-in-Charge, St. Cyprian's Episcopal Church,
Pensacola, Fla., 1951-58; Priest in Charge, St. Luke's
Episcopal Church, Knoxville, Tenn., 1958---; teacher,
W.P.A. Adult Education, 1936-38; Raleigh, N.C. Mem.
Chr., Fricker Rec. Center Board, Pensacola, Fla.
1952-53; Pres., Knoxville Branch NAACP, 1961; Sec.
Exec. Comm. Associated Council for Full Citizenship,
Knoxville, Tenn., 1960-61; Advisory Board, Homemakers
service, State Dept. Public Welfare, Tenn.; Urban League
Award; Home: 2201 McCalla Ave., Knoxville, 15, Tenn.;
600 Chestnut St., Knoxville 14, Tenn.

JONES, Robert L., b. Elizabeth, New Jersey, July 29,
1936; s. Samuel O. and Eva (Taylor) J.; B.A., Atlantic
Union College, 1959; M.A., Andrews Univ., 1961; m. Dawn
Lee Reynolds. Conducted evangelistic crusade, 1963;
Lake Region Conf. of Seventh-Day Adventists, 1961; as-
sistant pastor, Benton Harbor, Michigan; present: pastor,
Seventh-Day Adventist Church, Kalamazoo, Pontiac and
Millan, Michigan. Phi Delta Chi Society; Urban League.
Home: 3263 Avon Manor, Rochester, Michigan, Office:
London S.D.A. Church, London, Michigan.

JONES, Sercy Leonard, b. Conroe, Tex., Nov. 7, 1917;
s. John and Ella Foster; Samuel Houston Coll., 1940; A.
B.; Gammon Theological Seminary, B.D.; Drew Univ.,
graduate study, 1943; S.T.M., Temple Univ., 1943; m.
Mary Elizabeth Randolph; children---Randolph L., Car-
roll W., Carroll W., Iris Faye, Francis Robert, Marcus
Edwin; pastor, Woodbury Methodist Church, 1944-45;
Delair, N.J., 1945-47; Fordville, N.J., 1947-49; Chester,
Siloam, 1949-55; Cambridge, Maryland, 1955-61; Haven
Meth. Church, Philadelphia, Pa., 1961---; Mem., Bd. of
Managers of YMCA, Chester & Phil., Pa.; Board of
Managers, Columbia Branch YMCA; Bd. of Directors,
Inter-church Child Care Society; Citizens' Advisory Com-
mittee of The Dept. of Public Assistance of the City of
Philadelphia; Mem., Omega Psi Phi; Home: 6700 Cresheim
Rd., Phil., Pa. 19119; Office: 23rd and Oxford St., Phila.
Pa., 19121.

JONES, Vernon Algernon, Jr. chaplain; b. Brunswick County,
Virginia, Sept. 19, 1924; s. Vernon A. and Harriet
(Rhodes) J.; A.B., Virginia Union University, Richmond,
Va., 1941-45; B.D., Bishop Payne Divinity School (Vir-

ginia Theol. Sch., Alexandria), 1945-48; m. Lillian Li-
ressarine Clark; children---Frances Cecilia, Harriet
Ethelyn, Lillian Vernelle; pastor, St. Andrew's, Danville,
Chirst, Halifax, St. Luke's Chatham (Virginia), 1948-49;
pastor, St. James, Emporia, Va. and St. Thomas',
Freeman, Va., 1949-53; pastor, St. Stephen's, Peters-
burg, Virginia, 1953-57; rector, St. Andrew's Church,
Tuskegee Institute, Alabama, 1957---; Episcopal Chaplain
to Students, Tuskegee Institute - with counseling and
Hospital Ministry Assignments; Member, Tuskegee Civic
Association, Omega Psi Phi Fraternity; Mason; Home:
301 Neal Street, Tuskegee Institute, Alabama; Office: 429
Montgomery Road, Tuskegee Institute, Alabama.

JONES, William Clarke, Church official; b. Detroit, Michigan,
Sept. 18, 1927; s. Gilbert Emmanuel and Lue Alma (Clarke)
J.; Oakwood Academy, 1944-45; B.A., Oakwood College,
1949; m. Doris Willia Mae Kimble; children-William
Clarke, Jr., Cynthia R. Merret; Southwest Reginal Conf.
of Seventh-Day Adventist, 1949- ; Pastored: Lubbock,
Texas, 1950-53; Fort Worth, Texas, 1953-57; Tyler,
Texas, 1957-62; San Antonio, 1962-63; present: secretary,
Sabbath School and Home Missionary, of S.A.D. Church,
Dallas, Texas. Office: 1900 South Blvd., Dallas, Texas.

JONES, William Ronald, b. Louisville, Ky., July 17, 1933;
s. Henry Wise, Jr. and Lannie Belle (Brogsdale) J.;
1955, A.B. Howard Univ.; 1958, B.D. Harvard Univ.,
1960, Candidate for Ph.D., Brown Univ. m. Lauretta
Adalyne (Hicks) J. Children: Jeffrey; Current; Asst. Minister,
First Unitarian Church, Providence, R.I.; Teacher Asst.
Brown Univ.; present prof. philosophy, Howard Univ., Wash.
D.C.; Phi Beta Kappa; National Defense Education Act Fellowship; Rockefeller Brothers Theological Fellowship; Rockefeller Doctoral Fellowship in Religion; Office: Dept. of Philosophy, Howard Univ., Wash. 20001, D.C.

JORDAN, Frederick Douglass, bishop; b. Atlanta, Ga.,
Aug. 8, 1901; s. D.J. and Carrie (Thomas) J.; A.B.,
Northwestern Univ.; B.D., Garrett Theol. Sem.; Graduate
work: Chicago Theol. Sem., Univ. of Chicago; D.D.
(hon.), LL.D. (hon.), Wilberforce Univ., Payne Sem.,
Campbell Coll., Morris Brown Coll., Kittrell Coll., Allen Univ., Monrovia Coll., Liberia; m. Artishia Wilkerson; dean of Sch. of Rel., dean of Coll., organizer and
pres., Bishop Wms. Sch. of Rel., Western Univ.,

Quindaro, Kans.; dean, International Council of Religious
Education; pastor, St. Paul African Methodist Episcopal
Church, South Chicago; St. Paul A. M. E. Ch., Moline,
Ill.; Carey Temple and St. Mary A. M. E. Ch., Chicago,
Ill.; First A. M. E. Church, Gary, Ind.; Bethel A. M. E.
Ch., Leavenworth, Kans.; Bethel A. M. E. Ch., Kansas
City, Mo.; 1st A. M. E. & Ward A. M. E. Ch., Los
Angeles, Calif.; Episcopal supervision: Union of S. Africa,
Central African Federation Ghana, Liberia, Sierra Leone
and Nigeria, on the West Coast of Africa; Fifth Episcopal
District: Missouri, West to Calif.; Eighth District; La.
and Miss. -forced to leave the latter because of integration
activities, voter registration and etc.; Mem., Exec. Bd.
of NAACP Committee of Management, YMCA, Los Angeles;
National Advisory Committee of CORE; Urban League;
Southern Christian Education Committee; American Civil
Liberties Union; American Christian Palestine Com.;
Exec. Com. and Chairman, Race Relations Commission
of Los Angeles Ch. Federation; Mason; Alpha Phi Alpha;
Sigma Pi Phi; NAACP; Home: 5151 Franklin Ave., Hollywood 27, Calif.

JORDAN, Robert Lee, b. Knoxville, Tenn., May 20, 1906;
s. Henry and Emma (Matteney) J.; Va. Union Univ., 1928-
30; A. B., Chapman Coll., 1936; Univ. of Southern Calif.,
1932; M. A., Univ. of Mich.; m. Maisie Norman; children
Robert Lee, Emma Goldie, Kenneth Samuel; asst. supt.,
West Side Community Center, Los Angeles, Calif., 1933-
35; chmn, Com. on Friendly Relations, Christian Churches,
1934-36; asst. pastor, Hooper Ave. Christian Ch.; current
pastor, United Christian Ch., Detroit, Mich., 1937---;
pres., Nat. Christian Missionary Cov., 1958-60; chmn,
Social Action Com., Christian Ch., 1954-58; Bd. Mem.,
Detroit Council of Churches, 1958-60; Bd. Mem., Delta
Home for Girls, 1956-58; Program chairman, Denominational Ministerial Alliance, 1963---; Mem., Selective Rat-
ings Group of Negro Preachers of Detroit, Mich.; Award:
25 year citation for serving one church, Detroit Ministers Conf.; pres., West Side Pastors Union, Detroit;
Interdenominational Ministers Alliance; Kappa Alpha Psi;
author: Two Races in Fellowship; Negro Disciples in
Michigan; former manager, Western Challenger (newspaper,
Los Angeles); Home: 2421 W. Forest, Detroit 8, Mich.;
Office: 2415 W. Forest, Detroit 8, Mich.

JOSEPH, Charles David, b. Centerville, Ala., July 30,
1936; s. Walsh and Avie (Smelley) J.; B. S., Oakwood

College, 1957; B.A., Oakwood College, 1961; M.A.,
Andrews Univ., 1962; m. Vivian Holland. Seventh-Day
Adventist Church - intern work in Gary, Indiana, 1961-
62; intern work in Chicago, Ill., 1962; intern work in
Minneapolis, Minn., 1962; present: pastor, Greenwood
S.D.A. Church, 1962-   . Teacher of Academy science
and College biology, 1960-61. Home: 1016 Eastlawn Dr.,
Greenwood, Miss.

JUSTISS, Jacob, Jr., Church official, College professor;
    b. Mount Pleasant, Texas, May 2, 1919; s. Jacob and
    Beatrice (Price) J.; University of Toledo, 1937-39; Jr.
    College; B.A., Emmanuel Missionary College, 1939-42;
    Wayne University, Detroit 1943; M.A., Seventh-Day Ad-
    ventist Theological Seminary, 1944-45; S.D.A. Theological
    Seminary, 1945-46; advanced work toward B.D., Harvard
    Univ., Summer 1950, Pastoral Training; Ohio State Univ.,
    1951-52, Grad. Doctoral work toward Ph.D. in History;
    m. Mae Elizabeth Smith; children-- Joan Andree and
    Jacob III. Michigan Conference of S.D.A., pastor-evange-
    list, 1942-44; S.D.A. Theological Seminary, 1944-45;
    Head of History Department, Pine Forge Institute, Pine
    Forge, Pa., 1946-48; Associate in History Dept., Oak-
    wood College, 1948-50; Principal, Washington Union
    Academy, Washington, D.C., 1950-51; pastor, Columbus,
    Ohio, 1951-1953; pastor, Cincinnati, Ohio, 1958-62; pres-
    ent: chairman of Youth Activities, Alleghny Conf. of S.
    D.A., Chaplain, National Service Organization, and
    Temperance Coordinator, Pine Forge, Pa., 1962-   .
    Marriage Counselor; Chairman of the Board of Directors,
    Christian Benefit Association. Member - Executive Com-
    mittee of Allegheny Conference, 1960-62; Executive Board
    of Pine Forge Institute, 1958-62; Chaplain, Hadley Memor-
    ial Hospital, Washington, D.C., 1956-58; Chaplain, Ad-
    visory Committee, Metropolitan Boys Club, 1956-58; Chap-
    lain, Advisory Committee, Metropolitan Boys Club, 1956-
    58. Author: History of Health Work of Seventh-Day Adven-
    tist Among Negroes; History of Riverside Sanitarium and
    Hospital to 1945. Home: Post Office Box #21, Pine Forge,
    Pa. Office: Allegheny Conf., Pine Forge, Pa.

KEARNS, Curtis Andre, b. Charlotte, N.C., Aug. 29,
    1916; s. Andrew B. and Belle Harrell; A.B., Johnson C.
    Smith, Charlotte, N.C., 1935-39; B.D., Theological
    Seminary, 1939-42; Graduate work Union Seminary,
    Richmond, Va., 1949; m. Laura Lee Henderson; children

---Ida Isabella, Curtis A., Jr., Ronald; college pastor
and rel. ed. teacher Mary Allen Jr. College, Crockett,
Texas, 1942-43; pastor Pine St. Presby. Ch., Purham,
N.C., 1943-44; Davie St. Presby. Ch., Raleigh, N.C.,
1944-54; Fifth Ave., Presby. Ch., Roanoke, Va., 1955-
pianist Roanoke Minister's Conference; pres. Clergy Club
(Inter-Faith - Inter-racial); State clerk Presbytery of
Southern Va.; mem.: YMCA, NAACP; Home: 311 Patton
Ave., N.W., Roanoke, Va.

KELLER, Cyrus Samuel, Sr., b. Lake Charles, La., Jan.
9, 1920; s. Cyrus S., II, and Bertha (Scott) K.; B.A.,
Univ. of Calif., Los Angeles, 1940; Christian Ed., Bible
Institute of Los Angeles, 1943; Theology, Noah Williams
School of Religion, 1946; m. Hazel Maurie Tackett; chil-
dren--- Edward, (deceased) Juliebeth Maurie, Cyrus
Samuel, Jr., Marjo Renee, Michelle Evon; pastor, Bethel
A.M.E. Church, Elwood, Kansas, 1943-45; pastor, Allen
Chapel, Salina, Kansas, 1946-48; Quinn Chapel, Inde-
pendence, Kans., 1948-51; Ward Chapel, Kansas City,
Mo., 1952-56; St. John A.M.E. Church, Topeka, Kans.,
1956-58; Cain Memorial A.M.E. Church, Bakersfield,
Cal., 1956-58; St. Andrew's A.M.E. Church, Sacramento,
Calif., 1958---; Examining chaplain for the Annual Confer-
ence A.M.E. Ch. since 1952; Pres., Sacramento Minister-
ial Alliance, 1961; Advisor, Youth Council, Council of
Churches, K.C. Mo. Bakersfield, Cal., Sacramento, Cal.;
Trustee member, Payne Theological Seminary, 1951-56;
Member, Committee of Administration Douglas Hospital,
1953-56; Trustee Board (same), 1943-56; Western Univ.
Holding Corporation, 1958-64; Member, NAACP since 1951;
currently President Sacramento Branch, NAACP; Member,
Human Relations Committee, Sacramento; Chairman, Conf.
Relig. & Race; Member, Division of Christian Education;
Mem., National Council of Churches; Democrat; Southern
Christian Leadership Conference (western sec.); prepared
and presented Radio and TV programs for the Councils of
Churches and the ministerial alliances; Home: 3825 44th St.,
Sacramento, Calif. 95820; Office: 2131 8th St., Sacramento,
Calif. 95818.

KELLOGG, Reginald John, teacher; b. Ann Arbor, Mich.,
July 2, 1933; s. Francis Bernard and Anna Theresa
(Roney) K.; Assumption Seminary, 1955-61; Our Lady of
Carey Seminary, 1953-55; Laval Universite, 1961-63; Or-
dained priest, Rom. Cath. Ch., 1961; Teacher, Religion,
French, Central Cath. High Sch., Toledo, Ohio Study and

teach, Universite Laval, Quebec, Canada, 1961-63; French
teacher, Our Lady of Carey Sem. & Coll., Carey, Ohio,
1963-64; Home: 2425 Cherry, Toledo, Ohio, 43608. Office:
Mt. St. Francis, Mt. St. Francis, Indiana, 47176.

KENNARD, Messie Lewis, Jr., b. Chicago, Ill., Oct. 23,
1918; s. Massie L. Kennard and Helen Q.K.; University
of Illinois, 1935-36; 1941-42 Roosevelt University 1946-
47 BA; Garrett Biblical Institute-1947-50; B.D. Chicago
Lutheran Theological Seminary, 1956-57; pastor, Concordia Lutheran Church, Buffalo, N.Y., 1959---; Member, Alpha Phi Alpha; Home: 426 Northampton St., Buffalo
8, New York; Ch.: 400 Northampton St., Buffalo 8, New
York.

KENT, Reginald H., b. Virginia; s. Basil and Bettie (Coleman) K.; St. Paul's College, 1933-36; A.B., St. Augustine's College, 1941-43; B.D., Virginia Seminary, 1943-
46; Courses: Union Seminary, Columbia University;
Graduate study: Univ. of Penn.; m. Mrs. Reginald H.;
children-four boys; pastor, St. Matthew's, Detroit; St.
Cypice, Detroit, St. James, Philip; St. Luke, Virginia;
St. Marks, St. Mary's, St. Matthew's and St. John's, St.
Matthew's Prot. Episcopal Church, South Hill, Va.; current rector, St. Mary's Prot. Episcopal Church, Chester,
Pa.; Hospital chaplain; Member, NAACP; Home: 1905 W.
4th St., Chester, Pa.; Office: 7th & Edwards Sts., Chester
11, Pa.

KEYES, Wilbert David, b. Jamesville, N.C., May 17, 1913;
s. Ivory V. and Nancy Daisy (Barber) K.; 1962-63, Shaw
Univ. (Roanoke Institute); 1963-64, Goldsboro Christian
Institute, Goldsboro, N.C.; m. Tyress Maryland Wilkins;
pastor: 1951-57, Promise Land Christian Church, Jamesville, N.C.; White Oak Chapel Church, Bath, N.C.; 1958-
64; Antioch Christian Church, Hookerton, N.C.; Speller's
Chapel Church, Windsor, N.C.; Union Chapel Christian
Church, Roper, N.C.; Zion Grove Christian Church, Co-
lumbia, N.C. Minister's Institute, Roper, N.C.; statisti-
cian, Washington-Norfolk District Assembly; President,
Joint union, Washington-Norfolk District; General secre-
tary, General Assembly (Eastern Seaboard); Consultant,
Interracial Consultation, College of the Bible, Lexington,
Ky. Consultant on Negro Evangelism at United Christian
Mission Society Indianapolis, Ind.; Democrat; Mason;
Home: P.O. Box 72, Roper, N.C.

KIBBLE, Harvey Ward, Church official; b. Huntsville, Ala.,

Jan. 28, 1908; s. Edward and Mittie (Livingston) K.;
Oakwood College, 1928; Andrews University (Extension
Division), 1962; m. Thelma Lois Winston; children-
Harvey, Jr., Herman Loris, William Harold, Marie Lois
(Mrs. Edward Robinson), Ann La Verne, Alvin Maurice.
Pastor: Seventh-Day Adventist Churches in Houston, Tyler,
and San Antonio, Texas, 1929-35; Newark, Jersey City,
Montclair and Englewood, New Jersey, 1935-42; Chicago,
Ill., 1942-48; Brooklyn, N.Y., 1948-1951; Radio broad-
cast (weekly) WAIT, Chicago, Ill., 1943-45; president,
Lake Region Conference - Seventh-Day Adventist, Chicago,
Ill., 1951-62. Present: chairman, Lake Region Conference
Executive Committee, Chicago, Ill. Radio and TV devo-
tional messages (The Department of Radio and TV of the
Church Federation of Greater Chicago over NBC Channel
#5 and WGN radio)- "Time to Reflect" and WGN TV Chan-
nel #9, "Five Minutes to Live By", 1960-61. Member:
Oakwood College Board, 1951-62; Riverside Sanitarium and
Hospital Board, Nashville, Tenn., 1951-62; Hinsdale Sani-
tarium and Hospital Board, 1951-62; Emmanuel Missionary
College Board, 1951-62; Andrews University Board, 1960-
62; Urban League Board, Newark, N.J., 1938-1942;
Boy Scouts Council Committee, Newark, N.J., 1941. S.
D.A. Ministerial Fellowship Council member, Chicago,
Ill.; Republican; contributing editor to "The Message"
magazine, Nashville, Tenn., 1951-62. Home: 782 Janos
Lane, West Hempstead, N.Y. Office: Northeastern Confer-
ence Seventh-Day Adventist, 560 West 150th St., New
York 31, N.Y.

KILGORE, Claude Columbus, teacher; b. Macon, Georgia,
Dec. 1, 1921; s. Jackson and Alice (Smith) K.; B.S.,
Hamton Institute, 1942-47; B.C., Lincoln University,
1948-51; Post-Graduate Work in Religious Education,
Evangelical & Reformed Seminary, Lancaster, Pa. (1952-
53); Adjunct Fellow, Department of Urban Studies, Rutgers
Univ., (1963-64); m. Mildred Elizabeth Holmes; children--
Darryl, Lynda, Robert, and David; Member of Personnel
Staff, Hampton Institute (1946-48), Lincoln University
(1948-49); pastor Faith Presby. Ch., York, Pa. (1951-56)
Fabricating Inspector, York-Hoover Body Corp., York,
Pa. (1951-57); Minister-To-Migrants, Penna. Council of
Churches (1954-55-Summer); Thirteenth Ave. Presby.
Ch., Newark, N.J. (1956-63); Westminster-Bethany United
Presby. Ch., Brooklyn, N.Y. (1963-).; teacher Summer
Camps and Conference, Synod of New Jersey; former vice
Moderator Presbytery of Newark, N.J.; rep. of radio-TV,

Synod of New Jersey and the New Jersey Council of Churches;
chairman General Missions Interpretation Committee,
Presbytery of New York City; Member of N.Y.C. Pres-
bytery's Committee on Candidates and Church Vocations;
mem.: Urban League of Essex Co., Newark, N.J.; Committee of Management of Jones Street YMCA, Newark,
N.J.; Board of Directors of Planned Parenthood Assoc.,
Clergy Advisory Comm. to the Mayor's Commission of
Human Rights, Newark, N.J.; sec. The Red Shield Boys'
Club, Brooklyn, N.Y. (1964-); Local School Bd. -
Districts 32, 33, 34-Bklyn., N.Y. (Appointment from
June 31, 1964 to July 1, 1969); The Omega Psi Phi Fra-
ternity; Elks, Masons; Originated the community radio
show- "Perspective"-a program dealing with the Lives of
the minorities in urban New Jersey; Guest Soloist with
the Religious Television Show-"The Evangel Hour, Station
WPIX, New York; Guest Preacher for the Protestant
Council of New York City on the program-"Morning Medi-
tations," WPIX; Scholarship recipient-To act and study
Drama In The Church-Wagner College, Staten Island, New
York (1964) as a result of amateur and professional acting
experience. Home: 555 Bainbridge St., Brooklyn 33, New
York, N.Y.; Office: Howard Ave. and McDonough St.,
Brooklyn 33, New York, N.Y.

KILGORE, Thomas, Jr. b. Woodruff, S.C., Feb. 20, 1913;
s. Thomas and Eugenia (Langston) K.; A.B., Morehouse
Coll., 1935; Howard Univ. Sch. of Religion, 1944; D.D.
(hon.), Shaw Univ., 1956; B.D., Union Theol. Sem., 1957;
D.D., Morehouse Coll., 1963; m. Jeannetta Scott; chil-
dren---Lynn Elda; Jini Medina; pastor, New Bethel Baptist
Church, Asheville, N.C., 1936-38; Friendship Bapt. Ch.,
Winston-Salem, N.C., 1938-47; Exec. sec., North Caro-
lina General Bapt. Convention, 1945-47; pastor, Friend-
ship Bapt. Ch., New York City, 1947-63; Second Bapt.
Church, Los Angeles, Calif., 1963---; chaplain, Winston-
Salem Teachers Coll., 1942-44; Mem. Bd. of Trustee,
National Trade and Professional School, Wash., D.C.;
YMCA Service Award, Harlem Branch, N.Y., 1963; Mem.,
Chi Alpha (Ministers Fraternity): Omega Psi Phi; Home:
1238 Westchester Pl., Los Angeles, Calif, 90019; Office:
2412 Griffith Ave., Los Angeles, Calif. 90011

KINARD, David Lee,b. South Carolina, June 5, 1915; s.
Wymon C. and Julia (Glover) K.; m. Ruth Taylor K.;
children: Ruthalie, (Mrs. James Wooten Jr.), Helen
(Mrs. Joseph S. Solomon), Magdalen (Mrs. Rodgers L.

Shelton), Patricia, Sandra, David Lee, Jr.; pastor:
1942-50, Calvary Christian Church, Brooklyn, N.Y. Current: 1953, St. Phillips Christian Church, Brooklyn, N.
Y.; Activities: President, Eastern Seaboard Christian
Convention, 1949-1956; Home: 304 Kosciusko St., Brooklyn,
N.Y. 11221; Church: 345 Throop Ave., Brooklyn, N.Y.
11221

*KING, Dearine Edwin, b. LaGrange, Tenn. Feb. 9, 1910;
s. Martin A. and Effie K.; A.B., LeMoyne Coll.,
Memphis, Tenn.; B.D., M.A., Howard Univ. Sch. of
Rel.; m. Mae Evelyn Rudder; children---Dearine Ed.,
Michael Earl, Maderia Evonne; coll. minister and instruc-
tor, Ala. State A & M Coll., 1942-43; pastor, Wash. St.
Bapt. Ch., Paducah, Ky., 1942-46; Zion Bapt. Ch.,
Louisville, Ky., 1946-63; current, Friendship Bapt. Ch.,
NYC, 1963---; former sec., Nat. Bapt. Conv., USA;
Exec. Bd., Louisville Area Council of Churches; Chair-
man, Advisory Bapt. Fellowship Center; Mem., Bd. of
Trustees, Nat. Trade & Professional Sch., Wash., D.C.;
Bd. of Dir., Nat. Council of Churches, 1953-58; Institu-
tion rep., Boy Scouts; Bd. of Directors, Red Cross
Hospital; Trustee, Simmons Univ.; Mem., NAACP;
Omega Psi Phi; Mason; Published Sermon: The Shepherd
Heart; Office: 144 W. 131st St., New York City, N.Y.

KING, John Lucas, Jr. b. Greenville, Miss., April 14,
1920; s. John Lucas K. Sr. and Lena (Coleman) K.; A.B.,
Rust Coll., 1938-42; B.D., Gammon Theol. Seminary,
1943-45; m. Madice Nickson; children--- Matie Channice,
Claude Raymond, Madice Eileen, Mable Maxine, Claudette
Denise; pastor, Columbus Ct., Columbus, Miss., 1946-
49; St. Paul Methodist Church, Moss Point, Miss., 1949;
St. Stephens Methodist Church, Yazoo City, Miss., 1949-
53; St. Paul Meth. Ch., Biloxi, Miss., 1953-55; Lynch
Chapel Methodist Church, Forest, Miss., 1955-58; St.
Mark Methodist Church, Dekalb, Miss.,1958-59; Franklin
La., 1959-62; St. James Methodist Church, Shreveport,
La., 1962---; teacher, Related Subjects, Columbus Veteran
School, Columbus, Miss., 1946-49; Bd. of Education,
Louisiana Annual Conf., 1959---; Board of Ministerial
Training, La. Annual Conference, 1959---; Mem. NAACP,
Shreveport, La. Chapter; Parliamentarian; International
Ministerial Alliance; Home: 945 Lewis Pl., Shreveport,
La. 71103; Office: 850 Hope St., Shreveport, La. 71101

KING, Martin Luther, Jr., civil rights leader; b. Atlanta,
Ga., Jan. 15, 1929; s. Martin Luther, Sr. and Alberta
(Williams) K.; A.B., Morehouse Coll., 1948; B.D.,
Crozer Theol. Sem., Chester, Pa., 1951; Univ. Pa.,
1950-51; Harvard Univ., 1952-53; Ph.D., Boston Univ.,
1955; D.D. (hon.), Chicago Theol. Seminary, 1957; Boston Univ., 1959; Springfield Coll., 1964; Wesleyan Univ.,
1964; LL.D. (hon.), Morgan State Coll., 1958; Howard
Univ., 1957; Lincoln Univ., 1961; Univ. of Bridgeport,
1961; Yale Univ., 1964; Jewish Theol. Sem., 1964; L.H.
D. (hon.), Morehouse Coll., 1957; Central State Coll.,
1958; D.C.L., Bard Coll., 1962; D.L., Keuka Coll.,
1963; m. Coretta Scott; children---Yolande Denise, Martin Luther III, Dexter Scott, Bernice Albertine; co-pastor,
Ebenezer Bapt. Bh., Atlanta, Ga.; pres., Southern Christian Leadership Conf., Atlanta, Ga.; pres., Emeritus,
The Montgomery Improvement Assn; Gallup Poll revealed
that he was one of the most admired religious leaders in
the world, 1957; In 1957 Time Magazine selected him as
one of the ten most outstanding personalities of the year.
Received more than 125 citation awards for his work in
civil rights; In a poll conducted by Link Magazine of New
Delhi, India, he ranked as one of the sixteen world leaders who contributed most to the advancement of freedom
during 1959; In 1963 Time Magazine selected him as its
37th Man of the Year, stating that he had become ''The
unchallenged voice of the Negro people and the disquieting
conscience of the white;'' Nobel Peace Prize, 1964; author:
Stride Toward Freedom, 1958 (The book received the Ains-
field-Wolf Award as the best book in race relations in 1958);
The Measure of a Man, 1959; Strength To Love; 1963; Now
is the Time; 1964; Why We Can't Wait, 1965; Mem.,
NAACP; Alpha Phi Alpha; Sigma Pi Phi; Elk; Office: 407-13
Auburn St. NE, Atlanta, Ga.

KING, Robert Henry, b. Sunny South, Ala., April 1, 1922;
B.D., Immanuel Lutheran Seminary, 1949; m. Ed., Univ.
of Pittsburg, 1956; m. Edna Jean McCord; children---
Jocelyn, Jann, Roger; pastor, Victory Lutheran Church
Youngstown, Ohio, 1949-57; pastor, St. Philip's Lutheran
Church, Chicago, Ill., 1957---; pastoral advisory, Walther
League of Northern Illinois, District of Lutheran Church-
Missouri Synod, 1961-63; Home: 6731 Eberhart, Chicago,
Ill.; Ch.: 6732 Eberhart, Chicago 37, Ill.

KING, William Herbert, sem.prof.; b. Atlanta, Ga., Mar. 27,
1906; s. William Huel and Margaret Willie Anna (Nesbitt)

K.; A.B., Morehouse Coll., 1927; A.M., Columbia Univ.
1929; B.D., Union Theol. Sem., 1930; S.T.M., Oberlin
Grad. Sch. of Theol., 1934; Ed.D., Columbia Univ.,
1950; Minister, Plymouth Cong. Ch., Wash., D.C.,
1930-33; Plymouth Cong. Ch., Det., Mich., 1933-35;
Grace Cong. Ch., New York, N.Y., 1946-58; Assoc.
Chaplain, Hampton Institute, Va., 1935-37; Nat. Assoc.
Sec'y Student YMCA, 1936-43; Lecturer, Psych. and Soc.
N.Y. City Dept. of Health, 1943-52; prof. of Preaching,
McCormick Theol. Sem., 1958---; Instr. and Counselor
in Rel. Ed., Columbia Univ. and Union Theol. Sem.,
Summers 1939, 40, 41; mem. Adult Ed. Assn. USA;
Amer. Assn. of University Professors; Assn. of Semin-
ary Professors in the Practical Fields; N.A.A.C.P.; Nat.
Assoc. Biblical Instructors; Nat. Educ. Assoc.; Soc. for
the Scientific Study of Religion; Soc. of Biblical Lit. and
Exegesis; United Presbyterian Church in the U.S.A.
Home: 800 W. Belden Ave., Chicago, Ill., 60614. Office:
McCormick Theol. Sem., Chgo., Ill.

*KING, William Joseph, chaplain; b. Selma, Ala., July 21,
1921; s. Joseph and Lillian (Davis) K.; A.B., Talladega
Coll., 1943; B.D., Howard Univ., Sch. of Rel., 1946;
m. Clariee Robinson; children--- Eris Evermont; Home
Missions Councils of North American Chaplain to migrant
workers, 1946-48; pastor, Third Baptist Church, Suffield,
Conn., 1948-51; current chaplain, US Air Force, 1951---;
Mem., Alpha Phi Alpha; Mason; Home: 5312 Arnold Ave.
Otis AFB, Mass.

KING, Willis Jefferson, bishop; b. Rose Hill, Tex., Oct. 1,
1886; s. Anderson William and Emma (Blackshear) K.;
A.B. Wiley Coll., Marshall, Tex., 1910; S.T.B., Boston
U. School of Theology, 1913, Ph.D., 1921; hon. D.D.,
Boston U., 1933; student Harvard Divinity School; m. Per-
mella J. Kelly, (died Feb. 23, 1943); children-- Velma
Norine, Eloise Aurora, Grace Evangeline; married 2d,
Emma Clarissa Arnold, June 28, 1944. Entered ministry
M.E. Church, 1908; pastor Greenville, Tex., 1908-10;
asso. pastor St. Mark's Ch., N.Y.C., 1911; pastor
Fourth Ch., Boston, St. Paul Ch., Galveston, Tex.,
Trinity Ch., Houston, until 1918; prof. O.T. and Christian sociology, Gammon Theological Sem., Atlanta, 1918-
30, pres., 1932-48, lectr. 1953; elected bishop, 1944, assigned to Liberia, W. Africa; reassigned, 1948; assigned
to La., Miss. and Upper Miss. Confs., 1953; resident
bishop New Orleans area, central jurisdiction The Meth-

odist Church, 1956- . President of Samuel Houston College, 1930-32. Fellow Julius Rosenwald Fund, for research, Oxford Univ. and Palestine, under auspices Am. Sch. of Oriental Research (on leave of absence from Gammon Theol. Seminary), 1929-30. Represented Negro students at World's Student and Christian Federation, Peking China, 1922. Recipient of the Great Band of the Humane Order of African Redemption, Liberia, 1956; Knight Commander of the Order of African Redemption, Knight Commander Order of African Pioneers, Member General Conf. M.E. Ch., 1924, 28, 32; del. to Conf. on Life and Work, Oxford, Eng., 1937; del. to World Council Meth. Ch., Oxford, 1951; rep. Bishop's Council to Africa Central Conf., Belgian Congo, 1952; mem. Nat. Preaching Mission Staff, 1936-37; Commn. of Unification of Meth. Chs. in Am.; Atlanta Sch. of Social Work; Commn. on Interracial Cooperation since 1940; Am. Oriental Soc., Southern Sociol. Soc., Am. Acad. Polit. and Social Science, Omega Psi Phi. Republican. Author: The Negro in American Life, 1926. Collaborator: Personalism in Theology and Christian Bases of World Order, 1943. Address: 631 Baronne St., New Orleans.

KIRKENDOLL, Chester Arthur, coll. president; b. Searcy, Ark., June 3, 1914; s. Chester Arthur and Mattie (Wyatt), K.; A.B., Lane Coll., 1938; M.A., Northwestern Univ., 1941; Littl.D., Texas Coll., 1957; D.D., St. Andrew's Seminary, 1962; m. Alice Elizabeth Singleton; children-- Chester Arthur III, Loretta Jean, Leland Kapel; Director of Leadership Ed., General Bd. of Religious Education, Christian Methodist Episcopal Church, 1940-50; pastor, St. Paul C.M.E. Church, Bolivar, Tenn.; Lane Chapel C.M.E. Church, Whiteville, Tenn.; Walls Chapel C.M.E. Church, Chicago, Ill.; pres., Lane College, 1950---; Board of Directors, United Negro College Fund, Inc., 1950---; Tennessee Council on Human Relations, 1957---; Omega Psi Phi Achievement Award, 1952; Alpha Phi Alpha; Mason; author: Improving the Education Program of the Local Church; Home: 566 Lane Ave., Jackson, Tenn.; Office: Lane Coll., Jackson, Tenn.

KIRTON, Edwin Eggliston, b. Trinidad, B.W.I., Dec. 13, 1907; s. Christopher and Lucretia (Hope) K.; B.S., College of the City of N.Y., 1932; New York Law School, 1938; General Theological Seminary, 1948-49; m. Eunice Brothwaite; children---Eunice, Edwin E., Jr., Elsie Elise; vicar, St. Michael Prot. Episcopal Church, Med-

ford, N. Y. , 1949-51; rector, St. Mark's Prot. Episcopal
Church, Wilmington, 1951---; Mem. : Deputy to General
Convention Protestant Episcopal Church, 1961; Executive
Council-Diocese of East Carolina, 1963-65; Chairman,
Dept. of Missions-Diocese of East Carolina, 1963-65; staff
member, St. Augustine's Summer School, 5 years, of
Religious Education; Wilmington-New Hanover Bi-Racial
Committee, 1963---; Mental Health Advisory Council,
1963---; Board of Directors, New Hanover County Mental
Health Ass'n, 1958-63; Community Council, City of Wil-
mington, 1961---; Governor's Committee on Juvenile
Delinquency and Youth Crime, 1962---; Named Citizen
of the Year 1958 and cited for Humane Service by Omega
Psi Phi Fraternity; Mem. : Polemarch-Wilmington Alumni
Chapter, Kappa Alpha Psi Fraternity, Alumnus-College of
Preachers, Wash. , D. C. ; delegate to the Provincial Synod-
4th Province, 1954, 55, 63; director of Oceanside Episcopal Youth Camp, 1953---; Member, Dept. of Christian
Education; Member, Committee on Camps and Conferences; Home: 601 Grace St. Wilmington, N. C. ; Office:
6th and Grace Sts. , Wilmington, N. C.

KNOX, Wilbur Benjamin, author; b. Smith, S. C. , Nov. 25,
1912; s. Milas J. and Carrie (Minor) K. ; A. B. , B. D. ,
Johnson C. Smith Univ. , 1950; m. Susie Boulware; chil-
dren---Kathleen, Wilbur, Jr. , Paul; pastor, First Washington Baptist Ch. , Lancaster, S. C. , currently, writing
plays and speeches, addresses for special days and all
special church occasions; teacher, public school, 1941-
43; pres. , NAACP, Rock Hill, S. C. ; Mem. , Phi Beta
Sigma; contributor: The 1949 Anthology of Poetry and The
1950 Gold Medal Series of Contemporary Poets; Home: 307
W. Moore, Rock Hill, S. C. ; Office: 123 Pleasant Hill,
Lancaster, S. C.

LAMBERT, Rollins Edward, b. Chicago, Ill. , March 3,
1922; s. Monroe E. and Martha (Rollins) L. ; A. B. , U. of
Chicago, 1942; M. A. and S. T. L. , St. Mary of the Lake
Seminary, 1942-49; Asst. Pas. St. Malachy Ch. , Chicago,
1949-57; Asst. Pas. , St. Dorothy Ch. , Chicago, 1957-61;
Asst. Cath. Chaplain, U. of Chicago, Illinois Inst. of
Tech. , 1961---; Mem. Board, Adult Education Center,
Archdiocese of Chicago; Chicago Conf. on Rel. and Race.
Home: 5735 University Ave. , Chicago, Ill. , 60637; Office:
Calvert House, 5735 University Ave. , Chicago, Ill. 60637.

LAKEY, Othal Hawthorne, b. Shreveport, La., Apr. 6,
1936; s. Clarence J. and Zandree (Ashley) L.; B.A.,
Whitman Coll., 1954-57; B.D., Drew Univ., 1957-60; m.
Narsis Beard; children---James Othal; pastor, St. James
Christian Methodist Episcopal Church, Pasco, Washington,
1954-57; asst. pastor, Salem Methodist Church, New York,
1958-60; pastor, Allen Temple Christian Methodist Episco-
pal Church, Portland, Oregon, 1960-63; Williams Memor-
ial C. M. E. Church, Shreveport, La., 1963---; chief
sec., Louisiana Annual Conf., C. M. E. Church; chairman,
Educational Comm., Portland Branch NAACP, 1961-63;
Board of Directors, Portland Urban League, 1960-63; Pi
Kappa Delta National Forensic Honorary; National Thespian
Society; pres., Albina Community Council, Portland, 1962-
63; vice pres., Greater Portland Council of Church;
Board of Directors of the Oregon Council on Alcoholic
Problems, 1961-63; Standards Committee for Child-Caring
Institutions of the Oregon State Public Welfare Commis-
sion, 1963; Board of Trustees, Mississippi Industrial Coll.,
Holly Spring, Miss.; Home: 1853 Logan St., Shreveport,
La.; Office: 1501 Peabody St., Shreveport, La.

LATTA, William Clarence, teacher; b. Oxford, N. C., Feb.
20, 1932; s. Wilber E. and Lulamiller (Allen) L.;
Cortex W. Peters Business School, 1952-53; Washington
Bible College, 1956-60; B.A.; m. Lelia Mae Turner;
children--- William Clarence, Jr.; pastor, The Bible
Way Church, Columbus, Ohio, 1960-63 (Bible Way
Churches of our Lord Jesus Christ World-Wide, Inc.),
teacher, The Aenon Bible School, Columbus, Ohio, 1960-
63; US Forces, 1954-56; National Defense Service Medal;
Army of Occupation Medal (Germany); Good Conduct
Medal; Mem., Local Minister's Fellowship, Columbus,
Ohio; Home: 685 So. Highland Ave., Columbus 23, Ohio
43223; Office: 453 So Wheatland Ave., Columbus 4, Ohio.

*LAVALL, John W., b. Charleston, S. C., Jan. 17, 1893;
s. Jacob and Melissa (Ross) L.; Th.B., Howard Univ.,
Sch. of Rel., 1928; m. Blanche Etta Stuart; current pastor,
Shiloh Baptist Church, Middleburg, Va., 1964---; teacher,
Church History, Frelinghuysen Univ., Wash., D. C.,
1931-42; Home: 1227 Walter, Wash. D. C. 20003; Office:
Shiloh Baptist Church, Middleburg, Va.

LAVALAIS, Joseph George, teacher; b. Mansura, La.,
Drpy. 13, 1913; s. George J. and Mary (Lucendia); St.
Paul's Lutheran Elementary school, Mansura, La., 1919-

27; Luther College, New Orleans, La., 1927-31; Lutheran
University, Baton Rouge, La., 1931-34; Immanuel Luther-
an College & Seminary, Greensboro, N.C., 1934-37; m.
Elizabeth L. Smith; children---George, Juanita, Gwendolyn;
teacher, Ala., 4 years; Services in parishes: Kingslanding
Lutheran Church, Maplesville, Ala., 1937-38; Montrose,
Ala., 1938-39; Kinbrough, Ala., Lamison, Alabama, 1939-
41; Pine Hall Lutheran Church, Arlington, Ala., Abshi,
Ala., Vineland, Ala., 1941-43; St. Philip's Lutheran
Church, Pa., 1943---; Member serving as Circuit Coun-
selor, Philadelphia Circuit, Eastern District, Lutheran
Church-Missouri Synod; Missionary Board of the Lutheran
Synodical Conference Youth Conservation Association;
Commission on Human Relation, Lutheran Church-Missouri
Synod (Eastern District); Home: 533 N. 56th St., Phila-
delphia, Pa.; Ch.: 53rd & Wyalusing Ave., Phila., Penna.

LAWSON, James Morris, Jr., church official; b. Uniontown,
Pa., Sept. 22, 1928; s. James Morris and Philane May
(Cover) L.; A.B., Baldwin-Wallace Coll., Berea, Ohio,
1947-52; Oberlin Coll., Graduate School of Theology,
1956-58; S.T.B., Divinity School, Vanderbilt Univ.,
1958-60; Boston Univ.; m. Dorothy Dolores Wood; chil-
dren---John Clifford L., III; vice pres., National Conference of Methodist Youth, 1949-53; chairman, National
Methodist Youth Fellowship Commission, 1948-49; field
worker, International Christian Univ. of Japan, 1950-51;
pastor, Turner Chapel Methodist Church, 1950-51; Methodist Missionary in India, 1953-56, Hislop Coll., Nagpur,
India.; pastor, Scott Methodist Church, 1960-62; Centenary
Methodist Church, Memphis, Tenn., 1962---; special consultant, Southern Christian Leadership Conference, 1960
---; southern sec., Fellowship of Reconciliation, 1958-
60; editorial contributor: Fellowship Magazine; Office:
Centenary Methodist Church, 653 Alston Ave., Memphis,
Tenn.

LAWSON, William Alexander, Jr., b. June 28, 1928; s.
William A. Sr. and Clarisse L.; A.B., Tenn. A & I State
Univ., 1950; b.D., M. Th., Central Bapt. Theol. Sem.,
1953, 55;Candidate Ph.D., Univ. of Chicago, 1961; m.
Audrey Ann Hoffman; children--- 3 daughters and 1 son;
pastor, Mt. Hebron Bapt. Ch., 1952-55; director, Bapt.
Students and Prof. of Bible, Tex. Southern Univ.; cur-
rent pastor, Wheeler Ave. Bapt. Ch.,Houston, Tex.,
1962---; organizer, United Ministers, Tex. Southern
Univ.; chairman of Chaplains, 1963---; Mem., Alpha

Phi Alpha; Danforth Foundation; Missions and Evangelism
Assignments, Southeast Asia, Middle East; speaker, Bapt.
World Alliance Youth Conf., Beirut, Lebanon, 1963; fre-
quent speaker, Coll. and Univ.; Office: 3124 Wheeler
Ave., Houston, Tex. 77004

LEDBETTER, Theodore S., b. Goliad, Texas, Jan. 15,
1910; s. Caesar S. and Maggie (Clemons) L.; A.B.
Atlanta Univ., 1932; B.D., Oberlin Grad. Sch. of Theol.
1935; m. Orelia Washington: 3 children-- Theodore S.,
Jr., Leslie M., Charles A.; Plymouth Cong. Ch.,
Louisville, Ky., 1937-47; Dixwell Ave. Cong. Church,
New Haven, Conn., 1947-58; Plymouth Cong. United Ch.
of Christ, Wash., D.C. 1958-; Dir., Plymouth Social
Settlement, Louisville, Ky., 1937-47; Dean of Men,
Tillotson College, Austin, Texas, 1935-37; Del. Nat.
Dem. Conv., 1960; Mem. Dem. Central Committee, D.
C., 1960-64; Trustee, United Planning Organization;
Mem., Public Welfare Advisory Board; Assoc. Moderator,
Middle Atlantic Conference, UCC; Assoc. Mod., Washing-
ton Assoc., UCC; Vice-Chmn., Comm. on Amendment to
Constitution, UCC; mem., Kappa Alpha Psi. Home: 1737
Webster, N.W., Wash., D.C. Church: 5313 N. Capital,
Wash., D.C.

LEDOUX, Jerome Gaston, educator; b. Lake Charles, La.,
February 26, 1930; s. Peter Louis and Gastonia (Petrie)
L.; St. Paul's College, Epworth, Iowa, 1949-51; St.
Augustine's Major Seminary, 1951-1957; J.C.D. and S.
T. L., Gregorian University (Rome); Ordained priest, Ro-
man Cath. Ch., 1957; Author: doctoral thesis, "Coarctatio
jurisdictionis sacramentalis", 1962, (a study of sacramen-
tal jurisdiction as restricted by the Code of Canon Law.);
"Defender of the Bond" for the marriage tribunal of the
diocese, Natchez-Jackson, Miss.; Home and Office: Divine
Word Missionaries, Bay St. Louis, Mississippi.

LEE, Carleton Lafayette, coll. prof.; b. Clayton, N.C.,
March 30, 1913; s. Frank Joshua and Aurelia Gertrude
(Hill) L.; A.B., Talladega Coll.; M.A., Univ. of
Chicago; B.D., Chicago Theol. Sem., 1937; Ph.D.,
Univ. of Chicago, 1951; m. Maggie Ada Latta; children
---Carleton Henry; pastor and teacher, Midway Congre-
gational Church and Dorchester Academy, McIntosh, Ga.;
1935-37; Lincoln Congregational Ch., Kings Mountain, N.C.,
1937-38; Case-Aide, Chicago Relief Administration, 1938-
39; assoc. sec., Southern Area Council, YMCA, Atlanta
Ga., 1939-44; acting dean, Turner Theol. Sem., 1944-

45; Research and Survey National Council, YMCA, 1946-
47; Chaplain, Tuskegee Institute, 1947-53; Fraternal
Worker, World Council of Churches, Mainz Kastel am
Rhein, 1953-55; Professor of Philosophy, Tougaloo College,
Miss., 1955-57; director, Religious Life & Prof., Phil.,
Central State Coll., Wilberforce, Ohio, 1957---; Mem.,
Advisory Committee NCCF, 1951-53; Mem., Kent Fellow,
1949---; former pres., Exec. Com., National Assn of
Coll. and Univ. Chaplains; Coll. Language Assn (Mem.),
Mem., Assn of Social Science Teachers; Assn for the
Study of Negro Life and History; NAACP; Mason; Alpha
Phi Alpha; Alpha Phi Gamma; Phi Alpha Theta; A.A.U.P.;
contributor: Assuring Freedom for the Free, ed. by
Arnold Rose, 1963. Home: Box 187, Wilberforce, Ohio;
Office: Central State Coll., Wilberforce, Ohi.

*LEE, Gabriel S., Jr., b. Junction City, Ark., July 6,
1922; s. Gabriel S. and Mollie Elder L.; B.A., Bishop
Coll., Marshall, Tex., 1949; B.D., Howard Univ. Sch.
of Religion, 1954; m. Leona Jean Williams; pastor, Fellowship and New Land Bapt. Churches, Lillie, La., Bernice, La., 1949-51; Hollywood Hghts. Presby. Ch.,
Shreveport, La., 1956-60; co-pastor, Beacon & Glenham
Reformed Churches, Beacon, N.Y., 1960-62; current
pastor, Nazareth Bapt. Ch., Washington, Pa., 1965---;
director, Men's and Boys' Work, Westminster House,
Buffalo, N.Y., 1954-55; caseworker, Erie County Dept.
of Social Welfare, Buffalo, N.Y., 1962-65; mem., NAACP;
Ad. Bd., Child Welfare, Washington County, Dept. of
Welfare, Washington, Pa.; US Army, 1942-46; awards:
Good Conduct Medal; Asiatic-Pacific Campaign Medal;
W.W. II Victory Medal; mem., Phi Beta Sigma; Washing-
ton, Pa. Lions Club; director, Former Buffalo Host Club
International; Home: 143 Eichestnut St., Washington, Pa.
15301; Office: 123 N. Lincoln St., Washington, Pa.,
15301.

LEE, Morris William, b. Isle of Wright County, Va., Oct.
19, 1935; s. Peter Haywood and Mannie (Crocker) L.;
A.B., B.D., Va. Union Univ., 1958, 1960; pres., Student Participation Ass'n of Va.; At. coll., chief justice
of Student Court; pres., Lyceum, Bartone Soloists,
narrator of Choir, Basileus of Zeta Chapter, Omega Psi
Phi; Licensed to ministry, May 30, 1953; called to
pastorate of Jerusalem Baptist Ch., Doswell, Va., 1957;
current pastor, Third Baptist Ch., Youngstown, Ohio,
1960---; Mem., Mahoning County Welfare Board; Exec.

Comm. Citizens Ass'n; Youngstown; pres. , Youngstown
Ministerial Ass'n; Mem. , Exec. Comm. of Youngstown
Council of Churches; Home: 1175 Park Hill Drive, Youngs-
town 2, Ohio; Office: 1177 Park Hill Drive, Youngstown 2,
Ohio.

LEE, Willie Samuel, Church official; b. Dothan, Alabama,
May 29, 1915; Oakwood College, 1936; m. Ruth Althea
Reid; children-- Althea Grace (Mrs. Arthur Kennedy),
Willie Samuel, Jr. , Brenda Ruth; Pastored: five Seventh-
Day Adventist Churches, Oklahoma City District, 1936-
40; S.A.D. Churches in Tampa, Fla. , 1940-43; Jacckson-
ville, Fla. , 1946-50, New Orleans, 1950-55, Ephesus-
New York, 1955; Regional Secretary, Pacific Union Con-
ference, Seventh-Day Adventist Church. Home: 2283
El Sereno Avenue, Altadena, California. Office: P.O. Box
146, California. California.

LEHMAN, Harvey John, teacher; b. Mansura, Louisiana,
Oct. 10, 1905; s. Paul Marius and Harriett (Thompson)
L. ; Lutheran Parochial School, 1911-1920; Luthern
College, New Orleans, La. , 1920-24; Immanuel College
and Seminary, Grennsboro, N.C. , 1925-30; children---
Harvey J. Jr. , Lillian E. , Philip M. ; Ordained into the
ministry, Jul. 5, 1930; pastor, Trinity Lutheran Church
Selma, Alabama; pastor, St. Paul and Christ congregation,
Oak Hill and Rosebud, Alabama, 12 years; pres. , Ala-
bama Conference; pastor, Matthews Baltimore; current
pastor, The Lutheran Church of Our Savior, Buffalo, N.
Y. ; teacher, Lutheran Parochial School, Ala. ; Service
on the Mission Board of the Southeastern District; Service on the Profession Youth Board, Buffalo, N.Y. , 1960--;
part-time chaplain, the Erie County Home, Alden, N.Y. ;
Home: 30 Brunswick Blvd. , Buffalo 8, N.Y. ; Office: 26
Brunswick Blvd. , Buffalo 8, N.Y.

LESSER, Leo, Jr. ; b. Indianapolis, Ind. , Apr. 28, 1928;
s. Leo, Sr. and Katie (Jones) L. ; B.S. , Indiana Univ. ,
1950; B.Th. , Burton College 1958; B.D. , Burton College,
1960; D.D. , Monrovia College, 1959; D.D. , Chicago
Divinity College, 1962; pastor, Parks Chapel A.M.E.
Church, Chattanooga, Tenn. , 1957-61; pastor, St. John
A.M.E. Church, 1961-62; pastor, Greater St. James A.
M.E. Church, Louisville, Ky. , 1962; Professor, Business Dept. Zion Coll. , Chattanooga, Tenn. ; administrative
assistant to president, Zion Coll. , Chattanooga, Tenn. ;
chaplain, Geriatric Unit Central Hospital, Anchorange,

Ky.; appointed by governor as member of Kentucky Commission on Aging Director of Research and Training for
St. James Literacy Center, Louisville; Served in ETO
1945, Served in Korea 1961; Outstanding contributions in
the field of illiteracy, establishing centers in Louisville
and throughout the state of Kentucky; Mem.: Exec. Bd.
NAACP, Institute of Pastoral Care, Academy of Religion
and Mental Health, Mason; National Council of Senior
Citizens, Urban League; YMCA; Boy Scouts of America;
paper-Ministry for Mental Health, Publication-A Program
for the Church and It's Senior Citizens, paper read at
Governors Conf. on Aging-The Church and the Ministry
to The Old Member, Column - "In Times Like These;"
Home: 2104 West Oak St., Louisville 10, Ky.; Office:
2100 W. Oak St., Louisville 10, Ky.

LEWIS, Alexander Leonard, chaplain; b. St. Pauls, N.C.,
Dec. 10, 1910; s. Wase and Emma J. (Davis) L.; Red-
stone Academy, 1931; A.B., Johnson C. Smith Univ.,
1935; B.D., Theol. Seminary, 1941; Boy Scouts National
School, Mendam, N.J., 1944; m. Addie J. Jones; chil-
dren--- Alexander L., Jr., Gertrude L.; pastor Salem
Presbyterian Church, Anderson, S.C., 1941; Washington
Avenue Presby. Ch., 1942-44; Boy Scout Field Executive,
Mason, Ga.; mem. of YMCA Council; chmn. Youth Com-
munity Center and other community organizations principal
Panthersford School, Buies, N.C., 1935-36; principal
Fremnt Negro High School, 1936-39; chrm. Robeson
County School Master Organization, 1935-36; mem. Boy
Scouts of American, Honolulu, Hawaii, 1962; counselor,
USA Stockade Scho Bks, Hawaii, 1963; chaplain US Army,
1st Lt., 1944; Capt., 1946; Major, 1952. Served as chaplain in both theaters of war, First Ch to enter Korea
during the occupation 1946, POW Camp in Kojedo, Korea,
1950-52; Stockade Ch., Port Ch., Bn Ch., Regimental
Ch, Sub Area Ch, Post Chaplain, Fort Hampton, N.Y.,
1957-59; Asst. Div. Chaplain, Schofield Barracks, Hawaii,
1952-60; hospital chaplain in Germany; school counselor
and school officer for Kassel Sub Area, Kassel, Germany; Youth Counselor to the Youth Center, AYA officer
and advisor; athletics dir. for both youth and soldiers;
being in service, Boy Scout Master, Chrm. of Boy Scout
Committeeman, Cub Scout Den Dad, Cub Scout Committeeman in Kassell, Germany; chrm. Social and Civic Comm.
of the five nations located in that area: Americans, French,
German, English and Belgium Forces; mem.: Phi Beta
Sigma, Alpha Epsilon Chapter, Cosmopolitan Consistory

#291, Honolulu, Hawaii, Cosmopolitan Lodge #82, Hono-
lulu, Hawaii, local YMCA, The Lions' Club, pres. the
Leilehua High School PTA, Eastern Star, the Mental Health
Society of Honolulu, Hawaii, NAACP, State of Hawaii PTA;
Home: 110 South Cane St. Wahiawa, Hawaii.

LEWIS, Mahlon Montgomery, contractor; b. Bedford, Va.,
July 29, 1890; s. Chas. Shepherd and Mary (Ellen) L.;
C. N. & I. Dept. Wilberforce, Univ., Payne Theological
Seminary, Wilberforce, Ohio, B.D., 1916; D.D. (hon.),
Payne Theological Seminary, 1936; m. Cornelia B. Reed;
55 years an ordained Itinerant Elder; 40 years in the
A. M. E. Church. Resigned from A. M. E. Church, 1949;
Organized Greater Saint Matthew Independent Church,
Phila., Pa.; Builder of St. Matthew A. M. E. Church;
Mahlon M. Lewis Boys Club; Builder of Bethel A. M. E.
Church, Ardmore, Pa.; contractor and builder, built
Bethel A. M. E. Church, Walnut Ave., St. Matthew A. M. E.
Church, 1939; Member, Mason; Mem., Crime Prevention
Committee, Phila., Pa.; Office: Greater St. Matthew In-
dependent Church, Race and Vadges Sts., Phila., Pa.

LEWIS, Willie, b. Gainsville, Fla., July 29, 1939; s. Willie
and Bessie (Jones) L.; B.A., Oakwood College, 1960;
M.A., Andrews Univ., 1961; m. Barbara Ann Stokes; 1
son: William Stokes. Present: South Atlantic Conf. of
Seventh-Day Adventist, Atlanta, Georgia, 1961-   . Home:
1302 Heidt St., Columbia, S.C. Office: 1750 McFadden St.,
Columbia, S.C.

LEWIS, Willie B., b. Nash Co., N.C., Sept. 17, 1925;
s. Willie and Hazel L.; A.B., B.D., Shaw Univ., 1945-
53; m. Lillie Hilliard; children--- Lileta Ynettee,
Wilhelmia; pastor, Wake Chapel Bapt. Ch.; Bethlehem
Bapt. Ch.; current pastor, Fayetteville St. Bapt. Ch.,
Raleigh, N.C.; teacher, Nat. Bapt. Sunday School and
Training Union Cong.; organizer, Voters League, Fayette-
ville Bapt. Ch.; Home: 1013 South person St., Raleigh,
N.C.; Office: 751 Fayetteville St., Raleigh, N.C.

LIGGIN, Carl Crutcher, b. Louisville, Ky., Feb. 20, 1929;
s. Clyde A. and Jennie (B.) L.; Tuskeegee Institute,
1946-47; Kentucky State Coll., 1947-49; Wilberforce Univ.
& Payne Theo. Sem., 1952-53; m. Lois Jean Gray;
children--- Karen Renee, Katrina Rochelle, Karl Clyde;
Entered ministry of African Methodist Episcopal Church,
Quinn Chapel, Louisville, Ky., 1950; director, Youth Work,

A. M. E. Church; appointed to Clayborn Chapel Mission,
Lexington, Ky., 1951; Ordained Deacon; pastor, St. John
A. M. E. Church, Louisville, 1956; current pastor, Ebene-
zer, Clarksville; one of organizers, School of Practical
Nursing & Business, 1958; director, Ebenezer Kindergarten-
Nursery & Business Enterprises, 1961---; dean, Louis-
ville School of Religious Education, Louisville Council of
Churches, 1960---; director, Citizen's Committee of Local
Affairs; Vice pres., Clarksville Christian Leadership Corps,
NAACP, Kappa Alpha Psi, Democratic Party, League of
Montgomery County, Interdenominational Ministerial Al-
liance; current conducting, religious census and voter's
registration survey, Clarksville, Tenn.: Home: 131 Ed-
mondson Ferry Road, Clarksville, Tenn.; Office: 129
Edmondson Ferry Road, Clarksville, Tenn.

LIGGINS, Lyman William, teacher; b. Gallipolis, Ohio,
Jan. 12, 1921; s. Elmer Lewis and Irene (Smith) L.;
University of Toledo, Toledo, Ohio, 1940; Howard Uni-
versity, 1941-43; Ohio State Univ., A. B., 1946; M. A.,
Ohio State Univ., 1951; Ohio State Univ. work towards
Ph. D.; m. Grace Elizabeth Busby; children---Denis,
Cheryl; asst. pastor, Minister Allen Temple A. M. E.
Church, Cincinnati, Ohio, 1956; pastor, Quinn Chapel
A. M. E. Church, Wilmington, Ohio, 1957-63; current
pastor, Holy Trinity, Wilberforce Univ., Wilberforce,
1963---; visiting lecturer, Philosophy of Law, Wilberforce
Univ., 1951; visiting lecturer, Philosophy of Religion,
Payne Seminary, Wilberforce, 1960-61; visiting lecturer
Pastoral Psychology, Payne Seminary, Wilberforce, 1960-
62; Staff Position, Juvenile Diagnostic Center, Columbus,
Ohio, 1952-55; Full time Consultant, Legislative Service
Commission, State of Ohio, 1955; conducted statewide
study of Juvenile Delinquency; Research Consultant, Ohio
Dept. of Mental Hygiene & Correction, 1956; Directed
statewide evaluation of the effectiveness of tranquilizing
medications; Research Statistician, Ohio Bureau of Un-
employment Compensation, 1957; Employment trends for
U. S. Dept. of Labor; Assistant Research Sec. Governor's
Advisory Commission on Civil Rights, 1958; Statewide
statistical study of employment patterns; Mem., Alpha
Phi Alpha; Home: 742-B North Nelson Rd., Columbus
19, Ohio; Office: Wilberforce Univ., Wilberforce, Ohio.

LIGGINS, Thomas Elmer, b. Wolfdale, Pa., Nov. 10, 1935;
s. Edward S. and Eura Maxine (Patterson) L.; Ohio
State Univ., Columbus, Ohio; Payne Theol. Sem., Wilber-

force, Ohio; m. Mary Frances Slade; children---Thomas
E., Threase E., Terri E., Toni E., Timothy E.; pastor,
Bethel African Methodist Episcopal Ch., Westerville, Ohio,
1955-56; St. John A. M. E. Ch., Worthington, Ohio, 1956-
57; current pastor, Zion A. M. E. Ch., Marysville, Ohio,
1957---; Allen Chapel A. M. E. Ch., Marysville, Ohio,
1957---; visiting minister, Ohio Reformatory for Women,
Marysville, Ohio; Mem., Liberty Community Center Bd.,
Delaware, Ohio, 1960---; Red Cross Bd. Delaware County,
1961-63; chrm., Delaware Civil Rights Com., 1963---;
Mem., Mental Health Bd., Delaware County, 1964---; Outstanding Citizen Award by the Human Relation Council of
Delaware, Ohio; Mem., Mason; Ohio Republican Council;
Kiwanis International; NAACP; Home: 81 Park Ave.,
Delaware, Ohio; Office: 140 South Washington St., Dela-
ware, Ohio.

LIGGINS, Wendell, b. Xenia, Ohio, Oct. 21, 1914; s. Frank
Mr. and Aroma H. L.; A. B., Denver Univ.,; B. D., Payne
Theol. Sem., Wilberforce Univ.; course on Th. D.,
Iliff School of Theology; D. D. (hon.), Ark. Bapt. Coll.,
Little Rock, Ark.; m. Louise Helen; children---Wanda
Faye; current pastor, Zion Bapt. Ch., Denver, 1940---;
Mem., Library Commission, Denver, Colo.; former
pres., Western Bapt. Convention; General Bd., National
Council of Churches; editorial writer, National Bapt. S. S.
Publishing Bd.; instructor, Nat. Sunday School and Baptist
Training Leadership Union Congress; Exec. Mem., Bd. of
National Trade & Professional School, Wash., D. C.;
former member, Speaker Bureau, Republican State Com-
mittee of Colo.; Mem., Phi Beta Sigma; Writer of De-
votional Literature, Nat. Bapt. S. S. Publishing Bd.;
former religious column writer, The Denver Call; Home:
3200 Monaro, Denver 7, Colo.; Office: 933 E. 24th
Denver 7, Colo.

LIGHTSEY, Joseph Hancock, b. Irwin County, Ga., March
1, 1909; s. John W. and Cora Bell (Mclain) H.; Holsey
Cobb Institute, Cordele, Ga., 1922-30; inservice training - Bennett College, 1948; A & T College, 1954; University of N. Carolina, 1962-63; m. Ruth Mozella Martin;
children--- Malvea Joan, Joseph Martin, Phoebe Mozella.
Pastor, Mt. Calvary Christian Methodist Episcopal Church,
Bridgeport, Conn., 1933-36; pastor, North Carolina Annual Conf. C. M. E. Church, 1940-64; Conf. director,
Christian Education, 1949-58; present: presiding elder,
Durham District, North Carolina Conference, 1961- .

North Carolina Council of Churches; Durham Ministers Association; Mason; N. A. A. C. P. Home: 510 S. Alston St. ,
Durham, N. C. Office: 510 S. Alston St. , Durham, N. C.

LINCOLN, C. Eric, author, coll. prof. ; b. Athens, Ala. ,
June 23, 1924; A. B. , Lemoyne Coll. , 1947; A. M. , Fisk
Univ. , 1954; B. D. , Univ. of Chicago, 1956; Ph. D. , Bos-
ton Univ. , 1960; M. ed. , 1960; m. Lucy Cook; children--
Cecil Eric, Joyce Elaine, Hilary; pastor, John Calvin
Presbyterian Church, Nashville, 1953-54; Director of
Public Relations, Lemoyne Coll. , 1950-51; asst. person-
nel dean, asst. prof. , rel. & philosophy, Fisk Univ. ,
1954-57; resident chaplain, Boston Univ. Sch. of Theology,
1958-59; director of panel of Amer. , Human Relations
Center, 1958-60; assoc. professor and asst. to pres. ,
Clark Coll. , 1961-63; current prof. and director, Institute
for Social Relations, 1963---; decorations: John Hay Whit-
ney Fellow; Crusade Fellow; Eli Lilly Fellow; Mem. , Soc.
Psychological Study of Social Issues; Nat'l Association of
Univ. Prof. ; Nat'l Ass'n of Intergroup Relations Officials;
American Academy of Political and Social Science; Kappa
Alpha Psi; Frontiers; guest appearances on several local
TV and radio shows in Boston, Y. U. , St. Louis, Mem-
phis, Atlanta, Chattanooga, Cleveland; lecturer, univer-
sities and learned societies; author: The Black Muslims in
America, 1962; My Face Is Black, 1964; A Meaning of Mal-
colm X, 1964; The Nation of Islam, The Black Muslims in
America; The Encyclopedia Britanica, 1963; Has contributed
to many books and periodicals, such as The Reporter, The
New Englander, New South, The Negro Digest, The Journal of
Social Issues, Phylon, Christian Century and many others:
Home: 2937 Collier Drive, NW, Atlanta, Ga. ; Office: Clark
Coll. , Atlanta, Ga.

LINDSEY, Merrill Winston, teacher; b. Holly Springs, Miss. ,
Feb. 21, 1911; s. Albert and Molly (Burns) L. ; A. B. ,
Rust Coll. , 1948; M. A. , Denver Univ. , 1953; D. D.
(hon.), Rust Coll. , 1956; m. Alberta Lee Michael; chil-
dren---Merill W. , William Bernard, Delores Elnora (Mrs.
Roland McJunkins), Masheetta Uylanda, Michael Forsythe;
pastor, Algoma, Miss. , 1933-36; Ripley, Miss. , 36-41;
Griffin Church, Starkville, Miss. , 1941-46; Haven Church,
Clarksdale, Miss. , 1946-50; Wesley Church, Greenwood
Miss. , 50-60; Asbury Church, Holly Springs, Miss. ,
1960-62; current, District Supt. , Aberdeen Dist. Upper
Miss. Conference, Methodist Church; teacher, City and
County Schools of Tippah County, Miss. , 1941-46; profes-

sor, Coahoma Jr. Coll., Clarksdale, Miss., 1948-50;
professor, Sociology, Miss. Vocational Coll., Itta Bena,
Miss.; guest lecturer, Grad. School, Jackson State Coll.,
Jackson, Miss.; Rust Coll., 1960-62; candidate for Con-
gress, First Congregational Dist., Miss., 1962; Mem.,
Advisory Staff, Democratic Party; Home: 425-5th St., West
Point, Miss.

LINK, John Lewis, b. Milton, N.C., Sept. 4, 1884; s.
Stephen and Susan L.; B.A., Lincoln Univ., 1909; S.T.B.,
Lincoln Univ. Theol. Seminary, 1912; Derrick Business
School, 1921; journalism, Univ. of Pa., 1936; Crozer
Seminary, 1938; m. Nora Helen Cameron Watson; pastor,
African Methodist Episcopal Church, Shippensburg, Pa.,
1912-13; Downingtown, Pa., 1914-17, Columbia, Pa.,
1917-20, Media, Pa., 1920-25; Murphy Church, Chester,
Pa., 1925-33; presiding elder, Delaware Conference,
1933---; Mem., Chester City School Bd., 1947-63; pres.,
Inter-Racial Treasurer Branch YMCA, Chester, Pa.;
Mem., Lincoln Univ. Alumni Ass'n; Mason; Home: 524
Flower St., Chester, Pa. 19013; Office: 524 Flower St.,
Chester, Pa.

*LINSEY, Nathaniel, b. Atlanta, Ga., July 24, 1926; s.
Sam and L.E. (Forney) L.; A.B., Paine Coll., 1948;
B.D., Howard Univ., 1951; m. Mae Cannon Mills; chil-
dren---Nathaniel L., Ricarldo Mills, Julius Wayne;
pastor, Halifax Circuit, 1949-51; National Youth Director,
Christian Methodist Episcopal Church, 1951-52; pastor,
Walterboro Circuit, Walterboro, S.C., 1952-53; presiding
elder, Greenville District, S.C., 1953-54; pastor, Vander-
horst Memorial C.M.E. Church, Charleston, S.C., 1954-
55; pastor, Mattie E. Coleman Church, Knoxville, Tenn.,
1955-62; pastor, Thirgood C.M.E. Church, Birmingham,
Ala., 1962---; Birmingham District, Director of Evangelism, C.M.E. Church; pres., NAACP, Knoxville, Tenn.,
1960; chairman, Board of Management, YMCA, Knoxville,
1961-62; Mem., Mayor's Bi-racial Committee, Knoxville,
Tenn., 1960-62; Community Service Award 1964 Zeta Phi
Beta Sorority, Birmingham, Ala. Rec'd Citation in Religion
from Pi Lambda Sigma Honor Society, Birmingham, Ala.,
1963; Ala. Christian Movement for Human Rights; Strategy
Committee YMCA; Advisory Committee of Planned Parenthood; Mem., Ministers and Laymen's Council, C.M.E.
Church; Home: 932 Center Pl., S.W., Birmingham, Ala.;
Office: 1029 7th Ave., N. Birmingham 3, Ala.

LITTLE, John Franklin, b. Rock Run, Ala., Mar 5, 1908;
s. Hampton Wiley and Lula (Thomason) L.; B.S., Blue-
field State Teacher's College, W. Va., 1940; B.D.,
Payne Theological Seminary, Wilberforce, Ohio, 1935;
Further study: Denver Univ., 1960 and Pittsburgh Univ.;
m. Mabel Sterns; children---Marjorie Loretta (Mrs.
Howard Cockrell); Laura Jane (Mrs. John Okumu), Jo-
Anne Murray; pastor, A.M.E. Churches, Ohio, West Va.,
Pa., Liberia, 1931-62; Professor, Univ. Of Liberia, 1953-
56; pres., Monrovia Coll. & Industrial Training Sch.,
1953-60; teacher, Capte Palmas High School and A.M.E.
Day School, Harper City, Liberia, 1961; current pastor,
Trinity A.M.E. Church, Pittsburgh, Pa.; pres., United
Nations Organization, Harper City, Liberia; preached in
John Wesley Chapel, London, Eng., July 31, 1951;
preached and lectured in Germany, 1951; Home: 560
Clow Ave., Newcomerstown, Ohio; Office: 2702 Wylie Ave.,
Pittsburgh 19, Pa. 15219.

LLOYD, Gil Burton, b. Nashville, Tenn., Nov. 9, 1916;
s. Grant, Sr. and Johnella (Stewart) L.; A.B., Fisk Univ.,
1939; B.D., Chicago Seminary, 1941; m. Doris Watts;
children---Doris Diane; asst. pastor, Sylvan St. Baptist
Ch., Nashville, Tenn., 1935-37; pastor, St. Mary Congregational Ch., Abbeville, La., 1938; chaplain, US Army,
1942-46; pastor, Mt. Zion Baptist Church, Seattle, Washington, 1955-57; exec. director, Englewood Christian Center, 1957-59; pastor, Cherry Hill Baptist Church, Seattle,
Washington, 1959---; associate director, Parkway Community House, Chgo, Ill., 1946-47; community worker, Southside Community Comm., Chgo., Ill., 1948-52; Chaplain
1st Lt., Chaplain Corps, 1942-46; Bronze Star Medal; Mem.,
American Public Welfare Ass'n; 1st Vice pres., North
Pacific Baptist Convention; Bd. of Home Missions, National
Baptist Convention, USA, Inc.; former editor, The FACTS,
Northwest weekly, Seattle, Wash.; Home: 325 19th Ave.,
East Seattle, Wash. 98102. Office: 700 22nd Ave., Seattle
Wash. 98122.

*LOCKMAN, Irvin Charles, b. Baltimore, Md., June 22,
1929; s. William and Elizabeth (Griffin) L.; A.B., Morgan
State Coll., 1952; B.D., Howard Univ. Sch. of Rel.,
1955; m. Joan Carroll; Ordained Methodist Ch., 1952;
pastor, John Mann Methodist Ch., Winchester, Va., 1952-
56; St. Matthew's Meth. Ch., Baltimore, Md., 1956-58;
Epworth Meth. Ch., Bronx, New York, 1958-63; current
pastor, Mt. Calvary Meth. Ch., New York City, 1963---;

Mem., Bd. of Directors, Bethel Meth. Home, Ossining,
N.Y.; Church Campaign Com., YMCA, Harlem Branch;
Protestant Federation of Welfare Agencies; sec., Metro-
politan Sub-district Meth. Minister's Fellowship; treas.,
Meth. for Ch. Renewal, N.Y.; sec., Interdenominational
Chaplain, N.Y. Chapter; Howard Univ. Alumni; Home:
227 W. 149th St., New York, N.Y. 10039; Office: 116
Edgecombe Ave., New York, N.Y. 10030

LOGAN, John Richard, Jr., chaplain; b. Phila. Pa., May
12, 1910; s. John R., Sr. and Mary L. (Harbison) L.;
Lincoln Univ., 1930-34; Philadelphia Divinity, 1934-37;
m. Sarah U. (Johnson); children---John R., III; present
rector, St. Simon Cyrenian Prot. Episcopal Church;
Member, The Executive Council; Mem., Board of Missions; Board of Triers of the Diocese of Pa.; Episcopal
chaplain, the Mercy-Douglas Hospital; Board of Directors
of the Christian Street Branch of the YMCA; St. John's
Settlement House; The American Red Cross; advisor,
Reed Street Community Council; Awards rec'd from American Red Cross, Christian Street YMCA, Point Breeze
Community Council, Boy Scouts of Amer.; Mem.: Sigma
Pi Phi, Alpha Boule; Alpha Phi Alpha; Mason; Elks; Home:
1230 So. 21st. Phila. 46, Pa.; Office: 2122 Reed Phila.,
46, Pa.

LOGAN, Thomas W.S., b. Philadelphia, Pa., Mar. 19,
1912; s. John Richard and Mary (Harbison) L.; A.B.,
Lincoln Univ., 1935; General Theol. Sem., 1938; S.T.B.,
Phila. Divinity School, 1941; m. Hermoine Hill; 1 son:
Thomas W.S., Jr.; deacon, Phila., Pa., 1938; priest,
Phila., Penna., 1939; vicar in charge, St. Augustine's
Protestant Episcopal Ch., Yonkers, N.Y., 1938-39; cur-
ate, St. Philip's Parish, N.Y.C., 1938-39; vicar, St.
Michael's Chapel, Phila., Pa., 1940-45; current rector,
Calvary P.E. Ch., Pa., 1945---; dean, School of Religion,
Methodist Ch., Wilmington, Del., 1951---; dean, Summer
School of Religion, St. Paul's Coll., 1944-46; chaplain,
Summer School, St. Augustine's Coll., 1947-49; former
pres., National Church Workers Conf. of Episcopal Ch.,
1952-61; and the Hampton Interdenominational Conf., 1961-
62; Distinguished Service Certificate, American Legion of
Pa., 1960; Distinguished Service Award, Prince Hall
Masons, Pa., 1961; Distinguished Service Award by Afro-
American, 1945; Mem., Alpha Phi Alpha; Elks; Mason;
Democrat; former pres., local and present chaplain of
Frontiers of America; Home: 46 Lincoln Ave., Yeadon,

Penna.,Office: Calvary Episc. Ch., 814 N. 41st St.,
Phila., Pa.

LOVE, Edgar Amos, bishop; b. Harrisburg, Va., Sept. 10,
1891; s. Julius C. and Susie (Carr) L.; Morgan Academy,
1905-09; A.B., Howard Univ.,Sch. of Rel.; 1913; B.D., 1916;
S.T.B., Boston Univ., 1918; D.D. (hon.), Morgan Coll., 1935;
Gammon Theol. Sem., 1946; Boston Univ., 1956; m.
Virginia Louise Ross; children---Jon Edgar; Ordained to
ministry, Meth. Ch., 1915; principal, academy, Morgan
Coll., Balt., 1920-21; coll. prof., 1919-21; pastor,
Washington, Pa., 1921-26, Annapolis, Md., 1926-29,
Wheeling, W. Va., 1929-31; 1931-33; dist. supt., Wash-
ington Dist., Washington Conf. Meth.Ch., 1933-40; supt.
dept. Negro Work Bd. Missions, Meth. Ch., 1940-52;
bishop since 1952, assigned Balt. area; sometime lecturer,
numerous Colls. and Univs.; Trustee, Morgan Coll.; Mem.,
Bd. of Governors, Gammon Theol. Sem., Atlanta, Mor-
ristown Jr. Coll.; Bd. Missions; vice pres., Bd. Evange-
lism, Coordinating Council of Meth. Ch.; Meth. Com. on
Chaplains; Gen. Com. on Chaplains; Nat.Council Chs. of
Christ in U.S.A.; Mem., Omega Psi Phi; Elk; Mason;
Frontiers of America (Balt.); Retired 1964; Home: 2416
Montebello Terrace, Balt. 17, Md.

LOWE, Richard A., chaplain, editor; b. Cleveland, Ohio,
June 12, 1898; s. Robert B. and Martha (Lane) L.; B.
Th., Wilberforce Univ., 1917; B.S., Univ. of Chicago,
1926; Lewis Institute, Chicago; Harvard Univ., 1940; D.D.
(hon.), Texas Bapt. Coll.; m. Ruth Wheeler (1st), Catherine Redman (present) children---Anna Belle, Richard,David;
field missionary, Western Bapt. Convention, 1919-21; Ordained A.M.E. Elder, 1922; pastor, African Methodist
Episcopal Churches, 1922-30; associate pastor, Shiloh
Bapt. Ch., Cleveland, Ohio, 1930-35; Providence Bapt.
Ch., 1935-37; Greater El Bethel Bapt. Ch., Dallas, Tex.,
1937-41; current, Mt. Zion Bapt. Ch., Newark, N.J.;
public relations practitioner, 1926-40; public relations
consultant, 1940---; editor, Missionary Bapt. Digest, official organ New England Bapt. Convention and Amer.
Negro Missionary Bapt., 1956---; Public Relations Counsel: Nat'l Negro Independent Civic & Political Ass'n,
Inc., 1952---; US Veteran, World War I, 1918-19; Chaplain, US Army, 1941-43; 1st Lt.; Mem., Mason; Commissioner of Public Relations, General Baptist Convention;
editor, These Changing and Clashing Worlds 1948; Home: 214
W. Market St. (Apt. 5), Newark, N.J.; Office: Third

Floor East, 160 Broadway, New York, N. Y.

LUCAS, Lawrence Edward, b. New York, N. Y., July 8,
1933; s. George Alvin and Miriam (Grant) L.; Cathedral
College, N. Y., 1947-53; St. Joseph's Seminary, Yonkers
College, 1953-59; Ordained Roman Catholic priest; St.
Joseph's Church, Croton Falls, N. Y., 1959; St. Peter's
Church, Barclay St., N. Y., 1959-61; Resurrection Church,
N. Y. C., 1961---; Bd. of Dir., Harlem Neighborhood Assn;
Mayors Comm. of Religious Leaders; Home and Office:
276 W. 151st., New York 39, N. Y.

LYLES, James V., coll. chaplain; b. Texarkana, Texas,
July 4, 1928; s. F. O. and Laura (Stucky) L.; B. A.,
Philander Smith Coll., 1952; B. D., Perkins Sch. of
Theology, Southern Methodist Univ., 1955; Further study:
Hogg Foundation on Mental Health; Univ. of Texas, 1960;
m. Shirley Robinson; children---Marquis Densell; youth
director, St. Paul Methodist Ch., Dallas, Texas, 1952-53;
Bd. of Evangelism of the Methodist Ch., 1953-54; Or-
ganized Golden Methodist Church, Memphis, 1954-56; US
Air Force chaplain, 1956-61; chaplain, pastor, teacher and
counselor of Bethel Church, Morristown Coll., 1961---;
registrar, East Tenn. Annual Conference, 1963---; Mem.,
Bd. of Managers, Gulfside Methodist Assembly School;
Cultural and Civic Comm. of the Morristown; Chamber
of Commerce; Democrat; American Philosophical Society;
42nd Bomb Wing Unit Citation; 5th Motor Transport Unit
Citation; B'nai B'rith Award for Outstanding Achievements
in the field of Social Ethics; Mem., Alpha Phi Alpha;
NAACP; Urban League; National Council of Christians and
Jews; Mem., Editorial Bd. of The Red Knight Journal;
Home: 307 East 6th St., North Morristown, Tenn.; Office:
Morristown Coll., Morristown, Tenn.

MALOY, Rufus Charles, b. Nashville, Tenn., Nov. 24, 1895
s. Henry and Hattie (Winston) M.; 1916, School for Blind,
Nashville, Tenn.; 1921-1922, post-grad. course at Knoxville, Tenn.; m. Robbie (Erzell); pastor, 1921-22, Christian Church, Strawberry Plains, Tenn.; 1923-40, Gay
Street Christian Church, Nashville, Tenn.; current: Alameda Street Christian Church, 1940; (Disciples of Christ);
awards: Disciples of Christ Service Pin (40 yrs. ministerial service 1957 and 1962; Oldfellows; Home: 333 21st
Ave. North Nashville, Tenn. 37203; Office: 2422 Alameda
St., Nashville, Tenn. 37208.

*MANGRAM, John Dee, coll. prof.; b. Pittsburg, Texas,
June 18, 1924; s. Ruther, Sr. and Viola Ruth (Reed) M.;
A.B., Jarvis Christian Coll., 1945; Howard Univ., Sch.
of Rel., 1948, B.D.; S.T.M., Yale Univ., 1958; presently, studying toward Th.D., at Pacific School of Re-
ligion, Berkely, California; m. Bobbye Ella Durham; assistant director, Social Studies, Pendle Hill, Wallingford,
Pa., 1948-49; univ. minister, Lincoln Univ., 1949-50;
coll. chaplain, Tougaloo Coll., Tougaloo, Miss.; assistant
professor of religion, Tougaloo Coll., 1950-61; pastor,
First Congregational Church, Meridian, Miss.; moderator,
Alabama-Miss. Conference of Congregational Christian
Churches, 1959-61; Trustee Convention of the South,
Greensboro, N.C., 1959-61; interim pastor, The Church
for the Fellowship of All Peoples, San Francisco, Calif.,
1963---; vice pres., Jackson, Miss. NAACP, 1954-61;
chairman, Board of Directors, Jackson, Miss. NAACP;
vice chairman, Southeastern Region NAACP, 1955-57;
Board Directors, Miss. Council on Human Relations,
1953-60; Board of Directors, Progressive Voters' League
of Miss.; advisor, Youth Chapters of NAACP, State and
Jackson, Miss. Branch, NAACP, 1953-61; awards:
Citizenship Award from Alpha Phi Alpha Fraternity,
Tougaloo, Miss., 1956; Danforth Campus Christian Worker
Fellowship to Yale Univ., 1957; Danforth Study Grant for
work toward Doctorate, 1961; Mem.: National Ass'n of
Coll. Univ. Professors; National Ass'n of Coll. and Univ.
Chaplains; Danforth Associates; Home: 1716 Routh St.,
Dallas 4, Texas, Office: The Church for the Fellowship
of All Peoples, 2041 Larkin St., San Francisco 9,
Calif.

MANIGO, George Franklin, Jr., b. Bamberg, S.C., Nov.
10, 1934; s. George Franklin and Etta Mae (Ramsey) M.;
Voorhees Jr. Coll., 1952-53; B.S., Claflin Coll., 1959;
B.D., Gammon Theol. Sem., 1962; m. Rosa Lee Lewis;
children---Marcia Benita; student work, Central Methodist
Church, Atlanta, Ga., 1959; pastor, Horst Memorial
Methodist Church, 1960-62; current pastor, St. Paul
Methodist Churches, Johnson City & Elizabethon, Tenn.,
1962; Clinical Training at High Spaulding Hospital, Atlanta,
Ga., 1960-62; Mem., Young Democrats of Johnson City;
Exec. Comm. of Local NAACP Chapter; US Forces, 1953-
56; National Defense Service Medal; Army Occupation
Medal Good Conduct Medal; Mem., Phi Beta Sigma; John-
son City Progressive League; Community Relation Com-
mittee; Democrat; Home: 402 Chilhowie Ave., Johnson

City, Tenn.

MARCUS, Chester Lee, church official; b. Swiftown, Miss.
Feb. 14, 1917; s. Frank and Eliza M.; B.S., Alcorn
A & M, 1940; B.D., Lincoln Univ., Pa., 1943; Albright
Coll., Pa.; m. Warnetta Patton (dec.); 1 son, Chester
Lee, Jr.; Ordained, Philadelphia Presbytery, 1943; pas-
tored, Washington Street Presbyterian Ch., Reading,
Pas., 1943-44; Sec., Racial and Cultural Relations of
E & R Church, Cleveland, O., 1954-62; Teacher and
Goodwill Ambassador, Ghana, 1960; Africa Secretary,
United Church of Christ, 1962, Named outstanding
alumnus, Alcorn A & M, 1962; Recipient, Africa Gold
Star for contribution to Labor understanding, Ghana, 1960;
Reading Fellowship Medal for contribution to Racial Under-
standing, 1954; Dir., Nat. Council of Churches Inst. on
Racial and Cultural Relations, 1957-58; mem. World
Council Comm. on Christian Ed.; mem., Phi Beta Sigma
Author, The Bible and Race, 1959; Home: 201 Irvington
Rd., Teaneck, New Jersey. Office: 475 Riverside Drive,
N.Y. 27, N.Y.

MARINO, Eugene Antonio, coll. prof.; b. Biloxi, Miss.,
May 29, 1934; s. Jesus Maria and Irene (Bradford) M.;
Epiphany Apostolic College, Newburgh, N.Y., 1952-55;
St. Joseph's Seminary, Washington, D.C., 1956-62; St.
Michael's College, Winooski, Vt., 1957-60; Loyola Univ.,
New Orleans, La., 1961-63; Ordained priest, Roman
Cath. Ch., Washington, D.C. (National Shrine of the
Immaculate Conception, 1962; Mem. Society of St. Joseph
of the Sacred Heart; Instructor: physical science, biology,
Catholic doctrine, Epiphany Apostolic College, Newburgh,
N.Y.; Mem. Amer. Assoc. for the Advancement of Science,
Home: and Office: Box 390, Newburgh, N.Y.

MARSH, Clinton McClurkin, church administrator, b. Anne-
manie, Ala. Oct. 28, 1916; s. Thomas P. and Sadie; A.
B., Knoxville College, 1939; B.D., Pittsburgh-Xenia
Theological Seminary, 1944; D.D. (hon.), Knoxville Col-
lege, 1955; Graduate courses: Univ. of Pittsburgh; m.
Dorothy Cosby; children---Walter Francis; pastor United
Presby. Ch., Chase City, Va., 1944-45; Witherspoon U.
Presby. Ch., Indianapolis, Ind., 1946-63; Director of
Evangelism, North Central Area, United Presby. Ch.;
pres. Indianapolis Ch. Fed. Bd. of Dir., Indianapolis
Council of Churches Gen. and vice pres. Bd. Nat. Council
of Churches; Bd. of Dir. Eastside Ch. Center of In-
dianapolis. Bd. Dir. Indianapolis Center Senior Citizens.

Bd. Dir. Indianapolis Health and Welfare Council. Bd. of
Nat. Missions, United Presby. Ch., U.S.A.; Mem.:
Counseling Comm. on Church and Society, U.P.U.S.A.;
Advisory Bd., Marion County Tuberculosis Assoc.,
Government's Youth Council; Comm. on Segregated Pres-
byteries and Synod., Moderator, Indianapolis Presbytery;
pres. Indianapolis Ministeries Assoc.; moderator Second
Synod, U.P.C.; chairman Christian Ed., Indianapolis
Presbytery; pres. Lord's Day Alliance of Indiana; Bd.
Weekday Rel. Ed. of Marion County, Indiana. Home:
436 W. 25th St., Indianapolis, Ind.

MARSHBURN, J. Dett, b. Maple Hill, N.C.; B.D., D.D.
(hon.), Va. Union Univ., Richmond, Va.; Union Theol.
Sem., N.Y.C.; pastor, Wine St. Bapt. Ch., 1932-36;
Zion Bapt. Church, Phoebus, Va., 1936---; Bd. of
Directors, Bapt. Children's Home, Petersburg, Va.;
chairman, Prov. of Ch. supported Schools & Coll., Na-
tional Bapt.; dean, Lebanon Va. Bapt. Ass'n; current
pastor, Antioch Baptist Ch. and Zion Baptist Ch., Phoebus,
Buckroe, Va., 1937---; organizer, Phoebus Comm. Cen-
ter, 1942, Louise Davis Playground, Phoebus, Va.; Mem.,
Coord. Comm., Lower Peninsula Voters League; Exec.
Bd. Mem., King Street Communication Center; Candidate
City Council, 1955 and 1961; delegate, Bapt. World Al-
liance, 1948, Copenhagen, Denmark; Mem., Mental Health
Bd., Lower Peninsula Assn. for Mental Health; Mem.,
Omega Phi Psi; Mem., Peninsula Ministerial Alliance;
Office: 11 North Hope St., Phoebus, Va.

MARTIN, Richard Beamon, teacher; b. Peak, South Carolina,
Feb. 23, 1913; s. Benjamin Butler and Violet (Glasgow)
M.; A.B., Allen University, 1933-37; B.D., Bishop Payne
Divinity School, 1939-42; Graduate School of Theology
University of the South, 1962; Union Theological Seminary,
1958; m. Annella Hoover; children---Richard Beamon, Jr.,
Garnett Hoover; Priest-in-charge, St. Augustine's, Sumter
County and Church of the Good Shepherd, Sumter, S.C.,
1942-44; Rector, Grace Church, Norfolk, Va., 1944-63;
Archdeacon, Diocese of Southern Virginia; Rector, St.
Philip's Church, Brooklyn, N.Y., 1963---; Public School
Teacher, Howard High School, 1937-39; teacher, Morris
College, Sumter, S.C., 1943-44; Former Member of
Board of Directors, Norfolk Journal & Guide; American
Church Institute; St. Paul's College, Lawrenceville, Va.;
Youth Consultation Service, Diocese of Long Island;

Brooklyn Tuberculosis & Health; Presiding Bishop's Com-
mittee on Racial Minorities; Member, Alpha Phi Alpha;
Former Weekly Column in Norfolk Journal and Guide,
Norfolk, Va.; Home: 195 Willoughby Ave., Brooklyn,
N.Y.; Office: 265 Decatur St., Brooklyn, N.Y.

MARTIN, Samuel Joseph, b. Huntsville, Ala., June 5,
1905; s. John Thomas and Hubbard (Dorrence); B.S.,
Boston Univ.; Tufts College, Chicago University; B.D.,
Institute of Technology 1933; Episcopal Seminary, 1930;
S.T.M., Seabury Theological Seminary, 1935; D.D.,
Seabury Western Seminary, Evanston, 1954; m. Clarice
White; children --- Annette, John Craighead, Samuel
Martin, Jr.; pres. Standing Committee, Diocese of
Chicago; Member, Diocesan Council, Diocese of Chicago;
current, Dean of the Chicago Deanery Diocese of Chicago;
director, NAACP, Chicago Branch; Founder, Saint Ed-
munds Parochial School; Distinguished service cross for
outstanding service to Diocese presented by Bishop Steward,
1936---; Bishop Payne Episcopal Seminary; Numerous
articles in "The Living Church" Episcopal Weekly; Home:
8515 Indiana Ave., Chicago, Ill.; Off.: 6105 Michigan Ave.,
Chicago 37, Ill.

MASHAW, Samuel Jones, b. Pickneyville, Ala., Nov. 25,
1891; s. Benjamin Frank and Luella (Wilson) M.; A.B.,
Miles Coll., Birmingham, Ala., 1937; B.D., Miles Coll.,
1938; Study in Rel. Education Tuskegee Institute, 1942;
Study in Religious Education Fisk Univ., 1944; m. Addie
Earnestine Reynolds; children---Mattie (Mrs. Theodore
Douglas Gill); pastor, 7 years in Ohio; 19 years in Ala.;
current pastor, St. Peter Christian Methodist Church,
Kansas City, Kansas, 12 years; elected to Judiciary
Court of C.M.E. Church, 1950; elected Chief Justice of
the court, 1962; delegate, C.M.E. General Conf., 1930,
34, 38, 42, 46, 50; Mem., Commission from C.M.E.
Church of the state of Kansas to Council of Churches on
Political Action at Univ. of Nebraska, 1963; Mem., Bd.
of Dir., Douglas Hospital, Kansas City, Kansas; Board
of Trustee, Miles Coll.; Trustee of Phillips School of
Theology, Atlanta, Ga.; Republican; Exec. Bd. of NAACP
Kansas City, Kansas; Home: 743 Oakland Ave., Kansas
City, Kansas 66101; St. Peter C.M.E. Church 8th Oakland
Kansas City, Kansas 66101.

MASON, Cleveland L., b. Daingerfield, Texas, Jan. 23,
1908; s. Thomas and Bessie (Whitmore) M.; A.B., 1949;

Extension School, Prairie View College, Prairie View,
Texas; m. Evelyn D. Burgess; children--- Cleveland L.
Jr., Oland D., Oreantha D. Pastor, Mt. Zion Christian
Methodist Episcopal Church, Daingerfield, Texas, 1915-
30; Pastor, Miles Chapel C. M. E. Church, Norfolk, Va.,
1930-59; present: pastor, St. John C. M. E. Church, Petersburg, Va., 1959-   ; former teacher, Veteran's School,
and insurance agent, 1933-40. U. S. Army, Ft. Sill, Okla.
1941-44; Europe, 1944-45; 5 battle stars, 1 bronze star
medal, unit citation. Member, N. A. A. C. P., Y. M. C. A.;
Mason; Democrat. Office: St. John C. M. E. Church, 428
St. Mark St., St. Petersburg, Virginia.

MAYES, Allen Mercer, church official; b. Jefferson, Texas,
Sept. 20, 1920; s. F. D. and N. Allen; B. S., Wiley Coll.,
1941; B. D., Gammon Theol. Sem., 1944; S. T. M., Bos-
ton Univ. Sch. of Theol., 1946; Additional study: Harvard
Univ., 1945-46; m. LaVerne Hadnott; children---Janis
Alene; supervisor, Migrant Ministry in New York State,
National Council of Churches, 1944-45; pastor, Asbury
Methodist Church, Houston, Tex., 1946-50; St. James
Methodist Church, Beaumont, Tex., 1950-63; current,
asst. sec., General Bd. of Pensions of Meth. Ch., Evanston, Ill., 1963---; dean, New Orleans Area Pastors'
School, 1960---; sec., Central Jurisdictional Conf., 1964
---; Mem., Bd. of Managers, General Bd. of Missions
of Meth. Ch., 1960-64; sec., Section of Church Extension, General Bd. of Missions, 1960-64; Joint Committee
of Missionary Personnel, Bd. of Missions, 1960-64; Bd.
of Directors, Wesley Foundation, Texas Southern Univ.;
delegate, Methodist World Conf., 1956; Reserve Delegate
to General Conference, Meth. Church, 1956-, 60; Conference Bd. of Ministerial Training, 1946---; chairman, Texas Conference Bd. of Education, 1948---; Texas Conf.
Missionary Secretary, 1948-64; Home: 2416 Crain St.,
Evanston, Ill. 60202; Office: General Board of Pensions
of Methodist Church, 1200 Davis St., Evanston, Ill.

MAYS, Benjamin Elijah, coll. pres., sem. dean, author; b.
Epworth, S. C., Aug. 1, 1895; s. S. Hezekiah and Lou-
vania (Carter) M.; A. B., Bates Coll., 1920; M. A., Univ.
of Chicago, 1925; Ph. D., 1935; D. D. (hon.), Howard Univ.,
Wash., D. C.; Bates Coll., Lewiston, Maine, 1947; Buck-
nell Univ., Lewisburg, Pa., 1954; Berea Coll., Berea,
Ky., 1955; Kalamazoo Coll., Kalamazoo, Mich., 1959;
LL. D. (hon.), Denison Univ., Granville, Ohio, 1945; Va.
Union Univ., Richmond, Va., 1945; Univ. of Liberia,

Monrovia, Liberia, 1960; St. Augustine's Coll., Raleigh,
N. C., 1963; LH. D. (hon.), S. C. State Coll., Orangeburg,
S. C., 1946; HH. D. (hon.), Boston Univ., Boston, Mass.,
1950; DH. L., Keuka Coll., Keuka Park, N. Y., 1962; Ed.
D. (hon.), St. Vincent Coll., Latrobe, Pa., 1964; m.
Sadie Gray; prof., Morehouse Coll. and pastor, Shiloh
Baptist Church, Atlanta, Ga., 1921-24; instructor, S. C.
State Coll., 1925-26; Exec. sec., Tampa Urban League,
Fla., 1926-28; National Student Sec., YMCA, 1928-30;
director, a study of Negro Churches in the US under the
auspices of the Institute of Social and Religious Research,
N. Y. C., 1930-32; dean, Howard Univ. Sch. of Rel., 1934-
40; author: The Negro's Church (co-author); The Negro's
God; Seeking to be Christian In Race Relations; A Gospel
for the Social Awakening; Has written many chapters in
books, articles in 69 magazines as Christian Century,
Crisis, Journal of Negro Education in Life, Presbyterian
Outlook and many others; Kent Fellow of National Council
on Rel. in Higher Education; Represented the YMCA of
America the Plenary Session of the World Com., Stock-
holm, Sweden, 1938; Represented the US at the Oxford
Conf. on the Ch., Community and State, Oxford Univ.,
England, 1937; leader, Youth Conference at Amsterdam,
Holland, 1939; Mem., Delta Sigma Rho, the Delta Theta
Chi, the Omega Psi Phi Fraternities, and Phi Beta Kappa
Society; Southern Education Foundation; contributing editor,
Journal of Negro Education; Mem., Theol. Discussion
Group; Bd. of Nat. YMCA; vice pres., The World Student
Service Fund; delegate, World Council of Churches,
Amsterdam, Holland, 1948; Mem., Central Com., World
Council of Churches, 1949-53; Central Com. Meeting of
the World Council of Churches, Chichester, England,
1949; Attended the meeting of the Central Com. of World
Council of Churches, Rolle, Switzerland, 1951; delegate
and leader, Bapt. World Alliance Assembly, Cleveland,
Ohio, 1950; Attended the Meeting of the Central Committee
of World Council of Churches, Lucknow, India, 1952-1953;
Attended meeting of the Commission on the Church Amidst
Racial and Ethnic Tensions, Geneva, Switzerland, 1953;
Bd. Mem., Institute of International Education; Bd. Mem.,
Booker Washington Agricultural and Industrial Institute of
Liberia; Trustee, National Fund for Medical Education;
Trustee, Danforth Foundation; Bd. Mem., Southern Assn
of Colleges and Schools; vice pres., The Federal Council
of the Churches of Christ, USA, 1944-46; Named on the
Schomberg Honor Roll of Race Relations, 1944; Recipient
of LETTER AWARD from Letter Magazine, Ada P. Mc

Cormick, editor; Named "The Alumnus of the Year" by
the Div. Sch. of the Univ. of Chicago; Recipient of the
2nd Annual State Fair Negro Achievement Award of Texas,
1950; The Distinguished Service Award for effectiveness in
public speech given by Delta Sigma Rho at its 50th Golden
Jubilee; pres., The United Negro Coll. Fund, Inc., 1958-
61; Advisory Council of the US Com. for the UN, 1959;
Mem., National Advisory Council to the Peace Corps,
1961; Mem., United States National Commission for
UNESCO; Represented the United States at the State Funeral of Pope John XXIII, 1963; Home: 820 Fair St., NW,
Atlanta, Ga. 30314; Office: 223 Chestnut St., Atlanta,
Ga.

MAYS, Willie, b. New Orleans, La., May 14, 1927; s.
George and Ruby M.; B.S., Grambling Coll., 1959; B.D.,
Interdenominational Theol. Center, 1962; m. Queen Eliza-
beth Coleman; children--- Wayne Wendell; ordnance worker,
Port Chicago, Calif., 1950-51; current pastor, Christian
Meth. Ch., 1954---; pres., Bd. of Directors of the Cal-
casieu Co-ordinating Council, 1963---; chairman, The
World Service Comm., YMCA, 1963---; Mem., Mason;
Home: 308 South Lyons St., Lake Charles, La.; Office:
1439 Winterhalter St., Lake Charles, La.

MAYSON, Henry Irving, b. Cleveland, O., Feb. 1, 1925;
s. Edwin Lawson and Josephine Bell (Hill) M.; 1948,
B.A. St. Augustine's College; 1951, B.D. Bexley Hall,
Divinity School, Keynon College; m. Alma Marie (Harris)
M.; m. Heather Kim; Founder and rector, St. Philip's
Episcopal Church, Akron, O., 1951---; Akron Chapter of
Core (Exec. Board); Omega Psi phi; Urban League (Exec.
Bd.) 1957-61; NAACP. (Exec. Bd.) 1960; Y.M.C.A.:
Glendale Bd., 1951; Metropolitan Bd.; Ohio, W.Va. Area
Council; National Council; Frontiers of America, 1951;
Council of the Diocese of Ohio, 1960; Home: 885 Storer
Ave., Akron, O. 44320; Church: St. Philip's, 1130 Mercer
Ave., Akron, O. 44320.

MEACHEM, Robert Allen, teacher; b. Warren, Ark., Nov.
21, 1926; s. Allen Scott and Wheatley Joina (Todd) M.;
B.A., Johnson C. Smith Univ., 1949; B.D., 1958; Graduate Work: Univ. of Mich.; m. Jean Frances Jackson;
children--- Sherry Lynn, Robert Lynnette; pastor Freedom
East Church, Mt. Olive UP & Mars Hill United Presbyterian Ch., 1956-57; Caldwell & Miranda UP Churches,
1958; Catawba UP Church, 1959---; teacher, Mary Homes

Jr. College, West Point, Miss., 1954; typing instructor
1952 Hugo, Oklahoma, dir. of Recreation Center, Charlotte,
N.C., 1957-63; Service in USAF Control Tower Operator;
mem.: Certified Recreator State of N.C., American
Recreation Society; Kappa Alpha Psi Fraternity, Pole-
march '57 Johnson C. Smith Univ., Ministerial Relations
Committee; Catawba Presbytery of the UP Ch., USA;
Home: 3033 Bellaire Drive, Charlotte 8, N.C.; Ch.:
Rte #2, Box 105 Huntersville, N.C.

MEDFORD, Hampton Thomas, bishop (retired); b. Marion,
N.C., Jan. 29, 1887; s. Charles M. Greenlee and
Cecelia Godfrey Greenlee; Livingstone College, 1909-20;
D.D. (hon.), 1920; m. Elizabeth Kemp; children---
Booker T., Alma, Cordella, Thomas A.; pastor, A.M.E.
Zion Church, Cherryville, N.C.; Morris Chapel, Salis-
bury, N.C.; Jacob St. Church, Louisville, Ky.; Logan
Temple, Knoxville, Tenn.; John Wesley A.M.E. Zion
Church, Washington, D.C.; General Sec. of Foreign Mis-
sions, A.M.E. Zion Church, 1930-50; Bishop to Africa,
1950-54; Retired as bishop, 1960; Member, Board of
Trustee, Livingstone College; Editor of "From The Depths",
"From Rags to Riches"; Home: 4615 16th NW, Washington,
D.C.; Office: 1421 U St. NW, Washington, D.C.

MERCER, William Summer, b. Providence, R.I. October 1,
1917; s. Miah William and Abelle (Seter); B.A., Lincoln
Univ., 1941; S.T.B., Lincoln Seminary, 1944; M.A.,
McCormick Theol. Sem.- Chicago, 1948; D.D., Knoxville
College, 1964; m. Cecilia McCoy; Sunday School Mission-
ary, Southern Va., 1944-45; pastor and larger parish
director Burke County Georgia, 1945-46; social group
worker Neighborhood House, Buffalo, N.Y., 1946-47;
Director of Goodwill Larger Parish-Sumter, Lee and
Clarendon Counties South Carolina, 48-53; pastor Redcliffe
United Presby. Ch., Atlanta, Ga., 1953- ;moderator
Knox-Hodge Presbytery; moderator Atlantic Synod; chmn.
Christian Ed. Knox-Hodge; Evangelism chmn. Knox-Hodge
Presbytery; chmn. The Advisory Comm. of Boggs
Academy Keysville, Ga.; Bd. Mem. of Gate City Nursery
Assoc., Atlanta; D.D., from Knoxville Coll.,1964; mem.:
Alpha Phi Alpha; exec. comm. Southern Christian Leader-
ship Conference; exec. comm. N.A.A.C.P. Home: 284
Hightower Rd. NW., Atlanta 30318 Georgia; Ch.: 290
Hightower Rd., N.W., Atlanta, Ga.

MEYERS, Samuel David, b. New York City, N.Y., November
26, 1925; s. Theodore Troup and Louvenia (Meyers) T.;
B.S., Emmanuel Missionary College, 1947; m. Gloria
Lee Vaughn; children- Anthony Lloyd, Pamela Marie,
Charles Weldon, Donna Louise, Sibyl Diane. Southwest
Region Conference of Seventh-Day Adventists, Hq. in Dal-
las, Texas, pastored, 1947-52, in New Orleans and Baton
Rouge, La., & Dallas and Forth Worth, Texas; Central
States Conference of Seventh-Day Adventists, Hq. in Kan-
sas City, Missouri, pastored, 1952-60; in Kansas City,
Kansas, and Omaha, Nebraska; Lake Region Conference
of Seventh-Day Adventists, Hq. in Chicago, Ill., present-
ly pastor, S.A.D. Church, Chicago, Ill. Home: 7020 South
Michigan Ave., Chicago 37, Ill. Office: 7008 South Michigan Ave., Chicago 37, Ill.

MICHAEL, Euilious Raphael, b. Rutherfordton, N.C.,
March 6, 1907; s. John Wiley and Margaret A.; A.B.,
Livingstone College, 1927-31; D.D., Hood Seminary,
Livingstone College, 1960; Special studies: Harvard Uni-
versity Divinity School, 1961-63; m. Elizabeth Lee Arnold;
children--- Margaret Anna, Vernoca Louise; pastor, A.
M.E. Zion Church, Indianapolis, Ind., 1933-36; Kentucky,
6 years; North Carolina, five years; New York, six years;
Massachusetts five years; New Jersey: two years; Penn.,
three years; author, in Ebony Magazine, Oct. 1957,
"A Historic Pulpit Swap with Rev. Wilson Bridge of the
United Church Lachute, Quebec, Canada."; Present pastor,
Big Wesley African Methodist Episcopal Zion Ch., Phila.
Pa.; Member, Board of Managers YMCA Charlotte, N.C.
Branch, three years; Pres., P.T.A. Northwest Jr. High,
two years; Mem., Elk, Mason; Home: 4918 Walnut St.,
Philadelphia Pa., 19139; Office: 1500 Lombard, Philadel-
phia, Pa., 19146.

MICHAUX, Solomon Lightfoot, b. Buckroe Beach, Va.; m.
Mary E.; Entered ministry, 1917, Hopewell, Va.; Here
began to broadcast services over local radio station; Established the Church of God (Gospel Spreading Assn); Has
large coast to coast audience C.B.S. radio net work.

MICKLE, John Charles, b. Birmingham, Ala., Dec. 3,
1914; s. John Charles and Ethelyn (Simmons) M.; Ala.,
A & M Coll., 1931-32; A.B., Talladega Coll., Ala.,
1936; Howard U. Sch. of Rel., 1936-37; B.D., Chicago
Theol. Sem., 1939; U. of Chgo. Divinity Sch., 1939-
40; m. Sadie Blanche Thomas; children: Elva Louise,

Blanche Naomi;   Gregory Thomas; Dir. of Rel. Ed.,
Church of the Good Shepherd, Chgo., 1940-41; Pastor,
Mt. Zion Cong. Ch., Cleveland, O., 1941-47; (co-), South
Berkeley Community Cong. Ch., Calif. 1947-55; Second
Congregational Church, Memphis, Tenn., 1954---; Per-
sonnel Counselor, LeMoyne College, Memphis, 1954---;
mem. Exec. Comm., Memphis Comm. on Community Re-
lations, Exec. Comm., Budget Comm., United Church of
Christ; Publications Comm., United Church Herald;
Southern Personnel and Guidance Assoc.; Pres., Memphis
Interdenominational Ministers Alliance; Home: 762 Walker
Ave., Memphis 6, Tenn. Office: 764 Walker Ave. Memphis,
Tenn.

MIDDLETON, James Peter, Jr. b. South Carolina, April 12,
1928; s. James Peter and Joetta (Chaplin) M.; B.A.,
Oakwood College, 1951; m. Marilyn Lindsay; children--
Yvonne, Elizabeth, James, Eric., Arizona Conference of
Seventh-Day Adventist, 1951; built and pastored the Sharon
Seventh-Day Adventist Church in Tucson, Arizona, 1954-
61; Present: pastor, Beacon Light S.D.A. Church, 1961- ;
taught school for the Arizona Conf. of Seventh-Day Adventist, 1951-1953; member: N.A.A.C.P. Board, 1958-61;
Tempe Hospital Board, 1962; Indian School Board, 1959-
62; Urban League, 1963- ; member: executive committee
of Arizona Conf. of S.D.A. since 1958; Men of Tomorrow
Group, 1963-   ; Church Interracial Committee for State
of Arizona, Nevada, Utah, California, Hawaii. Home:
1424 E. Granada Rd., Phoenix 6, Arizona. Office; 963 E.
Monroe St., Phoenix, Arizona.

*MILES, Henry, b. Heflin, La., July 4, 1919; s. Mack C.
and Vila (Bailey) M.; A.B., Morehouse Coll.; B.D.,
Howard Univ., Sch. of Rel; American Univ., Wash.,D.C.;
m. Mary Goggins; chaplain and counselor, Migrant Work-
ers, N.Y. State; assoc. pastor, 19th Street Baptist Church
Wash., D.C., 1954-58; asst. pastor, Third Baptist Church,
Wash., D.C., 1959; acting pastor, Third Baptist Church,
1960; current pastor, Third Baptist Church, 1960---; Mem.
Board of Directors, Stoddard Baptist Home, 1959---;
Brightwood Civic Ass'n, 1962; Neighbors, Inc.; NAACP;
YMCA; US Army, 1941-45; 1st Sergeant; Mem., Exec.
Board, Lott Carey Baptist Foreigh Mission Convention;
Exec. Committee, Baptist Minister's Conference of Wash.,
D.C. and Vicinity; Civil and Social Committee of the Conf.,
Wash., D.C.; Morehouse Alumni Club; Phi Beta Sigma;
Home: 1355 Tewkesbury Pl., NW, Wash. 12, D.C.; Of-
fice: 5th and Que Sts. NW, Wash. 1, D.C.

MILLER, Clyde Horace, Jr., b. Middlesboro, Ky., Dec. 9,
1927; s. Clyde Horace, Sr. and Daisye (Anderson) M.;
Kentucky State Coll., 1945-47; A. B., Talladega College,
Ala., 1954; B. D., Chicago Theol., Sem., 1958; m. Eva
Whitlock;children: Claire, Joy; Military service, 1950-52;
Pastor, Church of the Good Shepherd Congregational,
Chicago, 1958---; mem. The Church Federation of Gtr.
Chgo., 1964--; Home: 5132 S. Greenwood, Chicago 15,
Ill. Office: 116 S. Michigan, Chicago 3, Ill.

MILLER, Roy L., b. Newberry Co., S. C., May 22, 1915;
A. B., Allen Univ., 1940; B. D., Wilberforce Univ., 1945;
Graduate study, Duquane Univ.; Univ. of Pittsburgh; D. D.
(hon.), Allen Univ., 1960; LL. D. (hon.), Shorter Coll.,
1962; m. Evelyn L. Davis; children--- Roy Lynn, Jr.,
James Furman; Ordained itinerant elder, African Methodist
Episcopal Church, 1939; pastor, S. C., Mich., Ohio, Pa.,
Bermuda and Indiana; current pastor, Greater Institution-
al A. M. E. Church, Chicago, Ill., 1954---; Office: 8610
S. Vernon Ave., Chicago, Ill.

MILLS, Cedric Earl, bishop; b. Hartford, Conn., Dec. 17,
1903; s. Patrick Henry and Sophannia (Blount) M.; A. B.,
Lincoln Univ., 1926; S. T. B. Phila. Divinity School, 1929;
M. A., Univ. of Penn. 1929; D. D. (hon.), Lincoln Univ.,
1946; D. D. (hon.), Phila. Div. Sch., 1960; LL. D. (hon.),
Saint Augustine's Coll., 1963; m. Rebecca Esther Taylor;
children---Damon Foster; vicar, Chapel of Ascension,
West Chester, Penn.; vicar-in-charge, St. Cyril's Mission,
Coatsville, Penna.; St. Mary's Church, Chester, Penn.;
chaplain, Episcopal students, Lincoln Univ., Cheyney State
Teacher's Coll. and Downingtown Industrial Sch., 1929-
37; comdt. of boys and teacher of math. and science,
Downingtown School; rector, St. Mark's Church, Plainfield,
N. J., 1937-40; rector, St. James' Church, Baltimore, Md.
1940-63; bishop, The Missionary District of the Virgin
Islands, 1963---; Mem., Exec. Council of the Diocese of
Md., 1944-50, 1954-57; sec., The Army and Navy Com-
mission of the Diocese of Md. during World War II; pres.
Md. Clericus, 1950; chairman, Adult Education in the
Diocese of Md.; deputy, General Convention, 1961; Stand-
ing Committee of the Diocese of Md., 1958-63; chmn.,
The Associate Study Comm. of the Diocese of Md.,;
charter mem., Balt. Chap. of the Frontiers of Am.,
Inc.; Bd. of Directors, NAACP; The Governor's Comm.
on Problems Affecting The Colored Population; Bd. of

Directors, Balt. Council of Social Agency's, 1951; chairman, Survey Comm., PTA Fred. Doug. H.S., 1952; chairman, Parent's Citizens Com. on Edn.; Bd. of Managers, The George F. Bragg Fund; Bd. of Directors of Mental Hygiene Society of Greater Balto.; Adv. Com. Henryton Practical Sch. Nursing; vice pres., Bd. of the Citizens Planning and Housing Assn; vice pres., Bd. of Directors, Balto. Urban League; Trustee, Provident Hospital; Mem., Harlem Park Neighborhood Council; counselor student nurses, Provident Hospital and chairman, Bd. of Directors, The Lafayette Square Community Center; Home: P.O. 1589 Charlotte Amalie St. Thomas, US Virgin Island.

MILLS, William G., fieldwork teacher; b. Newport, Rhode Island, Aug. 30, 1906; s. Laurence and Essie (Gray) M.; Hampton Institute, 1926; New York City College, 1928; Oakwood College, 1933; Andrews Univ., 1963; m. Cora Reid Davis; children--- William Laurence, Eleanor (Mrs. Aaron R. Wright), Aaron N., Phyllis a., Earl N.; Pastored: 1933-43, Seventh-Day Adventist Churches, Alabama, Mississippi; 1944-45, Florida, Arizona; 1956, Indiana, Michigan; present: pastor, S.D.A. Church, Calvin Center Road and Cossopolis, Michigan; member: 1948-52, Arizona Academy School Board; field work teacher for Seminary students (Andrews Univ.); American Red Cross, First Aid instructor, 1953-63; N.A.A.C.P., Community Chest leader. Home: 1708 S. 3rd Street, Niles, Michigan. Office: 215 Johnson Street, South Bend, Indiana.

MITCHELL, Henry Bryant, hospital chaplain; b. Ahoskie, N.C., Nov. 12, 1918; s. Bryant M. and Mary (Lewter) M.; B.S., Hampton Institute, 1939; Va. Theol. Sem. (Episc.), Alexandria, Va.; Yale Univ., School of Alcohol Studies, 1960; m. Gertrude Marion Phillips; children--- Carolyn P., Henry Bryant. Teacher, School for Blind and Deaf, Raleigh, N.C., 1939-41; employee, Norfolk Navy Yard, 1941-42; postal employee, Newport News Post Office, 1942-54; vicar, Danville Cure, 1957-58; rector, Trinity Episc. Ch., Charlottesville, Va., 1958-present. Real Estate Broker, 1950-54; pastoral clinical training (advanced), Univ. of Virginia Hospital, 1963. President, Charlottesville Ministerial Assoc., 1962-63; executive board of Charlottesville Branch, N.A.A.C.P., 1963-present; vice-chairman, Charlottesville Bi-racial Comm., 1963-present; pres., Council of Human Relations, 1962-

63; mem., board of Charlottesville Mental Health Assoc.
and board of Virginia Skyline Council of Girl Scouts, 1963.
Omega Psi Phi Fraternity. Home: 415 10th St., N.W.,
Charlottesville, Va. Office: Trinity Episcopal Ch., 10th
St. at Grady Ave., Charlottesville, Va.

MITCHELL, James Carl, b. Greenville, Ga., Oct. 20, 1900;
s. Richard Calvin and Laura (Bowles) M.; A.B., More-
house Coll., 1925; B.D., Va. Union Univ., 1935; M.A.,
Marshall Univ., 1953; LL.D. (hon.), Monrovia Coll.,
Liberia, W. Africa; m. Ora Esttels Fain; pastor, Flaggs
Chapel Baptist Ch., 1929-31, Milledgeville, Ga.; Va.
Union Univ., 1931-33; current pastor, Sixteenth St. Bap-
tist Ch. and Community Center, Huntington, W.Va.,
1933---; pres., Bapt. State Ministers Union, 1934-35;
pres., W.Va. Baptist State Convention, 1935-40; pres.
Baptist Ministers (Inter-racial); pres., Tri-State Baptist
Brotherhood, 13 years; pres., Huntington Branch, NAACP,
14 years; sec., State Conference of NAACP; organizer,
Guardian Nursing Home, Inc.; pres., Negro Co-operative
Olan, Inc.; Guardian Securities Co.; Exec. Bd., Mental
Health Ass'n; delegate, Nat'l Republican Convention, 1948;
vice chairman, County Republican Exec. Committee;
Mem., City Council, Huntington; former basileus, Omega
Psi Phi; Mem., Mason; Elk; Psi Chi National Honorary
Society (Psychology); Home: 1653 9th Ave., Huntington
3, W.Va.; Office: 1647 9th Ave., Huntington 3, W. Va.

MITCHELL, James William, b. Boston, Mass., July 3,
1898; s. James Dennis and Julia (Linehan) M.; Bates
College. Boston Univ. Bishop Payne Divinity School; m.
Martha Jefferson 2nd. Eleanor M. Brown; children---
Mary, Elyne, Michael, Sherri, Jacqueline, Peter, James,
David, William; pastor, St. John's P.E. Church, Wash.,
D.C., 1928-30; pastor, St. Mary's, Wash., D.C.,; pastor,
St. Bartholomew Cambridge, Mass; Retired as Rector,
1963---; Grace Church, Millers Tavern Va.; Home: 216
Blue Hill Ave., Dorchester 25, Mass.

MITCHELL, Kelly Karnale, Sr.; b. Atlanta, Ga., May 18,
1928; s. Jerry C. and Marie T.M.; B.A., Fisk Univ.,
1952; Alabama State Coll., 1961-62; m. Audrea Marie
Martin; children--- Kelyne Andrienne, Kelly Karnale, Jr.;
pastor, Green Street Church of Christ, Nashville, Tenn.,
1951-54; current pastor, Holt Street Church of Christ,
Montgomery, Ala., 1955---; former asst. manager,
Martin's Funeral Home, Nashville, Tenn.; staff writer,

Christian Echo; Mem., Advisory Board for the Foundation
for Christian Education; National and International Evangelist; Phi Beta Sigma; Alabama State Teacher's Ass'n; National Teacher's Ass'n; Dansforth Foundation Honor Roll for
Leadership; Ministerial Alliance, Montgomery, Ala.; Home:
3404 Santee Drive, Montgomery, Ala. 36108; Office: 726
Columbia, Montgomery, Ala. 36108

MITCHELL, Raymond S., b. Morton, Pa., Nov. 6, 1918;
s. Howard and Edna B. (Scott) M.; B.S. Ed., Cheyney
College; S.T.B., Phila Div. School (Episcopal); m.
Mildred S. Johnson; children--- Monica, Ingrid; pastor,
St. Cypriani, Phila., 1947-54; St. Philip's, Syracuse,
N.Y., 1954-57; St. Augustine, Norristown, Pa., 1957-61;
present, St. Philip's Prot. Episcopal Church, Richmond,
Va., 1961---; Former teacher (Language-French, Ger-
man), Organist, Pianist, Clinical Training (Mentally ill);
chaplain, Crouse Irving Hospital, 1954-57; pres. Eastside
Comm. Council, Syracuse, N.Y.; Member, Board of
YMCA; Escru;NAACP; Child Therapy Center, Richmond,
Va.; Honorable discharge, World War II. Clericus of
Richmond-Race Relations Consultant; Richmond Va. Board
Director (US); Home: 614 Overbrock Rd., Richmond 22,
Va.; Ch.: 2900 Hanes Ave., Richmond 22, Va.

MITCHELL, Roscoe Marron, b. Greenville, S.C., Oct. 5,
1908; s. William E. and Mary E. (McWilliams) M.;
Shelton Coll., New York; Burton Coll.; B.Th., Th.M.,
D.D. (hon.); m. Bessie Louise Gillard; children--- Mary
Alice (Mrs. Benjamin Warren), Roscoe M., William Allen;
pastor, Shiloh Bapt. Ch., Southhold, N.Y., 1929; Mt.
Pleasant Bapt. Ch., N.Y.C., 1930-34; Ebenezer Bapt.
Ch., Newbough Bapt., Ch., N.Y., 1934-41; New Hope
Bapt. Ch., Tarrytown, N.Y., 1941-55; current pastor,
Faith Bapt. Ch., Buffalo, N.Y., 1955---; instructor, Na-
tional S.S. & B.T.U. Congress; pres., Faculty Club;
Republican; Mem., YMCA Bd.; Welfare Bd., Buffalo &
Erie County; Exec. Bd., Local NAACP; moderator, Great
Lakes Bapt. Assn. of Western New York; Mason; author:
Principles of Stewardship; Stewardship for Today; Home:
630 Humboldt St., Buffalo, New York. 14211; Office:
626 Humboldt St., Buffalo, New York, 14211.

MITCHELL, Wallace Jefferson, b. North Birmingham, Ala.,
Apr. 27, 1916; s. Doss and Georgia (Dix) M.; B.A.,
Oakwood College, 1948; m. Charlotte Rebecca Boysaw.
Pastor: Seventh-Day Adventist Churches in Tennessee,

Alabama, Mississippi and Kentucky; present: pastor, University Avenue S. D. A. Church, Knoxville, Tenn. and S. D. A. Churches in Morristown, Harriman and Greenville, Tenn., 1948- . Member of Ministers Council, Seminar and Supervisor of youth activities; field representative of Bible Schools - Voice of Prophecy, Southern Union School of Bible Prophecy and Faith for Today Telecast. Voluntary active when requested for: Heart Fund, March of Dimes, Civic Moral Booster for God. U. S. Army, 1943-45; ETO. Honorable Discharge in 1945; Good Conduct Ribbons in U. S. Army; Beyond the Call of Duty Ministerial activities; Ambassador for Good Will and Peace, for the Cause of God. Independent political affiliations; Biblical research on Truth not Theory. Home: Racuule Village, Rt. 5, Milroy Lane, Knoxville, Tenn. Office: University Avenue S. D. A. Church, 1300 University Ave., Knoxville, Tenn.

MONTGOMERY, Leroy Jeremiah, author; b. Crockett, Texas, Sept. 12, 1902; s. Walter and Fanny (M.); A. B., Morris-Brown College, 1925; S. T. B., Boston University, School of Theology, 1928; S. T. M., Union Theological Seminary, 1930; m. Beatrice Duren. Pastored: Methodist Churches in Danbury, Conn., 1954-1956, and Buffalo, N. Y., 1956-60; William Temple C. M. E. Church, Phila., Pa., 1960-62; Russell Temple C. M. E. Church, Alexandria, Va., 1962-64. Author: The Race Problem, Two Distinct Religions, and My Trip Abroad. Home:1930 Mississippi Ave., S. E., Washington, D. C. Office: 507 North Alfred St., Alexandria, Va.

MONTGOMERY, Simon Peter, church official; b. Pineville, S. C., Feb. 12, 1922; s. Lee and Lizzie (Jenkins) M.; B. D., Cummings Theol. Sem., 1946; Benedict Coll., 1946-47; Claflin Coll., 1958-59; A. B., Garrett Biblical Institute, 1952-53; M. A., Boston Univ., 1955; m. Bessie Mathilda Allen; children--- Simon Peter, Jr., Vernita Renee, Keith Allen; pastor, Rock Hill Methodist Church, 1947-49; Gaffney Methodist Church, 1949-50; director, Christian Education, Mobile Unit South Fla. Conf. Methodist Church, 1950-52; Old Mystic Meth. Ch., 1955-57; Rockville Meth. Ch., 1957-59; current, exec. director and pastor-at-large, Inner City Parish, Stamford-Darien Council of Churches, 1959---; principal, Chesney School, Chesney, S. C., 1949; instructor, Norwich Tech., 1955-56; director, Intercultural and Interfaith project at Emmanuel Lutheran Church, Boston; First Negro chaplain of the Connecticut Gen'l Assembly, 1957-58; pres., Stamford

Alumni Chapter Claflin Univ., 1959---; chairman, Social
and Economic Committee of N. E. Southern Conf., Meth.
Ch., 1956-59; Mem., Commission of Social Concern, N.
E. Southern Conf., 1959-64; consultant, Young Adult Fellowship Week-end Retreat, summers of 1956-59; staff
mem., Northern N. E. Sch. of Religious Education, 1956-
62; special consultant, The Congregational Family Conf.
of Connecticut Conference, 1964; current, Exec. Bd. of
the West Main Street Community Center; Tuberculosis &
Health Assn., Southern Fairfield County; Psychiatric
Clinic for Children, Stamford-Darien New Canaan Heart
Assn; Conn. Heart Assn; Stamford-Darien Council of
Churches; NAACP Stamford Chapter; Committee on Re-
ligion and Race, Conn. Council of Churches; Bd. of
Directors, Conn. Council of Churches, 1955-58; vice
pres., Stamford-Darien Ministerial Assn, 1963; Mem.,
Exec. Bd. Senior Citizens Assn., Stamford; Award from
Conn. State for outstanding service as a Chaplain in the
House of Representatives; Certificates of Appreciation for
faithful service from the Norwich Lions Club, Rockville
Rotary Club; Research developer of the Inner City Parish
of the Stamford-Darien Council of Churches; Home: 36
Bonner St., Stamford, Conn.

MOORE, Arthur Chester, b. Philadelphia, Pa., Jan 4, 1894;
s. James Henry and Anna (Brice) M.; S.T.B., Temple
Univ., Philadelphia, Div. School of Episcopal Ch., 1924;
Th. M., Temple Univ., 1940; m. Marguerite Carmen
Young. Pastored: St. Cyprian's Ch., Phila.; St. Mary's
Ch., Chester; St. Monica's Church, Phila.; St. Luke's
Ch., N. Y. City, 1945-51; present: St. Simon's Protestant
Episcopal Ch., New Rochelle, N. Y., 1951---. Chairman,
Church School Teachers Training School under the New
Rochelle Council of Churches, 1961. Member: New Ro-
chelle Chapter of N. A. A. C. P.; New Rochelle Hospital
Assoc.; Council of Unity, New Rochelle; Urban League
of Westchester. Award for Philadelphia Afro-American
for Better Housing; Governor Award for Civilian Defense
in State of New York. President, Protestant Ministers'
Assoc. of New Rochelle, N. Y., 1962 and Interdenominational Minister's Alliance, 1963-present; member and
chaplain, Alpha Phi Alpha, Westchester Chapter; member
and former secretary, Westchester Clericus of Episcopal
Clergy; member, Department of Christian Education
Diocese of Penna. and Dept. of Christian Social Relations;
secretary, Convocation of West Philadelphia. Home: 135
Remington Pl., New Rochelle, N. Y. Office: 133 Reming-

ton Pl., New Rochelle, N.Y.

MOORE, Ezra Julius, businessman; b. Maysville, N.C.,
Apr. 30, 1922; s. George Israel and Everlenner (Ash-
wood); B.S., A & T College, 1953; B.D., Johnson C.
Smith Univ., 1960; m. Lula Mae Stanton; children---
Michael Julius, Ezra Maceo, Beverly Joanne; Cashier and
Bookstore Manager: Claflin College, 1953-57; pastor,
Macedonia First Presbyterian Ch., 1957; Sadalia Congre-
gational, Haw River, N.C. and Sedalia Congregational
Sadalia, N.C., 1958-60; current pastor Brooklyn United
Presbyterian Ch., 1960---; mem. Bd. of Dirs., Char-
lotte Council on Alcoholism, Bd. of Dirs., Mecklenburg
Girl Scouts Council; chrmn. Housing Committee of Mecklen-
burg Organization on Political Affairs; Active service in
the US Navy, 1940-46; mem.: Kappa Alpha Psi Fraternity,
Second Ward High School PTA, YMCA, YWCA, Northwest
Junior High PTA; University Park, PTA; NAACP; Democratic Party, etc. Boy Scouts; Home: 2027 Syracuse Drive,
Charlotte 8, N.C.; Ch.; 418 South McDowell St., Charlotte 4, N.C.

*MOORE, Jerry A., coll. chaplain; b. Minders, La., June
12, 1918; s. Jerry A., Sr. and Mae Dee (Abner) M.;
B.A., Morehouse Coll., 1940; B.D., Howard Univ. Sch.
of Rel., 1943; M.A., 1957; post graduate: Univ. of
S.C. and American Univ.; m. Ettyce H. Hill; children---
Jerry A., III, Juran D.; pastor, 19th Street Baptist
Church, 1946---; Baptist Univ. Chaplain, Howard Univ.,
1956---; Mem., Republican State Committee, D.C.;
Exec. Committee Baptist World Alliance; National Comm.
For Support of Public Schools; Phi Beta Sigma; Baptist
Minister's Conference, D.C. & Vicinity; Home: 1612
Buchanan St. NW, Wash., D.C. 2004; Office: 19th Street
Baptist Church, 19th & Eye Sts., NW, Washington, D.C.
20009.

MOORE, Jesse Lee, b. York County, Rock Hill, S.C.
Sept. 1, 1929; s. Albert and Sadie (Ervin) M.; A.J.,
Johnson C. Smith Univ., 1957; B.D., Johnson C. Smith
Univ.; Charlotte, N.C., 1960; pastor The Grandview
United Presby. Ch., Chesterfield, S.C.; The Pageland
Second United Presby. Ch., Pageland, S.C.; chairman,
The Upper Fairfield-McClelland Larger Parish; chair-
man The Chesterfield Community Civic Club; mem.:
Alpha Phi Alpha Fraternity; N.A.A.C.P. Home: P.O.
Box 72, 203 Mill St. Chesterfield, S.C.; Church: P.O.

Box 72, 203 Mill St., Chesterfield, S. C.

MOORE, John Dewey, b. Macon, Ga., Feb. 18, 1904; s.
John and Annie M.; Hampton Institute, 1919-26; B.D.,
Gammon Theol. Sem., 1930-33; B.S., Clark Univ.,
1927-30; B.D., Oberlin Divinity Sch., 1933-34; m.
Frankie Reid Neal; children--- Evelyn Dametta Evans,
Cevil Evans, Karna Lotthene; pastor, Evergreen congre-
gational Ch., Beachton, Ga., 1932; First Cong. Ch.,
Florence, Ala., 1934-35; Joe Wheeler Dam Office Inter-
viewer, 1935-36; current pastor, Pilgrim Cong. Ch.,
1936---; Omega Man of Year; Boy Scouts "Silver Beaver"
Girl Scouts "Thank You Badge"; Mem., Omega Psi Phi;
YMCA; NAACP; Independent (politics); pres.,P-T.A. Coun-
cil Harris County; vice pres., State P.T.A.; vice pres.,
W. L. Davis Boy Scouts; Treas., Houston Assn, United
Ch. of Christ; pres., Turner P.T.A.; Mem. of Bd.
Houston Tillotson Coll.; Eden Home for Aged; San Jacinto
Girl Scouts of America; Houston Assn of Churches; T.S.
U. Conference Ministers of United Ch. of Christ; Human
Relations, Planned Parenthood; Home: 3547 Rosedale Ave.,
Houston 4, Tex.; Office: 3519 Live Oak St., Houston 4,
Tex.

MOORE, Noah Watson, Jr., bishop; b. Newark, New Jersey,
March 28, 1902; s. Noah W. Moore, Sr., and Eliza A.
M.; A.B., Morgan College, Baltimore, Md., 1926; B.D.,
Drew University, Department of Theology, 1931; Graduate
Study, Crozier Theological Seminary, 1945-46; D.D.,
Gammon Theological Seminary, 1951; LL.D., Morgan State
College, 1961; m. Carolyn W. Lee; children--- Carolyn
O.; Ministry: New Rochelle, New York, 1930-31; Upper
Hill, Maryland, 1931-35; Fairmount Circuit and Upper Hill,
Maryland, 1935-37; Camphor Memorial, Philadelphia,
Penna., 1937-41; St. Daniels, Chester, Penna., 1941-43;
Superintendent of the Eastern District, 1943-47; Tindley
Temple, Philadelphia, Penna., 1949-60; Activity: Trustee
and Vice-President, Morgan College Corporation, 1950-
60; Trustee, Morristown College, Morristown, Tennessee,
1956-60; Member, Methodist Council on World Service and
Finance, 1960; Member, The World Methodist Council and
Executive Committee; Chairman, Commission on Higher
Education, Delaware Conference Baltimore Area, 1949-
60; Member, The Masonic Order; Member, Omega Psi
Phi Fraternity; Board Member and Secy.-Treasurer,
Philadelphia Housing Authority; Member, Board of Managers, Christian Street YMCA, Phila., Penna.; Member,

Frontiers of America; Trustee, United Fund, Phila. and
vicinity; Three times member, General and Jurisdictional
Conference, The Methodist Church, Southern Area Phila.
Health and Welfare; Elected Bishop, The Methodist Church;
Cleveland, Ohio, July 14, 1960; consecrated July 17,
1960; Assigned to New Orleans Area (Consisting of Louisiana, Texas, and West Texas Conference); Publications
and lectures: Selected articles in Central Christian Advocate and The Church School Journal, including Book Reviews; Articles and Lenten Messages in the weeklies and
the Philadelphia daily papers; Teacher and lecturer at
Pastors' Schools, including Bennett College, Emory and
Henry College; Lenten Series speaker for eight consecutive
years for Wilmington Council of Churches and Council of
Churches of Pulaske, New York, and Ogdensburg, New
York; Study Tour of West Germany and Berlin, as guest
of the government of the Federal Republic of Germany -
one of nine clergymen (Protestant, Catholic and Jewish)
from the United States, 1959; Elected president of College
of Bishops, 1962; Home: 631 Baronne St., New Orleans
12, La.

MORGAN, Frank Douglas, b. Durham, N.C., Sept. 26,
1917; s. Walker Hargrove and Maggie Daisy; A.B.,
Johnson C. Smith Univ., 1949; B.D., 1950; Graduate
study Yale University; m. Ida Lee Coleman; pastor First
Congregation Church, 1953-63; current pastor Goodwill
Presbyterian Ch., 1963---; moderator of Conference,
1953-59; chmn. March of Dimes, 1957-60; Member, the
Executive Branch of the Florida Council on Human Rights;
pres. of the Interdenominational Ministers Alliance,
1953-58; Certificate of Award from the National Foundation of Infantile Paralysis; mem.: Democrat, Omega Fraternity, Master Mason; Home: 516 North 8th Street, Fort
Pierce, Florida.

MORGAN, Philip Henry, b. Birmingham, Ala., July 28,
1914; s. Philip M. and Belle (Palmore) M.; Oakwood
College, Huntsville, Alabama; Andrews University, Mich-
igan; m. Rosolia Clark; children-Philip H., Jr., Willie
Charles, Rosalyn L., Maurice C. Pastor: Seventh-Day
Adventist Churches, 1938-60, in Columbus, Ga., Knox-
ville, Tenn., Albany, Ga., Raleigh, N.C., Durham, N.
C., Columbia. S.C., Tulsa, Oklahoma, and Los Angeles,
Calif. Present: pastor, S.D.A. Church, Palmdale, Calif.,
1960- . Teacher, Columbus, Ga., 1938-40; secretary,
Negro Chamber of Commerce, Knoxville, Tenn., 1941-

43; president, Interdenominational Ministerial Alliance, Albany, Ga.; secretary, N.A.A.C.P., Albany, Ga., 1947-
48; former member, Georgia State Negro Democratic Committee. Home: 234 W. 124th Street, L.A. 61, Calif. Office: 1007 Aves. St., Little Rock, Calif.

MORRIS, John Batiste, b. Gretna, La., April 3, 1920; s.
Amos F. and Agnes (Shorter) M.; A.B., Leland Coll.,
1943; B.D., Oberlin Graduate School of Theology; m.
Gloria Butler; children--- Deborah Gail; pastor, First
Free Mission Baptist Ch., New Orleans, La., 1945; in-
structor, the Layman's Dept. of the National Baptist Con-
vention, 1946; instructor, National Baptist Sunday Sch. and
B.T.U. Congress, U.S.A. Inc.; teacher, Dept. of Chris-
tian Education, State Convention; Mem., Interracial and
Interfaith Clergy Fellowship; chairman, Religious Life
Committee of Interdenominational Ministerial Alliance;
Devotion Leader for the Youth Encampment; pastoral ad-
visor, Dillard Univ. Student Union; current pastor, First
Free Mission Bapt. Ch., New Orleans, La.; Mem., Bd.
First Dist. Missionary Baptist Ass'n; Bd. of Management,
Dryades St. YMCA; The Urban League of Greater New
Orleans; vice chairman, The Citizen's Committee; Desire
St. Project Special Committee; delegate, Baptist Alliance,
London, England, 1955; Mem., Frontiers of America;
NAACP; Mason; Home: 7612 Zimple St., New Orleans,
La. 70118; Office: 919 Adams St., New Orleans, La.
70118.

MORRIS, Lloyd Belton, b. Charlotte, N.C., Nov. 21, 1938;
s. John Henry and Grace (Henderson); B.A., Johnson C.
Smith Univ., 1955-59; B.D., 1959-62; Summer Service
Projects: Matton United Presbyterian Ch., Washington,
D.C.; Ordained by the Fairfield McClelland Presbytery;
Pastor Hermon United Presbyterian Ch., Rock Hill, S.
C. in 1962; vi. pres. Rock Hill NAACP, youth advisor
NAACP Youth Branch, dir. Negro Voter Registration
Campaign in York County, S.C.; mem.: Phi Kappa Alpha,
Humanities Honor Society, Omega Psi Phi Fraternity;
Home: 442 South Trade Street, Rock Hill, S.C.; Ch.: 446
South Trade St., Rock Hill, S.C.

*MORRIS, Ronald Elliot, b. Malden, Mass., Nov. 20, 1931;
s. Stanley C. and Dorothy Mae M.; B.B., Boston Univ.,
1952; B.S., Boston Univ., 1954; B.D., Howard Univ.,
Sch. of Rel., 1962; chaplain, New York State Council of
Churches, Migratory Ministry, 1960-62; Director of Re-

ligious Education, Mt. Zion Congregational Church, Cleve-
land, Ohio, 1963; pastor, Antioch United Church of Christ,
Suffolk, Va., 1964; chairman, Suffolk-Nansemond Coordinat-
ing Committee; vice pres., Suffolk, Ministerial Alliance;
US Air Forces, 1954-58; Good Conduct Medal; Mem.,
Omega Psi Phi; Home: 24 Deckard, Boston 21, Mass.;
Office: 424 Smith, Suffolk, Va.

MORRIS, Samuel Solomon, Jr., coll. prof., b. Norfolk, Va.
Nov. 1, 1916; s. Samuel Solomon and Mamie (Lawson) M.;
B.S., Wilberforce Univ., 1937; B.D., Yale Univ., 1940;
D.D. (hon.), Shorter Coll., 1946; LL.D., Monrovia Col-
lege, 1952; LL.D., Kitrell College, 1962; m. Ermine M.
Smith; children---Joyce Lynn; Ermine Laurel; Samuel
Solomon III; pastor, St. Luke A.M.E. Church, Gallatin,
Tenn.; St. John A.M.E. Church, Springfield, Tenn.,
1940-41; pastor, St. Paul A.M.E. Church, Nashville,
Tenn., 1943-46; associate pastor, Bethel A.M.E. Church,
Detroit, 1948-49; pastor, First A.M.E. Church, Gary,
Ind., 1949-56; pastor, Coppin A.M.E. Church, Chicago,
1956---; prof., Church History, Payne Theological Semin-
ary, Wilberforce, Ohio; instructor, Wilberforce University,
1941-43; pres., Shorter College, North Little Rock, Ar-
kansas, 1946-48; pres. of Chicago Branch NAACP, 1961-
63; Member, Frontiers Club; Member, Executive Comm.
on Educational Institutions of the A.M.E. Church, 1960---;
Trustee of Camp Baber, Cassopolis, Mich.; Outstanding
Minister Award, Payne Theological Seminary, Alumni
Assoc.; Member: Alpha Phi Alpha; Mason; Urban League;
Church Federation of Greater Chicago, National Council of
Churches; author: An African Methodist Primer; Editor-
ial staff, Division of Christian Education, A.M.E. Ch.,
African Meth. Episcopal Christian Recorder; Home: 5621
So. Michigan Avenue, Chicago 37, Ill.; Office: 5627 South
Michigan Ave., Chicago 37, Ill.

MORRISON, James W., b. Pinehurst, N.C., June 26, 1918;
s. Levi W. and Mary (Baldwin) M.; B.A., Johnson C.
Smith Univ., Charlotte, N.C., 1952; B.D., Hartford Sem.
Foundation, 1961; m. Lorenza Pauline Fuller; children---
Patricia Louise; pastor, Red Hill Christian Church, Clay-
ton, N.C., 1949-53; Children's Chapel, United Church of
Christ, Graham, N.C., 1953---; sec., Convention of the
South United Church of Christ, 1951-58; chairman, Comm.
on Christian Social Action, Conv. of the South, 1963---;
Exec. vice sec., Alamance County Committee on Civic
Affairs, 1962; Mem., Human Relations Council, 1964---;

US Army, 1942-46; 4 Bronze Stars; Mem., Kappa Alpha
Psi; Mason; NAACP; Farmers and Home Makers Conf.
of N.C.; Home: 324 E. Harden St., Graham, N.C.

MORSE, Savarhett, b. Jacksonville, Fla., July 30, 1910;
s. Richard and Mamie (Sims) M.; B.Th., Wilberforce
Univ., 1945; A.B., Howard Univ., Washington, D.C.,
1950; m. Elaine Weyms; children---Sharon Elett, Savar-
hett, Jr., Raymond Ellis; pastor, St. Paul A.M.E. Church,
Danville, Va., 1951-55; Trinity A.M.E. Church, Norfolk,
Va., 1956-58; Ebenezer A.M.E. Church, Hagerstown, Md.,
1959-62; current, Pilgrim African Methodist Episcopal
Church, Washington, D.C., 1963---; Mem., Phi Beta
Sigma; Republican; Home: 718 19th NE, Washington 2,
D.C.; Office: 700 17th NE, Washington, 2, D.C.

MORTON, Charles Evans, coll. prof.; b. Bessemer, Ala.,
Jan. 31, 1926; s. Hodge M. and Mary M.; B.A., More-
house Coll., 1943-46; B.D., Union Theol. Sem., N.Y.,
1949; Heidelberg Univ., Germany, 1955; Garrett Biblical
Institute of Northwestern Univ., 1956; Ph.D., Columbia
Univ., 1958; m. Jean Estelle Braboy; children--- Joan
Maria, Carla Estelle; youth director, Greater New York
Interracial Fellowship, 1947-48; student minister, St.
James Presbyterian Church, 1946-47; instructor, More-
house Coll., Atlanta, Ga., 1949-51; pastor, Ebenezer Bapt.
Ch., Poughkeepsie, New York, 1951-53; assoc. prof.,
Knoxville Coll., Knoxville, Tenn., 1953-57; chairman, Div.
of Humanities and prof. of Rel. & Philosophy, Dillard
Univ., New Orleans, La., 1957-62; academic dean, Fayet-
teville State Coll., Fayetteville, N.C., 1962-63; current
pastor, Metropolitan Baptist Church, Detroit, Mich; as-
soc. prof., Albion Coll., Albion, Mich., 1964---; Mem.,
Mayor's Exec. Committee on Voters Registration; Wayne
County Commission on Juvenile Delinquency; Bd. of Di-
rectors, Detroit Branch, NAACP; The Founders Society,
Detroit Institute of Arts; chairman, Detroit Branch NAACP
membership campaign, 1964; The Ministerial Advisory
Committee, Detroit Planned Parenthood Assn; Detroit
Protestant Council of Churches; Committee on Radio & TV
Communication and co-chairman of the Ministerial Com-
mittee of the African Art Gallery Fund; Phi Beta Sigma
Award for Service to Education, New Orleans, 1962;
NAACP Membership Campaign Award, Detroit, 1962;
Pittsburgh Courier's Ministerial Award, 1964; Mem., Phi
Beta Sigma; Urban League; NAACP; National Council of
Churches & World Council of Churches; Article, The South

Today; author: The Teaching of Religion in Church Related College, Bd. of Higher Ed., The Meth. Church,
Nashville, Tenn., 1962; Home: 17510 Ohio Ave., Detroit
21, Mich.; Office: 13110 14th St., Buena Vista, Detroit
38, Mich.

MOSELEY, Alexander Dumas, b. Lewiston, N.C., Jan. 20,
1915; s. Samuel Henderson and Burnettie (Wiggins) M.;
A.B., Shaw Univ., 1948; M.A., Univ. of Denver, 1953;
N.C. Coll., Durham, N.C., 1950; Union Theol. Sem.
N.Y.C., 1959; D.D. (hon.), Kittrell Coll., 1960, Neotar-
ian Coll. of Philosophy, 1961; m. Earle Cleaves; children:
--- Alexis Earle; teacher, Public School, N.C., 1935-41;
pastor, New Sawyer Creek Bapt. Ch., Bell Cross, N.C.,
1947-51; Union Bapt. Ch., Tarboro, N.C.; St. John Bapt.
Ch., New Bern, N.C., 1951-56; First Bapt. Ch., Weldon,
N.C., 1956-61; Mt. Gilead Bapt. Ch., Durham, N.C.,
1961---; director, Christian Education, Old Eastern Ass'n,
Greenville, N.C., 1950-57; Exec. secy., Eastern Bapt.
Dist. Convention and Aux. to The General Bapt. State Conv.
of N.C., Inc., 1950-61; director, Veterans Training Program, P.S. Jones High School, Washington, N.C., 1952-
55; Commissioner of Civil Liberties, N.C., 1950-60; pres.,
Walker-Lassiter Defense Fund, Weldon, N.C., 1957-61;
chairman, Fuller School Precinct, Durham, N.C., 1962
---; pres., Durham Ministerial Ass'n, 1964; vice pres.,
General Bapt. State Conv., N.C., Inc., 1960---; Exec.
Durham Committee on Negro Affairs, 1962---; Exec.
Bd., John Avery's Boys Club, Durham, N.C., 1962---;
NAACP, CORE, SCLC; US Air Forces, 477th Bomb Group,
1945; Cited for Meritorious Service; Mem., Neotarian Fel-
lowship; Alpha Phi Alpha; Mason; Elk; Pythian; Eastern
Star; Democrat; Office: 401 Dowd St., Durham, N.C.

MOSES, Jesse Daniel, teacher, b. San Antonio, Texas,
Dec. 18, 1914; s. Jesse Daniel and Veinita (Bryan) M.;
B.A., Univ. of Redlands, 1937; M.A., B.D., Berkeley
Baptist Divinity Sch., 1937-40; Univ. of Southern Calif.;
Th.D., 1945-55; m. Regenia Andrey Payne; children---
Jesse Daniel, Jeffrey Dennis; secy., Gleiss Center, De-
troit, Michigan, 1941-42; US Army chaplain, 1942-45; pas-
tor, St. Barnabas Church, Pasadena, 1915-50; asst. pastor,
St. Paul's Cathedral, L.A.; teacher, Pasadena City Schools,
1950---; teacher and vice principal, Jr. High School,
Pasadena, Calif., 1949---; pres. Pasadena Education Assn.
2 terms; pres. California Teachers Assn.-Southern Section;
Member, Urban League, Red Cross, 1942-45; Member,

Alpha Phi Alpha, Phi Delta Kappa; Home: 1148 Wotkyns
Drive, Pasadena 3, Calif.: Office: 325 South Oak Knoll,
Pasadena, Calif.

MOSS, Otis, Jr. b. La Grange, Ga., Feb. 26, 1935; s.
Otis, Sr. and Magnolia (R.) M.; B.A., Morehouse Coll.,
1956; B.D., Morehouse School of Religion, 1959; m.
Sharon Joann Howell; children--- Daphne Rachelle; pastor,
Old Mt. Olive Bapt. Ch., La Grange, Ga.; Providence
Bapt. Ch., Atlanta, Ga., 1956-61; current, Mt. Zion
Bapt. Ch., Ohio, 1961---; former vice pres., Atlanta
Branch, NAACP; former sec., Atlanta Council on Human
Relations; area representative, Southern Christian Leader-
ship Conference, Cincinnati, Ohio; Mem., Alpha Phi
Alpha; Home: 69 Chestnut, Cincinnati 15, Ohio; Office:
325 N. Wayne Ave., Cincinnati 15, Ohio.

MOUCHETTE, Edward Donley, chaplain; b. Bermuda B.W.I.,
May 27, 1930; s. Brownlow and Blanche (C.) M.; A.B.,
Wilberforce Univ., 1955; B.D., Payne Theol. Seminary,
1953-56; m. Anna Mary Shipes; children--- Franscine,
Edward Dowley III, Sherri Lynn; pastor, Bethel African
Methodist Episcopal Ch., Shelley Bay, Bermuda, 1956-58;
First United A.M.E. Church, Lockport, N.Y., 1958-59;
Bethel A.M.E. Church, Bay Shore, N.Y., 1959-61; Allen
Memorial A.M.E. Church, Brooklyn, N.Y., 1961-62; US
Army Chaplain since 1962; pres., NAACP, Bay Shore, N.
Y. Branch, 1961-62; Foundation for Mentally Retarded
Children, Suffolk County, N.Y., 1960-62; German Occupa-
tion Ribbon and Medal; Mem., Alpha Phi Alpha; Zeta
Sigma Phi; National Social Science Honor Society; Ass'n
of Military Chaplains; Contributor: The A.M.E. Christian
Recorder; Home: 319-1 Pollan Ft. Riley, 66442, Kansas;
Office: 2nd Bde, St. Inf. Div., Ft. Riley, Kansas.

MURCHISON, Elisha P., bishop, prof.; b. Fort Worth, June
18, 1907; s. Elisha P., Sr. and Gertrude (Moore) M.;
A.B., Clark Coll., 1929; B.D., Gammon Theol. Sem.,
1930; A.M., Boston Univ., 1932; Univ. of Chicago, 1932-
34; 1939-40; D.D. (hon.), Paine Coll., 1958; m. Imogene
Ford; children--- Ellen, Jrs. Joseph Pierce; Licensed
preacher, Christian Methodist Episcopal Ch., 1921; pastor,
Churches in Texas, Ga., Mass. and Ill.; director, Leader-
ship Education, C.M.E. Ch., 1935-38; dist. supt., Chicago
District, 5 years; editor, The Christian Index, 1946-54;
Elected bishop of the C.M.E. Church, Fifth Episcopal
District (Ala., Fla., Ghana, Nigeria), 1958---; prof.,

Texas Coll., 1932-35; Missionary to Africa; chairman,
Bd. of Trustees, Miles Coll.; Bd. of Trustees, Phillip's
School of Theology; vice pres., National Fraternal Coun-
cil of Churches; Mem., 1st World Council of Churches
Assembly; National Council of Churches; Exec. Mem.,
National Conference on Race and Religion; Omega Psi Phi;
Established Historical Library of the C. M. E. Ch.; Re-
search in field of Psychology of Religion; chairman, Pub-
lic Resolutions C. M. E. Church; Home:308 Tenth Ave.,
West Birmingham 4, Ala.

MURPHY, Maximilian Edward, b. Dallas, Texas, December
4, 1902; s. Robert Louis and Viola (Wiley) M.; St. Augus-
tine Seminary, Bay St. Louis, Miss.; St. Patrick's Sem-
inary, Menlo Park, Calif.; Charles University, Prague,
Czechoslovakia, 1930-34; Ordained priest, Roman Cath.
Ch., 1930; Dean, Trinidad, B. W. I., 1935---; Canon,
Metropolitan Cathedral, Port of Spain, Trinidad, 1961---;
Chrmn, Aquinas Sponsoring Scholarship Committee; Regu-
lar contributor to German language papers; Home and
Office: The Presbytery, Chaguanas, Trinidad, British
West Indies.

MURRAY, Chasteen Theophilus, b. Va., Sept. 16, 1887;
s. Fountain and Casanda (Mont) M.; A. B., B. D., D. D.
(hon.), Va. Seminary and Coll., 1911-18; Th. M., Zenia
Seminary, Pittsburg, 1927-28; m. Sadie Jeneva Reynolds;
children---Chasteen T., Jr., Gregory Carlyle, Rosalyn
Jeneva (Mrs. Harold Minor), Windell Contee; James Ham-
ilton; Sadie Evelyn (Mrs. Harold Menor); pastor, Dearing-
ton Hill Baptist Ch., 1914-19; Loyal Baptist Ch., Danville,
Va., 1920-24; Carron Baptist Ch., Pittsburg, Pa., 1925-
29; Vermont Ave. Baptist Ch., Wash., D. C., 1929-64;
Mem., General Board Nat'l Council of Churches; Bd. of
Directors, Lott Carey Foreign Mission Convention; Bd. of
Directors, Council of Churches National Capitol Area;
Crime Council-Precinct No. 2, Wash., D. C.; Republican
State Committeeman; Mason; pres. (former), Baptist Con-
vention, Wash., D. C. and Vicinity; National Fraternal
Council of Churches; Home: 1001 3rd St. SW, Wash. 24,
D. C.; Office: 1630 Vermont Ave. NW, Wash. 9, D. C.

MURRAY, Earl, church official; b. Lapine, Ala., June 2,
1922; s. William and Maggie (Trotter) M.; B. D., Daniel
Payne Sem.; children---Earl, Willie L. Thomas L.,
Samuel J., Gloria E.; pastor, Eleventh St., Christian
Ch.; Pres., Christian Missionary Conv., Jefferson Co.,

Ala., 1953-63; vice pres., Ala. Christian Missionary
Conf., 1957-63, and current pres., 1962---; Mem., Bd.
of Trustees, YWCA, Birmingham, Ala.; chmn, Auxiliary
Bd., Amer. Cast Iron Pipe Co., 1961---; Mem., Recommendation Com., International Conv. of Christian Churches;
US Forces, 1944-46; Home: 10 So. 20th Court St., Birmingham 5, Ala.

MCCALL, Aidan Maurice, coll. prof.; b. Washington, D.C.,
July 25, 1926; s. Henry A. and Eva (Thompkins) M.; B.
A., St. John's Univ., 1950; A.M., U. of Michigan,
1959; Ordained priest, Roman Cath. Ch., 1954; Instructor;
Latin, St. John's Prep Sch., 1950-54; Latin & Scripture,
St. Augustine's College, Nassau, Bahamas, 1954-57; Latin
& Greek, St. John's University, 1957---; Asst. Prof., St.
John's U., 1962---; Mem. Linguistic Society of Amer.,
Classical Assn. of Midwest & South, Minnesota Classical
Conference; Home and Office: St. John's University,
Collegeville, Minnesota.

McCALLUM, James Hector, teacher; b. Robeson County,
N.C., Sept. 23, 1918; s. P. Jefferson and Jackie Anne
(Anderson) M.; B.S., Fayetteville State Coll., Fayette-
ville, N.C., 1942; M.S., A & T Coll., Greensboro, N.
C., 1953; Th.M., American Divinity School, Chgo., Ill.
1963; m. Wilhelmenia Powell; children--- Rachelle; pastor,
Methodist Church, North Carolina Conference, 21 years:
10 years in Maxton and surrounding areas, 8 years in
Laurinburg and surrounding areas, 3 years Fayetteville,
N.C.; teacher, public schools 20 years; pres., Local
Teachers Ass'n; Mem., State Nominating Committee;
Mem., NAACP; NCTA; NEA; Home: 806 Frolic St.,
Fayetteville, N.C.; Office: 616 Cumberland St., Fayette-
ville, N.C.

McCLAIN, Herbert Linton, chaplain; b. Decatur, Georgia
Apr. 14, 1920; s. Herbert and Frances (Beasley); B.A.,
Johnson C. Smith Univ., 1946-49; B.D., 1949-51; US
Army Chaplaincy, Ft. Slocum, N.Y., 1949; m. Rebecca
Washington; children--- Sharon, Carolyn, Leroy; chaplain
US Army Chaplain serving both Far East and Europe,
1952-58; Dir. of Camp and Rel. Ed.,Westminster House,
Buffalo, N.Y., 1958-61; Dir. of Community Center, Bethel
United Presbyterian Church, Phil.,Pa., 1963-   .; Sec.
for 22 District of Youth Conservation Service sponsored
by the Dept.; Served as Private and Chaplain Asst. with
Grade of Technician 5th Grade, 1941-45; Bronze Star Medal

for Meritorious Service during the Korean War., 1953;
Certificate of Meritorious Service from Philadelphia Dept.
of Police (Juvenile Aid Division), June 1963; mem.: Alpha
Phi Omega Scout Fraternity, Phi Beta Sigma Fraternity,
The Fraternity of the Humanities at Johnson C. Smith
University, Alpha Kappa Mu National Honor Society,
United States of America Chaplain Military Association,
Washington, D. C.; Home: 5933 N. 21st St., Phil. 38,
Pa.; Bethel Center, 19th and York Street, Philadelphia
32, Pa.

*McCLELLAN, James F., Jr. coll. prof., dean; b. Nash-
ville, Tenn., Sept. 24, 1925; s. James F. and Robbie
(Bell) M.; B.S., Tenn. A & I State Coll., 1944; Howard
Univ., Sch. of Rel., B.D., 1947; American Univ., sum-
mer session, 1946; Teachers Coll., Columbia Univ.,
M.A., 1951; Ed. D., 1956; m. Lois Jean Dedeaux; chil-
dren---Jean Elizabeth; pastor, Faith Presbyterian Church,
Pine Bluff, Ark., 1961-62; Washington Heights Church of
Christ, New York, N. Y., 1949-51; Release-Time Teacher,
City Mission Society New York, N. Y., 1948-49; pastor,
Migrant Laborers, New Jersey Council of Churches,
Princeton, New Jersey, 1948; pastor, Harlem Church of
Christ, New York, N. Y., 1948; asst dean and prof. of
Education Psychology, Kentucky State Coll., Frankfort,
Ky., 1963---; professor of education, Arkansas A. M. &
N. Coll., Pine Bluff, Ark., 1954-63; director of student
personnel, Ark. A. M. & N. Coll., Pine Bluff, Ark.,
1959-60; associate in student personnel, Ark. A. M. &
N. Coll., Pine Bluff, Ark., 1956-59; counselor, Liberal
Arts Counseling Service, Howard Univ., Washington, D. C.
1953-54; educational director, George W. Cook Hall,
Howard Univ., Washington, D. C., 1951-53; Bd. Mem.,
Pine Bluff NAACP (incl. Chairman, Education Committee;
chairman, Legal Redress Committee); secy., State Conf.
(Ark.) NAACP: Bd. Mem., Arkansas Council on Human Re-
lations; chairman, Citizenship Committee; Delta Sigma
Lambda Chapter; Alpha Pha Alpha; Townsend Park School
Award for Outstanding Community Service (Pine Bluff,
Ark., 1961); Tennessee A & I State Univ. Golden Anniver-
sary Alumni Award, Nashville, Tenn., 1962; Pine Bluff
Branch NAACP Citizenship Citation (Pine Bluff, Ark.,
1963); Delta Sigma Lambda Chapter; Alpha Phi Alpha Fra-
ternity Service Ward (Pine Bluff, 1963); Mem: Alpha
Kappa Mu National Honor Society; Kappa Delta Pi Honor
Society in Education; Phi Delta Kappa Honor Fraternity
in Education; American Ass'n of Univ. Professors; Amer-

ican Teachers Ass'n; Ass'n of Higher Education; Nat'l Ed.
Ass'n; Coll. and Univ. Personnel Ass'n; National Ass'n of
Personnel Workers; Southern Coll. Personnel Ass'n; Alpha
Phi Alpha; Unpublished Doctoral Project: Seminary Train-
ing in Pastoral Counseling; Home: Kentucky State Coll.,
Frankfort, Ky.; Office: Student Personnel Off., Kentucky
State Coll., Frankfort, Ky.

McCLONEY, Leon H., coll. pres.; b. Beaumont, Tex.,
Aug. 27, 1924; s. Robert, Sr. and Minnie M.; A.B., The
Coll. of Emporia, Emporia, Kansas; B.D., Western Univ.
Sem.; D.D. (hon.), Paul Quinn Coll.; Wilberforce Univ.;
m. Juanita; children--- Bruce Alan, Brena Ann; pastor,
Wayman Temple African Methodist Episcopal Church, Troy,
Kansas, 1943-44; Bethel A.M.E. Ch., Elwood, Kansas,
1945; Quinn Chapel A.M.E. Ch., St. Louis, Mo., 1945-
47; Mt. Olive A.M.E. Ch., Emporia, Kansas, 1947-52;
Brooks Chapel A.M.E. Ch., Corpus Christi, Tex., 1952-
58; St. Luke A.M.E. Ch., Waco, Texas, 1958-62; cur-
rent, pres., Paul Quinn Coll., Waco, Tex.; Mem., City
of Waco Advisory Committee; The Budget Comm. of the
Waco United Fund; The Board of Directors of the Doris
Miller YMCA; Waco Urban Renewal Commission; Waco
Progressive Council; Education Comm. of the Waco Chamber of Commerce; Office: Office of President, Paul Quinn
Coll., Waco, Texas.

McCLOUD, J. Oscar, b. Waynesboro, Georgia, April 10,
1936; s. George and Sophronia (Foley) Mc.; 1954-56;
Warren Wilson Junior College; 1956-58 B.A. Berea Col-
lege; 1958-61 B.D. Union Theological Seminary (NYC);
m. Robbie Juanita (Foster) children: Ann Michelle. As-
sistant pastor, 1951-61; Willis Avenue Methodist Church,
Bronx, N.Y.; 1961-The United Church, Raleigh, N.C.
(White); 1961 present, Davie Street United Presbyterian
Church, Raleigh, N.C. mem. 1962, Bi-racial Committee,
Raleigh, N.C.; 1963, Vice President, Raleigh Branch
NAACP; President, Ministerial Alliance; Psi Chi Honor
Society (Psychology); North Carolina Young Democrats
Club; Home: 913 S. East Street, Raleigh, N.C. 27601;
Church: Corner Davis and Person Street, Raleigh, N.C.
27601.

*McCOY, Cleo Milam, coll. chaplain; b. Winnfield, La.,
Sept. 29, 1912; s. Matt Milam and Hattie McCoy (Lee)
M.; A.B., Paine Coll., Augusta, Ga., 1939; B.D.,
Howard Univ., Sch. of Rel., 1942; courses: A & T Coll.,

McCray, M.E. 263

N.C.; m. Mabel Amelia Madden; children--- Ellen O'
Hear, David Madden; U.S. Civil Service, Wash. D.C.,
1942-46; chaplain & teacher of philosophy, religion, history
and social science, A & T Coll. of N.C., Greensboro,
N.C., 1946---; Organized Dir., Town & Rural Ministers
Institute; Director of Christian Education, N.C.Annual
Conf. Christian Methodist Episcopal Ch.; Mem., Div. of
Christian Ed.; National Council of Churches; Contribution
in the area of community leadership during the civil rights
demonstrations crisis of 1963 resulted in the creation of
The Greensboro Community Fellowship, a nonsectarian,
non-political, interracial fellowship; Mem.: The Ass'n
for the Coordination of Univ. Religious Affairs; National
Ass'n of Chaplains and Directors of Religious Life; The
N.C. Ass'n of Teachers of Religion; N.C. Christian Stu-
dent Workers Ass'n; The Institute of Religion, Howard
Univ., Wash. D.C.; The Greensboro Ministers' Fellow-
ship; The Pulpit Forum of Greensboro and Vicinity; The
Ass'n of Social Science Teachers; The Greensboro Citizens
Ass'n; The Greensboro Community Fellowship, vice pres.;
The Greensboro Community Council; Rural Church Com-
mittee, N.C. Council of Churches; Committee on Continu-
ing Education For Town and Country Pastors; Land grant
Univ.; Home: 10009 Martin St., Greensboro, N.C. 27406;
Office: Box H-23, A & T Coll., 312 N. Dudley St., Greens-
boro, N.C. 27411

*McCray, Maceo Edward, librarian; b. Bucksport, S.C.,
Feb. 10, 1935; s. Vetus C. and Grace (Wallace) M.;
B.S., S.C. State Coll., 1956; B.D., Howard Univ. Sch.
of Rel., 1962; Drexel Institute of technology, School of
Library Science, Summers of 1963-64; Ordination, 1961;
Served with several Churches in the Washington area,
South Carolina and Springfield, Mass.; Asst. Pastor, Mt.
Sinai Baptist Ch., 1959-63; Chaplain to Migrants in western
New York, summers of 1960-61; asst. circulation librarian,
Howard Univ., 1962-65; Serials Librarian, Howard Univ. Den-
tal-Medical Library; Mem., Washington Urban League; Visit-
ing Nurses Assn; the Howard Univ. Library Assn; D.C. Library
Assn; Omega Psi Phi; Home: Route 1, Box 14, Bucksport,S.C.;
Office: Dental-Medical Library, Howard Univ.,Wash.,D.C.

McDONALD, Harry James, b. Grafton, W.Va., Dec. 17,
1905; s. John Wesley and Henritta (Watson) M.; A.B.,
Clark Univ., 1931; B.D., Gammon Theol. Sem., 1938;
m. Nellie Janet; pastor, St. Mary's County, Md. - Park
Hall Charge, 1931-32; Marlington, W.Va., 1933-34;

Bridgewater, Va., 1935; Charlestown, W. Va., 1936-38;
Boyds, Md., 1939-41; Lexington, Va., 1941-45; Clarks-
burg, W. Va., 1945-48; Lynchburg, Va., 1948-53; St.
Marks, New York City, 1953-55; Epworth, Bronz, N. Y.
City, 1955-58; Bel Air, Md., 1958; Meth. Ch., Asbury
Frederick, Md., 1959-64; Mem., Church District Bd. of
Trustees, W. Baltimore Dist., 1962---; Trustee Bd.
Washington Annual Conference, 1961-64; Home: 200
West All Saints St., Frederick, Md.; Office: 100 W. All
Saints St., Frederick, Md.

McDOWELL, Henry Curtis, b. Epes, Ala., Feb. 7, 1894;
s. Lorenzo and Louvenia M.; A. B., Talladega College,
Ala., 1915; B.D., Talladega College, 1917; Hartford
Seminary, Conn., 1930; D. D. (honorary), Talladega Coll.,
1937; 2 sons, Curtis F. and Elmer Hugh; Pastor, 1st
Cong. Ch., Chattanooga, Tenn., 1917-18; Dixwell Ave.
Cong. Ch., New Haven, Conn., 1944-47; Church of the
Open Door, Miami, Fla., 1959---; Chaplain, Talladega
College, 1918-19; Missionary, Angola West Africa, 1919-
37; 1947-59; Prin., Lincoln Academy, Kings Mt., N. C.,
1937-44; Visiting Lecturer, Hartford Sem., 1944-47;
1952-53; Voluntary Chaplain, World War I, Camps Chica-
mauga and Oglethorpe; Recipient Harmon Award, field of
Religion, 1930; Mason; Home: 6001 N. W. 8th Ave.,
Miami, Fla., 33127.

McFARLANE, Percival Alan Rex, b. Montreal, Canada,
Jan. 25, 1928; s. Clarence Percival and Irene Louise
(ne Arnold) M.; McGill School Certificate, 1947; Epis-
copal Seminary, Haiti; St. Peters College, Jamaica,
B. W. I.; McGill University (Certificate in Theology),
1951; Columbia University, B. S. & M. A., 1962; curate,
St. Boniface Church, Assiniboia, Canada, 1951-52; curate,
St. Paul's Cathedral, Regina, Canada, 1952-55; Vicar,
St. Thomas Church, Red Bank, N. J., 1955-58; curate,
All Soul's Church, N. Y. C., 1958-60; curate, St. Philip's
Church, Brooklyn, N. Y., 1961---; chaplain, Anglican
Young People's Association for Alberta, Manitoba, Saskat-
chewan, Canada, 1953-55; current, study director, Cam-
pus Ministry Study, Institute of Urban Studies, Teachers
College, Columbia University; sec. Columbia University
Student Council, Head of Columbia University Delegation
to 1963 United States National Student Association Con-
gress; Off.: Institute of Urban Studies, Teachers College,
Columbia University, New York 27, N. Y.

McGEE, Lewis Allen, chaplain; b. Scranton, Penna., Nov.
11, 1893; s. Charles A. and Gay (Ruth) M.; University of
Pittsburg, 1912-13; B.D., Payne Theological Seminary
Wilberforce, O., 1916; Loyola Univ., Chicago, 1933-1935;
B.A., Carthage College, Illinois, 1936; Meadville Theol.
School, Chicago, 1946-47; m. Mary Marcella Walker;
children--- Lewis A., Jr. (deceased), Charles E., Mrs.
Jacob Downs. Pastor, AME Church, Parkersburg, W. Va.
1916-17; instructor, Kittrell College, N.C., 1917-18; U.
S. Army Chaplain, 1918-19; AME minister, Cleveland, O.
Morgantown and Charleston, W. Va., 1919-25; instructor,
Edward Waters Coll., Fla., 1925-27; social worker with
Illinois Childrens Home and Aid Soc., 1927-31; Chicago
Municipal Court, 1931-37; AME minister, Chicago, Ill.
and Gary, Ind., 1937-43; U.S. Chaplain, 1943-45; minis-
ter, All Souls Unitarian Ch., Chicago, 1947-53; Admin.
Asst., American Humanist Assoc., Yellow Springs, Ohio,
1953-57; associate minister, First Unitarian Ch., L. A.,
1958-61; Minister, Unitarian Fellowship, Chico, Calif.,
1961-62; interim minister, Orange County Unitarian Ch.,
Anaheim, Calif., 1962-63; Minister of Education, Throop
Mem. Unitarian-Universalist Ch., Pasadena, 1936-present.
President, American Civil Liberties Union, Yellow Springs,
Ohio, 1956-57. Alpha Phi Alpha; Mason; American Legion
and American Veterans Committee; American Association
of Social Workers; Democrat. Home: 4384 Risinghill Road,
Altadena, Calif. Office: 300 S. Los Robles Ave., Pasadena,
Calif.

McKENNEY, Martin Luther, Jr., b. Charles County, Md.,
May 12, 1933; s. Martin Luther and Ahean (Frazier) M.;
A.B., Morgan State Coll., 1959; S.T.B., Wesley Theol.
Seminary, 1962; m. Dorothy Ross; served, Westminster,
Md., 1961-63; asst. pastor, Metropolitan Methodist,
Baltimore, Md., 1963-64; US Air Force, 1951-55; Good
Conduct Medal; Mem., Mason; Home: 3009 Lyttleton Rd.
Baltimore 16, Md.; Office: Metropolitan Methodist Church,
Baltimore, Md.

McKINNEY, Richard Ishmael, educator; b. Live Oak, Fla.,
Aug. 20, 1906; s. George P. and Sallie R. (Ellis) M.;
A.B., Morehouse College, 1931; B.D., Andover Newton
Theol. Sch., 1934; S.T.M., Andover Newton, 1937; Ph. D.,
Yale University, 1942; Added study, Pendle Hill, U. of
Chgo., U. of Paris, Columbia U.; m. Phyllis Vivian
Kimbrough, 1933; 1 son, George K., 1 dau. Mrs. Osban
W. Bynum, Jr. (Phyllis); Pastor, Pond Street Bapt. Ch.,

1934-35; Dir., Rel. Activities and Asst. Prof., Phil. and
Rel., Va. Union U., Richmond, Va., 1935-42; Dean, Sch.
of Rel., Va. Union U., 1942-44; Pres., Storer College,
Harpers Ferry, W. Va., 1944-50; Actg. Dir., Rel. Activi-
ties, Va. State Coll., Petersburg, Va., 1950-51; Head,
Dept. Phil., Morgan State College, Baltimore, Md.,
1951---; Mem., Summer Sch. Grad. faculties, Texas
Southern U., Florida A & M U., Southern U.; Visiting
Lecturer, American Friends Service Committee; Mem.,
Bd. Dirs., Baltimore Urban League, 1956-59; Mem. Bd.
Trustees, Union Baptist Church, 1961---; mem. Phi Sigma
Tau Nat. Honor Soc. (past pres.); Amer. Phil. Assoc.,
Nat. Soc. for Rel. in Higher Education; Alpha Kappa Mu
Honor Soc.; Amer. Assoc. Univ. Profs.; Soc. for Existen-
tial Phil, and Phenomenology; Institute of Religion; Mason;
Omega Psi Pni; Sigma Pi Phi; Author: Religion In Higher
Education Among Negroes, 1945; Contributor, The Chris-
tian Way in Race Relations, 1948; Home: 2408 Overland
Ave., Baltimore, Md. 21214. Office: Morgan State College,
Baltimore, Md. 21212.

McKINNEY, Samuel Berry, b. Flint, Mich., Dec. 28, 1926;
s. Wade Hampton and Ruth (Berry) M.; A.B., Morehouse
Coll., Atlanta, Ga., 1952; B.D., Colgate-Rochester
Divinity School; m. Louise Jones; children--- Lora Ellen,
Rhoda Eillen; Inner-Mission of Rochester, N.Y. and stu-
dent asst. minister, The Aenon Baptist Church, Providence,
R.I., 1954-58; current pastor, Mt. Zion Baptist Ch.,
Seattle, Wash., 1958---; pres., North Pacific Baptist
Convention, 1960-63; vice pres., Washington-Northern
Idaho Council of Churches, 1964-65; Mem., Mayor's
Human Rights Commission; US Forces, World War II;
Mem., Alpha Phi Alpha; Home: 828 33rd Ave., Seattle
22, Wash.; Office: 1634 19th Ave., Seattle 22, Wash.

McKINNON, Snowden Isaiah, b. Streetman, Navarro County,
Texas, Nov. 17, 1913; s. John Marshall Ewatt and Ardella
Edna (Orange) M.; A.B., Fisk Univ., 1950; B.D., Louis-
ville Presbyterian Theol. Sem., 1953; m. Linda Rhoda
Samuels; children--- Snowden, Isaiah, Jr.; pastor, St.
James Bapt. Ch., Chattanooga, Tenn., 1954-58; pastor,
Hope Presbyterian Church, Dallas, Texas, 1958-61; cur-
rent, pastor, Highland Hills Presbyterian Church, USA,
Dallas, Texas; sec., Local Baptist Ministers Union;
YMCA Youth Committee, Dallas, Tex.; Boy Scouts of
America; "Certificated" teacher, Bapt. Bible Center,
Chattanooga and Tenn. State Baptist Education Training,

Memphis; Owen Jr. College; Bd. of Directors, Moorland
Branch, YMCA, Dallas; USAAF, 1942-46; Awards: Good
Conduct Medal; United Negro College Fund, College Division Award; Mem., Alpha Phi Alpha; Home: 7334 Vecino
Dr., Dallas, Texas 75241; Office: Highland Hills Presbyterian Church, 6352 Bonnie View Rd., Dallas, Texas,
75241.

McKINNON, Udalga Zorosha, prof.; b. Corsicana, Texas,
Oct. 9, 1903; s. John M.E. and Ardella Edna (Orange) M.;
A.B., Texas Coll., 1927; A.B., Clark Coll., 1944; B.
D., Gammon Theo. Seminary, 1945; A.M., Drew Univ.,
1950; D.D. (hon.), Miss. Ind. Coll., 1949; Graduate stud-
ies in Perkins School of Theology, S.M.U., summer
1952; Special study in Human Relations, Boston Univ.,
summer, 1962; m. Beatrice Winifred Smark; teacher,
public schools of Ellis Co., Texas, 1929-31; pastor,
Christian Methodist Episcopal Churches, Texas, Ga. and
Tenn.; presiding elder, 1957-58; professor, rural work,
Phillips School of Theology, Jackson, Tenn., 1946-51;
Exec. Dean, 1954-59; Director of Extension, Interdenominational Theol. Center, 1959---; Mem., Local Sec. &
Pres., NAACP since 1946; vice pres., Tenn. State Council of Branches, NAACP, 1948-49; Candidate for State
Constitutional Convention in 1952; the first Negro to seek
office in Jackson, Tenn. since reconstruction; Mem.,
Mason; Alpha Phi Alpha; Democrat; Adult Education Ass'n
of America; Master's thesis on Study of Financial Methods
of Negro Churches for Drew Univ. Edited booklet on
Stewardship in the Church; wrote and published booklet
on Achieving a Minimum Salary for full time pastors in
our Church (1949) & Handbook for Recruiting for the Christian Ministry (1960); Home: 641 Beckwith St., SW, Atlanta,
Ga. 30314; Office: 671 Beckwith St., SW, Atlanta, Ga.
30314.

McKISSICK, John Henry, Jr., teacher; b. Pickens, S.C.,
Dec. 1, 1913; s. John Henry, Sr. and Mary (Allen) M;
A.B., Benedict Coll., 1938; B.D., Benedict School of
Theology; D.D. (hon.) Allen Univ., Columbia, S.C.; m.
Willie Pearl Hazzard; pastor, Green Bethel Baptist Ch.,
1939-42; Shiloh Baptist Ch., Saluda, S.C., 1941, Second
Baptist, Aiken, S.C., 1943-59; Jerusalem Bapt. Church,
Ridge Spring, S.C.; current, First Baptist Ch., St. Augus-
ta, Fla., 1957---; teacher, Bible, Bettis Jr. Coll., Tren-
ton, S.C., 1948-50; Public School, Lawrens County, 1935-
37; Public School Aiken County, 1950-55; pres., NAACP,

1960-62; Trustee, Morris Coll., 1945-56; pres., Coopera-
tive Baptist State Convention, S.C., 1953-56; Nathan W.
Collier Award, 1962; Mason; Democrat; Home: 81 St.
Francis St., St. Augustine, Fla.; Office: 83 St. Francis
St., St. Augustine, Fla.

McLEAN, Edward Clifton, b. Harnett Co., N.C., May 30,
1928; s. Alexander and Gertrude S.M.; B.A., Livingstone
Coll., Salisburg, N.C.; B.D., Hood Theol. Sem., Salisbury, N.C.; m. Mildred Ennis Raye; children--- Edward
C., Jr., Michael Eldred; pastor, African Methodist
Episcopal Zion Church, 1928---; Mem., Minister's &
Laymen Assn, A.M.E. Zion Ch., 1954---; Present
pastor, Old Ship A.M.E. Zion Ch., 1964---; Interdenom-
inational Ministerial Alliance, 1963---; Durham Minister-
ial Assn, 1963---; Religious Affiliate, Redevelopment
Commission, 1963---; NAACP; NCTA, 1958-60; NEA,
1958-60; Committee on Negro Affairs, 1963---; United
Campus Ministry, 1963---; N.C. Coll., 1963---; US
Forces, 1949-53; Mem., Sigma Rho Sigma; Omega Psi
Phi; Democrat; Home: 120 Mildred St., Montgomery 8,
Ala.; Office: 483 Holcombe St., Montgomery 8, Ala.

*McNEIL, James Henry, teacher; b. Ennis, Texas, Sept.
21, 1915; s. Jake N. and Haydie (Johnson) M.; B.S.,
Prairie View A & M Coll., 1947; Howard Univ., Sch. of
Rel., B.D., 1950; summer of Graduate Study in Educa-
tion, North Texas State Univ., Denton, Texas; m. Bessie
Velton Mellon; children--- James M., Mimi Vern, Lini
Fern; student council advisor & teacher of social studies,
Turner High School, Waxahachie, Texas, 1950---; pastor,
Fourth Ward Baptist Church, Ennis, Texas, 1956---; di-
rector, Youth Dept., North Texas District Missionary
Baptist Ass'n, 1963---; dean of chapel, Religious Counse-
lor & Special Lecturer, Prairie View A&M Coll., Texas,
summer 1952; US Navy, company officer & yoeman, 1943-
45; Mem.: State Teachers Ass'n, Texas; North Texas
Teachers Ass'n; National Education Ass'n; Waxahachie
Classroom Teachers Ass'n; Ministers Conf. of North
Texas Missionary Baptist District Ass'n; Interracial Min-
isters Alliance, Ennis, Texas; Home: 1006 N. Kaufman
St., Ennis, Texas 75119; Office: 1301 N. Shawnee St.,
Ennis, Texas.

McNEIL, Jesse Jai, sem. prof.; b. North Little Rock, Ark.,
Feb. 24, 1913; s. Henry Bishop and Serveller (Edwards)
M.; B.S., M.A., Ed.D., Columbia Univ., 1938, 41, 43;

Certificate (Ecumenical Studies), Bossey, Celigney,
Switzerland, 1959; courses: Union Theol. Sem.; D.D.
(hon.), Va. Union Univ., 1959; m. Pearl Lee Walker;
children--- Jesse Jai, Jr., Kenneth Ross, Genna Rae,
Brenna Jean; pastor, First Community Bapt. Ch., New
York City; Spruce St. Bapt. Ch., Nashville, Tenn.; asst.
sec., Christian Education, S.S. Publishing Bd., Nashville,
Tenn.; dean, Sch. of Rel., Bishop Coll., Marshall, Tex.;
current pastor, Metropolitan Bapt. Ch., Pasadena, Calif.,
1961---; head of dept., Religious Education, California
Bapt. Theol. Sem., Covina, Calif., 1964---; Mem., Summer Faculty, Young Life Institute, Colorado Springs,
Colo.; director of publication, S.S. Pub. Bd., Nat. Bapt.
Conv., USA, Inc.; lecturer and leader, The International
Congress on Christian Education, Mexico City and Cuerna-
vaca, Mexico, 1943; lecturer and leader, the World Conference of Christian Youth in Oslo, Norway, 1947; Key-
note speaker and discussion leader, The Third World Bapt.
Youth Congress, Stockholm, Sweden, 1949; discussion
leader, the International Conference on Christian Educa-
tion, Toronto, Ontario, Canada, 1950; consultant, Second
Assembly of the World Council of Churches, Evanston,
Ill., 1954; former vice pres., Detroit Pastor's Union;
Michigan Council of Churches; Mem., Uniform Lessons
Series Committee, Division of Christian Education, Na-
tional Council of the Churches of Christ, USA; Education-
al Commission, National S.S. and B.T.U. Congress,
Nat. Bapt. Conv., USA, Inc.; Exec. Bd., Tri-County Dist.
Assn; Exec. Bd., Western Bapt. State Conv; Cited by
Omega Psi Phi, Detroit Chapter, 1951; Cited by the
Booker T. Washington Trade Assn, Detroit, Mich., 1954;
Recipient Freedom Award for distinguished service in the
field of public affairs, from the British Amer. Assn. of
Windsor, Ontario, Canada; Certificate of Service from Bd.
of Education, Detroit, 1958; Travel and study missions
for the World Council of Churches in Europe in 1949, 51,
53; Mem., Bd. of Directors, State YMCA; chmn, Com.
on Higher Education, State YMCA; Corporate Mem.,
Family Service Society, Detroit; vice chairman, Michigan
Corrections Commission, 10 years; author: Things That
Matter Now, 1946; The Church Working With Boys, 1947;
Your Church, 1955; A Present Help, 1958; Abounding In
Hope, 1959; Men In The Local Church, 1960; As Thy
Days So Thy Strength, 1960; A Minister's Service Book
for Pulpit and Parish, 1961; The Preacher-Prophet In
Mass Society, 1961; Moments In His Presence, 1962;
Home: 2021 No. Arroyo Blvd., Pasadena, Calif.; Office:

California Bapt. Theol. Sem., Covina, Calif.

McPHATTER, Thomas Hayswood, teacher; b. Lumberton,
North Carolina, Oct. 8, 1923; s. Thomas Matthew and
Elizabeth (Morrisey) Mc.; 1948 A.B. Johnson C. Smith
University; 1951 B.D.; m. Genevieve Redona Bryant; dau.
Mary Elizabeth; Doretha; sons Thomas Jr., George Howard,
Joseph D.; 1951-58; Pastor, St. Paul's Presbyterian
Church, Kansas City, Missouri, 1958-63; U.S. Navy Chap-
lain; Certified teacher, graduate, Presbyterian Institute,
of Industrial Relations; mem. Hearing Boards, Naval Re-
pair Facility, San Diego, Calif.; Advisor, Equal oppor-
tunities committee (same installation); Penal counseling
U.S. Navy Brig., San Diego, 1962-63; Urban League;
Wheatly Hospital; Paseo Branch YMCA; Linwood YMCA;
NAACP; Wayne Minor Post American Legion 149, and
5th District Chaplain; 1958, Vice President, Council
Churches of Greater Kansas City; Vice President, Mis-
souri State Conference NAACP; Moderator, Presbytery
of Kansas City; 1955-57, Human relations committee-
Council Church; 1956 Commissioner to General Assembly
of the Presbyterian Church in USA; 1958, President Eisen-
hower Minority Leaders Conference; Mili. rec.-1944-46,
Sergeant, U.S. Marine Corps; 1945, World War II, at
Iwo Jima and in the occupation Japan; 1958-63, U.S.
Navy Chaplain, Lieutenant; Awards: Presidential Unit
Citation; expert rifleman; Navy Unit Citation; WW II Medal;
Occupation Medal-letter of appreciation outstanding serv-
ice, U.S. Navy Brig, San Diego, Calif.-Letter of com-
mendation for serving a Hearing Board Member (Industrial
Relations); Citations, Boys Scouts of America; Misato
Church of Christ (Okinawa-Civic) mem. Omega Psi Phi
fraternity, (social); Sigma Rho Sigma (professional).
Democrat. 1957-58, Articles published in Kansas City in
Civil Rights Struggle- "A Passport to Eat"; "Abuse of
Authority". Home: 902 Ballensacher Street, San Diego,
California, 14. Office: U.S. Naval Station, San Diego,
Calif., Box 139 (92136).

McQUEEN, Charles Waldo, b. Montgomery, Ala., April 25,
1916; s. J.W. and Maggie (Broodenax); A.B., Miles Coll.,
Birmingham, Ala.; B.S., Ala. State Coll., Montgomery,
1941; Seabury-Western Theol. Sem., Evanston, Ill., 1948;
Univ. of Cincinnati, 1949-50; Univ. of Southern California,
1953-54; m. Ruby Phifer; children--- Gwendolyn Yvonne,
Charles W., Jr., Barbara Ann, Henry, William Earl;
headmaster-priest-in-charge, St. Christopher Episcopal

Ch., Columbus, Ga., 1950-53; curate, St. Philips, Los
Angeles, Calif., 1953-54; chaplain-priest-in-charge, Bethune
Cookman Coll., 1954-56; current priest-in-charge, St.
Mathews, Debray, St. Mary, Deerfield Beach; St. Cuth-
berts, St. John, St. Cuthbert's, Baynter Beach, Fla.,
1956---; instructor, High School, Debray Beach, Fla.;
US Forces, 1941-48; Home: P.O. Box 1412 Debray Beach,
Fla.; Office: P.O. Box 1412, Debray Beach, Fla.

NABRIT, H. Clarke, sem. prof.; b. Augusta, Ga.; s. James
M. and Gertrude (West) N.; A.B., Morehouse Coll.,
1937; B.D., Crozer Theol. Sem., 1942; D.D. (hon.),
Simmons Univ., 1957; m. Vernice Smith; children--- H.
Clark, Jr., Barbara Anne, Charles M.; prof., Church
History, American Baptist Theol. Sem., 1942; pastor,
Ebenezer Baptist Ch., 1942-45; editor, Young Adult and
Senior Quarterlies, 1950-58; current pastor, First Baptist
Church, Memphis, Tenn., 1947---; instructor, Owen Coll.,
Memphis, Tenn., 1960-61; director, Negro Work in Edu-
cation-Northern Baptist, W.Va., 1946-47; Mem., Bd. of
Directors, National Training School, Nashville, 1948-60;
pres., Memphis Chapter Frontiers of America, 1960-63;
chairman, Legal Redress Committee; Mem., NAACP;
chairman, Freedom Committee, NAACP, Memphis Branch,
1960---; Mem., Omega Psi Phi; Home: 682 So. Lauderdale, Memphis 38105 Tenn.; Office: 807 E. McLemore,
Memphis, Tenn. 38106.

NEAL, Warren Joseph, b. Columbus, Ohio, Feb. 10, 1921;
s. Porter A. and Charlotte (Rivers) N.; B.A., Oakwood
College, 1949; Post-graduate work at La Sierra College,
1961, and Andrews Univ., 1962-63; m. Roberta Mae (N);
children-- Brian L.; Warren A.; Pastor, Blythe,
California, 1950-52; associate pastor, San Diego, Calif.,
1952-54; present: pastor, Emmanuel Seventh-Day Adventist
Church, Riverside, Calif., 1954- . Youth counselor in
junior camps; Army Air Force - hospital orderly, 1942-
46; Good Conduct medal - World War II. Home: 7446
Lincoln Ave., Riverside, Calif. Office: Emmanuel S.D.A.
Church, 2719 - 11th St., Riverside, Calif.

NELSON, Clarence Theodore Roosevelt, b. Little Rock, Ark.,
July 5, 1903; s. Duncan William and Lydia (Durant) N.;
A.B., Philander Smith Coll., Little Rock, Ark., 1920;
B.D., Garrett Theol. Sem., Evanston, Ill., 1932; M.A.,
Northwestern Univ., Evanston, Ill.; D.D. (hon.), Philander
Smith Coll., 1959; m. Juanita Jackson; children--- Lydia

Juanita, Sandra Diane; pastor, Taylor Methodist Ch.,
Batavia, Ohio, 1932-34; Broaddus Methodist Ch., Spring-
field, Ohio, 1934-35; Pennsylvania Avenue and Lincoln
Heights Methodist Churches, Columbus, Ohio, 1935;
Braden Meth. Ch., Toledo, Ohio, 1935-38; Camphor Me-
morial Meth. Ch., St. Paul, Minn., 1938-47; Exec. sec.
Lexington Conference   (The Methodist Church) Board of
Education, 1947-52; McKinley Meth. Ch., Dayton, Ohio,
1952-55; superintendent, The Columbus Dist. of the Lex-
ington Conference, 1955-61; Scott Memorial Meth. Ch.,
Detroit, Mich., 1961---; director, Public Relations and
Correspondent for Meth. Information of the St. Louis
Area of The Methodist Ch., 1951-64; National chairman
of Operation Freedom (a civil rights organization); vice
pres., Meth. Federation for Social Action of The Meth.
Ch.; co-chmn, The Religious Freedom Com., Inc.; life
mem., The Ohio Pastor's Convention; former sec., Ohio
Council of Churches, 1959-61; mem., Phi Beta Sigma;
author; The Romance of the Negro and the Meth. Ch.
(to be published); home: 262 East Boston Blvd., Detroit,
Mich., 48202; Office: 609 East Kirby St., Detroit, Mich.,
48202.

NELSON, James Herbert, I. b. Ridgeway, S.C. Jul 7, 1919;
s. Warren Julius and Maggie Sarah (Grant) N.; A.B.,
Johnson C. Smith, 1940; B.D., Johnson C. Smith Univ.,
1949; m. Johnalee Barnes; children--- Louise Ja Malla
James Herbert, II; pastor Congruity Westminster P.
Churches; current pastor St. Luke U. P. C., Orangeburg,
S.C.; dir. Westminster Foundation, S.C. State College;
teacher Sumter County Public Schools, S.C.; Morris
College, Sumter, S.C.; Atlantic Presbytery Co-director,
Goodwill Larger Parish, United Presbyterian Ch., S.C.;
mem.: S.C. Council on Human Relations, Southern Re-
gional Council; exec. comm. Orangeburg; N. A. A. C. P.;
US Army, World War II, Pacific Theatre 372nd Infantry
Div.; award: Omega Man 9th year; mem.: Mason, Omega
Psi Phi Fraternity; Home: Box 1574 State College, Orange-
burg, S.C.; Ch.: Lowman at Amelia, Orangeburg, S.C.

NELSON, R. Wendell, b. Charlotte, N.C., Apr. 18, 1916;
s. Arthur and Anna May (Stephens) N.; B.A., Pacific
Union College, 1941; courses: University of Southern
California, Pacific School of Religion, Loma Linda University and Andrews University; m. Margaret Ellen Perry;
children--- Marilynn Elaine, R. Wendell, Jr., Walter
Ronald. Regional evangelist, Texico Conference of the

Seventh-Day Adventists, 1941-45; district pastor-evangelist
Lake Region Conf. of S.D.A., 1945-46; pastor-evangelist,
North Calif. Conf. of S.D.A., 1946-57 . Market St. S.
D.A. Church, Oakland, Calif.; present: pastor-evangelist,
South Calif. Conf. of S.D.A., Sunset Avenue Seventh-Day
Adventist Church, Pasadena, Calif., 1957- . Member:
Conf. Executive Committees of Texico Conference, 1945,
North Calif. Conf., 1948-54; South Calif. Conf., 1959-63.
President, Ministerial Fellowship - North Calif. Conf., in
Oakland, California; chairman, Yosemite Nature Camp,
1952-61; member, South Calif. Conf. Ministers' Chorus
(2nd Bass Sect.), 1958-present; member, Southern Har-
monious Quartet, 1939- present. Home: 1530 Poppy Peak
Drive, Pasadena, Calif. Office: 1281 Sunset Ave.,
Pasadena, Calif.

NELSON, William Stuart, univ. vice pres.; b. Paris, Ky.,
Oct. 15, 1895; s. William Henry and Emma (Kersands)
N.; A.B., Howard Univ., 1920; LL.D. (hon.), 1936;
Union Theol. Sem., New York, 1920-21; B.D., Yale Univ.
1924; grad. student, Sorbonne and Protestant Theol. Sem.,
Paris, 1921-22; Univ. of Marburg and Univ. of Berlin,
1922-23, 25, 26; LL.D. (hon.), Shaw Univ., 1936; LL.D.,
Daniel Payne Coll., 1962; m. Blanche Louise Wright; in-
structor, Howard Univ., 1924-26; asst. prof., 1926-29;
assoc. prof. and asst. to pres., 1929-31; pres. Shaw
Univ., Raleigh, N.C., 1931-36; pres., Dillard Univ.,
New Orleans, La., 1936-40; dean, Sch. of Rel., Howard
Univ., 1940-49; dean, 1948-61; vice pres., Howard Univ.,
1961-; US Army, 1st Lt.,; Fullbright research fellow to
India, 1958-59; Mem., Conference on Science, Philosophy
and Religion; Fellow National Council of Rel. in Higher
Education; Religious Educational Assn; Acad. Polit. Sci-
ence; Omega Psi Phi; editor: The Christian Way in
Race Relation, 1948; Journal of Religious Thought; Lec-
ture at Univs. in India, 1947-48; author: Bases of World
Understanding, 1949; La Race Noir Dans La Democratic
Americaine, 1921; Contributor-Articles and book reviews to
journals and newspapers; Home: 1722 Varnum St., NW, Wash.,
D.C. 20001; Office: Howard Univ., Wash. D.C.

NEWBERRY, Earl Edward, b. Wilcox Co., Ala., June 2,
1918; S. Frank and Mollie Josephine (N.); A.B., Morris
Brown Coll., 1951; B.D., Gammon Theological Sem.,
1954; m. Inez Platt; children--- Edward Bernard, Brenda
Y., Beucenia D.; organizer, pastor, Trinity Presbyterian
Ch., Decatur, Ga., 1943-56; current pastor, S. Tryon

Presbyterian Ch., Charlotte, N.C., 1958---; principle,
Public Sch.; director, City recreation; leader, Boys Club;
pres., Decatur Civic Club, 1953-55; counselor, Housing
Projects; Mem., Phi Beta Sigma; Home: 2201 English Dr.,
Charlotte 8, N.C.; Office: 2616 S. Tryon St., Charlotte 3,
N.C.

NEWBOLD, Robert Thomas, Jr. coll teacher; b. Miami,
Fla., Feb. 26, 1920; s. Robert Thomas, Sr. and Irene
(Johnson) A.B., Florida A.& M. University, 1942; B.D.,
The Theological Seminary, Lincoln Univ., Pa., 1945; M.
A., McCormick Theological Seminary, Chgo., 1946; m.
Ann Worrell; pastor, Second Presbyterian Ch., Brunswick,
Ga., 1944-46; pastor, Radcliffe Mem. Presbyn. Ch.,
Atlanta, Ga., 1946-53; pastor, Grace United Presby. Ch.,
Baltimore, Md., 1953-   ; lecturer, Homiletics, Gammon
Theological Seminary, Atlanta, Ga., 1948-53; lecturer,
Public Relations, Cortez Peters Business School, Balti-
more, Md., 1955-58; instructor, Philosophy, Morgan
United Presbyterian Ch., Baltimore, Md., 1953---;
mem., Bd. of Strategy, Baltimore Presbytery, 1962---;
mem. Comm. on Nominations, Baltimore Presbytery,
1962---; mem. Comm. on Race and Religion, General
Assembly; mem. Bd. of Dirs., Wilson Leadership School,
mem. Bd. of Dirs. Baltimore Urban League; mem. Bd.
of Dirs. Patuxent Institution; mem., Mayor's Representa-
tive-Steering Committee Human Renewal Commission;
mem.: YMCA, NAACP, Urban League, Frontiers of
America, Citizens Planning and Housing Assn., The
Governor's Comm. on Juvenile Delinquency, Interdenomina-
tional Ministers' Alliance, Theodore R. McKeldin Republi-
can Club, Northwestern United Protective Assn., Pi Omega
Chapter, Omega psi Phi Fraternity, Clergy Visiting Staff-
Baltimore City Hospitals, Member of the Balto. Grand
Jury, the Federal Grand Jury, The Baltimore Petty Jury,
Na. Rehabilitation Assn., Adult Education Assn., Col-
umnist-Afro-American Newspapers, Bd. of Dirs.-Maryland-
Delaware Council of Chs., Clergy Council of the Urban
League, Bd. of Dirs. Baltimore Urban League, Bd. of
Dirs. Patuxent Institution, the Mayor's Representative-
Steering Committee Human Renewal Commission; Home:
3610 Grantley Rd., Baltimore, Md.; Church: Dolphin and
Etting Streets, Baltimore, Md.

*NEWBORN, Ernest J., teacher; b. Whiteville, Tenn., Mar.
19, 1927; s. James H. and Josephine (McKinney) N.; A.
B., Tenn. State Univ., 1951; B.D., Howard Univ. Sch.

of Rel., 1954; Kent State (Ohio) Univ., 1962---; m.
Janice Robinson; children--- Ernest J. Jr., Mary-Jo;
pastor, Gay-Lee Christian Church, Nashville, Tenn.,
1950-51; chaplain, Migrant Farm Workers, Pa., N.C.
Ohio, 1954-55; current pastor, Cherry Christian Church,
Canton, Ohio, 1954---; teacher, Social Science, Canton,
Ohio, 1956---; dean, Christian School of Religion for
Community Leadership School, Canton, Ohio; Bd. Mem.,
YMCA; Ohio Society of Christian Churches; treasurer,
Canton Leadership Council; Advisory Board; Canton Urban
League; Stark County Ministerial Ass'n; Canton Profession-
al Educators Ass'n; National Ed. Ass'n; Home: 2118 17th
St. NE, Canton, Ohio 47705; Office: 1217 Cherry Ave.,
SE, Canton, Ohio 47707.

NICHOLS, Roy, b. Hurlock, Md., Mar 19, 1918; s. Roy
and Mamie (Waters) N.; Lincoln Univ., 1941; Pacific
Sch. of Religion, Berkely, Calif., 1947; D.D. (hon.),
Univ. of the Pacific, 1961; Pacific Sch. of Rel., 1964;
m. Ruth Richardson; children--- Melisance, Allegra,
Nathan; pastor, South Berkely Community Ch., Berkely,
Calif., 1943-46; Downs Memorial Meth. Ch., Oakland,
Calif., 1949-64; current pastor, Salem Meth. Ch., N.Y.
City, 1964---; delegate, Meth. General Conf., 1960,
1964; pres., Berkely Bd. of Education, Berkely, Calif.,
1963-64; Mem., Alpha Phi Alpha; author: Motivation For
A New Age, 1964; Home: 240 Nagle Ave., New York City,
N.Y.; Office: 2190 7th Ave., New York City, N.Y.

*NOISETTE, Ruffin Nichols, b. Summerville, S.C., Mar.
20, 1923; s. Joseph Edward and Louise (Nichols) N.;
A.B., Howard Univ., 1946; B.D., 1949; D.D. (hon.),
Wilberforce Univ.; m. Thelma Irene Anderson; children
--- Shelley, Karin, Robin, Louis; asst. dean of chapel,
Fisk Univ., 1949-50; pastor, Ebenezer African Methodist
Episcopal Church, Rahway, N.J., 1950-51; Bethel A.M.
E. Church, Wilmington, Del., 1951---; Volunteer Religious
Instructor, Ferris School for Delinquent Boys, Wilm.,
1958-61; Woodshaven Kruse School for Delinquent Girls,
1961-62; pres., Wilmington Ministerium, 1955-57; pres.,
Wilmington Council of Churches, 1959-61; Mem., Board
of Directors, Walnut St. Branch YMCA, Wilmington;
pres., East Center City Protestant Churches of Wilming-
ton, 1962---; Outstanding Citizen Award, 1959; Red cross
Outstanding Service Certificate, 1957; Mem., NAACP;
YMCA; Alpha Phi Alpha; Boy Scouts of America; Mayor's
Committee on Housing; Bi-Racial Committee; Home: 905

N. Rodney St., Wilmington, Delaware 19806; Office: Walnut St., Wilmington, Delaware 19801.

NORTHCUTT, Robert Robinson, Prairie View Univ.; Perkins Sch. of Theology; Christian Methodist Episcopal Churches, 32 years; current pastor, Be Bee Tabernacle C. M. E. Ch., 1950---; Mem., Interdenominational Ministerial Alliance; Houston Ministerial Assn. of Greater Houston; treas., The Texas Annual Conf.; The Judiciary Court of the C. M. E. Ch.; Alumni Assn. of Texas Coll., Tyler, Tex.; Trustee and Exec. Mem., Texas Coll.; instructor, Pastor's School, 10 years; Mem., Long Range Planning Com., C. M. E. Ch.; Mem., United Fund and the Red Cross Committee; YMCA; Office: Be Bee Tabernacle C. M. E. Ch., 822 West Dallas Ave., Houston 3, Tex.

NORWOOD, John Fredrick, Church official; b. Darlington, S. C., Nov. 28, 1927; s. John Ruben and Benzena (Mc Curry) N.; B. A., Claflin Coll., Orangeburg, S. C., 1951; B. D., Gammon Theol. Sem., Atlanta, Ga., 1957; m. Zanthia L. Bush; children--- John Fredrick Jr., Iris Regina; Served four charges in South Carolina and one charge in the Central Alabama Conf. of The Meth. Ch., 1951-56; Dist. Supt., The Huntsville Dist., The Meth. Ch., Huntsville, Ala.; Mem., Exec. Com., General Bd. of Lay Activities of The Meth. Ch.; delegate, Jurisdictional Conf. of the Central Jurisdiction, Meth. Ch.; Mem., General Bd. of Missions of The Methodist Ch.; principal, Hickman Elementary School, Kershaw County, Camden, S. C.; volunteer chaplain, Macon County Jail, 1957-62; Mem., NAACP; Tuskegee Civic Assn; Alabama Provisional Council of Churches; Exec. Com., Citizen Service Com., Huntsville, Ala.; The Voters League; Award: "Ruptured Duck"; Mem., Mason; Madison County Mental Assn; Ministerial Alliance; Home: 1605 Armstrong St. NW, Huntsville, Ala.; Office: P. O. Box 1454, Huntsville, Ala.

OBEY, Edward Rudolph, b. Olivia, North Carolina, Dec. 2, 1927; s. James Edward and Viola (Johnson) O.; 1944-1948, B. A. Johnson C. Smith University, Charlotte, N. C.; 1948-51; B. D. (Theology); m. Elizabeth Ann (Frazier) O. Children--- Vickie Lynn, Valerie De Anna, Veronica Elizabeth; 1951-53; Pastor, Lenoir North Carolina and Morganton, Lenoir and Morganton Presbyterian Churches; 1953-Aug. 1955, Lincolnton and Shelby North Carolina

(Presbyterian Churches); Director, Friendship House, Lackawanna, N.Y.; 1955-59; 1959-60 Associate Pastor, Bethel Presbyterian Church, Lackawanna, N.Y.; Pastor, Cherry Hill Community Presbyterian, Baltimore Md.; 1960---; mem. Baltimore, Md. Coordinating Council of Cherry Hill; Big Brothers of Baltimore; Synod Westminster Foundation Committee, Ministers Alliance of Baltimore, Inner City Council; Omega Psi Phi Fraternity; Home: 2516 Terra Firma Rd., Balto. 25, Md. Church: 819 Cherry Hill Rd., Baltimore 25, Maryland.

*OGLESBY, Jacob C., b. May 13, 1918; s. John and Ida Mae; A.B., Lane Coll., 1940; M.A., B.D., Howard Univ. Sch. of Rel., 1942, 44; D.D. (hon.), Birmingham Bapt. Coll., 1963; m. Anne H.; Courses for Th.D., Sch. of Religion, Boston Univ., 1963; m. Anne H. Harris; children--- two sons; chaplain, Fla. Normal and Industrial Coll., 1944; teacher, Lane Coll., 1945-47; pastor, Bapt. Ch., Tenn., 2 yrs; Fla., 3 yrs; current pastor, Christ Bapt. Ch., Detroit, Mich., 1956---; Bd. mem., Detroit Council of Churches; Great City Projects for New Schools; awards: NAACP award; "Minister of the Week" (Michigan Chronicle), 1963; Presented Plaque for Community Service by Eta Phi Beta Sorority, 1964; dean, Bapt. Training Sch.; past pres., Bapt. Ministers Conf. of Detroit and Vicinity mem., Commission for Establishment of a Seminary for Detroit (Detroit Council of Churches); Alpha Phi Alpha; Home: 4428 Burns St., Detroit 14, Mich.; Office: 3544 Iroquois Ave., Detroit, Mich.

OLIVIER, Leonard James, administrator; b. Lake Charles, La., October 12, 1923; s. James Lawrence and Mathielde (Rochon) O.; St. Augustine's Seminary, 1939-41; St. Mary's Seminary, Techny, Ill., 1942-46; St. Augustine's Sem. Phil. and Theol., 1946-52; M.A., Catholic University of Amer., 1961; Asst. Dean of Students, St. Augustine's Sem., Bay St. Louis, Miss., 1952-56; Head Dean, St. Augustine's, 1956---; Mem. Nat'l. Bd. of Education, Society of the Divine Word (S.V.D.); Nat'l Cath. Educational Assoc.; Miss. Education Assoc.; Nat'l Assoc. of Secondary School Principals; M.A. Thesis: "History of the Origin and Development of Saint Augustine's Seminary"; Home and Office: Ullman Ave., Bay St. Louis, Mississippi 39520.

OLIVER, William Raoul, educator, teacher; b. New Orleans, La., August 17, 1928; s. Henry J. and Iola V. (Duvernay)

O.; M.A. Soc. Sc., Catholic University of America;
Xavier University; Instructor; Seminary Divine Word
Fathers, Riverside, Calif., 1959-60; Asst. Dir., Holy
Rosary Institute, 1960-62; Dir., Holy Rosary Institute,
1962---; Home and Office: Holy Rosary Institute, P.O.
Box 2219, Lafayette, La.

OWEN, Samuel Augustus, b. Stanton, Tenn., July 21, 1886;
s. Henry Clay and Fannie (Ware) G.; Roger Williams
Univ., Nashville, Tenn.; Walden Univ., Nashville, Tenn.;
A.B., Atlanta Bapt. Coll., 1911; M.A., Morehouse Coll.,
Atlanta, Ga., 1922; D.D. (hon.), Roger Williams Univ.,
1922; Graduate work, Divinity Sch., Univ. of Chicago,
1920-35; m. Mary Jane Wood; children---Samuel Augustus,
Jr.; teacher, Fla. Institute, Live Oak, Fla., 1912-17;
pres., Fla. Memorial Coll., Live Oak, Fla.; pastor,
Jethro Bapt. Ch., 1913-16; pastor, Mt. Bethel Bapt. Ch.,
Daytona Beach, Fla., 1917-30; pres., Roger Williams
Coll., Nashville, Tenn., 1920-23; pastor, Metropolitan
Bapt. Ch., Memphis, Tenn., 1923-63; moderator, West
Tenn. B.M. & E. Assn., 1928-61; pres., Tenn. Bapt.
M. & E. Convention, Inc., 1936-63; chairman, Bd. of
Directors, Griggs Business Coll.; chairman, Bd. of
Directors, Owen Jr. Coll.; vice chairman, Bd. of Trus-
tees, LeMoyne Coll., Memphis; vice pres.-at-large, Na
tional Bapt. Convention, Inc., 1953-57; Designated minis-
ter of the year in Memphis, 1953; US Army Chaplain,
World War II, 1942-44; Captain; Mem., Mason; Odd Fel-
lows; Knights of Pythians; Republican; Phi Beta Sigma;
Home: 761 Walker Ave., Memphis 6, Tenn.; Office: 767
Walker Ave., Memphis 6, Tenn.

PAIGE, Charles Thomas, professor; b. Phoebus, Va., Sept.
25, 1911; s. Charles Henry and Ethel (Webb) P.; A.B.,
Hampton Institute; B.D., Virginia Union Univ.; current
student for S.T.D., Temple Univ.; m. Mary Elizabeth
Manning; children--- Milton Thaddeus, Helen Elizabeth,
Jeanette Claire, Sarah Ethel, Inena Mae, Carlena Faye,
Vivian Jo-Ann, Robert Charles; instructor, Religion &
Acting Chairman of Religion Dept., Bishop Coll., Marshall
Tex.; coll. minister and chairman of religion, Owen Coll.,
Memphis, Tenn.; pastor, Riverview Christian Church;
chaplain, Western State Hospital; teacher, Shelby County,
Tenn.; Gloucester & Warwick Counties, Va.; chmn., Bd.
of Helping Hand Assn, 1958-60; bus. manager, Zuber
Bymun Council, 1960-62; Mem., Kappa Alpha Psi; Tenn.

Chaplain, Mental Hospital; Home: 1120 South Lauderdale
St., Memphis 6, Tenn.; Office: 1982 Riverside Blvd.,
Memphis 9, Tenn.

*PAIR, James David, b. Wake County, N.C., Aug. 31, 1873;
s. Harmon and Alie (Lassates) P.; A.B., Shaw Univ.,
1898; B.D., Howard Univ. Sch. of Rel., 1911; m. Lula
N. Thornton; children--- Clarence A., James M. Hubert
B., Lois (Mrs. John Turner) Virginia (Mrs. Peter Ridley, Sr.)
Harmon E.; Ordained Baptist Minister, 1912; pastor, Churches,
Va. and Md., 1912-58; Retired, 1958; Mem., Federation Civic
Assn, 1924--; sec., North Carolina Bapt. Sunday School Con-
vention, 1897-1904; vice pres., D.C. Bapt. Sunday Sch.
Conv., 1906-10; pres., Wash., D.C., Congress of Par-
ents and Teachers, 1932-34; Mem., Chairman, Dist. of
Columbia Selective Service Draft Bd., 1940-45; Mem.,
and sec., D.C. Selective Draft Bd., 1948-64; Financial
director, D.C. Nat. Congress of Colored Parents and
Teachers (Atlanta, Ga.); Special awards from Presidents,
Truman, Eisenhower, Kennedy for service to the nation
in selective service system, 1940-63; Mem., Mason;
former vice pres., Interdenominational Ministers Alliance,
Wash. D.C.; Pastor-Emeritus, First Bapt. Ch., North
Brentwood, Md.; Home: 745 Girard St., Wash., D.C.
20001.

*PARKER, Charles Edward, b. Annapolis, Md., Oct. 18,
1923; s. John Wesly and Carrie (Parker P.; B.S. Ed.,
Wilberforce Univ., Ohio, 1953; M.S. Ed., Loyola Coll.,
Baltimore, Md., 1957; B.D., Howard Univ. Sch. of Rel.,
1960; m. Joan Isaacs; children--- Tanya, Toxcy, JoAnn;
teacher, Kittrell Coll., pastor, Galatia African Methodist
Episcopalian Ch., Nashville, N.C., 1953-55; Exec. officer,
Service Co., US Army and between 1955 and 1957 did
graduate study at Loyola Coll., Baltimore, Md. and
worked at North Carolina Mutual Insurance Co.; pastor,
Ebenezer A.M.E. Ch., Washington, D.C., 1957-60; East-
minster-Woodville Interracial Parish, Richmond, Va., 1961-
63; current, Bethel Presbyterian Ch., Alexandria, Va.;
Trustee, Wilberforce Univ. Foundation; Mem., Church and
Civil Rights Committee, Presbytery of the Potomac; Ad-
visory Bd., YMCA, Alexandria, Va.; Christian Ed. Com.,
Hanover Presbytery, Richmond, Va.; US Army, 2nd Lt.,
Infantry and Engineer Corps, 1953-55; Republican; Mem.,
Omega Psi Phi; Zeta Sigma Phi; Sen Mer Rhek; pres.,
Zeta Sigma Phi; Mem., NAACP; Home: 605 South Fayette
St., Alexandria, Va.; Office: 634 North Patrick St.,

Alexandria, Va.

PARKER, Fred William, b. Tampa, Fla., Dec. 18, 1924;
s. William and Amanda (P.); A.B., Oakwood College,
1949; m. Mildred P.; children- Fred W., Willie Samuel,
Walter Wayne, Yvonne. Pastor, Seventh-Day Adventist
Church, Fayetteville, North Carolina; substitute-teacher,
elementary school; U.S. Navy, 1944-46. Home: 1874
Gola Drive, Fayetteville, N.C. Office: 330 Old Wilmington Rd., Fayetteville, N.C.

PARKER, Lynnwood, church official; b. Arrow Rock, Mo.,
June 19, 1920; s. Henry and Sophia P.; B.S., Univ. of
Nebraska, 1948; M.S., Univ. of Omaha, 1951; B.D.,
Gammon Theol. Seminary, 1958; Univ. of Nebraska,
1959-60; m. Gertrude Elizabeth Jones; children--- Lynette;
exec. sec., Central West conference Bd. of Education,
St. Louis, Mo. 1958---; pastor, Clark Meth. Church,
McMinnville, Tenn., 1955-58; teacher, English & Social
Studies, Chrispus Attucks High Sch. in Adult Education
Dept., Indianapolis, Ind., 1954-55; director of guidance,
Washington Technical High School & Substitute Teacher in
English & Social Studies Adult Education Dept., St. Louis,
Mo., 1952-53; Exec. Sec., The Urban League, Lincoln,
Nebraska; editor, The Omaha Star (Weekly Newspaper),
Omaha, Nebr., 1950-51; Boys counselor, Boys Town,
Nebr.; Battalion Adjutant, The Infantry School, Fort Ben-
ning, Ga., 1944; Christian Education in all Central Juris-
diction Churches in the states of Missouri, Kansas,
Colorado, Nebraska, Ill., Iowa; Bd. of Managers, and
Dean of St. Louis Area Leadership School; Mem., Gen-
eral Comm. on Family Life of the Meth. Church; Inter-
conference Commission on Student Work of Mo.; Greater
Kansas City Metropolitan Area Planning Comm.; Missouri
Council of Churches; Set up workshops & clinics to pro-
vide camping and conference opportunities for youth and
young adults; Former Mem., Nebraska Comm., White
House Conference on Children & Youth; Lincoln, Nebraska:
Mayor's Comm. on Human Relations; Nebraska Social
Action Council; Nebraska State Parole Board; National
Methodist Scholarship Award; Mem., Alpha Phi Alpha;
Mason; Home: 4324 Marcus St., St. Louis 15, Mo.; Of-
fice: 4903 Delmar Blvd., Suite 201 St. Louis 8, Mo.

*PARKER, Sidney Bayne, teacher; b. Jamaica, West Indies,
July 13, 1922; s. Luther Augustus and Rachel (Salmon) P.;
Mico T. College 1941-43; Howard Univ., Sch. of Rel., 1945-

52; B. S. 1949; M. A. 1953; Louisiana State M. S. 1954;
Nashotah House, Wisconsin 1960; General Theo. Sem.,
N. Y. C. S. T. B. 1961; m. Bernice Eleanor Martin, March
19, 1948; children--- Philip Sidney, Cynthia Victoria
Elaine; High school teacher, Jamaica 1944-45; Member,
American Univ. faculty in social science, 1952-53; vicar,
St. Michael's Episcopal Church, Baton Rouge, La., 1953-
57; Monclair, N. J., 1957-61; rector, Trinity Episcopal
Church, Montclair, N. J., 1961---; Substitute teacher,
High schools, East Orange, N. J.; Member, Bd. of Trus-
tees, Visiting Nurse Association of Montclair; Member,
Mayor's Committee, United Nations; President of Student
Behaviour Committee, Montclair; Instructor, Leland Col-
lege, Baker, La., 1954-57; Member, The Fellowship of
the Institute for Religious & Social Studies; Home: 43
Gates Avenue, Montclair, New Jersey: Office: 19 North
Willow Street, Montclair, New Jersey

PARKER, Walter Procter Hall, b. Philadelphia, Pa., Sept.
23, 1919; s. William Edward and Blanche Hall; B. S.,
Temple Univ., 1938-41; S. T. B., Temple University,
1943-45; m. Christine Rider; children--- Carolyn, Janet,
William, Gloria; vicar, Chapel of the Ascension, West
Chester, Pa. & St. Cyrill's Chapel, Coatesville, Pa.,
1946-50; priest-in-charge, St. Philip's Church, Syracuse,
New York, 1950-54; rector, The Church of The Holy
Cross, Pittsburgh, Pa., 1954-; youth advisor, Diocese of
Central New York, Syracuse, N. Y., 1952-54; Executive
Council, Diocese of Pittsburgh, Pa., 1957-60; Mem.:
Pittsburgh-Board of Directors, Lemington Avenue for
Aged, Pgh., Pa.; Homewood-Brushton; Community Im-
provement Assn.; Homewood-Brushton Renewal Council;
Religious Advisory Comm. Planned Parenthood Assoc.;
Negro Foster Home Adoption Committee; Family and
Children's Service; 1962 Simon Gratz Distinguished Serv-
ice Award; Mem.; Omega Psi Phi Fraternity; NAACP;
Frontiers of America; Mason; Home: 7507 Kelly St.,
Pittsburgh 8, Penna.; Office: same.

PARRIS, Henry Phares, b. Holly Grove, Ark., Nov. 17,
1906; s. John and Ivory Dove P.; Minister's Institutes,
Langston Univ., & Bishop Coll.; m. Marry Alice Lemons;
pastor, Oklahoma, in the following churches: Mt. Olive
Baptist Ch., Chickasha, 1931-34; New Bethel Bapt. Ch.,
Blanchard, 1935-38; Mt. Olive Bapt. Ch., Chickasha,
1939-40; First Bapt. Ch., Purcell, 1940-43; First Bapt.
Ch., Kingfisher, 1943-47; Union Bapt. Ch., Shawnee,

1947-49; current pastor, Union Bapt. Ch. , Lawton, Okla. ,
1949---; director of education, New Hope Bapt. Ch. ,
Chickasha, Okla. ; dean, Chickasha Dist. Congress; dean,
Western Dist. Congress, four years; pres. , three Minis-
terial Alliances; current pres. , Lawonview Improvement
Ass'n; moderator, Western Dist. Bapt. Ass'n; 1st vice
pres. , Okla. Bapt. State Congress on Christian Education;
State vice pres. , Nat'l Baptist Congress; author: History of
Chickasaw District Bapt. Ass'n; Home: 1606 Garfield, Lawton,
Oklahoma; Office: Union Baptist Ch. ,16th at Farfield, Lawton,
Okla.

PATTERSON, Bernardin Joseph, teacher; b. Clarksdale,
Arkansas, December 24, 1924; s. Alonzo and Johnnie
(Wilson) P. ; B. A. Philosophy, B. A. Classics, St. John's
Univ. , Collegeville, Minn. , 1949; J. C. B. , Catholic Univer-
sity, 1958; J. C. L. , Catholic University, 1959; Ordained
priest, Roman Cath. Ch. , 1954; Instructor: Classics,
St. John's U. , 1949-53; Classics and Linguistics, St.
John's U. , 1953-55; Greek and Latin, St. Maur's Semin-
ary, South Union, Ky. , 1955-57; Cannon Law, Moral
Theol. , St. Maur's Sem. , 1959-63; Asst. Superior, St.
Maur's Interracial Seminary, South Union, Ky. , 1960-63;
First Negro Superior of Catholic Institute In U. S. , South
Union, Ky. , Dec. 1963; Founder, Nat'l Institute for Race
and Religion, So. Union, Ky. , 1963; Pres. , St. Maur's
Interracial Seminary, 1963---; Pres. , Mid-West Clergy
Conf. on Negro Welfare, 1963; Home and Office: Saint
Maur Interracial Seminary, South Union, Ky. , 42283.

*PATTERSON, Rossie L. , b. Abbeville, Ala. , Nov. 26,
1918; s. Hezikiah and Lucy (Panty) P. ; B. S. , Alabama
State Teachers Coll. , 1947; B. D. , Howard Univ. Sch. of
Rel. , 1951; m. Mattie Martha Pringle; children--- Mar-
ilynn, Carolynn, Leonard; director of Christian Education,
Mt. Carmel Baptist Ch. , Wash. , D. C. , 1951-55; pastor,
First Institutional Bapt. Ch. , Winston-Salem, N. C. ,
1955-59; current pastor, Mt. Carmel Bapt. Ch. , Wash. ,
D. C. , 1959---; pres. , Bapt. Ed. Congress of D. C.
Vicinity; sec. , Bd. of Trustees, Wash. Bapt. Sem. ,
Wash. , D. C. ; auditor, Progressive National Bapt. Con-
vention; Mem. , Com. of 100 Clergymen; US Forces,
1942-45; Mem. , Mason; Democrat; NAACP; Southern
Christian Leadership Conference; Home: 1728 Webster St.
Wash. , D. C. 20011; Office: 3rd and Eye Sts. , Wash. ,
D. C. 20011.

PAYNE, Arthur Jerome, b. Baltimore, Md., Nov. 1894;
s. James Henry and Maggie (Bonaparte) P.; Wayland
Academy of Va. Union Univ., 1918; A.B., Morgan Coll.,
1928; A.M., Columbia Univ., 1939; D.D. (hon.), Va.
Union Univ., 1936; m. Elizabeth Welch; (2nd) Odell Watkins;
children--- Arthur Jerome, Jr.; Ordained Baptist ministry,
1915; pastor, Union Bapt. Ch., Ekridge, Md., 1913-14;
Good Hope Bapt. Ch., Baltimore, Md., 1914-15; asst.
pastor, Abyssinia Bapt. Ch., New York, N.Y., 1920-23;
current pastor, Enon Bapt. Ch., Baltimore, Md., 1923--;
former pres., Council of Churches and Christian Education of Maryland and Delaware; director, Dept. Store,
Baltimore, Md.; pres., United Baptist Convention, Md.,
1929; vice pres., National Baptist Convention, Inc.,
1929; Trustee, Northern Univ., Long Branch, N.J.; Mem.,
Bd. of Directors, Mt. Bethel Ass'n; Bd. of Directors,
Urban League; NAACP; YMCA; Rec'd Boy Scouts Silver
Beaver Minister of the Year; New England Baptist Conven-
tion, 1960; Certificate of Merit from the city of Balto.
for service in the Civilian Mobilization during 1945; Wel-
fare Ass'n; Alpha Phi Alpha; Vocational Guidance Group;
Baptist World's Alliance; Republican; Bd. of the Morgan
Coll. Christian Center; Bd. of Provident Hospital, Balto.
Md.; author: Bible Meditations; Church Programs and
Parent Education; Distinctive Characteristics of American
Public Education; dean, Preachers of Baltimore, Md.;
Home:5901 Old Frederick Rd., Baltimore, Md. 21228;
Office: Edmondson Ave. and Schroeder St., Baltimore,
Md. 21223.

PAYTON, Benjamin Franklin, sem. prof.; Orangeburg,
S.C., Dec. 27, 1932; s. Leroy R. and Sara Mack P.;
South Carolina State Coll., 1955; B.D., Harvard Univ.,
1958; M.A., Columbia Univ., New York City, 1960;
Ph.D., Yale Univ., New Haven, Conn., 1963; m. Thelma
Plane; pastor, Friendship Baptist Ch., Orangeburg, S.C.,
1951-55; Savannah Creek Bapt. Ch., Ehrhardt, S.C.,
1952-55; asst. pastor, Ebenezer Bapt. Ch., Boston, Mass.
1955-58; asst. pastor, The Riverside Ch., New York
City, 1958-60;   Head, The Dept. of Sociology of
Religion and Social Ethics in The Howard Univ. Sch. of
Rel.; director, The Howard Univ. Community Service
Project;-Mem., American Society of Scholars; Society
for Religion in Higher Education; Alpha Phi Alpha; Amer.
Sociological Ass'n; NAACP; The Wilkinson High Sch. National Honor Society; Alpha Kappa Mu Honor Society; Danforth Graduate Fellowship to study for Doctorate, Harvard

Univ.'s Billings Prize, First Place, 1957; Nathan W.
Scott Award for Meritorious Service from Fla. Memorial
Coll., Augustine, Fla.; Home: 101 G. St. SW, Wash.,
D.C.

*PEARSON, Augustus Japheth, b. Pine Bluff, Ark. Oct. 29,
   1916; s. Carl W. and Bessie (O.) P.; A.B., Ark. A.M.
   & N. Coll., 1939; B.D., Howard Univ., Sch. of Rel.,
   1940; M. ed., M.A. Fisk Univ., 1947; Univ. of Arkansas,
   1954; m. (Jane) Lee Nichols; children--- Rosylyn, Jessie
   Y., Augustus J., Marguenrite D., Nichola; pastor, Shiloh
   Baptist Church, Camden, Ark., 1942-47; Ninth Street
   Baptist Church, Ft. Smith, Ark., 1947-60; Shiloh Baptist,
   Topeka, Kans., 1960---; teacher, Lincoln High School,
   Camden, Ark., 1942-47; counselor, Arkansas Baptist Coll.,
   1956-57; Second Negro elected to Central Democratic Committee, Ark., 1956-58; chairman, Housing Committee,
   NAACP, Topeka, Kans.; Mem., Mason: author: Literature
   for the Senior High Baptist Sunday School; Home: 1211 W.
   12, Topeka 3, Kansas; Office: 1202 Buchanan St., Topeka
   3, Kansas.

PEARSON, George Isaac, teacher; b. Steelton, Pa., Feb. 3,
   1930; s. William H.W. and Lassie (Adams) P.; St. Phillips
   College, 1956; B.A., Oakwood College, 1959; M.A.,
   Andrews University, 1960; m. Lou Ethel Duckworth; Teach-
   er, Dupont Park High School, Washington, D.C. 1960-62;
   Pastor, Greenville District, Miss. South Central Confer-
   ence of Seventh-Day Adventist, 1962-present. U.S. Air
   Force, Jan. 18, 1952 - Aug. 17, 1956; National Defense
   Service Medal, Good Conduct Medal. Member of Green-
   ville Ministerial Association. Home: 328 South Ninth St.,
   Greenville, Miss. Office: Cateley at Belle Aire, Green-
   ville, Miss.

PEAY, Ralph Preston, b. Greensboro, N.C., Jan. 31, 1931;
   s. John Henry and Mary (Irby) P.; A.B., Oakwood College, Huntsville, Ala.; A.M., Andrews University, 1954;
   m. Erma Juanita Jackson; 1 daughter; Ralita Alene.
   Seventh-Day Adventist pastoral-evangelist since 1954;
   pastored in Alabama, Mississippi (Delta Area), Kentucky,
   Chattanooga; present: pastor, Seventh-Day Adventist Church,
   Memphis, Tennessee. President, Interdenominational Ministers Alliance in Chattanooga. Tenn.; member, Mayor's
   Committee for Desegregation of Public Schools, Chattanooga.

Tenn. Frequent contributor to the "Message Magazine".
Home: 4922 Ortie Dr., Memphis 9, Tenn. Office: 1051
Mississippi Blvd., Memphis, Tenn.

*PENN, Leon Sinkler, Sr., b. Wash., D.C., Aug. 21, 1905;
s. Robert Sinkler and Nannie B. (Austin) P.; Th.B.,
Howard Univ. Sch. of Rel., Wash., D.C., 1927; D.D.
(hon.), Kittrell Coll., Kittrell, N.C., 1959; m. Myra
Virginia Gibson; children---Leon S., Jr., Edward N.,
Nanita (Mrs. Donald G. Riddick), Joseph A., Ruth C.;
pastor, Seaton African Methodist Episcopal Church, Lin-
coln, Md., 1931-33; Petersville Circuit, A.M.E. Church,
Petersville, Md., 1933-36; Mt. Pleasant Circuit, A.M.E.,
Church, Frederick Co., Md., 1936-39; Bethel A.M.E.
Church, Chestertown, Md., 1939-44; Wright's A.M.E.
Church, Elkton, Md., 1944-45; Robinson A.M.E. Church,
Grasonville, Md., 1945-48; Bethel A.M.E. Church, Easton,
Md., 1948-49; presiding elder, Easton District, Baltimore
Conference, A.M.E. Church, 1949-52; Quinn A.M.E.
Church, Frederick, Md., 1952-53; St. Paul A.M.E.
Church, Raleigh, N.C., 1953---; vice pres., Ministerial
Alliance, Easton, Md.; vice pres., Raleigh Ministerial
Alliance; Mem., Troop Com. Boy Scouts, Easton, Md.;
Treas., Crosby-Garfield School P.T.A., Raleigh, N.C.;
Mason; former associated editor, The Allen Christian En-
deavor Quarterly (A.M.E. Church); vice pres., Raleigh
Council of Churches; Mem., Christian Social Action Com-
mittee, N.C. Council of Churches: Home: 217 East
Lenoir St., Raleigh, N.C. 27601; Office: 407 W. Edenton
St., Raleigh, N.C.

PENN, Robert Earl, b. Keystone, W.Va.; s. George and
Phoebe E. (Dickenson) P.; A.B., Clark Univ., 1938;
B.D., Gammon Theol. Sem., 1941; Th.M., Th.D., Cen-
tral Baptist Theol. Seminary; m. Lois Henrietta Neale;
children--- Barbara Jeanne, Robert Earl, Jr.; teacher,
Extension Dept., Clark Univ., 1939-40; Newton County
Public Sch., 1939-40; pastor, New Hope Baptist Ch.,
Covington, Ga.; First Baptist Church, Nacon, Ga., 1942;
US Army, 1942-46; Pleasant Green Baptist Ch., Kansas
City, Kans., 1946-52; current, First Baptist Ch., Gary,
Ind., 1952---; Mem., NAACP; Alpha Phi Alpha; pres.,
Baptist Ministers Conference; Board of School Trustees,
Gary, 1956-60; Board of Trustees, Amer. Baptist Theol.
Sem., 1956-62; Bd. of Directors, Campbell Friendship
House; Gary Neighborhood House; Advisory Bd., Gary Ur-
ban League; Mayor's Advisory Commission on Sch. Bd.

Appointments, 1964; chairman, United Negro Coll. Fund;
Man of The Year Award; Mem., Fellowship of Gary Min-
isters, Gary Conf. on Rel. & Race; Home: 537 W. 19th
Pl., Gary, Ind.; Offiee: 626 W. 21st Ave., Gary, Ind.

PEOPLES, Robert Hayes, b. Hollywood, Miss. Jan. 25,
1903; A.B., Eureka Coll.; Univ. of Chicago, 1 year;
Christian Theol. Sem., Indianapolis, Ind. 2 years; m.
Zellie M. Simpson; children--- Perle Peoples Fowler
(Mrs.); United Christian Missionary Society, 16 years;
teacher of Religion, Jarvis Christian Coll., Hawkins,
Tex., 8 years; Field Sec. for Negro Churches of Chris-
tian Church, 8 years; current pastor, Second Christian
Church, Indianapolis, Ind., 1923---; sec., Church Federa-
tion of Greater Indianapolis; vice pres., Church Federa-
tion; Home: 2700 North Capitol, Indianapolis, Inc., 46208;
Office: 2901 No. Kenwood Ave., Indianapolis, Ind. 46208.

PERRY, Harold Robert, Bishop;b. Lake Charles, La., Oct. 9,
1916; s. Frank J. and Josephine (M.) P.; Divine Word Seminary, Bay St. Louis, Miss.; St. Mary's Seminary, Techny, Ill.;
Holy Ghost Seminary, East Troy, Wis.; Ordained priest,
Roman Cath. Ch.; Pastoral work: Lafayette, La., St. Martinville, La., Mound Bayou, Miss., Broussard, La., Pine Bluff,
Ark., 1944-58; Rector, Seminary at Bay St. Louis, Miss.,
1958-63; appointed auxiliary Bishop of the New Orleans Archdiocese Oct. 1965-; Nat'l Chaplain, Knights of St. Peter Claver; Mem. Exec. Bd., Catholic Interracial Council; Home and
Office: St. Augustine Seminary, Bay St. Louis, Miss.

PERRY, Michael, church official; b. West Point, Miss.,
Feb. 27, 1909; s. Will and Lucy (Collins) P.; Rust Coll.;
Jackson State Coll.; m. Lula Tuy; children--- Lucille
Walker, Meredith P. Blanks (Albernia) Hollimon, Michael
Sr.; pastor, Srong Hill Baptist Ch.; pres., NE Miss.
State Sunday School and B.T.U. Congress; Mt. Olive
Dist. S.S. & B.T.U. Congress; principal, Southside
Elementary Sch.; instructor, Dept. of Rel. Education,
Ministerial Institute & Coll.; Trustee, M.I. & I. Coll.
& West Point Municipal Schools; Mem., Modern Math.
Club; Mason; Home: 319 Moore West Point, Miss.; Office:
Box 515 West Point, Miss.

*PERRY, Nathaniel Patrick, church official; b. New Orleans,
La., Mar. 17, 1912; s. Willie and Esther Redd (Bums);
B.A., Dillard University, 1935; B.D., Howard Univ.,
1937-40; Master Social Work, Howard Univ., 1951-52;

55-56; m. Clytie Fears; pastor, John Wesley Methodist
Ch., Washington, Pa., 1940-42; pastor, Mt. Zion Methodist Church, Silver Spring, Md., 1942-46; Exec. Sec.,
Louisiana Conf. Methodist Ch., 1946-52; Dist. Supt.,
Louisiana Conf. Methodist Church, 1952-54; pastor,
Trinity Methodist Ch., New Orleans, La., 1954-55;
pastor, Cherry Hill Methodist Ch., Baltimore, Md., 1956-
64; Social Worker State of Maryland, including 3 1/2 years
of supervisory status, 1964---; teacher and principal, West
Baton Rouge Parish, La., 1 year; teacher in Adult Education in East Baton Rouge Parish, La., 1 year; Supervisor
of Students in field work at Maryland Training School for
Boys from Howard Univ., Sch. of Social Work and Univ.
of Pa. Sch. of Social Work; Dir. of leadership training for
Washington Conference of Methodist Ch.; Participated in
survey on Social and Religious Status of Rural Negro
in Md. by Univ. of Md.; Vice pres., Cherry Hill Co-
ordinating Council, 1959-64; Mem.: Methodist Conference
on Christian Education; Academy of Certified Social Workers; National Association of Social Workers; NAACP;
YMCA; Mason; Omega Psi Phi; Several articles on Christian Ed. in Methodist periodicals; Home: 946 No. 23rd
Baton Rouge La.; Office: 544 Government St., Baton
Rouge, La. 70802.

PETERSEN, Claude Tedford, chaplain; b. St. Croix, Virgin
Islands, July 21, 1927; s. Hugh Valdemar and Petrina
(Edney) P.; B.A., Inter-American University, Puerto
Rico; B.D., Lutheran Theological Seminary, Phila., Pa.;
m. Anna Marynda Dorsey; children--- Diane Elizabeth,
Trina Marie; associate pastor, Bethany Lutheran Church,
Bronx, N.Y., 1958-61; pastor, Christ Lutheran Church,
Phila., Pa., 1961---; protestant chaplain, Phila. Gen.
Hospital, 1962---; pres. Board of Directors Christ- Beth-
lehem Community Center, 1962-63; Central District Steward-
ship Representative Eastern Pa. Synod, 1962-64; Service
during Korean Conflict as supply specialist, 1952-54; Home:
3008 W. Diamond, Phila., Pa.; Church: 3006 W. Diamond,
Phila., Pa.

*PHIFER, Solomon Crooms, b. New Bern, N.C., July 12,
1931; s. Willie and Mary (Bryce); Md. State Coll., Prin-
cess Anne, Md., 1954-56; B.A., B.D., Howard Univ.,
Wash., D.C., 1958, 1961; certificate, Council for Clinical
Training, 1961; m. Elizabeth Louise Tracy; children---
Solomon C., Jr.; asst. pastor, Antioch Baptist Church,
Cleveland, Ohio, 1962; pastor, Washington Park Baptist

Church, Seattle, Washington, 1963---; dean, Seattle Baptist Ministers Institute, Volunteer Chaplain for Seattle Council of Churches; Mem., NAACP; US Marine Corps, 1951-53; Korean Presidential Unit Citation; United Nations Campaign Medals; Three Battle Stars; Mem., Phi Beta Kappa; Kappa Delta Phi; Phi Alpha Theta; Seattle Baptist Ministers Council; contributor to: Missions Magazine; Home: 3115 East Madison St., Seattle, Wash. 98102; Office: 624 Lake Washington Blvd., Seattle, Wash. 98102.

*PHILLIP, Lee C., coll. chaplain; b. Harrison County, Texas, Sept. 15, 1902; s. Alex Phillip and Julian (Bradley) P.; B.S., Prairie View A & M Coll., 1924-28; B. D., Howard Univ., 1928-31; M.A. Rel. Ed., Howard Univ., 1939; m. Jimmie Ruth McDonald; children--- Jimmie Lee (Mrs. Poindexter), Cecelia (Mrs. Bolden); Prof. Philosophy & Ed. Prairie A & M Coll., 1932---; mem. of Ex. Comm. Nat. Assn. of Univ. and Coll. Chaplains (4 yrs); mem. Nat. Ed. Assn.; St. Teacher's Assn.; Area Council of the Southwest Y.M.C.A.; Cited by Prairie View A & M Coll. for outstanding work in public relations and human relations; Home: Box 2002 Prairie View A & M Coll., Prairie View, Texas.

PHILLIPS, Channing Emery, educator; b. Brooklyn, N.Y., Mar. 23, 1928; s. Porter W. and Dorothy (Fletcher) P.; Carnegie Institute of Technology (Art Scholarship); U. of Utah, 1945-46; A.B. Soc., Virginia Union U., 1947-50; B.D., Colgate Rochester Div. School, 1950-53; Grad. Studies, Drew Univ., 1953-55; Candidate Ph.D. New Testament, Drew U.; Teaching Ministry: Instr. N.T., Howard U., Sch. of Religion, Wash., D.C., 1956-58; Vstg. Lec. Greek, Prot. Episcopal Sem., Alex., Va., 1958; Vstg. Lec., N.T., Amer. U.Wash., D.C., 1957-58; Pastorates: Educ., Ch. of the Open Door, Brooklyn, N.Y., 1956; Interim, Plymouth Cong. Ch., Wash., D.C., 1958; Assoc., Grace Cong. Ch., N.Y., N.Y., 1958-59; Lemuel Haynes Cong. Ch., Jamaica, Long Island, N.Y., 1959-61; Current pastor: Lincoln Memorial Cong. Temple, Wash., D.C., 1961---; M. Jane Celeste Nabors, 1956; Children--- Sheilah Nahketah, Tracy Jane, Channing Durward; Mem., Natl. Assoc. Biblical Instructors, Soc. of Biblical Lit. and Exegesis, Institute of Religion, Alpha Phi Alpha, Alpha Kappa Mu Honor Society, NAACP; Ordained, Baptist Minister, 1952; Rec'd. Colgate Rochester Graduate Scholarship Tipple graduate Fellowship, Drew Univ. 1953-55; Home: 1232 Fairmont St., NW, Wash., D.C.; Office:

1701 11th St., N. W., Wash., D. C.

PHILLIPS, Ernest Blake, b. Banks, Ark., Mar. 9, 1906;
s. Joe and Mattie (Green) P.; Ideal Bible Coll. Corres-
ponding, 1937; D. D. (hon.), Natchez Coll., Natchez,
Miss., 1950; Courses: John W. Wilkerson Bapt. Institute,
St. Louis, Mo., 1930-34; m. Cortie Golden Timms;
children---Lorenza, Steve; pastor, Pleasant Land Bapt.
Ch., 1934-41; St. Louis, Mo.; St. Paul Bapt. Ch., Terre
Haute Indiana, 1941-53; current pastor, The Greater Gali-
lee Bapt. Ch., Milwaukee, Wisconsin, 1953---; vice pres.,
General Bapt. State Conv., Wisconsin; pres., Baptist
Ministers Conference; chairman, Public Relations Com.,
Interdenominational Ministers Conference; chairman,
Greater Milwaukee, Council of Churches Evangelistic
Com.; Mem., NAACP; Urban League; North Town, Com-
munity Organization; Near Northside Non-Partisan Confer-
ence "Young Men's" Christian Assn; Home: 628 W. Wright
St., Milwaukee, Wisconsin, 53212; Office: 2432 N. Teu-
tonis, Milwaukee, Wisconsin. 53212.

PHILLIPS, Porter William, Jr., b. Washington, D. C.,
May 24, 1925; s. Porter W. Sr., and Dorothy (Fletcher),
P.; A. B., Soc., Virginia Union U., 1949; B. D., Union
Theol. Sem., N. Y., 1952; M. Dorothy Bobo, 1950; chil-
dren: Stephanie Laverne, Adrienne Lorraine, Claudia
Leslie, Dorothy LaNell; Pastor, Humboldt Parkway Baptist
Ch., Buffalo, N. Y., 1953---; Pres. Bapt. Ministers Conf.
Buffalo and Vicinity; Pres., Council of Churches of Buffalo
and Erie County; Mem. Citizens Council of Human Rela-
tions, Psychiatric Clinic of Buffalo, Hickory Street Chris-
tian Center, Buffalo Bapt. Assoc.; Office: 794 Humboldt
Pkwy., Buffalo 11, N. Y.

PHILLIPS, Porter William, Sr., b. Little Richmond, N. C.,
Oct. 7, 1897; s. John Emery and Mollie Belle (Davis) P.
Slater State Normal; A. B., Virginia Union Univ.; M. A.
Columbia Univ.; B. D., Union Theol. Sem.; D. D. (honor-
ary), Virginia Union University; m. Dorothy Anne Fletcher,
1924; children: Marie Belle Cary, Treadwell Oliver,
Wendell Harrison, Fletcher Allison, Porter William, Jr.,
Channing Emery; Pastorates: Trinity Baptist Church, New-
port News, Va., Brown Memorial Church, Brooklyn, N. Y.,
Carrone Baptist Church, Pittsburgh, Pa., 1938---; Dean,
Fort Greene Teachers Training Sch., Brooklyn; Chrmn.,
Comm. of Labor and Management, Natl Bapt. Conv. of
Amer., Inc., Mem. Exec. Bd., YMCA and NAACP; Pres.,

Homewood Brushton Council of Churches; Mem. Executive
Bd., Allegheny Union Association and Pa. Bapt. State
Conv.; "Father of the Year" Award, 1958 Pittsburgh
Courier; Home: 312 Lowell St., Pittsburgh, Pa. Office:
7119 Frankstoun Ave., Pittsburgh, Pa.

PHILLIPS, Wendell Harrison, b. Brooklyn, N.Y., Nov.
19, 1934; s. Porter Wm., Sr. and Dorothy (Fletcher) P.;
Pa. State Univ., B.S., Virginia Union U., 1956; Howard
U. Grad. Sch. (Physiology); B.D., Colgate Rochester
Divinity School, 1961; Univ. of Rochester Grad. School.
m. Dorothy Harris. Pastor, Second Baptist Church, Mum-
ford, N.Y.; Mem. Exec. Bd., Rochester NAACP; Mem.
Social Action Comm., Monroe Bapt. Assoc., Mem. Alpha
Phi Alpha Fraternity; Home: 937 George St., Mumford,
N.Y.

PIERCE, Isaiah Benjamin, presiding elder; b. Winfall, N.C.,
Sept. 28, 1907; s. William Dallas and Annabelle (White)
P.; B.A., Knoxville College, 1932; S.T.B., Pittsburgh
Theological Sem., 1935; M.Th., 1947-49; M. Ed., Uni-
versity of Pittsburgh; advance work toward Ph.D., 1950;
D.D., Livingstone College, 1957; m. Carrie Bedgette;
children--- Isaiah B., Jr., Jane Carolyn Cook, William
D. II; A.M.E. Zion Church (Presiding Elder), Mason,
Borough Park Comm., Sewickley, Pennsylvania; chaplain
U.S.A.R., 1951---; served W.W. II in Europe and Africa,
rec'd Bronze Star Medal, w/4 battle stars; Lt. Col., U.S.
A.R. Chaplain Corps; Author: My Church Believes,
booklet, 1956; Worship in the A.M.E. Zion Church,
1946, revised 1954; life's work with A.M.E. Zion Church;
presiding elder, 10 yrs.; pastor, Knoxville, Tenn.; Pitts-
burgh, Pennsylvania; Uniontown, Pa.; Sunbury, N.C.;
Newport News, Virginia; Youngstown, Ohio; Sewickley,
Pennsylvania; At present, pastor of Jones Tabernacle A.
M.E. Zion Church, Indianapolis, Indiana, 1960---; Host
to the 37th Quadrennial General Conference A.M.E. Zion
Church May 6020, 1964; Member, the General Board Na-
tional Council of Churches, also Religious & Race; author:
Ushers In Our Church, 1960;   Why We Worship as We
Do,   1962; President of the Interdenominational Ministers
Alliance of Greater Indianapolis and Vicinity, 1964-65;
Home: 135 W. 43rd St., Indianapolis 8, Inc.; Office:
440 N. Blackford, Indianapolis 4, Ind.

PINDER, Nelson Wardell, b. Miami, Fla., July 27, 1932;

s. Geo. L. and Colleen (Saunders) P.; Bethune-Cookman
Coll., Daytona Beach, Fla., 1956; Nashotah House Sem.,
Nashotah, Wis.; m. Marian E. Grant; children--- Gail
Yvonne; current pastor, The Episcopal Church of St. John
the Baptist, Orlando, Fla., 1959---; state officer, Fla.
Congress of Parents and Teachers Assn, 1961-62; US
Army, 1953-55; Home: 438 Cottage Hill Rd., Orlando,
Fla.; Church: 1000 Bethune Drive, Orlando, Fla.

*PITTS, W. Lyndsai, b. Essex Co., Va., Oct. 18, 1912;
s. William Albert and Lettie (Washington) P.; B.S.,
Howard Univ., 1945; B.D., 1951; M.A., 1957; Coll. of
Divine Metaphysics, 1959; Doctor of Psychology; Yale
Univ., 1959; Northwestern Coll., 1959; D.D. (hon.); m.
Annie B. Cain; children--- Brenda L.; W. Lyndsai Pitts,
Jr.; asst. pastor, Mt. Lebanon Baptist Church, 1940-46;
asst. pastor, Metropolitan Baptist Church, 1946-47;
Minister-in-charge, First Mt. Calvary Baptist Church,
1947-48; pastor, First Mt. Calvary Baptist Church, Balto.,
Md., 1948---; teacher, Md. Baptist Center, 1953-56;
professor, Mt. Royal Coll., Balto., Md.; lecturer, Coppin
State Coll.; Mem., Phi Beta Sigma; Big Brothers of Balti-
more; Interdenominational Ministerial Alliance; Baptist
Ministers Conference; YMCA; Baltimore Area Council of
Alcoholism; Howard and Yale Univs. Alumni Assn; Home:
2916 Auchentoroly Terrace, West, Balto., Md. 21217;
Office: 1142 N. Fullton Ave., Balto. 21217, Md.

POGUE, King David Solomon, chaplain; b. Sumter, South
Carolina, Aug. 21, 1912; s. Solomon and Mary Elizabeth
(Pearson) P.; 1930-34; A.B. and 1934-37, B.D. Johnson
C. Smith University; 1959, D.D. Burton Theological
Seminary; m. Ruby Louise (Mitchell) P.; children---
David Eugene; Pastor, 1937-41, Salem United Presbyter-
ian Church, Anderson, S.C.; 1946-48, Sargeant Memorial
Presbyterian Church, Washington, D.C.; Chaplain, 1941-
45, Lieutenant Colonel, U.S. Army; 1958-1963; Veterans
Administration Hospital, Tuskegee, Alabama; mem. 1958-
63 Advisory Board of YMCA-YWCA, Tuskegee Institute,
Alabama; 1958, served as Consultant for establishing De-
nominational Chaplaincy at The John A. Andrew Hospital
of Tuskegee Institute; mili. rec., 1941-43 Regimental
Chaplain, 99th CA(AA) U.S. and Overseas; 1944-45, Regimental Chaplain, 27th Troop, 2D Calvary Division; 1944-
45, Regimental Chaplain, 371st Infantry, 92D Infantry
Division U.S. and Overseas; Awards: Mediterranean Battle
Stars and Commendation for Italian Campaign; mem. The

Academy of Religion and Mental Health; Omega Psi Phi;
Tuskegee Civic Association; Home: 121 Colvert Street,
Tuskegee Institute, Alabama; Office: Veterans Administra-
tion Hospital, Tuskegee, Alabama.

POLK, Robert Lawrence, b. Chicago, Ill., May, 1928; s.
Tillman and Lilly (Bell) P.; Wilson Junior College, Chgo.,
Ill.; B.A., Doane College, Crete, Neb.; B.D., Hartford
Theol. Sem.; Pastor, Berthold Cong. Ch., Berthold, N.
D., 1955-57; Youth Work Sec., YMCA, Minot, N.D.,
1957-60; Minister to Youth, The Riverside Church, New
York City, 1960---; Office: 490 Riverside Drive, N.Y.
27, N.Y.

POLLAR, Alfred, b. New Orleans, La., Oct. 1, 1927; s.
Henry and Isabell (Russell) P.; A.B., Clark Coll., 1949;
B.D., Gammon Theol. Seminary, 1955; m. Barbara Lee
Walker; children--- Alfred, Jr.; Columbus Charge, 1958-
59; Commerce-Lawrenceville Charge, 1959-63; pastor,
Palen Methodist Ch., Savannah, Ga., 1963---; Mem.,
Board of Frank Callen Boy's Club; US Army, 1952;
Mem., Alpha Phi Alpha; Home: 1907 Burroughs S.,
Savannah, Ga., 31401; Office: Palen Methodist Church,
601 W. 35th St., Savannah, Ga. 31401.

POOLE, John Douglas, b. Greensville, S.C., May 25, 1927;
s. Theodore T. Morehead and Emily E. Morehead; Lutheran Junior College, 1946-48; Immanuel Seminary, 1948-52;
m. Myrtice Hicks; pastor, St. James Lutheran Church,
Southern Pines, N.C., 1951-52; pastor, Mt. Calvary
Lutheran Church, Kannapolis, N.C., 1952-53; pastor, Mt.
Marks Lutheran Church, Atlanta, Ga., 1953-59; pastor,
St. John's Lutheran Church, Salisbury, N.C., 1959---;
chairman, Program Committee of N.C. Sunday School
Convention, N.C.; contact pastor, The Stewardship De-
partment for Churches in this circuit; Member, the Luther-
an Human Relation of America; Member, Rowan County
Civic League; Home: 623 W. Horah St., Salisburg, N.C.;
Ch.: Cor. S. West & W. Innes Sts., Salisbury, N.C.

PORTER, Herman Anthon, b. Chicago, Illinois, Feb. 8, 1917;
s. Shirley and Ellen (Moreland) P.; Loyola Univ., 1941;
B.A., Sacred Heart Monastery, 1947; M.A., U. of Notre
Dame, 1952; Dean of Studies, Divine Heart Sem., Donald-
son, Ind., 1952-60; Asst. Pastor, Sacred Heart Ch.,
Sterling, Ill., 1960-63; Dir., Cath. Info. and Counseling
Ctr., Chaplain, Cath. Interracial Council, Rockford, Ill.,

1963---; Author, 25 article series on the Catholic Church
and the Negro, The Steubenville Register, Steubenville,
Ohio, 1964; Home and Office: Catholic Information and
Counseling Center, 1722 Chestnut St., Rockford, Ill.

PORTER, Richard Sylvester, teacher; b. Gloster, Miss.,
June 9, 1923; s. Ishop and Bertha (Lusk) P.; Amite
County Training School; A.B., Leland Bapt. Coll., Baker,
La., 1949-53; m. Annie Mae Matthews; children--- Louise,
Dorothy, James, Shirley, Richard, Linda, Patricia, Eric,
Laura, Lawrence; pastor, First Bapt. Ch., Gloster, Miss.,
1949-53; Owens Chapel Bapt. Ch., Columbia, Miss.,
1953-59; First Union Bapt. Ch., Meridian, Miss., 1959--;
teacher, Public School System of Miss., 1953-57; dean,
Harper Bapt. Sem., Magnolia, Miss., 1957-59; Associate
Bd. Men., Leland Bapt. Coll., 1953-1955; Bd. of Trustees,
Meridian Bapt. Sem.; 1st vice pres., East Miss. Bapt.
State Conv.; organizer and pres., Meridian and Lauderdale
County Human Rights Assn; Council of Federated Organiza-
tion; Veteran of World War II, European Theatre of Opera-
tion; Bronze Stars; Mem., National Bapt. Conv., U.S.A.,
Inc.; 2nd New Hope Consolidated Bapt. Assn; Leland Coll.
Alumni Assn; NAACP; Mason; Home: 602 39th Ave., Mer-
idian, Miss.; Office: 610 38th Ave., Meridian, Miss.

POTTER, William Abraham, teacher; b. Demopolis, Alabama,
April 18, 1916; s. William A., Sr. and Mary G.P.; B.S.,
Alabama State College, 1938- ; B.D., Gammon Theologi-
cal Seminary, 1948; Courses: Oberlin College, Oberlin,
Ohio; m. Sadye Mae Watson; children--- Savannah, Sadye;
principal, Jr. High School, Tuscaloosa, Ala., 1932-40;
Field Scout Executive-Boy Scouts of Alabama, 1940-42;
minister, North Alabama Conference; teacher, Caner Vo-
cational School, 1946-63; pastor, Shaw Tenyle A.M.E.
Zion Church, Atlanta; Ga., 1951--; asst. chaplain, Grady
Hospital, Atlanta, Ga., 1958-64; pres., Atlanta Minister-
ial Alliance; Mem., Executive Board, Ga. Council of
Churches; Mem., Operation Bread Basket, Atlanta, Ga.;
Member, Civic Liberties Association; chaplain's assistant
in US Forces; Mem.: Elks, Mason, Phi Beta Sigma,
YMCA; Member, General Conference A.M.E. Zion Church,
Home: 38 Hightown Rd. NW, Atlanta 11, Ga.

POULARD, Grady Emory, b. Crowley, La., Aug. 15, 1936;
s. Grady E., Sr. and Leola (Green) P.; Temple Univ.,
Phila., Pa., 1953-54; A.B. Southern Univ., Baton Rouge,
La., 1957; B.D., Yale Univ., 1960; Courses on Ph.D.,

Columbia Univ., New York; m. Marguerite Marie Brown;
children--- Michael; pastor, Second Bapt. Church, Greenfield, Mass.; interim minister, Dixwell Ave. Congr'l
Ch., New Haven, Conn.; Migrant chaplain, Pa.Council of
Churches; camp counselor, Camp Cononicus, Worwick,
Rhode Island; associate minister, Concord Bapt. Ch.,
Brooklyn, New York; field representative, National Student
Christian Federation, Commission on World Mission; visiting traveling field sec., World Student Christian Federa-
tion, Europe and the Middle East; chaplain, Christian Med-
ical Coll., Vellore, South India; field sec., National Coun-
cil of Churches, Commission on Religion and Race; current
pastor, People's Congregational Ch., Washington, D.C.;
Awards from: Who's Who Among Students in American
Coll. and Univ.; "Debater of the Year", Southwest Forensic Conference; Award of Merit for role as Student Body
President, Southern Univ.; Mem., Alpha Phi Alpha;
Home: 6005 Eastern Ave., Hyattsville, Md.; Office: 4704
13th St. NW, Washington. 11, D.C.

POWELL, Adam Clayton, Jr., congressman, author; b. New
Haven, Conn., Nov. 29, 1908; s. Adam Clayton and
Mattie Fletcher (Schafer) P.; A.B., Colgate U., 1930;
M.A., Columbia U., 1932; D.D., Shaw U., 1935; LL.D.,
Va. Union U., 1947; m. Isabel Geraldine; Washington,
Mar. 8, 1933 (separated Nov. 1944); married 2d, Hazel
Scott, Aug. 1945 (divorced); one son, Adam Clayton III;
married 3d, Yvette Diago. Minister, Abyssinian Baptist
Ch., 1937-60; elected to City Council of New York, 1941;
founder People's Voice, editor in chief, co-publisher,
1942; elected to Congress Nov. 1945; mem. 79th-87th
Congress from New York 16th District, chairman com.
on education and labor. Del. Parliamentary World Govt.
Conf., London, 1951-52, Int. Labor Organization Conf., Geneva, Switzerland, 1961. Decorated Knight of the Golden
Cross, Ethiopia, 1954, Mem. World Assn. Parliamentarians
on World Govt. (v.p.) Author: Is This a White Man's War?
1942; Stage Door Canteen, 1944; Marching Blacks, 1945,
Adam Clayton Powell, 1960. Office: U.S. House of Representatives, Wash. D.C.

POWELL, John Lewis, b. McKeesport, Pa., Nov. 2, 1902;
s. John and Rachel (Deering) P.; A.B., Johnson C.
Smith Univ., 1931; B.D., 1934; M. Ed., Univ. Of Pittsburgh, 1947; D.D. (hon.), Johnson C. Smith Univ., 1956;
m. Ruth Marie Davidson; pastor, Friendship Baptist Ch.,
Charlotte, N.C., 1932-47; teacher, Social Sciences, Unity

High School, Statesville, N.C., 1944-47; professor, Chris-
tian Education, Church History, Dean of Students, Amer-
ican Theol. Sem., Nashville, Tenn., 1947---; pastor,
Progressive Baptist Ch., Nashville, Tenn., 1950---;
director, Extension Classes of Amer. Bapt. Theol. Sem.,
Nashville, Tenn.; Board of Directors, South St. Community
Center, 1950-58; Bd. of Director, Bethlehem Community
Center, 1958---; pres., Nashville Ministers Conference;
Mem., NAACP; NCLC; Democratic League of Voters; Na-
tional Ass'n of Coll. Deans & Registrars; Alpha Phi Alpha;
Mason; Home: 611 Young's Lane, Nashville 7, Tenn.;
Church: 1419 12th Ave., South, Nashville 8, Tenn.

POWELL, Robert Bernard, sem. prof.; b. Petersburg, Va.
Nov. 2, 1894; s. Henry William and Hattie Rebecca
(Valentine) P.; A.B., Virginia Union Univ., 1923; B.D.,
Oberlin Graduate Sch. of Theology, 1926; D.D. (hon.),
Simmons Univ., 1948; m. Maggie Webster Winstead; chil-
dren--- Clara Margaret (Mrs. Willie B. Satterfield),
Elfrida Roberta (Mrs. John Henry Scott, Jr.), Gloria
Violet (Mrs. Norman M. Winsmore, Jr.), Chrystal Gar-
rell (Mrs. Chrystal Powell Tibbs); pastor, Mt. Zion
Baptist Ch., Oberlin, Ohio, 1924-26; Shiloh Baptist Ch.,
Southold, L.I., NY, 1927-28; Ebeneza Bapt. Ch., Williams-
port, Pa., 1928-38; Macedonia Bapt. Ch., Wheeling, W.
Va., 1938-42; chaplain, US Army, 1942-46; professor,
Bible and English, Lynchburg Sem. and Coll., Va.,
1947-48; director, Negro and Interracial Work, W. Va.
Baptist Convention, 1948-61; Serve as Interim Pastor
where needed; director, Christian Education for West Va.
Baptist State Convention and the Mt. Zion Dist. Baptist
Convention, 1948---; Mem., Bd. of Directors Planned
Parenthood Ass'n; Brotherhood Activities Committee;
Governor's Human Rights Commission, 1963; Alpha Phi
Alpha; Masons; American Legion; Home: 1325 Oak St.,
Parkersburg, W. Va.

POWELL, Robert Meaker, b. Cumberland, Md., April 23,
1930; s. William Edward and Edna (Williams) P.; A.B.,
Morgan State Coll., Baltimore, Md., 1954; B.D., Vir-
ginia Protestant Episcopal Theol. Sem., Alexandria, Va.,
1957; vicar-in-charge, Holy Trinity Episcopal Church,
Baltimore, 1957-58; General Diocesan Missionary, Diocese
of Maryland, 1958-63; Exec. Director, Lafayette Square
Community Center, Baltimore, 1958-63; asst. priest, St.
James Episcopal Church, Balto., associate priest, St.
James' Episcopal Church, Baltimore, 1958---; Mem.;

Maryland Commission on Interracial Problems and Relations; Christian Social Relations Commission of the Diocese of Md.; Citizen's Planning and Housing Ass'n; Harlem Park Urban Renewal Exec. Council; Volunteer Consulting Staff at Rosewood State Training School; Md. Council of Churches; Bd. of Directors, Lafayette Square Community Center; Citation by the Balto. Junior Ass'n of Commerce for its Distinguished Service Award, 1961; Citation by the Baltimore Afro-American News; Home: 827 North Arlington Ave., Baltimore 17, Md.; Office: St. James' Episcopal Church, 827 North Arlington Ave., Balto. 17, Md.

POWELL, W. J., b. Montgomery County, Alabama, Nov. 2, 1908; s. Joseph and Bertha (Lee) P.; A.B., Livingstone College, Salisbury, N.C., 1947; B.D., Hood Seminary, 1950, Salisbury, N.C., 1950; m. Bessie Ford; Worked as common laborer during high school days with the American Cast Iron Pipe Shop of Birmingham, Ala., 1925-27; Served as YMCA Secretary in Birmingham after graduation from Industrial High School, 1927-42; Began preaching, 1942; pastor, Birmingham, Ala., Cheeryville, N.C., Charlotte, N.C., Salisbury, N.C., Montgomery, Ala.; eurrent pastor, African Methodist Episcopal Church, Montgomery, Alabama; One of the organizers of Montgomery Improvement Association. Served as secretary, 1st Vice President, Chairman of Program Committee, etc.; Served as President Montgomery Emancipation Committee; Board member branch YMCA; Member, Local Bi-Racial Comm.; Sec. Board of Trustees, Lomax-Hannon College, Greenville, Ala.; Home: 120 Mildred St., Montgomery 36104 Alabama; Office: Holcombe St., Montgomery 36104, Alabama.

PRESSLEY, Calvin Oliver, b. New York, Nov. 10, 1937; s. George W. and Pansy C. P.; B.A., Drake Univ., 1959; B.D., Drew Univ., 1962; m. Iona Adams; pastor, Metropolitan Community, The Meth. Ch., 1961-62; Church of The Open Door, 1963---; New York City Board of Education, Local School Bd., 1925-1927; Lay Advisory Bd. Cumberland Hospital, Brooklyn; Community School Zoning Committee, Faregist-Hights; Mem., Chi Iota Phi; Home: 175 Willowby St., Brooklyn, New York; Office: 201 Gold St., Brooklyn 1, New York

PRICE, Alonzo, b. Pittsburgh, Penna., May 1, 1933; s. Alonzo and Bessie (Shannon); B.A., San Francisco State College, 1954-58; B.D., Church Divinity School of the

Pacific, 1958-61; Youth director, St. Johns Episcopal
Church, San Francisco, 1961; Missionary, Diocese of
Alaska, 1962; Asst. rector, St. James Episcopal, San
Francisco, 1962; present, deputy organist & asst. minis-
ter, Grace Cathedral, San Francisco, 1963---; US Air
Force, 1949-53; Member, Phi Mu Alpha-Musical Frater-
nity; Home: 625 Scott-Apt. 301, San Francisco 15, Calif.;
Office: 1051 Taylor, San Francisco, Calif.

PRIMES, Joseph Ronald, b. Akron, Ohio, Sept. 11, 1926;
s. George Walter, Sr., and Annabelle (Holsey) P.; Kent
State Univ., 1948; A.B., Claflin Univ., 1955; B.D.,
Gammon Theo. Seminary, 1958; m. Minerva Hollaway;
children--- Joseph Ronald, Jr.; pastor, Haven Methodist
Church, Dadeville, Ala., 1956; Richards Chapel Meth.
Church, Troy, Ohio, 1958; Cory Meth. Church, Cleveland,
Ohio, 1960; pastor, St. Paul Meth. Church, Cleveland,
Ohio, 1961---; Mem., Phi Beta Sigma; Home: 16408 Tel-
fair Ave., Cleveland 28, Ohio; Office: 4720 Lee Rd.,
Cleveland 28, Ohio.

PRIMM, Howard Thomas, bishop; b. Brentwood, Tenn.,
June 23, 1903; s. Zack and Addie (Curtis) P.; A.B.,
Wilberforce Univ. (Ohio), 1924; B.D., Payne Theol.
Sem., 1927; D.D. (hon.), Wilberforce Univ., 1940; LL.
D. (hon.), Edward Waters Coll., 1944; m. Edythe Mary
Hailey; children--- Rita Mae; pastor, Trinity African
Methodist Episcopal Church, 1926-28; Gilchrist A.M.E.
Church, Memphis, 1928-29; Allen A.M.E. Church, Mem-
phis, 1929-31; Bethel A.M.E. Church, Alexanda, La.,
1931-32; St. Peter A.M.E. Church, Port Gibson, Miss.,
1932-33; Union A.M.E. Church, Arkansas, 1933-35;
Visitors' Chapel A.M.E. Church, Arkansas, 1935-41;
Union Bethel A.M.E. Church, New Orleans, 1941---;
Elected bishop, 1952; currently serving the 5th Episcopal
Dist.; Organized the Sarah Allen Child Welfare Station,
New Orleans, 1942; Sunday School Board, 1930; Book Con-
cern, 1940; Trustee of Shorter Coll., 1936-39; Campbell
Coll., 1939---; pres., General Board of the A.M.E.
Church, 1962-64; Secy. Council of Bishops, 1963; pres.,
Council of Bishops, 1964; Builder of Denomination's First
Home for Senior Citizens Kansas City, Kansas, 1964;
chairman, Minimum Salary Commission A.M.E. Church;
Mason; NAACP, Urban League; delegate, World Confer-
ence of Christian Youth, Amsterdam, Holland, 1939;
Mem., Omega Psi Phi; Home: 1724 Villa Place, Nash-
ville, Tenn.

PRITCHETT, Clayton Robinson, b. Felton, Delaware, Apr.
20, 1927; s. Alvin and Annie (Harris) P.; B.A., Oak-
wood College, 1949; m. Jessie Vivinee Raymond; chil-
dren-- Jerald David, Cherrie Elaine, Steven Lloyd.
Teacher-Pastor, Southwest Region Conf. of Seventh-Day
Adventists serving in private schools in Houston and Dal-
las, Texas, 1949-52; teacher, denominational schools in
Pasadena and Los Angeles, 1952-54; present: pastor, Santa
Monica and Monrovia, 1954-   ; member, Prohibitionist
Political Party. Home: 144 E. Evergreen St., Monrovia,
Calif. Office: 1003 So. Ivy Ave., Monrovia, Calif.

PROCTOR, Samuel Dewitt, coll. pres., church official, govt.
official; b. Norfolk, Va., July 13, 1921; s. Herbert Q. and
Velma G. P.; Va. State Coll., Petersburg, Va., 1937-39;
United States Naval Apprentice School, 1939-40; A.B., Va.
Union Univ., 1940-42; B.D., Crozer Theol. Sem., 1945;
Univ., of Pa., Graduate, 1944-45;Graduate Sch., Yale Univ.,
1945-46;Th. D., Boston Univ., 1950; pastor, Pone Street Bapt.
Church, Providence, Rhode Island, 1945-49; professor, Va.
Union Univ., 1949-50; dean, Sch. of Rel., Va. Union Univ.,
1950-55; vice pres., Va. Union Univ., 1953-55; Va. Union
Univ., 1955-60; pres., A.T. Coll. of N.C., 1960-61; Peace
Corps Representative to Nigeria, 1962; associate director,
Peace Corps, 1963---; Assoc. Gen. Sec. for Communication
Nat. Coun. Chs. 1964-; Mem., Exec. Bd., Southern Regional
Council; General Bd. of National Council of Churches; Na-
tional Committee 1960 White House Conference of Children
and Youth; Commission on Liberal Education of the Assn. of
American Coll.; Sigma Pi Phi; Kappa Alpha Psi; Outstanding
Alumnus Award, Sch. of Theology, Boston Univ.; Mem., Bd.
of Trustees, Crozer Theol. Sem.; Bd. of Managers, Amer.
Bapt. Bd. of Education and Publication; 1965 elected v.p.
Amer. Bapt. Conv.; Office: 457 Riverside Drive, N.Y. 27, N.Y.

PUGH, Alfred Lane, b. Pleasantville, N.J., May 31, 1927;
s. Wilfred B. and Mamie P.; A.B., Lincoln Univ., 1944-
48; B.D., Theol. Sem., Lincoln Univ., Pa., 1948-51;
Rutgers Univ., N.J.; m. Cleora; children---Kevin,
Karen; pastor, Mt. Ararat Baptist Ch., Rutherford, N.J.,
1951-56; Second Baptist Ch., Asbury Park, N.J., 1956--;
pres., Asbury Park, Shore Area Branch, NAACP, 1957-
60; Home: 158 Fisher Ave., Neptune, N.J.; Office: 120
Atkins Ave., Asbury Park, N.J.

PUGH, Thomas Jefferson, sem. prof.; b. Lewiston, N.C.

Oct. 25, 1917; s. John David and Otebia (Parker)P.;
A.B., Clark Coll., 1940; B.D., Gammon Theol. Sem.,
1942; M.A., Atlanta Univ., Ga., 1947; Drew Univ.,
1948; Ph.D., Boston Univ., 1955; m. Lillian Ruth Raper;
children--- John Raper; director, Rel. Education to Migrants, Jas. Andrew Farm, Hurlook, Md., 1942; principal, Dickens County Jr. School, Tate, Ga., 1942-44;
pastor, Bethesda Baptist Ch., Americus, Ga., 1943-45;
teacher, Bryant Theol. Sem., 1944-47; chaplain, Albany
State Coll., Ga.; 1948-58; current associate prof. and
pastor, Interdenominational Theol. Center, Atlanta, Ga.,
1958---; consultant, Human Relations, Miles Coll., 1960;
Worship Leader to worship in Secondary Education for the
Philip States Fund, 1960; consultant, Pastoral Counseling
to In-service Ministers, Christian Methodist Episcopal
Church, 1961; counselor, Alcoholics Helping Hand Society,
Atlanta, Ga.; Mem., Alpha Phi Alpha; International Theo-
logical Scholastic Society; The Academy of Religion &
Mental Health; The National Society for the Scientific Study
of Religion; The American Psychological Ass'n; American
Ass'n of Univ. Professors; Home: 2806 Engle Rd. NW,
Atlanta, Ga. 30318; Office: 671 Beckwith St., Atlanta,
Ga. 30314.

RAND, David George, b. Indianapolis, Indiana, Jan. 26,
1930; s. Frank and Helen (Ubanks) R.; A.B. Emmanuel
Missionary Coll., 1957; M.A., Andrews University,
1959; m. Martha Nola Wideman; principal, Church School
and Asst. Pastor, Seventh-Day Adventist Church, Gary,
Indiana, 1959-61; present: pastor, Battle Creek, Jackson
and Kalamazoo, Michigan Seventh-Day Adventist Churches,
1961- ; U.S. Army, 1951-53; Home: 320 N. Washington
Ave., Battle Creek, Michigan 49017. Office: 420 W. Van
Buren, Battle Creek, Michigan.

RANDALL, Eugene, b. New Orleans, Louisiana, Nov. 19,
1927; s. Wilson and Calvie (Haughton)R.; 1949, B.S.
Tuskegee Institute, (Ala.) 1963, B.D. Johnson C. Smith
University, Charlotte, N.C.; m. Helen Juanita (Rudisell)
R.; Supply Minister, 1963, Ebenezer Presbyterian Church,
Morven, N.C.; Greenstreet Presbyterian Church, Morganton, N.C., 1963---; Relocation Director, Charlotte, Redevelopment Commission; Secretary of Executive Board,
Charlotte, NAACP; Organized the Brooklyn Day Care Center in Charlotte for deprived children; 1955-
56, Corporal, U.S. Army Second Armored Division,

48th Medical Battalion (Germany); Home: 1900 Aileen Dr.,
Charlotte, N.C.

RANGE, King Solomon, business man; b. Lexington, Miss.,
April 3, 1893; s. Ambrose M. and Dycie (Archer) R.;
Henderson Business Coll., Memphis, Tenn., 1915-17;
Moody's Bible Institute, Chgo., Ill., 1923-25; m. Mar-
guerite Washington; children--- Margueritte Range Chap-
man, Warren C. Chapman, Dycolene Range Bland, Oscar
Bland, Thelma Range Smith, Chester Smith; asst. pastor,
Olivet Bapt. Ch., Chgo., Ill., 1936-39; organizer and
founder, Range Memorial Baptist Ch., 1949, Chgo., Ill.;
founder, King S. Range Real Estate Co., 1929; founder,
Ill. Federal Savings Loan Co., Chgo., Ill.; Mem., Bapt.
Ministers Conference; Pastors Conference of Chicago &
Vicinity; Chaplin, Frederick Douglas Republican League;
2nd & 6th Wards Republican Organization; US Army,
1918-19; Mem., Elk; Mason; publisher, First Negro Greet-
ings Cards; Home: 1318 72nd St., Chgo. 53, Ill.; Office:
3808 Indiana, Chgo. 15, Ill.

RANSOME, William Lee, sem. prof.; b. Nottoway Co., Va.
Mar. 7, 1879; s. George W. and Lucy (Fowelks) R.;
A.B., Va. Union Univ.; M.A., Va. Union Univ.; B.D.,
LL.B, D.D. (hon.), Va. Union Univ.; Th.M., Union
Theological Sem., Richmond, Va.; m. Mary E. Wingfield,
Mary M. Cobb; children--- Esther (Mrs. Miller), Clarence,
(Mrs. Miller), George W., Mary E., J. Rodman; pastor,
Shiloh Baptist Ch., Fredericksburg, Va.; teacher, Freder-
icksburg High Sch., 1906-20; pastor, First Bapt. Ch.,
So. Richmond, Va., 1920---; teacher in Va. Univ., 22
years; pastor, White Rock Bapt. Ch., Durham, N.C.
(one year); pres., NAACP, Richmond; founder, Richmond
Civic Council Candidate for Richmond City Council; Va.
State Legislature; (former) Grand Master Prince Hall
Grand Lodge of Masons; present, editor and founder of
Masonic Organ the "Bee Hive;" pres., Baptist General
Assn, 7 years; chmn, Lott Carey Bapt. Foreign Mission
Society; Ed. Bd., Nat. Bapt. Convention; co-organizer and
sec., Goodwill Bapt. Conv., Va.; Mem., Phi Beta Sigma;
author: Stewardship and Negro Baptists; "Old Story for
This New Day", Central Publishing Co., 1954; Home: 1507
Decatur St., Richmond, Va. 23224; Office, 1501 Decatur
St., So. Richmond, Va.

*RASBERRY, Hosea, b. Idabel, Oklahoma, April 17, 1914;

s. Richard and Currie (Moore) R.; A.B., Clark College,
Atlanta, Georgia, 1942; B.D., Howard University, School
of Religion, 1945; m. Ozella Smith; children--- Richard;
pastor, Milton Congregational Christian Church, Milton,
Delaware, 1942-44; pastor, Graham Congregational Christian Church, Beaumont, Texas, 1945-47; Pioneer Presbyterian Church, Beaumont, Texas, 1947---; organized in
1950 as the second Negro Presbyterian Church, U.S. of
the state of Texas. 1956 delegate General Assembly of
the Presbyterian Church, UU.S., representing the Synod
of Texas, have served on various committees on the
Presbytery and Synod level. (Committee of Christian Education and Printed minutes); teacher of school, 1947-49,
1950-63 served as counselor or director of summer camp,
Camp Cho Yeh, Livingston, Texas; Volunteer worker for
the United Appeals, 1960-62; Institutional representative
for the Boy Scouts - Trinity Neches Council of the Boy
Scouts of America, 1959; Chairman of Board of the Beaumont Council of Campfire Girls of Beaumont, Texas, member of the Beaumont Minister's Association; Member of
the Minister's Discussion Group-This Group has contributed much in the smooth integration of many of the public
facilities of the public facilities of the city (public parks
and swimming pools, theatres, clerks in the department
stores, etc.) Mem.: Alpha Phi Alpha; Y.M.C.A.; Minister's Association of Beaumont; Minister's Discussion
Group; Home: 2480 Houston, Beaumont, Texas; Office:
3520 Pine St., Beaumont, Texas.

*REDD, Albert Carter, b. Columbia, S.C., March 13, 1917;
s. Curtis and Polly (Carter) R.; A.B., Benedict Coll.,
1948; B.D., Howard Univ. Sch. of Rel., 1951; m.
Georgia Geneva Harrison; children--- Althea Brenda,
Albert Carter Jr.; exec. sec., South Conference NAACP,
1951-54; pastor, Trinity Christian Methodist Episcopal
Church, Columbia, S.C., 1954-55; St. James C.M.E.
Ch., Winter, Haven, 1955-56; St. James C.M.E. Ch.,
Tallahassee, Fla., 1955-56; William Temple C.M.E.
Church, Winter, Haven, Fla., 1956-57; Turner Chapel
C.M.E. Ch., 1957-60; Womack Temple C.M.E. Ch.,
1960-62; current pastor, Grace C.M.E. Ch., Inskter,
Mich., 1962---; Church Sec., State Conference NAACP,
Fla., 1954-56; mem., Ad. Bd. Inter City Council, Talla-
hassee, Fla., 1954-55; US Army, 1941-46; award: Amer-
ican Defense SV Medal; American Theatre S.V. Ribbon;
World War II Victory Medal; EAMET Service Medal; Good
Conduct Medal; mem., Alpha Phi Alpha; compiled the last

research work for the Clarendon County School case lead-
ing up to the 1954 Court Decision; home: 661 Edison St.,
Detroit, Mich.; Office: 11346 Oakland Ave., Detroit, Mich.

REDDICK, Albert Joseph, b. Madison, Fla., Aug. 2, 1921;
s. Albert and Josie (Dixon) R.; A.B., Edward Waters
College Jr. 1941; A.B., Morris Borwn College, 1944; B.
D., Hamma Divinity School, 1947; D.D., Monrovia College, 1956; L.L.D., Campbell College; m. Clara Louise
Roberts; children--- Cleo Alberta, Patricia Louise, Marian Joanne; pastor, St. Paul A.M.E. Church, Dallas,
Georgia, 1942-43; Allen A.M.E. Church, Milford, Ohio,
1944-45; Allen Chapel A.M.E. Church, Williston, Fla.,
1947-49; Hurst Chapel A.M.E. Church, Orlando, Fla.,
1949-52; St. James A.M.E. Church, Miami, Fla., 1952-
58;Bethel A.M.E. Church, Tallahassee, Fla., 1958-61;
Bethel A.M.E. Church, St. Petersburg, Fla., 1961---;
teacher, Public schools, Levy County, Fla., 1947-49;
Seminole County, Fla., 1949-52; Former State President,
NAACP; Delegate and Secy. to 1956, 1960, 1964 General
Conference of the A.M.E. Church; Member, Advisory
Board of FAMU University, 1959-61; Member, Board of
Management & Trustee Board of Edward Waters College;
Mem., Knights of Pythian, Elks, Alpha Phi Alpha; Edi-
torial staff, A.M.E. Christian Recorder; author: The
History of the Negro Branches of Methodism; Home:
912 3rd Ave. No. St., Petersburg, Fla., 33705; Office:
3rd Ave. & 10th St. No., St. Petersburg, Fla.

REECE, John Henry, Jr., b. New York, N.Y., Jan 16,
1919; s. John H. and Lenora (Smith) R.; Government
Schools, Nassau, Bahamas, 1925-36; Bishop Payne
Divinity School, Petersburg, Va., 1945-48; Asst.teacher,
Nassau, Bahamas, 1937-39; headmaster, Bahamian Schools,
1939-45; Ordained deacon, Jan. 19, 1949; priest, Jan.
21, 1950; deacon and priest-in-charge, All Saints' Clarks-
burg, W.Va., 1949-50; present, vicar, St. Peter's, Key
West, Fla., 1950---; Mem., Republican Mason, NAACP,
ACV; Home: 800 Center Key West, Fla.; Office: 800
Center Key West, Fla.

REED, Carother N., b. Hayesville, Louisiana, May 5,
1911; s. Judge T. and Suddie (White) R.; A.B., Texas
College, Tyler, Texas, 1950; S.M.U., Perkin School
Theology; D.D., Union Baptist Seminary, 1955; L.L.D.,
Texas College, 1957 (honorary Degree); widower; 1 son;
Winston D.; Dean and Minister of Texas College; member

Board of Trustees and Executive Committee of Board,
Texas College; member, Commission on Organic Union of
Churches C. M. E.; treasurer, New York Washington Conf.,
C. M. E.; present: pastor, Holsey Temple Christian Meth-
odist Episcopal Church, Phila., Pa. Consultant, National
Council of Churches; certified instructor, Board of Chris-
tian Education. Man of the Year, Citizens' League, Hous-
ton, Texas, 1950; National Negro Business League's
Award for work done at S. M. U., Dallas, Texas, 1951;
Mason, Member, National Negro History Society. Home:
1631 W. Grange St., Phila., Penna. Office: 1641 W. Hunt-
ing Park Ave., Phila., Pa.

*REID, Edgar Leroy, b. Brownsville, Tenn., July 7, 1925;
s. Robert L. and Annie (Morgan) R.; A. B., Lane Coll.,
1950; B. D., Howard Univ., Sch. of Rel., 1955; m.
Christene Crues; children--- Rita A.; asst. pastor,
Walker Memorial Baptist Church, Wash., D. C.; pastor,
Oakrum Baptist Church, Thoroughfare, Va., 1957-58;
pastor, Second Baptist Church, Jefferson City, Missouri,
1958---; pastor, advisor, Baptist Student Union, Lincoln
Univ.; voluntary worker, Intermediate Reformatory for
men, Jefferson City, Mo.; Trustee, Western Baptist Bible
College, Kansas City, Mo., 1962; pres., Jefferson City
Branch NAACP, 1963-64; pres., Jefferson City Minister-
ial Alliance, 1963-64; US Navy, 1944-46; Home: 505 Mon-
roe St., Jefferson City, Mo.; Office: 501 Monroe St.,
Jefferson City, Mo.

REID, George Ransom, b. Louisville, Ky., Oct. 30, 1932;
s. Frank Madison and Veatrice Victoria (Andrews) R.;
A. B., Allen Univ., Columbia, S. C., 1953; ST. B. Boston
Univ.; Union Theological Seminary; m. Mary Ann Brown;
children--- Gina Ann, George R.; pastor, Calvary African
Methodist Episcopal Ch., Louisville, S. C.; Campbell,
A. M. E. Church, Washington, D. C.; St. Paul
A.M.E. Church, Washington, D. C.; St. Paul A. M. E. Church,
Washington, D. C., 1956-64, Bethel A. M. E. Ch., Ardmore,
Pa.; dean of religion, Kittrell Coll., Kittrell, N. C., 1957-
64; counselling staff, Boston, Mass. General Hospital; Mem.
Alpha Phi Alpha; Mason; Home: 208 Simpson Rd., Ardmore,
Pa.

REID, Robert Edward, presiding elder; b. Como, Miss.,
Sept. 13, 1903; s. John Jackson and Laura Ann (Danner)
R.; A. B., Lane Coll.; B. D., Gammon Theol. Sem.; m.
Alyce W. Monroe; children--- Orien E.; pastor, Christian

Methodist Episcopal Churches, Ga. , Tenn. ; presiding elder, Topeka, Kansas; dean, Leadership Sch. , C. M. E.
Ch. , 4 years; vice pres. , City Alliance, Topeka, Kans. ,
sec. , representative, Council of Churches, Council of
Rel. and Race; attended Seminary, Hebrew Sem. , Jerusalem, Israel, 1964; Mem. , NAACP; Home: 3344 So.
Benton St. , Kansas City, Mo.

REUBEN, Odell Richardson, coll. pres. , b. Silverstreet,
S. C. , June 21, 1918; s. James and Matilda (Stewart) R. ;
A. B. , Benedict Coll. , 1942; B. D. , Benedict Coll. , 1954;
S. T. M. , Oberlin Coll. , 1947; LL. D. , Allen Univ. (hon-
orary), 1955; Pd. D. (hon.), Benedict Coll. , 1959; m.
Anna Daniels; children--- Wilhelmina, Lucy, Anna Maria,
Odell, Kayne, Janice Reuben; pastor, Happy Home Baptist
Ch. , Allendale, S. C. ; Dunn Creek Baptist Ch. , Ware
Shoals, S. C. ; instructor, Theology, Morris Coll. , 1947-
48; pres. , Morris Coll. , 1948---; secy. , S. C. Christian
Action Council Bd. ; Member: Community Hospital Sumter,
S. C. ; Penn Community Service, St. Helena Island, S. C. ;
Council on Human Relations; Mem. , NAACP, Odd Fellows;
Mason; American Academy of Political Sciences, etc. ;
Office: Morris College, Sumter, S. C.

RICE, George Edward, b. Perryman, Md. , April 13, 1919;
s. Andrew A. and Villa (Johnson) R. ; A. B. , City Coll.
of New York and Roosevelt Univ. , Chicago, Ill. , 1948;
B. D. , Drew Theol. Sem. , Madison, N. J. , 1951; m.
Birdie Beamon; children--- Edythe, Linda, Jocelyn;
pastor, Cory Meth. Church, Cleveland, Ohio, 1951;
Second Meth. Ch. , Elyria, Ohio, 1952; St. James Meth.
Ch. , Pine Bluff, Ark. , 1953-54; Kelly Meth. Ch. , Chicago,
Ill. , 1954-61; Centennial Meth. Ch. , Kansas City, Mo,
1961---; teacher, St. Louis Area Pastors' School; US
Army, 2nd Lt. , 1941-45; military award: North African
and Sicilian Campaigns; Home: 4042 Coll. , Kansas City
30, Mo. ; Office: 1834 Woodland, Kansas City 8, Mo.

*RICE, James Donald, sem. prof. ; b. Union, S. C. , Oct. 6,
1926; s. J. D. and Mildred (Rosborough) R. ; A. B. , S. C. ,
State Coll. , 1950; B. D. , Howard Univ. , Sch. of Rel. ,
1953; m. Ellen Vincienne Smithwick; children--- Donnelida
L. , James Donald, Jr. ; chaplain, National Council of
Churches; N. Y. City Mission Society; chaplain & teacher,
Leland Coll. , Baton Rouge, La. ; coll. minister & teacher,
Morris Coll. , Sumter, S. C. ; pastor, Enon Baptist Church,
Sumter, S. C. ; pres. , Western Baptist Seminary (Bible

Coll.), Kansas City, Mo.; current pastor, Roanoke Baptist Church, Hot Springs National Park, Ark., 1962---;
occasional teacher, Religious Institutes; guest lecturer &
religious emphasis Week Leader on various Coll. campuses; Mem., Board of Community Council for Social
Action of Greater Kansas City, 1960-62; First Vice Pres.,
Kansas City, Mo., Branch NAACP; currently: pres.,
Hot Springs National Park Branch, NAACP, & Chr. Legal
Redress Comm., Ark. Conf., NAACP; S. W. Regional
Church Sec. of NAACP; Mem., Kansas City Council Exec.
Bd., Council of Churches, 1958-62; World War II veteran,
served overseas; 1961 Phi Beta Sigma Award, Kansas City,
Mo.; Man of the Year for work in desegregation; Mem.,
Phi Beta Sigma; Home: 737 Pleasant Hot Springs National
Park, Ark.; Office: Roanoke Baptist Church, P.O. Box
1201, Hot Springs, Ark.

RICE, Warner Myron, Church official; b. Minneapolis, Minn.,
Oct. 29, 1932; s. Warner E. and Myra (Riley) R.; Oakwood Coll., 1954-57; Washington Missionary Coll., 1957-
58; Union Coll., 1958- 1959- B.A.; Drake Univ., postgraduate courses, 1963 - ; m. Shirley I. Smith; one son:
Lowel V.; Assistant pastor, Seventh-Day Adventist Church,
Wichita, Kansas, 1959-60; Pastor, Compress Road S.D.A.
Church, Sikeston, Mo., 1960-62; and Philadelphia S.D.A.
Church, Des Moines, Iowa, 1962-63;
Central States Conf. of Seventh-Day Adventists, Kansas
City, Mo.; Park-time teacher, 1960-61; vice-president,
N.A.A.C.P., 1961, Sikeston, Mo.; secretary, Interdenominational Ministers Alliance, Sikeston, Mo.; vicepresident, Interdenominational Ministers Alliance, Des.
Moines, Iowa, 1963- present. Cub-scout master, Sikeston, Mo., 1961. Home: 1433 Fremont St., Des Moines,
Iowa. Office: 1150 13th St., Des Moines, Iowa.

RICHARDSON, Ben, A.B. Florida A & M, 1936; S.T.B.,
Harvard University, 1939; Certificate in Education,
Newark State Teachers College, 1948; Pastor, Presbyterian Churches, 1940-54; director, Erie Neighborhood
House, Chicago, Ill. Office: 1347 W. Erie St., Chicago,
Ill.

RICHARDSON, Harry Va., sem. dean; Jacksonville, Fla.,
June 27, 1901; s. Martin V. and Bertha I. (Witsell) R.;
A.B., Western Reserve Univ., 1925; S.T.B., Harvard
Univ. Divinity Sch., 1932; Ph.D., Drew Univ., 1945;
D.D. (hon.), Wilberforce Univ., 1941; m. Selma T.

White; chaplain, Tuskegee Institute, Ala., 1934-48; pres.,
Gammon Theol. Sem., 1948, 1959; pres., Interdenomina-
tional Theol. Center, 1959---; mem., Bd. of Directors,
Southern Regional Council, Inc.; mem., Nat. Council of
Churches of Christ in the U.S.; Southern Advisory Com.,
General Bd.; mem.-at-large, Greater Atlanta Council of
Churches; mem., Bd. of Directors, Atlanta Urban League;
mem., Citizens Advisory Com. for Urban Renewal of
Atlanta; Bd. of Directors, Atlanta Tuberculosis Assn;
Assn. of Methodist Theol. Schs., pres. of the Assn., 1955;
Exec. Com. of the American Assn of Theological Schs.;
mem., Bd. of Directors of the Community Chest; Bd. of
Directors, Georgia Assn for Pastoral Care; Mayor's Com.
of the Atlanta Coordinating Council; Bd. of Directors of
Family Service Society, Public Relations Com.; Council
of Evangelism of the Methodist Ch.; Bd. of Managers,
Gulfside Pastors School, Meth. Ch.; chmn, Negro Division
of Community Services Campaign; Field Director of Program for Training of the Negro Rural Ministery under the
auspices of Home Missions Council of North America and
the Phelps-Stokes Fund. author: Dark Glory: A Study of
the Rural Church; Contributor to: Best Sermons, The
Christian Way in Race Relations, Journal of Religious
Thought, Opportunity, New York Times Magazine, The
Negro Educational Review, The Central Christian Advocate, The Upper Room, Ebony, and others; Office: 671
Beckwith Street, SW, Atlanta 14, Georgia.

RILEY, Negail Rudolph, sem. prof., b. Oklahoma City,
Okla., Sept. 15, 1930; s. Tilton and Estella Lucille
(Sneed) R. Caruthers; B.A., Howard Univ., 1952;
B.D., Perkins Sch. of Theology, Southern Methodist
Univ., 1955; Boston Univ., 1955- candidate for Th.D.;
m. Gwendolyn Maurine Allen; children--- Beryl Elise;
asst. pastor, St. Paul Meth. Church, Dallas, Texas,
1952-55; interim director, Brooks Memorial Community
Center, Jamaica, Long Island, N.Y., 1955; director,
Christian Education, Church of All Nations, Boston,
Mass., 1955-57; director, Morgan Memorial Youth and
Children's Settlement House, Boston, Mass., 1958-62;
interim pastor, Union Baptist Church, Cambridge, Mass.,
1962; pastor, Wesley Chapel Meth. Church, Little Rock,
Ark., 1962---; asst. professor, Religion and Sociology,
Philander Smith Coll., Little Rock, Ark., 1962---; Mem.,
Bd. of Directors, Carver Branch YMCA, Little Rock,
Ark.; Bd. of Dir., Urban League of Greater Little Rock;
Bd. of Dir., Ark. Council on Human Relations; Bd. of

Riley, S.M.   307

Dir., Aldersgate Meth. Camp, Little Rock, Ark.; first
vice pres., Ark. Council of Churches; vice pres., Little
Rock Council on Community Affairs; treasurer, Little
Rock Interracial and Interdenominational Ministerial Al-
liance; Exec. Comm., Professors of Religion Section,
Meth. Conf. on Christian Education; Alpha Phi Alpha;
Articles: The Christian Advocate; Power Magazine; The
Annals of Political and Social Sciences; Together Maga-
zine; Home: 1113 State St., Little Rock, Ark. 72202;
Office: 1109 State St., Little Rock, Ark. 72202.

RILEY, Sumpter Marion, Jr., church official; b. Greenwood,
S.C., June 10, 1903; s. Sumpter Marion and Amy Jane
(Fisher) R.; A.B., DePauw Univ., 1926; B.D., Garrett
Biblical Institute, 1930; S.T.M., Boston Univ., 1938;
Completed the Residence for Ph.D., 1941; D.D. (hon.),
Philander Smith Coll., 1952; m. Varina Wilhelmenia Lone;
children--- Phyllis (Mrs. Richard Willimas); pastor,
Browns Methodist Ch., Ill.; Patoka Methodist Ch., Ind.,
1926; 2nd Methodist Church, Princeton, Ind., 1927; asst.
pastor, South Park Methodist Ch., Chicago, Ill., 1928-30;
asst. director, Negro Work of Board of Home Missions
and Church Extension, 1930-31; Phil., Pa.; pastor, Cen-
tenary Methodist Church, Akron, Ohio, 1931-32; Scott
Methodist Church, Denver, Coll., 1932-34; Burns Meth.
Ch., Des Moines, Iowa, 1934-36; LaSalle Meth.Ch., St.
Louis, Mo., 1936-37; 4th Meth. Ch., Boston, Mass.
1937-42; Asbury Meth. Ch., Columbus, Ohio, 1942-44;
Berea Meth. Ch., Detroit, Mich., 1944-45; Gorham Meth.
Ch., Chicago, Ill., 1945-51; District Superintendent of
Chicago Dist., 1951-57; pastor, Cory Meth. Ch., Cleve-
land, Ohio, 1957---; Mem., Mason: Alpha Phi Alpha;
Democrat; Home: 10515 Grantwood Ave., Cleveland 8,
Ohio; Office: 1117 East 105th St., Cleveland 8, Ohio.

RIVERS, Clarence Joseph, educator, teacher; b. Selma,
Ala., Sept. 9, 1931; s. Clarence R. and Lorraine
(Echols) R.; B.A., The Athenaeum of Ohio, 1952; M.A.
Philosophy, 1956; Grad. Studies, Xavier (Ohio) and Yale
U., Eng. and Lit; M.A. Drama, Catholic U. of Amer.,
1964; Ordained priest, Roman Cath.Ch., 1956, Arch-
diocese of Cincinnati; Asst. Pastor, St. Joseph's Church,
Cin., 1956 and Church of The Assumption, Walnut Hills,
1962; Instr. of Eng. and Dept. Head, Purcell High School,
Cin., O., 1956-63; Dir. The Queen's Men Drama Guild,
1956-63; Composer, An American Mass Program"; Narrator, A.B.C. Network Documentary "We Should Be

Heard". (History of Civil Rights Movement). Organizer
and Director: School for Cantors, Lectors and Commenta-
tors. Home: 1935 Hackberry St., Cincinnati, Ohio. 45206.

ROBERT, James Deotis, Sr., sem. prof.; b. Spindale, N.
C., July 12, 1927; s. J.C. and Edith (Goode) R.; A.B.,
Johnson C. Smith, 1947; B.D., Shaw Univ., 1950; B.D.,
Hartford Theol. Sem., 1951; S.T.M., Hartford Theol.
Sem., 1952; Ph.D., Edinburgh Univ.,Scotland, 1957; m.
Elizabeth Caldwell; children: James Deotis,Jr.; Edin Char-
maine, Carlita Rose; pastor, Union Bapt.Ch., Tarboro, N.C.,
1947-50; asst. pastor, Union Baptist Ch., Hartford, Conn.,
1950-52; dean, Religion, Georgia Bapt. Coll., Macon,
Ga., 1952-53; assoc. prof. and chaplain, Shaw Univ.,
1953-55; 57, 58; current prof. Theology, Howard Univ.
Sch. of Rel.; Mem., Institutional Ministry Committee,
Council of Churches, National Capital Area; Kappa Alpha
Psi; Alpha Kappa Nu National Honorary Society; Amer.
Ass'n of Univ. Professors; author: Faith and Reason; Com-
parative Study of Pascal Bergson and James. Home: 1428
Whittier Pl. NW, Wash. D.C. Office:Sch. of Rel., Howard
Univ., Wash. 1, D.C.

ROBERTS, Joseph Lawrence, Jr., b. Chgo., Ill., Feb. 17,
1935; s. Joseph L.; B.A., Knoxville Coll., 1956; B.D.
Union Theol. Sem., 1959; m. Esther Jean; children---
Cheryl, Cynthia; field worker, Church of the Master,
N.Y.C., 1956-58; First Church, Hoboken, N.J.; pastor,
Weequahic Church, Newark, N.J., 1959-62; Elmwood
United Presby. Church, East Orange, N.J., 1962---;
Mem., Presbyterian Comm. on Ecumenical Mission &
Relations; vice chmn., Synod's Com. on Rel., and Race;
vice pres., Ministerial Assn. of Oranges & Maplewood,
N.J.; Office: Elmwood United Presby. Church; Elmwood
Ave. & Epppert Sts., East Orange, N.J.

ROBERTSON, Benjamin William, Sr., b. Roanoke, Va.,
Apr. 6, 1931; s. Clarence and Anna (Holland) R.; A.B.,
Va. Union Univ., Richmond, Va., 1954; B.D., Va.
Seminary & Coll., Lynchburg, Va., 1956; D.D. (hon.),
Va. Sem. & Coll., Lynchburg, Va., 1959; m. Dolores
Wallace; children--- Benjamin W., Jr.; pastor, First
Union Baptist Ch., Chesterfield, Va., 1950-52; Piney
Grove Bapt. Ch., Princess Anne, Va., 1952-55; current,
Cedar Street Memorial Bapt. Ch., Richmond, Va.;
founder and director, The Robertson Kiddie Kollege which
is a Child care and Day Nursery Center; Trustee, Va.
Sem. & Coll.; Trustee, East End Masonic Home; Trustee,

Baptist Negro Children's Home; Advisory Bd. , Union Mutual Savings & Loan Ass'n; Exec. Bd. of the Va. State
Chapter of Southern Christian Leadership Conf.; field sec. ,
Va. State B.T.U. Convention, 1950-55; pres. , Va. State
B.T.U. Convention, 1958-63; state secy. , Foreign Mis-
sion Bd. of the Nat'l Baptist Convention of America; state
representative, The Foreign Mission Bureau, 1962---;
Alpha Phi Alpha Citizenship Award for Outstanding Com-
munity Leadership, 1959; East End Civic League Citizen-
ship Award, 1960; Mem. , Mason; vice pres. , East
End Ministerial Alliance; treasurer, Richmond
Baptist Ministerial Conference; treasurer, Va. Baptist
State Convention; Exec. Bd. of the Virginia Council of
Churches; national secy; Progressive Nat'l Sunday School
and Baptist Educational Congress; special research, Negro
Gospel Singing and Singers; Home: 716 North 24th St. ,
Richmond, Va.; Office: 24th & N St. , Richmond, Va.

ROBERTSON, Burnell Jacob, b. Patterson, La. , June 13,
1924; s. Jacob and Alma Bridget R.; Southern Univ.;
Campbell Coll. , Miss.; Lampton Sem.; R.R. Wright Sch.
of Religion; m. Gaynell Blake; children--- Jocelyn Ann,
Lorraine Theresa, Emily Marie; Ordained, 1957; pastor,
St. Paul (Congregational) United Church of Christ, New
Iberia, 1956; current pastor, Teche United Ch. of Christ,
Iberia, La.; chaplain, New Orleans. Council Parent Teach-
er Assn, 1942-45, 1950-52; awards: Good Conduct: Three
Battle Campaign Stars; Boy Scout Eagle Badge; Mem. , La.
Public Health Assn; Boy Scout Troop Scoutmaster; Home:
1920 N. Mao New Orleans, La. 70119; Office: Teche
United Ch. of Christ, New Iberia, La.

ROBINSON, Arthur Alexander, Jr. b. Napoleonville, La. ,
Feb. 20, 1928; s. Arthur Alexander and Odessa (Noel) R.;
A.B., Dillard Univ.; B.D., Gammon Theol. Seminary,
1954; US Army Chaplain School; m. Jeanette Wyne; chil-
dren--- Adrienne A. , Arthur A. , III, Anthony A.; Angeli-
que A.; pastor, Camphor Memorial Methodist Church,
Baton Rouge, La. , 1954-56; Philips Memorial Meth. Ch. ,
New Orleans, La. , 1956-60; Baynton Meth. Ch. , Gretna,
La. , 1948-51; Kynett Meth. Ch. , Forsyth, Ga. , 1952-54;
current pastor, St. James Meth. Ch. , 1962---; substitute
teacher, Pine Bluff, Ark. Public School system; adult
organizer and adviser, Pine Bluff Student Movement,
1963; Mem. , New Orleans Interdenominational Ministers
Alliance, 1956-60; Scotlandville Branch, NAACP; Baton
Rouge Interdenominational Ministers Alliance; US Navy,

1943-46; US Army, 1960-62; US Army Chaplain, Fort
Lee, Va.; US Navy Unit Commendation Award, 1944;
Stars for four battles, World War II; Democrat; chairman, Bd. of Pension of the La. Conference of the Meth.
Church and Bd. of Ministerial Training of the same Conf.,
Called a boycott of the merchants of downtown Pine Bluff
and the shopping center area which led to interracial
negotiation, March 1963; Led and called the first march
over 500 people in the downtown area of Pine Bluff seeking equality for all the races. St. James Meth. Ch. where
he was the pastor was bombed because of its integration
activities; Home: 314 South Poplar, Pine Bluff, Ark.;
Office: 316 South Poplar, Pine Bluff, Ark.

ROBINSON, Dillard, b. San Antonio, Texas, June 8, 1934;
s. Dillard and Naomi (Richardson); Diploma, Phillis High
School, 1951; A. B., Drew Univ., 1955; Saint Augustine's
College, Raleigh, N. C., 1951-52; S. T. B., Berkeley
Divinity, 1958; priest-in-charge, St. Philip's Episcopal
Church, San Antonio, Texas, 1959---; Attended the Col-
lege of Preacher, Washington, D. C., 1963; represented
the Diocese of West Texas at Provincial Synod, 1963;
Board Member, San Antonio, Visiting Nurses Associa-
tion, Pres. East Terrace Neighborhood; Member of
Diocesan, Youth Division, Christian Education Division,
Adult Leadership Division, Race Relations Division;
Member, The Board of Welcome Home for the Blind and
Aged-Allied Children's Service; Home: 427 Dorie St., San
Antonio, Texas; Office: 1310 Artesia Dr., P. O. Box
10078, San Antonio, Texas, 78210.

ROBINSON, Hubert Nelson, bishop; b. Urbana, Ohio, April
28, 1912; s. John H. and Rovilla Ontario (Hill) R.; A.
B., Ohio State Univ., 1935; B. D., Hamma Divinity Sch.,
1934; Univ. of Pittsburgh, 1945; Wilberforce Univ., D.
D. (hon.), 1943; D. D., Allen Univ., 1952; m. Mary Isley;
children--- Cassandra Lee; Entered African Methodist
Episcopal Church ministry, 1930; Elder's ordination,
1934; pastor, Smithfield A. M. E. Ch., Ohio, 1935; Jones
Tabernacle A. M. E. Ch., Cincinnati, Ohio, 1935; Steuber-
ville A. M. E. Ch., Ohio, 1938; St. Paul A. M. E. Ch.,
Col., Ohio, 1940; St. James A. M. E. Ch., Pittsburgh,
Pa., 1944; St. James A. M. E. Ch., Cleveland, Ohio,
1948; Ebenezer A. M. E. Ch., Detroit, Mich., 1955-64;
Elected bishop, A. M. E. Ch., Cincinnati, Ohio, May 1964;
teacher, Payne Sem., Wilberforce Univ., 1943; lecturer,
Minister's Seminars at Paul Quinn Coll., Texas 1950-

53; Edward Waters Coll., Jacksonville, Fla., 1960-63;
Bd. of Education, A. M. E. Ch., 1944-60; Trustee Bd.,
Wilberforce Univ. and Payne Seminary; vice pres., De-
troit Council of Churches; pres., Detroit Metropolitan
Pastor's Union; Gov's. Commission on Traffic Safety,
Mich., 1962-64; Gov's. Commission on Traffic Safety,
Mich., 1964; Mem., Kappa Alpha Psi; Mason; Elks;
NAACP; Urban League; Frontier Club of America; Bd.
of Dir., Children's Adoptive Agencies, Cleveland, Ohio.
Detroit, Mich.; Home: 131 Arden Park, Detroit 2, Mich.;
Office: 5151 W. Chicago Blvd., Detroit 4, Mich.

*ROBINSON, G. Dewey, chaplain; b. Sumter Co., S.C.,
Feb. 22, 1910; s. Powell and Carrie (James) R.; A.B.,
Allen Univ.; B.D., Howard Univ. Sch. of Rel., Wash.
D.C.; further study: Harvard Univ., Cambridge, Mass.;
m. Darrie Mae Chandler; pastor, Young Chapel, S.C.;
Little Mountain Circuit, S.C.; Burlington Ct., N.C.;
Allen African Methodist Episcopal Church., Baltimore,
Md.; Ward Memorial A. M. E. Church, Wash., D.C.;
Campbell A. M. E. Church, Washington, D. C.; Waters,
A. M. E. Church, Baltimore, Md.; Present pastor,
Metropolitan A. M. E. church, Wash., D.C.; US Army
Chaplain, 1941-44; Mem., Religious Committee, YMCA,
Balto.; Christian Education Committee Urban League,
Balto., Md.; Trustee, Kittrell Coll.; treasurer, Kittrell
Coll.; Trustee & treasurer, Baltimore Conference; Mem.,
Board of Directors, Council of Churches; National Coun-
cil of Churches; World Council of Methodism; treasurer,
Washington Conf. A. M. E. Church; Mem., Mason; Phi
Beta Sigma; author: What We Believe and Why We Believe
It (African Methodism); Home: 1715 Webster St., NW,
Washington, D.C.; Office: 1508 M. St. NW, Wash., D.C.

ROBINSON, J.E., coll. prof.; b. Drawdy, S.C.; A.B.,
Paine Coll.; B.D., Howard Univ., Sch. of Rel.; Resi-
dential work for M.A., Howard Univ.; M.A., Drew Univ.;
two children; asst. pastor, Wash., D.C.; Tenn.; pastor,
Christian Methodist Episcopal Churches, S.C., Delaware,
Va., Tenn; presiding elder, Jackson-Memphis Annual
Conf. (C. M. E. Church); current pastor, Miles C. M. E.
Church; head of dept. of rel., Miles Coll., Birmingham,
Ala.; administrative asst to Bishop E. P. Murchison
(C. M. E. Church); dean and registrar, Phillips Sch. of
Theol. Seminary, 6 years; dean, Leadership Training
Sch., Tenn. 4 years; Mem., C. M. E. Ministers' Alliance;
Birmingham Brotherhood of Clergymen; Alabama Council

on Human Relations; Lesson Writer, General Bd., Chris-
tian Education (C. M. E. Church). pres., Birmingham
Brotherhood of Clergyman; Mem., YMCA; Mason; Alpha
Phi Alpha; Office: Miles College, Birmingham, Alabama.

ROBINSON, James Herman, consultant, State Dept.; b.
Knoxville, Tenn., Jan. 24, 1907; s. Henry John and
Willie (Banks) R.; A. B., Lincoln Univ., 1935; B. D.,
Union Seminary, 1938; D. D. (hon.), Wesleyan Univ.,
1957, Dartmouth College, 1963; LL. D., Lincoln Univ.,
1949; LH. D., New School for Social Research, 1958;
D. D., Occidental College, 1964; m. Gertrude Cotter;
Youth Dir., NAACP, 1938-40; pastor Church of the Mas-
ter (N. Y. C.), 1936-61; Dir. Morningside Comm. Center,
Inc., 1936-61; Emeritus Church of the Master, 1957-
present; consultant on Africa for United Presbyterian
Church; consultant on African Desk, Dept. of State;
vice chmn., Nat. Advisory Comm. to Peace Corps;
mem.: Bd. of Syndenham Hospital; Boys' Club of New
York; Greater New York; Safety Council; Former Member;
Bd. of NAACP; Nat. Urban League; author: Road Without
Turning; Tomorrow is Today; Adventurous Preaching;
Love of This Land; Africa at the Crossroads; Home: 549
W. 123rd St., New York, N. Y.

ROBINSON, Paul Mitchell, b. High Point, N. C. June 23,
1928; s. Carrows William and Senas (Barnes) R.; A. B.,
B. D., Johnson C. Smith University, 1952; m. Maggie
Lee Brown; children--- Carolyn, Veatrice, Paul Jr.,
Kevin, Twila; pastor, The Bethel and Shinnecock Presbyn.
Ch., Southampton, Long Island, New York, 1952---; also
moderator Long Island Presbytery, 1959; chairman South
Fork Migrant Committee, Eastern Long Island, 1956-60;
chairman Long Island Presbytery's Comm. on Bill &
Overtures, 1955-61; pres. Community Improvement As-
sociation, Southampton, New York; 1960; Selected "Man
of the Year", 1959, Southampton, New York; chaplain
Tyre Lodge #91 Riverhead, N. Y. Mem. Mason, 1956-61;
Office: Shinnecock Indian Reservation, Southampton, L. I.,
New York.

RODNEY, John Joseph, b. Chicago, Illinois, June 4, 1931;
s. Onazie Joseph and Blanche (Young) R.; St. Paul's
College, Epworth, Iowa, 1952-54; St. Mary's Seminary,
Techny, Ill., 1954-60; B. A., 1956; 10 summers, Loyola
Univ., Chicago, M. A. 1964; Ordained priest, Roman
Cath. Ch., 1960; Asst. Pastor, St. Anselm's Church,

Chicago, 1960-61, Our Lady of the Gardens Ch., Chicago, 1961-63; St. Nicholas Church, St. Louis, Mo, 1963---; Chicago Urban League, Council of Religious Leaders, 1961-62; March on Wash. for Jobs and Freedom, Aug. 1963; Home: 18th and Lucas St., St. Louis 3, Mo.

*ROGERS, Jefferson Paramore, b. Quincy, Fla., Jan. 27, 1918; s. Jefferson and Dovie R.; A.B., Florida A&M College, 1940; M.A., Howard University, Religious Education, 1949; B.D., Yale Univ., 1947; m. Mary Grace Harris; children--- Anita Darrielle, Alain Burghardt, Weldon Douglass; Dir. Christian Ed., Jones Tabernacle, A.M.E. Ch., Philadelphia, Pa., 1944; pastor, St. Jones A.M.E. Ch., Philadelphia, Pa., 1945; pastor, Bethel A.M.E. Ch., New Haven, Conn., 1945-46; Race Relations Sec., Evangelical and Reformed Ch., Cleveland, O., 1947-54; pastor, Plymouth Congregational Church, Washington, D.C., 1954-57; founder & pastor, Church of Redeemer Presbyterian Church, Washington, D.C., 1957 ---; president, D.C. Chapter Southern Christian Leadership Conf., 1964; Organizing member, Fellowship of Concern, Presbyterian Church, U.S.A., 1963---; Religious editor, Philadelphia Tribune, 1945; columnist of Religion in Modern Times, Philadelphia Tribune, 1945-47; staff mem. editorial Bd. of Social Action, monthly organ of Congregational Churches. Organizer, New Haven Social Action Com., 1945; mem. NAACP; race relations div., Federal Council of Churches; Comm. on Christian Social Action of the Evangelical and Reformed Ch.; bd. of Natl Missions of Evangelical and Reformed Ch.; Inst. of Religion, Howard U.; Home: 4340 Argyle Terrace, NW, Washington, D.C., 20011; Office: 15th at Girard St., NE, Washington, D.C.

ROGERS, Leslie Thomas, teacher; b. San Jose, Calif., December 31, 1929; s. Clovel and Alice (Berry) R.; B.A., Maryknoll College, Glen Ellyn, Ill., 1954; M.R. E, Maryknoll Seminary, Maryknoll, N.Y., 1959; Ordained, Roman Cath. Ch. priesthood June 13, 1959; Teacher, Minor Seminary, Musoma, Tanganyika, E. Africa, 1959-61; Asst. Pastor, Komuge Cath. Ch., Musoma. Home: U.S. Maryknoll, P.O., New York; Office: Komuge Catholic Church, P.O. Box 109, Musoma, Tanganyika, East Africa.

ROLAND, Garther William, b. New London, N.C., Feb. 12, 1911; s. Arthur and Mary (Smith) Owens (adopted parents);

Slater State Normal Sch. (Now Winston-Salem State Coll.),
1927; B.S., Piedmont Bible Institute, 1953; m. Daisy Lee
Chavis; children--- Mary Deloise (deceased), James
Peters, Alphonzo Crosby (foster children); pastor, Middle
Fork Christian Church, Winston, N.C., 1934-48; Little
Salem Christian Church, Reidsville, N.C.; current, 1st
Christian Church, Concord, N.C.; teacher, Religion &
Bible Ed., Winston-Salem & Reidsville, N.C., 2 years;
pres., Piedmont Tri-State District Convention, 2 years;
chmn., Bd. and sec.-treas., Dixie Shores Realty Co.,
Inc.; consultant, Interracial Consultation; Ministers of the
South, Lexington, Ky. (Coll. of the Bible); Home: 2309
E. 1st St., Winston-Salem, N.C.; Office: Mahan & Rone
Sts., Concord, N.C.

ROLLINS, Joseph Metz, Jr. teacher; b. Newport News, Va.,
Sept. 8, 1926; s. Joseph Metz and Alice (Clements) R.;
1943-44, Hampton Institute, 1944-47, Johnson C. Smith
Univ., A.B.; B.D. 1947-50; Johnson C. Smith Seminary;
m. Julia May (Boone) R., June 18, 1950; children:
Cecelia Rose, Joseph Metz, III; Ordained by Presbytery
Southern Virginia, 1950; 1950-53; Instructor of Relation
Ed., College of Liberal Arts, Johnson C. Smith Univ.,
Charlotte, N.C.; 1953-58 Organizing pastor, Trinity
Presbyterian Church, Tallahassee, Fla.;1958-63, Special
Field Director in Race Relations, United Presbyn. Church,
Nashville, Tenn; Sept. 1963, Associate Director Commis-
sion on Relations and Race, United Presbyterian Church;
mem. Treasurer, Inter-City Committee, Tallahassee,
Fla.; leader of Tallahassee Bus Boycott, 1956; vice-
pres., Nashville Christian Leadership Council, Nashville,
Tenn.; Awards: Citizen of the Year; Graduate chapter
Omega Psi Phi, Tallahassee, Fla.; Davidson County In-
dependent Political Council, Board member, Nashville,
Tenn. Author-articles on the racial situation in the South,
published in Presbyterian Life; Home: 90 LaSalle St.,
Apt. 10D, New York 27, N.Y.; Office: Rm. 367, 475
Riverside Drive, N.Y. 27.

ROLLINS, Richard Albert, educator; b. Phila., Penn., Nov.
30, 1927; s. Nathaniel and Alyce R.; A.B. Lincoln U.,
Pa., 1952; B.D., Union Theol. Sem., N.Y., 1955; S.T.
M., Boston U. Sch. of Theol., 1960; m. Audrey Joan
King; Assoc. Minister, Enon Tabernacle Bapt. Ch.,
Phila., 1949-52; Asst. Minister, Cornerstone Bapt. Ch.,
Brooklyn, 1954-55; Youth Dir., Manhattanville Neighbor-
hood Center, N.Y.C., 1952-53; Interim Pastor, Park

Manor Presbyterian Ch., N.Y.,1953-54; Bishop College:
Dean of Men, 1955-58; Instr., Div. Rel. and Phil.,
1955-57; Asst. Instr., Div. Rel., 1957-59; Dean of the
Chapel, 1959-64; Asst. Dir. Rel. Ed., Jerusalem Baptist
Ch., Marshall, Tex., 1959-61; Assoc. Prof. and Chmn.,
Div. of Rel. and Phil., Bishop College, 1959; Author:
Principles and Procedures in Improving Prayer in Pub-
lic Worship, 1955; Education; Mem. Nat. Assoc. of Col-
lege and Univ. Chaplains; Amer. Soc. Society; Amer.
Assoc. of Univ. Profs.; Texas State Teacher's Assoc.;
Nat. Assoc. of Biblical Instrs.; Amer. Psychological
Society; Amer. Bapt. Education Assoc.; Kappa Alpha
Psi, Nat. Urban League, NAACP, YMCA; Dir. Nat.
Bapt. Survey (Texas), 1964; College Advisory, United Na-
tions Week, 1960; Danforth Teacher, 1964; Home: 2371
E. Ledbetter Dr., Dallas, Texas. Office: 3837 Simpson
Stuart Rd., Dallas, Texas.

*ROLLINS, Robert Lee, b. Louisa Col., Va., Nov. 17,
1903; s. William and Sallie; A.B., Storer Coll., Harpers
Ferry, W.Va.; B.D., Howard Univ. Sch. of Religion,
1941; D.D. (hon.), Va. Theol. Sem., 1948; m. Geneva
C. Gillis; children--- Elois Villa (Gibson); pastor, Fla.
Ave. Bapt. Ch., Washington, D.C., 1938---; teacher,
Bible Course in the Nat. Bapt. Congress; statistician,
New England Bapt. Missionary Conv., 1950-63; Mem.,
Ledroit Civic Assn; Mason; former pres., D.C. Bapt.
Educational Congress; Outstanding alumnus award from
Storer Coll., 1950; Mem., National S.S. Publishing Bd.;
Home: 720 Quebec Pl., Wash., 10, D.C.; Office: 623
Fla. Ave. NW, Wash., D.C.

*ROMAN, Gus, chaplain; b. New Orleans, La., Dec. 20,
1932; s. Gus and Mary (Ballard) S.; Dillard Univ.,
1952-54; Va. Union Univ. 1956;Sch. of Rel. A.B.,B.D., Howard
Univ.,Wash.D.C.,1956,1959; m. Eunice Helena Matthews;
children: Marcus, Tonai, Derrick; assoc.pastor, Sixth Mt.
Zion Baptist Church, Richmond, Va., 1954-56; assoc.pastor,
Mt. Pleasant Baptist Church, Wash., D.C., 1956-59;
present, pastor, First Baptist Church, Baltimore, Md.
US Army Chaplain, 1959-62; Commendation Medal; Home:
1710 N. Broadway, Baltimore, Md. 21213; Office: 525-
27 N. Caroline, Baltimore, Md. 21205.

ROOKS, C. Shelby, administrator; b. Beaufort, N.C., Oct.
19, 1924; s. Shelby A. and Maggie (Hawkins) R.; B.A.
Va. State Coll., 1949; B.D., Union Theol. Sem., N.Y.,

1953; m. Adrienne Martinez; children--Laurence Gaylord;
Carol Ann; Minister, Shanks Village Protestant Ch.,
Orangeburg, N.Y., 1951-53; Lincoln Memorial Cong.
Temple, Wash., D.C., 1953-60; Assoc. Dir., The Fund
For Theol. Educ., Inc., Princeton, N.J., 1960---; U.S.
Army, 1943-46, Overseas (Guadalcanal & Philippines),
Staff Sargeant; Nat. Council of Churches, Dept. of the
Ministry, Commission on Higher Education; Bd. of Dirs.,
United Southern Chrtn. Fellowship; Theol. Commission,
United Church of Christ; Del., World Congregational
Council, Rotterdam, Holland, 1962; Moderator, Middle
Atlantic Conference, UCC; Bd. of Dirs., Middle Atlantic
Conference, UCC (Pres., 1960-62); Adv. and Study Comm.
on Realignment of Middle Atlantic Area, UCC; Steering
Comm. of Consultation on Theol. Sch. and Student Finan-
cial Aid; Advisory Bd., author: Christianity and Crisis Maga-
zine: Author, "The Image of the Ministry in the Protestant
Fellowship Program", "A Cross To Bear", The Journal of
Religious Thought; "We Can't Ignore The Negro Campus",
Presbyterian Survey; The Shortage of Negro B.D. Stu-
dents", Union Seminary Tower; Surveys, Rockefeller
Doctoral Fellows, Negro Ph.D.'s and Th.D.'s, 1953-63,
and Negro B.D. students enrolled in Amer. Assoc. of
Theol. Schools. Home: 152 Guyot Ave., Princeton, N.J.
Office: 163 Nassau St., Princeton, N.J.

ROSS, Solomon David, b. Sumpter Co., Ga., Aug. 29,
1886; s. Esquire and Haggar; A.B., Morehouse Coll.,
Atlanta, Ga.; Univ. of Chicago; m. Lucinda Moore (deceased), Mary Olivia Brookins; children--- Abigail, Jud-
son, William, Angelene, Darene McKinney; principal,
High School, Griffin, Ga., 3 years; High School, Sardis,
Miss., 5 years; pastor, Bapt. Ch., Pelham, Ga., 3
years; Second Bapt. Ch., Savannah, Ga., 6 years; current pastor, Shiloh Bapt. Ch., Detroit, Mich., 1929---;
moderator, Metropolitan Assn. (Detroit), 8 years; chairman, Race Relations Com., Nat. Bapt. Conv.; officer,
Bapt. World Alliance; Mem., National Council of Churches,
Nat. Sunday Sch. & Baptist Training Union Congress; Detroit Council of Churches; Testimonial Resolutions, Detroit City Council, 1959; Mem., Omega Psi Phi; Home:
584 Arden Pk., Detroit 2, Mich.; Office: 557 Benton,
Detroit, Mich.

ROSTON, David Williamson, b. Milledgeville, Ga., Sept. 8,
1904; s. John Maxwell and Anna (Williamson) R.; Tuskegee
Normal and Industrial Institute, 1921; National Bible In-

stitute, New York, 1935; m. Hattie Foster (divorced);
children--- Philip, Robert. Pastored Christian Methodist
Episcopal Churches in New Haven, Syracuse, N.Y.,
Bridgeport, Conn., Boston, Mass., 1936-40; pastored
C. M. E. Churches in Apex-Fuquay-Varina, Greesnboro,
Chapel Hill, Washington and Gastonia, North Carolina,
1941-54; present: pastor, C. M. E. Churches in Allendale
Lexington, Spartanburg, Saluda and Estill, South Carolina,
1955-   ; Secretary to Bishop H. P. Porter, 1937-38;
secretary, Washington-Virginia Conf. C. M. E. Churches,
1938-40; secretary to Bishop C. H. Russell, 1943-48;
secretary, N. Carolina Conf., 1942-54; secretary, S.
Carolina Conf., 1955- present. Substitute teacher, Estill
Training School, S. Carolina; Member: Knights of Pythians;
Masons; N. A. A. C. P., 1930-64; Democratic Executive
Committee, Greensboro, N. C., 1944-47; Democratic
Executive Committee, Columbia, S. C., 1956-58; vice-
president, Ward 9, County Democrats, 1956-58; dele-
gate, Richland City Conf., Spartaburg, S. C., 1960.
Home: P. O. Box 703, Estill, S. C., Office: Wilmot St.,
Estill, S. C.

ROUSSEVE, Maurice Louis, educator; b. New Orleans, La.
Sept. 22, 1906; s. Bartholomew Abel and Valentine Marie
(Mansion) R.; Xavier Prep., 1918-20; St. Augustine's
Seminary 1920-34; Ordained priest, Roman Catholic Ch.,
May 23, 1934, first class of Negro S. V. D.; Pastoral
work 1934-50; 1952-64; Teacher, Asst. Provincial and
Master of Clerical Novices, 1950-52; Mem. Knights of
Peter Claver, 4th Degree; Home and Office: St. Joseph
Church, Box 278, Julien Rd., Broussard, La.

ROUTTE, Jesse Wayman, b. Macon City, Mo., June 13,
1906; s. Louis William and Lu Lu Belle (Smith) R.;
B. A., M. A., Augustana College, 1929; B. D., Augustana
Seminary, 1932; m. Enid Gomez; children--- Luther,
Jess (deceased), Enid, Carmen; Ordained New York
Synod, 1932;pastor, Holy Trinity Church, Jamaica,
Queens, 1934---; pres. Queens Lutheran Pastors Assoc.;
mem. Advisory Committee on Juvenile Delinquency,
Jamaica, N. Y.; Home: 111-46 167th St., Jamaica, New
York: Ch.: Holy Trinity Luth. Ch., 162-28 Mathies Ave.,
Jamaica, N. Y.

RUFFIN, Andrew Jackson, b. Lisman, Ala., Nov. 11,
1893; s. Spencer P. and Dora Ann R.; A. B., State
Teachers Coll., 1918; B. S., Morehouse Coll., 1929;

B. Th. , Western Bapt. Coll. , 1937; m. Jennie Roberts;
minister, Religious Education Dept. , Pilgrim Bapt.
Church, Chgo. , Ill. , 1930-42; supply pastor, Bethel Bapt.
Ch. , Dayton, Ohio, 1943-45; pastor, Jerusalem 2nd Bapt.
Ch. , Urbana, Ohio, 1946---; teacher, Nat'l Sunday
School & B. T. U. Congress 1943; Ohio State S. S. & B.
T. U. Congress, 12 years; Trustee, Champaign County
Home Hospital, 1960---; Mem. , Urban Bi-Racial Comm. ;
pres. , NAACP; Home: 127 Hill St. , Urbana, Ohio,
43078.

*RYCE, Amos, II, b. Fort Valley, Ga. ; A. B. , Paine Coll. ,
Augusta, Ga. ; B. D. , Howard Univ. , Sch. of Rel. , Wash-
ington, D. C. ; Special Study: University of Wisconsin,
Madison, Wisconsin; D. D. (hon.), Eden Theol. Seminary,
1964; pastor, Holsey Temple C. M. E. Church, Atlanta,
Ga. ; Trinity C. M. E. Church, Augusta, Ga. ; Israel
Metropolitan C. M. E. Church, Gary, Ind. ; Lane Taber-
nacle Christian Methodist Episcopal Church, St. Louis,
Missouri since 1954; Industrial sec. of Atlanta Urban
League, Atlanta, Ga. ; principal, Austell Georgia Public
School; pres. , Holsey Institute, Cordele, Ga. ; Initiation
and supervision of building od dormitory, Holsey Institute,
Cordele, Ga. ; Remodeling and renovation of Israel Metro-
politan C. M. E. Church, Gary, Inc. , 1954; present pastor,
Lane Tabernacle C. M. E. Church, St. Louis, Mo. , 1955
---; Mem. : Former First Vice-President Metropolitan
Church Federation; Former Executive Board of NAACP;
Clergy Advisory Comm. of Planned Parenthood; Board
of Family and Children's Service; Exec. Bd. of Ferrier
Harris Home For Aged; Dialogue Group of Catholics-
Protestants-Jews; Frontier's of America Choice for Man
of Year Award, 1961; Executive Board of Conference on
Religion and Race; chosen one among the delegation of
18 to travel one month in the Mid-East to study the
socio-economic and political impact of the Israeli-Arabic
conflict; Home: 4353 Enright Ave. , St. Louis, Mo. ; Office: Lane Tabernacle C. M. E. Church, 916 N. Newstead
Ave. , St. Louis, Mo.

SABOURIN, Clemonce, b. New Orleans, La. , October 6,
1910; B. D. , Immanuel Lutheran College, Greensnboro,
N. C. , 1935; A. B. , Johnson C. Smith Univ. , 1939; LL.
D. , Valparaiso University, Indiana, 1963; m. Glenice
James; children--Clemonce James; asst. pastor Grace
Lutheran Church, Concord, N. C. ; pastor, St. Paul's

Lutheran Church, Charlotte, N.C., 1936-39; pastor,
Grace-Luther Memorial Lutheran Church in Greensboro,
N.C., 1939-44; pastor, Mt. Zion Lutheran Church, N.Y.
C., 1947---; dir. Mt. Zion's Parochial school; sec.
General Conference (a National organization of Synodical
Conference Negro Lutheran congregation); pres. General
Conference of Synodical Conference Negro Lutheran con-
gregation; Member, the Synodical Conference Survey
Committee; Member, the first board of directors of
Lutheran Interracial Service, now a department of Luther-
an Social Service in New York City; Member, the Bd. of
Directors of Lutheran Child Welfare Assn. in NYC; Member, Bd. of Dirs. of Adopt-A-Child; sec. Lutheran Welfare Council; pres. Lutheran Human Relations Ass'n;
pres. the Bronx-Manhattan-Westchester Pastoral Conference; author: Let the Righteous Speak; Home: 421 West
145th St., New York 31, N.Y.

SALMON, Harold Anthony, teacher; b. New York, N.Y.,
Nov. 17, 1929; s. Harold and Dorothy (Henderson) S.;
St. Joseph's Seminary & College, 1950-56; Asst. Dir.,
Mission of Immaculate Virgin, Staten Island, N.Y.,
1956-59; Teacher, English & Religion, Cardinal Hayes
High School, Bronx, N.Y.; Chrmn, Family Life Council,
Harlem-Washington Heights Area; Mem. Committee of
Religious Leaders of N.Y.C., N.A.A.C.P., Catholic
Interracial Council, Nat'l Council of English Teachers;
Home: 650 Grand Concourse, Bronx, N.Y., 10451.

*SAMPSON, Frederick George, b. Port Arthur, Texas,
Aug. 9, 1925; s. Frederick and Florence S.; A.B.,
B.Th., Bishop Coll., 1946, 1947; B.D., Howard Univ.,
Sch. of Rel., 1950; D.D. (hon.), Va. Theol. Seminary
& Coll.; Bishop Coll.; m. Earlene Zone Harrison; chil-
dren--- Frederick G., III, Freda Gelene; director, Re-
ligious Life & Teacher, Bishop Coll., 1947; acting pastor,
Coll. Hill Baptist Church, Ark., 1946-47; asst. pastor,
Shiloh Baptist Church, 1948-52; pastor, High Street Bap-
tist Church, Roanoke, Va., 1952-60; current pastor,
Mt. Lebanon Baptist Church; Faculty member, Ky. State
S.S. & B.T.U. Congress, National S.S. & B.T.U. Con-
gress; lecturer, National Baptist Convention, U.S.A., Inc.
Women's Auxiliary; Mem., Alpha Phi Alpha; consultant
to Governor of Kentucky on Human Relations; Worship
Leader, Women's Missionary State Convention; Mem.,
YMCA; YWCA; Home: 950 SW Parkway, Louisville, Ky.
40211; Office: 2224 Chestnut St., Louisville, Ky.

SAMS, Roosevelt, coll. prof.; b. Lee Co., Texas, Feb.
15, 1923; s. Teb and Joe (Anna) S.; B.S., Paul Quinn
College, 1949; M. ed., Texas Southern University,
1953; Texas College-Special Study, 1964; m. Izetta Christ-
man; children--- Donna Jeanine, Cynthia Gale; Interim
minister Church of Christ, Waco, Texas, 1951-52; Conducted Gospel meeting in many cities in Texas & Oregon,
lecturer, The Annual Lectureship in many states, Texas,
Ill., Tenn., Calif.; US Army, 1943-55; current pastor,
College Church of Christ, Terell, Tex.; dean, Southwestern Christian Coll., Terrell, Tex.; teacher, 6 years,
Paul Quinn Coll.;   broadcast radio station, 1 year KTER,
Terrell, Tex.; Awards: three battle stars (Europe),
Marksman and Good conduct Medal; Member, Texas State
Teachers Assoc.; Texas Association of Colleges and Uni-
versities Registrars; Home: 605 West End, Terrell,
Texas; Office: 205 West End, Terrell, Texas.

SARGENT, Charles Jackson, Jr. b. Hampton, Va., Oct.
23, 1927; s. Charles J., Sr. and Ruth (Jackson) S.;
B.A., Va. Union Univ., 1944-49; B.D., Drew Theol.
Sem., 1949-52; Biblical Seminary of New York; m. Vir-
ginia Adele Evans; children--- Hope Irene; pastor, Mi-
grant Laborers, Va. Council of Churches, 1950-51; First
Baptist Ch., Madison, N.J., 1952-55; Ebenezer Baptist
Ch., Poughkeepsie, N.Y., 1955-59; current, Union Bap-
tist Ch., Stamford, Conn., 1959---; vice pres., The
Lott Carey Baptist Foreign Mission Convention, Conn.;
moderator (former), The Duchess Baptist Ass'n of the
American Baptist Convention; 1965 Nominating Committee
of the American Baptist Convention; Mem., Omega Psi
Phi; Home: 15 Fifth St., Stamford, Conn.; Office: 28
Adams Ave., Stamford, Conn.

SATTERWHITE, John H., sem. dean, prof.; b. Newberry,
S.C., Jan 1, 1913; s. Modock and Lucretia S.; A.B.,
Benedict Coll., 1934; B.D., S.T.M., Oberlin Graduate
Sch. of Theology, 1937, 38; Th.D., Boston Univ. Sch.
of Theol., 1947; D.D. (hon.), Johnson C. Smith and
Benedict Coll., 1959, 64; m. Lucille C. Mills; children
--- Joan C. (Mrs. Cartwright), John M.; instructor,
Livingstone Coll., Salisbury, N.C., 1938-40; dean Hood
Theol. Sem. and prof. of theol., 1940-57; prof. Syste-
matic Theol. and Ecumenics, Wesley Theol. Sem.,
Wash., D.C., 1958---; pastor, African Methodist Epis-
copal Zion Church; Mem., Philadelphia-Baltimore Conf.;
director, The American Society of Christian Social Ethics;

Council of Churches of Greater Washington; Exec. Com-
mittee: Dept. of Racial and Cultural Relations, National
Council of Churches; Howard University Institute of
Religion; NAACP; Fellowshio of Professors of Ecumenics
and Missions; Interreligious Committee on Religion and
Race; Inter Church Club of Wash., D. C.; Ministerial
Assn. of Greater Washington; Chairman of Committee on
Ecumenical Education, Council of Churches of Greater
Washington; author: Christian Action in Racial and
Ethnic Relations: Its Biblical and Theological Basis.
Dept. of Racial and Cultural Relations, National Council
of Churches, New York City, 1963; Home: 3208 19th St.,
NW, Wash., D. C. 20010.

SAUNDERS, Lenwood Daniel, clergyman; b. Richlands,
Mar. 21, 1927; s. Louis Johnson and Hanah (Cox) S.;
B. Th., Kittrell Coll., Kittrell, N. C., 1956; s. Lena
Malie Davis; children--- Alinda, Gwendolyn, Louis,
Zrank, Wayman; pastor, Dak Chapel A. M. E. Church,
Warrenton, N. C.; pastor, Shocco A. M. E. Church,
Bethel A. M. E. Church both at Spring Hope, N. C.;
Enfield, N. C.; current pastor, Mt. Olive African Meth-
odist Episcopal Church, Wilmington, N. C.; Mem.,
Exec. Bd. of Gegony Elementary Sh.; Treasurer, Inter-
denominational Alliance; Member, Ministerial Ass'n;
Member, Fannis Nawood Home Board Directions; Mem.
Exec. Board, NAACP; Mem., Civic League; Vice Chair-
man, 5th Ward, 2nd Precinct (Wil., N. C.); Good Con-
duct Medal, US Army; Member, Mason; Home: 712
Wright St., Wilmington, N. C.; Office: 1001 Seventh St.,
Wilmington, N. C.

*SAUNDERS, Monroe Randolph, bishop; b. Florence, S. C.,
April 13, 1919; s. Lawrence and Millie (Fleming) S.;
Va. State Coll., 1937; A. B., B. D., Howard Univ., 1953,
1957; m. Alberta Brockington; children--- Monroe Randolph Jr.; Jackquelin Faye; Esther Karen, Adrian Jason;
pastor, Rehoboth Church of God (Apostolic), Wash., D. C.
1953---; Gen. sec., Church of God In Christ Jesus
(Apostolic), 1954---; presiding bishop, The Central District of the Church of God in Christ Jesus (Apostolic),
1957---; Ex. Dir., Rehoboth Education and Welfare Center, Sykesville, Md.; director, Rehoboth Bible Institute,
Balto., Md.; special consultant, Presiding Bishop of
the Church of God In Christ Jesus (Apostolic) on Ministerial Training and Youth Affairs; Editor, 'The Rehoboth Beacon," official publication of the denomination;

pres., Clergymen's Ass'n for Social Service in the Sec-
ond Precinct, D.C.; Mem., Policy Committee of the
Community Service Project, Howard Univ., 1962-63;
Chairman, Housing Committee, Clergymen's Ass'n,
1964; chaplain, Apostolic Students, Morgan Coll.; Mem.,
Christian Council of Morgan Coll., 1962---; US Army,
1942-45; Good Conduct Medal; Mem., Alpha Kappa Delta,
Honorary Sociological Fraternity; NAACP; Home: 3002
N. Hilton St., Baltimore 16, Md.; Office: 700 Poplar
Grove St., Baltimore 16, Md.

SAVAGE, Horace C., author; coll. pres.; b. Portsmouth,
Va.; M.A., New York Univ., 1948; LL.D., Lane Coll.,
1959; pastor, Christian Methodist Episcopal Ch., Goolet-
tsville, Tenn.; Mission Church, Haiti; Foreign Mission-
ary, Haiti and Cuba; professor, Lane Coll., 1952-54;
Tennessee State Univ., 1954-64; pres., Texas Coll.,
Tyler, Tex., 1964---; Mem., Assoc. for study of
Negro life and history; Miss. Valley Historical Society;
Tenn. Educational Congress; Southern Historical Society;
Ass'n of Univ. Professors; Mason; Democrat; author:
Life and Times of Bishop Issac Lane; co-publisher &
founder, Capitol City Defender (newspaper), Nashville,
Tenn.; Office: Texas Coll., Tyler, Texas.

SAVOY, Clarence Monroe, Church official; b. Croom, Md.,
July 1, 1924; s. Walter and Mary (Pinkney) S.; A.B.,
Lane College, Jackson, Tenn., 1954; B.D., Gammon
Theological Seminary, 1957; m. Florence Louise Penn.
Pastored: Bowden Hills Chapel Christian Methodist Epis-
copal Church, 1953-54; Rock of Ages C.M.E. Church,
Augusta, Ga., 1957-59; Hamlet Chapel, Stanton Memor-
ial C.M.E. Chs., Pittsboro, N.C., 1959-63; Calvary
C.M.E. Church, Jersey City, N.J., 1963-64; chaplain,
migrants summers of 1956-57; present: Episcopal Direc-
tor, Christian Education for the Seventh Episcopal District
of the C.M.E. Church, 1959-   . U.S. Marine Corps,
1943-46. Omega Psi Phi. Home: 25 Oak St., Jersey City,
N.J. Office: 27-29 Oak St., Jersey City, N.J.

SCALES, William Clinton, Jr. b. Charleston, W.Va.,
March 18, 1935; s. William Clinton and Myra (Davis)
S.; B.A., Oakwood Coll., 1956; M.A., Andrews Univ.,
1958; m. Lois Nila Ruth Yates; Sedalia, Mo. Seventh-
Day Adventist Church, Sedalia, Missouri, 1958-60;
Prospect Avenue S.D.A. Church, Springfield, Mo., 1960-
1961; Phila. S.D.A. Church, DesMoines, Iowa, 1961-

62; present: pastor, Bethel S. D. A. Church, Kansas City,
Kansas, 1962-   ; Teacher of various Bible classes
regularly and counseling from time to time: ministerial
alliance. Home: 645 Oakland Avenue, Kansas City, Kansas 66101. Office: 713 Freeman Ave., Kansas City, Kansas 66101.

SCOTT, Claude Caesar, teacher; b. Lenoir, N. C., Dec.
25, 1894; s. William Barham and Tempie E. S.; A. B.,
Kittrell Coll., Shaw Univ., 1925; D. D. (hon.), 1933;
m. Margaret Helen Deloatch; children--- Claude, Jr.
and Zenobia Mae; Ordained Elder 1922 in A. M. E. Church
at Morganton, N. C.; pastor, St. James A. M. E. Church,
1925; pastor, St. Paul A. M. E. Church, 5 yrs.; St.
James A. M. E. Church, Winston-Salem, 7 1/2 yrs; St.
Paul A. M. E. Church, Raleigh, 7 years; Bethel A. M. E.
Church, Greensboro, 3 yrs; Present, St. James A. M.
E. Asheville, 15 years; principal, The Orange Co. Tr.
School, Chapel Hill, N. C., 3 yrs; Mem., The Trustee
Board and Board of Control, Kittrell Coll; current,
Director of Religious Education, 2nd Epis. District A.
M. E. Church; pres., Interdenominational Alliance of
Winston Salem, Raleigh and Asheville, N. C.; Sec., Ash-
ville and Buncombe Citizens Organization; pres., Citizens
Civic Organization, Winston Salem, N. C., 1933-34; Home:
2001 McConnell Rd., Greensboro, N. C.; Office: 134
Broad St., Asheville, N. C.

SCOTT, Julius Samuel, Jr., coll. chaplain, church official;
b. Houston, Tex., Feb. 26, 1925; s. J. S., Sr. and
Bertha (Bell) S. ; A. B., Wiley Coll., 1945;
B. D., Garrett Biblical Institute, 1949; M. A., Brown
Univ., 1964; Ph. D. Candidate, Boston U., 1956-60; m.
Ianthia Lucille Harrell; children--- Julius S. III, David
Kumar; Missionary to India, 1949-52; director, Public
Relations, Wiley Coll., 1952-55; Methodist Chaplain,
Brown Univ., 1958-60; Methodist Chaplain, MIT, 1961;
dir. Wesley Foundation, Texas Southern Uni., 1961-63;
Exec. sec., Brown Univ. Christian Assn., 1963---;
lecturer, World Religions, Boston Univ., 1958-60; lec-
turer, World Religions, Boston Adult Education Center,
1958-60; Mem., Omega Psi Phi; Democrat; FOR; CORE;
NAACP; Home: 95 Brown St., Providence, R. I. 02906;
Office: Brown Univ., Providence, R. I. 02912.

SCOTT, Nathan A., Jr., College professor, author; b.
Cleveland, Ohio, Apr. 24, 1925; s. Nathan A. and

Maggie (Martin) S.; A. B., Univ. of Michigan, 1944;
B. D., Union Theological Seminary, 1946; Ph. D.,
Columbia Univ., 1949; m. Charlotte Hanley; children---
Nathan A. III, Leslie Kristin. Ordained Protestant Epis-
copal priest; member of faculty, Howard Univ., Division
of General Education Program in the Humanities, 1948-
55; present: Professor, Theology and Literature, Divinity
School, Univ. of Chicago, 1955-   . Major Publications:
Rehearsals of Discomposure: Alienation and Reconcilia-
tion in Modern Literature (King's Crown Press, 1952);
The Tragic Vision and the Christian Faith (Associated
Press, 1957); Modern Literature and the Religious
Frontier (Harper & Bros., 1958); Albert Camus (Hillary
House, 1962); Reinhold Niebuhr (Univ. of Minnesota
Press, 1963); The New Orpheus: Essays Toward a Chris-
tian Poetic (Sheed & Ward, 1964); The Climate of Faith
in Modern Literature (Seabury Press, 1964); Samuel
Beckett (Bowes & Bowes Ltd., 1964); Forms of Ex-
tremity in the Modern Novel, Man in the Modern Theatre,
and Four Ways of Modern Poetry (to be published simul-
taneously by John Knox Press, 1965). Contributor: Re-
ligious Symbolism (Harper & Bros., 1955); Literature
and Belief (Columbia Univ. Press, 1958); Symbolism in
Religion and Literature (George Braziller, Inc., 1960);
Christian Faith and the Contemporary Arts (Abingdon
Press, 1962); Society and Self (Free Press); Graham
Greene: Some Critical Considerations (Univ. of Kentucky
Press, 1963); Nature and Grace (Harper & Row, Inc.,
1964); The Search for Identity: Essays on the American
Character (Harper & Row, Inc., 1964); Religion in American Literature (Univ. of Washington Press, to be published Spring 1965); The Christian Doctrine of Man (Sea-
bury Press, to be published, Spring, 1965). Has contributed articles to numerous scholarly periodicals. Home:
5242 S. Greenwood Ave., Chicago 15, Ill., Office: The
Divinity School, Univ. of Chicago, Chicago 37, Ill.

SEWELL, George Alexander, coll. prof.; Newnan, Ga.,
Oct. 12, 1910; s. J. Otis and Pearl (Clark) S.; A. B.,
Morris Brown College, 1934; S. T. B., Boston Univ.,
1944; S. T. M., Boston Univ., 1946; Ph. D. Boston Univ.,
1957; LL. D., Monrovia Coll., 1956; m. Lillie Mae White;
children--- Annita Pearl (Mrs. Marvin Oliver); pastor,
Decatur Mission A. M. E. Church, Decatur, Ga., 1933-
34; Post Oak Mission, Sneads, Fla., 1934-36; Greenwood-
Neal's Landing Circuit, Jackson Co., Fla., 1936-42; St.
Andrews Methodist Church, Worcester, Mass., 1942-44;

Trinity A. M. E. Church, Atlanta, Ga.; Gaines Chapel
A. M. E. Church, Waycross, Ga., 1951-52; Steward
Chapel A. M. E. Church, Macon Georgia, 1952-57; Spring
Bethel A. M. E. Church, Louisville, Ga., 1960-62; Coll.
minister, LeMoyne College, Memphis, Tenn., 1944-45;
Coll. minister, instructor Bible & Religion, Morris
Brown College; Coll. minister & Dean of Men, Arkansas
A. M. & N. Coll., Pine Bluff, Ark.; Dean: Turner Theol.
Seminary, Atlanta, Ga., 1957-62;   Pro-
fessor Sociology, Alcorn A&M College, Lorman, Miss.,
1962---; Distinguished Community Service Award
(Plaque) Interracial group, Macon, Georgia, 1956; Mem.,
A. M. E. General Conference, 1954---; Mem.: Society
Biblical Literature; Secy., General Board of Education
A. M. E. Church, 1962---; Delegate (Youth Section) 2nd
Assembly National Council of Churches, Evanston, Ill.,
1957;   Mason; author: A Motif for Living and Other
Sermons, Vantage Press, NYC, 1963; Home: 74 Ashby
St., Atlanta, 14, Ga.; Office: 409 Church St., Port
Gibson, Miss.

SHANNON, David Thomas, sem. prof.; b. Richmond, Va.,
Sept. 26, 1933; s. Charlie Lee and Phyliss (Gary) S.;
A. B., Va. Union Univ., 1954; B. D., Va. Union Univ.
Sch. of Rel., 1957; S. T. M., Oberlin Graduate Sch. of
Theol., 1959; Union Theol. Sem., 1960---; m. Averett
Powell; children--- Vernitia Averett, Davine Berlinda;
Licensed, Baptist Ch., 1950; Ordained, 1954; pastor,
Fair Oaks Bapt. Ch., Fair Oaks, Va., 1954-57; student
asst. pastor, Antioch Bapt. Ch., 1957-59; Ebenezer Bapt.
Ch., 1960---; prof., Va. Union Univ., 1959---; Women's
Leadership Training Sch., Bapt. Ch., 1960-63; ch. chmn,
NAACP, 1960; Mem., Exec. Com. Richmond Chaplaincy;
vice pres., Area of Allied Bodies of Va., 1962---;
Exec. Com., Lott Carey Foreign Mission Convention,
1961---; Com. on Theol. Ed., 1962---; American Bapt.
Conv., 1962---; 2nd vice pres., Baptist Ministers Conf.
of Va., 1963---; Phi Beta Sigma; Y Men's International
author: The Life and Teachings of Paul, Townsend Press,
Nashville, Tenn.; Meditations - Upper Room Disciplines;
contributor to: The New Testament Image of the Re-
deemed Community, ed. by Jessie Jei McNeil, 1962;
Home: 2712 Seminary Ave., Richmond 20, Va.; Office:
Ebenezer Bapt. Ch., 216 W. Leight St., Richmond 20,
Va.

SHAW, C. Alexander, b. Cleveland, Ohio, Apr. 4, 1927;

s. Edward E. and Curlie A. (Brocks) S.; A.B., Wilber-
force Univ., 1953; B.D., Payne Theological Seminary,
1956; m. Marjorie B. (S.); children-- Bonita Elaine.
Pastored: Miles Chapel Christian Methodist Episcopal
Church, Fairmont, W.Va.,; Peoples Community C.M.
E. Church, Dayton, Ohio; Phillips Chapel C.M.E.
Church, Springfield, Ohio; St. Phillips C.M.E. Church,
Hamilton, Ohio. Phi Beta Sigma. Home: 64 Hanover St.,
Charleston, S.C. Office: 66 Hanover St., Charleston,
S.C.

SHAW, Harry Wilbert, Church Administrator; b. Mayesville,
Sumter County, Sept. 3, 1907; s. Benjamin and Alice
(Monroe) S.; 1942, A.B. and 1949 B.D. Theological
Seminary, Johnson C. Smith University; m. Rosetta L.
(White) S. Children--- Harry Eugene, Michael Monroe,
Jacquelyn Yvone, James Wilbert; pastor, 1947-50;
Salem U. Presbyterian Church, Anderson, S.C.; 1950-
56, Goodwill U. Presbyterian Church, Fort Pierce, Fla.;
1956-62; Trinity U. Presbyterian Church, Key West,
Florida; Sunday Schools Missions and Mobile Ministries
with Board of National Missions; Sunday Schools Missions:
Dyersbury, Tenn.; Miller, Miss.; Selma, Ala.; Camden,
S.C. Current: 1962, Director Community Center for
Youth and Adults, James Island, Charleston, S.C. Begin-
ning Oct. 1963, called to pastorate of St. James United-
Presbyterian Church; Director of Youth Work, Mem.,
Omega Psi Phi ; Ministerial Alliance; Mason;
NAACP; Democrat; Home: 1008 Park Ave., Charleston,
S.C.; Office: Route #5, Box 286, Charleston, S.C.

SHAW, Talbert Oscall, b. Jamaica, W.I., Feb. 28, 1928;
s. Albert and Albertha S.; B.A., Emmanuel Missionary
Coll., 1960; M.A., BD., Andrews Univ., 1963; m.
Lillieth Hamilton Brown; Pastored: East Jamaica Conf.
of Seventh-Day Adventist, Kingston, Jamaica, 1952-55;
Bahamas Mission of Seventh-Day Adventists, Nassau,
Bahamas, 1956-58; present: Lake Region Conference of
Seventh-Day Adventist Church while pursuing studies at
the Univ. of Chicago on doctoral program. Former chair-
man, School Board, Nassau, Bahamas; social worker with
Cook County Public Assistance, Chicago, Ill. Home: 5427
University Ave., Chicago, Ill. Office: 8517 South State
St., Chicago 19, Ill.

SHEPPARD, Garrett Augustus Hobart, b. Greenville, Tex.,
Feb 9, 1897; s. A.D. and Susie (Greesy) S.; B.Th.,

Bishop Coll., 1930; B.R.E., Hartford Seminary, 1931;
B.D., Yale Univ., 1934; Th.D., 1936; D.D., Arkansas
Baptist Coll., 1940; LL.D., Bishop Coll., 1961; m.
Bertha Mae Watson; pastor, Antioch Baptist Church,
Maxia, Texas, 1934-38; Sunset Baptist Ch., Texarkana,
Tex., 1938-41; secy., American Bible Society, Dallas,
Div., 1941-45; pastor, Greater Bethlehem Baptist Ch.,
Dallas, Tex., 1946---; current pres., B.M.&E. State
Congress of Texas, since 1936; pres., St. Paul Jr.
Coll., Mexia Tex., 1936-38; Trustee, Bishop Coll., Dal-
las, Tex., 1961---; Mem., Bd. of Directors, Dallas
Negro Chamber of Commerce, 1963---; Committeeman,
Boy Scouts of America, Circle Ten Council; Life Mem.,
NAACP; Mem., Mason; Kappa Alpha Psi; Epsilon Delta
Chi Religious Society; The American Academy of Political
and Social Science; Mem., Editorial Bd., Western Star;
author: Several Booklets; many News articles; Home:
2808 Sutton St., Dallas 10, Tex.; Office: 4401 Spring
Ave., Dallas 10, Tex.

SHEPPARD, Marshall Lorenzo, b. Oxford, N.C., July 10,
1890; s. Robert and Pattie (Gilliam); Va. Union Univ.,
Richmond, Va.; Pendle Hill Quaker Grad. Center, Wallingford, Pa.; m. Willie L. Owens; children--- Marshall,
Jr.; asst. pastor, Abyssinian Baptist Ch., 1923-26; pastor, Mt. Olive Tabernacle Baptist Ch., Phila., Pa.,
1926---; rel. work sec., 135th St. Branch YMCA, NYC,
1922-23; Bd. of Directors, Christian St. YMCA, Phila.,
Pa.; Mem., Comm., Div. Christian Life & Work, National Council of Churches; Pa. State Legislature, 1934-
36-40; recorder of deeds, Wash., D.C., 1944; recorder
of deeds, Phila., Pa., 1951; councilman-at-large, Phila.,
Pa., 1955-59-64; delegate and speaker, World Baptist
Alliance, Copenhagen, Denmark, 1947; Mem., Alpha Phi
Alpha; Mason; Elks; Home: 1331 N. 57th St., Phila.,
Pa.

SHERARD, Robert Douglas, educator; b. Memphis, Tenn.,
June 10, 1922; s. Major James and Elizabeth (Perkins)
S.; A.B., Morehouse Coll., Atlanta, Ga., 1949; B.D.,
Gammon Theol. Sem., Atlanta, Ga., 1952; m. Lois
Johnson; children--Robert Douglas, Jr., Lynn
Chase, Dawna Jean; Teacher, Carver Vocational High
School, 1949-52; Minister, Beecher Memorial United
Church of Christ New Orleans, La., 1953-58; Corona
Cong. Ch. (UCC), Corona, NY, 1958---; mem., Mayor's
Task Force for Youth, NYC., Mayor's Comm. on Ex-

ploitation, NYC, State Social Action Comm., N.Y. State
Conference, United Church of Christ; Co-chairman, Civil
Rights Comm. for Conference on Rel. & Race for NYC;
Sponsor, Northeast Queens Fair Housing Comm., NYC;
Bd. of Dirs., NYC Assoc. of Cong. Churches; Pres.,
Corona-East Elmhurst Br. NAACP, 1959---; Chrmn. Bd.
Independent Citizens for Good Government, Corona, N.Y.
Bd. Mem., Community Council of Corona, NY; First
Class Petty Officer, U.S. Navy, 1942-45; Recipient, 4
Battle Stars for European Theatre of Operation; Human
Relations Award, North Shore Bus. & Prof. Women's
Club, N.Y., 1962; Community Interest Award, Elmview
Women's Club, N.Y., 1963; Mem., Omega Psi Phi;
Home: 27-21 99th Street, East Elmhurst, N.Y., 11369
Office: 102-18 34th Avenue, Corona, N.Y. 11368.

SHERMAN, Odie Lee, bishop; b. Jacksonville, Tex., 1897;
Texas Coll.; A.B., Shorter Coll., 1927; D.D. (hon),
Shorter Coll.; Wilberforce Univ.; m. Ruth Andy Jones,
Edna Othenia Daniels; children--- John Oliver Davis,
Mary Etta; pastor, African Methodist Episcopal Churches,
Arkansas; presiding elder, Augusta, Arkansas, Camden,
Central Ark. Conf., Hot Springs; Elected bishop, 1956;
Now presiding bishop 10th Dist., A. M. E. Ch.; Award
for outstanding services during the integration crisis,
Little Rock, Ark.; Mem., NAACP; manager, State cam-
paign for ex. governor McMath; State Bd. of Directors,
Girls Industrial Sch., Fargo, Ark.; chairman, Civil
League, Little Rock; pres., Publication Bd., A. M. E.
Church; Home: 128 Garrison St., Waco, Texas.

*SHIELDS, Landrum Eugene, coll. prof.; b. Winston-Salem,
N.C., Mar 17, 1927; s. Joanna (Berry) S.; A.B., Lin-
coln Univ., Pa., 1949; Oberlin Graduate School of
Theology, 1950-51; B.D., Howard Univ. Sch. of Rel.,
1958; M.R.E., Christian Theol. Sem., 1960; Candidate
for Ph.D., Indiana Univ.; m. Marjorie Earley McDaniel;
children--- Landrum Eugene Jr., Sharyn Camille, Laurita
Eileen; pastor, First Congregational Ch., Greensboro,
N.C., 1952-55; YMCA sec., Adult Program, Indianapolis
YMCA, 1955-57; asst. pastor, Witherspoon Presbyterian
Ch., Indianapolis, Ind., 1959-61; current, Adult Educa-
tion Specialist, Bd. for Fundamental Education, Indiana-
polis, Ind., 1963---; prof., Indiana Central Coll., 1963
---; Democrat; Alpha Phi Alpha; Mem., Adult Education
Assn, U.S.A.; American Society of Training Directors;
Mason; Indianapolis Presbytery; Home: 1055 Pomander

Pl. , Indianapolis, Ind. 46208

SHOCKLEY, John Richard, b. Fruitland, Md. , Jan. 18,
1914; s. John Wilmore and Effie (Allen) S. ; Clark Col-
lege, Atlanta, Ga. and Gammon Theological Seminary,
Atlanta, Ga. Diploma, 1933-36; m. Edith Matthews;
children: Richard, Carol, Zarina, Audrey; ministry:
Wachapreague, Va. 1936-39, St. Andrews Methodist
Church, Upper Hill, Md. 1939-1942, Shiloh, Crisfield,
Md. , 1942-49, Waugh, Cambridge, Md. , 1949-55, Ezion
Wilmington, Del. 1955-61, District Superintendant, Wil-
mington District, Delaware Conference of The Methodist
Church, 1961 to present; Member: Phi Beta Sigma;
Home: 412 N. Clayton Street, Wilmington, Delaware,
Zip 19805.

SHORTS, Robert Buell, presiding elder; b. Gloster, Miss. ,
Dec. 10, 1905; s. Nathan and Eliza S. ; A. B. , Miss.
Industrial Coll. , 1930; B. D. , Gammon Theol. Seminary,
1934; m. Helen Jenetta Clift; teacher, Public School,
Miss. , 5 years; pastor and presiding elder Christian
Methodist Episcopal Church; Present pastor, Linden
St. C. M. E. Church, Atlanta, Ga. ; Mem. , Fulton County
Democratic Club; Leadership Summit Conf. , Atlanta,
Ga. ; Advisory Committee, National Conf. ; Georgia Coun-
cil of Churches; Voter's League; NAACP; Mason;
Democrat; Home: 601 Hightown Rd. NW, Atlanta
18, Ga. ; Office: Linden Street Institutional C. M. E.
Church, 286 Linden Ave. , NE, Atlanta, Ga.

SHUTTLESWORTH, Fred Lee, civil rights leader; b. Mug-
gler, Ala. , Mar. 18, 1922; s. Will and Alberta (Robertson) S. ; Cedar Grove Institute; Mobile, Ala. ; A. B. ,
Selma Univ. ; B. S. , Ala. State Teachers Coll. ; m. Ruby
Keller; children--- Patricia (Mrs. Eugene Barnes), Ruby,
Fredricka, Carolyn Fred, Jr. ; pastor, First Bapt. Ch. ,
1952-55; Bethel Bapt. Ch. , Birmingham, Ala. , 1957-60;
current, Revelation Bapt. Ch. , Cincinnatti, Ohio, 1960
---; organizer and pres. , Ala. Christian Movement for
Human Rights, Birmingham; pres. , Southern Conf. Edu-
cational Fund; Sec. , Southern Christian Leadership Conf. ;
Mem. , Nat. Advisory Bd. of Core; Nationwide speaker
for Civil Rights Movement; awards: National Newspaper
Publishers Assn. for Russwurm Award, 1958; display of
self sacrifice, gallantry and bravery, Cincinnati Business
League, 1963; tribute to brave leadership, Back Our
Brothers, Inc. , 1963; humanitatian award, Maryland St.

Conf. NAACP Branch, 1962; Capital Press Club Award
for Human Relations, 1962; distinguished citizen award,
Birmingham Frontier's Club, 1962; for self sacrifice in
field of human rights, Honors & Awards Commission:
ACMHR, 1962; admiration, Cincinnati Newswomen, 1963;
personal contribution and leadership in fight for human
dignity, Cincinnati Branch NAACP, 1964; Home: 965
Dana St., Cincinatti 29, Ohio; Office: 1556 John St.,
Cincinatti 29, Ohio.

SHY, P., Randolph, bishop; b. Kelly, Jasper Co., Ga.,
May 5, 1898; A.B., Paine Coll.; M.A., Fisk Univ.;
M.A., Columbia Univ.; Coll. prof., Miles Coll., Bir-
mingham, Ala., 10 years; pastor, Christian Methodist
Episcopal Churches, Decatur, Athens and Birmingham,
Ala.; pastor, Capers Memorial C.M.E. Ch., Nashville,
Tenn., 1940-48; academic dean, Lane Coll.; pastor,
St. Paul C.M.E. Ch., Jackson, Tenn.; Elected 30th
bishop C.M.E. Ch., May, 1958---; Represented C.M.E.
Ch. Conv. on Christian Education, Mexico City; Mem.,
Alpha Phi Alpha; Home: 2780 Collier Dr. NW, Atlanta,
Ga.

*SIDEBOARD, Henry Yergan, church official; b. Centerville,
Miss., Oct. 9, 1909; s. Richard and Mary L. (Mont-
gomery) S.; A.B., Paine Coll., 1935; B.D., Howard
Univ., Sch. of Rel., 1938; m. Christina White; children
--- Jean Carolyn, Rosemary, Cheryl Ann; pastor, Chris-
tian Methodist Episcopal Church, Georgia, Virginia,
New Jersey, South Carolina; Ordained Elder, 1938; cur-
rent pastor, Sidney Parker C.M.E. Church, Columbia,
S.C.; Director, Christian Education, C.M.E. Church;
principal, Holsey-Cobb Academy, Cordele, Ga., 1940-
42; dean, Leadership Training School, N.C., S.C.; US
Army Chaplain; Bronze Star Medal, Korea; Mem., Omega
Psi Phi; Home: 1108 Blanding, Columbia, S.C.; Office:
1114 Blanding, Columbia, S.C.

SIMMONS, Dimpson Waycross, b. Atlanta, Georgia, April
21, 1917; s. Dean E. and Minnie B.S.; B.A., Lane College, 1955-59; B.D., Interdenominational Theological Center, 1960-63; m. Lillie V. Wallace; children--- Mrs.
Benton Strode, Mrs. Paul Boyd, Mrs. Geraldyne Johnson; pastor, St. Paul Methodist Church, Paris, Tenn.;
Burdettes Chapel Methodist Church, Capleville, Tenn.;
1951-55; St. Paul Methodist Church, Dover, Tenn., 1949;
Clark Methodist Church, McMinnville, Tenn., 1959; pre-

sent pastor, Pickett Chapel Methodist Church, McMinnville, Tenn., 1960---; Home: 207 East Market St.,
Lebanon, Tenn.

SIMMONS, Julius Caesar, b. New Rochelle, N.Y., Nov.
24, 1925; s. Charles and Priscilla (Dilligard) S.; A.B.,
Va. Union Univ., 1952; B.D., Va. Union Univ. Sch. of
Rel., 1955; further study: Fort Valley State Coll., m.
Alma Alexander; children--- Patricia Diane, Julius C.,
Jr.; christian social worker, Dayton Christian Center,
Dayton, Ohio, 1955-57; director, Religious Activities,
Fort Valley State Coll., 1957---; pastor, Trinity Baptist
Ch., Fort Valley, Ga., 1957---; vice pres., Southern
Regional Va. Union Univ. Alumni Ass'n, 1959---; pres.,
Fort Valley Minister's Alliance, 1959---; Mem., Fron-
tiers International; nat'l and regional officer, Phi Beta
Sigma (former); US Navy, Pacific Theatre of War, 1944-
46; World War II Medal; Pacific Battle Ribbon; Honor
Man during Boot Training; Mem., National Ass'n of
Univ. and Coll. Chaplains; Progressive Nat'l Baptist Con-
vention; Ass'n of Coll. Personnel Workers, Baptist Stu-
dent Union; advisor, YMCA; Home: Fort Valley State
Coll., Fort Valley, Ga.

SIMMS, David McDaniel, research asst.; b. Richmond, Va.,
Aug. 28, 1933; s. Obadiah B. and Rebecca (McDaniel)
S.; A.B., Virginia Union Univ., 1950-54; B.D., Protestant Episcopal Theological Seminary, Va., 1955-58;
New York University, 1960---; (Ph.D. candidate); chaplain Dept. of Correction, NYC, 1960---; Chapel of Inter-
cession (Curate), Trinity Parish, NYC, 1961-62; Research
asst., Bureau of Research and Survey, National Council
of Churches, USA, 1962-63; Mem: Society for Scientific
Study of Religion; Associate, American Sociological Association; Member, Academy of Religion and Mental Health
author: "Understanding the Adolescent Offender," Journal
of Pastoral Care, Summer, 1961; "Communicating With
the Adolescent Delinquent," Journal of Educational Sociology, Summer, 1962; "The Liturgical Movement in the
Roman Catholic Church: Path to Dialogue?", Journal of
Religious Thought, No. 2, 1962-63; Home: 45 Tiemann
Place, Apt. 4A, New York 27, N.Y.

SIMS, George Turner, b. Thebes, Ga., July 23, 1897; s.
Felix R. and Emma (E.) S.; A.B., Morris Brown Coll.,
1915-19; B.S.T., Lincoln Univ., 1920-23; D.D. (hon.),
Wilberforce Univ., 1960; m. Beatrice Childs (1924),   .

(1924), Victoria Hargon (1060); children--- George Turner,
Jr.; Ordained A. M. E. Ch., 1920, to the deaconate; Ordained A. M. E. Church to the eldership, 1923; pastor,
African Methodist Episcopal Ch., Muskogee, Okla.,
1925-27; Pine Bluff, Ark., 1928-31; Hot Springs, Ark.,
1931-35; presiding elder, Cleveland, Ohio, 1935-39;
pastor, St. John A. M. E. Church, Cleveland, 1950-55;
current coll. prof., Campbell Coll., and presiding elder,
A. M. E. Ch., 1963---; sec. Bd. of Wilberforce Univ.,
1955-61; teacher, Campbell Coll., 1963; Office: Campbell Coll., Jackson, Miss.

*SIMMS, Virgil Andrew, social worker; b. Ronceverte, W.
Va., Aug. 5, 1931; s. Edward F. and Evelyn (Peck) S.;
A. B., West Va. State Coll., 1954; B. D., Howard Univ.,
School of Religion, 1958; present-Sch. of Social Work,
Howard Univ., 1962---; m. La Verne Wilmer; children
--- Dwayne Kerin, Deborah Leyna; teacher, The Lewisburg, W. Va., 1954-55; counselor, to Delinquent Boys,
1955-58; pastor, First Bapt. Church, Lex., Va., 1955-
62; teacher, Rockbridge, West Va., 1960; counselor to
delinquent children, Wash., D. C., 1962-64; psychiatric
social worker, St. Elizabeth Hospital, 1962-63; associate
pastor, Second Bapt. Ch., 1951-53; US Forces, 1952;
Home: 5017 The Alemeda, Baltimore 12, Md.

SIMON, Joseph Donald, teacher; b. Natchitoches, La., June
30, 1932; s. Charlie and Ida (LaCour) S.; St. Mary's
Seminary, Techny, Ill., 1951-53; St. Paul's Seminary,
Epworth, Iowa, 1953-55; L. C. H., Gregorian Univ.,
Rome, 1961-63; Ordained priest, Roman Cath. Ch.,
1961; Teacher, Church History, American and World
History, St. Augustine's Seminary, Bay St. Louis, Miss.,
1963---; Home: St. Augustine Seminary, Bay Saint Louis,
Miss.

SIMPSON, William Bratton, b. St. Louis, Missouri, Aug.
26, 1933; s. Wm. Emanuel and Lillian Mae (Bratton) S.;
Wayne Univ., Detroit, Mich., 1952-55; B. A. Wilberforce
Univ., Wilberforce, Ohio, 1962-64; m. Anna Christie
Brown: asst. pastor, Ward A. M. E. Church, Los Angeles,
Calif. 1959-61; pastor, Primm Tabernacle, A. M. E.
Church, Pomona, Calif., 1961-62; pastor, Shorter A. M.
E. Church, So. Charleston, Ohio, 1962-63; asst. pastor,
St. John A. M. E. Church, Xenia, Ohio, 1963---; US Navy,
1955-57; Member, Alpha Phi Alpha; Home: Emery Hall,
Wilberforce U., Wilberforce, Ohio.

SIMS, David Henry, bishop; b. Ala., July 18, 1886; s. F.
R. and Evelyn S.; A.B., Ga. State Coll., 1905; A.B.,
Oberlin Coll., 1909; B.D., Oberlin Theol. Sem., 1912;
A.M., Univ. of Chicago; D.D. (hon.) Allen Univ.; Mor-
ris Brown Coll.; Wilberforce Univ.; Livingstone Coll.;
m. Mayme; children--- Careve S. Dudley, Mayme Anna;
pastor, African Meth. Episcopal Churches, Painesville,
Ohio, Rhode Island; pastor, Morris Brown Coll., Green-
wood, S.C.; Elected bishop, 1932; Has served as bishop,
South African, Alabama, 1936-40; retired, 1940; prof.,
Morris Brown Coll.; dean, Allen Univ.; director, Citi-
zens & Southern Bank & Trust Co., Phila., Pa.; director
Phila. Tribune (Weekly newspaper); director, Union Mutual Life Ins. Co.; Mem., Elk; Mason; Alpha Phi Alpha;
Knight of Pythias; author: History of the A. M. E. Church
in the 14th District; The Function of the Presiding Elder;
The Office of Presiding Elder; Religious Education in
Negro Colleges; The Function of Worship; Home: 211 N.
53rd St., Phila., Pa.

SINGLETON, George Arnett, author; s. George Condon and
Lou (Zaney) S.; A.B., Allen Univ., 1915; Boston Univ.,
B.U.S.T., 1922; A.M., Univ. of Chicago, 1929; B.D.,
1930; LL.D., Edward Waters College, Jacksonville, Fla.
LL.D., Payne Coll., Birmingham, Ala.; LL.D., Mon-
rovia, Liberia; D.D., Wilberforce Univ., Ohio; m. Ettie
Ruth Cochran; pastor, A.M.E. Church, Chelsea, Cam-
bridge, Mass., Greenwood, S.C., Paducah, and Lexing-
ton, Ky., Springfield, Ill., and Des Moines, Iowa; edi-
tor, THE CHRISTIAN RECORDER, 1936-44; editor, THE
A.M.E. REVIEW, 1951---; Dean, The Graded High School,
Bishopville, S.C.; Professor, Allen Univ.; Dean Turner
Theological Seminary, Atlanta, Ga.; Pres., Paul Quinn
College, Waco-Texas; Professor, West Kentucky College,
Paducah, Ky.; Dean, Jackson Theological Seminary,
Little Rock, Ark.; US Army, Philippine Island, 1912,
1915 in the 24th Infantry; Served in New Mexico, and
Texas; 1st Lt. chaplain & served in France World War I;
AME Review & Life Member of the NAACP; Mem., Alpha
Phi Alpha; Mason, Northern Jurisdiction;
Veterans Administration; a Life Member, The Alumni
Association, Univ. of Chicago and Boston Univ.; author:
The Romance of African Methodism, Sarah Allen
Heroine Mother of African Methodism,   The Life Exper-
ience and Gospel Labors of Richard Allen,   The Life
and Labors of Jordan Winston Early,   cooperator in writ-
ing 3 vol. of "The History of American Methodism;"

Home: 5828 Race St., Phila., Pa. 19139; Office: same.

*SINGLETON, William Matthew, b. Conway, S.C., Oct. 11,
1920; s. George W. and Elizabeth S.; A.B., Virginia
Union Univ., 1943; Howard Univ., Sch. of Rel., B.D.,
1946; D.D. (hon.), Western Baptist Bible Coll., 1964;
m. Florence Revels; children--- Margout Ann, Elizabeth
Ann, William M., Jr.; pastor, Bethlehem Baptist Church,
Tyler, Tex., 1947-49; First Baptist Church, Madison,
N.J., 1961-52; Second Baptist Church, Minova, Mo.,
1957-62; director, Religious Activities, Butler Coll.,
Tyler, Tex., 1946-50; teacher, Bible, Butler Coll.,
Tyler, Tex.; dean, Western Baptist Bible Coll., 1958-
61; pres., Western Baptist Bible Coll., 1962---; Mem.,
Independent Voters League, Kansas City, Mo., 1951;
Lincoln Community Council, 1963---; Trustee Board
Western Baptist Bible Coll., Kansas City, Mo., 1961--;
Special supervisor, Surgeon General's Office, Wash.,
D.C., 1945-46; Kansas City Theological Society; YMCA;
Urban League, NAACP; Ministerial Alliance, Kansas City,
Mo.; Religion and Labor Foundation; Omega Psi Phi;
author: History of Missouri Baptist State Convention,
1964; Home: 2119 Tracy, Kansas City 8, Mo. 64108;
Office: 2119 Tracy, Kansas City 8, Mo. 64108.

SKEETE, F. Herbert, b. New York, N.Y., Mar. 22,
1930; s. Ernest A. and Elma I.S.; A.B., Brooklyn Coll.,
1959; B.D., Drew Univ. Theol. Sem., 1962; graduate
work towards M.A., New Sch. for Social Research; m.
Shirley Clarissa Hunte; children--- Michael Hervert,
Mark Curtis; student asst., Metropolitan Community,
Meth. Ch., New York City; student pastor, Union Meth.
Ch., New York; Ordained Elder, New York Conference,
1962; pastor, Union Methodist Ch., South Ozone Park,
New York; social investigator, New York City Dept. of
Welfare, 1959; Mem., Exec. Bd., Education Chairman,
United Neighbors Civic Assn., 1961-64; Mem., Exec.
Com., Second Van Wyck Civic Assn. co-chmn, Queens
Assn. for Integrated and Quality Education; membership
chmn, Exec. Com., South Ozone Park Coordinating Coun-
cil, 1962---; Mem., N.Y. Conf. Bd. of Social Concerns
of The Meth. Ch., 1962-64; Mem., Committee on Health
Care Agencies, New York Conf. of The Meth. Ch.,
1964; vice chmn, New York Chapters of Meth. for Church
Renewal, 1963; chmn, Ed. Com., Queens Interfaith
Clergy Council, 1964; Chapel Com. at Kennedy Airport,
1964; Evangelism Com., Queens Federation of Churches,

1962; US Air Forces, Aptitude Testing Unit; director, Emergency Youth Work Project in Bedford-Stuyvesant, Brooklyn, New York, 1964; Home: 130-32 149th St., South Ozone Park 36, New York; Office: Union Meth. Ch., 150 St. Rockaway Blvd., South Ozone Park 36, New York.

SKINNER, John Thomas, chaplain; b. Jackson, Ala., July 15, 1915; s. Hayes W. and Bettie (Dickinson) S.; B.D., Lutheran College, 1934-40; m. Lai Levonne Ramsey; pastor Calvary, Holy Cross, St. Mark's, Gethsemane, Christ, St. Paul's Lutheran Ch., Alabama, 1940-48; Mt. Calvary, Konnapolis, N.C., 1948-55; Calvary, Memphis, Tenn., 1955-59; Trinity Lutheran Church, Montgomery, Ala., 1959-62; Bethlehem Lutheran Church, New Orleans, La., 1962-63; Institutional chaplain, New Orleans, 1963-   ; Dept. of English-Alabama Lutheran Academy, 1946-48; secy. of Bd. of Control, Immanuel Lutheran College, Greensboro, N.C., 1953-58, Institutional chaplain, Charity Hospital, New Orleans; Mem.: NAACP; Democrat; Home: 4402 Anthony Ave., New Orleans, La.; Office: Charity Hospital, New Orleans, La.

SMITH, Benjamin Julian, bishop; Barnesville, Ga., Dec. 27, 1899; s. Rev. John Benjamin and Martha Angeline (Thomas) S.; A.B., Howard U., 1924; B.D., Garrett Theol. Sem., 1927; student Northwestern U.; D.D., Lane Coll., 1944; m. Hermion V. Jackson; children-- Roy Morgan, Carol Susan (Mrs. Earle Anthony), Benjamin Julian. Ordained to ministry Christian Meth. Episcopal Ch.; asst. pastor Israel Met. Ch., Washington, 1922-24; pastor New Hope Ch., Evanston, Ill., 1924-28; Dir. religious edn. 8th Episcopal Dist., acting pastor, Williams Institutional. Ch., New York City, 1928-29; pastor Jubilee Temple, Chgo., 1929-30; Jamison Temple, Kansas City, Mo., 1930-35; gen. sec. bd. religious edn. C.M.E. Ch., 1935-54, bishop, 1954 --; pres. bd. Christian edn.; v.p. Interdenomination Theol. Center, Atlanta, Mem. Nat. Council Boy Scouts; Pres. bd. trustees Lane Coll., Jackson, Tenn.; trustee Miss. Industrial Coll.; dir. Rockefeller Brothers Fund for Theological Edn. Mem. Nat. Council Chs. Christ U.S. (v.p.), World Council Christian Edn. and Sunday Sch. Assn. (v.p.), World Council Chs. (exec. com. U.S. conf.), So. Conf. Human Welfare, N.A.A.C.P., Phi Beta Sigma. Author, Educational Opportunity of the Local Church; Educational Evangelism; The Church at the Cross Roads; Home: 8128 S. Calumet Ave., Chgo. 19.

SMITH, Charles Mifflin, b. Wilmington, Del., Jan. 10,
1921; s. W. Hibberd and Louise Coursey S.; A.B.,
Livingstone Coll., 1962; m. Theodora Shippy; children
--- Charles Mifflin Jr., Edgar Hibberd; pastor, Ernest
Robinson Mem. African Methodist Episcopal Zion Ch.,
Chester, Pa., 1950-52; Alloyne Mem. AME Zion Ch.,
Phila., Pa., 1952-55; Union Chapel AME Zion Ch.,
Albemerle, N.C., 1955-57; Russell Chapel AME Zion
Ch., Rogersville, Tenn., 1957-59; Mount Zion AME
Zion Ch., Lancaster, S.C., 1959---; teacher, Public
School, Albemarle, N.C., 1 year; Lancaster, S.C., 1
year; Trustee, Clinton Coll.; mem., Connectional Dept.
Budget Bd. AME Zion Ch.; mem., Alpha Psi Alpha;
NAACP; author: Our Heritage, 1867-1958; Home: 401
Clinton Ave., Lancaster, S.C.

SMITH, Charlie Jasper, b. Angelus, S.C., Nov. 12, 1929;
s. Charlie and Eula (McQueen) S.; A.B., Claflin Coll.,
Orangeburg, S.C., 1959; B.D., Gammon Theol. Sem.,
Atlanta, Ga.; m. Doris Frances Webb; pastor, Landrum
and Inman Meth. Ch., 1951-53; McBee Meth. Ch., S.
C., 1953-54; York Meth. Ch., 1954-60; Spartanburg Meth.
Ch., 1960-62; District Supt. of the Sumter Dist., The
Meth. Ch., 1962---; chmn, The Com. on Urban Work;
vice chmn, Bd. of Ministerial Training and Qualification;
Mem., The Commission on World Service and Finance
in the S.C. Conference; vice chmn, The Sumter Move-
ment; Democrat; Mem., Alpha Phi Alpha; Odd Fellows;
Masons; Home: 514 S. Main St., Sumter, S.C. 29151.

SMITH, Ernest Clarence, sem. prof.; b. Cumberland, Va.
Jan. 16, 1897; s. Booker and Alice (Epps) S.; A.B.,
Va. Union Sem. & Coll., 1923; A.B., B.D., Va. Union
Univ., 1926, 1929; Union Theol. Sem., N.Y., 1936;
DD. (hon.) & LL.D. (hon.), Va. Seminary, 1953; D.D.
(hon.), Va. Union Univ., 1940; m. Dorothy B. Butler;
children--- Oswald C., Ernest C., Jr.; pastor, Mt.
Carmel Bapt. Ch., Lynchburg, Va., 1919-24; second
Bapt. Ch., S. Richmond, Va., 1924-28; pastor, Metro-
politan Bapt. Ch., Wash. D.C., 1928---; instructor,
Howard Univ. Sch. of Univ., 1935-58; lecturer, Bapt.
Sunday School Congress; Home: 1551 Henlock NW, Wash.
D.C.

SMITH, George Walker, b. Montgomery, April 28, 1928;
s. Will and Amanda (Tyler) S.; B.S., Knoxville Coll.,

Tenn.; B.D., Pittsburgh Theol. Sem., 1956; m. Elizabeth Hightower; children--- Anthony Tyrone, Carolyn
Yvonne, Joyce Lorpaine; youth director, Third United
Presbyterian Ch., Pittsburgh Pa., 3 years; current
pastor, Golden Hill United Presbyterian Ch., 1956---;
vice pres., Bd. of Education; Mem., Advisory Bd. of the
Salvation Army; Bd. of Directors, San Diego County Coun-
cil of the Boy Scouts of America; Resolutions Committee
of the California School Bd. Assn, 1964---; Bd. of
Directors, The Big Brothers of San Diego, Inc.; Bd. of
Directors, USO Council of San Diego; Civil Service Oral
Review Bd.; chmn., Support of Churches Commission for
Southeastern Kiwanis Club; Bd. of Trustee, Univ. Re-
ligious Foundation, Univ. of Calif., San Diego; chmn.,
Bd. of Managers, Southeast YMCA; Mem., Metropolitan
Bd., San Diego City-County YMCA; San Diego Mental
Health Com.; supt., Schools Commission dealing with the
culturally handicapped; San Diego Unified School District
Bd. of Education; Outstanding Young Clergyman of the
Year, by the Jr. Chamber of Commerce, San Diego;
Outstanding Young Men of America, by the Nat. Bd. of
Directors of the Jr. Chamber of Commerce; Home: 5514
Mira Flores Dr., San Diego 14, Calif.; Office: 2130
Market St., San Diego, Calif.

SMITH, Herald Leonydus, church official; b. Smithfield,
Ohio, Apr. 20, 1907; s. Ira Rufus and Mary (West) S.;
B.D., Payne Theological Seminary, 1945; m. Dorothy
Irene McClinton; children--- Herald Smith, Jr., Verl
Rosalie Foster, David; Assigned to St. Andrew Coshocton,
1939; St. Paul London, 1941; Quinn Chapel Ironton, 1945;
St. Paul, Cincinnati, 1953; Asst. pastor, St. John Cleve-
land, 1957; Quinn Chapel, Cleveland, 1962; Chief Secy.
of South Ohio, Ohio Conference from 1943-57; Secy. of
Tawawa School of Religion, District Conference, Vice-
president of Tawawa School of Religion, Editor of Tawawa
and a Trustee of North Ohio Conference, instructor of
Seminary sponsored by Ministers in Cleveland; Secy.,
Methodist Ministers Alliance, A. M. E. Fellowship, Treas-
urer of Methodist Alliance, 2nd Vice-pres. of NAACP of
Cincinnati, Ohio, Active in Community Work in Cincin-
nati, Masonic Lodge, Boy Scouts Institutional and Regional
Representative; Director of Religious Education; Social
Relation of Council of Churches in the City of Cleveland;
Mem.,   Bd. of Kinsman Area Recreational Building;
Award given in 1950 for best letter on theme "My City"
in Ironton, Ohio; Many other citations; Royal Cresent

Club of Wilberforce, Sphinx Club Republica; Liter-
ary Societies; Columnist in the Call & Post, Negro
Weekly of Cincinnati, "Extending the Pulpit Beyond The
Sanctuary", Cincinnati Enquire, Cleveland Press, Metro
Forum and others; Home 3359 142nd Cleveland, Ohio:
Office: 3241 130th Cleveland, Ohio.

SMITH, James Wynetotte, b. Cherokee County, S. C., Mar.
15, 1893; s. Cooper Samuel and Nancy (Meachem) S.;
A. B., Johnson C. Smith Univ., 1920; B. D., J. C. Smith
Univ., 1923; D. D., Johnson C. Smith Univ., 1945; m.
Margaret Arthur;children--- James Wynetatte, Jr., Wil-
liam Arthur, Estelle Ida Mae (Mrs. William Gayman),
Gloria Margaret (Mrs. James Thomas Burch); pastor
East Vine Avenue Presbyterian Ch., Knoxville, Tenn.;
Davie St. Presbyterian Church, Raleigh, N. C.; (cur-
rent) Seventh Street Presbyterian Ch., Charlotte, N. C.;
Secretary Trustee Board, Johnson C. Smith Univ., Char-
lotte, N. C.; Mem. Trustee Board, Barber Scotia Col-
lege, Concord, N. C.; chairman, National Missions Com-
mittee, Catawba Synod; First Class Private, World War
I, 1918-1919; 1961 "Father of the Year" by W. P. O. of
Seventh Street Presbyterian Ch.; Mem.: Mason, Finance
Committee Order Eastern Star, Executive Board, Council
of Christians and Jews, Commission on Church Relations,
Presbyterian Ch.; Home: 1901 Patton Ave., Charlotte 8,
N. C.; Church: 406 N. College St., Charlotte, N. C.

SMITH, John Conway, Church official, b. Little Rock, Arkansas, Jan. 4, 1927; s. John C. Smith; B. A., Oakwood
College, 1950; m. Helen L. George; children--- Laura
Janet, Jonathan C. Publishing Secretary, Southwest Region Conf. of Seventh-Day Adventists, 1952; Home Missionary - S. S. secretary, Southwest Region Conf., Dallas, Texas, 1962; pastor: Phil. S. D. A. Church, Shreveport, La., Ephesus S. D. A. Church, San Antonio, Texas;
present: pastor, Bethel S. D. A. Church, Toledo, Ohio,
1963-   . U. S. Army, World War II. Home: 1703 Park-
dale St., Toledo, Ohio. Office: 660 Vance St.,Toledo,
Ohio.

SMITH, Kenneth Bryant, b. Montclair, N. J., Feb. 19, 1931;
s. William and Dorothy (Jackson) S.; B. A., Virginia
Union U., 1953; Grad. Work, Drew Univ., 1953-54;
B. D., Bethany Biblical Sem., 1960; m. Jacqueline
Fielder; 1 son, Kenneth Byrant, Jr.; YMCA, Summit,
N. J., 1953-54; Assoc. Youth Worker, YMCA, Chgo.,

Ill., 1954-57; Assoc. Minister, Cong.Ch. of Park Manor,
Chgo., 1957-61; Organizing Minister, Trinity United Church
of Christ, Chgo., 1961---; Mem., Religious Leaders
Council, Chgo. Urban League; Bd. of Dirs., Chatham
YMCA, Chgo., Adv. Bd., Roseland District, United
Charities, Chgo.; Chgo. Cong. Christian Assoc.; The
Cong. and Christian Conf. of Illinois: Chrmn., United
Church Fellowship for Racial Justice Now; Home: 9704
S. Emerald Ave., Chicago, Ill., 60628.

*SMITH, Lawrence Benjamin, b. Washington, D.C., Nov.
2, 1925; s. Alice Smith; A.B., Dickinson Coll., Carlisle,
Pa.; B.D., Howard Univ. Sch. of Rel.; m. Estelle
Augusta Holsey; children--- Jonathan Darryl, Lawrence
Benjamin, Jr., Kevin Augustus (Jameson), Timothy
Bruce; pastor, Mt. Zion Methodist Ch., Silver Spring,
Md., 1951-52; Nottingham-Croom Charge, The Methodist
Ch., Nottingham and Croom, Md., 1955-56; chaplain to
students, Wesley Foundation, Howard University, Wash.
D.C., 1953-54; Metropolitan Community Meth. Ch., New
York City, 1957-59; pastor, Trinity Meth. Ch. of Mor-
riania, Bronx, New York, 1959---; chmn, Children's
Work Committee, The Protestant Council of The City of
New York, 1958-59; chmn, Christian Education Com-
mittee, The Protestant Council of The Bronx, 1961-63;
Chaplain Ten Mile River Scout Camps, Narrowsburg,
New York, 1960-63; Mem., Bd. of Directors, Clare-
mont Neighbor Community Centers, Inc.; Clergy Advisor,
Parents for Leadership and Action Now (Public School
action group organized May 1964); US Army, Overseas
duty in Italy, Germany and France, 1944-46; Ehrenfeld
Service Award; Affiliated in active capacity and role with
Bronx Council of Greater New York Councils, Boy Scouts
of America; Home: 1074 Washington Avenue, Bronx, New
York 10456; Office: 1076 Washington Avenue, Bronx,
New York 10456.

*SMITH, Oswald Garrett, b. Richmond, Va., April 17,
1925; s. Ernest Clarence and Odile (Davis) S.; B.A.,
B.D., Howard Univ., Wash., D.C., 1947, 1950; M.A.
Columbia Univ., N.Y., 1951; D.D. (hon.) Va. Theol.
Seminary & Coll., 1954; m. Berta Elizabeth Mills; chil-
dren--- Oswald, Jr. Alicin Odile; current, Director
Activities & Asst. Pastor, Metropolitan Baptist Church,
Wash., D.C., 1947---; pastor, Mt. Zion Baptist Church,
Arlington, Va., 1952---; lecturer, Lott Carey Summer
Conference, 1954; instructor, National Baptist Sunday

School & B. T. U. Congress; instructor, District Baptist
Educational Congress; pres., Capitol Funeral Service
Inc., 1959-62; vice pres., Reynolds Smith Investment
Co.; Mem., Board of Civic Welfare; Baptist Ministers
Conference; US Army, 1944-46; Good Conduct Medal;
Expert Rifleman Award; Board of Directors, Veterans'
Memorial Y. M. C. A.; Board of Directors Lott Carey
Foreign Mission Convention; Board of Directors, Northern
Virginia Baptist Ass'n; Arlington Ministerial Ass'n; Fam-
ily Services of Northern Virginia; Southern Christian
Leadership Congress; Home: 1938 Bunker Hill Rd., NE.,
Wash., D. C.; Office: 19th South Glebe Rd., Arlington,
Va.

*SMITH, Perry Anderson, III, b. Mount Bayou, Miss., May
16, 1934; s. Perry Anderson and Elease (Williams) Wilson S.; A. B., B. D., Howard Univ., Wash. D. C., 1955,
1958; pastor, The First Baptist Church, North Brentwood, Md., 1958-65; appointed Ex. Director Poverty Program
Prince Georges County, Md.; pres., Prince Georges Md.
NAACP; vice pres., Md. State Conference NAACP Branches,
1961--; Freedom Rider, CORE, 1961; Arrested 23 times;
Mem., Alpha Phi Alpha; Home: 1227 Kenyon St., NW, Wash.
10, D. C.; Office: 4009 Wallace Rd., North Brentwood, Md.

SMITH, Robert, b. Birmingham, Ala., July 2, 1933; s.
Eddie and Malissa S.; B. S., Tuskegee Institute, 1955;
B. S. T., Boston Univ. Sch. of Theol., 1958; m.
Gwendolyn J. Bailey; children--- Robert E., Caryolyn J.;
asst. pastor, St. Mark Cong. Ch., Boston, Mass., 1956-
58; Lab. Director, Church Surveys Dept., Boston Univ.
Sch. of Theol., 1955-59; current pastor, Riverside Park
Meth. Ch., Indianapolis, Ind., 1959---; Mem., Bd. of
Trustees, Meth. Hospital, Ind.; Conf., Bd. of Christian
Social Concerns, NW Indiana; PTA; NAACP; National
Foundation, Non-Partisans for Better Schools; Home:
1517 W. 25th St., Indianapolis, Ind.; Office: 2440 N.
Harding St., Indianapolis, Ind.

SMITH, Roland, b. Decatur, Ga., Feb. 26, 1902; s. Ander-
son and Mattie S.; A. B., Morehouse Coll., 1929; A. M.
Atlanta Univ., 1961; D. D. (hon.), Selma Univ., Selma,
Ala.; Allen Univ., Columbia, S. C.; Morris Brown Coll.,
Atlanta, Ga.; L. L. D. (hon.), Arkansas Bapt. Coll.,
Little Rock, Ark.; Monrovia Coll., Liberia, W. Africa;
m. Mary S.; pastor, Metropolitan Bapt. Ch., Columbus,
Ga., 1929-31; First African Bapt. Ch., Tuscaloosa, Ala.,

1931-36; First Bapt. Ch. , Macon, Ga. , 1936-37; First
Bapt. Ch. , Little Rock, Ark. , 1947---; statistician, Na-
tional Bapt. Convention, U.S.A. , Inc. 1932-54; sec. ,
Negro Work, Home Mission Bd. , Southern Bapt. Con-
vention, 1938-49; sec. , National Bapt. Training Union
Bd. , National Bapt. Convention, U.S.A. , Inc. , 1954-
57; editor, The Georgia Bapt. (Paper) 1941-49; Mem. ,
National Council of Churches of Christ in America;
Former Mem. , Joint Commission of Public Affairs, Na-
tional Baptist , Southern Baptist, and American Bapt.
Conventions; former sec. , Joint Commission on Minister-
ial Education and Race Relations, American, Southern
and National Baptist Conventions; Mem. , World Baptist
Alliance Executive Committee, Copenhagen, Denmark,
1947; World Baptist Alliance Relief Commission, 1947-50;
director, Citizens Trust Company, Atlanta, Ga. ; director
South Eastern Fidelity Fire Insurance Company, Atlanta,
Ga. ; Mem. , Kappa Alpha Psi; Delta Sigma Rho Honorary
Society; Mason; former chairman, Bd. of Trustees, Ark.
Baptist Coll. , Little Rock, Ark. ; pres. , Arkansas Christian Movement (Led in the declaring of all four segre-
gated laws nullification by the Supreme Court of State
of Arkansas as proposed by Governor Oval E. Faubus);
Home: 613 West 7th St. , Little Rock, Ark. ; Office: 7th
S. Gaines St. , Little Rock, Ark.

SMITH, Thomas, Jr. b. Ansonville, N.C. , July 15, 1922;
s. Thomas, Jr. and Callie (Windfield) S. ; B.S. , St.
Paul's Coll. , 1946-50; S.T.B. , Philadelphia Divinity
School; Temple Univ. Sch. of Theol. , 1950, 1953; Coll.
of Preachers, 1960, 60; m. Mary Jackson; children---
Carolyn, Clarise, Cynthia, Thomas, III; priest-in-charge,
St. James Prot. Epis. Church, Emporia, Va. , St.
Thomas Prot. Epis.Church, Freeman, Va. , 1953-57;
current vicar, St. Stephen's Church, Winston-Salem, 1957
---; chaplain, Episcopal Faculty and Students, Winston-
Salem State Coll. and the School of Nursing and the Kate
Bitting Reynold's Hospital; Mem. , Executive Council of
the Diocese of N.C. Dept. of Missions, Christian Social
Relations, Dept. of College Work; chairman, YMCA Fund
raising campaign, Winston-Salem, 1962-63; Group Chairman of United Fund, Business Section, 1963; co-chairman, The Congress of Racial Equality, Winston-Salem,
1963; Exec. Bd. of the NAACP, 1961-62; US Army,
1941-45; Good Conduct Medal; Campaign Medals for the
Pacific operation with five battle stars; Mem. , Financial
Com. , Democratic Party, Winston-Salem, N.C. ; Home:

810 North Cameron Ave., Winston-Salem, N.C.; Office:
1104 North Highland Ave., Winston-Salem, N.C.

SNELL, Simon, b. Rosenberg, Ft. Bend Co. Texas, Feb.
8, 1912; s. Isome and Marcella (Stewart) S.; Wiley Col-
lege, Marshall, Texas, A.B. Clark College, Atlanta,
Ga., 1949, B.D. Gammon Theological Seminary, Atlanta,
Ga., Further study: Atlanta University. m. Mary Lee
Tinner; children: Dr. Edna Faye Snell Houston, (Dr.
Sam Houston); ministry: Warren Methodist Church,
Macon, Ga., 1949, Porch Chapel Methodist Church,
Calhoun, Ga., 1950, First Pastor of Bowen Methodist
Church, Atlanta, Ga. 1951-52, Lawrenceville Circuit,
Lawrenceville, Ga., 1953-59; St. Paul Methodist Church,
Texarkana, Texas, present: Pastor of Methodist Church,
Marshall, Texas; Member: Conference Board of Educa-
tion, Asst. Sec., Board of Directors of The Wesley
Foundation, Chairman, Conference Commission on Evan-
gelism; Teacher in the District Institute, Marshall,
Texas; Substitute teacher, Texarkana Public School Sys-
tem; Member, Y.M.C.A., Red Cross; Citizens Com-
mittee; Chairman, Ministerial Committee; Member,
Political Action Committee of N.A.A.C.P., Civil Defense,
U.S. Army, 1941-44; served in North Africa, Italy,
France. Received the EAME Campaign Medal with four
bronze stars, good conduct medal, victory ribbon, one
service stripe, four overseas bars; Member: Phi Beta
Sigma, American Woodmen; Home: 908 Whetstone Street,
Marshall, Texas.

SOMERSILLE, James Humphries, b. Albay, Legaspi,
Philippines, June 27, 1915; s. Albert E. and Maude
(Humphries) S.; A.B., Capital University, 1937-40; B.
D., Capital University Theol. Seminary, 1940-43; Courses
in Psychology and Social Work in Howard University;
m. Elizabeth Beatrice Adams; pastor Evangelical Lutheran Church of Our Redeemer (LCA), 1943---; Home:
3644 13th St. NW, Washington, D.C.; Office: 2 Rhode
Island Avenue, NE, Washington, D.C.

SOMERVILLE, Wendell Clay, sem. prof.; b. Reidsville,
N.C., Mar. 10, 1900; s. Addie Louise Brown; A.B.,
1929, B.D., 1931, Shaw Univ.; A.M., Graduate Sch.
of Theol., Oberlin Coll., 1939; D.D. (hon.) Shaw Univ.,
1943; LL.D. (hon.), Howard Univ., 1960; m. Alice E.
Cooper; Exec. sec., General Bapt. State Conv., N.C.,
Exec. sec., Lott Carey Bapt. Foreign Mission Con-

vention, 1940---; visiting prof., Sch. of Rel., Howard
Univ.; US Navy, World War I; Certificate of Achievement,
Washington Afro-American, 1941; Mem., The Omega Psi
Phi; author: Around The World For Others, 1960; Home:
4408 16th St., Wash. 11, D.C.; Office: 1501 11th St.,
Wash. 1, D.C.

SPARROW, Eugene, educator; b. Clinton, Mass., Oct. 6,
1921; s. William N. and Mae (Chant) S.; A.B., Michigan
Univ., Ann Arbor, Mich., 1946; S.T.B., Tufts Coll.,
Crane Theol. Sch., 1949; Harvard Divinity School, Cambridge, Mass., 1946-47; m. Divorced; children--- Debra,
Rebecca; dean of men, Texas Coll., Tyler, Tex.; acting
head, Social Studies Dept., Jarvis Christian Coll.,
Hawkins, Tex.; teacher, Elementary School, Plainville,
Conn., 1953-56; acting director, Urban League, Springfield, Mass., 1956-58; director, Field Service, Unitarian Universalist Conference; present asst. director,
Mayor's Friendly Relations Committee, Cincinnati, Ohio;
consultant, The Midwest Unitarian Fellowship Committee;
camp director, 1957-58; Mem., Mayor's Committee,
Springfield, Mass., 1957-58; US Air Force; Mem., National Educational Assn; Unitarian Universalist Ministerial Assn; National Assn of Intergroup Officials; Weekly
column, Daily Newspaper, Cincinnati, Ohio; Home: 1491
Baymiller Walk, Cincinnati 14, Ohio; Office: 909 Plum
St., Cincinnati, Ohio.

SPEAKS, Ruben Lee, sem. prof.; b. Lake Providence, La.,
Jan. 8, 1920; s. Benjamin and Jessie B.S.; A.B.,
Drake Univ., Des Moines, Iowa, 1946; B.D., Drew Univ.,
Madison, New Jersey, 1949; S.T.M., Temple Univ.,
Phila., Pa., 1952; Duke Univ., Durham 1960-61; m.
Janie Angeline Griffin; children--- Robert, Joan Cordelia,
Faith Elizabeth; pastor, St. Thomas African Methodist
Episcopal Zion Church, Somerville, N.J., 1946; Wallace
Chapel A.M.E. Zion Ch., Summit, N.J., 1947; Varick
Memorial A.M.E. Zion Ch., Phila., Pa., 1950; St.
Mark A.M.E. Zion Ch., Durham, 1956; First Church
Brooklyn, N.Y.; 1964; professor, Hood Theol. Sem.;
Livingstone Coll., Salisbury, N.C., 1959-64; Mem.,
Commission on the Education of Exceptional Persons;
National Council of Churches, USA; Episcopal Committee,
A.M.E. Zion Ch.; Durham Committee on Negro Affairs,
N.C.; Trustee, Lincoln Hospital, Durham, N.C.; NAACP;
Citation and plaque, Outstanding community service to
city of Durham; Democrat; Mem., Mason; editorial staff,

devotional book, Strength of My Life; Home: 1455 Carroll, Brooklyn 13, N.Y.; Office: 480 Tonpkins Ave., Brooklyn, New York.

SPIVEY, Bennett, b. Newmarket, Tenn., Aug. 30, 1932; st. Joseph's Jr. College, 1953-55; A.B., Philosophy, Our Lady of Angels Seminary, 1956-58; St. Joseph Major Seminary, 1959---; 1963, victim of multiple sclerosis.

SPOTTSWOOD, Stephen Gill, bishop; b. July 18, 1897; s. Abraham Lincoln and Mary Elizabeth (Gray) S.; Albright College; Gordon Divinity School; Yale University; D.D. (hon.), Livingstone College, 1939; m. Viola Estelle Booker (deceased); 5 children; pastor, 34 years, Washington, D.C., Buffalo, Indianapolis, Winston-Salem, New Haven, Portland, Maine, West Newton & Lowell, Mass., Elected 58th Bishop of the African Methodist Episcopal Zion Church, 1952---; (District, Alleghany, Ohio, Michigan and Indiana Conference); pres. NAACP (Washington, D.C. Branch), 1947-52; member, National Board of Director, NAACP, 1954-61; pres. Board NAACP, 1961---; Chairman, Board A.M.E. Zion Church, Board of Finance; Transportation and Statistics; Commission on Chaplains; General Conference and Contennial of Freedom Campaign; Member, World Methodist Council; National Council of Churches; Board of Trustees, Livingstone College, N.C.; Home: 1931 16th St. NW, Washington 9, D. C.

STANLEY, Alfred Knighton, b. Greensboro, N.C., July 15, 1937; s. Rev. and Mrs. J. Taylor S.; A.B., Talladega Coll., 1959; B.D., Yale U. Divinity Sch., 1962; Ordained minister, Cong. Ch., 1962; m. Beatrice Alice Perry; Dir. Jr. Youth Act. and Asst. Minister Bunker Hill Cong. Ch., Waterbury, Conn., 1959-60; Consultant for Youth Work, Wider City Parish, 1960-61; Grad. Asst. Assoc. Chaplain, Yale University, 1961-62; Summer Assistant, Central Cong. Ch., N.O., La., 1959-62; Minister-Director, United Southern Christian Fellowship Foundation, North Carolina A & T Coll., 1962-64; Mem. State Advisory Committee of all Civil Rights organization; Appointed to Greensboro Human Relations Commission, 1962 (Chrmn. Comm. on Progress and Information); mem. Regional Board of Selections, North Carolina Volunteers (state Peace Corp type organ.); Assoc. Minister, Plymouth Cong. Ch., Det., Mich., sum. 1964; Asst. Prof. Phil. and Rel., Bennett Coll., Greensboro, N.C., (beg.

Sept., 1964); Mem. Alpha Phi Alpha; Recipient,
Sumner and DeForest Scholarships; Buel Gallagher Award;
Avery Speech Award; Woodrow Wilson Fellowship; Rocke-
feller Theological Fellowship; Author: "Freedom and Re-
sponsibility in Religious Perspectives", "The Current
Crisis in the Negro State Supported University" and sev-
eral other articles; Listed among 100 Negro leaders in
The Negro Revolution in America (Newsweek publication);
Address: Bennett Coll., Greensboro, N.C.

STANLEY, Othello Doremus, b. Beaufort, N.C., July 4,
1904; s. John B. and Annie (Gibble) S.; St. Augustine's
Coll., 1925-27; B.A., Lincoln Univ., 1930; Univ. of
Penna., 1932-1933; Th.B., Philadelphia Divinity School,
1933. Pastored: St. Titus' Episcopal Church, Durham,
N.C., 1933-45; St. Cyprian's Ch., Oxford, N.C., 1943-
52; vicar, St. Matthew's Ch., Baltimore, Maryland,
1953-55; present, pastor, St. Cyrpian's Ch., N. Carolina, 1956-   . Home: 404 Granville St., Oxford, N.C.
Office: 408 Granville St., Oxford, N.C.

STANLEY, Walter Payne, b. Balto, Md., Feb. 18, 1890;
s. Wm. and Grace (Carroll) S.; B.D., Lincoln Univ.,
(Pa.) Pittsburg Seminary; m. Edythe (Hume) S.; chil-
dren--- Edythe Powell, Patricia, Walter; pastor, Pro-
testant Episcopal Churches in New York, Kentucky,
Toledo, Luisville; Retired in 1954 as rector of St.
Augustine's Protestant Episcopal Church, Youngstown,
Ohio.; Mem.: School Board, Toledo; Former Pres.-
Douglas Community Center, Toledo, Ohio; Welfare
Board. YMCA secy. (14 months); pres. Ministerial As-
sociation, Youngstown; Mason Elks; Democrat; Organist;
Home: 703 Parmalee St., Youngstown, Ohio.

STEVENS, Junius Ray, b. Hugo, Okla., July 4, 1914;
s. Joe and Lula B.; Howard Univ., 1948-51; Graduate
courses: US Dept. of Agriculture, Wash., D.C., 1952-
54; m. Esther Bowers; children--- Justice Bowers; assoc.
pastor, Church of Christ, 13th & Irving Sts., Wash., D.
C., 1952-55; pastor, Davisville Ch. of Christ, Hopewell,
Va., 1955-62; current pastor, East Capital St. Ch. of
Christ, Wash. D.C., 1962---; teacher, Camp Mawava,
Front Royal, Va.; Home: 100 Madison NW, Wash., D.
C. 20011; Office: 5026 East Capital, Wash., D.C.
20019

STEVENS, Robert Matthew, coll. pres.; b. Quincy, Fla.;
s. W. S. and Annie (Kent) S.; A. B., Fisk Univ.; B. D.
Payne Theol. Sem.; D. D. (hon.), Wilberforce Univ.,
1954; LL. D., Monrovia Coll., 1955; m. Dorothy Chappell;
one son; Mem., General Bd., African Methodist Episcopal Ch.; former pastor, African Meth. Epis. Ch.; presiding elder, A. M. E. Ch.; dean, Theol. Sem.; current
pres., Campbell Coll.; Mem., Mason; Kappa Alpha Psi;
NAACP; Home: 1352 Alamo, Jackson, Miss.; Office:
1500 W. Lynch, Jackson, Miss. 39203.

STINSON, Olden Hixon, b. Woodbury, Ga., Oct. 25, 1905;
s. Edd L. and Carrie (Hixon) S.; A. B., B. D., Morehouse Coll. and Morehouse Sch. of Religion, 1927, 1949;
post graduate study, Univ. of Chicago, 1951; m. Eddie
Bay Curgil; children--- Jeanne M., Olden Edward; pastor,
Mt. Zion First Baptist Ch., Griffin, Ga., 1943---; pres.
New Era Missionary Bapt. Convention, Ga., 1961---;
instructor, New Testament, Extension Dept. of the Interdenominational Theological Center, Atlanta, Ga., 1962---;
pres., Citizens Improvement League of Griffin and Spald-
ing County; clerk, Cane Creek and Cabin Creek Baptist A
Ass'n; Mem., Griffin Staff on Alcoholic Rehabilitation
Service, Counseling; former sec., Republican Party,
Spalating Co.; author: Handbook, A Brief Glimpse of
Negro Baptists In Georgia; Home: 123 S. 4th St., Griffin,
Ga.; Office: Mt. Zion Baptist Ch., Corner of East Taylor
and 4th Sts., Griffin, Ga.

STITH, Forrest Christopher, b. Marshall, Texas, May 18,
1934; s. Forrest M. and Daisy L.; B. S. University of
Nebraska, 1955, B. D. Drew Theological Seminary, 1958;
m. Josephine Mitchell; children: Lori Crystal; ministry:
Douglas Memorial Methodist Church, 1958 to present
(Washington, D. C.) Treasurer, Area P. Board - Commissioner's Youth Council, Washington, D. C., Chaplain,
Public Interest Civic Assoc. member: Sigma Theta Epsilon, Washington Ministerial Union, Washington Methodist
Ministers Group; Capitol Hill Ministerial Assoc.; Home:
1700 Otis Street, N. E., Washington, D. C. Office: 11th
and H Streets, N. E. Washington, D. C. 20002.

STITT, Robert Elemaker, b. Charlotte Courthouse, Va.,
June 8, 1909; s. William Banks and Alice (Morris) S.
1940, B. S., Lane College, Jackson, Tenn.; 1947; B. D.,
Lincoln University; m. Wilhemenia Gertrude Christmas;
children--- Robert Elemaker, Jr.; Pastor, United Pres-

byterian Church, U.S.A., 1940---; Mem. Moderator of
Cape Fear Presbytery (1 yr.); chairman of Ecumenical
Mission and Relations Committee (10 yrs); chairman of
Ministerial Relations Committee; mem. Phi
Beta Sigma; Ancient Egyptian Arabic Order; Nobles of
The Mystic Shrine of North and South America; Home:
P.O. Box 524 Lillington, N.C.

STOKES, Frank Agustus, b. Griffin, Georgia, Nov. 13,
1916; s. Frank and Pauline S.; B.A., Oakwood College,
1951; M.A., Oakwood College, 1952; m. Ruth Bracy;
children- Barbara, Lewis, Edward, Frank III, Paul;
pastored: Atlantic City, New Jersey; Rome, Georgia;
Greenville, S.C.; West Palm Beach, Florida. Present;
Mt. Sinai Seventh-Day Adventist Church, Orlando, Florida.
Chaplain, Dr. Phillips Hospital, Orlando, Fla.; served
on Mayor's Committee, Urban Renewal Committee and
Voters' League; Executive vice-president, N.A.A.C.P.
Former member, Civil Service Board of Palm Beach
County; active duty in World War II, Okinawa and
Phillipines. Home: 2316 W. South St., Orlando, Fla.
Office: 514 South Parramore Street, Orlando, Fla.

STOKES, Rembert Edwards, coll. pres.; b. Dayton, Ohio,
June 16, 1917; s. William Otis and Hoyel Marie S.;
B.S., Wilberforce Univ., 1940; S.T.B., Boston Univ.;
TH.D., Boston Univ.; Studies in Harvard Univ.; m.
Nancy Philips; children--- Linda, Deborah, Celesto;
pastor, A.M.E. Church, Jamestown, Rhode Island,
Cambridge, Mass., Canton, Ohio; Dean, Payne Theologi-
cal Seminary, 1951-56; Pres., Wilberforce Univ., Wilber-
force, Ohio, 1956---; Member, Administrative Council,
Ohio Council of Churches, Faith and Order Conference,
World Council of Churches, Board of Trustees, National
Conference of Christians and Jews; Member, Governor's
Commission on Aging; Ohio Commission on Aging; Greene
Montgomery County Red Cross Board;   Alpha Phi
Alpha; Frontier International, Dayton, Ohio; Home: P.O.
Box 453, Wilberforce, Ohio 45384; Office: Office of the
President, Wilberforce Univ., Wilberforce, Ohio 45384.

STONE, Lee Owen, b. Lexington, Ky., April 27, 1903;
s. Walter and Lillace (Peasons) S. 1936, B.D. Bishop
Payne Divinity; 1944, B.S. Lewis and Clark College; m.
Eva Lena Wilson, 1926-28; Teacher, Kentucky House of
Reform; 1936, Vicar, St. Philips Episcopal Church,

Portland, Ore. 1936; Board of Portland Urban League, 1946-
50; Board, Portland Council of social agencies, 1950-
56; Board, Portland, U.S.O., 1946-58; Deputy to General
Convention of Episcopal Church, 1952-62; Home: 6920
27th Ave. N.E., Portland 11, Oregon. Office: 120 Knott
St., N.E., Portland 12, Ore.

STRASSNER, William Russell, coll. administrator; b. Mor-
rilton, Ark.; A.B., Ark. Bapt. Coll.; B.D., Va. Union
Univ.; M.S.T., Andover Newton Theol. Sem.; further
study: Union Theol. Sem. and Teachers Coll., N.Y.;
D.D. (hon.), Shaw Univ.; LL.D. (hon.), Va. Union Theol.
Sem., 1962; student pastor, Zion and Galilee Ch., W. Va.;
Zion Bapt. Ch., Boston; pastor, Mt. Zion Bapt. Ch.,
Charlottesville, Va., 7 years; current co-ordinator, Coll.
Community Relations, Hampton Institute, 1962---; dean of
Religion, Bishop Coll.; dean of Sch. of Rel., Shaw Univ.,
Raleigh N.C.; pres., Shaw Univ., 1951-62; Mem., Fel-
lowship of Southern Churchmen; Southern Regional Educa-
tional Bd.; Va. Teachers Ass'n; Nat'l Ed. Ass'n; Joint
Committee on the Negro Baptist; YMCA; Alpha Phi Alpha;
Odd Fellows; organizer, Civil League, Inter-Fraternal
Council, Recreational Center, Charlottesville, Va.; Of-
fice: Hampton Institute, Hampton, Va.

STREET, John Franklin, b. Millsboro, Del., Jan. 8, 1906;
s. Gardner Ross and Della (Norwood) S.; Oakwood Junior
College, Huntsville, Ala., 1936; m. Ruth Evelyn Burton;
children-- Della Ruth Evelyn. Pastor: Seventh-Day Ad-
ventist Churches, Alabama, Mississippi, Arizona and
South Atlantic Conferences, 1939-1959; present: pastor,
Alleghney Conference, 1959- ; Farm Superintendent,
Oakwood College, 1936-39. Home: 532 E. Commerce St.,
Bridgeton, New Jersey.

STRINGER, Emmett James, chaplain; b. Yazoo Co., Miss.
Sept. 16, 1919; s. Young Marion and Janie (Hargove) S.;
B.S., Alcorn Coll., Alcorn, Miss., 1937-41; D.D.S.,
Meharry Medical Coll., Nashville, Tenn., 1946-50;
m. Flora Charlene Ghist; US Army, 1941-46; stenographer,
The Veterans Administration, 1946; Engaging in the prac-
tice of General Dentistry in Columbia, Miss., since
1950; current pastor, Mt. Olive Missionary Bapt. Ch.,
Boligee, Alabama, 1959---; vice moderator, Mt. Olive-
Green County, Ala., Baptist District Assn; faculty mem-
ber, National Bapt. S.S. and B.T.U. Congress, U.S.A.
Inc., 1961---; chaplain, National Dental Assn, 1962---;

Advisory Com. of Mary Holmes Jr. Coll., 1962---; pres.
NAACP, Columbus, Miss., 1953-58; pres. Miss. State
Conf. of NAACP Branches, 1953-54; The first Negro
since reconstruction days to register to vote in Lowndes
County, Columbus, Miss., 1952; chaplain, treas., Co-
lumbia Negro Assn for Retarded Children; pres., Dental
Section, John A. Andrew Clinical Society, Tuskegee,
Ala.; Man of the Year, 1960, by Miss. Regional Council
of Negro Leadership; Dentist of the Decade Award from
the Dental Class of 1950 of Meharry Medical Coll.; pres.
Miss. Dental Society, 1961-62; pres., North Miss. Medi-
cal, Dental, Pharmaceutical and Nurses Society, 1960;
Mem., Mason; Elk; Phi Beta Sigma; Home: P.O. Box
146 Columbus, Miss.; Office: 114 1/2 South 4 th St.,
Columbus, Miss.

SUMPTER, Augustus Cicero, teacher; b. Sumter County, S.
C., 1895; s. Marcus J. and Ella (Dorothy) S.; Allen
Univ., Columbia, S.C.; Wilberforce Univ., Wilberforce,
Ohio; Howard Univ., Washington, D.C.; Tuskigee Insti-
tute; D.D., Payne Theol. Seminary; m. Mary Maude
Brown; principal, Bishopville High School, S.C.; pastor,
Bethel African Methodist Episcopal Ch., Conway, S.C.;
Bethel A.M.E. Church, Dillon, S.C., 3 years; Allen
Temple, Greenville S.C., 5 years; Allen Temple, Cin.
Ohio, 7 years; Mt. Vernon A.M.E. Church, Columbus,
Ohio, 4 years; Exec. Committee, National Council
Churches, 1950-57; current pastor, St. James A.M.E.
Church, Pittsburgh, Pa.; Mem., Board of Directors,
Council of Churches of Pittsburgh Area; US Forces,
World War I, 8 months; Home: 7334 Monticello, Pitts-
burgh 8, Pa.; Office: 208 North Euclid Ave., Pittsburgh
6, Pa.

SUMPTER, Benjamin Franklin, presiding elder; b. Sumter,
S.C., Mar. 11, 1916; s. M.J. and Cleopatra S.; Allen
Univ.; Dickerson Theological Seminary; D.D. (hon.),
Allen Univ., 1954; D.D., Monrovia Coll., West Africa,
1954; m. Thelma O. Brown; children--- two sons and
five daughters; pastor, St. Peters African Methodist
Episcopal Church, Cameron, S.C., 1938-40; pastor,
Miller Chapel A.M.E. Church, Newberry, S.C., 1940-
46; pastor, Mt. Zion A.M.E. Church, Charleston, S.C.,
1946-59; current, presiding elder, The Manning & Wateree
Districts, 1959---; principal, Junior High School, Newberry, S.C., 1942-46; First Negro Commissioner of the
city of Charleston; Chairman, Board of Reid House of

Christian Service; pres., NAACP (Charleston, S.C.);
Mem.: Alpha Phi Alpha, Mason, Elk; Home: 193 Smith
St., Charleston, S.C.

SWANN, Melvin Chester, b. Baltimore, Md., Nov. 6, 1914;
s. Isaiah and Grace Viola (Chester) S.; A.B., Clark
Univ., Atlanta, Ga.; D.D., Allen Univ.; Kittrell Jr.
Coll.; m. Dorothy Elizabeth Whitaker; children--- Melvin
Chester, Jr.; pastor, Hosana A.M.E. Church, Berkley,
Md.; Hemingway Temple, A.M.E. Church, Baltimore,
Md.; Bethel A.M.E. Church, Greensboro, N.C.; cur-
rent pastor, St. Joseph's A.M.E. Church, Durham, N.
C., 1957---; Trustee, Kittrell Jr. College, Kittrell,
N.C.; US Army, captain, 3 years (chaplain); chairman,
vice pres., Durham Minister Ass'n; Mem., Exec. Comm.,
Durham Committee on Negro Affairs; co-director, Audio-
Visual and Radio Education, A.M.E. Church; Audio and
Radio Education Comm. of the National Council of
Churches; General Board of the A.M.E. Church. Home:
806 Fayetteville St., Durham, N.C.; Office: 804 Fayette-
ville St., Durham, N.C.

SWEET, Henry Beauregard, b. Augusta, Ga., July 8,
1902; s. Henry B. and Grace (Brown); Lincoln Univer-
sity, Penna., 1924; A.B., B.D., McCormick Sem.,
1953; Graduate study-Univ. of Chicago; m. Sarah Evelyn
Christian; children--- Fred S. Cummings, Rene, Alan
Lloyd; pastor, Second Presbyterian Church, Oxford, Pa.,
1951-53; pastor, Church of the Master, New York City,
1953-54; current pastor, Westhills Presbyterian Church,
U.S.A., Atlanta, Ga., 1954---; Boys Worker, Jones
Memorial Community Center, 1946-48; Chicago Heights,
Illinois; Sec. Atlanta Chapter-Lincoln Univ. Pa. Alumni;
Chaplain, Eta Landa Chapter, Alpha Phi Alpha, 1959;
Stated clerk, Ga.-Carolina Presbytery, 1957-62; Home:
3518 Fairburn Place, Atlanta 31, Ga.; Office: 1745
Springview Rd., Atlanta 14, Ga.

TALBOT, David Arlington, coll. administrator; b. British
Guiana, Jan. 25, 1916; s. David Patterson and Maude
(Roberts) T.; certificate, Queen's Coll., of British Guiana-
Oxford and Cambridge School; B.A., Morris Brown Coll.,
1935-39; Turner Theol. Sem., 1938-40; Columbia Univ.,
1940-42. M.A., 1951; m. Phyllis Snow Willis; children
--- David Arlington, Jr., James Patterson, Eric Maurice,
instructor, Morris Brown Coll., 1939-40; circulation man-

ager and assoc. editor, Tan Town Stories, 1945-46;
social worker, Dept. of Welfare, New York City, 1947-
51; coll. minister and chairman, Division of Languages,
Literature and Art, Shorter Coll., 1952-57; pastor,
Bethel African Methodist Episcopal Church, Blytheville,
Ark., 1954-57; chaplain, A.M. & N. Coll., 1957---;
Psychometrist, A.M. & N. Coll., 1957-60; current dean
of students, A.M. & N. Coll., 1960---; Mem., Bd. of
Directors, Tiny Tim School, Pine Bluff, Ark.; US Army
1942-45; Sgt. Major; Bronze Star Medal, 1945; Mem.,
American Coll. Personnel Assn; National Assn. of Per-
sonnel Workers; Southwestern Regional Assn. of Guidance
Workers; author: Comparative Study of Freshmen Enter-
ing A.M. & N. College from 1957-62; Home: Box 154,
A.M. & N. Coll., Pine Bluff, Ark.; Office: 1300 Magnolia
Street, Pine Bluff, Ark.

TAYLOR, G. Herfin, b. Shreveport, La., Apr. 7, 1911;
s. Hezekiah and Lillie (Morris) T.; A.B., Dillard University, New Orleans, La., 1935; m. Evelyn Smiler;
children- G. Herfin, Jr., Raymond A., Barbara A.,
Brenda A. Colorado Conf. of Seventh-Day Adventists,
Denver, Colo., 1946-48; Central States Conf. of S.D.A.,
1948-63; Pastored: Denver Beth Haven, Denver, Colo.,
1946-51; New Hope, S.D.A. Church, Pueblo, Colo., and
Sharon S.D.A. Church, Omaha, 1951-59; New Hope,
S.D.A. Church, Sioux, Iowa; Allon Chapel, Lincoln,
Nebraska, 1959-60; present: Beacon Light S.D.A. Church
and Berean S.D.A. Church, St. Louis, Mo., 1960- .
Y.M.C.A. Service award, 1957, Omaha, Nebr. Home:
5440 Clemens Ave., St. Louis, Mo. Office: 1244 No.
Union Blvd., St. Louis, Mo.

TAYLOR, Gardner Calvin, b. Baton Rouge, June 18, 1918;
s. W.M. and Selma G. (Taylor) T.; A.B., Leland Coll.,
1937; D.D. (hon.), 1944; B.D., Oberlin Grad. Sch.
Theology, 1940; m. Laura Scott; children--- Martha Lyn;
Ordained to ministry Bapt. Church, 1939; pastor, Elyria,
Ohio, 1938-40; New Orleans, 1941-43; Baton Rouge,
1943-47; Brooklyn, N.Y., 1948---; former pres., Pro-
testant Council, New York City; vice pres., Bd. of
Directors, Urban League Greater New York; vice pres.,
Progressive National Baptist Convention, Inc.; Mem.,
Bd. of Education, New York City; Kappa Alpha Psi;
Mason; Home: 833 Marey Ave., Brooklyn, New York
City, N.Y.

TAYLOR, Julian Augustus, church official; b. Hertford, N.
C., May 14, 1903; s. William A. and Roberta (Fortune)
T.; B.A., B.D., Howard Univ., Univ. of Chicago, Co-
lumbia Univ.; D.D. (hon.) Northern Sch. of Religion; m.
Margaret Pauline Morris; children--- Mauryne Brant,
Doris Kaith, Jewells Gibbs, Julian, Jr., Shirlee Haizlip,
Patricia Williams; pastor, Ebenezer Baptist Ch., Martins-
burg, W. Va., 1927-30; First Baptist Ch., Stratford,
Conn., 1933-38; Macedonia Baptist Ch., Ansonia, 1938
---; Pres., New England Baptist Training Union, 1950--;
pres., Conn. Baptist Missionary Convention, 1956---;
pres., Tri-County Interdenominational Ministers Alliance;
Mem., Bd. Conn. Council of Churches; Advisory Bd.
Salvation Army; Bd. of Directors, Nat'l Baptist Conven-
tion, USA, Inc.; Bd. of Amer. Baptist Theol. Seminary,
Nashville; hearing examiner, Civil Rights Commission,
Conn., 1955---; chairman, Ansonia Municipal Planning
Comm., 1955---; organizer, president, Ansonia Branch
NAACP, 1944---; Mem., Mason; Kiwanis International
Administrative Consultant Sen. Abraham Ribicoff; special
commission from Nat'l Baptist to Liberian Government,
1961-62; delegate-at-large, 1960 Nat'l Democratic Con.;
delegate-at-large 1964 Nat'l Democratic Con.; Home: 133
West Park Ave., New Haven, Conn.; Office: 24 Clifton
Ave., Ansonia, Conn.

TAYLOR, Paul Lawrence, college prof.; b. Darien, Ga.,
Oct. 26, 1913; s. Joseph David and Martha (Covington)
T.; A.B., J.C. Smith Univ.; M.A., Hartford Sem.
School of Religion; B.D., McCormick Theol. Seminary;
M. Th., Western Theological Seminary; Ed. D., Indiana
University, 1933, 1936, 1938, 1949 and 1958 respectively;
m. Bessie Carpenter; pastor, Laura Street Presbyterian
Church, U. S. A., Jacksonville, Fla., Trinity Presbyter-
ian Church, Smithfield, N. C., 1937-39; 1939-41; US Army
chaplain, 1941-46; pastor, Faith Presbyterian Church,
Pine Bluff, Ark., 1952-57; Dean of Instruction, Barber-
Scotia College, Dir. of Testing & Guidance, Savannah
State College; Dir. Student Personnel, Alabama A. &M.
College, Chairman Dept. Education, Miss. Vocational
College, Itta Bena, Miss.; decorations: Five Battle Stars,
was chosen along with five other chaplains to study the
crimes of the Army personnel and make recommendation;
Mem.: APGA-Phi Delta; Masons; Omega Psi Phi; Ab-
stract of Doctoral Dissertation was published-"An Analysis
of Religious Counseling Practices of Nine Selected Negro
Colleges" - Master Thesis "The Social Teaching of St.

Paul"; Home: P.O. Box 446 Itta Bena Miss.

TAYLOR, Prince Albert, Jr. bishop; b. Hennessey, Okla.,
Jan. 27, 1907; A.B., Samuel Huston Coll., Austin,
Tex., 1931; B.D., Gammon Theol. Sem., Atlanta, Ga.,
1931; M.A., Columbia Univ., New York, 1940; Ed.D.,
New York Univ., New York City, 1948; D.D. (hon.),
Rust Coll., Holly Springs, Miss., 1949; Gammon Theol.
Sem., 1950; LL.D., Philander Smith Coll., Little Rock,
Ark.; Ordained, 1931, elder, N.C. Conference; pastor,
Kernersville, N.C., 1931; N.W. Greensboro, N.C., 1931-
34; St. John Meth. Ch., Thomasville, N.C., 1934-37;
East Calvary, N.Y.C., 1937-40; St. Mark's Meth.Ch.,
N.Y.C., 1940-42; 1945-48; Elected a bishop of The
Methodist Ch. at the Central Jurisdictional Conf., New
Orleans, La., 1956; Assigned to: Monrovia, Liberia
Area; New Jersey Area; instructor and asst. to the pres.,
Bennett Coll., Greensboro, N.C., 1940-43; Head of Dept.
Christian Ed. and Psychology, Gammon Theol. Sem.,
1943-48; Exchange teacher, Clark Coll., Atlanta, Ga.,
1943-48; adult counselor, Central Jurisdiction National
Meth. Student Com., 1944-48; director, Correspondence
Sch. for Commission on Ministerial Training, Central
Jurisdiction, 1945-48; editor, Central Christian Advocate,
New Orleans, 1948-56; president, Designate Council of
Bishops; Mem., Com. on the Structure of Meth. Over-
seas; General Bd. of Missions; Com. for Ecumenical Af-
fairs; Trustee of several educational institutions; Phi
Beta Sigma; mem. Advisory Coun. of the International move-
ment for Atlantic Union; Awards: Gov. of Liberia for dis-
tinguished service, twice; The Venerable Knighthood of the
Pioneers; Highest Decoration given by the government, second private citizen to receive it; Recipient St. George's
Award given by Old St. George's Ch., Phila., Pa. Mem: State
Youth Com., N.J.; Citizen's Council for Economic Opportunity, N.J.; Home: 70 Nassau St., Princeton, N.J. 08540.

*TAYLOR, Rafe Monroe, b. Clearview, Okla., May 10, 1931;
s. Cary and Mary Keller (Mayo) T.; Oklahoma School of
Religion & Langston Univ., 1954-56; Bishop Coll., 1956-
58, B.A.; B.D., Howard Univ., Sch. of Rel., 1962; m.
Bennie Jewel Shaw; children--- Rafe M. Jr., Ralph
Philander; pastor, Mt. Olive Baptist Ch., Marshal, Texas,
1957-58; pastor, Shiloh Baptist Church, Wash., D.C.
(Student assist.) pastor, Antioch Baptist Church, King
George, Va., 1960-62; current pastor, Faith Tabernacle
Baptist Church, Stamford, Conn., 1962---; Mem., Board

of Directors for Friendship House; Mem., Eight Charter
Revision Commission; Mem., Mayor's Committee on Hu-
man Rights; Exec. Board of Stamford Branch of NAACP;
Exec. Board of Stamford-Darien Council of Churches;
US Army, 503 Field Artillery Bn, 2nd Infantry Div.,
1948-53; Medal of Valor from Oklahoma State; 3 Battle
Stars; United Nations Medal of Honor; Good Conduct
Medal; also Prisoner of War in Korea; Omega Psi Phi;
Home: 38 Standish Rd., Stamford, Conn..; Office; 16
Greyrock Place, Stamford, Conn.

TEAMER, James William Robert, educator; b. Greenville,
S.C., Jan. 3, 1908; s. Jesse and Minnie (Evans) T.;
A.B., Johnson C. Smith Univ., 1943; B.D., 1945;
Courses: Moody Bible Institute; Gammon Theol. Sem.,
Turner Theol. Sem.; Morris Brown Coll,; D.D. (hon.)
James W. Tramer School of Religion, 1958; pastor in
North Carolina, South Carolina and Georgia; current
pastor, Cosmopolitan Community Ch. (non-denominational),
Charlotte, N.C.; Founder, James W. Teamer School of
Rel., Teamer School of Education, Teamer School of
Commercial Education; Boys Scout Commissioner, 3
years; Chairman, Board of Management, Henry Lawrence
McGorey, YMCA; Mem.: Democrat;   Mason;
NAACP; Phi Beta Sigma; Home: 2524 Newland Road,
Charlotte, N.C.; Office: 2600 Newland Road, Charlotte,
N.C.

*TERRELL, Leonard Earl, coll. dean; b. Montgomery Co.,
Miss., Jan. 27, 1908; s. William H. and Addie V.T.;
A.B., B.D., Howard Univ., Wash. D.C., 1935; Drew
Univ., Madison, N.J.; M.A., New York Univ., 1959;
Ph.D. candidate, Drew Univ.; m. Louise F. Moorhead;
children--- Leonard Howard; acting dean, Chapel of
Howard Univ., 1938-39; pastor, New Hope Bapt. Ch.,
Hackensack, N.J., 1939-46; pastor, Bethel Bapt. Institu-
tional Ch., Jacksonville, Fla., 1946-52; pres., Storer
Coll., Harpers Ferry, W.Va., 1952-55; director, Religious Activities, Va. State Coll., Petersburg, Va.,
1955-63; current, Union Bapt. Ch., New York, 1963---;
prof., Sch.of Rel., Howard Univ., 1937-38; Va. State
Coll., 1952-53; organizer and treas., Civic League, Jacksonville, Fla., 1949; Trustee, Bd. of Fla., Normal & Industrial Coll., St. Augustine, Fla., 1946-52; Citation
from Fla. Normal and Industrial Coll., 1951; Mem., Phi
Beta Sigma; NAACP; Southern Christian Leadership Conference; Religious Education Assn; Bd. of Sloane House,

YMCA; Supervisory Com. over Chaplaincy, New York City;
Home: 408 Tecumseh Ave., Mt. Vernon, N.Y.; Office:
240 W. 145th St., New York, N.Y. 10039.

THOMAS, Clarence Harris, coll. teacher; b. Mooresville,
N.C., June 19, 1924; s. Theodore Roosevelt and Lovell;
A.B., Johnson C. Smith Univ., 1944-50; B.D., 1950;
Th.M., Union Theological Seminary 1957-58; m. Adelaide
Maxwell; children--- Deborah Carol; pastor, Chase City
United Presbyterian Ch., Chase City, Va., 1950-56; Hay-
mount Presbyterian Ch., Fayetteville, N.C., 1956---;
teacher, Fayetteville State College, 1960---; Founder of
and Advisor to Chase City Service Club, moderator Tenn.
Presbytery, 1953; Treasurer Mecklenburg County, Va.,
Branch NAACP, 1954-56; Mem.: North Carolina Teachers
Assn., NEA; ATA, Alpha Phi Alpha; Home: 420 Chatham
St., Fayetteville, N.C.: Ch: 611 Hay Street, Fayetteville,
N.C.

THOMAS, Cornelious Egbert, coll. prof.; b. Marion, Ala.,
May 4, 1923; s. James A. and Serna (A.) T.; A.B.,
Daniel Payne College, 1946; B.D., Gammon Theol.
Seminary, 1949; D.D. (hon.) Payne Coll., 1954; m. Susie
Mae Jamar; children--- Cornelia S., James E.; pastor,
St. Mark A.M.E. Church, Dora, Ala., 1943-49; pastor,
Bethel A.M.E. Church, Ensley, Ala., 1949-52; pastor,
St. John A.M.E. Church B'ham, Ala., 1952---; part time
instructor, Daniel Payne Coll., Birmingham, Ala.; Trus-
tee, Daniel Payne Coll., Mem. General Citizens Federa-
tion; Member, Board of A.M.E. Church; Mem., Ad-
visory Board, Savings & Loans; Mem., Progressive
Democratic Party; Mem., Mason; Mem., Knight of
Pythians; author: As He Spoke To Me; Home: 431 12
Ter. Birmingham 4, Ala.; Office: 708 15th No. Birmingham
4, Ala.

THOMAS, George, b. Pittsburgh, Pa., Jan 8, 1931; s.
David Prince and Georgia (Bailey) Ware; B.A., U. of
Toledo, 1954; Western Reserve U., Cleveland, Ohio,
B.D., Oberlin College, 1958; m. Delores Mabel Shoe-
craft; children--Sheila Delores, George David,
Anthony Adrian; Dir., Chagrin Falls Park Community
Center, 1957-60; Pastor, Coronado Cong. Chrtn. Ch.,
Norfolk, Va., 1960-61; Pastor, St. Mark Cong. Church,
Boston, Mass., 1961---; Sec.-Treas., Boston Conf. on
Rel. and Race, 1964-65; Bd. Mem., Roxbury Comm.
Council; Mem., United Comm. Services-Special Service

Committee; Life Member NAACP; Home: 34 Elm Hill Ave.,
Boston, Mass., 02121 Church: 210 Townsend St., Boston.
Mass.

THOMAS, James J., church official; b. Charleston, S. C.;
s. Joseph J.; St. Colmes Theol. Sem., 1943; B. D.,
Lincoln Univ., Pa., 1946; M. A., Drew Univ., 1950;
M. A., Union Theol. Sem., 1954; D. Ed., Teachers
Coll., Columbia Univ., 1957; m. Winell Mae (Thorpe);
children--- Ralph, Joy, Howard; Presbyterian minister
(United), 1945; pastor, Mott Haven Reformed Ch. in
America, 1953-61; area sec., Japan and Southeast Asia
areas (Reformed Church in America); Mem., Com. on
Ministry Personnel in Far East; China Com.,
Overseas Union Churches; The East Asian Christian
Conf. Com.; The Japan Com., S. E. Asia Com., Nat.
Council of Churches; Com. on Christian Higher Ed.,
Southeast Asia; pres., Synod Reformed Ch., in America,
New York area; Mem., Bd. of Trustees, Western and
New Brunswick Theol. Sem.; Mem., Bd. of World Mis-
sions; Home: 3216 Paulding Ave., Bronx, New York,
10469; Office: 475 Riverside Dr., New York City, N. Y.

THOMAS, James Samuel, bishop; b. Orangeburg, S. C.,
April 8, 1919; s. James Samuel Sr. and Dessie (Merks)
T.; A. B., Claflin Coll., 1939; B. D., Gammon Theol.
Sem., 1943; M. A., Drew Univ., 1943; Ph. D., Cornell
Univ., 1953; D. D. (hon.), Claflin Coll., 1953; LL. D.
(hon.), Bethune Cookman Coll., 1963; m. Ruth Naomi
Wilson; children--- Claudia, Gloria, Margaret, Patricia;
principal, Hickson Grove School, Florence Co., S. C.;
pastor, Orangeburg Co., S. C.; chaplain, S. C. State
Coll.; pastor, York, S. C.; prof., Gammon Theol. Sem.;
associate director, Division of Higher Education, Metho-
dist Bd. of Education; prof., Friendship Union Coll.,
1947; visiting prof., Southern Methodist Univ., 1958; elected
Bishop, The Methodist Ch., June, 1964-; Mem., Bd. of Trus-
tees, Bennett Bethune Cookman Coll., Claflin Coll., Clark
Coll., Houston Tillotson Coll., Philander Smith Coll., Rust
Coll., Wiley Coll., Paine Coll.; Kappa Delta Pi; Phi Kappa
Phi; Consultant, Danforth Foundation; Home: 3500 Kingman
Blvd., Des Moines, Iowa 50309; Office: 508 Tenth, Des
Mones 9, Iowa.

THOMAS, Nathaniel Charles, Church official; b. Jonesboro,
Ark., June 24, 1929; s. Willie James and Linnie (T.);
Mississippi Industrial College, 1951; A. B., Lincoln Univ.

1954; B.A., Lancaster Theological Seminary, 1953; m.
Juanita Fannie Jefferson; children-- Gina Charlise. Migrant Ministry (student) in Oxford, Pa., 1953-54; director,
Christian First Episcopal District C.M.E. Church (comprising Arkansas and Oklahoma), 1955; pastor, Cottrell
C.M.E. Church, Hot Springs, Ark., 1957-60; vice-president, youth section of the Division of Christian Education,
National Council of Churches, 1959; pastor, Bullock Temple C.M.E. Church, Little Rock, Ark., 1960-62; secretary, Interracial Ministers' Alliance, Little Rock, Ark.,
1961; present: Director of Christian Education, and Administrative Assistant to presiding Bishop, C.M.E.
Churches (Arkansas and Tennessee), 1962- . Member:
Interracial Council, Lancaster, Penna., 1953-55; Steering Committee, National Conf. of Religion and Race,
1961- ; Steering Committee, Little Rock Conf. on Religion and Human Relations, 1963- ; director of Leadership Training for C.M.E. Churches in Oklahoma, Arkansas and Tennessee, 1954-58. Distinguished Service award
by Y.M.C.A., Little Rock, Ark., 1961. Member: C.M.
E. Ministers Alliance of Greater Memphis Area; Interdenominational Ministerial Alliance, Memphis, Tenn.;
General Board of Christian Education, C.M.E. Church;
chairman, Committee on location of the C.M.E. General
Conference. Published Christian Youth Fellowship Guide
(1st in C.M.E. Church), 1956; edited and compiled three
publications for Board of Christian, 1957, 1959, 1960;
author, Living Up To My Obligations of Church Membership, 1963. Home: 664 Vance Ave., Memphis, Tenn.
38126.

*THOMAS, William Neamon, b. Malvern, Ark., Aug. 18,
1927; s. Felix Neamon and Arvilla T.; A.B., Storer
Coll., Harpers Ferry, W.Va., 1953; B.D., Howard Univ.
Sch. of Rel., 1959; m. Elsie Virginia Tucker; children
--- Deborah, William; current pastor, Zion Baptist Ch.,
1954---; Mem., Com. on Racial Unity, 1963; Democratic
Committeeman, 1962; chmn, CORE, 1963; Mem., Bd. of
Directors, NAACP, Alexandria, Va.; US Forces, 1946-
49; Outstanding Citizens Award, 1963, Alexandria, Va.;
Democrat;   Mason; Home: 916 Queen St., Alexan-
dria, Va.; Office: 114 S. Lee St., Alexandria, Va.

THOMPSON, Albert A., educator; b. South Carolina, May
14, 1909; s. T.A. and Mary (Gill) T.; A.B., B.D.,
J.C. Smith U., 1936; Ph.D., Harvard Univ., 1952;
m. Willie Mae Callaham; children-- Gloria, Albert;

Pastor, Laura St. Presbyterian Ch. , Jacksonville, Fla. ,
1940-41; Faith Cong. Church, Hartford, Conn. , 1960---;
Head, Science Dept. , Tenn. State U. , 1953-60; Adjunct
Prof. of Hist. , U. of Hartford; Mem. , Citizens Charter
Committee, Family Service, Hospital Chaplains Assoc. ;
Home: 87 Rosemont, Hartford, Conn. Church: 2030
Main, Hartford, Conn.

THOMPSON, Floyd Wm. , b. Columbia, S. C. , May 19,
1900; s. Thomas Wm. and Mary (Rowls); B. D. , Allen
Univ. , 1923; D. D. (hon.) Campbell Coll. , 1951; m.
Juanita Lancaster; children--- Floyd W. Jr. ; Mary E. ,
Leon W. , Vivian; pastor, Jones Tabernacle African Methodist Episcopal, 1945-50; Grace A. M. E. Church, Warren
Ohio, 1951-57; Brown Chapel A. M. E. Church, Pittsburgh,
1958-59; St. Paul A. M. E. Church, Washington, 1959-63;
current pastor, St. Paul A. M. E. Church, Lima, Ohio,
1963---; Mem. , NAACP Family Service Board, Washington, Pa. ; Hospital chaplain; Mem. , Elks; Masons; Home:
1328 W. Elm, Lima; Office: 1103 Spring St. , Lima,
Ohio.

*THOMPSON, John Andrew, b. McCool, Miss. , Dec. 24,
19   ; s. Isaac J. L. and Susie T. ; A. B. , Jackson Coll. ,
Jackson, Miss. , 1933-40; Atlanta Univ. , Atlanta, Ga.
1942; Univ. of Chicago, 1945, 46, B. D. , Howard Univ.
Sch. of Rel. , 1950; m. Maudie Louise Lee; children---
John Andrew, Karl Anthony; principal, Weir Jr. High
School, 1941-44; principal, Oakland Jr. High School,
1946-47; College Hill High School, Pontotoc; Homes Co.
Tr. Sch. Durant, Lawrence Co. Tr. Sch. ; pastor, First
Baptist Church, Ronceverte, W. Va. , 1947-50; Tabernacle
Bapt. Ch. , West Palm Beach, Fla. , 1951; Bethel Bapt.
Ch. , Omaha, Nebr. , 1952-54; current, Corinth Memorial
Bapt. Ch. , 1955---; Bd. Mem. , NAACP; Exec. secy. ,
New Era Baptist State Convention of Nebr. ; founder and
pres. , International League for Brotherhood and Peace,
1962---; Bd. Mem. , Omaha Council of Churches, 1953-
63; director, Western Bapt. Bible Coll. (Omaha Center),
1964---; Home: 2709 Spaulding St. , Omaha, Nebr. 68111.

THURMAN, Howard, sem. dean, author; b. Daytona Beach,
Fla. , Nov. 18, 1900; s. Saul Solomon and Alice (Ambrose) T. ; A. B. , Morehouse Coll. , 1923; D. D. (hon.),
1935; B. D. , Rochester Theol. Sem. , 1923; D. D. , Wesleyan Coll. , Conn. , 1946; D. D. (hon.), Lincoln Univ. ;
Howard Univ. , 1955; LL. D. (hon.), Ohio Wesleyan Univ. ,

1954; LL.D., Washington Univ., 1955; Allen Univ., 1954;
Litt.D. (hon.), Tuskegee Institute, 1956; D.D., Oberlin
Coll., 1958; LL.D., Va. State Univ., 1959; m. Sue E.
Bailey; children--- Anne, Olive; Ordained to ministry,
Baptist Church, 1925; pastor, Mt. Zion Bapt. Ch.,
Oberlin, Ohio, 1926-28; prof., Morehouse Coll., 1928-
31; prof. and dean of chapel, Howard Univ., Wash. D.C.,
1932-44; pastor, Church for Fellowship of All Peoples,
San Francisco, 1944-53; dean, Marsh Chapel; prof.,
spiritual disciplines and resources, Boston Univ., 1953
---; lecturer, on immortality of man, Harvard Univ.,
1947; Merrick lecturer, Ohio Wesleyan Univ., 1953;
Mem., Bd. of Directors, Urban League Greater Boston,
Inc.; director, Travelers Aid Society; Mass. Commn.
Against Discrimination; Bd. of Nat. Mental Health Assn;
National Council, Religion in Higher Education; American
Academy of Arts and Sciences; Alumni Assn. Colgate
Rochester Division School; Fellowship of Reconciliation
Clubs; Book of California, Mass. Schoolmasters Com-
monwealth; author: The Greatest of These, 1945; Deep
River, 1946, 1955; Meditations for Apostles of Sensitive-
ness, 1947; The Negro Spiritual Speaks of Life and Death,
1947; Jesus and the Disinherited, 1948; Deep is the
Hunger, 1951, Meditations of the Heart, 1953; The Crea-
tive Encounter, 1954; Apostles of Sensitiveness, 1956;
The Growing Edge, 1956; Footprints of a Dream, 1959;
contributor to: Interpreter's Bible, Vol. 7; Inward Journey,
1961; Mysticism and the Experience of Love, 1961;
Disciplines of the Spirit, 1963; The Luminous Darkness,
1965; Home: 184 Bay State Rd., Boston 15, Mass.; Office:
Marsh Chapel, Boston Univ., Boston, Mass.

TIEUEL, Robert C.D., Jr. b. Boley, June 26, 1914; s.
Robert C.D. and Nodie E. (T.); Lane College, 1930-32;
Tennessee State College, 1932-33; LeMoyne College,
1933-34; Special study at Harvard Divinity School, 1934-
36; A.B., Texas College, 1950; m. Mary Porter. Pre-
sent: pastor, Brown Chapel Christian Methodist Episcopal
Church, San Angelo, Texas, 1946-   ; director, Public
Relations of Eighth Episcopal District C.M.E. Church,
including States of Texas and Kentucky. Member: Hobbs
Chamber of Commerce and Board of Christian Education
of the Northwest Texas-New Mexico Conference C.M.E.
Church; chairman, Executive Committee of the Progressive
Citizens League, Inc. of New Mexico. Candidate, State
representative in 1958 Democratic primary race (Lea
County, New Mexico). Cited by President Eisenhower -

efforts in building Christian inter-racial goodwill and relations as editor of the magazine, Christian Call. Executive Member, N. A. A. C. P., San Angelo Branch, Texas;
editor, Who's Who in the C. M. E. Church, 1962; publisher, Christian Call, publication of C. M. E. Church.
Home: 914 S. Dal Paso St., Hobbs, New Mexico. Office:
200 West 14th St., San Angelo, Texas.

*TILLMAN, Eugene C., b. West Palm Beach, Fla., Apr.
  10, 1926; s. William and Laura T.; A. B., Howard Univ.,
  1948; B. D., Howard Univ. Sch. of Rel., 1951; m. Vivian,
  children--- Eugene C., Jr., Thurmond Neil; Ministers to
  the Migratory Farm Workers, Pompano, Fla. and Bridge-
  ton, N. J., 1948-54; pastor, Mt. Bethel Baptist Church,
  Daytona Beach, Fla., 1954-63; pres., The Sunday School
  and B. T. U. Congress, Fla. East Coast Ass'n, 1962--;
  Instructor, Sunday School and B. T. U. Congress, State
  Convention, Fla., 1951---; Instructor, National Sunday
  School and B. T. U. Congress, 1952---; present pastor,
  Shiloh Baptist Church, Brunswick, Ga. One of two
  Negroes appointed to the State Bi-Racial Committee of
  Governor Leroy Collins; Mem., The Florida Advisory
  Committee to the Federal Civil Rights Commission, ap-
  pointed by the late John F. Kennedy; The Urban Renewal
  Board, Daytona Beach, Fla.; State-wide co-
  ordinator for Negro and minority vote to elect Mayor
  Robert King High of Miami for Governor, Fla.; US
  Naval Reserve, 1944-46; Many citations from human re-
  lations groups, NAACP Groups, colleges, fraternities;
  Mem., Phi Beta Sigma; Exec. Bd., Fla. Council on
  Human Relations; Bd. of the NAACP, State of Fla.; Home:
  1221 Egmont St., Brunswick, Ga.

TIMPSON, George William, teacher; b. Frederick, Md.,
  August 16, 1927; s. James Thomas and Cora Bell (Leeks)
  T.; B. S., 1952, Oakwood College, Huntsville, Ala.; m.
  Cynthia Eleanor Knight; children-- Dane Anthony. Pastored:
  First Seventh-Day Adventist Church, Ellenville, N. Y.,
  1959-60; Bethesday S. D. A. Church of Amityville, N. Y.,
  1960-61; Mount Zion S. D. A. Church of New Haven, Conn.,
  1961- . Principal, Ephesus Junior Academy, Birming-
  ham, Ala., 1952-53; teacher, Bethel Elementary School,
  Brooklyn, N. Y., 1953-61; U. S. Navy combat - Okinawa,
  1944-46; awarded a life-time teaching certificate from the
  General Conference Educational Department of S. D. A.,
  Wash., D. C.; member, Ministerial Alliance of New Haven,
  Conn. Home: 79 Thompson St., New Haven 11, Conn.

Office: 64 Marlboro St., Hamden, Conn.

TIVY, Cleveland Burie, College professor; b. Kingston,
Jamaica, West Indies, June 19, 1916; s. Charles Caleb
and Doris (Roslyn) T.; Oakwood College, Huntsville,
Ala., A.B., 1950; m. Gloria Olena Bonterre; children-
Julie Lillian, Janice Oleana, Joy Linda. Pastored
Seventh-Day Adventist Churches;   Richmond, Peters-
burg, Crewe, Virginia, 1950; Dayton, Germantown,
Springfield, Ohio, 1955; Jersey City, Englewood, Mont-
clair, New Jersey, 1958; present: Pine Forge, Pa.,
1959-   . Teacher of Bible courses, Pine Forge Institute,
Pine Forge, Pa., 1959-   . U.S. Army, 1942-1945.
Home: Box 34, Pine Forge, Pa.

TOATLEY, Robert George, missionary; b. Irmo, S.C.,
May 6, 1922; s. Robert Nelson and Lottie (Watts) T.;
A.B., B.D., Johnson C. Smith Univ., 1943, 1946; m.
Juanita Bernice (Williams) T.; children--- Johnie Mae,
Robert George Jr., Juanita Laverne; supply minister,
Pleasant Ridge Presby. Ch., Lancaster, S.C., 1944-45;
Lincoln Academy (Congregational), King Mountain, N.C.,
1945-46; Calvary and Shiloh Presby. Chs., Winsboro,
S.C., 1946-47; missionary, Fairfield-McClelland Pres-
bytery, Atlantic Synod, 1957; instructor, Veteran Farm
Training Program, New Home School, 1948-52; co-di-
rector, Audio-Visual Workshop, Atlantic and Catawba
Leadership Training Sch., Johnson C. Smith Univ., Char-
lotte, N.C., 1957---;   Presbytery chairman of
Com. on Social Education and Action, 1957-60; sec.,
Local Com. for Promotion of Human Rights, 1960; Mem.,
Phi Beta Sigma; Home: 927 Crawford St., Rock Hill,
S.C.

TONEY, Patrick W., educator; b. Mayesville, S.C., Nov.
1, 1897; s. Gaston and Virginia (Ceasar) T.; A.B., B.
D., Johnson C. Smith Univ.; m.Albertha (Plowden); T. chil-
dren--- Lydie (Mrs. Kearns), Patrick W. Jr., Boyd G.,
Lloyd; pastor, Trinity Presby. Ch., Marion, N.C.,
1920-22; Green St. Presby. Ch., Morganton, N.C.,
1920-22; Faith Presby. Ch., Aberdeen, N.C., 1923-30;
Good Will Presby. Ch., Ft. Pierce, Fla., 1930-33; current pastor, Mt. Sinai and Mt. Lisbon Presby. Chs.,
1933---; principal, Kisler Academy, Morganton, N.C.,
3 yrs; principal, Sarah Lincoln Academy, Aberdeen, N.
C.; principal, Curry High Sch., St. Charles, S.C.,
15 yrs.; Mem., Masons; Sons and Daughters of Job,

St. Charles, S.C.; Office: Mt. Sinai and Mt. Lisbon Un.
Presby. Ch., St.Charles, S.C.

TRAYLOR, Horace Jerome, coll. pres.; b. La Grange, Ga.,
March 15, 1931; A.B., Zion Coll., Chattanooga, Tenn.,
1953; B.D., Gammon Theol. Sem., 1958; Graduate study:
Atlanta Univ., 1956; Univ. of Chattanooga; m. Thelma
Dennis; children--- Sheryl Lynn; Linda Gail, Yohanna Fayl,
Chequeta Renee, Tonya Yvonne; prof., Zion Coll., 1951
---; Administrative Asst., Zion Coll., 1951-54; dean,
1954-59; current pres., Zion Coll., 1959---; current
pastor, First Congregational Ch., 1958---; chairman,
Commission on Resolutions, Tenn. Ky. Conf., Congrega-
tional Christian Churches, 1959-61; pres., Council for
Cooperative Action; Mem., Auditorium and Tivoli Bd.;
The Adult Educational Council; Bd. of Chattanooga Area
Literacy Movement; Bd. of Family Service Agency;
Mayor's Bi-Racial Committee; Chattanooga Chamber of
Commerce. Selected as one of seven outstanding men
from Chattanooga area by Jr. Chamber of Commerce,
Chattanooga, Tenn., May 1964. Office: Zion Coll.,
Chattanooga, Tenn.

TUCKER, Charles Eubank, bishop; b. Baltimore, Md.,
Jan. 12, 1896; s. William A. and Elivia (Clark) T.;
m. Amelia Moore, 1922; one child: Bernice; ed. Beck-
ford and Smith's Coll., Jamaica, B.W.I., 1913; Lincoln,
U., Pa., 1917; Temple U., 1919; read law under Hon.
Charles Gogg, Pt. Pleasant, Va. pastor, A.M.E. Zion
Ch., Middletown, Pa., 1916; Delta, Pa., 1917; Salem
Ch., Williamsport, Pa. 1919; Hilliard's Chapel, Mont-
gomery, Ala., 1920-22; A.M.E. Zion Ch., Sharon,
Miss., 1922-23; Mt. Zion Ch., Augusta, Ga., 1923-27;
Cornish Temple Ch., Key West, Fla., 1927-29; Stoner
Memorial Ch., Key West, Fla., 1927-29; Stoner Memor-
ial Ch., Louisville, Ky., 1929-30; Jones' Temple Ch.,
New Albany, Ind., 1930-31; Elder, Philadelphia and
Baltimore Conf., A.M.E. Zion Ch., 1918-19; presiding
elder, South Ga. Conf., 1923-27; became presiding elder,
Madisonville District, Ky., 1931; began criminal law prac-
tice, Louisville, Ky., 1929; candidate, assembly, Louis-
ville, Ky., 1933; mem. Lincoln Bar Assn., NAACP, Inde-
pendent in pol.; present, Bishop, A.M.E. Zion Ch.,
Seventh Episcopal District; Home: 1625 West Ky. St.,
Louisville, Ky.

*TURNER, David, Jr. chaplain; b. Anderson, Texas, May

12, 1930; s. A.B. and Bertha W. (Lewis) T.; B.S.,
Prairie View A.&M. Coll., Texas, 1953; B.D., Howard
Univ., Sch. of Rel., 1959; m. Sylvia Larkins; children
---; David Fernando, Frank Lenous; pastor, First Baptist
Church, Anderson, Texas, 1955; Tabor Presbyterian
Church, Washington, D.C., 1955-56; asst. pastor, First
Baptist Ch., Wash., D.C., 1956-61; counselor, Depart-
ment of Public Welfare, Wash., D.C., 1956-61; associate
protestant chaplain, Dept. of Correction, 1961---; US
Army Chaplain, 1959---; Certified as a Clinically Trained
Clergyman, Board of Directors, National Council for
Clinical Training, USA, 1962; National Defense & Good
Conduct Medal; Mem., US Army Reserve Officers Ass'n
Home: 3208 Park Place NW, Wash., D.C.; Office: Box
25, Dept. of Corrections, Lorton, Va.

TURNER, Eugene Burns, b. Goldston, N.C., Sept. 16,
1924; s. Samuel David and Ollie (Emerson) T.; A.B.,
Shaw Univ., 1947; B.D., Shaw Divinity Sch., 1950;
M. Th., Midwestern Graduate Bible Sch., 1954; D.D.
(hon.), Friendship Coll., 1963; m. Georgia Anna Mc
Neil; children--- Andrea Lisa, Rosalyn Arlene; pastor,
First Baptist Ch., 1948---; moderator, Robeson Baptist
Union, 1959-63; pres., Lumberton Civic Comm., 1958-63;
chairman, Central Divisional Comm. Boy Scouts of Amer-
ica, 1963; Mem., Exec. Comm. Lott Carey Foreign Mis-
sion Convention, USA; Sunday Sch. Bd. National Baptist
Convention, 1961; Exec. Comm. General Baptist State
Convention of N.C.; recording secy., General Bd., Gen.
Baptist State Convention; Bd. of Directors, Robeson
County T.B. Ass'n; Chaplain's Advisory Comm., South-
eastern General Hospital;North Carolina Council of
Churches; N.C. Comm. on Religion and Race; Lumberton
City Council, 1961; registrar, Voting Precinct No. 6;
Mem., Precinct Committee No. 4; delegate, State Demo-
cratic Convention, 1964; Community Service Award, 1962;
Mem., Mason; N.C. Municipal Ass'n; N.C. Ass'n of Li-
censed Day Care Facilities; Child Welfare League of
America; author: A Biography of William Henry Knuckles,
1962; The Pastor's Helper, 1961; Home: 139 Spruce St.,
Lumberton, N.C.; Office: 504 West 2nd St., Lumberton,
N.C.

TURNER, Jury Ethward, b. New Albany, Miss. Aug. 15,
1915; s. Rogers G. and Rena (Jackson) T.; Fisk University, 1934-36; B.S. A.& T. Coll. Greensboro, N.C.
B.D. Gammon Theological Seminary, Atlanta, Ga. 1947,

Graduate Study: University of Southern California, Los
Angeles, Calif. 1942-43; Cornell University, Ithaca,
N.Y. 1961; m. Ophelia Turner; children: Joyce, Rena,
Floy Christina, Jaunell Denitra, Lyris Agvett; Ministry:
Clark Chapel Methodist Church, 1943-46; McMimmville,
Tenn., Stone River Circuit, Murfreesboro, Tenn., 1946-47,
Patterson Memorial Methodist Church, Nashville, Tenn.,
1947- present; Principal, Bernard High School, McMimm-
ville, Tenn., Mathematics Teacher, Cameron H.S. Nash-
ville, Tenn., (18 years); Member: Methodist Minister's
Alliance, Treas. N.A.A.C.P., Nashville Christian Leader-
ship Council; Tennessee Educational Congress; Middle
Tennessee Teachers Assoc., Tennessee Mathmatics Assoc.,
N.E.A. Mathematics Assoc., Kappa Alpha Psi; Home:
1111 32nd Ave. N Nashville, Tenn. Office: 316 Whitsitt
St., Nashville, Tenn. 37211.

TURNER, Maynard Philip, Jr. sem. pres.; b. St. Louis,
Mo.; b. Maynard Philip and Alma Elizabeth; A.B.,
Fisk Univ., 1934; B.D., Eden Theol. Sem., Webster
Grove, Mo.; Th.D., Central Bapt. Theol. Sem., Kansas
City, Kans.; m. Edna Earl Hall; science instructor,
Western Coll., Kansas City, Mo.; dean, Western Bapt.
Sem., Kansas City, Mo., 1944-49; dean, Sch. of Rel.,
Bishop Coll., 1949-50; pres., Western Bapt. Sem.,
1950-55; pastor, Mozart Bapt. Ch., Chgo., Ill., 1957;
Mt. Zion Bapt. Ch., Nashville, Tenn., 1960---; vice
pres., Interdenominational Minister's Fellowship; vice
pres., Middle Region, Tenn. Bapt. Miss. & Ed. Conven-
tion; former mem., Committee on Theol. Education, Nat'l
Bapt. Convention, USA, Inc.; Mem., Div. of Christian Ed-
ucation, Nat'l Council of Churches; Mayor's Committee
on the Aging; Committee on Churches, Nashville Branch,
NAACP;   Bd. of Nashville Christian Leadership
Council; chairman, UNGF Drive, Nashville, 1964; Mem.,
Alpha Phi Alpha; Frontiers International; Society of Biblical
Lit. & Exegesis; Sigma Rho Sigma; Kappa Delta Pi; Articles and Address, Bulletin of Negro History; Congression-
al Record; Laymen S.S. Informer; Home: 1910 15th Ave.,
South Nashville, Tenn.; Office: 1112 Jefferson St., Nash-
ville, Tenn.

*TURNER, Samuel, Jr. coll. prof.; b. Memphis, Tenn., Aug.
21, 1935; s. Samuel and Lelia (Bland) T.; B.S., Le Moyne
Coll., 1958; B.D., Howard Univ., Sch. of Rel., 1961; m.
Naomi Turner; children--- Samuel III, Ruth E.; pastor,
Hollywood Heights Presbyn. Ch., Shreveport, La., 1961-

62; dean of instruction, Butler Coll., Tyler Texas,
1962---; Mt. Olive Baptist Church, Winona, Texas,
1964---; Mem., NAACP; Democrat; Home: Butler Coll.,
Tyler, Texas.

TURNER, William Davis, b. Charleston, S.C., Jan. 4,
1911; s. Richard M. and Lillie (Davis) T.; A.B., St.
Augustine College, 1934; Bishop Payne Divinity School,
Petersburg, Va.; S.T.B., Temple Univ., Divinity School,
1948; m. Dorothy Virginia Norris; children--- Anne
Yvonne (Mrs. Anthony Avelino), Alice Patricia, William
Davis, Jr. Vicar: Church of the Good Shepherd, Sumter,
S.C.; St. Augustine's Church, Sumter County, 1938-40;
St. Stephen's Church, Savannah, Ga., 1940-42; rector:
St. Stephen's Protestant Episcopal Ch., Petersburg, Va.,
1942-43; St. Augustine's P.E. Ch., Phila., Pa., 1943-
present; Member, board of directors, Volunteers in
Sickle Cell Anemia, Phila., Pa. Humanitarian Award,
Volunteers in Sickle Cell Anemia, 1960. Home: 3825
Pulaski Ave., Phila., Pa. Office: 27th St. and Girard
Ave., Phila., Pa.

*TYMS, James Daniel, sem. prof.; b. Aberdeen, Miss.,
Jan. 2, 1905; s. Lawrence and Nancy T.; A.B., Lin-
coln Univ., Jefferson City, Mo., 1934; B.D., Howard
Univ. Sch. of Rel., 1937; M.A., Graduate School,
Howard Univ., 1938; Ph.D., Boston Univ., 1942; D.D.
Western Baptist Seminary, Kansas City, Mo., 1958; m.
Brittie Ann Martin; pastor, New Hope Baptist Ch., Win-
chester, Mass., 1940-42; teacher, Morehouse Coll.,
1942-47; School of Rel., Howard Univ., 1947---; Fellow,
General Education Board, 1944-45; Mem., Religious Ed-
ucation Ass'n; Ass'n Seminary Professors in Practical
Field; Institute of Religion; Fullbright Research Scholar,
Gold Coast, W. Africa. Lecturer, State Dept. (U.S.).
Institute Foreign Affairs on Christian Ed. in Ghanain
Culture. Book review editor, Journal of Religious Thought;
Author, The Rise of Religious Education Among
Negro Baptists; Home: 1729 Varnum St. NW,
20011, Wash., D.C.; Office: School of Religion, Howard
Univ., Wash., D.C. 200011.

TYSON, Charles Edward, b. Asheboro, N.C., July 25,
1925; s. Levy and Martha Ellen (Chrisco) T.; B.S.
Agricultural & Technical Coll., Greensboro, N.C.,
1960, B.D. Southeastern Baptist Theological Seminary,
Wake Forest, N.C., 1964; m. Maude Lee Brady; chil-

dren: Angeline Alfredda; Ministry: Wilkesboro Circuit,
St. Homes Methodist Church, Wilkesboro, N.C., Phila-
delphia Methodist Church, Stoney Point, N.C., 1958-62;
Asbury Temple Methodist Church, Durham, N.C., 1962
to present; Candidate for School Board, Asheboro, N.C.,
1956, Candidate for City Council, Asheboro, N.C. 1958,
Member: Negro Affairs Committee of Asheboro, N.C. by
appointment by Mayor (6 years); U.S. Navy, 1943-46,
Korean Service, 1950-51; Member: Mason; Republican;
Home: 1407 Lincoln Street, Durham, N.C.

UPSHAW, Robert Lee, presiding elder; b. Union Springs,
Ala., Sept. 28, 1900; s. William and Lucretia U.; A.
B., B.D., Payne Seminary, 1939; D.D. (hon.), Mon-
rovia Univ., W. Africa; m. Sylvia A. Matthews; chil-
dren--- Robert C., Connie M.; Teacher, Pike County,
Houston County, Bullock County, Ala.; dean, Central
Coll., Birmingham, Ala.; vice pres., Ministers Confer-
ence Hampton, Va., 2 years; presiding elder, The Al-
legheny District, African Methodist Episcopal Ch.;
Home: 1322 Sylvan Ave., Homestead, Penna.

UPTON, Milton Leon, educator; b. Sweetwater, Tenn., Nov.
23, 1925; s. Elihu Howard and Hattie (Cleveland) U.;
A.B., Knoxville Coll., 1950; B.D., Gammon Theol.
Sem., 1956; Grad. Studies, Gammon Theol. Sem. and
Altanta U. toward S.T.M., Soc. of Rel.; m. Marcella
Ellis; children-- Linda Carol, Mildred Elain;
Leander Howard; Pastor, Freedmen Cumberland Presby-
terian Ch., Athens, Tenn., 1947-50; St. James C.P.
Church, Cleveland, Tenn., 1948; Pulpit Assoc., 1st
Cong. Ch., Atlanta, Ga., 1954-56; Minister, 1st Cong.,
Marietta, Ga., 1955-56; Rush Memorial Cong., Atlanta,
1956-58; present, Beecher Memorial Cong. Ch., New
Orleans, La., 1958---; Dean of Men & Instructor, Al-
corn A. & M. Coll. (Miss.), 1950-53; Research Asst.,
Ford Foundation, Dillard Univ.; Mem. Bd. Dirs., Met.
Assn. for Blind, Carriet Steele Pitts Children's Home
(Atlanta), 1957-58; Camp Fire Girls of America, Atlanta,
1956-58; Bd. Mem., NAACP, New Orleans, 1959-63; Commun-
ity Relations Council of N.O., 1964; N.O. Urban League,
1960---; Dir. Voter Reg., Coord. Council of N.O., 1961;
Vice-Pres., Interdenom. Ministerial Alliance, N.O.;
Chrm. Soc.Action Comm., South Central Conf., UCC,
1963---; U.S. Navy, Seaman 1st Class, 1944-46; Recipient, Victory Medal, Battle of Phillipines, et. al.,

Baden Powell Statuette; Outstanding Citizen Award, Radio
Station WYLD; Outstanding Civic Leader Award, New
Orleans AME Church; Citizenship Award, Omega
Psi Phi; Mem., Omega Psi Phi; Mason; Frontiers
International; YMCA; Toastmasters Club, Y's Men's
Club, Consumers League of N.O., Greater New Orleans
Assoc. of Day Care Centers; sec., Christian Communi-
cations Fellowship of New Orleans; Partial research for book,
The Negro Leadership Class, Thompson, D.C.; Contribu-
tor to Church Journals; Home: 1912 N. Miro St., New
Orleans, La. 70119. Church: 1914 N. Miro St. New
Orleans, La.

VAN CROFT, William Arthur, Jr., b. William Arthur and
Gertrude Dillon V.; A.B., St. Augustine's Coll., Raleigh,
N.C., 1946-49; S.T.B., The General Theological Semin-
ary, 1949-52; Shaw University, summer 1948; m. Ruby
May Rainey; children--- William Arthur III; Ordained in
Diocese of Newark, 1952; Curate, St. Luke's Episcopal
Ch., Washington, D.C., 1952-62; current rector, St.
Luke's Epis. Ch., 1962---; chaplain, D.C. National
Guard, 1955---; chaplain, Boys Village of Maryland,
1953---; Mem., Bd. of Directors, Northwest Settlement
House, 1962---; Diocesan Com., State of the Church;
Com. on the Deacons Training Program; Com. on the
Dio. of Wash.; Summer Urban Program; Staff member on
Summer Conf. for Diocesan Youth Conf.; Dept. of Chris-
tian Ed. (Diocese of Wash.); US Army, overseas in N.
Africa, Italy, France, Germany, 1943-45; awards: Four
bronze stars; Good Conduct Medal; Meritorious Service
Award; mem., Omega Psi Phi; Home: 2705 13th St. NE,
Washington, D.C. 20019; Office: 1514 15th St. NW, Wash-
ington, D.C. 20005.

*VAUGHAN, Alfred Austin, b. Beckley, W.Va., June 6,
1922; s. Charles and Lillian (Poney) V.; B.A., More-
house Coll., 1946; B.D., Howard Univ. Sch. of Rel.,
1952; Courses M.A.; m. Martha Butterworth; children--
Michael Phillip, Charles, Mechele; pastor, Cherry Hill
Meth. Ch., Baltimore, Md., 1954-56; Prince Frederick
Methodist Charge, 1956-60; Union St. Meth. Ch., West-
minster, Md.; current, Union Methodist Ch., Aberdeen,
Md., 1961---; teacher, Jr. High School, Elbert Co.,
Ga., 1946-47; dean of chapl. teacher, Fla. Industrial
Coll., St. Augustine, Fla., 1949-50; Mem., NAACP;
Hartford County Human Relations Council; Methodist

Ministers Assn; Home: Old Post Rd., Box 9, Aberdeen,
Md.

*VEAZEY, Carlon Wadsworth, b. Memphis, Tenn., May 9,
1936; A.B., Arkansas AM & N Coll., Pine Bluff, Ark.;
B.D., Howard Univ., Sch. of Rel.; m. Eva Earlene
Marshall; children--- Michael Vincent; National Council
of Churches, Md., 2 years; present pastor, Zion Baptist
Church, D.C., 1960---; substitute teacher, Public Schools
of Wash., D.C.; counselor, Juvenile Delinquents; Advi-
sory Council of Wash., D.C.; Home: 6009 Eastern Ave.,
NE 20011 Wash., D.C.; Office: 4850 Blagden Ave. NW,
Wash., D.C.

VERRETT, Joseph C., educator; b. New Orleans, La., Jan.
17, 1930; s. Joseph C. and Mary Stella (Smith) V.;
Epiphany Apostolic College, Newburgh, N.Y.; St. Joseph's
Seminary, Wash., D.C.; B.S. Ed. Loyola Univ., New
Orleans, La., 1958; S.T.L., Angelicum Univ., Rome,
1962; J.C.B., Catholic Univ., Wash., D.C., 1963; M.A.
Ed., Xavier Univ., 1964; Ordained priest, Roman Cath.
Ch., 1955; Instr., Engl. Lat., Dramatics, St. Augustine
H.S., New Orleans, 1959-60; Asst. Prin., 1960-61; Instr.
Latin & Eng., Couns-teach., Moderator of Dramatics,
Asst. Princ., St. Augustine H.S., New Orleans, La.,
1963---; Mem. Nat'l Cath. Theatre Conf., Nat. Council
Teachers of Eng.; A member of the Josephite Fathers;
Home: St. Augustine High School, 2600 London Ave.,
New Orleans, La., 70119.

WADSWORTH, James Edward, Jr.; b. Indianapolis, Ind.,
May 17, 1923; s. James Edward and Catherine (Carpen-
ter) W.; Va. State Coll., 1942-47; B.S., Butler Univ.,
Indianapolis, Ind., 1948-49; B.D., Pittsburgh Theol.
Sem., 1949-52; pastor, First United Presbyterian Ch.,
Tenn., 1952-53; St. Mark's Community Ch., Detroit,
Mich., 1953---; corrections commissioner, Michigan
Dept. of Corrections; pres., Detroit Branch, NAACP;
Commissioner, Fair Election Practices Commission,
1964; An active participant in the selective buying program
sponsored by the Negro Ministers of Detroit; Mem., De-
troit Pastor's Union; Detroit Interdenominational Minister-
ial Alliance; Kappa Alpha Psi; Democrat; Guardian Club;
NAACP; Pioneer Club; Thursday Luncheon Club; Home:
2212 Atkinson, Detroit 6, Mich.; Office: 9321 Twelfth
St., Detroit 6, Mich.

WALDEN, Charles Eugene, Jr., b. Washington, D.C., Feb.
2, 1922; s. Charles Eugene and Lillian (Coleman) W.;
Wilberforce Univ., 1937-38; A.B.,
Howard Univ., 1941; B.D., Graduate School of Theology,
Oberlin Coll., 1943; graduate work, Drew Univ.; m.
Wilhelmina Brower; children--- Charles Clayton, Karen
Laverne, Deborah Hean, Frances Marlene, Stephanie
Charlene. Prof., Rural Sociology & Church Administra-
tion, Turner Theol. Seminary, Morris Brown Coll.,
Atlanta, Ga., 1945-46; pastor, Trinity A.M.E. Ch.,
Ridgely, Md., 1947-50; assistant to vicar, Atonement
Episcopal Chapel, 1950-52; present: vicar, St. Philip's
Episc. Ch., 1952- . Visiting lecturer, Rural Ch. Ex-
tension Program, Phelps-Stokes Fund (N.C. - Shaw Univ.
& Livingstone Coll.; Ala., Miss., Tenn., (Fisk Univ.)
Kentucky, Fla., Va., Ga. (Ga. State Coll.); visiting
preacher, D.C. Village; counselor, Diocese of Washing-
ton Youth Conf., 1953; member, Dept. of Promotion,
1956-58; Member, Ch. School Division, Dept. of Chris-
tian Education, 1960-62. Chaplain & Board member, Whip-
per Home for Unwed Mothers, 1958-60; chairman, Area
Commissioners' Youth Council, 1956-58; board mem.,
Planned Parenthood Assn. of D.C., 1959-61; mem.,
Clergy Advisory Committee, Planned Parenthood;
Parents' Advisory Committee, Ripon Coll., Wisconsin,
1962-64; chaplain (captain), Nat'l Capital Wing, Civil
Air Patrol; pres., Davis School PTA, 1961-62;
Advisory Committee, Special Services, D.C. Tuberculosis
Assn; program chairman, Potomac Area Council, Camp Fire
Girls of America, 1961; merit badge counselor, Nat'l Capital
Council, Boy Scouts of America. Citation: J. Finley Wil-
son Mem. Lodge No. 1371, IBPOE of W: "for effective
performance measuring to the high standards in commun-
ity service ... sharing skills and knowledge...", 1958.
Omega Psi Phi. Home: 1200 45th Pl., S.E., Wash., D.
C. Office: 2431 Shannon Pl., S.E. Wash., D.C.

*WALKER, Arnold George, b. Talladega, Nov. 9, 1935;
s. Arnold George and Doris (Vick) W.; B.S., B.D.,
Howard Univ., Wash., D.C., 1956, 1959; chaplain-
trainee, D.C. General Hospital, 1959; chaplain intern,
Medical Coll., Va. Hospital Div., 1960; pastor, Bethany
Presbyterian Church, Lumberton, N.C., 1962---; pres.
Lumberton Citizens Civic Committee; Good Neighbors
Council, 1964; sec., Lumberton Ministerial Ass'n,
1963---; Mem., Omega Psi Phi; Lumberton Interracial
Organization; Home: 523 Ninth Lumberton, N.C.; Office:

Elizabethtown Rd. , Lumberton, N. C.

WALKER, George David, b. Enterprise, Miss. 1920; s.
William Riley and Sussieanna (McCormick) W. ; A. B.
Clark Coll. , 1944, B. D. Gammon Theological Seminary
1947, Further study: Atlanta University, Chicago U. and
American U. ; m. Cornelia Anita Williams; Children:
Julia Anntionett, Rosella Anita, Mirlenda Louise; Minis-
try: Bude, Miss. , 1940, Mt. Olive, Atlanta, Ga. 1941,
Cedartown, Ga. 1941-42, Carrolton, Ga. 1942-46, Rome,
Ga. , Metropolitan Methodist, 1946-55; Savannah, Ga.
Asbury Meth. 1955-61; Present: Chattanooga, Tenn.
Wiley Memorial Methodist; High School Principal,
Georgia (ten years); Candidate for Alderman, Savannah,
Ga. 1958, Trustee Board of Clark College, 1955-61.
Mem. , Masons, Phi Beta Sigma, Home: 504 Lookout
Street, Chattanooga 3, Tenn.

WALKER, Henry W. B. , b. Charlotte Co. , Va. , Sept. 27,
1903; s. Charlie and Lucy Walker (Slaughter); A. B. , Va.
Seminary; B. D. , Temple Univ. ; S. T. M. , Union Seminary,
N. Y. ; Completed work for Th. D. from Temple Univ. ; m.
Anita Freeman Barettee; children--- Mrs. Helen Hunt
(adopted); pastor, Mt. Zion Bapt. Church, Appomattox,
Va. ; Brooksville Bapt. Ch. , Lynchburg, Va. ; Bapt.
Church, Piedmount, Yanceys, Mills, Va. ; Mem. , Mason;
Elk; Phi Beta Sigma; teacher and dean of the Theol. Dept.
of Va. Seminary and Coll. , 9 years; current pastor,
Second Calvary Bapt. Church, Norfolk, Va. ; pres. , The
Bapt. Ministers Conference of Norfolk, Portsmouth and
Vicinity; vice pres. , Inter-Racial Ministers Assn; pres. ,
Civic League, 2 years; Mem. , Hampton Minister Confer-
ence Bd. ; vice-pres. , Va. Bapt. Conv. ; National Bapt.
Convention of America; vice-pres. , Trustee Bd. , Va.
Seminary, Lynchburg, Va. ; US Chaplain, 1941-44; Captain;
Home: 6740 Newtown Rd. , Va. 23452; Office: Croprew and
Godfrey Ave. , Norfolk, Va.

WALKER, John Thomas, b. Barnesville, Ga. , July 2,
1925; s. Joseph and Mattie (Wyche) W. ; B. A. , Wayne
State Univ. , Detroit, Michigan, 1951; B. D. , Episcopal
Theol. Sem. , Alexandria, Va. , 1954; m. Rose Maria
Flores; children--- Thomas Peyton; pastor, St. Mary's
Prot. Epis. Ch. , Detroit, Mich. ; teacher, St. Paul's
Sch. , Concord, New Hampshire, 1957-64; Mem. , New
Hampshire Advisory Com. of the US Civil Rights Commis-
sion; Office: St. Paul's School, Concord, New Hampshire.

WALKER, William Raphael, b. Clarksville, Texas, May 26,
1918; s. George Henry, Sr. and Nettie (Burks) W.;
B.S., Wilberforce Univ., Ohio, 1950; B.D., Payne
Theol. Seminary, Wilberforce, Ohio, 1951; m. Vera
Marie Fossett; children--- Vicki Sue, William Jr.,
John Edward, George Henry, Vera Marie, Vivian Kaye;
pastor, Quinn African Methodist Episcopal Ch., Wilming-
ton, Ohio, 1947-51; St. Paul A. M. E. Church, Bellaire,
Ohio, and Wayman A. M. E. Church, Martins Ferry,
Ohio, 1951-61; current pastor, Trinity A. M. E. Church,
Springfield, Ohio, 1961---; chairman, Inter-racial Com-
mittee Clark County, Ohio; Sec., Board of Directors,
Grace Tatum Nursery Sch.; Board of Directors, Union
Settlement House, Mem., Budget Committee of the
United Appeals Fund of Clark Country;   Trustee
Board of the United Appeals Fund of Clark County, Ohio;
US Air Forces, staff sergeant, 3 years; Certificate of
Merit Third Episcopal District, African Methodist Church
for Distinguished and Unselfish Service, for Faithful De-
votion to Duty, for Loyalty to the cause of Christian Ed-
ucation, 1954; Mason; pres., Inter-Denominational Al-
liance of Springfield, Ohio; Chief sec., Ohio Annual
Conf., Trustee,   Ohio A. M. E. Church Annual Con-
ference; Trustee Payne Theological Seminary; Home: 506
West Southern Ave., Springfield, Ohio; Office: Trinity
A. M. E. Church, 554 Selma Road, Springfield, Ohio.

WALKER, Wyatt Tee, civil rights leader; b. Brockton,
Mass., Aug. 15, 1929; s. John Wise and Maude (Pinn)
W.; B.S., Va. Union Univ.; B.D., School of Religion,
Va. Union Univ.; m. Theresa Edwards; children--- Anne
Patrice, Wyatt, Jr., Robert, Earl; pastor, Gillfield
Bapt. Ch., Petersburg, Va., (8 years); exec. asst.,
Southern Christian Leadership Conf.; vice pres., in
charge of marketing & service, American Education
Heritage, Inc., (For two years on loan from Southern
Christian Leadership Conf. to help in developing and dis-
tributing Negro History Library; to help diminish the
"cultural block out" that has been imposed on the Negro
community in Amer.); pres., NAACP, Va. 5 years;
state director, CORE; National Bd. Mem., Southern
Christian Leadership Conf.; Trustee, Va. Theol. Sem.
& Coll.; pres., P.T.A.; Visitors League; pres. & Bd.
mem., Va. Council on Human Relations; Elks Awards;
National Civil Rights Award; Mem., Alpha Phi Alpha;
Office: American Educational Heritage, Inc., 733 Yonkers
Ave., Yonkers, N. Y.

WALLACE, Eustace Fieldings; b. Bearden, Arkansas, Nov.
23, 1896; s. Christopher C. and Mary (Walker) W.;
attended Philander Smith College, 1937 and 1951-54; m.
Mamie Swinger, 1928; children: (Mrs. Elren Hutchinson,
(Mrs. Edith Harris), Mrs. Agnes Myers, Marion; Ministry: Pastor in Arkansas 1927-48; District Superintendant
1948-54, pastored in Oklahoma, 1954-61, pastored in
Arkansas 1961-62, present District Superintendant of the
Little Rock District, Arkansas,   The Methodist Church,
1962; Taught public school, 1916-1918; Mason; member: Republican Party; Home: 3215 Arch Street, Little
Rock, Arkansas.

WALLS, William Jacob, bishop; b. Chimney Rock, N.C.,
May 8, 1885; s. Edward and Harriet (Edgerton) W.;
A.B., Livingstone Coll., Salisbury, N.C., 1908; B.D.,
Hood Theol. Sem., 1913; D.D. (hon.), Livingstone Coll.,
1918; LL.D. (hon.), 1943; A.M., Univ. of Chicago,
1941; m. Dorothy Louise Jordan; pastor, Cleveland,
N.C., 1905-07; Lincolnton, N.C., 1908-10; Salisbury,
N.C., 1910-13; Louisville, Ky., 1913-20; editor, Star
of Zion, Charlotte, N.C., 1920-24; bishop, African
Meth. Episcopal Zion Ch., 1924; chairman, Bd. of Publ.,
1930; chairman, Bd. of Home Missions, Resident in
Chicago, 1930; chaplain, World War I; chairman, Bd.
of Trustees, Livingstone Coll.; Trustee, Gammon Theol.
Sem.; chairman, African Methodist Episcopal Zion Ses-
quicentennial, 1946; delegate, Gen. Con. M.E. Ch.,
South, 1918; M.E. Church, 1928; del. Ecumenical Meth.
Conf., London, England, 1921; Atlanta, Ga., 1931;
Springfield, Mass., 1947; Oxford, Eng., 1951; vice pres.,
World Meth. Conf., 1951; Mem., president's and war
secretary's Am. Clergymen's Com. to occupied countries
in Europe, 1947; Mem., Exec. Bd. National Council of
Churches of Christ in USA; Mem., Commn. Cultural
and Human Relations, 1954; del., World Council of
Churches, Amsterdam, Holland, 1948; Mem., Message
and Central Committees since 1948; Exec. Committee,
World Methodist Council, 1956; delegate, World Christian
Education and Sunday School Convention, Tokyo, 1958;
vice pres., Divinity Sch.; Trustee, United International
Christian Endeavor Society; Mem., Religious Educational
Assn.; International Council Religious Education; World's
Sunday Sch. Assn; National Council of Churches of Amer-
ica; Mem., NAACP; Amer. Academy Political Science;
chaplain, National Negro Business League; Mem., Phi
Beta Sigma; Republican; Mason; Odd Fellow; K.P.; Elk;

author: J. C. Price Educator and Race Leader; Pastorates
and Reminiscences; What Youth Wants; The Dream of
Youth; The Romance of A College; Home: 4736 South
Parkway, Chicago 15, Ill.; Office: 151-3 West 136th St.,
New York 30, N. Y.

WALLS, William Roscoe, b. Winston Salem, N. C., Nov. 3,
1926, s. Porvioys and Nannie (Barber); W.A.B., Johnson
c. Smith Univ., B.D., J.C. Smith U., 1949 & 1952
respectively; m. Gertrude Hines; pastor Philadelphia
Methodist Church, Rockingham, N. C., 1952-53; Laughton
Methodist Church, Greensboro, N. C., 1953-55; Broad
Presbyterian Ch., Statesville, N. C.; 1955-61; Timothy
Darling Presbyterian Ch., 1961---; Oxford, N. C.; Mem.
The Mayors bi-racial Comm.; Home: 121 Halifax St.,
Oxford, N. C.

WAMBLE, Amos Sylvester, Sr. b. Warren, Arkansas,
s. James Oscar and Lula (Dorn) W.; B.Th.
Western College, Kansas City, Mo. 1951, attended Rock-
hurst Coll. Kansas City, Mo. 1951-52; m. Earlene
(Collins) Wamble; Children: Edwin, Brneda, John, Amos,
Jr., Marcus, Minnie, Carl, Theresa, Phillip, Angelia,
Eunice; Ministry: Young's Chapel, Blackburn, Mo.,
Crutchfield Chapel, Malta Bend, Mo., White Oak, Inde-
pendence, Mo., Grace Methodist, Kansas City, Mo., St.
James Methodist (formerly Kelly Chapel) Kansas City,
Mo., St. James Methodist, Coffeyville, Kansas, Second
Methodist, Independence, Kansas, Present: Quayle Meth-
odist, Oklahoma City, Okla; Government Employee,
1946-55, Inc. Post Office, Veterans Administration,
Gov't. Ser. Assoc. C. C.C., Quartermaster, all in Kan-
sas City, Mo.; Mem.: Census Board, Independence,
Mo., Planning Board Committee, Coffeyville, Kansas,
1960; U.S. Army, July 3, 1940-Sept. 11, 1945, Honor-
able Discharge; Good Conduct Medal, 4 Campaign Rib-
bons; Sec. of Southwest Conference of The Methodist
Church, member: Oklahoma Council of Churches, Sec.
of Interdenominational-Interracial Alliance, member,
N. A. A. C. P., Urban League, YMCA & YWCA, Chmn.
Conference Board of Promotion & Cultivation; Chmn.
Conference Board of Publications, Edit and Publish An-
nual Conference Minutes and Journal; Home: 2801 N.
Missouri Street, Oklahoma City, Okla. 73111.

*WARD, Charles W., b. Georgia, Nov. 1915; s. Willie
and Cerrender (R.) W.; A.B., Morehouse Coll., 1942;

B.D., Howard Univ., Sch. of Rel., 1946; certificate,
Psychosomatic medicine, Bowman Gary School of Medi-
cine; m. Roberta Earnestine Gore; children--- Charles
Winfred, Jr.; pastor, West End Baptist Ch., Winston-
Salem, N.C., 1944-49; Rising Star Baptist Ch., Walnut
Grove, N.C., 1946-52; Executive secy., Georgia Mis-
sionary and Educational Convention; current, First Baptist
Ch., Raleigh, N.C., 1959---; Mem., YMCA Boards;
United Fund Drives; Ministerial Ass'n; Human Relation
Committee; State-Wide chairman of Voter-Registration
for N.C.; NAACP, 1964; Young Democratic Club of N.C.;
Delegate To State Democratic Convention, 1964; Home:
501 S. Bloodworth St., Raleigh, N.C.; Office: 101 S.
Wilmington St., Raleigh, N.C.

WARD, Eric Calvin, college professor; b. Los Angeles,
California, Nov. 11, 1924; s. Galbourne A. and Estelle
(W.) W.; Los Angeles Union Academy, 1936-40; Lyn-
wood Academy, 1940-42; Th.B., Pacific Union College,
1946; m. Gwendolyn M.; children--- Carolyn, Prince,
Golbourne, Beverly, Linda, Della. Pastor, South Atlantic
Conf. of Seventh-Day Adventist, Atlanta, Ga., 1946-53;
Southern Union Conf.; evangelist, Seventh-Day Adventist,
Atlanta, Ga., 1954-63; present: pastor, 31st Street
Seventh-Day Adventist Church, San Diego, Calif., 1963-.
Instructor for Field School of Evangelism and Pastoral
Care, Andrews Univ., June 1963 - Sept. 1963; visiting
lecturer on Pastoral and Evangelistic methods for Oak-
wood College, 1953-62; special articles for "The Mes-
sage" magazine and "The Ministry" magazine of Wash-
ington, D.C. Home: 422 Los Angeles Place, San Diego
14, Calif. Office: 414 So. 31st St., San Diego, Calif.

WARD, Martin DePorres, teacher; b. Boston, Mass., Mar.
20, 1918; s. William Henry and Clara (Irby) W.; Ordained Franciscan Friar, 1955; Prof. English. Prof.
of Com. English, Prof. of Sacred Music; Franciscan
missionary in Brazil; Has formed choirs for execution of
Gregorian chant; Home: Ginasio Santo Antonio, Sao Luiz
Gonzaga, Rio Grande DoSul, Brazil, S. Amer.

WARREN, Charles Lacy, ch. official; b. Victoria, Tex.,
Aug. 1, 1911; s. John W. and Helen (Coffey) W.; A.B.,
Houston-Tillotson Coll., 1933; B.D., Gammon Theol.
Sem., 1936; S.T.M., Boston Univ. Sch. of Theol.,
1937; D.D. (hon.), Houston-Tillotson Coll., 1948; D.D.,
Gammon Theol. Sem., 1950; m. Alice H. Jones; chil-

dren--- Charles Lacy, Oscar Wesley, Madelynn Louise;
pastor, Taylor Memorial Me. Ch., 1940-58; St. Mark's
Meth. Ch., New York City; current Dist. Supt., Metropolitan Dist., New York Conf., The Meth. Ch.; former
vice pres., Oakland Council of Ch., Dept. of Human Re-
lations; Mem., Bd. of Directors, Welfare Bureau; dele-
gate, Western Jurisdictional Conf., Meth. Ch., 1948,
52, 56; delegate, General Conf., Meth., 1952; delegate,
NE Jurisdictional Conf., 1964; Mem., Exec. Com.,
Dept. of Racial and Cultural Relations, Nat. Council of
Churches, Com. of Religious Leaders, New York City;
Harlem Hospital Advisory Bd.; Advisory Bd., Sydenham
Society; Advisory Bd., Harlem Branch, YMCA; Clergy
Com., Sch. Dist. 12, 13, 14; Bd. of Directors of Meth.
Deaconess Home; Bd. of Directors, New York City
Society; New York Region Personnel Com., Bd. of World
Missions; In the New York Annual Conf. the chairman of
the Interboard Council; Mem., Urban Life Com.; vice
pres., Bd. of Missions; Mem., British-American
Preachers Exchange Preaching, Scotland and England,
1961; Chi Alpha; Alpha Phi Alpha; Mason; Home: 72
Holls Terrace N. Yonkers, New York; Office: 475 River-
side Dr., New York City, N.Y. 10027.

WASHINGTON, Curtis Thomas,   missionary; b.
   Coconut Grove, Miami, Fla., April 5, 1917; s. Marion
   and Rhoda (Smith) W.; St. Emma High School Academy,
   Rock Castle, Va., 1936; St. Mary's Philosophate, Techny,
   Ill., 1943; Finished coll. course, theology course, philosophy course at Bay St. Louis, Miss., 1949; Ordained
   1949; Built churches and academic primary, high schools
   and colleges and doing social work in credit unions,
   hospitals and family welfare in Africa; local manager of
   schools in Ghana, West Africa in the Diocese of Accra
   within the Krobo, Adwamu, Shai, Osuduku educational
   districts; award: expert rifle medal; Mem., International
   Religious Society of the Divine Word; Home: St. Mary
   Seminary, Techny, Ill.; Office: Catholic Church, Ago-
   manya, Odumase-Krobo, Ghana, West Africa.

WASHINGTON, Dennis Comer, church official; b. Hale Co.,
   Ala., Aug. 15, 1905; s. William H. and Mary (Scott) W.;
   B.S., Ala. State Teacher's Coll., Montgomery, Ala.;
   Selma Univ., Selma, Ala.; D.D. (hon.), Selma Univ.,
   1947; LL.D., Selma Univ., 1954; m. Bessie Randall;
   children--- William M., Bessie W. Jones, Dennis C.,
   Jr., Harold, E.; pastor, Bapt. Church, Ala., 1924-38;

17th St. Baptist Ch., Anniston, Ala., 1938-59; asst. secy.,
National Bapt. Convention, USA, Inc., 1957-59; Exec.
Director, Sunday School Publication Bd., National Bapt.
Convention, USA, Inc., 1959---; vice moderator, Snow
Creek Bapt. Dist., Ass'n, Ala.; Mem., Exec. Bd., Ala.
Baptist State Convention, 18 years; official delegate,
Anniton Chapter NAACP; White House Conference on Civil
Rights, 1956; teacher, Calhoun Co. Training School;
Trustee, Selma Univ.; Trustee, American Bapt. Theol.
Sem., Nashville, Tenn.; Trustee, Anniston Fed. of
Colored Women's Clubs; Democrat; Mem., NAACP; Na-
tional Bapt. Convention, USA, Inc.; Office: 330 Charlotte
Ave., Nashville, Tenn.

WASHINGTON, Emanuel Ezra, b. Hoboken, N.J., Dec. 24,
1920; s. George Edward and Mary (Cook) W.; A.B.,
1949, B.D., 1951, Johnson C. Smith University, Char-
lotte, N.C.; M.Th., Texas Christian University (Brite
College); m. Mildred Katherine Chisholm; children---
Emanuel, Jr., Ronald Phelton, Granville Calvin; Sabbath
School Missionary - Presbyterian Ch., U.S.A., 1951-
54; pastor, St. James Presbyterian Church, Kingsport,
Tenn., 1954-58; current pastor, St. Peter Presbyterian
Church, U.S.A., Ft. Worth, Texas, 1958---; US Air
Force, 1942-45; Mem., Phi Beta Sigma, Mason, Boy
Scouts of America, Boys Club; Home: 5549 Patton Drive,
Ft. Worth 76112, Texas; Office: 5801 Truman Dr., Ft.
Worth 76112, Texas.

WASHINGTON, James Augustus, b. Marion, South Carolina,
Sept. 9, 1932; s. John and Nancy (Glover) W.; B.A.,
Oakwood College, 1954; M.A., Andrews Univ., 1956;
m. Sarah Elizabeth Costen; children-Costena Marie,
Sarah Elizabeth, Nancy Ann. Pastored Seventh-Day Adventist Churches in: Atlantic City, N.J., 1954-55; Akron
and Canton, Ohio, 1956-59; Roanoke, Danville, Virginia,
1959-63; present: pastor, Columbus, Ohio, 1963- .
1955-56 Assistant pastor, Dupont Park S.D.A. Church,
Washington, D.C., Lecturer and public evangelist;
secretary, Roanoke Ministerial Alliance, 1962-63;
former member, City of Roanoke Bi-Racial Council; research on Negro History Pre- and Post Slavery Era.
Home: 2110 Maryland Ave., Columbus, Ohio. Office:
2171 E. Fifth Ave., Columbus, Ohio.

WASHINGTON, Joseph R., Jr. chaplain, author; b. Iowa
City, Iowa, Oct. 30, 1930; s. Rev. and Mrs. Joseph

W.; B.A., Univ. of Wisconsin, 1952; B.D., Andover
Newton Theological School, 1957, Andover Newton Theo.
School, 1957-58; Th.D., Boston Univ. Sch. of Theology,
1961; m. Sophia May Holland; children--- Bryan Reed;
Ordained minister, The Central Pennsylvania Conf., The
Methodist Church; asst. pastor, First Baptist Church,
Woburn, Mass., 1954-56; pastor, West Newfield, Maine,
Congregational Ch., and Newfield, Maine, Methodist
Church, 1956-57; students pastor, The Baptist Church,
Brookline, Mass., 1957-58; assoc. Protestant chaplain,
Boston Univ., 1958-61; dean of chapel, Dillard Univ.,
New Orleans, 1961-63; chaplain, Dickinson Coll., 1963
---; US Army Corps of Military Police, 1952-54; 1st Lt.,
Univ. of Wisconsin's Iron Cross, honorary society which
annually elects twelve men who have contributed signifi-
cantly to the Univ. during their undergraduate years,
1952; author: Black Religion: The Negro and Christianity
in the United States; Articles: Central Christian Advocate,
Mar. 1962; Motive, Jan., 1963; Theology Today, Apr.
1963; Religious Education, June, 1963, Sept. 1963, Mar.
1964; Foundations, Jan., 1964; Office: Chaplain to the
Coll. and Assistant Professor of Religion, Dickinson Coll.,
Carlisle, Pa.

WASHINGTON, L. Barnwell, chaplain; b. March 16, 1910;
s. William and Nancy (Fludd) W.; A.B., Johnson C.
Smith Univ., 1935; B.D., 1938; M.A., Howard Univ.,
Courses on Ph.D., Union Theol. Sem.; m. Vivian
Beatrice Shute; 1939-42; Instructor Rel. Ed. and Regis-
trar, Student pastor, Coulter Jr. Coll. and Asst. Dir.,
Cheraw Larger Parish, Cheraw, S.C, pastor Calvary
Presbyn. Ch., Kannapolis, N.C.; 1942 - ; chaplains
school, Ft. Benjamine Harrison, Ind. Served: 583 FABn,
92 Div.; Served Com. and Port Battallions, Indiantown
Gap, Pa.; 1943-44, Duty S.W. Pacific Chaplain, 97 Ing.
Active reserve to 1955; Part time instructor, Johnson
C. Smith Univ., 1946-49; Current pastor, New Life
United Presby. Ch., Boston, Mass.; 1946-54; pastor
Wilson M.P.C., Awards: Campaign, Asiatic Pacific
Campaign, U.S.A. World War II Medal, 1941-45.
Certificate of Award for Meritorious Service and Bronze
medal for Devoted service by the General Assembly of
the United Presbyterian Church, U.S.A. Mem: 1949-58
Academy Pol. Science; Nat. Travelers Club, N.Y.C.
Phi Beta Sigma: Coordinator and member P.L.C. (Presby.
Inter-racial Council Clergy Comm.) Wash. Park Re-
development Assoc. Comm.; twice to Church's Highest

Court, The General Assembly of the U. Presbyterian
Ch., U.S.A., 1946; represented Presby. Boston 175th
General Assembly, Des Moines, Iowa; Comm. World
Responsibility; Mass. Council of Churches; Author:
Prayers Before Meals for Record American; sermonettes
for "Boston Herald." Church: #1 Gore St., Boston (Rox-
bury) 20, Mass.

WATKINS, Readus Joseph, b. Pensacola, Florida, July 13,
1931; s. Edward Francis and Berlina (Pickens) W.; B.
A., Gordon Coll., 1956; S.T.B., Boston Univ., 1959;
Ed. M., Boston Univ., 1960; m. Deborah M. McClure;
children--- Bryan Joseph, Dana Linn, Geoffrey Read;
associate pastor, East Saugus Meth. Ch., Saugus,
Mass., 1956; pastor, Pleasant St. Bapt. Ch., Westerly,
Rhode Island, 1958; Head of Counselling & Guidance Dept.,
Achimoto Coll., Ghana, W. Africa, 1959; pastor St. Luke's
Meth. Ch., New Rochelle, New York, 1962-65; current, First
Meth. Ch., New Milford, Conn. Mem., Advisory Bd., Plan-
ned Parenthood, Southern West-Chester Chapter;Exec. Com.,
New Rochelle Council of Churches;Bd. of Education, New York
Annual Conf., The Meth. Ch.; Bd. of Directors, Adoption
Service of Westchester County, New York; vice pres., Amer-
ican Red Cross Society, City of New Rochelle, New York;
sec., Protestant Ministers' Assn, City of New York; Home:
32 Lakeside Drive, New Rochelle, New York; Office: St.
Luke's Meth. Ch., 108 Guion Place, New Rochelle, New York.

WELLS, Gerald Nathaniel, b. Boca Raton, Fla., August 2,
1934; s. Gerald Godwin and Tarrah Lee (Jackson) W.;
B.A., Oakwood College, 1959; M.A., Andrews Univ.,
1960; m. Beverly Jean Porter; children-- Desrea Lunn.
Pastored: Independence Blvd. Church, Chicago, Ill.,
1960-61; Berean S.D.A. Church, South Bend, Ind., 1961-
62; present: Trendley Ave. S.D.A. Church, E. St.
Louis, Ill., 1962- ; National Service medal and the
Good Conduct medal. Home: 605 Tulane Drive, East St.
Louis, Ill. Office: 2000 Trendley Ave., E. St. Louis,
Ill.

WEST, James Oliver, Jr.; b. Richmond, Va. March 2,
1918; s. James O. and Cynthia E. (W.); B.A., Va.
Union Univ., 1936; B.D., Va. Episcopal Theol. Sem.,
1939; S.T.M., Hartford Theol. Sem., and Foundation,
Hartford, Conn., 1940; m. Maxie B. Pearson; children
--- Brenda; Paula; Served 1 year in four mission chapels;

Alexandria, Va. Berryville, Va., Millwood, Va.; Sem-
inary, Va., 1940; current rector, Calvary Protestant
Episcopal Ch., Wash. D.C., 1941---; Mem., Christian
Ed., Social Action and Social Casework Com. of the
Episcopal Diocese of Wash.; Radio and TV Com. of the
Wash. Federation of Chs.; Bd. of Directors, D.C.
Tuberculosis Assn; Area P. Bd. of D.C. Commissioners
Youth Council; award: Outstanding Achievement in Re-
ligious Education from the Omega Psi Phi, 1953; Out-
standing citizen award from the Y's Men's Club of
Wash., 1962; Mem., Omega Psi Phi; D.C. Chapter of Va.
Union Univ. Alumni Assn; Democrat; Home: 509 Eye St.,
Wash., D.C. 20002; Office: 820 6th St., Wash., D.C. 20002.

WESTON, M. Moran, b. Iarbori, N.C.; s. Milton M. and
C. Cornelia (Perry) W.; A.B., Columbia Univ.; B.D.
Union Theol. Sem.; Ph.D., Columbia Univ.; D.D. (hon.),
Epis. Theol. Sem. (Alexandria, Va.), 1964; New school
for social research, 2 years; m. Miriam Yvonne Drake;
children--- Karen Yvonne, Philip Gregory Moran; business manager & curate, St. Phelp's Epis. Ch., N.Y.C.,
1948-51; exec. sec., Div. of Christian Citizenship,
National Council of Prot. Epis. Church, 1951-57; current rector, St. Philips Ch., 1957---; social worker; real
estate salesman; public relations; founder & mem., Bd.
of Directors, Carver Fed. Savings & Loan Assn; Bd. of
Directors, Community Council of Greater New York; New
York City Mission Society; Council on Religion in Independent Schs.; Child Adoption Service; State Charities
Aid Assn; Harlem Neighborhood Assn; Harlem Youth Op-
portunities Unlimited; District 10 Planning Council; Man-
hattan Borough President's Office; Urban League; Elder
Craftsman's Shop; New York Clergy Study Com. on Al-
coholism; Bd. of Directors, Leake and Watts Children's
Home; Mem., Administrative Com. Federation of Prot.
Welfare Agencies (N.Y.C.); Kappa Alpha Psi; Elks; Pol.
Independent; author: Social Policy of the Epis. Ch. in the
Twentieth Century, Seabury Press, 1964; Episcopalians
at Work in the World, 1952; Chapter in: Man at Work in
God's World, ed. by Cannon G.E. De Mille; Chapter in:
Committment and Community in the Schools; frequent
speaker at Diocese Conventions and on College Campuses;
Home: 253 Blvd., New Rochelle, N.Y.; Office: 215 W.
133rd St., New York City, N.Y.

WHITE, Albert McNeil, chaplain; b. S.C., Dec. 29, 1910;
B.S., B.D., Allen and Wilberforce Univ.; Graduate study

Boston Univ.; D.D. (hon.), Campbell Coll., 1951; LL.
D. (hon.), Kittrell Coll., 1955; m. Aleane Beatrice; chil-
dren--- Sylvester Jeradin, Ralph McNeil, Francese
Renee, Sara Anne; pastor, African Methodist Episcopal,
Churches, Fla., La., Pa., Mass., Rhode Island, Ohio,
since 1925; principal, High School, S.C.; teacher, Edward
Waters Coll., Jacksonville, Fla.; US Army Chaplain serving in ECOM, FECOM, and PTO during WW II and Kor-
ean Conflict; 10 1/2 years American Campaign Service
Medal; European-African-Middle East Service Medal;
Asiatic Pacific Service Medal; Distinguished Service Ribbons; Five Battle Stars; Mem., Phi Beta Sigma; Elks;
Mason; American Legion; YMCA; A.M.E. Ministers' Alliance; A.M.E. Chaplains' Organization; editor, From a
Chaplain's Point of View; Pastoral Counseling; The Pulpit Led Church; Home: 1233 Melon St., Phila., Pa.; Office: Mt. Pisgah A.M.E. Church, 519 East Washington,
Lake City, Fla.

*WHITE, Andrew, editor, ch. official; b. Moncks Corner, S.
C., March 8, 1912; s. Andrew and Annie (Reed) W.;
Avery Institute, 1928-32; A.B., Howard Univ., 1936-40;
B.D., Howard Univ., Sch. of Rel., 1940-43; M.A., Fisk
Univ., 1954-55; D.D. (hon.), Monrovia Coll., 1955; m.
Edith Burrel; children--- Andrew N. III, Edith Anne;
pastor, Basil African Methodist Episcopal Ch., Cockeys-
ville, Md., 1940-43; St. James A.M.E. Ch., Covington,
Ky., 1943-48; St. Paul A.M.E. Ch., Nashville, Tenn.,
1948-49; Salem A.M.E. Ch., Nashville, Tenn., 1949-56;
administrative asst. and editorial associate, Division of
Christian Education, A.M.E. Ch., Nashville, Tenn.,
1948-56; editor-in-chief, Religious Literature, Division of
Christian Education, A.M.E. Ch., Nashville, Tenn.,
1956-60; exec. sec., Division of Christian Education, A.
M.E. Ch., Nashville, Tenn., 1960---; Mem., CIO Poli-
ticical Action Com., Cincinnati Branch, 1943-48; Com.
J.C. Napier Division Boy Scouts of America, Nashville,
Tenn., 1950-56; founding mem. and sec., Nashville,
Christian Leadership Council, 1958-64; pres., Nashville,
Christian Leadership Council, 1964---; mem., Exec. Bd.,
Southern Christian Leadership Conf., 1963-64; 1964-65;
mem. Exec. Bd., Division of Christian Education,
National Council of Churches; editor, The Journal of Re-
ligious Education, A.M.E. Ch.; publish manuals and
work books for use in local churches; Home: 1621 Haynes
Meade Circle, Nashville, Tenn. 37207; Office: 414 8th
Ave., South Nashville, Tenn. 37203.

WHITE, Edward Augustus, b. Muskogee, Oklahoma, Jan.
25, 1934; s. Joseph and Effie (Huddleston) W.; B.A.,
Pacific Union Coll., Angwin, Calif., 1958; M.A., S.D.
A. Theological Seminary, Washington, D.C., 1959; m.
Fleda Toliver; children-- Darrell, Janie, Susan. Pas-
tored Seventh-Day Adventist Church, Oakland, 1960;
present: pastor, Pittsburgh S.D.A. church, Pittsburgh,
Calif. and Berea S.D.A. Church, Valleje, Calif. 1961- .
Home: 535 Ridge Ave., Valleje, Calif. Office: 833
Louisiana St., Valleje, Calif.

WHITE, Joseph Douglas, jr. bishop; b. Mason, Ga., Dec.
25, 1904; s. Isaac and Estella W.; Church of Christ
Bible Institute, N.Y.C., 4 years; Bible Way Training
Sch., Wash., D.C., 3 years; m. Geneva Sylvia
Strothers; children--- Joseph D. Jr., Shirley M., Isaac
M., John H., Reginald J.; Licensed for Ministry, 1935;
Ordained 1938; pastored churches in Atlanta, Ga. (Bible
Way Church of our Lord Jesus Christ World-Wide, Inc.)
Baltimore, Md., Greensboro, N.C.; current pastor,
Kernersville, N.C. and Director of Religious Education
in Western N.C., Ga., Florida; Junior bishop over the
same area; teacher, Bible Way Training Sch., Wash., D.
C.; One of organizers and director of political action,
United Cafeteria Workers Union, Wash., D.C.; US Army,
1923-31; Former editor, Bible Way News Voice, Bible
Way Church-Wash., D.C.; former vice pres., Bible Way
Training Sch., Bible Way Church-Wash., D.C.; Home:
181 1/2 Nelson, Kernersville, N.C.; Office: 181 Nelson,
Kernersville, N.C.

WHITE, Kenneth, chaplain; b. Miami, Fla., Jan 1, 1906;
s. Boyer and Millie (J.) W.; Edward Waters Coll. Lee
Seminary, Jacksonville, Fla., B.D., 1940-44; Courses:
Howard Univ. Sch. of Rel., Wash. D.C.; Graduate Cortez
Peters Business Sch., Wash., D.C., 1956; m. Lillie
H.; children--- Kenneth Jr., Margaret Alston, Henry
Patricia, William Alston; teacher, Taylor Co., Perry
Fla., 1937-39; pastor, African Methodist Episcopal
Churches, Fla., 1936-44; chaplain, US Army, 1944-52;
Captain; pastor, A.M.E. Churches, Maryland; current
pastor, Reid Temple A.M.E. Church, Wash., D.C.,
1964; Chaplain, American Legion, James Reese Post No.
5, D.C.; Victory Medal, SWP, Japan, Korea; Home: 1519
Queen, Wash. 2, D.C.; Office: 1335 Michigan Ave.,
Wash., D.C.

*WHITE, Lanneau L., b. Marion Co., S.C., July 13,
1910; s. Claren A. and Lou W.; A.B., Agri. & Tech.
Coll., Greensboro, N.C.; B.D., Howard Univ. Sch. of
Rel., 1936; M. Re., Union Theol. Sem., N.Y.C.; D.D.
(hon.), Reed Coll. of Rel., Oregon; m. Bernice Cald-
well; children--- Lanneau, Jr., Franklin Leslie, Robert,
Joy Kathleen; pastored Meth. Churches, Wash., D.C.;
Collesville, Md.; Roanoke, Va.; current pastor, Holman
Meth. Ch., Los Angeles, 1947---; Elected delegate to
the General Conf. of The Meth. Ch.; pres., Los Angeles
Council of Churches; chmn, Architectural Guild of Amer-
ica, 1958; Omega Psi Phi Achievement Award; Masonic
Award; Local Council of Churches Award; Mem., Omega
Psi Phi; 1965 Alumni Achievement Award in Religion,
Howard Univ.; Home:4292 Don Carols Dr., Los Angeles
8, Calif.; Office: 3320 West Adam Blvd., Los Angeles
16, Calif.

WHITE, Leamon Whitfield, b. Holly Hill, S.C., Sept. 10,
1910; s. Capus C. and Rebecca (Daley) Jaquse W.;
Allen Univ., Columbia, S.C., 1929; Washington Bapt.
Sem., 1943; m. Catherine Arnold; children--- Eloyce L.,
Neil (Mrs. Brooks), Kathy, David, Lydia; pastor, Silver
Hill Bapt. Ch., Morrisville, Va., 1945-50; Goldvain, Va.
1948-50; current pastor, Mt. Bethel Bapt. Ch., Wash.,
D.C., 1950---; sec., Northern Minister's Conf., 1948-
50; pres., Bapt. Minister's Conf., 1962 (Wash.D.C.);
vice pres., Bapt. Convention of D.C., 1956---; Trustee,
Stoddard Bapt. Home, Wash. D.C., 1952, 1964; Mem.
Mason; various Boards for Assn, 1964; Mem., The
Bloomingdale Assn; Chaplain, The Edgewood Civic Assn;
Official Watcher For Democratic Party Precinct No. 42,
1964; Civilian Award from Dept. of Navy, 1945; Home:
630 Edgewood St. NE, Wash. 17, D.C.; Office: 1915
First St. NW, Wash. 1, D.C.

WHITE, Major Cornelius, b. Muskogee, Oklahoma, May 13,
1926; s. Joseph and Effie (Huddleston) W.; Pacific Union
College, A.B., 1948; Univ. of the Pacific, 1963 - working on M.A.; m. Rue Pearl Haynes; children.--- Major
Aurelius, Marvin Eugene, Maurice Norvette. Pastorates -
Seventh-Day Adventist Churches: Tucson, Arizona, 1948-
51, Richmond, California, 1951-61; present- Stockton,
California, 1961- . Member, Board of Directors, Easter
Seal Society, Contra Costa County, California; Vice president, Easter Seal Society, 1957; Home: 1952 South California St., Stockton 6, Calif. Office: 2290 E. Market

St. , Stockton, Calif.

WHITE, Walter Syrus, chaplain; b. Sparr, Fla. , Sept. 4,
1907; s. Rifus Feldo and Ellen Gloria W. ; A.B. , B.D. ,
Wilberforce Univ. & Payne Seminary; Further study:
Bethune-Cookman Col. , Fla. , A&M Univ. , Northwestern
Univ. , Chap. Sch. ; m. Thelma Lee Skrine; children---
Patricia Ellen, Walter Syrus, Thelma Lee, Gwendolyn
Yvonne, pastor, South Charleston Mission, A. M. E.
Church, Ohio; Bethel A. M. E. Church, Keywest, Fla. ;
Allen Chapel, Melbourne; Mt. Zion, Ocala; St. Andrews,
Palmotto; Allen Chapel, New Smyrna Beach; St. James,
Sanford; Mt. Olive, Orland; Allen Chapel, Pompano
Beach; Greater Bethel, Gainesville; presiding elder, A.
M. E. Church; US Army, World War II, 29 months over-
seas; also Chaplain, Korean War, 36 months overseas;
Total service 8 years; Rank: Major; current, Inactive
Reserve; current pastor, Greater Bethel A. M. E. Church,
Gainsville, Fla. ; Four Battle Stars; Mem. , Omega Psi
Phi; Mason; Knights of Pythians; Home: 922 6th St. ,
West Palm Beach, Fla. ; Office: 753 NW 8th St. , Gaines-
ville, Fla.

WHITE, William Henry, church official; b. Cynthiana, Ky. ,
Aug. 3, 1897; s. William and Fannie (Alexander) W. ;
A. B. , B.D. , Wilberforce Univ. and Payne Theol. Sem-
inary, 1925-28; B.D. , Coll. of the Bible, 1955; D.D.
(hon.), Monrovia Coll. , West Africa, 1955; m. Frozene
G. Campbell (deceased); Vivian M. Miller; Mrs. George
Alston; pastor, African Methodist Episcopal Churches,
Ky. ; current pastor, St. James A. M. E. Church, Coving-
ton, Ky. ; Thirteenth Episcopal District A.M.E. Church
Director of Christian Education; vice pres. , Kentucky
Council of Churches; Mem. , Christian Education Comm. ;
Ky. Council of Churches and Norther Ky. Ass'n of
Protestant Churches, pres. , Interdenominational Minister-
ial Alliance; Exec. Comm. , NAACP; Mem. , Northern Ky.
Protestant Ass'n Commission on Religion and Race; chair-
man, Education Committee, NAACP; US Army, World
War I;Testimonial for 25 years service as director of
Christian Education Thirteenth Episcopal District A. M. E.
Church; Mem. , Mason; Alpha Phi Alpha; Republican;
lesson writer, Sunday School Literature A. M. E. Church;
Home: 118 E. Lynn St. , Covington, Ky. ; Office: 120 E.
Lynn St. , Covington, Ky.

*WHITTEN, Bennie Edward, Jr. b. Shreveport, La. , June

26, 1933; s. Bennie Edward and Leoma (Pryor) W.;
A. B., Texas Coll., 1952; B. D., Howard Univ., Sch. of
Rel., 1958; m. Gwendolyn Marie Pearson; children:-
Leslie Michelle, Bennie Edward, III. Chaplain resident,
St. Elizabeths Hospital, Washington, D. C., 1958-60;
present: pastor, First Reformed Ch. (United Church of
Christ), Cincinnati, Ohio. Chairman, N. A. A. C. P. Hous-
ing Committee, 1963- present; Advisory Committee,
Better Housing League, 1963-present; trustee, Mayor's
Friendly Relations Comm., 1963-present. U. S. Army,
Anti-aircraft Artillery Intelligence, 1953-55. Mem., Assn.
of Mental Hospital Chaplains; Kappa Alpha Psi. Home:
1512F Dudley St., Cincinnati, Ohio. Office: 1809 Freeman Ave., Cincinnati, Ohio.

WHITLOW, Charles Williams, b. Clinton, Okla., Nov. 23,
1925; s. Coleman and Luvina (Johnson) Reece W.; A. B.,
Langston Univ., 1951; B. Th., Okla. Sch. of Religion,
1957; graduate work: Okla. Univ.; m. Juanita Lewis;
children--- Michael, Rubie; pastor, Mt. Olive Baptist
Ch.; St. Paul Baptist Church; Bethlehem Baptist Church;
pres., Western Dist. Sunday Sch. & B. T. U. Congress,
1949-61; pres., Chickasaw Dist. Congress, 1963---;
principal and teacher, Lakeview, Tex., 1951-53; caseworker, 1953-55; vice pres., Ministerial Alliance, Interracial Committee, 1962-63; Advisory Comm., Mental
Health Program, P. T. A.; NAACP; Democrat; Urban
League; US Navy, 1943-45; Mem., Alpha Phi Alpha;
Home: 311 N. Birch, Pauls Valley, Okla.; Office: same.

WILKES, William Reid, bishop; b. Patnam Co., Ga., April
10, 1902; A. B., Morris Brown Coll., 1928; B. D., 1933;
D. D. (hon.), Morris Brown Coll.; LL. D. (hon.), Wilber-
force Univ.; m. Nettie Julia Adams; children--- William
Reid Jr., Alfred Weyman; coll. pastor, Morris Brown
Coll.; pastor, African Methodist Episcopal Churches,
Atlanta, Ga., director, Leadership Educa-
tion and Ministers' Institute (for the episcopal district);
Elected bishop, 1948; presiding bishop 6th Dist., A. M.
E. Ch.; pres., Council of Bishops; Mem., Bd. of Trus-
tees, Morris Brown Coll.; sec., Interdenominational
Theol. Center; Mason; Phi Beta Si; Mem., Mayor's Com.
on Urban Renewal, Atlanta, Ga.; Mem., Citizens Com-
mittee; chairman, General Conf., Committee on Finance,
A. M. E. Ch.; 1st vice pres., General Bd., A. M. E. Ch.;
Mem., Door of Hope, Atlanta, Ga.; author: Christian
Education in the Local Church; Home: 11009 Wade Park

Ave., Cleveland, Ohio. 44106.

WILLI, Eddie James, chaplain; b. St. Petersburg, Fla.,
Jan. 5, 1925; s. Eddie James Rivers and Rosa Dennis
Forman; A. B., Clark Coll., 1949; B. D., Gammon Theo.
Seminary, 1958; m. Ida Mae Gates Rivers; children---
Jeffrey James, Brenda Rose; asst. pastor, Warren Me-
morial Methodist Church, Atlanta, Ga., 1947-48; Pastor,
Pleasant Hill Methodist, Arcadia, Fla., 1952-55; Steward
Memorial Meth. Ch., Daytona Beach, Fla., 1955-61;
current, Ebenezer Methodist Ch., Jacksonville, Fla.,
1961---; chairman, Fla. Conference Bd. of Education,
Meth. Ch.; director of music, Fla. Conference, Metho-
dist Ch.; Associate Bd. Trustees, Bethune Cookman
Coll., 1959; current chaplain, Bd. of Directors, Brewster
Methodist Hospital; Awards: United Negro College Fund,
Religion and Human Relations from Bethune Cookman Col-
lege; Mem., YMCA; Mason; Knight of Pythian; Democrat;
Home: 431 W. Ashley St., Jacksonville 2, Fla.

WILLIAMS, Arthur D., chaplain, author;b. Abingdon, Va.,
July 22, 1895; s. Arthur C. and Hattie (Ellison) W.; A.
B., Lincoln Univ., 1922; S. T. M., Temple Univ., 1949;
Th. D., Harvard Univ., 1955; post graduate, Yale Univ.,
American Bible School, Chicago; m. Cleo Dix; children--
Arthur F., John Mark, Burton D., Dorethea W., (Mrs.
Anderson), Sadie W. (Mrs. Snead), Harriette W. (Mrs.
Batipps); Ordained Meth. Ch., 1923; pastor, Second
Presby. Ch., West Chester, Pa., 1920-23; Meth. Ch.,
Pocahontas, Va., 1924-30; Meth. Ch., Hot Springs, Ark.,
1930-33; Clark Memorial Ch., Nashville, Tenn., 1933-
35; Exec. sec., Nashville YMCA, 1935-38; Faith Presby.
Ch., Pa., 1945-50; Second Presby. Ch., West Chester,
Pa., 1953-57; teacher, Phila. Public Schs. of retarded
educables; current chaplain, The Eastern State Peniten-
tiary, Phila., Pa., 1960---; assoc. director; Skidmore
Vocational Sch.; founder, Hattie Pation Williams Clinic;
US Military Chaplain, 1941-47; pres., Nat. John Brown
Assn; Mem., West Chester, Chamber of Commerce; Nat.
Pastoral Counciling Assn., Phila.; Nat. Writers Assn;
awards: The George Washington Medal of Honor for an
outstanding accomplishment in helping to achieve a better
understanding of the American way of life by sermon, "All
or Nothing," 1964; First prize by Saturday Evening Post
for the Year, 1962; First prize in book writing contest
Random House Publishers for US Fourth Class Citizens,
1963; First Prize, Nat. Hospitalized Veterans Contest,

1962; First prize for NAACP Essay Contest (essay: "The
Economic Element in Lynching and Mob Violence"; author:
Another Simon of Cyrene; It will Show In Your Face
(poem); Jacob's Ladder; Snow and Ice Service (plays);
Home: 2017 W. Girard Ave., Phila., Pa. 19130.

WILLIAMS, Clarence Joseph, b. Huntsville, Ala., Aug. 14,
1919; s. James Albert and Ida (Marshall) W.; A.B.,
Oakwood College, 1952; Northwestern Univ., 1949; Andrews University Extension, toward M.A., 1960-63; m.
Sara Marguerite Collins; children--- Sheryle Elaine,
Patricia Ann, Marguerite Rugh, Joyce Marie. Joined
Ministerial Force of Southeastern California Conf. of
Seventh-Day Adventist in 1954; pastor, San Bernardine,
1954 (3 months); associate pastor, San Diego Church,
1954-57; present: pastor, Fontana Juniper Ave. S.D.A.
Church, 1957-   . Youth Camp counsellor, Guest speaker
for Ministerial Associations, city functions and community
organizations; conducted evangelistic campaigns in Chicago,
San Bernardine, San Diego, and Fontana. Home: 7348
Juniper Ave., Fontana, Calif. Office: 7347 Juniper Ave.,
Fontana, Calif.

*WILLIAMS, W. Clyde, youth worker, sem. official; b.
Cordele, Ga., Aug. 29, 1932; s. M.R. and Annie (Clude)
W.; A.B., Paine Coll., 1955; B.D., Howard Univ., Sch.
of Rel., 1959; M.R.E., Interdenominational Theol. center,
1961; m. Elaine Wade; children--- Joyce Lorraine, Clyde
Randolph; director of Boys Work, Bethlehem Community
Center, 1953-56; student missionary to Cuba, 1954; State
director of youth work, Sixth District Christian Methodist
Episcopal Ch., Ga., 1959-62; director of recruiting,
Interdenominational Theo. Center, 1962---; pastor,
Trinity C.M.E. Ch., Milledgeville, Ga., 1962-63; chmn.
com. on Youth Work, Ga. Council of Churches; chmn of
youth work, Bd. of Christian Education of the C.M.E.
Ch.; Citation for outstanding community service rendered
at Bethlehem Community in Center, Augusta, Ga., 1955;
Mem., Masons; YMCA; NAACP; Minister-Layman Council
of the C.M.E. Ch.; MRE Thesis: "The Nature and Development of Youth Work of the C.M.E. Ch., Ga.,
1945-61; Home: 461 Haldane Dr. SW, Atlanta 11, Ga.;
Office: 671 Beckwith St., Atlanta 14, Ga., (I.T.C.).

WILLIAMS, Curtis, teacher; b. Rhine, Ga., May 13, 1927;
s. John Luther and Grace (Harrell) W.; A.B., Western
Reserve, 1952; B.D., Payne Theol. Seminary, 1957;

Further study: Union Coll., Alliance, Ohio; Chicago Theol.
Seminary; m. Etta Belle Harris; children--- Gail, Deborah,
Peter, Byron, Faith; pastor, African Methodist Episcopal
Churches, Arizona; Ohio; current pastor, Bethel A.M.E.
Church, New Castle, Pa.; teacher, Ben Franklyn Jr.
High Sch., New Castle, Pa.; Dir. of Public Relations,
NAACP (New Castle, Pa.); US Air Force, 1945-48; Of-
fice: Bethel African Methodist Church, New Castle, Pa.

WILLIAMS, Dogan Wilford, b. Starkville, Miss., Feb. 18,
1920; s. Joseph S. and Penney (Robinson) W.; A.B.
Rust. Coll. Holly Springs, Miss. 1940-44, B.D.
degree, Gammon Theo. Seminary, Atlanta, Ga. 1944-47
M.A. Degree, Garrett Seminary, Northwestern U.,
Evanston, Ill., 1950-52; Children: Donna, Wilfretta,
Franklin Andrew, Penney Darlene; Ministry: Randolph
Street Methodist Church, Lexington, Va., 1947-57,
Wiley Memorial Meth. Ch., Chattanooga, Tenn. 1957-61;
Present: John Wesley Meth. Ch., Bristol, Va., Mem-
ber: Democratic Party, N.A.A.C.P., PTA, Fraternal
Organizations; Ministerial Association; Home: 427 Scott
Street, Bristol, Va. Office: 311 Lee Street, Bristol,
Va.

WILLIAMS, Donald James, b. San Bernardino, Calif., Jan.
26, 1928; s. Harry Howard and Violette Lenora (Reynolds)
W.; B.A., Oakwood College, 1950; M.A., Potomac Uni-
versity, Washington, D.C., 1960; m. Pearl Earnestine
Harvey. Pastor, Smyrna Seventh-Day Adventist Church,
Lynchburg, Virginia, 1960- present. U.S. Army, 1953-
55. Home: 818 8th Street, Lynchburg, Va. Office: 911
Taylor Street, Lynchburg, Va.

*WILLIAMS, Edward Samuel, b. Roanoke, Va., July 1,
1906; s. Edward and Nellie (Finney) W.; A.B., Johnson
C. Smith Univ., 1938; B.D., Howard Univ. Sch. of Rel.;
1950; m. Annie May Calloway; children--- Camille Adelle,
Marguerite May, Edward Samuel, Jr.; Jr. pastor, St.
Paul Methodist Ch., Roanoke, Va., 1942; pastor, John
Wesley Methodist Ch., Salem, Va., 1942-46; pastor, Mt.
Zion Meth. Ch., Silver Spring, Md., 1946-50; pastor,
Grace Meth. Ch., Fairmount Hqts., Md., 1950-59;
Associate pastor, Holman Meth. Ch., Los Angeles, Calif.
1959---; Chairman, Commission on Minimum Salary,
Chr. Committee on State of country, Treasurer's Asst.
Mem. of Committee on Worship and Fine Arts. Positions
held on Washington District: Director of Temperance,

Member of Committee on Ministerial Qualifications;
Treasurer, Local Chapter, NAACP, Salem, Va., 1944;
Director Wesley Foundation Howard University, 1951-53;
Mem. of the Board of Managers Wesley Foundation,
Howard University, Washington, D.C., 1953-59; Treasur-
er, Northeast Ministers Alliance, Washington, D.C.,
1957-59; Mem.: Omega Psi Phi; Urban League, NAACP;
Home: 4536 W. 17th St., Los Angeles 19, Calif.; Office:
3320 W. Adams Blvd., Los Angeles 18, Calif.

*WILLIAMS, Frank Leviticus, city official; b. Barnwell,
S.C., Oct. 12, 1917; s. Robert B. and Theodocia E.
(Wright) W.; Voorhees Jr. Coll., 1935-37; A.B., Claflin
Coll., 1937-39; B.D., Howard Univ., Sch. of Rel., 1939-
42; m. Ruth Estella Carr; children---Frank L. Jr.,
Beryl C., Cheryl R., Mark Robert; pastor, John Steward
Methodist Church, Wash., D.C., 1942-49; Christ Metho-
dist Church, Baltimore, Md., 1949-56; current pastor,
Metropolitan Methodist Church, Baltimore, Md., 1956--;
Trustee, Morristown Coll., Morristown, Tenn.; pres., In-
terdenominational Ministers' Alliance, Baltimore, Md.,
1960--; Phi Beta Sigma; appointed to Balto Community Relations Commission, 1964; Governor's Police Advisory Commission, 1964; Home: 1119 W. Lanvale St., Baltimore, Md. 21217;
Office: 1121 W. Lanvale St., Baltimore, Md. 21217.

WILLIAMS, Frederick Boyd, curate; b. Chattanooga, Tenn.,
April 23, 1939; s. Walter Howard and Matlyn (Goodman)
W.; B.A., Morehouse Coll., 1959; Howard Univ., 1959-
61; S.T.B., General Theol. Sem., 1963; Christiopher's
Chapel, N.Y.C. seminarian asst. 1960; curate, All Saints
Anglican Parish, St. Thomas, U.S. Virgin Islands, curate
summer 1962; St. Marks Episcopal Church, Mt. Kisco,
N.Y., 1961-63; St. Luke Protestant Episcopal Church,
Wash., D.C., 1963---; research assoc. mathematics,
Goddard Space Flight Center, NASA, Wash., D.C., 1960;
assoc. chaplain, Boy's Village, Cheltenham, Md., 1963--;
Mem., Delta Sigma Rho; Pi Mu Epsilon; Beta Kappa Chi;
Alpha Fhi Gamma; ESCRU, Kappa Alpha Psi; Home: 1
Hawaii Ave NE, Wash. 11, D.C.; Office: 1514 15th St.
NW, Wash 5, D.C.

WILLIAMS, Henry E. b. Charleston County, S.C., 1900.
s. Edward and Hannah (Bryon) W.; A.B., Johnson C.
Smith Univ., 1924-28; B.D., Johnson C. Smith Divinity
School, 1928-31; children--- Rose M. Chavis; L.G.
Chavis, Henry; pastor Mizpah Presbyterian Ch., South

Boston, Va. Ebenezer Presbyn Ch., New Bern, N.C.;
Mt. Pisgosh Presbyn Ch., Rocky Mount., N.C.; Free-
dom East Presbyn Ch., Raiford, N.C.; Marsh Hill
Presbyn Ch., Hope Mills, N.C.; Ogden Presbyn Ch.,
Charlie Hope, Va.; Great Creek Presbyn Ch., Brasey,
Va.; Principal & teacher Myzpah School, So.Boston, Va.
public school, Charlie Co., Va.; principal & teacher
Public School, Pamplico County, N.C.; principal &
teacher Public School, Nash Co., N.C.; principal &
teacher Public School, Hoka Co., N.C. mem. Unity
Lodge (Mason) #64 Rocky Mount, N.C. Phi Beta Sigma;
Home: 716 Atlantic Ave., Rocky Mount, N.C.; Church:
Ogden Church Charlie Hope, Va., Great Creek, Bracey,
Va.

WILLIAMS, John Francis, b. Pittsfield, Mass.; s. Joseph
and Blanche (Pegram) W.; B.S., S.T.B., Temple Univ.;
Union Theol. Sem., N.Y.; D.D. (hon.), Va. Union Theol.
Sem.; m. Mollye Virginia Jackson; pastor, Baptist
Churches, Phila., West Virginia, New Orleans, Va.; cur-
rent Pastor and Founder, Messiah Bapt. Church, New-
port News, Va.; former teacher, Marion, Va. High
School; chaplain, National Council of Negro Churches of
Christ of America; sec., Progressive Baptist Convention;
former pres., NAACP, 1949; pres., Tidewater District
Sunday School Convention; sec., Hampton Ministers Con-
ference; Trustee, Va. Sem.; Mem., Newport News, City
Council, Advisory Board Planning Committee; Home:
2815 Marshall Ave., Newport News, Va.; Office: Messiah
Bapt. Ch., 1152-24th St., Newport news, Va.

*WILLIAMS, John V., army chaplain; b. Wash. D.C.,
Aug. 30, 1930; s. Chancellor James and Mattie (McRae)
W.; B.A., Howard Univ., 1953; B.D., Howard Univ.,
Sch. of Rel., 1959; m. Beatrice E. Bryant; children--
John V., Jr. Gregory H., Kenneth T.; asst. pastor,
First Bapt. Ch., Deanwood, 1949-52; First Bapt. Ch.,
SW, 1952-54; 1956-59; US Chaplains Corps, 1959-62;
Serving currently in Mannheim, Germany, 1962---;
Pres. The Mannheim-Heidelberg Council for Retarded
Children; award: The Army Commendation Medal for
Meritorious Service; Mem., Military Chaplains Assn;
Home: 5000 Sheriff Rd. NE, Wash. 19, D.C., Office:
HQ 19th Ordnance Bn APO 166, New York, N.Y.

WILLIAMS, John Wesley, sem. prof.;b. Houston, Tex.,
Jan. 2, 1906; s. Briscoe W. and Annie W.; B.A.,

B. Th. , Conroe Normal & Industrial Coll. , 1928-35; D. D.
(hon.), Univ. of Kansas City, 1952; B. D. , Central Baptist
Theol. Seminary, 1952-57; Th. M. , 1954; Th. D. , 1957;
LL. D. , 1956, Union Theol. Sem. , Houston, Tex. ; m.
Marena Belle Wilson; John W. , Jr. , Marina Ann, Dorothy
Mae (Mrs. Warren McKeever); pastor, Concord Baptist
Ch. , Wharton, Tex. , 1929-32; St. Mary Baptist Ch. , Mart.
Tex. ; Mt. Salem Baptist Ch. , Victoria, Tex. , 1932; Union
Baptist Ch. , Galveston, Tex. , 1933-39; Toliver Chapel
Baptist Ch. , Waco, Tex. , 1940-41; St. John Baptist Ch. ,
Corpus Christi, Tex. , 1941-44; St. Stephen Baptist Ch. ,
Kansas City, Mo. , 1944---; instructor, Practical Theology,
Western Baptist Sem. ; pres. , General Baptist Convention
of Missouri-Kansas; pres. , Bd. of Management, Baptist
Convalescent Home; Life Mem. , NAACP; vice pres. ,
National Councils of Churches, USA, 1960-63; Mem. ,
Comm. of Religion and Race, N. C. C. U. S. A. ; Mem. ,
Exec. Comm. , Baptist World Alliance; pres. , General
Ministerial Alliance, Greater Kansas City; pres. , Greater
Kansas City Baptist and Community Hospital Ass'n; Meri-
torious Service Award from Urban League of Kansas
City, Mo. ; Meritorious Service Certificate In The Field
of Religion and Cummunity Civic Affairs, Kansas City
Call of K. C. , Mo. ; Certificate or Recognition from Who's
What and Why: Honor Award Given by Gen. Baptist Conv.
of Missouri and Kansas; Churchmanship Citation, Central
Baptist Theol. Sem. ; Minister of the Year, 1954, Baptist
Ministers Union; Scroll of Honor, Omega Psi Phi; Mem. ,
Omega Psi Phi; Wrangler's Intellectual Club; Lodge;
author: Ministry In A Secular Society; The Minister's Steward-
ship Ministry; contributing editor: The National Baptist
Brotherhood Manual; Home: 2904 Benton Blvd. , Kansas
City, Mo. 64128; Office: 1414 Truman Rd. , Kansas City,
Mo. 64106

WILLIAMS, Julian Leander, b. Albany, Georgia, Dec. 20,
    1908; s. James A. and Ida (Marshall) W. ; B. S. , Oak-
    wood College, 1951; m. Juanita C. Ward; children:- Irene
    (Mrs. Leanard Williams), Julian Leander, Jr. Pastored
    Seventh-Day Adventist Churches in: Huntsville, Ala. ,
    1951; Daytona Beach and Ocala, Fla. , 1956-60; Fayette-
    ville, N. C. , 1960-61; present: pastor, S. D. A. Church in
    Winston-Salem, N. C. , 1962- ; publishing secretary,
    South Atlantic Conf. , 1951-56; former chaplain, State
    School, Forest Hills, Fla. Corporal, U. S. Army, 1943-
    45. Home: P. O. Box 2755, Winston-Salem, N. C. Office:
    240 No. Dunleith Ave. , Winston-Salem, N. C.

WILLIAMS, McKinley, bishop; b. Albany, Ga., Feb. 17,
1901; s. John and Eliza; Albany State College; American
Bible College, 1950-53; Th. B. M. D.,; D. D. (hon.),
American Bible College; m. Ethel Mae Thomas; pastor,
The Refuge Church of Christ, Bible Way World Wide
Inc., Phila., Pa.; current, Board of Bishops-The Bible
Way Churches World-Wide Inc.; Mem., Board of Direc-
tors Carver Loan Investment Co., Columbia Ave., Phila.,
Pa.; Board of 500 Ministers Selective Service; The
Downingtown School Board; The George T. Mitchell B.
& L. Board of Directors; Home: 523 S. Lansdowne Ave.,
Yeadon, Pa.; Office: 52nd & Rose Sts., Phila. 39, Pa.

WILLIAMS, Robert Gilmore, b. Fredericksburg, Va., June
19, 1924; s. Charles Beale and Lelia (Wormley) W.; A.
B., Va. Union Univ., Richmond, Va., 1945; B. D., 1952;
Graduate courses: Boston Univ.; m. Doris Inez Brown;
children--- Robert Gilmore Jr., Denise Rozelle; pastor,
Zion Bapt. Ch., Petersburg, Va., 1947-62; Union Branch
Baptist Ch., Prince Ga., 1956-62; current pastor, Mt.
Moriah Bapt. Ch., Washington, D. C., 1962---; career
counselor, Va. High Schools; staff mem., Petersburg
Family Counseling Service; Mem., Exec. Bd., Southern
Christian Leadership Conf.; former mem., Bd. of Manage-
ment, U. S. O.; Exec. Bd. NAACP; Va. Council on Human
Rights, Va. Bapt. Children's Home, (all Petersburg, Va.);
former visiting lecturer, Va. Union Univ. and Va. State
Coll.; Va. State vice pres., Lott Carey and Nat. Bapt.
Conv., 1959-62; 1960-62; Trustee Bd., Va. Union Univ.,
1960-62; Elected pres., Bapt. General Assn, Va., 1960;
pres., Petersburg Improvement Civic Assn, 1961-62;
Citation from Central New Jersey Freedom Assn. (for
role in Civil Rights struggle); Mem., Mason; Omega Psi
Phi; Nat. Frontiers Club of America; leader and coordina-
tor, 1960 Pilgrimage of Prayer for public school support,
Va.; Jailed for seeking to use public library, integrate in
Petersburg, Va. Trailways Bus Terminals and eating
facilities; Home: 7617 12th St. NW, Wash., D. C. 20012,
Office: Mt. Moriah Bapt. Ch., 17th & East Capitol St.
NE, Wash., D. C.

WILLIAMS, Samuel, b. Brewton, Ala., Mar. 30, 1922; s.
James and Gertrude (Mobley) W.; Northwestern Jr. Coll.,
Orange City, Iowa, 1941-43; A. B. Central Coll., Pella.
Iowa, 1946-48; B. D. Western Theol. Sem., Holland,
Mich., 1948-51; m. Paulin Hendrieth; children--Marcia
Amelia, Wanda Sylvia, Paula Velucia, Samuel Lloyd;

sch. pastor-teacher-dean of boys, Southern Normal High
Sch., Brewton, Ala., 1951-60; Current pastor, Pem-
broke Community Reformed Ch., Saint Anne, Illinois,
1960-present; U.S. Army, taught basic reading, writing
and arithmetic, Fort Benning, Ga.; mem. Pembroke
Community Consolidated sch., PTA; mem., Saint Anne
Ministerial Protestant Assn., and Kankakee County Inter-
Faith Comm.; pres., Illiana Classics (Presbytery); mem
of the Board of North American Missions, Reformed Ch.
in Amer.; articles for CHURCH HERALD, REFORMED
CH. IN AMER. OFFICIAL MAGAZINE; Home: Route 1,
Box 113-A, Saint Anne, Illinois.

*WILLIAMS, Samuel Woodrow, coll. prof.; Sparkman, Ark.,
s. Arthur and Annie (Willie) W.; A.B., Morehouse Coll.,
1937; B.D., M.A., Howard Univ. Sch. of Rel., 1941,
1942; Courses completed Ph.D., Univ. of Chgo; D.D.
(hon.), Ark. Bapt. Coll., 1960; m. Billge Suber; chil-
dren--- Samuel Golar; chaplain and prof., Alcorn Coll.,
1942-44; chaplain and prof., Alabama AM&N Coll.,
1944-46; current prof., Morehouse Coll., 1946---;
pastor, Friendship Bapt. Ch., Atlanta, Ga., 1954---;
Home: 863 1/2 Fair St. SW, Atlanta 14, Ga.; Office:
437 Mitchell St., SW, Atlanta 13, Ga.

WILLIAMS, Smallwood Edmund, bishop; b. Lynchburg, Va.,
Oct. 17, 1907; s. Edmund and Mary (Broadus) W.;
Howard Univ. Sch. of Rel.; American Bible
Coll., Wash., D.C., 1948; D.D. (hon.); Va. Theol.
Sem. & Coll., Lynchburg, Va., 1950; m. Verna L.
Rapley; children--- Smallwood Jr., Pearl, Yvonne,
Wallace; Licensed to preach, 1923, Ch. of Our Lord
Jesus Christ Of the Apostolic Faith; organized Bible Way
Ch. of Our Lord Jesus Christ, Wash., D.C., 1925; cur-
rent senior bishop and pastor, Bible Way Ch., Washing-
ton, D.C.; Pres., Commission on Mental Retardation;
delegate, Democratic Convention, 1964; pres., Southern
Christian Leadership Conf., Wash., D.C.; Established
recreation center, summer camp, Welfare home under
sponsorship of Bible Way Ch.; Named most popular radio
minister newspaper poll, 1943; Mem., Exec. Committee,
NAACP, Wash., D.C.; Committee of Nat. Fraternal
Council of Churches in America; director, The Bible
Way News Voice (Bi-monthly); Founder and director
Bible Way Training Sch. For ministers and Christian
workers (1944). Founded school and mission in Liberia
(1958). Mem., Board of Directors Washington Home
Rule Comm., Chr. Inter-religious comm. on Race

Relations, (1963-64). Home: 4720 16th St. NW, Wash.,
D.C.; Office: 1130 New Jersey Avenue, Wash., D.C.

WILLIAMS, Wilbert Henry, b. Columbus, Ohio. Dec. 13,
1913; s. Iradell H. and Nina (Condiff) W; Attended Philander Smith Coll., Little Rock, Arkansas, Extension studies at University of Pittsburgh; m. Catherine Lois Palmer
Children: Wilbert A. Jr., Clarissa, Jerin, Gabriel Timothy, Stanley Jerome, Linda Joyce, Charles Wesley; Ministry: John Stewart Memorial Methodist Church, Marietta,
Ohio, 1943-46; Pennsylvania Avenue Meth. Ch., Columbus,
Ohio, 1946-49; Simpson Meth. Ch., Steubenville, Ohio,
1949-52; Wesley Memorial Meth. Ch., Jeffersonville,
Ind. 1952-56; St. Johns Methodist Church, Evansville,
Ind., 1956-57; Gunn Tabernacle Meth. Ch., Lexington,
Ky., 1957-63; York Street Meth. Ch., Cincinnati, Ohio,
1963 to present. Agent, Superintendent and Supervisor for
former Domestic Life and Accident Insurance Co. of
Louisville, Ky. (12 years); First Negro Jury Commis-
sioner, Steubenville, Ohio, elected as only Negro charter
commissioner of Steubenville, Ohio, 1952; Youth Presi-
dent, Junior chapter of N.A.A.C.P. Steubenville, Ohio;
Past Pres. of Inter-Group Goodwill Assoc. for Civic,
Social, Economic, and Cultural Progress, Steubenville,
Ohio, 1951; Home: 838 Clark Street. Apt. G, Cincinnati,
3, Ohio. Office: York St. Methodist Church, Cincinnati 14,
Ohio.

WILLIAMS, Willie George, b. Tupelo, Miss.; s. W. M. and
Josephine (Glass) W.; Western Baptist Coll., Kansas
City, Kansas; B.Th., Central Baptist Sem., 1946; B.S.,
Drake Univ., 1956; M.A. Central Bapt. Sem., 1957;
m. Sharlee Annatia West; children--- Jerome Lawrence;
supply pastor, First Baptist Church, Montserat, Mo;
First Bapt. Ch., Nicodemus, Kansas; Independent Bapt.
Ch., Leavenworth, Kansas, 1952-64; current pastor,
Calvary Baptist Church, Wichita, Kansas, 1964---; pres.,
Leavenworth County Ministerial Alliance; Mem., Planning
Com. for County Home; Resolutions Com., Nat. Bapt.
Convention, USA; vice pres., Nat. Congress; moderator,
Northeastern District; former moderator, Smoky Hill
River Dist.; instructor, Summer Retreat, Missionary
Bapt. Convention, Kansas; pres., State Baptist Congress,
Kansas; A Golden key from the Mayor City of Leaven-
worth; Home: 2344 East 25th St., Wichita, Kansas; Office:
601 Water St., Wichita, Kansas.

WILMORE, Gayraud Stephen, Jr., ch. official; b. Phila.,
    Dec. 20, 1921; s. Gayraud S., Sr. and Patricia (Gardner)
    W.; A.B., Lincoln Univ., Pa., 1947; B.D., Lincoln
    Univ. Theol. Sem., 1950; S.T.M., Temple Univ., 1952;
    D.D. (hon.), Lincoln Coll., 1960; post-grad., Drew
    Univ., 1961; m. Lee Wilson; children--- Stephen, Jac-
    ques, Roberta, David; pastor, Second Presby Ch., West
    Chester, Pa., 1950-53; regional sec., Student Christian
    Movement (mid-Atlantic Region), 1953-56; assoc. sec.,
    Social Ed. & Action, United Presby. Ch., 1956-60; asst.
    prof., Pittsburgh Theol. Sem., 1960-63; exec. dir.,
    United Presby. Commission on Religion and Race, 1963
    ---; consultant, Church and Economic Life, United Presby.
    Board of Christian Education, 1962; candidate for county
    office - Democratic Party of Delaware Co., Pa., 1960;
    Bd. of Directors, Neighborhood Centers, Inc., Pittsburgh,
    Pa., 1963; US Army T/4 371st Infantry, 92nd Div., Italy,
    1944-46; Mem., NAACP; Democrat; Presby. Interracial
    Council; Alpha Phi Alpha; editor: "Christian Perspectives
    on Social Problems" series of Westminster Press; author,
    The Secular Relevance of the Church, Westminster,
    1963; articles in various periodicals; home: Rd. #1,
    Skillman, N.J.; Office: Rm. 367 Interchurch Center,
    475 Riverside Dr. N.Y., N.Y.

WILSON, Donald Octavio, b. Port Limon, Costa Rica, Cen-
    tral America, Nov. 19, 1915; s. John Christopher and
    Jeanette Gaynor (Wilson) W.; B.A., Bloomfield College
    and Seminary, 1942; S.T.B., General Theological Sem-
    inary, 1945; Berkely Divinity School, 1945-46; Union
    Theo. Sem., 1951-52; Graduate Sch. of Theol., Temple
    Univ., 1960-62; m. Theda Isabell Morris. Locum Tenens
    St. Luke's Episcopal Ch., New Haven, Conn., 1945-46;
    Vicar, St. Simon the Cyrenian Ch., Springfield, Mass.,
    1946-51; and St. Matthew's Ch., Wilmington, Del., 1951-
    63; present: rector, St. James Ch., Baltimore, Md.,
    1963- . Chairman, United Negro College Fund Dr.,
    1952-54; Board of Directors, Child Guidance Center,
    Board of Directors, St. Matthew's Comm. Center; Mayor's
    Committee on Housing, Chaplain, Tuberculosis Hospital,
    1955-63; Mason, Alpha Phi Alpha. Home: 2701 N. Hilton
    St., Baltimore, Md. Office: 827 N. Arlington Ave.,
    Baltimore, Md.

WILSON, Edward John, teacher; b. Mobile, Ala., July 31,
    1932; s. Edward and Sally (Nobdy) W.; Our Lady of The
    Lake Seminary, 1952-55; Crozier House of Studies, 1956-

61; St. Francis College, Hastings College; Ordained priest,
Roman Cath. Ch., 1961; Taught St. Cecilia's H.S., Hast-
ings, Nebr.; Teacher, Stepinac H.S., White Plains, N.
Y.; Home: 30 Gedney Park Dr., White Plains, N.Y.;
Office: Archbishop Stepinac H.S., White Plains, N.Y.

WILSON, Frank Theodore, educator; b. Maxton, N.C., Jan.
1, 1900; s. James Jacob and Sudie Jane (Harris) W.;
A.B., Lincoln Univ., 1921; S.T.B., 1924; D.D. (hon.),
1952; M.A., Columbia Univ., 1932; Ed.D., 1937; D.D.
(hon.), Edward Waters Coll., 1953; m. Anna Lucretia
Dorsey; children--- Frank Theodore, Anne Elizabeth
(Mrs. Edgar M. Cole); nat. student sec., National Council, YMCA, 1924-36; dean of students, prof., Lincoln
Univ., 1936-49; director, Young People's Summer Confs.,
Blairstown, N.J., 1945-48; dean, Sch. of Religion, prof.
of Religious Education, Howard Univ., 1949-57; sec. for
Educational Commission on Ecumenical Mission and Relations United Presbyterian Church in U.S.A., 1957---;
guest lecturer, Yale Div. Sch., 1950-54; director, educational survey in Asia, Latin Am., Middle East; Mem.,
General Committee of World Student Christian Federation, Mysore, India. 1928-29; Mem., Bd. of Christian
Education; chairman, Social Education and Action Committee, Presbyterian Ch., USA; National Student Committee,
YMCA, 1940---; accredited visitor, World Council of
Churches, Evanston, Ill., 1954; Trustee, Lincoln Univ.,
1954---; Fellow Nat. Council on Religion in Higher Education; author: Unconditional Spiritual Surrender, 1947;
contributor: The Christian Way in Race Relations, 1948;
Home: 93 Kenilworth Place, East Orange, N.J.; Office:
Rm. 920, 475 Riverside Dr., N.Y., N.Y., 10027.

WILSON, Ivory W., b. Winsboro, La., June 16, 1916; s.
Lem and Cura (Reed (Carr) W.; Wilburton, Okla. High
School; Langston Theol. Sem., Langston, Okla. Univ.;
Bishop Coll., Marshall, Tex.; D.D. (hon.), International
Baptist Theol. Center, Houston, Tex.; m. Ollye Lelar
Ward; children--- Floyd, Cleaster, Larrayne; pastor,
Bethel Baptist Church, Las Vegas, Nevada; 1st vice pres.,
Constitutional Bapt. Conv.; 1st vice pres., Minister Assn
Clark Co.; Mem., Civil Service Bd., 1962-66; NAACP;
Council for Kit Carson School; 1st vice pres., Voter's
League; Mem., Mason; Democrat; Home: 1900 Hassell,
Las Vegas, Nevada; Office: 400 Adams & D. Las Vegas,
Nevada.

WILSON, Robert Henry, b. Columbia, S. C. , Aug. 1, 1924;
s. Riley and Ida W. ; A. B. , Benedict Coll. , 1944; B. D. ,
1949; D. D. (hon.), Edward Waters Coll. , Jacksonville,
Fla. , 1955; D. D. , Benedict Coll. , S. C. , 1969; m. Elise
Georgette Wider; children--- Roberta Elaine; Robert
Henry, Jr. ; asst. pastor, Zion Baptist Ch. , Coll. , S. C. ,
1940-49; pastor, St. Paul Baptist Ch. , Columbia, S. C. ,
1950-53; current, Bethel Baptist Institutional Ch. , Jacksonville, Fla. , 1953---; teacher, In-service Minister's
class, Jacksonville, Fla. Memorial Coll. , 1954-63; Mem. ,
Exec. Bd. , Brewster Methodist Hospital, 1958-60; Trustee Bd. , Fla. , Memorial Coll. , 1954---; vice chairman,
Jacksonville Community Relations Comm. , 1964; corresponding secy. , National Baptist Convention of America;
secy. , Foreign Missions Progressive Baptist State Convention, Fla. ; dean, Progressive Baptist State Sunday
School Convention, Fla. ; former treasurer, Masons;
Home: 1058 Hogan St. , Jacksonville 2, Fla. ; Office:
1058 Hogan St. , Jacksonville 2, Fla.

WILSON, S. Russell, b. Norfolk, Va. , Aug. 29, 1918;
s. Joseph and Maggie (Fuller) W. ; A. B. , Va. Union
Univ. , 1937; B. D. , Va. Theol. Sem. , 1940; M. A. ,
Drew Univ. , 1962; courses, St. Margaret's Coll. , Amer-
ican Armed Forces Univ. (Italy); m. Carrie Chambers;
children (adopted) --- Robert and Christopher. Pastor:
Protestant Episcopal Churches, Millers Tavern (Va.),
St. Anna's, Columbia, St. Thomas (S. C.), St. Monica's
(S. C.), St. Barnaba's (S. C.); present: rector, South Hill,
P. E. Ch. , South Hill, Va.; chaplain, Elizabeth State
Teachers Coll. (N. C.); Columbia, S. C. Peninteniary;
headmaster, John Moncure Sch. , Millers Tavern, Va. ;
boy's work secretary, Leigh St. , Y. M. C. A. , Richmond,
Va. Trustee, Voorhees Coll. , Denmark, S. C. , 1960-61;
Chaplain, U. S. Army: Anm. Officer - 601 Ord. ; 3 combat
stars - European-African, American. Mason, Kappa Alpha
Psi, N. A. A. C. P. , Southern Christian Leadership, Fellow-
ship of Reconciliation; Democrat. Home: P. O. Box 597,
South Hill, Va.

WILSON, William L. , b. Greenwood, S. C. , Apr. 30, 1908;
s. Isam and Susan Devore; A. B. , B. D. , D. D. (hon.),
Benedict Coll. ; D. D. (hon.), Morris Coll. ; m. Jessie
Mae Gibson; children--- one; pres. , Baptist Educational
and Missionary Convention of S. C. ; State vice pres. , National Baptist Convention, USA, Inc. ; moderator, Spartanburg County Ass'n; pres. , Interdenominational Ministerial

Alliance; grand director, Odd-Fellows of America and
Jurisdiction; pastor, Macedonia Baptist Church, Spartan-
burg; Trustee, Benedict and Morris Coll.; Mem.,
NAACP; Home: 164 Fremont Ave., Spartanburg, S. C.;
Office: 301 West Henry St., Spartanburg, S. C.

WILSON, Wylie Edward, presiding elder; b. Hampton
County, S. C., Aug. 29, 1913; s. William E. and Janie
L. W.; Paine Coll., 1937-38; Allen Univ., 1948-50; Mid-
western Graduate Bible School, 1955-60; B. D., M. Th.,
Gammon Seminary Summer-School, 1957, 1960; m.
Hattie Miles; children--- Janie, Willie Marvell, Jerelyn
Gayle. Pastor, 23 years, Christian Methodist Episcopal
Church; presiding elder, 1946-53; and 1955-62; present:
pastor, Mt. Carmel Church, Anderson, S. C. Insurance
agent during World War II; Member, Community Fund
Drive Committee (Chapel Hill, N. C.); N. A. A. C. P.,
working for better jobs for the Negro of the community.
Member, Epsilon Delta Chi; The Ministers' and Lay-
men's Council, C. M. E. Church. Democrat. Research:
"The Church and its Responsibility in Modern Society."
Home: 611 Cleveland Ave., Anderson, S. C. Office: 609
Cleveland Ave., Anderson, S. C.

WINKFIELD, Orange Willis, teacher; s. Joseph and Gena
(Owens) W., b. Union Springs, Ala., Sept. 15, 1885.
Courses: Poetry, literature, psychology. m. Lillian C.
Walls, July 19, 1917; children--- Clyde Julian. Ordained
in Cataba Presbytery, U. S. A. pastored in Oklahoma,
1914-23; founder New Vision Bible Church, Chgo. Hon.
Certificate, 1961 from Johnson C. Smith for 50 years
professional service. Home: 7648 Cottage Ave., Chicago
19, Ill.

WISNER, Roscoe William, b. Nixa, Mo., Apr. 20, 1894;
s. Frank and Julia W.; B. A., Western Univ., Kansas
City, Mo., 1926; Chaeffers Theol. Sch., B. D., 1926;
teaching certificate, Kansas State Teachers Coll., 1923;
D. D. (hon.), Allen Univ.; Kittrell Coll.; D. Ed., Mon-
rovia Coll., W. Africa; m. Glayds Vivian; children---
Elbert C., Roscoe W., Richard; pastor, African Methodist
Episcopal Church, Ogden, Utah; Salt Lake, Utah; Pueblo,
Colorado; Marshall, Mo.; current pastor, Bethel Ch.,
Hampton, Va.; pres., Kittrell Coll., Kittrell, N. C.,
10 yrs; former teacher, Public Schs; US Forces, 1918-
19; Home: 1422 E. Penbroke Ave., Hampton, Va.;
Office: 108 West Lincoln St., Hampton, Va.

WOMACK, Andrew Australia, b. Prospect, Va., Nov. 11,
1904; s. Lincoln and Virginia (Allen) W.; A.B., B.D.,
D.D. (hon.), Virginia Seminary and Coll.; m. Helen
Lightfoot; children--- Andrew A.; current pastor, Mt.
Haven Baptist Ch., Cleveland, Ohio; Mem., The Minis-
ters Conference; The Cleveland Baptist Ass'n; National
Baptist Convention; The American Baptist Convention;
teacher, The State Sunday School Congress; Mem.,
NAACP; Mason; financial sec., State Sunday School Con-
gress; chairman, The Finance Comm., Northern Ohio
Ass'n; Bd. of Trustee Bd., Virginia Sem., and Coll.,
Lynchburg, Va.; Home: 15915 Eldamere Ave., Cleveland
28, Ohio; Office: Mt. Haven Baptist Ch., Cedar Ave.,
Cleveland, Ohio.

WOOD, Marcus Garvey, b. Glucester, Va., June 18,
1920; s. Frank Tucker and Julia (Braxton) W.; A.B.,
Storer Coll., Harpers Ferry, W. Va., 1948; B.D.,
Crozer Theol. Sem., Chester, Pa.; m. Bessie Pendle-
ton; children--- Jeanetta W. (Mrs. Eugene Brown),
Marcus G.; pastor, Wainwright Baptist Church, Charles
Town, W. Va., 1945-48; Bethlehem Baptist Ch., Woodbury, N.J., 1948-52; Providence Baptist Ch., Baltimore,
Md., 1952---; director of promotions, Lott Carey Baptist
Foreign Missions Convention, 1963; Travels in the Area
of Missions; Made a tour of the Island of Haiti and
photographed work of mission stations, 1959; Spent two
weeks in Haiti with Work Team-living on the mission
field, 1962; Led a Survey Team to British Guiana in
South America, 1964; Home: 848 Edmondson Ave., Baltimore, Md. 21201; Office: 850 Edmondson Ave., Baltimore, Md. 21201.

WOODRUFF, James Edward, chaplain; b. Trinidad, B.W.I.,
March 2, 1936; s. James Edward and Carmen (Earle)
W.; B.S., State Univ. of N.Y., 1953-57; B.D. Seabury
Western Seminary, 1957-60; Vanderbilt Div., working on
S.T.M. In Pastoral Counseling, 1961---; m. Nancy Ann
Denson; children--- Mark Francis; director, YMCA Com-
munity Center in College, 1955-57; director, swimming
pool, Buffalo City; Scoutmaster and Cubmaster working
with teen-age and early adult; During seminary 1957-60
worked with underpriviledged children and gangs in N.Y.
C., at St. Christopher's Chapel, 48 Henry Street and at
the Church of the Epiphany, 111 So. Ashland in Chicago.
First pastoral duty was doing the type of work at St.
Thomas Church, 3801 So. Wabash Ave., Chicago; present,

Episcopal chaplain, Fisk University, Tenn. A & I Univ.,
and Meharry Medical College, 1961---; Member, Omega
Psi Phi Fraternity; Home: 2602 Morena Street, Nashville,
Tenn.; Office: 2008 Meharry Blvd., Nashville, Tenn.

WOODS, Abraham Lincoln, b. Birmingham, Ala., Oct. 7,
1928; A.B., Miles Coll., 1962; B.Th., Daniel Payne
Coll.; Birmingham Baptist Coll.; current pastor, First
Metropolitan Bapt. Church, Birmingham, Ala., 1952---;
professor, Social Science, Miles Coll., 1962---; director,
Miles Coll. Citizenship Work-Study Project, 1963---;
instructor, Mt. Pilgrim District Congress; sec., Birmingham Bapt. Ministers Conf.; Mem., Ala. State Teachers Ass'n; American Teachers Ass'n; vice pres., Ala.
Christian Movement for Human Rights, 1955---; deputy
director of the South, March on Washington; Mem.,
Group Relations Sub-Committee of Birmingham's Interracial Citizens Affairs Committee; Cited by 9th Congressional District, Ala. Coordinating Ass'n for Voter Registration; Cited by WENN Radio, Birmingham, for Voter
Registration; Led march in Ecorse and River Rouge,
Mich.; Home: 125 Kappa Ave. South Birmingham, Ala.

*WOOTEN, James Henry,b. Tarboro, N.C., April 30,
1922; s. Curfew and Dollie (Bridges) W.; A.B., Morgan
State Coll., Baltimore, Md., 1954; B.D., Howard Univ.,
Sch. of Rel., 1957; m. Lois Copeland; children--- Darryl
Eugene; pastor, Trinity Methodist Church, Clarksburg,
West Va., 1957-61; Milton Ave. Methodist Church, Balti-
more, Md., 1961---; Director, Adult Work, Washington
Annual Conference, Baltimore Area; protestant chaplain,
Baltimore City Jail; Mem., Executive Board NAACP,
Baltimore, Md.; visiting clergy staff, Johns Hopkins
Hospital, Baltimore; US Forces, 1943-46; Good Conduct
Medal; Eliza. J. Cummings Award as department scholar
at Morgan State Coll.; Mem., Alpha Phi Alpha; Mason;
Democrat, seeking nomination as delegate to State and
National Conventions; Home: 2312 E. Federal St., Balti-
more 13, Md.; Office: 1500 N. Milton Ave., Baltimore
13, Md.

WRIGHT, Byrl Fisher, b. Knoxville, Tenn., Dec. 13, 1913;
s. James and Beatrice W.; Stillman College & School of
Theology, 1937-40; D.D., Livingstone College, 1963;
m. Daisy Faucher; children--- Byrl Fisher, pastor, Oakland & Pakgrove A.M.E. Zion Church, Knoxville, Tenn.,
1940-43; Bethel A.M.E. Zion Church, Knoxville, Tenn.,

1943-50; Holiday Memorial A. M. E. Zion Church, Brad-
dock, Pa., 1950-60; St. Paul A. M. E. Zion Church,
Toledo, Ohio, 1960---; First vice pres., Toledo Branch,
NAACP; Mem., YMCA Board of Management: Courier-
Wamo Achievement Award, 1960; Home: 954 Belmont
Toledo, Ohio, 43607; Office: 958 Belmont, Toledo, Ohio
43607.

WRIGHT, Calvin, Luther, presiding elder; b. Dolomite, Ala.
July 17, 1888; s. Cull Lee and Elvira (Wiley) W.;
Payne Univ., 1917-20; post graduate work: Columbia
Univ., 1927-28; D. D. (hon.), Payne Univ., 1928; LL.
D., Payne Univ., 1955; children---Mabel W. Alexander,
Calvin Lee, Jr.; first pastorate, 1912; organized nine
African Methodist Episcopal Church; current presiding
elder, West Birmingham District; Former Trustee, Payne
Univ.; Home: 3517 65th St., N. Birmingham, Ala. 35212.

WRIGHT, Giles Robert, chaplain; b. Memphis, Tenn.,
March 3, 1906; s. Giles and Esther (Wells) W.; B. A.,
Clark Univ., 1930; B. D., Gammon Theological Seminary,
1933; M. A., Univ. of Kansas, 1942; Columbia Univ.,
Residential requirements for Ed. D.; m. Mae Cora Whiten;
children--- Grace Eloise, Giles Robert, Jr. United States
Army Chaplain, 1942-46 (overseas); Christian Methodist
Episcopal Church Minister for 32 years; Public School
Teacher for 5 years; present: pastor, Hopps Memorial
C. M. E. Church, Syracuse, N. Y. Director, Public Rela-
tions, Seventh Episcopal District, C. M. E. Church;
Mem. Mayor's Commission on Human Rights, 1963-   ;
director, Dunbar Center. Vice-president, director, Syra-
cuse Council of Churches; member, Inter-Faith Commis-
sion. European-African Middle Eastern Service medal.
Mason; president, East Side Corporate Council. Republi-
can. Home: 105 Elk Street, Syracuse, N. Y. Office: 707
South McBride St., Syracuse, N. Y.

WRIGHT, Leon E., prof.; b. Boston, Mass., Jan 20,
1912; A. B., Boston Univ., 1934; A. M., Boston Univ.,
1937; S. T. B., Harvard Univ., 1943; Ph. D., Harvard
Univ., 1945; m. Jesse Mae Wyche; children--- Richard,
Wesley; instructor, Morgan State Coll., 1937-40; guest
lecturer, Westminster Choir Coll., Princeton, N. J.;
professor, Howard Univ. Sch. of Rel., 1945---; visiting
lecturer Va. Prot. Episcopal Theol. Sem., assoc. editor,
Journal of Religious Thought; U. S. State Dept. & Cultural

Attache of Embassy, Rangoon, Burma, 1955-57; Continual
assignment as interracial lecturer in churches and groups
in and about, Wash., D.C.; Mem., National Council on
Religion in Higher Education; Com. for the Study of
Patristic Quotations, International Commission for New
Critical Apparatus to Greek New Testament; Roster of
Bd. of Examiners, Middle State Assn. of Secondary Schs.
and Coll.; Speakers Bureau, National Council of Churches,
Society of Biblical Literature and Exegesis; Washington
Seminar on Religion and Psychiatry; Phi Beta Kappa;
Awards: Boston Univ. Trustee Scholarship, 1930-34;
Graduate Fellowship, 1936-37; Rosenwald Fellow, 1941-
43; Fellow, National Council on Religion in Higher Edu-
cation, 1942; Cited for Hopkins Share, 1942-43; Howard
Univ.; General Education Bd. Fellow, 1944-45; Guggen-
heim Fellow, 1951-52; author: Alterations of the Words of
Jesus, as quoted in the literature of the second century,
Harvard Univ. Press, 1952; Liberty to the Captives: A
Study in the relationship between Religion and Parapsy-
chology (ready for publication); Mem., Phi Beta Kappa;
Board for Homeland Ministers, United Church of Christ;
Committee Board of Religion and Higher Education, United
Church of Christ; Urban League; NAACP; Assn. of Biblical
Instructors; National Council on Religion in Higher Educa-
tion; First American to be awarded a certificate to teach
Buddhist meditation, 1963; Home: 1726 Varnum St. NW,
Wash., D.C.; Office: Howard Univ. School of Religion,
Wash. 1, D.C.

WRIGHT, Nathan, author; b. Shreveport, La. 1923; B.D.,
Episcopal Theol. Sem., Cambridge, Mass.; S.T.M.,
Harvard Univ.; Ed. M., State Teachers Coll., Boston;
Ed. D., Harvard Graduate Sch. of Ed.; m. Barbara Tay-
lor; children--- 5; rector, St. Cyprian's Episcopal Ch.,
14 yrs; Protestant Chaplain, Long Island Hospital, Bos-
ton, 8 years; current exec. director, For Urban Work,
Episcopal Diocese of Newark; former teacher, Lasell Jr.
Coll., Newton, Mass.; consultant, Compensatory education
and staff assistant, Mass. Ed. Commission; Served on
Governor's Com. on Civil Rights; Mayor's Com. on Housing; former vice pres., Mass. Clerical Assn; vice
president, Ch. School Union; mem., American Prot.
Hospital Assn; former mem., Bd. of Directors, Boston
Branch, NAACP; Urban League; organizer and first field
representative for New England "Core"; author: The Riddle
of Life, 1952; The Song of Mary, 1958; One Bread, One
Body, 1962; Home: 412 Lawn Ridge Rd., Orange, New

Jersey.

WRIGHT, Richard Robert, Jr. , bishop, educator; b. Cuthbert, Ga. , Apr. 16, 1878; s. Richard R. and Lydia
Elizabeth (Howard) W. ; A.B. , Ga. State Industrial Coll. ,
1898; B.D. , Univ. of Chicago Theol. Sem. , 1901; A.M.
U. of Chicago, 1904; studied U. of Berlin, 1903, U. of
Leipzig, 1904; Ph.D. , U. of Pa. , 1911; LL.D. , Wilberforce U. , 1920; m. Charlotte Crogman, Sept. 8, 1909;
children--- Charlotte Ruth (Mrs. Hayre), Richard R. ,
Ill. , Alberta Lavina (Mrs. McClain), Grace Lydia (Mrs.
Kyle), Edith (dec.). Paymaster's clerk in Spanish-Amer-
ican War, 1898. Ordained ministry African M.E. Ch. ,
1901; asst. pastoral Institutional Ch. , Chicago, 1900-1;
instr. in Hebrew, Pane Theol. Sem. , Wilberforce, O. ,
1901-03; pastor, Elgin, Ill. , 2 mos. , 1904, Trinity Mission, Chicago, 1905; resident, 8th Ward Social Settlement, Phila. , 1905-07; research fellow in sociology, U.
of Pa. , 1905-07; field sec. Armstrong Assn. , 1908-09;
editor Christian Recorder, Phila. , 1909-36; Business mgr.
Book Concern A.M.E. Ch. , 1909-12, 1916-20; founder
Citizens and Southern Building and Loan Association;
president Citizens and Southern Bank and Trust Company
Member committee to draft new charter for City of
Philadelphia, 1917-19; com. to plan for celebrating 150th
Anniversary of the Declaration of Independence, 1921;
organizer of Social Service, City Dept. of Pub. Welfare,
Phila. , 1921; a founder of the Spring Street Settlement,
Richard Allen House; supervisor of social service for
A.M.E. chs. of Phila. and vicinity, 1923; pastor, of the
Ward A.M.E. Church, 1928-30, Morris Brown A.M.E.
Ch. , organizer of Jones Tabernacle, A.M.E. ch. , 1930-
32; pres. Wilberforce U. , 1932-36, acting pres. , 1941-
42; elected bishop African Methodist Episcopal Church,
1936, and assigned to South Africa, 1936-40; pressing
bishop 13th Episcopal Dist. (Ky. and Tenn.), 1940-48,
and presiding bishop of New York, N.J. , New England
Bermuda, 1946-48; presiding bishop 6th Episcopal Dist. ,
Ga. , 1948-51; 12th Episcopal Dist. , Ark. and Okla. ,
1951-52; bishop of West Indies and So. America, 1952-
56, 8th Episcopal District (Miss. and Louisiana), 1956-
57, 5th Episcopal District, 1957-60; historiographer of
the A.M.E. Church, 1960---. Founded R.R. Wright
School of Religion, Wilberforce Institute, South Africa,
1938; built 50 new schools in South Africa. Founder Sch.
of Religion, Memphis, 1944. Pres. Missionary Bd. of
A.M.E. Ch. , 1940-44 (pres. publ. bd. , 1946-48, chmn.

bur. History); chmn. A.M.E. com. Army and Navy chaplains since 1940. Exec. sec. Fraternal Cl. Negro Chs. Am. and Africa, 1940-48. Mem. Commn. for union of A.M.E. and A.M.E. Zion Chs., 1943---; pres. Bishops' Council, A.M.E. Ch., 1957-58. Mem. American Acad. Political and Social Science, American Sociological Society, N.E.A., American Negro Acad., Kappa Alpha Psi. Mason. Elk. Author: The Teaching of Jesus, 1903; The Negro in Pennsylvania 1911; Church Financiering, 1919; Social Service, 1922; My Church, Handbook of A.M.E. Church, 1944, Editor: Poems of Phillis Wheatley, 1929; Encyclopedia of African Methodism, 1916 and 1944; The Mission Study Course, 1943; Sermons and Addresses, 1943. Lecturer on "The Negro in America. The Bishops of the A.M.E. Ch., 1964. Delegate Ecumenical Meth. Conf., 1911, 21, 31, 47, 56, 61. Address: 554 N. 58th St., Phila.

WRIGHT, Samuel Ross, b. Ann Arbor, Mich., Jan. 10, 1915; s. George H. and Rose W.; A.B., Lincoln Univ., 1943; B.Th., Butler School of Theology, 1961; children --- 6 girls, 3 boys; pastor, Methodist Churches, Rolla, Mo., 1939-41; Chicago, Ill., 1943-48; Lexington, Ky., 1948-52; Fort Wayne, Ind., 1953-56; Indianapolis, Ind., 1956-61; current, Mt. Zion Meth. Church, 1961---; active with NAACP in political action; teacher, Public Schools, 1958-61; prof., Lincoln Univ. Sch. of Theology, 1961-62; chmn., Political Action Committee of NAACP, Fort Wayne, Cincinnati, Ohio; Mem., YMCA; Urban League, Boy Scouts; Ministerial Alliance; award from NAACP in political action; award from Omega Psi Phi in political action; Mem., Kappa Alpha Psi; Home: 705 So. Crescent 29, Ohio; Office: 865 Altoon, Cincinnati 6, Ohio.

*WYNN, Daniel Webster, chaplain, coll. prof.; b. Wewoka, Okla., Mar. 19, 1919; s. Phay Willie and Mary (Carter) W.; A.B., Langston Univ., 1941; B.D., A.M., Howard Univ., 1944, 1945; Ph.D., Boston Univ., Boston, Mass., 1954; D.D., Eden Theol. Seminary, Webster Groves, Mo., Profession Study, 1941; Additional Study: Harvard Univ., Cambridge, Mass., Professional Study, 1950; Hebrew Univ., Jerusalem, Israel, 1963; Colorado Coll., Colorado Springs, Col., 1959; m. Lillian Robinson; children--- Marian Danita, Patricia Ann; Acting Chaplain & Instructor of Sociology and Economics, Kentucky State Coll., Frankfort, Ky., 1945-46; Acting dean, School of

Religion, Bishop Coll., Marshall, Texas, 1946-53; Act-
ing chaplain, Tuskegee Institute, Tuskegee Institute, Ala.,
1953-54; Dean of Students, Langston Univ., Langston,
Okla., 1954-55; chaplain, Tuskegee Institute, Tuskegee,
Ala., 1955---; pastor, Shiloh Church, West Medford,
Mass., 1948-50; Mem.: American Ass'n of Univ. Pro-
fessors; National Ass'n of Biblical Instructors; National
Ass'n of Coll. and Univ., Chaplains; Religions Education
Ass'n; Institute of Religion, Howard Univ., Wash., D.
C.; American Philosophical Ass'n; Mason; Kappa Alpha
Psi; Tuskegee Civic Ass'n; NAACP; Ala. Council on Hu-
man Rights; Distinguished Alumnus Award, awarded by
Langston Univ., 1963; author: NAACP Versus Negro
Revolutionary Protest, 1955; The Chaplain Speaks, 1956;
Moral Behavior and The Christian Ideal, 1962; contribu-
tors: Journal of Religious Thought, Howard Univ. Press;
Messenger Magazine, Evangelical Reformed Church;
Royal Service Magazine, Southern Baptist Convention;
Home Missions Magazine, Southern Baptist Convention;
National Baptist Voice, National Baptist Convention, Inc.;
Central Christian Advocate, Methodist Publishing Board;
Scottish Rite Informer, Upper Room Disciplines, 1963;
Motive Magazine, Feb. 1964; Rel. Ed. Magazine, 1964;
editor: Developing A Sense of Community, Tuskegee In-
stitute Press, 1957; Major Issues In Human Relations,
Tuskegee Institute Press, 1961; The Chapel Bulletin,
Tuskegee Institute Press, 1953, 1955---; Newsletter, Na-
tional Ass'n of Coll. and Univ. Chaplains, 1960-63; Home:
P.O. Box 925, Tuskegee Institute, Ala.; Office: Office
of the Chaplain, Tuskegee Institute, Ala.

WYNN, Master Julius, sem. prof. and official; b. Chat-
tanooga, Tenn., Oct. 17, 1903; s. Clayton and Georgia
(Camp) W.; A.B., Clark Univ., 1939; B.D., Gammon
Theol. Sem., 1941; M.A., Atlanta Univ., 1957; D.D.
(hon.) Clark Coll., 1961; m. Hattie Elizabeth Broughton;
children--- George T. Sylvia E.; pastor, The Methodist
Ch., Ga. Conf., 1936-49; principal, Chattanooga County
Training Sch., Lyerely, Ga., 1942-47; chaplain, Bethune-
Cookman Coll., 1949-53; prof. and dean of students,
Gammon Theol. Sem., 1953-59; current president, Gam-
mon Theol. Sem., 1959---; chmn, Organizational and
Extensional Com., Boys Scouts of America; chaplain,
Inter-alumni Council, United Negro College Fund; Mem.,
YMCA; Omega Psi Phi; editor, "Foundation" magazine
published by Gammon Alumni; office: 653 Beckwill St.,
SW, Atlanta, Ga.; Home: 9 McDonough Blvd., Atlanta,

Ga.

WYNN, Otis James, b. Elizabeth City, N.C., Oct. 7,
1912; s. James Henry and Louise Virginia W.; A.B.,
Howard Univ., Wash., D.C., 1932-36; Atlanta Univ.,
Atlanta, Ga., 1939; B.D., Lincoln Univ. Sch. of Theology,
1946-49; m. Pauline D. Childers; teacher, Swift Memorial Jr. Coll., Tenn., 1938-40; current pastor, The First
United Presbyterian Ch., 1949---; current teacher, Crest-
wood Jr. High Sch., Chesapeake, Va.; principal, Water-
ford Elementary Sch., Norfolk, Va., 14 years; Mem.,
United Presbyterian Men; Va. Teachers' Assn; National
Teachers Assn and the American Teachers Assn; Democrat; chmn, National Missions Com. for So-Virginia Ch.;
moderator, Presbytery of Southern Virginia, 1958-59;
chmn, Com. on Veterans Affairs, South Virginia; US
Army, 1942-46; Asst. to the Division Chaplain; Medal
for Bravery (South Pacific Theater); Certificate of Award
(Chaplain); Letter of Appreciation from the Sec., of War,
1946; Mem., National Historical Society, Secondary
Teachers; Mason; contributor: "Garden of Prayer", Presbyterian Publication; Home: 860 Philpotts Rd., Norfolk
13, Va., 23513.

*YATES, Walter Ladell, Sr., coll. prof; b. Pine Bluff,
Ark., Dec. 12, 1912; s. Julias and Ednia (Wilkins) Y.;
A.B., Philander Smith Coll., 1942; B.D., Howard Univ.
Sch. of Rel., 1945; M.A., Graduate School, 1947; S.T.
M., Hartford Seminary Foundation, 1963---; working on
Ph.D. program currently; m. Victoria Prince; children
--- Walter Ladell, Jr.; Associate professor of Church
History and Missions, Livingstone Coll. & Hood Theol.
Seminary, Salisby, N.C.; prof., Bible, Livingstone
Coll., 3 years; counselor, College students, 15 years;
advisor, Overseas Students Club, Livingstone Coll.,
1955-60; Mem., Omega Psi Phi; Amer. Ass'n of Church His-
tories; Ass'n of Professors of Missions, N.C.; Unpublished
thesis: The History of the A.M.E. Zion Church, West
Africa, 1880-1900; Home: 512 Milford Hills Rd., Salis-
burg, N.C.; Office: Hartford Seminary Foundation, 55
Elizabeth St., Hartford 5, Conn.

YOUNG, Rutus King, professor; b. Dermott, Ark., May
13, 1911; s. Robert and Laura (Scott) Y.; A.B., Shorter
Coll., 1937; B.D., Payne Theological Seminary, 1940;
D.D. (hon.), Shorter College; m. Essie Mae Adams;

children--- Essie Mae (Mrs. Richard Norman), Rutus
King, Jr.; James Robert, Ellen Arneatha, Allena Ann;
pastor, African Methodist Episcopal Churches, Ark.,
La., Ala.; current pastor, Bethel A. M. E. Ch., Little
Rock, Ark.; dean, School of Religion, Campbell Coll.,
Jackson, Miss., 1940-44; pres., Daniel Payne Coll.,
Birmingham, Ala., 1948-50; instructor, Shorter College,
Little Rock, Ark., 1951---; Treasurer, Trustee Bd.,
Shorter Coll., 1953---; pres., Greater Little Rock Minis-
terial Ass'n, 1961-62; director, Christian Education,
Miss. & La., 1942-48; Ark. & Okla., 1953---; award:
Division Leader in Red Cross Campaign, Hot Spring,
1952; Mem., Alpha Phi Alpha; Mem., Mason, Non-parti-
san, North Little Rock Civic League, Little Rock Coun-
cil on Community Affairs; Articles on Christian Steward-
ship in A. M. E. Journal of Christian Education; Sermons
published in A. M. E. REVIEW; Articles to Church paper,
"Speaking For Myself;" Home: 5000 Glenview Blvd., N.
Little Rock, Ark. 72117; Office: 424 W. 9th St., Little
Rock, Ark. 72201.

Bibliography

Suggested sources for further information on ministers and denominations included in this volume.

AFRICAN METHODIST EPISCOPAL CHURCH

No written directory of all the churches and ministers since 1955. For current information contact:

> Bishop Sherman L. Greene, Senior Bishop
> 1105 Fountain Drive, S. W.
> Atlanta 14, Georgia

AFRICAN METHODIST EPISCOPAL ZION CHURCH

Most recent handbook published in 1960. For current information contact:

> Department of Records and Research
> 1326 U Street, NW
> Washington, D. C.

BAPTISTS

For a list of Negro ministers related to this convention contact:

> Dr. Edwin H. Tuller, General Secretary
> 475 Riverside Drive
> New York, New York

NATIONAL BAPTISTS CONVENTION OF AMERICA

Information concerning this group is issued yearly in an annual report contact:

> Rev. D. C. Cooksey, Recording Secretary
> 1227 North Greenwood Street
> Tulsa, Oklahoma

NATIONAL BAPTIST CONVENTION, USA INC.

National Baptist Convention, USA Inc. (cont.)

Record of minutes issued in September at annual meeting includes previous year proceedings, officers and members.

Dr. T.J. Jemison, General Secretary
915 Spain Street
Baton Rouge, Louisiana

PRIMITIVE BAPTIST

A group of Baptists, mainly through the South, who are opposed to all centralization. Fellowship between organizations is maintained by the exchange of minutes and delegates to annual meetings. For further information write:

Primitive Baptist Publishing House
Elon College
Elon, North Carolina

PROGRESSIVE NATIONAL BAPTIST CONVENTION, INC.

Organized as a separate baptist convention in 1962. Geographical lists of ministers may be secured from:

Rev. L. Venchael Booth, Executive Secretary
630 Glenwood Avenue
Cincinnati, Ohio

SOUTHERN BAPTIST CONVENTION

For Negro ministers affiliated with this group, contact:

Mr. Guy Bellamy,
Secretary of Department of Work with National
Baptist
1141 North Robinson Street
Oklahoma City, Oklahoma

BAPTISTS (Other Sources)

a. Minutes of annual sessions of the National Sunday School and Baptist Training Union Congress issued yearly and includes committees of ministers and laymen attending conference.

Baptists (Other Sources) cont.

b. Minutes of yearly meetings of the Lott Carey Baptist Foreign Missions. Convention of American Lists Committees, Ministers and Laymen attending annual meeting. For further information contact:

> Dr. Wendell C. Somerville
> 1501 Eleventh Street, NW
> Washington 11, D.C.

c. Illinois Historical Records Survey Directory of Negro Baptists Churches in the United States, 2 vols., Chicago, Ill. Issued in 1942 and lists all Negro Baptist Churches geographically by local association.

d. Booth L. Venchael, ed. Who's Who in Baptist America in the National Sunday School and Baptist Training Union Congress. Ohio. Printed by Western Printing Company, 1960.

BIBLE WAY CHURCH OF OUR LORD JESUS CHRIST WORLD WIDE, INC.

Issues yearly minute book. May be secured from:

> Bishop Smallwood E. Williams, Presiding Bishop
> 1130 New Jersey Avenue, NW.
> Washington, D.C.

CATHOLIC, ROMAN

Catholic Directory listing all priests issued yearly. For additional information contact:

> Rev. Harold Perry, SVD
> St. Augustine Seminary
> Bay St. Louis, Mississippi

CHRISTIAN METHODISTS EPISCOPAL CHURCH

Meeting of all ministers held every four years. Yearly meetings held for each district. Directory of all churches and ministers in preparation.

For information contact:

> Bishop Bertram W. Doyle, Senior Bishop

Christian Methodists Episcopal Church (cont.)

    1702 Herman Street
    Nashville, Tennessee

CHURCH OF GOD IN CHRIST (APOSTOLIC)

For information concerning churches and ministers contact:

    Bishop Monroe R. Saunders
    Rehoboth Church of God
    1101-8th Street, NW
    Washington, D. C.

CHURCHES OF CHRIST

Large group of churches, formerly Disciples of Christ, but since 1906 separate. Strictly congregational and have no organization larger than the local congregation. For further biographies of ministers see,

    Baxter, B.B. & Young, M., ed.
    Preachers of Today, V. 3
    Nashville, The Gospel Advocate, 1964

LUTHERAN CHURCH IN AMERICA

For directory material for ministers affiliated with this branch of the Lutheran Church, contact:

    The Board of Publication
    2900 Queen Lane
    Phila, Pa. 19129

LUTHERAN CHURCH-MISSOURI SYNOD

Yearbook Issues. Contact:

    The Lutheran Annual
    Concordia Publishing House
    St. Louis 18, Missouri

METHODIST CHURCH

Directory material may be found in the General Minutes of the Annual Conferences, issued yearly. Addresses of ministers are not included, write to:

Methodist Church (cont.)

    Section of Records
    Research and Statistics
    1200 Davis Street
    Evanston, Illinois

The Methodist Church Directory 201-8th Avenue, Nashville, Tenn. Board of Publication of the Methodist Church,
Inc. c. 1965. contains names and addresses of all officers
in the church.

PRESBYTERIAN CHURCH IN THE US

A Branch of the Presbyterian Church established in separate existence in 1861. Sometimes called the "Southern "
Presbyterian Church. For directory material write:

    Rev. L. W. Bottoms
    Division of Home Missions
    Board of Church Extension
    341-B Ponce De Leon Avenue, NE
    Atlanta 8, Georgia.

UNITED PRESBYTERIAN CHURCH IN THE UNITED STATES OF AMERICA

Lists of churches, ministers and other directory material
may be secured from:

    Ministers of the General Assemly of the U. P. O.,
    Part III, Statistics
    Office of the General Assembly
    Witherspoon Building
    Philadelphia 7, Pa.

PROTESTANT EPISCOPAL CHURCH

For lists of Negro clergy, contact:

    Rev. Tollie L. Caution, Associate Secretary
    Home Department
    National Council of Episcopal Churches
    815 Second Avenue
    New York 17, New York

REFORMED CHURCH IN AMERICA

Reformed Church in America (cont.)

This body was established by the earliest Dutch settlers of New York as the Reformed Protestant Dutch Church in 1628. It embraces many of the historic colonial churches of New York and New Jersey and today has many strong churches in the middle and far west.

For yearbook, which lists ministers, contact:

General Synod
475 Riverside Drive
New York 27, N.Y.

SEVENTH-DAY ADVENTISTS

For information on Negro clergy contact:

Elder H.D. Singleton
General Conference of Seventh-Day Adventists
6840 Eastern Avenue, NW
Washington 12, D.C.

UNITARIAN UNIVERSALIST ASSOCIATION

Yearbook issued. Information secured from:

Mr. Leon C. Fay, Director, Department of the Ministry
25 Beacon Street
Boston 8, Mass.

UNITED CHURCH OF CHRIST

Constitution adopted in 1961 uniting the Evangelical and Reformed Church and the Congregational Christian Churches. Yearbook issued with information for previous year. May be secured from:

The United Church of Christ
297 Park Avenue, South
New York 10, New York. Price $1.75

Appendix

Adams, B. T.,
P. O. Box 552,
Ferris, Tex.
Adams, J. J.,
Rt. 1, Box 139,
Casdade, Va.
Alexander, E. D.,
Corpus Christi, Tex.
Allen, L. B.,
P. O. Box 4191
Beaumont, Tex.
Anderson, E. S.,
Rt. 4,
Lewisburg, Tenn.
Appleberry, C. E.,
733 First St.,
Cleveland, Tenn.
Ardrey, Wm. C.,
11359 Dexter,
Detroit, Mich.
Bailey, Alma,
706 Hackberry St.,
Brady, Tex.
Bailey, C. M.,
2123 Cornell Drive,
Albuquerque, New
Mexico
Bailey, H. L.,
15 Hampton St.,
Metuchen, N. J.
Baker, D. B.,
511 South 18th St.,
Temple, Tex.
Baker, W. W.,
530 South Denton St.,
Mexia, Tex.
Baptiste, Louis J.
P. O. Box 10693
Charlotte, N. C.
Barnes, W. B.,

Statensburg, N. C.
Bateman, G.,
333 Anderson St.,
Americus, Ga.
Beal, Z. N.
310 South Jackson St.,
Palestine, Tex.
Belcher, McKinley,
Box 474,
War, W. Va.
Bennett, L. K.,
General Delivery,
Jacksonville, Tex.
Berry, Lincoln,
Huntingtown, Md.
Bishop, Elmer A.,
Box 32,
Christianburg, Va.
Black, Jackie,
P. O. Box 149,
Clarksville, Texas
Black, J. C.,
1010 E. O'Conner St.,
Fitzgerald, Ga.
Black, Steward Earnest,
Box 114,
New River, Va.
Blakeney, Cooper L.,
1517 Jasper Ave.,
Knoxville, Tenn.
Blow, Leslie, R
Rt. 1, Box 36 C.
Greenville, N. C.
Boling, B. A.,
Box 483,
Ahahuac, Tex.
Bonner, C. N.,
908 Whetstone St.,
Marshall, Tex.
Bookman, Bozie,

413

Bookman, B. (cont.)
  Box 806,
    Huntsville, Tex.
Broadnax, Dennis D.,
  95 Grandfield Ave.,
    Bridgeport, Conn.
Broach, T.C.,
  Amos Temple CME,
    1500 10th Ave.,
      East Oakland, Calif.
Brown, C.R.,
  428 E. Palmetto St.,
    Florence, S.C.
Brownlow, W.L.,
  1103 3rd St.,
    Orange, Tex.
Burks, O.A.,
  Box 1265,
    Logan, West, Va.
Buchanan, James,
  P.O. Box 1134,
    Bryan, Tex.
Buckley, S.E.,
  Box 34,
    Willis, Tex.
Bullock, David,
  Rt. 3, Box 146,
    Stantonsbury, N.C.
Burroughs, William,
  14 Quincy St.,
    Roxbury, Mass.
Byrd, F.G.,
  504 West 8th St.,
    Hearne, Tex.
Cade, W.V.,
  810 East Main St.,
    Waxahachie, Tex.
Calvin, J.C.,
  601 Market St.,
    Opelousas, La.
Carruthers, J.H.,
  130 H. Mesquite St.,
    San Antonio, Tex.
Carter, Joe H.,
  1342 N.W. 12th St.,
    Amarillo, Tex.
Carter, W.C.,
  510 Lindsey St.,

  Americus, Ga.
Champion, M.,
  613 West 7th St.,
    Georgetown, Tex.
Christopher, O.W.,
  400 Thayor St., P.O. Box
    6132-
      New Orleans 14, La.
Clever, S.M.
  408 Dearborn St.
    Waco, Tex.
Cleaves, J.C.,
  Lexington, Tenn.
Cochran, Edward F.,
  1636 Mabry St.,
    Knoxville, Tenn.
Coe, O.B.,
  408 S. Polaris St.,
    San Antonio, Tex.
Coffey, William Leroy,
  General Delivery,
    Bristol, Va.
Colander, Obadiah,
  431 Hull St.,
    Suffolk, Va.
Cole, Ernest Ovis,
  Box 209
    Caretta, W. Va.
Cooper, Warren,
  615 Clay St.,
    Tarboro, N.C.
Cox, Joseph F.,
  2130 Brooklyn St.,
    Beaumont, Tex.
Crenshaw, Mrs. Sallie A.,
  2008 Vine St.,
    Chattanooga, Tenn.
Crockett, Alex, Box 272
  Anderson, Tex.
Crockett, Martin N.,
  1808 Leota St.,
    Springfield, Tenn.
Crudup, G.,
  144 Oxonia Ave.,
    Asbury Park, N.J.
Curry, W.M.,
  406 Walnut St.,
    Wilmington, Del.

414

Curtis, S. W.,
920 Hines St.,
Waco, Tex.
Daniels, A. B.,
155 Johnson St.,
Newark, N. J.
Daniels, J. H.,
3322 O'Neal St.,
Columbus, Ga.
David, James E.,
Box 943,
Bluefield, W. Va.
Davis, Abraham E.,
1852 Abbie St.,
Shreveport, La.
Davis, I. T.,
Liberty, Tex.
Davis, W. H.,
121 Hyacinth St.,
St. Martinville, La.
Dawson, T. R.,
523 1/2 Jackson St.,
Danville, Ill.
Dennis, A., Jr.
1148 Coleman St.
Atlanta, Ga.
Deverreaux, M. M., Jr.,
1007 Chapline St.,
Wheeling, West Va.
Dickens, James,
Cenetoe, N. C.
Dykes, Dewitt, S.,
2139 Dandrige Ave.,
Knoxville, Tenn.
Easley, M. L., Jr.,
375 First St.,
Jackson, Tenn.
Edge, L. R.,
Oglethrope, Ga.
Elliot, John W.,
P. O. Box 331,
Columbus, Tex.
Ellison, William, Jr.,
1414 McKinley St.,
Austin, Tex.
English, James,
P. O. Box 58
Oglethrope, Ga.

Erwin, E. T.,
Rt. 2,
Lebanon, Tenn.
Espie, S. E.,
P. O. Box 152,
Ore City, Tex.
Everett, David,
507 East 22nd St.,
Bryan, Tex.
Faison, William,
825 E. 27th St.,
Norfolk, Va.
Feast, James F.,
4307 Whipprecht St.,
Houston 26, Tex.
Felder, L. B.,
2585 Franklin St.,
P. O. Box 4101,
Beaumont, Tex.
Fleshman, A. R.,
1124 Greenbrier St.,
Bluefield, W. Va.
Ford, W. F.,
P. O. Box 904,
Mexia, Tex.
Francis, B.
614 No. Maney Ave.,
Murfreesboro, Tenn.
Frank, H. D.,
524 Wharton St.,
Phila. 47, Pa.
Foy, R. L.,
Rt. 1 Box 71-D,
Grand Prairie, Tex.
Franklin, S. M.,
814 South Second St.,
Kingsville, Tenn.
Frazer, J. T.,
Blackwell Memorial AMEZ
Ch., 3956 S. Langley,
Chicago, Ill.
Freeman, M. A. L.,
33 West 14th St.,
San Angelo, Tex.
Fuller, E. T.,
P. O. Box 521,
Brownwood, Tex.
Gaddie, William L.

Gaddie, W. L. (cont.)
315 Penn Street
Cynthiana, Ky.
Gamble, Ira J.,
1015 Davis St.,
Aliquippa, Pa.
Garrett, F. G.
Rt. 1 Box 320
Cordova, Tenn.
Geeter, Fred A.,
1111 S. 10th St.
Temple, Tex.
Gibson, Thomas,
99 Lincoln Ave.,
New Rochelle, N.Y.
Gibson, W.M.,
758 Second St.,
Paris, Tex.

Goff, G.J.,
1210 Paul Guinn,
Waco, Tex.
Golden, Walter S.,
Box 215,
Pulaski, Va.
Gratten, J.S.C.,
523 Como St.,
San Antonio, Tex.
Gray, C. Jarrett
4042 College,
Kansas City, Mo.
Greer, I.C.,
808 West 2nd St.,
Cameron, Tex.
Hall, Junious,
3337 Aubert St.,
St. Louis, Mo.
Hamilton, H.D.,
Rt. 1, 64 A,
Riesel, Tex.
Hamilton, R.H.,
908 South 9th St.,
Waco, Tex.
Harkins, L.K.,
308 20th Aven.,

Springfield, Tenn.
Harris, Alexander Darden,
519 Albermade Ave.,
Rocky Mount, N.C.
Harris, Andrew,
1675 Brooklyn,
Beaumont, Tex.
Harris, W.H.,
280 Clay St.,
Parkersburg, West Va.
Harrison, Ernest L.,
105 Davis St.,
Kerrville, Tex.
Harvey, Jesse,
511 Rock St.,
Shelbyville, Tenn.
Hatley, L.D.,
General Delivery Rt. 2,
Hughes Springs, Tex.
Hayes, Robert E.,
1914 Blodgett Ave.,
Houston 4, Tex.
Hill, C.L.,
1822 Lincoln St.,
Port Arthur, Tex.
Hill, F.S.,
P.O. Box 2081,
Savannah, Ga.
Hill, P.H.,
P.O. Box 6,
Battleboro, N.C.
Hill, J.E.,
175 Central Ave.,
Cleveland, Tenn.
Hillard, Thomas E.,
Rt. 1,
Bellville, Tex.
Holden, A.C.,
1113 St. Andrew St.,
Gonzales, Tex.
Holmes, A.O.,
1035 Simpson Rd. NW,
Atlanta, Ga.
Holmes, Zan W., Jr.,
11881 Schroeder Rd.,
Dallas, Tex.
Houston, C.J.,

Houston, C. J. (cont.)
1226 Grant St.,
Harlingen, Tex.
Houston, D. W.,
P. O. Box 747,
Fairfield, Tex.
Howard, William O.,
Box 537,
Gary, W. Va.
Hunt, D. C.,
1806 St. Phillips,
Selma, Ala.
Hynson, Eddie,
Livingston, Tex.
Jackson, James R.,
P. O. Box 395,
Hempstead, Tex.
Jackson, Moses T.,
513 Main St.,
Lafayette, La.
Jamisen, C. H.,
Rt. 1, Box 224 A.,
Axton, Va.
Jimmerson, John H.,
New River, Tex.
Jobe, G. T.,
453 W. Hobbs,
Lebanon, Tenn.
Johnson, Frank D.,
710 Wesley Ave.,
Greeneville, Tenn.
Johnson, Harvey L.,
P. O. Box 81,
Pulaski, Va.
Johnson, G. L.,
514 E. Avenue C.,
Temple, Tex.
Johnson, H. J.,
P. O. Box 13,
Navasota, Tex.
Johnson, J. F.,
914 Adams St.,
Monroe, La.
Johnson, R. R.,
Miles Chapel Church,
Tyler, Tex.
Johnson, Robert R.,
175-46 Murdock Ave.,

St. Albans, 33, N. Y.
Johnson, R. W.,
918 Linn St.,
Waco, Tex.
Johnson, T. A.,
500 High St.,
Brenham, Tex.
Johnson, W. M.,
302 Buxtan Ave.,
Springfield, Ohio
Johnson, V. E.,
413 West Tyler St..
Teague, Tex.
Jones, Al,
122 West 4th St.,
Tucson, Arizona
Jordan, James,
26 N. Summit St.,
Harrisburg, Pa.
King, J. L., Jr.
850 Hope St.,
Shreveport, La.
King, Robert T.,
P. O. Box 424,
Lampasas, Tex.
King, Z. B.,
218 Alexander St.,
Belton, Tex.
Lamb, L. S.,
4110 Chapel St.,
Longview, Tex.
Lamb, M. D.,
Box 481,
Madisonville, Tex.
Lankford, A. W.,
225 Elliott St.,
Mineola, Tex.
Lawrent, Gulfrey N.,
3110 Bekleview Ave.,
St. Louis, Ill.
Lippett, E. K.,
422 Drummond Ave.,
Neptune, N. J.
Lockett, W. F.,
P. O. Box 527,
Jefferson, Tex.
Long, T. L.,
2618 Highway #3,

Long, T. L. (cont.)
    Dickinson, Tex.
Loud, J.S.,
    2408 E. 28th St.,
    Lubbock, Tex.
Lyles, Glenn L.,
    Watertown, Tenn.
Lyons, O.R.,
    304 N. Willow St.,
    Trenton, N.J.
Malone, Moses H.,
    4009 Kirtland Ave.,
    Chattanooga, Tenn.
Manning, John W.,
    320 Madison St.,
    Abingdon, Va.
Mayes, A.M.,
    Box 372,
    Fairfield, Tex.
Mayes, F.D.,
    701 Ave. E.,
    Conroe, Tex.
McElroy, Talmadge E.,
    402 Lawrence St.,
    Morgan City, La.
Marchbanks, Paul Y.,
    467 E. College,
    Murfreesboro, Tenn.
Mason, A.M.,
    504 Conoly St.,
    Marlin, Tex.
Matthews, J.A.,
    P.O. Box 6,
    Milford, Tex.
Mayberry, C.J.,
    Box 682,
    Dickinson, Tex.
McCarty, H.C.,
    1101 North Hall St.,
    Bryan, Tex.
McCarty, W.N.,
    570 Buford St., Starlight
    Bapt. Ch.,
    Beaumont, Tex.
McGee, V.L.,
    P.O. Box 442,
    Sealy, Tex.
Melton, Warren,

113 South Reid St.,
    Wilson, N.C.
Metcalf, C.C.,
    802 Flood St.,
    Wichita Falls, Tex.
Miller, M.G.,
    1310 14th St.,
    Huntsville, Tex.
Miller, R.,
    Rt. 2 Box 106,
    Culloder, Ga.
Minor, A.D.,
    619 N. Fanning St.,
    Denison, Tex.
Montgomery, E.D.,
    Rt. 2 Box 126,
    Diana, Tex.
Moon, James L.,
    P.O. Box 479,
    Bluefield, W.Va.
Moore, C.H.,
    P.O. Box 171,
    Pittsburg, Tex.
Mouring, Johnnie,
    Hobgood, N.C.
Norris, W.S.P.,
    1850 Logan St.,
    Shreveport, La.
Norwood, W.H.,
    1339 W. Hill Ave.,
    Valdosta, Ga.
Nunley, Roscoe,
    West Houston St.,
    Clarksville, Tex.
Owens, C.D.,
    421 Dearborn Ave.,
    Waco, Tex.
Owens, J.G.,
    2801 Peabody St., Box 1443,
    Dallas, Tex.
Owens, George W.,
    506 W. Tulpehocken St.,
    Phila., Pa.
Pace, H.D.,
    912 28th St.,
    Galveston, Tex.
Manigo, George F.,
    220 Myrtle Ave.

Manigo, G. F. (cont.)
  Johnson City, Tenn.
Pacely, Homer,
  3432 E. Wyoming Ave.,
  El Paso, Tex.
Palmer, R. L.,
  226 W. 6th St.,
  San Angelo, Tex.
Pannie, R. L.,
  R. F. D. Box 581,
  Bassett, Va.
Parker, Jacob,
  Burlison, Tenn.
Parker, Jonah,
  5451 28th St.,
  So. Cremento, Calif.
Payton, G. C.,
  527 B. Boyd Ave.,
  Greenville, N. C.
Pegues, B. S.,
  541 Laclede,
  Memphis, Tenn.
Perry, Lawrence P.,
  Grace Church,
  Raleigh, N. C.
Peyton, C. H.,
  P. O. Box 733, 201 San
  Ford St.,
  Marshall, Tex.
Phoenix, J. B.,
  Rt. 3, Box 58,
  Hubbard, Tex.
Pitts, Albert S.,
  3021 Missouri Ave.,
  El Paso, Tex.
Procter, L. R.,
  2019 9th St.,
  Waco, Tex.
Polk, R. E.,
  P. O. Box 341,
  Centerville, Tex.
Rahming, L. G.,
  611 South 13th St.,
  Wilmington, S. C.
Reed, M. T.,
  2304 Cedar Ave.,
  Lubbock, Tex.

Reid, C. H.,
  1608 Edmondson St.,
  High Point, N. C.
Reid, Lawrence,
  6234 Manchester St.,
  Wilson, N. C.
Rhodes, J. A.,
  P. O. Box 2,
  Pittsburgh, Tex.
Richardson, J. B.,
  760 Mill Ave.,
  Seguin, Tex.
Revis, Robert,
  Rt. 3 Box 67A,
  Wilson, N. C.
Roberts, V. L.,
  2221 East Ute Place,
  Tulsa, Oklahoma
Robinson, L. P. M.,
  Humboldt, Tenn.
Robinson, R. M.,
  Rt. 2,
  Lebanon, Tenn.
Rogers, E. A.,
  702 1/2 E. Murphy St.,
  Odessa, Tex.
Rogers, Joseph L.,
  110 Poplar St.,
  Elizabethton, Tenn.
Rosborough, B. H.,
  Rt. 1 Box 436,
  Marshall, Tex.
Ruckner, I. O.
  P. O. Box 74,
  Hawkins, Tex.
Saunders, Frank,
  1307 Irby St., Ext.,
  Florence, S. C.
Scales, Levi,
  Rt. 2 Box 184,
  Sandy Ridge, N. C.
Scott, Peter J.,
  307 Avenue J.,
  Conroe, Tex.
Scipio, Isaiah,
  8715 Woodward St.,
  Detroit, Mich.

419

Silas, T. J.,
Box 66,
Spring, Tex.
Sims, Joseph,
P. O. Box 742,
Daingerfield, Tex.
Simms, Samuel R.
16 Perkins St.,
Nashville, Tenn.
Sink, Henry H.,
12 Tuckerman St. NW,
Washington, D. C.
Slaughter, Elbert L.,
1409 Wadsworth St.,
Radford, Va.
Smith, Earnest A.,
Rust Coll.,
Holly Springs, Miss.
Smith, Isaiah,
504 So E. 13th St.,
Gainsville, Ga.
Smith, LaFayette,
2312 W. 13th St.,
Texarkana, Tex.
Smith, Nathaniel,
P. O. Box 154
Watertown, Tenn.
Smith, R. J.,
215 North Tex. Ave.,
Palestine, Tex.
Snell, Howard,
Box 26,
Kendleton, Tex.
Snell, Thomas,
Hempstead, Tex.
Spearman, E. S., Jr.
Rt. 1 Box 168,
Fitzgerald, Ga.
Stearn, C. S.,
1906 Adams St.,
Monroe, La.
Steward, R. A.,
656 Chambers St.,
Gallatin, Tenn.
Sykea, John,
2500 Kabsubg Ave.,
Portsmouth, Va.
Stokes, Hobart,

Rt. 42,
Rock Island, Tenn.
Street, Lonnie T.,
517 Warren St.,
Bluefield, W. Va.
Stripling, J. C.,
726 W. 9th St.,
Port Arthur, Tex.
Tanner, E. J.,
313 N. Carver St.,
Edna, Tex.
Tatum, J. W.,
1114 Kellum St.,
Waco, Tex.
Taylor, Ezekiel,
105 S. 5th St.,
Conroe, Tex.
Taylor, H. M.,
P. O. Box 547,
Jasper, Tex.
Teague, L. C.,
Mansfield, Tenn.
Tervalon, Wilfred J.,
98 Harris St.,
Atmore, Ala.
Tiffany, Clarence W.,
300 Vine St.,
Bluefield, W. Va.
Timbers, S. W.,
Rt. 1,
Washington, Va.
Townsend, S. L.,
Dist. Supt., Meth. Ch.,
723 Walnut St.,
Lawrenburg, N. C.
Tunstall, J. E.,
410 N. Market St.,
East St. Louis, Ill.
Yarbough, E. Y.,
R. F. D. 2, Box 202,
Seary, Ga.
Wade, Robbie Lowell,
171 Magazine St.,
Pulaski, Va.
Walker, D.
329 Millde St.,
Macon, Ga.
Walker, D. L.,

Walker, D. L. (cont.)
  Hempstead, Tex.
Walker, Martin J.,
  115 Juarez St.,
    Beeville, Tex.
Ward, Benjamin,
  2640 Market St.,
    East St. Louis, Ill.
Washington, J. R.,
  200 Jones St.,
    Bluefield, W. Va.
Washington, L. D.,
  P. O. Box 113,
    Jefferson, Tex.
Weaver, W. M.,
  1906 E. Wilson St.,
    Tarboro, N. C.
Webb, W. A.,
  423 Kerr St.,
    Sherman, Tex.
Webster, Charles S.,
  68 High St.,
    Princeton, W. Va.
Welles, James W.,
  Greater St. Peters,
    4400 Mt. Elwt St.,
      Detroit, Mich.
White, Josiah,
  Rt. 3, Box 234,
    Independence, Va.
White, Saul A.,
  1308 East Pulaskie St.,
    Fort Worth, Tex.
White, T. E.
  109 K. St.,
    Martin, Tenn.
Whitten, Lunn P.,
  1217 N. Church St.,
    Kalamazoo 4, Mich.
Williams, Dogan W.,
  427 Scott St.,
    Bristol, Va.
Wilkes, W. G.,
  P. O. Box 321,
    Cairo, Ga.
Wilson, Jimmie,
  Rt. 1 Box 110,
    Cascade, Va.

Wilson, J. E.,
  1227 13th St.,
    Huntsville, Tex.
Young, Henry,
  Box 178
    Spring, Tex.